MW01089790

EVERLASTING DOMINION

EVERLASTING DOMINION

A Theology of the Old Testament

EUGENE H. MERRILL

NASHVILLE, TENNESSEE

Ten-Digit ISBN: 0-8054-4026-7
Thirteen-Digit ISBN: 978-0-8054-4026-3

Published by Broadman & Holman Publishers
Nashville, Tennessee

Dewey Decimal Classification: 230
Subject Heading: THEOLOGY / BIBLE—STUDY

1 2 3 4 5 6 7 8 9 10 11 12 • 15 14 13 12 11 10 09 08 07 06
LB

Contents

Preface . . . . **xv**

Acknowledgments . . . . **xvii**

CHAPTER ONE

Introduction: The Origins, Nature, and Present State of Old Testament Theology **1**

History of the Biblical Theology Movement
Defense of a New Biblical Theology
Statement of Presuppositions
Theological Method

PART ONE

God: His Person and Work 35

CHAPTER TWO

The Autobiography of God **37**

The Setting of the Narrative
The Nature of God
The Sovereignty of God
The Omnipotence of God
The Omniscience of God
The Eternality of God
The Character of God
The Holiness of God

The Righteousness of God
The Justice of God
The Love of God
The Pity of God
The Grace of God
The Compassion of God
The Covenant Fidelity of God
The Dependability of God
The Patience of God
The Anger/Wrath of God
The Forgiveness of God

CHAPTER THREE
The Revelation of God 75
Revelation by Word
Revelation by Visions and Dreams
Revelation through the Angel of Yahweh
Revelation through the Divine Names
Revelation through the Prophets
Revelation through Signs
Revelation through Lots

CHAPTER FOUR
The Works of God 101
Creation
Judgment
Salvation and Deliverance
Redemption

CHAPTER FIVE
The Purposes of God 127
Israel and the Purposes of God
The Reigning of God
Creation and Divine Sovereignty
History and Divine Sovereignty
The Territory of Divine Sovereignty
The Hierarchy of Divine Sovereignty
God's Fellowship with Mankind
Fellowship as a Creation Motif

Fellowship in the Wake of the Fall
Fellowship through Human Government
Fellowship through a Chosen People

PART TWO
Mankind: The Image of God 163

CHAPTER SIX
The Creation of Mankind **165**

The Creation and Purpose of Mankind
- The Creation Narratives
- The Image of God
- The Fashioning of Man

The Nature of Mankind
- The Theology of the Individual
- The Theology of the Community
- The Theology of the Clan
- The Theology of the Tribe
- The Theology of the Nations
- The Theology of Mankind

CHAPTER SEVEN
The Fall of Mankind **199**

The Narrative of the Fall
- The Possibility of a Fall
- The Result of the Fall
- The Identity of the Tempter

Death and the Hereafter
The Fall and Human Sinfulness
- The Alienation of Sin
- The Technical Terms for Sin
- Sin and Competing Dominions

CHAPTER EIGHT
The Redemption of Mankind **227**

The Principle and Practice of Sacrifice
The Material of Sacrifice
Covenant and Redemption

The ***Protevangelium***
Conclusion

CHAPTER NINE
The Creation of a Nation 251

The Promise of a Special People
The Founding of the Nation
The Deliverance of the Nation
The Significance of the Plagues
The Covenant at Sinai

PART THREE
The Kingdom of God 275

CHAPTER TEN
God and the World 277

The Concept of the Kingdom
The Concept of Sacred Space
The Garden of Eden
Eviction from Sacred Space
Eschatological Renewal of Sacred Space
Altars and Shrines as Sacred Space
The Temple as Sacred Space
The Mediation of the Kingdom
The Concept of Covenant
Resistance to the Kingdom by the Nations
The Kingdoms of the World
The Prophets and the Nations
Amos
Isaiah
Nahum
Jeremiah
Zephaniah
Ezekiel
Daniel
Reinstitution of the Kingdom
The Psalms of Yahweh's Kingship
The Royal Psalms
Conclusion

CHAPTER ELEVEN
God and Israel 325

The Mosaic Covenant
The Ten Commandments
The First Commandment
The Second Commandment
The Third Commandment
The Fourth Commandment
The Fifth Commandment
The Sixth Commandment
The Seventh Commandment
The Eighth Commandment
The Ninth Commandment
The Tenth Commandment
The Book of the Covenant
The Altar Law
Other Laws
The Covenant Ceremony
Israel as a Cultic Community
Sacred Space
Sacred Persons
Sacred Times
The Sabbath
The Passover and Unleavened Bread
The Festival of Harvest
The Festival of Ingathering
The Festival of Trumpets
The Day of Atonement
The Sabbatical and Jubilee Years
Sacred Acts
Ritual and Liturgy
Liturgy and Holiness
The Categories of Sacrifice
Miscellaneous Sacred Acts

CHAPTER TWELVE
Deuteronomy and Covenant Renewal 383

The Pre-Deuteronomic History
Deuteronomy as a Covenant Text

The Background of Its Stipulations
The Deuteronomic Decalogue
General Covenant Stipulations
Specific Covenant Stipulations
Implementation of the Covenant

CHAPTER THIRTEEN
The Deuteronomistic History 413

The Book of Joshua
Preparations for Conquest
Holy War
Covenant Renewal in the Land of Promise
The Books of Judges and Ruth
The Character of the Times
Yearnings for a King
Anticipation of Monarchy
The Books of First and Second Samuel
The Prophet Samuel: Preparation for Monarchy
Saul: Failed Monarchy
David: The Realization of True Monarchy
The Davidic Covenant
The Books of Kings
The Succession of Solomon
The Establishment of the Temple
The Dedication of the Temple
Royal Priesthood
The Temple and Sacred Space
Elijah and Elisha: Prophetic Confrontation
Jeopardy of the Kingdom Ideal

CHAPTER FOURTEEN
The Books of Chronicles, Ezra-Nehemiah, and Esther 465

The Books of Chronicles
Genealogies and Tribal Histories
The Reign of David
The Reign of Solomon
The Nature and Purpose of Sacred History
The Divided Monarchy

The Book of Ezra-Nehemiah
The Book of Esther

PART FOUR
The Prophets and the Kingdom 489

CHAPTER FIFTEEN
The Theology of the Eighth-Century Canonical Prophets 491

The Prophet Amos
The Prophet Hosea
The Prophet Jonah
The Prophet Isaiah
The Rebellion of Judah
The Judgment of Judah
The Restoration of Judah
The Messianic Servant and Savior
Oracles against the Nations
The Establishment of God's Kingdom
The Prophet Micah

CHAPTER SIXTEEN
The Theology of the Later Preexilic and Exilic Prophets 521

The Prophet Jeremiah
Judah's Covenant Unfaithfulness
The Judgment of Judah
The Judgment of the Nations
Restoration and Deliverance
The Prophet Nahum
The Prophet Habakkuk
The Prophet Zephaniah
The Prophet Ezekiel
The Disobedience of Israel
Judgment on the Nations
The Restoration of Israel

CHAPTER SEVENTEEN
The Theology of the Postexilic Prophets. 547

The Prophet Daniel
The Contest for Sovereignty
The Kingdoms of the World
The Kingdom of Heaven
God as Sovereign
The Prophet Joel
The Prophet Obadiah
The Prophet Haggai
The Prophet Zechariah
The Disobedience of Israel
The Judgment of Israel
The Restoration of Israel
The Judgment of the Nations
The Salvation of the Nations
The Coming Messiah
The Sovereignty of Yahweh
The Prophet Malachi

PART FIVE
Human Reflection on the Ways of God 567

CHAPTER EIGHTEEN
The Theology of the Psalms 569

God as King
Mankind as God's Viceroy
The Messianic King
The Kingdom Role of Zion
Life in the Kingdom
Difficulties in Kingdom Life
Hostility to the Kingdom
Yahweh's Faithfulness to the Kingdom

CHAPTER NINETEEN
The Theology of the Wisdom Literature 603

Introductory Observations
The Theology of the Book of Job

The Problem of the Human Predicament
God and the Human Predicament
The Resolution of the Human Predicament
The Theology of Proverbs
The Essence of Wisdom
The Expression of Wisdom
The Function of Wisdom
The Manifestations of Wisdom
Accessibility to Wisdom
The Theology of Ecclesiastes
The Theology of the Book of the Song of Songs

CHAPTER TWENTY
Conclusion 641

Theological Premises
Theological Method
The Theological Center
The Old Testament and the New Testament

Name Index 653

Subject Index 657

Scripture Index 665

Preface

For many years I have more than half seriously admonished my students that biblical theology is "an old man's game." By this I mean it presupposes so many other disciplines and so much accumulation of knowledge that few scholars are prepared to undertake the task unless they have invested long, hard years in preparation of its accomplishment. Biblical theology is rather like the pinnacle of a pyramid, the finishing touches on an edifice consisting of layer upon layer of strata of learning that provide it a foundation of method and meaning. First and foremost is a modicum of familiarity with the biblical content itself, a feel for both its wholeness and its particulars. If done well, it must be done by competent control of the languages of biblical texts; for a claim to an understanding of the literature that depends solely on the translations and interpretations of others, no matter how good, tends to vitiate any sense of authority the theologian brings to his or her assignment. Finally, sound principles of exegesis and hermeneutics are among other tools that must be brought to bear as well as a deep acquaintance with the environment of Old Testament Israel—its setting, its history, and its interaction with the peoples and cultures of the ancient Near Eastern world.

It would be presumptuous for me, on the one hand, to make the absurd claim to have mastered this disparate range of knowledge; but on the other hand, the now or never imperatives of life inexorably arrive when one must do the best he can with the resources at his disposal.

Many a theology has been born prematurely, not allowed the moderation and mellowing of full gestation, and therefore has fallen short of its potential. Others have never seen the light of day at all for (to continue the metaphor), though well conceived, they have expired in the womb, as it were, victims of a perception on the part of their begetters that the time had not yet come to bring their dreams to reality. There exists, then, a little window between the time when one believes he has fulfilled the requisite demands of scholarly and spiritual preparation and the time he must act before the ravages of mortality close the window forever. I write this preface on my seventy-first birthday, my God-given window, praying he will receive all glory and praise in the work that follows and that all my students—past, present, and future—will benefit from it even if only a fraction as much as I have benefited from their own contribution to my life and learning.

Eugene H. Merrill

Acknowledgments

An author's name on a book is almost a form of false advertising because it suggests that he or she alone is responsible for its existence. In reality, a host of individuals and institutions, like so many ghostwriters, share in the endeavor and, in fact, make it possible at all. These range from family and friends who offer encouragement and put up with prolonged absence and neglect to support staff who do the drudge work of typing, proofing, and indexing—unglamorous tedium to be sure—to editors and publishers who expect and demand high standards and who make available their resources to ensure the accomplishment of such a worthy end.

The impetus for this work originates in none of the above, however, but in the matrix of scores of graduate students at Dallas Theological Seminary who for over thirty years have challenged my assumptions, sharpened my critical thinking, and graciously endured my constantly evolving understanding of Old Testament theology. These fellow pilgrims, impossible to name here because of their multitude, hold me in their debt; and to them this work is affectionately dedicated.

Lest I rightly be thought to be remiss in failing to acknowledge my profound dependence on others as well, I wish to thank Mrs. Chris Wakitsch for her painstaking word processing, the administration of Dallas Theological Seminary for granting a sabbatical that allowed the time necessary to prosecute the project, and Broadman & Holman

Publishers—in particular Leonard Goss and John Landers—for their initial acceptance of the proposal, their enthusiastic support throughout the process, and their professional expertise in seeing it through to fruition.

May the God of Abraham, Isaac, and Jacob, the Father of our Lord Jesus Christ, be pleased with this offering; and may it redound to his everlasting glory and praise.

Eugene H. Merrill

Chapter One

Introduction: The Origins, Nature, and Present State of Old Testament Theology

To describe theology as "biblical" tends immediately to introduce ambiguity to the discipline, for the adjective seems to be either self-evident or redundant. How can theology be anything but biblical if it is Christian (or even Jewish) since these traditions regard the Bible as their authoritative witness to truth and since, one would think, theology is inseparable from the Bible? But the adjective is not at all superfluous, for it distinguishes biblical theology from other disciplines that are engaged in the theological enterprise—disciplines, for example, such as systematic and historical theology. The descriptors *systematic* and *historical* are also carefully chosen to suggest a certain aspect or thrust of theological study, the one emphasizing the logical categorizing of theological ideas into a coherent whole and the other the tracing of reflection on these ideas and their syntheses throughout the course of postbiblical history.[1]

Part of the terminological confusion has to do with the grammatical point as to whether *biblical* is subjective or objective in its connection

[1] For further helpful distinctions, see Richard B. Gaffin, "Systematic Theology and Biblical Theology," WTJ 38 (1976):281–99; Gerhard F. Hasel, "The Relationship between Biblical Theology and Systematic Theology," TJ 5 (1984):113–27.

to *theology.* That is, does *biblical* mean that the theology is in line with biblical truth or merely that it derives from the Bible? Though ideally these perspectives should result in one and the same conclusion as to biblical teaching, in actual practice this is often not the case because though a theology may be biblical in the sense that it is not anti- or unbiblical, it may contain ideas that are extra-biblical, that is, ideas drawn from philosophy, science, history, sociology, or any number of other sources. Biblical theology, when practiced best at any rate, limits its source material to the Bible, refusing to let the Bible say more than it intends and, at the same time, not denying its voice wherever it has a message to speak.

It is clear so far that we are speaking more of a method or strategy for doing theology than of theological texts and their exposition. The question is not whether a given theology is biblically defensible but whether it derives exclusively from the Bible and is in line with the Bible's own terms and intentions. To put it another way, a proper biblical theological method is (1) one that has no preconceived ideas about biblical truth, (2) one that refuses to read extraneous theological ideas into the text, and (3) one that allows the Bible to speak for itself at every stage of its development both canonically and historically.

This raises the question of a broader methodology with special attention to canon and history, matters introduced summarily here and developed more fully at a later point. Canon suggests something fixed and static, that is to say, something synchronic, whereas history, obviously progressive by definition, must be understood as diachronic. The canon of the Old Testament consists of a collection of sacred texts deemed by Judaism and the church to be divinely inspired and therefore authoritative but a collection that lies flat, as it were, with no obvious sign of movement or direction as a collection *per se.* A careful reading of these texts reveals, however, that they are far from lifeless and anything but fixed and frozen. They cannot, in the very nature of their status as revealed texts, be enlarged or diminished—in that sense they are inflexible—but they communicate from beginning to end a dynamic historical flow. The Old Testament on close inspection betrays itself for what it really is, a pulsating, life-changing narrative that has a beginning, a plot, a dénouement, and a (at least tentative) conclusion.

The synchronic (canon) and diachronic (history) must be recognized together as matching, complementary aspects of proper biblical theological method. We shall address method as a whole at a more appropriate point, but even at this early stage it will be helpful to offer at least brief definitions of key methodological terms and some hint as to how the concepts they represent relate to one another.

As soon as the term *canon* comes to the fore, several questions present themselves. What or whose canon is in mind? Can the various books and sections of the canon be dated and interrelated? Does it really matter how the previous questions are answered? In response to these queries, and in the order they have been posed, one must make hard and rather arbitrary decisions. As to the identity of the particular canon to be chosen, our view is that the Hebrew (so-called Massoretic) canon—as opposed, for example, to that of the Greek (Septuagint) tradition—is the only body of ancient writings that qualifies as divine revelation; and for that reason only they can provide the raw material for an Old Testament theology.[2] The Protestant canon is coterminous with the Hebrew (though it follows the order of the Greek canon for the most part) and thus forms the basis for our present work.

Claiming the Hebrew canon as sufficient may contribute to a solution of the synchronic problem, but the diachronic (historical) issue yet remains. A commitment to the principle of the progressive revelation of Old Testament teaching, a principle inherent in any view of gradual divine self-disclosure, is inseparable from the question of the authorship and dating of its several parts. There are hints in most of the books as to their origination; but modern critical scholarship challenges many of these assertions, thus leaving open the answers to these questions, at least in some quarters. Unless and until there is some consensus on the matter, the historical dimension of theological method will take on one or another shape depending on the model the theologian wishes to adopt. We shall address the fuller ramifications of these contingencies more adequately at a later point.

A further aspect of the adjectival *biblical* has to do with the larger canon, that is, the New Testament and its relevance to the possibility

---

[2] For a discussion of Old Testament canon in the early church, see E. Earle Ellis, *The Old Testament in Early Christianity* (Grand Rapids: Baker, 1992), 3–50.

of doing biblical theology. The title of our work contains the phrase "a theology of the Old Testament"; but since the Old Testament is only part of the Christian canon, in what sense can Old Testament theology be understood as "biblical" theology? It can, of course, if the Old Testament is construed only as a history of Israel's religion; but if the full canon, both Old and New Testament, is necessary to a totally satisfying biblical theology, then the term *biblical theology* is deficient to describe what we are doing here. We have therefore chosen to undertake a theology of the Old Testament alone, but in doing so we recognize that it is not "biblical" in the full diachronic sense even if it is biblical in its attention to Old Testament canonical and historical considerations. At the same time, the New Testament cannot be ignored, for only then can the Christian find full culmination of Old Testament theological themes and ideas that insistently point in that direction.

It might be helpful at the end of this brief consideration of definitional clarification to state our own understanding of the meaning and method of Old Testament theology: Old Testament theology is the study of biblical theology that employs the methods of that discipline to the Old Testament alone while being aware of the limitations inherent in not addressing the New Testament witness in any comprehensive way. This delimitation can be justified on the grounds that the Old Testament speaks its own message, one that is legitimate and authoritative in every sense of the term even if, from the Christian viewpoint, its message is not ultimately complete.

History of the Biblical Theology Movement

The history of a movement (if such this is) is a notoriously difficult thing to document. It is quite different from an event or even a trend since these usually have some discernible starting point or at least can be located within some kind of cause-and-effect nexus that gave rise to them with such effect as to have left their historical mark. Movements are more shadowy, appearing it seems out of nowhere, with no definitive points of origination.

This is clearly true of the history of biblical theology though certain dates, names, and circumstances are routinely cited as marking if not the beginning of the movement at least its critical turning points.[3] To begin with, the later Old Testament writings "theologize" the earlier ones; the extra-canonical Jewish literature does the same with the canonical; and the New Testament, in a sense, is a theology of the Old Testament. All postbiblical (hereafter suggesting post-Old Testament) writings that touch on the Old Testament in any way, especially in terms of exposition and theological interpretation, may, in a broad sense at least, be considered biblical theology.

Most scholars rightly distinguish between such a broad understanding of biblical theology and its modern technical usage, however, so it is best to consider the more recent turning points alluded to and see how and why biblical theology became a movement separate and distinct from theology in general. It is commonplace to begin with a young scholar from the University of Altdorf in Germany who, as part of his admission to the faculty of that institution, delivered a famous inaugural address titled "On the Proper Distinction between Biblical and Dogmatic Theology and the Specific Objective of Each" (March 30, 1787).[4] By "dogmatic" Johann P. Gabler meant what is usually called today "systematic" theology.

Gabler's central thrust and concern was the distinction between biblical and dogmatic theology, the former of which he clearly favored. He put it this way:

> There is truly a biblical theology, of historical origin, conveying what the holy writers felt about divine matters; on the other hand there is a dogmatic theology of didactic origin, teaching what each theologian philosophizes rationally about divine things, according to the measure of his ability or of the times, age, place, sect, school, and other similar factors. Biblical theology, as is proper to historical argument, is always in accord with itself when considered by itself—although even biblical theology when elaborated by one of the disciplines may be fashioned in one way by

---

[3] For a convenient and comprehensive history of the movement up to 1980, see John H. Hayes and Frederick Prussner, *Old Testament Theology: Its History and Development* (Atlanta: John Knox), 1985.

[4] See conveniently "Johann P. Gabler on Biblical Theology" in Ben C. Ollenburger, Elmer A. Martens, and Gerhard Hasel, ed., *The Flowering of Old Testament Theology* (Winona Lake, Ind.: Eisenbrauns, 1992), 492–502.

> some and in another way by others. But dogmatic theology is subject to a multiplicity of change along with the rest of the humane disciplines; constant and perpetual observation over many centuries shows this enough and to spare.[5]

So as not to misread Gabler, especially as a child of the eighteenth century, it is important to note that by such expressions as "historical origin" and "what the holy writers felt about divine matters," he is not denying the work of divine inspiration but rather is focusing on the fact that good theology should be grounded in history and based only on the teaching of the prophets. On the other hand, in an obvious overstatement he charges dogmatic theology with being perverted or even victimized by all kinds of philosophical and cultural influences from without. His fervent espousal of the methods of biblical theology no doubt fed his unfair caricature of any other approach. Nevertheless, his observations set forth here—no matter how simplistic—carried the day and more than any other factor gave rise to the biblical theology movement.

But Gabler was indeed a child of his age and breathed its philosophical and theological air. The Enlightenment was well under way by the time he delivered his essay; and, in fact, he shows awareness of the new way of thinking by various allusions to some of its spokesmen. A central premise of the Enlightenment was that embedded institutions, traditions, and worldviews need not be considered sacrosanct just because they were commonly held. And the underlying epistemology that could challenge the old and embrace the new was rationalism, the notion that only what can be believed must be believed.[6] A careful look at the quotation of Gabler above reflects this rationalistic spirit by its frontal attack upon the time-honored ways of doing and thinking theology. In the pre-Enlightenment world dogmatic theology reigned; now with the freedom gained by means of rational inquiry, dogmatism was dethroned and replaced by new ways of theologizing that were not bound to ecclesiastical tradition. One of these ways was biblical theology. Ironically, the very approach that

[5] John Sandys-Wunsch and Laurence Eldredge, "J. P. Gabler and the Distinction between Biblical and Dogmatic Theology: Translation, Commentary, and Discussion of His Originality," *Scottish Journal of Theology* 33 (1980):137.

[6] See, for example, W. T. Jones, *A History of Western Philosophy* (New York: Harcourt, Brace and Company, 1952), 805–10.

would open up the riches of God's revelation in previously unimaginable ways came as a by-product of a rational skepticism that included in its agenda a discounting of traditional (dogmatic) theological method.

At the same time, the Bible as a literary as well as a religious text was becoming subjected to critical analyses of authorship and dating as a by-product of the intellectual ferment that was sweeping over Europe and especially Germany.[7] Just twenty-four years before Gabler's address, Jean Astruc, a French layman, had proposed his novel idea that though Moses wrote the book of Genesis, he had used various preexisting documents to do so, and that these documents did not always agree with one another. J. G. Eichhorn and other critics followed this lead and expanded the documentary hypothesis to the point that none of the Pentateuch was attributed to Moses, all of it being considered a late patchwork of traditions edited by postexilic redactors. Julius Wellhausen, a century after Gabler, put the finishing touches on the hypothesis, one that still exercises enormous influence in Old Testament scholarship.[8]

The point must be made here that bibliology (the issue of the origin and nature of the Bible) cannot be separated from theology, a point to be further elaborated below under "Presuppositions." For now it is enough to observe that Gabler was impacted by the rationalism of his time and that much of his iconoclasm vis-à-vis dogmatic theology must be understood in light of his skepticism regarding the nature of the Bible as the Word of God. Moreover, he had mentors similarly affected to whom he was in debt and whom he acknowledged as such in his essay. Only a few of these need be mentioned in the following historical sketch.

Chief among these perhaps was S. F. N. Morus (1736–1792), described by Gabler as "that excellent man" who "has taught us what caution must be observed in interpreting the relationship amongst meanings of the same word."[9] This caution anticipated a similar argument made most forcefully in modern times by James Barr.[10] Continuing his praise

---

[7] For an adequate history of the so-called historical critical approach to the Old Testament, see R. K. Harrison, *Introduction to the Old Testament* (Grand Rapids: Eerdmans, 1969), 3–82.

[8] Julius Wellhausen, *Prolegomena to the History of Ancient Israel* (Cleveland: World, 1957, 1883).

[9] Sandys-Wunsch and Eldredge, "J. P. Gabler," 140.

[10] James Barr, *The Semantics of Biblical Language* (Oxford: Oxford University Press, 1961).

of Morus, this time for his renunciation of the allegorical and overly figurative exegesis common to the eighteenth century, he spoke of him as "a very great man whose reputation is his monument."[11] Gabler's most effusive expression of appreciation of Morus, however, concerned his theological method, one that argued for the notion that individual biblical texts must be examined for their universal ideas while at the same time being read against their own contextual and historical settings.[12]

Though Gabler cites Morus frequently in his address, careful study of his own methods and conclusions puts beyond doubt that his greatest debt was to G. T. Zachariä (1729–1777). A moderate rationalist, Zachariä held to the inspiration of Scripture and practiced a careful exegetical method in expounding its truth.[13] In presenting his own method, Gabler made three major points: (1) there must be a clear distinction between the divine and the human in Scripture; (2) there must be a distinction between biblical and dogmatic theology; and (3) "our philosophy" (that is, dogmatic theology) must be constructed upon the foundation of religion (that is, biblical theology).[14] "The late Professor Zachariae [*sic*] did this very capably," he said, "but I hardly need to remind you of the fact that he left some things for others to emend, define more correctly, and amplify."[15] In the remainder of his essay, Gabler did this very thing though he himself never wrote a full theology.

As for Zachariä, he, like his younger contemporary W. F. Hufnagel (1754–1830), was among the first to criticize the dogmatic approach to theology openly and to urge a theology based on exegesis, a case based already on previous work by J. S. Semler (1725–1791) and J. A. Ernesti (1707–1781) who stressed a purely historical and grammatical interpretation of the Bible as opposed to one that imposed a philosophically constructed grid upon the biblical text. Zachariä went so far as to state that proof texts—the common raw material of most dogmatic theology—must be subordinated to the whole thrust of biblical teaching even if this caused orthodox teaching to be undermined! What

[11] Sandys-Wunsch and Eldredge, "J. B. Gabler," 141.

[12] Ibid., 141–42.

[13] Gerhard Hasel, *Old Testament Theology: Basic Issues in the Current Debate* (Grand Rapids: Eerdmans, 1991), 14–15.

[14] Sandys-Wunsch and Eldredge, "J. B. Gabler," 138.

[15] Ibid., 138.

he meant was if "orthodox" teaching was based on faulty readings and interpretations of biblical texts, then it was not really orthodox after all but only philosophically driven dogma.

Gabler's theological successors carried out his methodological principles but from an increasingly rationalistic, anti-supernaturalistic viewpoint. C. F. von Ammon, in his work *Outline of a Pure Biblical Theology (Entwurf einer reinen biblischen Theologie),*[16] published in 1792, maintained that the only valid test of revelation was its rationality. Moreover, to von Ammon the New Testament was immeasurably superior to the Old. In terms of his use of proof texts, he represented a return to a pre-Gabler hermeneutic, thus betraying one of the key principles of the new biblical theology.

G. L. Bauer (1755–1806)[17] made a radical break between the Old Testament and the New Testament, denied the reality of the supernatural, and arranged all theology around theology proper and anthropology. He drew a clear line of demarcation between biblical theology and the history of Israel's religion, an important insight as it turned out later. As a student of the famous Old Testament critic J. G. Eichhorn, Bauer integrated his theology into the emerging analysis of the Old Testament now known as the historical-critical method. When applied rigorously, this method rearranges the biblical materials according to putative authorial and chronological adjustments thus leaving the Old Testament quite a different book from that of ancient tradition. A theology anchored to such a vastly different understanding of the origins and development of the Scriptures is bound to be a theology unlike that typical of the precritical era.[18]

G. P. C. Kaiser[19] was the most extreme exponent of the new skepticism, and in a major work published in 1813, he denied the possibility of divine revelation and attempted to distinguish in the Old Testament those ideas that were universal from those inferior concepts that were peculiar to Israel's life and times. Borrowing heavily from the mythologies and religious traditions of Israel's surrounding cultures, Kaiser ended up as

---

[16] Cited in Hasel, *Old Testament Theology,* 15.

[17] Hayes and Prussner, *Old Testament Theology,* 68–70.

[18] For an incisive support of this observation, see John H. Sailhamer, *Introduction to Old Testament Theology: A Canonical Approach* (Grand Rapids: Zondervan, 1995), 86–114.

[19] Hayes and Prussner, *Old Testament Theology,* 91–92.

a thoroughgoing universalist, thereby denying to the Bible any kind of unique message or pride of place.

Predictably, a reaction set in against the theological radicalism of the end of the eighteenth century, one led by moderates such as W. M. L. DeWette (1780–1849), C. P. W. Gramberg (1797–1830), and D. G. C. von Cölln (1788–1833). DeWette, in his *Dogmatics* (1813), tried to merge faith and piety with a rationalistic approach and in so doing became the first noteworthy scholar to impose a particular philosophical system (in his case Kantianism) on biblical theology. One result of his method was the bifurcation between the Hebrew religion and Judaism, the latter being nothing but "the unfortunate reinterpretation of Hebraism."[20] Such an attitude fed into a stream of anti-Semitism that eventually led to the horrors of the twentieth century.

Gramberg attempted to write an objective history of the development of Israel's religion without a previous commitment to either dogmatics or skeptical rationalism. In the strictest sense what he produced was not a theology at all but a history of Israel's religion, one that nonetheless took the Old Testament seriously as a record of that history. On the other hand, von Cölln urged that biblical theology should be done genetically, historically, on the basis of the Bible alone. Unfortunately, he embraced the principles of the religious evolutionism of his day that fit hand in glove with the various historical-critical hypotheses that were also gaining currency. Israel's religion thus had no real origin in revelation, certainly not in Mosaic revelation but gradually evolved from a pristine primitivism to its full-blown form in the exilic and postexilic periods.

Meanwhile, a number of philosophers, Georg Hegel chief among them, began to make their impact on biblical theology.[21] Hegel (1770–1831) laid the foundation for a cogent (to him) explanation of the origin and development of Israel's religion in the context of universal religious phenomena. He suggested three stages in this development:

1. The religion of nature—God is a natural substance.
2. The religion of spiritual individuality—God is a subject (Judaism).
3. The absolute religion (Christianity).

[20] Ibid., 100.

[21] R. G. Collingwood, *The Idea of History* (Oxford: Clarendon, 1946), 113–22.

Hegel's dialectical structure rehabilitated the Old Testament in the sense that the Old Testament could be seen as essential in the eventual emergence of the higher religion of the New Testament. This gave new impetus to Old Testament theological study, a jump-start to a movement that was in danger of stalling.

Seizing upon Hegel's construal of history, and especially of Israel's history, J. K. W. Vatke (1806–1882), the scholar from whom the later Wellhausen said he learned most and best, advanced his own theological position, one that promoted three key ideas:[22]

1. Biblical theology must show the development of religion and ethics in Israel's consciousness.
2. Revelation is indispensable, but it can be recognized and evaluated only along developmental (read "evolutionary") lines.
3. Evolutionary philosophy must undergird an interpretation of Old Testament history and religion.

Such an evolutionary way of viewing the development of Israel's religion was compatible with modern approaches to Old Testament study such as source- and redaction-criticism. In fact, it is quite clear that these and later criticisms found their genius and organizing principle in an evolutionary understanding of the development of Old and New Testament thought. The result for theology is that theology was forced into the mold dictated by the evolutionary model and therefore could no longer resemble the approach that had largely enjoyed favor prior to Hegel. The diachronic aspect of theology that viewed theology as springing out of Moses and the patriarchs in ancient times was substituted by one in which Moses played little or no role and which understood the great Mosaic ideas as products of late religious development.

These radical ways of understanding the Old Testament could not go unchallenged, and by the mid-1800s several champions of orthodoxy began to voice their opposition. Happily, this reaction came not only as a resistance to the radicalism of biblical criticism but also through the recognition that biblical theology as a method was not *per se* incompatible to orthodox faith.

---

[22] Hayes and Prussner, *Old Testament Theology,* 100–3.

One of the earliest proponents of the conservative renascence was Ernst W. Hengstenberg (1802–1869) who, in his massive *Christologie des Alten Testaments,*[23] reasserted the full inspiration of Scripture, rejected the historical-critical method with its evolutionary trappings, and, as the title of his work suggests, saw a fully developed messianic theology from beginning to end. His approach, however, largely discounted the principle of progressive revelation and thus the longitudinal or diachronic element essential to a true biblical theology. Hengstenberg had returned to a prebiblical theology dogmatic approach that could not advance the production of a true biblical theology.

J. C. F. Steudel (1779–1837), on the other hand, adopted the biblical theology method of Gabler but without the negative presuppositions held by most theologians of the time.[24] Steudel dealt with the Old Testament first genetically (that is, as a developing revelation) and then systematically, a method followed by most conservative scholars to this day. By "systematically" is meant simply the organizing of the biblical data into categories of similar or identical ideas, a matter to be pursued later on (see "Method"). To Steudel and his followers progressive revelation was seen as an essential key to proper interpretation. H. A. C. Hävernick also rejected the higher critical hypotheses and their subjectivism and in an important work published in 1848 argued that only an objectivism informed by spiritual understanding and by an organic (Steudel's "genetic") principle of Old Testament religious development would lead to a proper biblical theology. He saw the need to treat Old Testament theology in terms of its historical context.

A student of Steudel, G. F. Oehler (1812–1872), produced what many (conservative) scholars consider to be the greatest Old Testament theology of the nineteenth century. His major work (*Theologie des Alten Testaments,* 1873) insisted on the principle of the organic growth of Old Testament revelation, a principle he admitted he owed to Hegel and the philosophers of the history of religion school but which he "cleaned up" so as to avoid the humanistic aspects of the Hegelian worldview.[25] To

[23] Ernst W. Hengstenberg, *Christologie des Alten Testaments* (Berlin: L. Ohmigde, 1829–35).

[24] Hayes and Prussner, *Old Testament Theology,* 107–9.

[25] Gustave F. Oehler, trans. by George E. Day and republished as *Theology of the Old Testament* (Grand Rapids: Zondervan, reprint of 1883 edition).

Oehler the core of biblical truth around which all else is embellishment and amplification is the divine Spirit as fulfilled at last in the New Testament as Christ. This Idea (that is, the Spirit) must be discovered (though it be a datum of special revelation) by the application of the historical-grammatical method. Oehler's blending of the principle of progressive revelation (based on a biblical reading of history) and a proper exegetical method set the groundwork for a sound and sensible biblical theology.

By the end of the nineteenth century, Old Testament theology became eclipsed by an intense interest in the history of Israel's religion, a turn of events to be attributed to the continuing impact of a Hegelian historiosophy linked with the historical-critical approach to biblical studies. It was only after World War I that biblical theology was rediscovered, and this was largely due to (1) a general loss of faith in evolutionary naturalism; (2) a reaction against historical positivism (the view that historical truth could be attained by purely scientific objectivity); and (3) a return to the Reformation emphasis on the relevance, religiously and spiritually, of the Old Testament for Christian faith.

The first new work was by Eduard König who offered a polemic against the history of religions approach that had derailed serious work in Old Testament theology for several decades.[26] König objected to the evolutionary hypotheses that informed the history of religions method, and he insisted on the importance of objective, special revelation as opposed to comparative religious analogies from outside the Bible. At the same time he rejected the common spiritualizing of the text practiced in some circles and asserted the need for historical-grammatical exegetical method.

Otto Eissfeldt (1887–1973) suggested that Old Testament theology must differ from the history of the religion of Israel in that the former has religious faith for its unique organ of knowledge. He maintained moreover that one's theology is determined by his creedal presuppositions. That is, what one brings to his task of doing theology will affect the theological conclusions he reaches. To Eissfeldt, history is an object of knowledge, revelation an object of faith. The impact of Barthianism is quite apparent here.

---

[26] Eduard König, *Theologie des Alten Testaments Kritisch und vergleichend dargestellt* (Stuttgart: C. Belser, 1922).

Arguably the greatest biblical theologian of the twentieth century was Walther Eichrodt (1890–1978) whose major work first appeared in German in 1933.[27] Eichrodt defended the basic unity of thought of Old Testament religion throughout its history of development and contrary to Eissfeldt saw no need to separate faith from history. He maintained that the method of Old Testament theology must be empirical-historical and yet insisted that it cannot be done without consideration of the New Testament. As for a center or organizing principle, he proposed that the Old Testament revolved around the idea of covenant, the rubrics of which are a national God who reveals himself as the God of the world and of individuals. In developing this center, Eichrodt suggested a cross-section (i.e., synchronic) approach that lays bare the inner structure of the Old Testament religion.

Two other important theologians in the period between the World Wars were Ernst Sellin (1867–1945) and Ludwig Köhler (1880–1956).[28] Sellin attempted to bridge the gap between the history of the religion of Israel and Old Testament theology by building theology on a platform of history. In this respect he was very much an heir of the method espoused by Gustave Oehler in the nineteenth century. Sellin centered his work on the holiness of God and said that the Christian theologian could write an Old Testament theology only from the standpoint of the gospel. Köhler viewed the theme of the Old Testament as God's lordship and interpreted the Old Testament through the lenses of a Christian hermeneutic.

Following World War II, with all its jarring sociopolitical upheavals and call to serious theological introspection, the "history of Israel's religion school" came nearly to an end in favor of a theology that took the unity of divine revelation seriously and, for the most part, located its fulfillment in Christ and the New Testament. O. J. Baab (1896–1958), an American, reestablished Old Testament theology as a discipline entirely separate from the *religionsgeshichtliche* approach.[29] He saw the task of the theologian to be that of expounding the religious consciousness of Israel, which was centered in a unique and controlling experience of

---

[27] Walther Eichrodt, *Theology of the Old Testament,* 2 vols (Philadelphia: Westminster, 1961, 1967).

[28] For these, see Hayes and Prussner, *Old Testament Theology,* 184–86 and 186–87 respectively.

[29] Otto Baab, *The Theology of the Old Testament* (Nashville: Abingdon, 1949).

God. Historical continuity, to Baab, was the unifying principle in Old Testament theology. He maintained the independence of Old Testament theology from the New Testament and yet argued that Old Testament theology can be done properly only by a Christian.

Otto Proksch (1874–1947) wrote that Old Testament theology must be a "theology of history" which finds its fulfillment in Christ—"All theology is Christology."[30] Like Baab he asserted that theology can be done only by persons of (Christian) faith. The "history of religions" aspect is important, he says, but it must be subordinated to theology *per se*. It is important only as a base upon which to develop logical and systematic thought. T. C. Vriezen (1899–1981)[31] rejected the history of religions approach altogether because to him the proper concern of a theology of the Old Testament is the canonical Old Testament itself and not the hypothetical and imaginatively reconstructed development of Israel's religion. The French scholar Edmond Jacob proposed that the subject matter of theology is God and not institutions; Christology and not theory.[32]

Comparable to Eichrodt in his stature and influence is Gerhard von Rad (1901–1971). In opposition to Eichrodt, he resisted the so-called "crosscut" approach, advocating rather what may be called the "longitudinal" or "diachronic" method.[33] To von Rad, the concern of the theologian is not what really happened in history but Israel's understanding, interpretation, and proclamation of what happened. The two kinds of history need not necessarily coincide. At the heart of von Rad's thought is the idea that the Hexateuch (the Pentateuch plus Joshua) is in effect a cultic confession that can be reduced to brief creedal assertions that God, by a series of saving acts, had delivered his people and given them a land. Various covenant themes (such as the Sinai Revelation), patriarchal promises, and the primeval history (Gen. 1–11) were added later to support the creed at the core of the Hexateuchal tradition. A fair assessment of his work is that von Rad has produced in actuality a history of traditions rather than

---

[30] Otto Proksch, *Theologie des Alten Testament* (Gutersloh: C. Bertelsmann, 1950), 1.

[31] T. C. Vriezen, *An Outline of Old Testament Theology* (Oxford: Basil Blackwood, 1958).

[32] Edmond Jacob, *Theology of the Old Testament* (New York: Harper & Row, 1958).

[33] Gerhard von Rad, *Old Testament Theology*, 2 vols., trans. by D. M. G. Stalker (New York: Harper & Row, 1962).

a theology in the usual sense and that he is extremely skeptical about the history upon which the traditions are based.

Any survey of important twentieth-century biblical theologies would be remiss if it failed to include the work of the great Princeton scholar Geerhardus Vos, a work that has profoundly influenced the thinking of the present writer.[34] The genius of Vos's approach was his recognition of the organic nature of the revelation of God as he disclosed his kingdom purposes throughout history. Vos takes the Old Testament construal of history seriously and, like Oehler before him, sees it as the vehicle by means of which the saving message can be carried forward from creation through to the eschaton.

Finally, it will be helpful to look briefly at some contemporary theologians, not only to be able to appreciate their contributions but to provide a backdrop by which to judge the need for the present work. Unfortunately, the review here must be extremely selective both because of space considerations and the plethora of theological literature that has been generated in the last twenty-five years or so.

Walter C. Kaiser Jr., in his seminal work on Old Testament theology, centers his attention around the theme of promise, one he describes as "textually derived."[35] He traces this theme throughout the biblical epochs from the prepatriarchal to the postexilic periods. His method clearly takes the Old Testament's witness to its own historical development at face value and does not base it on some reconstruction of Israel's history derived from historical-critical hypotheses. As an evangelical, Kaiser is sensitive to the fact that Old Testament theology cannot be done without consideration of the New Testament, but he is also insistent that New Testament revelation must not be read back into the Old Testament in such a way as to distort the unique message of the Old Testament itself.

Elmer A. Martens organizes his theology around the concept of a grid for the Old Testament message as articulated in Exodus 5:22–6:8.[36] Like Kaiser, he traces this design historically throughout the Old Testament, finding in each era four elements: salvation, covenant community,

---

[34] Geerhardus Vos, *Biblical Theology: Old and New Testaments* (Grand Rapids: Eerdmans, 1948).

[35] Walter C. Kaiser Jr., *Toward an Old Testament Theology* (Grand Rapids: Zondervan, 1978), 33.

[36] Elmer A. Martens, *God's Design* (Grand Rapids: Baker, 1981).

knowledge of God, and land. His evangelical faith also propels him toward Christ and the gospel, so he sees in the New Testament (specifically in Matthew and Romans) the same pattern of divine design as in the Old Testament.

The theology closest in scope and method to the one being undertaken here is by the Australian evangelical William J. Dumbrell. His most important work on the subject, *Covenant and Creation,* organizes his theology around the creation mandate of Genesis 1:26–28, a mandate that, despite its difficulty of implementation because of mankind's sin and fall, continues in force and will do so until the great consummation of God's kingdom purposes at the end of the age.[37] It is a treatment which, though limited to the Old Testament, casts an eye forward to a fulfillment in the atoning, redemptive work of Jesus Christ.

One of the most significant and influential theological thinkers at the end of the twentieth century is Brevard S. Childs. His two major works, *Old Testament Theology in a Canonical Context*[38] and *Biblical Theology of the Old and New Testaments,*[39] make the case for a diachronic theology that takes as its raw material the Hebrew canon, and only that, as it left the hands of the final redactors of the sacred text. As can be seen from the title of the second volume, Childs is convinced that biblical theology can be done only by including the New Testament with the Old. In describing its task, he says that biblical theology must "explore the relation between these two witnesses [the Old Testament and New Testament], whereas the task of Old Testament theology is to reflect theologically on only the one portion of the Christian canon, but as Christian scripture."[40] This helpful distinction will inform to a great extent our own efforts to do a theology of the Old Testament alone.

Our brief history of the biblical theology movement comes to an end with a succinct overview of the creative and provocative theological

---

[37] William J. Dumbrell, *Covenant and Creation. A Theology of Old Testament Covenants* (Nashville: Thomas Nelson, 1984). Another approach similar to our own is Stephen G. Dempster, *Dominion and Dynasty: A Theology of the Hebrew Bible* (Downers Grove, Ill.: InterVarsity, 2003).

[38] Brevard S. Childs, *Old Testament Theology in a Canonical Context* (Philadelphia: Fortress, 1985).

[39] Brevard S. Childs, *Biblical Theology of the Old and New Testaments* (Minneapolis: Fortress, 1993). See also Sailhamer, *Introduction to Old Testament Theology.*

[40] Childs, *Old Testament Theology in a Canonical Context,* 9.

insights of Walter Brueggemann, especially as articulated in his *magnum opus, Theology of the Old Testament.*[41] Brueggemann erects a forensic model in which Yahweh, in a sense, is on trial and the Old Testament is a transcript of the court proceedings. These begin with Israel's core testimony in which Yahweh is described by his various attributes and characteristics. Then follows a countertestimony that appears to discount some of these positive features or at least raises questions about them. Israel, though troubled about certain issues relative to the affirmative side of the testimony, comes alongside Yahweh as a partner, bearing witness, as it were, to his integrity. Brueggemann concludes his theology proper by outlining the means by which Yahweh bears testimony to himself—through Torah, the monarchy, the prophets, the cult, and the sages.

The most helpful part of Brueggemann's endeavor is his bringing to light the dilemma posed to and by classical theology as to the negative or dark side of God and his dealings with his creatures. This is particularly the case in the wisdom literature and in many of the psalms. To see these writings as oftentimes a questioning of the justice and even the character of God, while yet remaining inspired revelation, is of immense theological value.

Defense of a New Biblical Theology

The previous historical survey of the biblical theology movement, though overly brief, is sufficient to show how prolific its contributors have been, especially since the 1970s. This gives rise to a reasonable question, namely, how can a new work in this area be justified? What can another publication add to the already overwhelming production of theological literature that will avoid mere replication on the one hand and make a significant contribution on the other?

Every work of an author—like that of a composer, an artist, or a sculptor—has a *Sitz im Leben,* a setting or matrix that has generated interest in the subject and impelled that interest to take formal shape. Some productions can be done early in one's life and career; others take much experience and many years of reflection before the author (or artist

[41] Walter Brueggemann, *Theology of the Old Testament* (Minneapolis: Fortress, 1997).

or composer) has sufficient skill and temerity to unburden himself of whatever has preoccupied his thoughts throughout the years.

An Old Testament theology is such an undertaking because by its very substance and nature it presupposes a range of scholarly disciplines that can be mastered in even minimal ways only after many years of careful attention. It is unthinkable that a theologian should address the task without competence in the language(s) of the original text and with little or no knowledge of the historical, cultural, and religious world of the Bible. Add to this a sensitivity to the literary qualities of the written Word and the exegetical and hermeneutical skills necessary to comprehend and expound its message. This is to say nothing of the need to have basic control of New Testament scholarship and to recognize above all the importance of dependence on the Spirit of God who, after all, inspired the sacred text in the first place.

Therefore, after three decades of reading deeply the relevant literature and teaching the subject of Old Testament theology at the graduate level, the time seems right to offer this as yet another attempt to come to grips with the important and admittedly elusive subject matter addressed by this book. In addition to this *apologia,* the following rationale may also clarify the author's impetus and motivation.

Until the publication of Walter Kaiser's work in 1978, the field of Old Testament theology had been dominated for the previous century largely by scholarship that held to either a totally dismissive view of Scripture as the inspired and authoritative Word of God or, at best, a position of moderate criticism that acknowledged the Bible's revelatory character in some respects while adhering to a historical-critical methodology that vitiated the Old Testament of any "face value," genuine historicity or integrity of attributed authorship and unity. Kaiser and a number of other evangelicals have weighed in since then but even so in comparatively small numbers. Clearly the need continues for a theology that embraces a high view of Scripture as well as sound methodology and a comprehensive, in-depth discussion.

An evangelical theology differs sharply from others in that it should at least take seriously the Bible's own claims as to its origins and nature and, along with that, confidence in its historical and cultural credibility, that is, the factual aspects of its testimony. As we have already suggested and shall demonstrate more at length, an Old Testament theology cannot be divorced from an Old Testament bibliology. How one understands the Bible as an artifact in itself will inevitably shape the theology based upon and derived from it. The present endeavor will thus make no pretense toward a tabula rasa approach that professes openness to all manner of opinions about the very character of the Bible. Like its evangelical predecessors it will be anchored to an authoritative text and by default distance itself from those works that eschew such a stance or at least make it seem unnecessary.

This being the case, why are existing evangelical theologies not adequate? Without entering into specifics at this point, we propose the following observations about publications of recent vintage:

1. Many of them, while not properly to be called "systematic" theologies, nevertheless embrace at least a form of systematizing that imposes on the text some kind of preconceived framework or grid. Some of these defend their grids as being derived from the text, but close analysis suggests that they verge dangerously close to a Procrustean bed in which the biblical materials are forced into a mold for which they were never intended.

2. Other theologies suffer from a center or organizing principle that is either so amorphous and general as to be of little practical value or so narrow as to be reductionistic to the point of inviting the grid suggested above. That is, they cannot account for all the diverse, multifarious strands of biblical revelation without bringing these strands, against their will, into a straitjacketed conformity. Or, even worse, they simply leave large parts of the canon out of the discussion precisely because they (the centers) cannot accommodate them. Some, recognizing the dilemma, have opted to have no center at all, an option which, though honest, seems to promote the notion that the Old Testament narrative has no plot and hence no thread of thought or objective that holds it together and provides its central story line. We hope to show how unlikely and unworkable that is (see "Statement of Presuppositions" below).

3. Many contemporary evangelical theologies are, in effect, theological surveys, summaries, or even outlines. They are unable or unwilling to invest the depth of treatment necessary to deal at all exhaustively with the vastness of the theological riches of the biblical revelation. This is not intended as a criticism, for all manner of constraints exist in undertaking

a project of this kind. Such inadequacies do, however, invite justification for a more synthetic examination and presentation.

4. Finally (and somewhat in line with point 1), a few recent theologies are so bound to either formal or informal creedal or confessional ecclesiastical traditions that they become in effect a subjective effort to shore up those traditions thus precluding the objectivity that is at the heart of authentic biblical theological method. In reality, of course, it is impossible to divest oneself of his or her ecclesiastical heritage and to be truly objective in dealing with the Old Testament data. There is no doubt that the present work will be charged with the same bias or precommitment, and fairly so. The effort must nevertheless be made to engage in the task with blinders on, as it were, so that the finished product can be judged to be biblical and not dogmatic.

The project undertaken here attempts to take seriously the following objectives in order to deliver it from either the onus of a preconceived, prepackaged enterprise or a legitimate accusation that it fails to address the tough questions of presupposition and methodology.

1. We must take the witness of the Old Testament text seriously, both in terms of its self-validating testimony as to its nature as divine revelation and its contents as inherently and designedly theological in character. This, indeed, is confessional, but as we shall argue next (see "Presuppositions"), such a stance is inescapable if theology is to be done at all.

2. Every effort is bent toward a proper biblical theological method, one sensitive to the very genius of the discipline itself as well as consciously distinct from what Gabler called dogmatic. We are certainly aware of how impossible it is to pursue this course rigidly and consistently, but we are equally convinced that the effort must be made.

3. The method will embody a commitment to the canonical model espoused by Childs and others (but with different critical assumptions) while being constantly informed by the principle of progressive revelation and historical development. In other words, we will be synchronic in the sense that the canon bears witness to Israel's last confession of her faith and self-understanding but diachronic in the sense of tracing the history of that revelation that culminated in its final, nonredactable form.

4. Finally, we will propose a theological center, one, we trust, narrow enough to be encapsulated into communicative propositional statements

and broad or comprehensive enough to account for the rich diversity of the Old Testament canon (see "Theological Method" below). How or if that succeeds is something that must be demonstrated and not merely asserted.

Statement of Presuppositions

To *presuppose* is, *inter alia,* "to require as an antecedent in logic or fact,"[42] so a presupposition is the required antecedent that makes logical development possible. Unfortunately, the term has come to mean the assertion of some *a priori* truth claim with little or no evidence to support it. One presupposes an idea only to have something to cling to absent any empirical or other confirmatory support. Then, so the argument goes, a whole system of belief is erected on the presupposed premise, a system sustainable only so long as the premise itself is correct.

In one respect this understanding of presuppositionalism is correct in that it proceeds from a rationally unproven and even unprovable hypothesis. In another respect it is deficient in that it takes no account of the testability of the presupposition once it has been embraced and found to be validated (or invalidated). As applied to theology, the discipline from beginning to end is syllogistically driven, for by definition *theology* is the "study of God." If there is no God (major premise) and theology devotes itself to the study of God (minor premise), then there is no theology (conclusion). Put another way, if theology is truly a legitimate exercise (major premise) and theology is the study of God (minor premise), then God must exist (conclusion).

Some will find this logically and philosophically unsophisticated, but it illustrates the process by which presuppositionalism must be an integral element of doing theology. We should not apologize for presupposing the very truths that theology is supposed to demonstrate, but neither should we assert presuppositions with no attempt to validate their assertions.

Two fundamental presuppositions, each with two opposite vantage points, undergird Old Testament theology: (1) God exists (or does not exist), and (2) God has revealed himself (or has not done so). A corollary to

---

[42] *Merriam-Webster's Collegiate Dictionary,* 11th ed. (Springfield, Mass.: Merriam-Webster, 2003), 984.

this second claim—one more specific and derivative—is held tenaciously by evangelical faith, namely, that God has revealed himself propositionally in Scripture as well as in nature or in the mere spirit or essence of the biblical message. These antipodal presuppositions will obviously dictate not only the description of a given theology but, more important, its authority. If one assumes there is no God, then Old Testament theology becomes only a history of Israel's religion. If there is no divine self-disclosure, then Old Testament theology becomes a testimony of ancient Israel as to what it believed about God and not what God believed about Israel and all other matters. More pointedly, if revelation is not in words of human language, Old Testament theology becomes no more than an attempt by the prophets to interpret the meaning of history or of God's mighty acts or of nature and the like. On the other hand, to embrace the opposite of all these is no more presuppositional than to embrace these denials themselves and clearly is far more rewarding and worthy of study.

Our theology confesses that God is and that he has revealed himself in many ways, particularly in and through the Old Testament text. This admitted assumption carries with it a host of implications about the nature, character, and purposes of God, all of which are the subject matter of the first major section of this work. At the risk of redundancy, if there is no God, then talk of who he is and what he is like is, of course, nonsense. But even if he exists, all that can be known of him with certainty is little more than that—he exists—unless there be some authoritative elaboration as to what that means.

It is possible even without Scripture to conclude not only that God is but also that he manifests certain traits or at least effects in or through the created order and perhaps even in the flow of history. All these testify to him unless one is open to some kind of dualistic worldview that can countenance God's real existence but maintain at the same time that things and events appear and occur apart from divine participation. In that case, theology would be so stultified as to move to the vanishing point of atheism. With that possible exception aside, a theology that is open to a cause-and-effect nexus in which God is the causer and all else the effect can recognize revelation on at least some level and scale.

One could conclude without much doubt that God is powerful, all-wise, self-sufficient, arbitrary, ubiquitous, capricious, resourceful, and possesses a host of other attributes both positive and negative. This is what the world looks like to the eye of the man or woman who knows nothing of God except by how God has impacted his own life and the lives of countless others who have borne testimony to his dealings with them. This kind of theological reflection would have to be empirically based, dependent entirely on history and experience. If good things happen, God must at times be good. If bad things happen, he must at times be evil.

Lost in all this is any comprehension of the finer attributes, those that can explain (or explain away) the moral and ethical conundrums that attach to a God known only through the prism of the human condition and interpretable solely in the crucible of birth, suffering, and death. There may be intimations from time to time of mercy, grace, faithfulness, and even love; but these seem all too rare and in any case far outweighed by the darker side of God. And yet, without further word and a different Word, this is the best that natural revelation can do. What is needed is a voice or at least—and as it turns out, for the better—an infallible account of who God really is (his essence), how he displays himself (his character), and what he intends for all creation and, more particularly, for the human race (his purposes). Wrapped up in that are insights into the nature of God impossible to be known with confidence apart from his own unveiling of himself. We can know him in the written Word and marvel at his unspeakable love and grace that, despite appearances to the contrary as seen in mere experience, become, if not fully comprehensible, at least endurable and with the promise of ultimate vindication.

Thus, the second great presupposition is that the Bible is the written Word of God through which he reveals himself and his attributes and purposes in ways indiscernible otherwise. This is an assertion of Scripture itself, of course, and one, like any other assertion, that can be either received as true or denied as special pleading (cf. 2 Tim. 3:15–17; 2 Pet. 1:20–21). How one perceives the Bible in this respect will determine not only how God himself is perceived but also how all of reality is to be understood. If the Bible contains only a witness to God in some vague or mystical sense, then the burden is on the reader to ferret out not only the kernel of truth that may be embedded there but its meaning as well. Worse still, if the Bible is in no sense revelatory but merely the religious reflections of an ancient Semitic tribal people, it hardly deserves serious theological inquiry. Like the great religious texts of the Egyptians, Mesopotamians, and Hittites, it may be of interest to students of comparative religion; but it can hardly qualify as authoritative for faith and life.

Attendant to the matter of the Bible's essential nature is the question of its authority, especially the authority of the Old Testament as it relates to the church. This will be fully addressed in part 5 of this theology, but for now it will be helpful to give it brief consideration as a presuppositional issue. Opinions on the matter have ranged all the way from extreme Reformed positions that consider the Old Testament to be the essential Word of God to which the New Testament serves as a commentary[43] to Marcionitic denials of the Old Testament as Scripture in light of the advent of the New Testament.[44] The working principle of our own effort here is that the whole Bible—both Testaments—is fully the Word of God and fully authoritative for Christian faith and practice. This is not to say, of course, that every part of the Old Testament is equally relevant to the life of the church in its originally intended meaning and application. By the same token, the principles derivative from all Old Testament texts without exception continue to remain binding and are necessary to the full understanding of divine revelation. That is to say, they can and must be "theologized" so that they can yield the fruit the divine Author intended to convey from the outset.

A logical and important corollary to the proposition that the Old Testament is authoritative revelation is the assertion that all it has to say about history is to be accepted as factual, assuming, of course, that it intends by form and declaration to be taken as historical narrative.[45] There obviously are passages which, while referring to historical events, are couched in highly poetic or figurative terms and therefore are not to

---

[43] Thus, e. g., A. A. van Ruler, *The Christian Church and the Old Testament* (Grand Rapids: Eerdmans, 1971).

[44] Rudolph Bultmann, "Prophecy and Fulfillment," *Essays in Old Testament Hermeneutics,* ed. Claus Westermann (Richmond: John Knox, 1963), 50–75.

[45] See Eugene H. Merrill, "Old Testament History: A Theological Perspective," *A Guide to Old Testament Theology and Exegesis,* ed. Willem A. VanGemeren (Grand Rapids: Zondervan, 1999), 65–82. See also Ferdinand Deist, "The Problem of History in Old Testament Theology," *OTWSA* 24 (1981): 23–39; John Goldingay, "'That You May Know That Yahweh Is God': A Study in the Relationship between Theology and Historical Truth in the Old Testament," *TynB* 23 (1972): 58–93.

be read as straightforward historiography. But the point remains that even these presuppose genuine historical events as their point of departure and not myth, saga, legend, or some other non- or even quasi-historical records. At the same time it is important to stress that the Old Testament is not fundamentally a work of history. At best it is a *Heilsgeschichte* or sacred history, to employ theological terms. It is not designed to provide a history of the world or even an objective history of Israel. Rather, its purpose is to narrate the dealings of the Lord with the world at large but through the prism of his chosen people Israel. Only what contributes to this narrative of ultimate salvation is considered pertinent and therefore included in the record.

Such a narrowing of the definition of Old Testament history should not be construed to mean that it can and does accommodate historical error or misinformation. Biased history need not be errant history. It only need be history that is selective in its subject matter, tendentious in its presentation, and pedagogical in its intent. The Old Testament reveals all that is necessary for one to know who God is and to understand his grand design for creation. It is history, indeed, but history that must be theologically interpreted if it is to communicate in a holistic and integrated manner the underlying message it intends to convey.

From another angle, the reason for an insistence on the historical integrity of the Old Testament is that a large part of the content of its theology is its interpretation of the meaning of historical events. Events did not occur and are not included in the record merely as random acts. They are part and parcel of the outworkings of a sovereign God who does all things ultimately as part of a grand design. But events are only that, brute facts that by themselves convey little or no meaning. They must be accompanied by a word of clarification, one that sets events in their contexts and elicits from them meanings that contribute to the overall biblical message.[46] Though some theologians propose that sacred history need not be based on authentic historical events but only on ancient Israel's perceptions of historical reality,[47] it is epistemologically and rationally absurd to suppose that interpretation of nonexistent acts

[46] For a critique of historical positivism that denigrates the need for contextual interpretation of facts, see Collingwood, *The Idea of History,* 126–33.

[47] Thus, e. g., von Rad, *Old Testament Theology,* vol. 1, 195–215.

can have theological power and validity. We will insist here that history as revealed in the Old Testament has at least two heuristic purposes: (1) It provides a time line against which the progress of divine revelation can be plotted, and (2) it supplies instances of events which, with the interpreting word, contribute to a fuller understanding of the nature of the Lord and of his workings among mankind.

A third presupposition informing this work is that the revelation of God in Scripture is coherent and telic; that is, it is unified around a central core idea and moves that idea forward to a completion or at least an anticipated completion. This core idea is variously designated as a center, a *Mitte,* an organizing principle, and the like. We choose the term *center,* recognizing at the same time that the word is freighted with difficulty as the ensuing theological exposition will make clear. Regardless of technical terminology, the main point is that if the Old Testament is indeed fundamentally a massive narrative (albeit a theological one) describing God, his creation, and his purposes, it follows that there must be a plot, a story line that along with numerous subplots guide the reader through the complicated maze of the revealed Word. This plot can also be called the center, for it is the pole around which and in the light of which the narrative communicates truth.

Most theologians who subscribe to a center (and many do not) identify it as a concept (e.g., covenant), an abstraction (e.g., God's holiness), or a confession or assertion ("I am Yahweh").[48] Others build their approach around a book (e.g., Deuteronomy) or even a single passage (e.g., Exod. 5:22–6:8). We ourselves have selected such a passage, namely, Genesis 1:26–28, defense for which will be elaborated in detail in our theological exposition. As critics of a "center centered" approach have noted repeatedly, centers often fail to be narrow enough to avoid tautology (e.g., God is the center of theology) or broad enough to incorporate all the multitudinous variety of the biblical texts and teachings. These criticisms are well taken, and we ourselves must and will proceed cautiously in advocating the particular core testimony that we have deemed to be most suitable.

---

[48] For the difficulties in this area, see Gerhard F. Hasel, "The Problem of the Center in the OT Theology Debate," *ZAW* 86 (1974): 65–82.

Theological Method

As much as one might like to think of theology as an abstraction or at best an intellectual and spiritual activity fraught with subjectivity, theology, like any other field of study, can and must be approached and carried out by a rigorous methodology.[49] Otherwise, its pursuit becomes *ad hoc* and undisciplined, reaching conclusions without rhyme or reason and with no just claim to credibility to say nothing of authority. This is not to say that a preconceived template, even methodological, is to be forced upon the theological enterprise; for theology is refractory, refusing to conform to agendas that are brought to it no matter how sound they might appear to be in principle. What is needed is a method of doing theology that is cognizant of the complexity of the material of the biblical text while acceding to the demand that it at least be attempted and that the attempt be in line with sound principles of investigation and analysis.

To speak of doing Old Testament theology begs the question raised already, what is the Old Testament? That is, what is the body of literature that constitutes the Old Testament? These questions have to do with canon, the collection of sacred texts deemed by the consensus of the community responsible for them to be divinely originated and therefore authoritative for faith and practice.[50] There is no need here for a detailed discussion of the content, extent, and order of the various ancient Hebrew and Greek canons, all of which has been done many times. Suffice here just to lay out the major issues as they affect theological method.[51]

The Hebrew (Masoretic) canon consists of twenty-two (or twenty-four) books divided into three major sections—Torah (the Pentateuch), Nebi'im (the Former Prophets [historical books] and Latter Prophets [the writing prophets]), and Kethubim (the Writings, i.e., poetry and wisdom). From the time of the earliest written compilation of these books,

---

[49] A. A. Anderson, "Old Testament Theology and Its Methods," *Promise and Fulfillment: Essays Presented to S. H. Hooke,* ed. F. F. Bruce (Edinburgh: T. & T. Clark, 1963), 7–19; J. J. Burden, "Methods of Old Testament Theology: Past, Present and Future," *ThEv* 10 (1977): 14–33; Ben C. Ollenburger, "Old Testament Theology: A Discourse on Method," *Biblical Theology: Problems and Perspectives,* ed. Steven J. Kraftchick, Charles D. Myers Jr., and Ben C. Ollenburger (Nashville: Abingdon, 1995), 81–103.

[50] See pp. 2–3, for a preliminary discussion of the matter.

[51] See Ellis, *The Old Testament in Early Christianity,* p. 3. The definitive treatment of canon now is Roger Beckwith, *The Old Testament Canon of the New Testament Church* (Grand Rapids: Eerdmans, 1985).

they have remained in a consistent order with few variations. With the translation of the Hebrew Bible into Greek (the Septuagint), however, the order of the books underwent a number of changes; and, in addition, other books were added (the Apocrypha), increasing the total at last to forty-six in the Roman Catholic Bible, seven more than in the Protestant canon. The thirty-nine of Protestantism are the same as the twenty-two of the Hebrew Bible, the latter being fewer because they join together books considered separate in the Greek and English Bibles.

Protestant scholars agree as to the content and extent of the canon; it is coterminous with the Hebrew collection. Catholics differ, of course, because of their commitment to the Greek and Latin traditions. What is common to all is the question of whether the Jewish tripartite division is sacrosanct and whether the order of the books between and within these divisions is also something to be emulated. These are not trifling matters, for they affect the way theology is to be done.

Two options present themselves. For lack of a better term, the first may be called the canonical approach, meaning that theological discourse should be sensitive to the ancient (or perhaps modern) canonical sequence of the inspired books and adhere to that sequence in the development of the theology. The question arises, of course, as to which canon one will adopt, the Hebrew or those inspired by the Septuagint such as all modern English versions. The other option is to proceed historically, that is, to locate the various books in their historical settings, date them as accurately as possible, and structure the theology in a diachronic fashion in accord with historical sequence. This has the benefit of accommodating the principle of progressive revelation. If God did indeed reveal himself in increasingly clear and complete ways from one age to the next, it is apparent that the books that record this revelation should be arranged chronologically so as to be able to trace it as it unfolded. The major problem with this—and it is not to be dismissed as trivial—is that not all the books can be dated, nor is it possible always to know which preceded which. And the problem persists within books, especially in Psalms and in the wisdom literature which are anthological in nature and frequently betray a singular lack of interest in chronological priority.

We propose that the best path through this conundrum of conflicting methods is the one we have chosen to adopt, namely, to pay serious attention to the canonical order, especially in the Hebrew version (which, after all, reflects ancient and perhaps even authoritative tradition), while attempting to adhere to the diachronic movement of the tradition so as to be respectful to the vitally important principle of progressive revelation.

Specifically we begin with the Pentateuch as it stands with its internal and external attestation of Mosaic authorship. A case can be made that Genesis was not the earliest of the Mosaic compositions; but canonical considerations should override questions of chronological priority, at least in this case, for reasons to be developed later. The Former Prophets—those known in other, non-Jewish circles as the historical books excluding Ezra-Nehemiah and Chronicles—will be traced through in their literary order which, in their case, is essentially identical to their chronological order. The Latter Prophets—Isaiah, Jeremiah, Ezekiel, and The Twelve—will receive attention in generally that order though clearly the minor prophets (i.e., The Twelve) in some cases precede Isaiah and follow Ezekiel historically. They will therefore be dealt with in chronological, not canonical sequence, in an attempt to give due consideration to the possibility of the dependence of the various prophets on antecedent revelation.

The same integrative approach will be taken with the Psalms and wisdom books. They were written at various times over the span of nearly a millennium though much of the production of this kind of material was clustered around the time of the United Monarchy in the tenth century B.C. Those psalms, proverbs, and other texts that give clues as to their authorship and dating can, of course, be studied in and as part of their context. Many, however, provide no such information and consequently cannot be viewed in terms of their contribution to the progress of revelation. Such anomalies suggest that the diachronic method, while to be preferred as an ideal, cannot be applied across the board. For these reasons it seems best to follow the canonical-historical approach suggested above.

Biblical theology originated as a method that if not in conflict with dogmatic (or systematic) theology was at least complementary to it. Gabler and his school attempted to point out the deficiencies of an approach that in his view was much too beholden to philosophy and creedalism and much too insensitive to the theology of the Old Testament texts themselves. But it is important also to remember that he saw biblical theology as a discipline leading to systematic theology without which it would lack order and structure.

Ideally biblical theology should yield its own structures and categories, but careful reading of the Old Testament makes crystal clear that this is far from the case. Nowhere is the Pentateuch, for example, organized systematically in its presentation of doctrine; for it, like the rest of the Old Testament for the most part, is narrative. It was not designed to provide an orderly account of theological propositions. Furthermore, the rest of the Old Testament shows no interest in systematizing the Pentateuch, to say nothing of developing its own internal logical and theological framework. Even the Psalms and wisdom books, where one might expect some kind of structuring of this kind, reveal little if any signs of deliberate organization of their theological assertions into anything resembling systematic theology.

This being the case, it might again seem that the best method of addressing the issue of Old Testament theology is to trace the flow of the biblical material *seriatim,* verse by verse and chapter by chapter, that is, from beginning to end, making theological observations along the way. This, in fact, is the model adopted by at least a few scholars, but in our view this is not theology but commentary. It lacks structure, direction, and coherence and in the final analysis yields little understanding of the totality of biblical teaching, an understanding that must be gained largely by the comparison and integration of texts to texts. In other words, biblical theology *must* be synthesized and systematized.

Thus, we will address (1) God and his person and work; (2) mankind as the image of God and implementer of his eternal purposes; and (3) the kingdom, that is, the arena in which the God and man cooperative program is enacted.

We admit at the outset that this has clear overtones of a structuring that some might call *systematic* theology. However, even to begin to think and express oneself in theological terms is to accede to the epistemological demands essential to the interpersonal communication of the abstract ideas that are at the heart of the theological enterprise. In other words, even biblical theology must be put into theological categories to some degree or other, a fact that all biblical theologians at least tacitly admit. The goal to which the theologian should aspire is to let the Bible yield its own categories and not to import them to the Bible from the outside.

A final methodological consideration also reverts back to an issue previously raised and that is the distinction between biblical theology and Old Testament theology. Old Testament theology obviously is limited to the Old Testament canon, and the term therefore is more descriptive of content than method. The term *biblical theology,* on the other hand, conjures up the idea of method and, in addition, invites attention to the New Testament as well since the New Testament, to the Christian at least, is also part of the Bible. Speaking practically, can a Christian do Old Testament theology by following a biblical theological method without at the same time giving due consideration to the New Testament?[52] Here we must choose our terms most carefully. The intent in this work is to provide only an Old Testament theology, not one of the whole Bible. But the approach will be biblical; i.e., it will pursue the method of biblical theology. Thus, content will create constraints upon the material to be covered, but method will break those constraints to the extent that the Christian theologian must recognize that his work cannot end at the end of the Old Testament canon, for the Old Testament itself is open to something beyond itself, namely, the New Testament.

This raises the important question as to whether biblical theology is possible at all to the Christian without the inclusion of the New Testament. God, after all, is the Author of the whole; and the Old Testament, though constituting more than three-fourths of the inspired canon, is an unfinished narrative without the New Testament climactic events that provide the Old Testament its ultimate meaning.[53] The answer may appear to be a quibbling no and thus the decision to call our work *Old Testament Theology.* However, by labeling it such we are not trying to be evasive of this extremely important matter of the relationship of the Testaments

---

[52] For this important issue, see Francis Watson, *Text and Truth: Redefining Biblical Theology* (Grand Rapids: Eerdmans, 1997), 276–320; Wolfhart Pannenberg, "Problems in a Theology of (Only) the Old Testament," *Problems in Biblical Theology: Essays in Honor of Rolf Knierim,* ed. Henry T. C. Sun and Keith L. Eades (Grand Rapids: Eerdmans, 1997), 275–80.

[53] For the shape of a Jewish (non-New Testament) biblical theology, see Elliot N. Dorff and Louis E. Newman, ed. *Contemporary Jewish Theology: A Reader* (New York: Oxford University Press, 1999); Isaac Kalimi, "History of Israelite Religion or Old Testament Theology? Jewish Interest in Biblical Theology," *JSOT* 11 (1997): 100–23; Matitiahu Tsevat, "Theology of the Old Testament—a Jewish View," *HBT* 8 (1986): 33–50; Tikva Frymer-Kensky, "The Emergence of Jewish Biblical Theologies," *Jews, Christians, and the Theology of the Hebrew Scriptures,* ed. Alice Ogden Bellis and Joel S. Kaminsky (Atlanta: Society of Biblical Literature, 2000), 109–21.

and of the New Testament as God's final word on the theological truths first raised in the Old Testament. We are simply trying to be honest about the complexity of what we are doing and to make the best effort possible to present the theological message of the Old Testament as discrete from the New Testament and yet in constant debt to it.

This rather lengthy introduction is intended to guide the reader to a better understanding of the nature of Old Testament theology and the method to be followed in laying it bare so that its profound, life-changing truths can be better apprehended and applied. The work to follow can lay no claim to being the last word on the subject for the inexhaustible riches of God's revelation can never be fully and finally plumbed by any human endeavor. It is hoped, however, that it will follow in the train of worthy works that have preceded it and that, with them and others yet to see the light of day, it will make some modest contribution to the end that God may receive glory and the church may be edified.

PART ONE

GOD: HIS PERSON AND WORK

Chapter Two

The Autobiography of God

The term *theology* most broadly connotes "the study of God." More precisely, when applied to the Scriptures—especially the Old Testament—it is better understood as the story of God. Scholars have come to emphasize especially recently that the Old Testament is a massive narrative, one with a clearly discernible setting, plot, and cast of characters, chief among whom is God himself. He appears first, is the force behind and within the action, and has the last word. It is not inappropriate to go even so far as to consider the Old Testament a biography, a history of God in Old Testament times.[1] Or to be still more accurate, it is an autobiography; for it bears consistent testimony that God himself is not only the chief character in the story but its author as well.[2]

The Setting of the Narrative

According to biblical tradition, the earliest part of the Old Testament narrative, the Torah (i.e., Pentateuch), achieved its final form at the hand

[1] Thus the provocative title by Mark S. Smith, *The Early History of God: Yahweh and the Other Deities in Ancient Israel,* 2nd ed. (Grand Rapids: Eerdmans, 2002).

[2] Walter Brueggemann, *Theology of the Old Testament* (Minneapolis: Fortress, 1997), 66–71.

of Moses in the plains of Moab just north of the Dead Sea (Deut. 1:1–2). Quite clearly he inherited earlier documents or oral traditions, specifically those comprising the book of Genesis and the early chapters of Exodus, which he edited into their present form.[3] As for the remainder of the Pentateuch, how and when it was completed is unclear except in the case of Deuteronomy which is presented as a work of Moses undertaken and completed in a brief span of time near the end of his life (Deut. 1:1; cf. 32:44–48).

The significance of this for Old Testament theology is to make the point at the outset that the original purpose of the Torah was not to provide to modern readers insight into creation or the flood or the other great turning points of prepatriarchal and patriarchal times but to address questions raised by Israel itself concerning its (then) present situation, what lay ahead, and, most important, its historical roots. Who are we? Why are we here? What purpose does God have in mind for us? How do we relate to the nations around us and, indeed, to the whole created order? Most fundamental of all were questions about the nature, the character, the works, and the purposes of God, especially as he made himself known to Israel.

Thus, the story of God is first of all the story of his relationship with Israel.[4] A theology that fails to acknowledge this is one that is insensitive to the Bible's own insistent testimony. Clearly God had revealed himself throughout the ages of antiquity but until the climactic event of the Moab convocation had never led a human author to collect the scattered memories and texts, add to them new and fresh divine self-disclosures, synthesize them into a cohesive narrative, and put into writing the whole as the first stage of a thousand years of inscripturated revelation.

In order for Israel to have a fuller understanding of its role as a kingdom of priests and a holy nation, Moses had to transport them back to the beginning—the absolute beginning—to creation itself. According to the purpose and terms of the Sinaitic covenant, Israel was called to be an instrument to communicate to alienated humanity the message of

---

[3] Duane Garrett, *Rethinking Genesis* (Grand Rapids: Baker, 1991), 191–94; Allen P. Ross, *Creation & Blessing* (Grand Rapids: Baker, 1988), 69–74.

[4] Vriezen, among others, views relationship—or "communion," to use his terminology—as the leading motif of Old Testament theology. Th. C. Vriezen, *An Outline of Old Testament Theology* (Oxford: Basil Blackwell, 1958), 131.

God's reconciling and restorative grace (Exod. 19:4–6). This being the case, Israel must know about the world and the nations, especially the patriarchal beginnings of its own history with all the glorious promises that God first enunciated then. Most important, Israel must know more about the Creator—his being, his acts, his plans and purposes. Genesis reveals something of these, albeit in broad and sweeping ways and primarily in deeds as opposed to specific theological utterance. For that, the remainder of the Old Testament must be brought to bear. What follows here is a brief overview of the Genesis account with special attention to the nature and character of God, and then an elaboration on those themes throughout the canon, particularly in the book of Psalms and in the Wisdom literature. When those texts themselves are examined and mined later on for theological content, they will yield their own theological insights into these matters but from the unique angle their respective authors bring to the task.

The Genesis narrative begins with the succinct but majestic declaration that "in the beginning God created the heavens and the earth" (Gen. 1:1). It makes no attempt to clarify when and how this was done but only affirms that all that exists is the product of God's omnipotent hand. In this respect the account is unique among the cosmologies of the ancient Near Eastern world for they know nothing of an immediate creation as opposed to a creation that makes use of preexisting matter.[5] The Hebrew verb *bārā'*, while not inherently denotative of *creatio ex nihilo,* bears that meaning in all its occurrences in the Genesis account.[6]

Central to the creation narrative is its dominant character, God himself, denominated here as Elohim. More an epithet than a name, *Elohim* derives from a Hebrew (and general Semitic) root meaning "power." It is used most commonly in contexts where his transcendent apartness or otherness is in view as opposed to his immanence or closeness, a relationship better described by the name *Yahweh.* With the advent of the historical-critical method in the eighteenth century and its division of the Pentateuch into hypothetical sources, Genesis 1:1–2:4a came to be attributed to a source

---

[5] See, for example, Charles Doria and Harris Lenowitz, ed. *Origins: Creation Texts from the Ancient Mediterranean* (Garden City, N.Y.: Doubleday, 1976); Barbara Sproul, *Primal Myths: Creating the World* (San Francisco: Harper & Row, 1979).

[6] Genesis 1:1, 21, 27; 2:3; 5:1–2; cf. 6:7; Raymond C. Van Leeuwen, ברא, *NIDOTTE* 1:732. For further development of the term, see pp. 101–9.

that knew God as Elohim (the E source, later assigned to P, Priestly) and 2:4b–25, the creation of mankind, to J (for the German Jahveh). Ignored by the hypothesis is the theological consideration that the divine names reflect aspects of the nature and character of the same God, Elohim being appropriate when describing creation cosmologically and Yahweh when speaking of it anthropologically.[7]

In the ancient Near East names represented more than mere labels to distinguish one person from another. They were descriptive of the individual named, expressing in effect the person's very essence. For example, Abram (great father) was thus named because of his eminent place in the patriarchal line; but he became Abraham (father of a multitude) in line with his new role as the ancestor of an innumerable covenant people that would spring from his loins. Moses' name, according to popular etymology, reflected the fact that Pharaoh's daughter had drawn him forth (*māšâ*) from the water (though more accurately it derives from the Egyptian word *mesu,* "child").

The emphasis on the transcendent power of God in the creation narrative of Genesis 1:1–2:3 is clear from the fact that the name *Elohim* occurs thirty-two times in a span of only thirty-four verses. He merely speaks and things come into existence, but there is no communion with the things he creates, no sense of intimacy even when mankind itself appears (vv. 26–30). He speaks about them and even to them but with a magisterial distance that hardly admits of response. It is not as though God is unmoved by what he does and sees, however, for he assesses it as being good (vv. 4, 10, 12, 18, 21, 25) or even very good (v. 31), thus revealing already an aesthetic aspect to his nature.

The power of God as a dominant part of his nature is combined in Genesis 2:4–25 with a focus on his intense involvement in his creation, especially in the mandate he had laid upon mankind to "be fruitful, multiply, fill the earth, and subdue it" (Gen. 1:28). Man's dominion was derivative and was to be expressed at first as a kind of trial run in which he would be assigned the management of the affairs of a mere garden. But he must always remember that he was in service to the Regent of the whole universe. The challenge to human hegemony came in the form of a reversal

[7] Umberto Cassuto, *The Documentary Hypothesis,* trans. by Israel Abrahams (Jerusalem: Magnes Press, 1961), 32–33.

of sovereignty spheres. An animal (in later revelation seen to be Satan; Rev. 20:2) questioned the limited role of man and woman, suggesting that God was jealous for undisputed sovereignty, guarding it selfishly against mankind. The first pair then disputed God's lordship by an act of rebellion against him, eating of the forbidden fruit. The result was man's fall, the serpent's subjugation, and man's banishment from the garden, the place which he had proved unable to govern as God's vice-regent.

Throughout the fall narrative of Genesis 3, a fundamental trait of God's identity—his covenant sovereignty—is underscored by the regular use of the name *Lord God* (vv. 1, 8–9, 13–14, 21–23). The notable exception is in verses 1–5 where the snake speaks, and there only the epithet *Elohim* occurs. The reason is apparent: though God's power as Creator must be acknowledged on empirical grounds alone, his sovereignty was not; in fact, both mankind and the serpent implicitly denied it.[8] Man, assigned dominion over the animal world, submitted to an animal; and he himself, who was created to serve and worship God alone, refused to do so, claiming for himself a prerogative that had never been granted him in the first place. This episode describing the first attempt to undermine the sovereignty of God sets the tone for all subsequent human history, for history, in the final analysis, is reducible to a record of human hubris and sin, a condition redeemable only by God's own gracious interposition.

As we have already noted, the autobiography of God, only introduced in Genesis, continues throughout the Old Testament record. For ease of elaboration, we shall develop it from this point forward under the broad rubrics of: (1) the nature of God; (2) the character of God; (3) the revelation of God; (4) the works of God; (5) the purposes of God; and (6) the kingdom of God. Beginning with the earliest occurrences of each of these, they will receive attention canonically and historically with a view toward constructing a full-orbed picture of God that is informed as much as possible only by the evidence of the text itself.

The Nature of God

To justify the approach just articulated, a brief reiteration of procedure will be helpful. We have already proposed that proper biblical theological

[8] Gordon J. Wenham, *Genesis 1–15*, WBC 1 (Waco, Tex.: Word, 1987), 73.

method demands adherence to the principle of inductive assimilation of the theological data as they appear in the text. At the same time, the task of addressing specific theological *topoi* requires that these data first be located in the text(s) and then collectively categorized in order for systematic discussion to be carried out in a coherent manner. To address the specific matter at hand, the nature of God, facets of this aspect of divine revelation presuppose the existence of others and in turn provide the platform for still others. Ultimately, of course, this approach is confessedly subjective for the arrangement of the divine attributes into relationships of priority and/or dependence one upon the other arises from the theologian's own perception as to how such things ought to be done. In other words, a certain idiosyncratic schema is necessary in order for any theologian to present a coherent synthesis of the vast and varied data at hand in the text. The method adopted here will call the reader back over and over to the foundational Genesis (and other) passages that form the springboard for the development of the larger theological picture. It also anticipates future treatment of the same themes and issues as elements of later revelation. Thus, discussion of God's nature and character, for example, while introduced here preliminarily, finds fuller expression in the later canon, particularly (as we have noted previously) in the Psalms and wisdom literature. This inevitably results in a certain degree of repetition of texts and yet from different vantage points.

The Sovereignty of God

The first and perhaps grandest of the descriptions that characterize the God of the Old Testament in the Genesis record is that of his sovereignty. Upon this facet of his nature rest all subsequent descriptions of him and, in our understanding, the whole edifice of Old Testament theology. This is implicit in both his work as Creator ("In the beginning God," Gen. 1:1) and in the mandate he issued to mankind to have dominion over all things as God's own image (Gen. 1:26–28). Beyond the observations previously made on these and other passages that provide the platform for all subsequent biblical teaching on the matter[9] a number of other texts are also highly informative. Some are in the nature of anecdotes whereas

[9] See p. 39.

others are declarative and theologically intentional in their assertions that God is sovereign.

One of the first narratives describing an affront to divine sovereignty is the account of the tower of Babel (Gen. 11:1–9). That this is at the heart of the matter is clear from the observation that the whole earth spoke one language, that all were gathered in one place, and that the intent of the whole affair was to preclude at least this segment of humanity from being "scattered over the face of the whole earth" (v. 4). This directly contradicted the creation mandate to "fill the earth" (Gen. 1:28) and thus constituted a challenge to God's own lordship. The builders wished to make a name for themselves (v. 4) rather than to submit to the name already linked to his sovereignty (Gen. 4:26).

Beyond Genesis the record continues to sustain this idea. Long ages after the Babel fiasco, Pharaoh asserted his independence of God's kingship by arrogantly asking, "Who is the Lord that I should obey Him by letting Israel go?" (Exod. 5:2), whereupon the Lord reminded Moses that once the exodus had occurred the Egyptians would know that he is Lord (Exod. 7:5). Indeed, after an initial series of plagues, Pharaoh's own magicians were forced to concede that "this is the finger of God" (Exod. 8:19). Even Pharaoh at last conceded reluctantly that he had sinned against "the Lord your God" (Exod. 10:16), thus tacitly confessing his subservience to the God of Israel.

In the days of the judges, Gideon achieved a smashing victory over the invading Midianites and was rewarded by the people's request that he rule over them and establish a dynasty of kings after him (Judg. 8:22). He responded in the negative, asserting that "the Lord will rule over you" (v. 23). In a similar vein, after the Israelites demanded a king like that of all the neighboring nations, Samuel protested until the Lord gave him permission to grant them one, with the sober reminder that "they have not rejected you; they have rejected Me as their king" (1 Sam. 8:7).

Three hundred and fifty years later the Assyrians came against Judah with their vast armies, and the envoys of Sennacherib challenged Yahweh's sovereignty by boasting how no other gods had been able to withstand the great king. Hezekiah responded to this arrogant ploy in a prayer in which he addressed the Lord as the one "enthroned above the cherubim," "God—You alone—of all the kingdoms of the earth" (2 Kings 19:15). Later still, mighty Nebuchadnezzar of Babylon, having been humbled by the power of Israel's God, confessed that "[Yahweh's] kingdom is an eternal kingdom, and His dominion is from generation to generation" (Dan. 4:3; cf. 4:34, 37; 6:26–27).

The most potent expressions of God's sovereignty came from the pens of inspired poets who articulated in a normative way how important this facet of God's nature was to the Old Testament community of faith. These are collected most clearly and conveniently in the so-called "psalms of Yahweh's kingship" (Pss. 47, 93, 95–99). They will receive detailed analysis at a more appropriate point,[10] so for now we only draw attention to the fact that the notion of divine sovereignty that finds its roots in Genesis and other early texts remains a dominant one throughout the canonical testimony.

The Omnipotence of God

Concomitant with God's sovereignty—indeed, flowing from it—are a number of corollary characteristics naturally and necessarily adjunct to that central aspect of his being. First among these in the inspired record is his illimitable power, what theologians commonly call his omnipotence ("In the beginning God *created,*" Gen. 1:1). One might argue that omnipotence is inherent in deity, but the Old Testament provides no sustained apologetic in defense of such a theological deduction; rather, it offers evidence of God's power through his mighty acts.

As noted already, these begin with the creation narratives, specifically with the disarmingly simple declaration, "In the beginning God created the heavens and the earth" (Gen. 1:1). With just seven Hebrew words the whole universe is encompassed and is said to have come into existence from nothing. God alone preexisted everything else, and by his power he created it all except himself. Beyond all this he did so merely by speaking the word, for the word, as an extension of himself (and in the fullness of New Testament revelation, identified with his very person [John 1:14]),

[10] See pp. 570–75.

possessed unlimited energy.[11] God's omnipotence expressed in his work of creation is elaborated in Psalm 89 where the poet affirms, "The heavens are Yours; the earth also is Yours. The world and everything in it—You founded them. North and south—You created them. Tabor and Hermon shout for joy at Your name. You have a mighty arm; Your hand is powerful; Your right hand is lifted high" (Ps. 89:11–13). Psalm 104, speaking of the great creatures of the sea, observes that they exist only by God's pleasure; and should he remove his sustaining hand, they would perish. On the other hand, they are created when he sends forth his life-giving Spirit (Ps. 104:25–30; cf. Job 33:4; Ezek. 37:9).[12]

Isaiah, of all the prophets, had most to say on the matter of God's omnipotence as manifest in creation. In a series of polemical diatribes, he compared the impotence (and, in fact, the nonexistence) of the gods of the heathen with Yahweh, the great God of Israel. These polemical discourses are found particularly in Isaiah 40–55.[13] Having drawn attention to man-made images with all their signs of instability and decay, the prophet urged his hearers to look up to the heavens above and see the stars and planets. "Who created these?" he asked. "He brings out the starry host by number; He calls all of them by name. Because of His great power and strength, not one of them is missing" (Isa. 40:26). The answer, of course, is self-evident. God created all these things and by naming them claims sovereign control over them.[14] These words were directed not to the heathen but to God's own people who were in danger always of lapsing into paganism. They must understand in their times of need especially that he, the Creator, is the one who could and would come to their aid (Isa. 41:20).

In support of the servant of the Lord in the first servant song (Isa. 42:1–9), the Lord promised to be with him in his challenging mission of

---

[11] For the ancient Near Eastern notion of the word as "the medium of powers which effectively influence events," see Walther Eichrodt, *Theology of the Old Testament,* vol. 2, trans. by John Baker (Philadelphia: Westminster, 1967), 69–71.

[12] Patrick D. Miller, "The Poetry of Creation: Psalm 104," *The Way of the Lord* (Tübingen: Mohr Siebeck, 2004), 178–92.

[13] Eugene H. Merrill, "Isaiah 40–55 as Anti-Babylonian Polemic," *Grace Theological Journal* 8/1 (1987): 3–18.

[14] Thus Gerhard von Rad, *Genesis: A Commentary,* trans. by John H. Marks (London: SCM, 1961), 81; for a different interpretation see George W. Ramsey, "Is Name-Giving an Act of Domination in Genesis 2:23 and Elsewhere?" *CBQ* 50 (1988): 24–35.

being a light to the nations by appealing to his own omnipotent power as Creator. "This is what God the LORD says—who created the heavens and stretched them out, who spread out the earth and what comes from it, who gives breath to the people on it and life to those who walk on it—'I, the LORD, have called you for a righteous purpose, and I will hold you by your hand'" (Isa. 42:5–6a). Here the call of God to service is undergirded by the awesome power he displayed in the creation of the world.

In a somewhat different sense, God also created Israel, that is, made Israel a people that had previously not been one. To assure his people that he would be with them and deliver them in a kind of second exodus, the Lord enjoined them not to fear, for he is "the One who created you" (Isa. 43:1). They are therefore his chosen, special people, the objects of his grace and love. They, the ones called by his name, would return safely home from Babylonian exile and even beyond; for, he says, they are "created for My glory" (v. 7).

The ironic side of Israel's having been created by God was the folly of her challenging the Creator like a clay pot might challenge its maker (Isa. 45:9–10). To do so would be to contend with the Almighty, the omnipotent One, who not only created Israel but also the earth and people to live on it. In fact, his sovereignty would extend to the point of raising up one (namely, Cyrus) who would emancipate God's captive people and allow them to return to their homeland.[15] All of this divine power was predicated on God's omnipotence. He said of himself, "It was My hands that stretched out the heavens, and I commanded all their host" (Isa. 45:12). Creation thus provided the credibility to believe God for not only the present but the future as well.

God's power in and over creation was celebrated as well. Job attributed to him the ability to calm the sea and to crush the head of the great sea monster, perhaps a reference to the mythical beast of chaos that was overcome at creation.[16] The same motif occurs in Psalm 74:13

---

[15] For so-called "creation theology" in Isaiah 40–55, see William J. Dumbrell, *Covenant and Creation* (Nashville: Thomas Nelson, 1984), 190–92.

[16] Job 26:12; cf. Isaiah 27:1; Ezekiel 29:3–5; 32:1–2. For a sensible view of mythic language in the Genesis creation accounts and elsewhere, see Richard E. Averbeck, "Ancient Near Eastern Mythography as It Relates to Historiography in the Hebrew Bible: Genesis 3 and the Cosmic Battle," *The Future of Biblical Archaeology,* ed. James K. Hoffmeier and Alan Millard (Grand Rapids: Eerdmans, 2004), 328–56.

which, speaking of God, says, "You divided the sea by your strength; You smashed the heads of the sea monsters in the waters." Jeremiah exclaimed that "He made the earth by His power" (Jer. 10:12) and on the basis of this great display of his might was able to say, "Nothing is too difficult for You!" (Jer. 32:17).

Most commonly the power of God is described almost as an epithet, a feature of the essence of God that is endemic to his nature. This is particularly the case in the poetic literature. Job observed that God is mighty in strength, one who cannot be challenged (Job 9:4). He himself had experienced that awesome power, much to his dismay (Job 10:16; cf. 30:18). It is part of who God is, he confessed (12:13), a characteristic he wanted to communicate to his companions (27:11). Elihu added to Job's testimony that "God shows Himself exalted by His power. Who is a teacher like him?" (Job 36:22). So vast is his power, in fact, that it cannot be imagined (37:23).

David testified that he gazed upon God's power in the sanctuary, a reference no doubt to the *shekinah* glory of God's presence there (Ps. 63:2). The same association occurs in Psalm 68 where David entreated God to manifest his power as he had in the past so that when the kings of the earth came to pay tribute to him at the temple they might see him in his awesome display of glory (v. 28). Moreover, he concluded the psalm with an exhortation that his hearers should proclaim abroad the power of God, a power once more linked closely to his sanctuary (vv. 34–35). In this psalm the power of God is not said to act but only to be. That is, God not only has power to create and accomplish mighty deeds, but he is the epitome of power. It is of his essence.

The prophets, too, marveled at God's omnipotence in history and human life. Isaiah, employing the language of holy war, warned that "the LORD God comes with strength, and His power establishes His rule" (Isa. 40:10). In this context and in many others, God's power is a fearsome thing because it is used to effect his wrath and punishment. More often, however, it is a positive thing, an asset to those who are weak and who need supernatural assistance. In this same literary context, the prophet promised that "He [the Lord] gives strength to the weary and strengthens the powerless" (v. 29). The power here is unspecified for God is what the weak need and is not just the purveyor of what he alone can give.

Jeremiah reinforced this idea when he expostulated, "LORD, there is no one like You. You are great; Your name is great in power" (Jer. 10:6). That is, God is power, and power is part of what constitutes his nature. Daniel, having prayed for wisdom to interpret Nebuchadnezzar's dream, praised God when the answer came and, like Jeremiah, affirmed that "wisdom and power belong to Him" (Dan. 2:20). He then went on to praise him further for having granted him the power to interpret dreams (v. 23).

The Chronicler recorded a prayer of David who, following the collection of materials for the projected temple, extolled the Lord for his greatness, power, glory, victory, and majesty (1 Chron. 29:11). He then proclaimed that "riches and honor come from You, and You are the ruler of everything. In Your hand are power and might, and it is in Your hand to make great and to give strength to all" (v. 12). The point is that all human power is derivative of the power of God who is the embodiment of such resources. More than a hundred years later Jehoshaphat, on the eve of a battle against an overwhelming coalition of forces, prayed publicly and addressed the Lord as the One who is powerful and mighty, against whom "no one can stand" (2 Chron. 20:6). It is his character to be mighty and therefore to be able to overcome all the obstacles his people will face. An unnamed prophet said this to King Amaziah of Judah: "God will make you stumble before the enemy, for God has the power to help or to make one stumble" (2 Chron. 25:8).

As awe inspiring as was the mere conception of God as omnipotent, even more so perhaps was the expression of his power in his mighty acts.[17] These were done not only to produce some great work on behalf of his people but to manifest his glory so that they and the peoples of the earth might see them and offer him the praise worthy of him. This is epitomized, for example, in the plagues visited upon Egypt in the midst of which Yahweh said to Pharaoh, "I have let you live for this purpose: to show you My power and to make My name known in all the earth" (Exod. 9:16). God's power, then, was evidentiary, designed to lead to

[17] For a theology grounded in God's deeds rather than in mere proposition, see G. Ernest Wright, *God Who Acts: Biblical Theology as Recital* (London: SCM, 1952).

his own glory. Psalm 77 makes the same point: "You are the God who works wonders; You revealed Your strength among the peoples" (v. 14). David likewise exclaimed, "They will proclaim the power of Your awe-inspiring works, and I will declare Your greatness" (Ps. 145:6). And the Psalter closes with the command to "praise Him for His powerful acts; praise him for his abundant greatness" (Ps. 150:2).

The paradigm historical event of the Old Testament was the exodus of God's people from Egypt, a deliverance so stupendous that it was marked by an annual festival—Passover and Unleavened Bread—and served as a prototype of God's salvific acts in the future. To this day observant Judaism traces its national roots to the exodus and the Sinai covenant that immediately followed. Of all the attributes of God celebrated by the exodus, none is as prominent as his omnipotence. Against all odds Yahweh delivered a disorganized mob of frightened and confused slaves from the clutches of the world's mightiest nation, Dynasty Eighteen of Egypt, and through the sea at that! No wonder the narrator noted that "when Israel saw the great power that the LORD used against the Egyptians, the people feared the LORD and believed in Him and in His servant Moses" (Exod. 14:31). The Song of Moses, composed in the aftermath of the crossing of the Sea of Reeds, proclaims, "LORD, Your right hand is glorious in power. LORD, Your right hand shattered the enemy" (Exod. 15:6; cf. v. 21). Later on, Moses, reflecting back on the exodus in the face of God's threat to destroy Israel for its idolatry, reminded the Lord that Israel was his special possession, one redeemed "through Your greatness and brought out of Egypt with a strong hand" (Deut. 9:26; cf. v. 29).

The Psalms also theologize the historical event of the exodus, especially Psalm 78 which, in effect, is a confession of Israel's faith in the God who, through mighty acts, made them into a covenant nation.[18] The poet pledged about the community that "we must not hide [these truths] from their children, but must tell a future generation the praises of the LORD, His might, and the wonderful works He has performed" (v. 4). The special focus is on the exodus (v. 13) and on God's goodness

---

[18] Hans-Joachim Kraus suggests that "Psalm 78 celebrates the great deeds of Yahweh. It never tires of describing the wonders of the basic historical activity of God." *Psalms 60–150,* trans. by Hilton C. Oswald (Minneapolis: Fortress, 1993), 130.

in providing for the tribes in the wilderness of Sinai (v. 26). Alas, all too soon, he lamented, "They did not remember His power shown on the day He redeemed them from the foe" (v. 42). Psalm 106 strikes the same refrain: "Our fathers in Egypt did not grasp the significance of Your wonderful works or remember Your many acts of faithful love; instead, they rebelled by the sea—the Red Sea. Yet He saved them because of His name, to make His power known" (vv. 7–8). Despite the many evidences of his omnipotence, these were not enough to bring God's people into perfect covenant faith and compliance.

The Omniscience of God

The creation narratives present the Lord not only as the omnipotent God but also as the all-knowing, all-wise God. He clearly had a plan for creation ("Let there be," "let us"); and as parts of that plan unfolded, they were assessed by him and declared to be good (Gen. 1:4, 10, 12, 18, 21, 25, 31). More specifically, the account of man's creation describes (among other things there) "the tree of the knowledge of good and evil" in the midst of the garden (Gen. 2:9). The combination "good and evil" seems not so much to suggest moral antitheses but comprehensiveness of knowledge, that is, omniscience. To eat of that tree would, it seems, acquaint mankind with the whole range of knowledge, if not cognitively, then at least experientially but certainly far short of divine omniscience.[19]

The serpent proposed, on the other hand, that God was jealous for his own omniscience and thus barred man from the tree to protect his uniqueness in that respect. "God knows that when you eat it your eyes will be opened," he said, "and you will be like God, knowing good and evil" (Gen. 3:5). To their immense chagrin and incalculable loss, all they learned once they ate of the forbidden fruit was that they were naked (v. 7). Far from achieving omniscience like God's, they came to know only the horrendous results of sin—abysmal ignorance and death.

The Old Testament is replete with references to the Lord as the bestower of wisdom, knowledge, and understanding—all of which presume that he possesses all of these as essential to his nature—but few texts actually explicitly describe him as wise or skillful. Mostly the

---

[19] Thus Gerhard von Rad, *Genesis,* 86–87.

wisdom and knowledge of God are inferential, logically derivative of his nature as God and deduced from the orderliness and perfection of his creation. Those few relevant texts are sufficient, however, to make the case that ancient Israel viewed their God as all-knowing.

Two key Hebrew terms are employed with reference to God's cognition, one usually translated *wise, wisdom (ḥkm, ḥokmâ)* and the other rendered *knowledge (daʿâ, daʿat)*.[20] The latter occurs in the song of Hannah in which she described the Lord as "a God of knowledge" (*ʾēl dēʿôt*; 1 Sam. 2:3), the grammar and context suggesting that he knows all things, in this case the heart of the prideful. Job asked if it is possible for anyone to teach God knowledge *(daʿat)* (Job 21:22). The insinuation is that one cannot since he already knows all things.

Elsewhere Job declared, "God is wise *(ḥăkam)* and all-powerful. Who has opposed Him and come out unharmed?" (Job 9:4). This sentiment was echoed by Isaiah who described God as wise *(ḥākām)* in his dealings with sinners (Isa. 31:2). Not surprisingly, however, the omniscience of God is most fully developed in connection with creation.[21] The psalmist cried out in wonder and joy, "How countless are Your works, LORD! In wisdom You have made them all; the earth is full of Your creatures" (Ps. 104:24). Even more explicit is the testimony of the sage who taught that "the Lord founded the earth by wisdom *(ḥokmâ)* and established the heavens by understanding *(tēbûnâ)*. By His knowledge *(daʿat)* the watery depths broke open, and the clouds dripped with dew" (Prov. 3:19). The allusion is to both creation and the flood, and in both cases the wisdom of an omniscient God is the only adequate explanation.

The prophet Jeremiah, in the midst of a polemical discourse against idolatry, said that contrary to the so-called gods, who did not make the heavens and the earth, the God of Israel "made the earth by His power, established the world by His wisdom *(ḥokmâ)*, and spread out the heavens by His understanding" *(tēbûnâ)* (Jer. 10:12). These words are repeated verbatim in Jeremiah 51:15. In the days surrounding the Babylonian exile when Judah would be thrust into the highly sophisticated and attractive polytheistic milieu of Babylon, it was urgent that the prophets contend

---

[20] See, respectively, Gerald H. Wilson, חכם, *NIDOTTE* 2:130–34; Terence E. Fretheim, ידע, *NIDOTTE* 2:409–14.

[21] Roland E. Murphy, *The Tree of Life* (New York: Doubleday, 1990), 118–21.

for the uniqueness of Yahweh as Creator and assert his omniscience in not only predicting such a turn of events but in guaranteeing its successful outcome.

An aspect of omniscience and evidence for it is God's foreknowledge, his ability to know the outcome of all future events without conditionality or qualification. As we have noted, Jeremiah tapped into this facet of God's nature to set him in opposition to the gods of the pagans who, in fact, know nothing at all, the least reason being their nonexistence. Isaiah, however, was most concerned of all the prophets to make the case that the God of Israel could and would bring his people back from Babylonian exile, for he knows the end from the beginning, unlike the gods of Babylon and other imaginary deities. In fact, the prophet staked Yahweh's reputation on his omniscient capacity to foretell the future. Should he fail to do so, he would be like the gods of all the other nations, impotent and ignorant. Should he succeed, Israel and the peoples of the earth would be forced to acknowledge his sovereignty and power.

The gauntlet was thrown down first in a trial speech in Isaiah 41:21–24. Speaking of the foreign gods, the Lord issued the challenge: "Let them come and tell us what will happen. Tell us the past events, so that we may reflect on it and know the outcome. Or tell us the future. Tell us the coming events, then we will know that you are gods. Indeed, do something good or bad, then we will be in awe and perceive. Look, you are nothing and your work is worthless. Anyone who chooses you is detestable" (Isa. 41:22–24). This stinging sarcasm dared not be uttered by one who had no confidence in his own God to reveal things to come.

In a second trial speech (43:8–15) the Lord challenged the nations to assemble together to hear his words. Once more the test was one of foreknowledge—who of all the gods can predict future events? The Lord himself asked of the idols, "Who among them can declare this, and tell us the former things? Let them present their witnesses to vindicate themselves, so that people may hear and say, 'It is true'" (v. 9). The rhetorical question, of course, expected a negative response. On the other hand, in the same passage the Lord makes the asseveration, "From today on I am He alone, and no one can take anything from My hand. I act, and who can reverse it" (v. 13)? God not only knows the future but in his sovereign power can bring it to pass.

Yet a third challenge was offered to the idols, this time explicitly affirming that they need not be feared, for in fact they do not exist (Isa. 44:6–8). The Lord, in a grand self-predication, claimed, "I am the first and I am the last. There is no God but Me. Who, like Me, can announce the future? Let him say so and make a case before Me, since I have established an ancient people. Let these gods declare the coming things, and what will take place. Do not be startled or afraid. Have I not told you and declared it long ago? You are My witnesses! Is there any God but Me? There is no other Rock; I do not know any" (vv. 6b–8).

All of this led up to the identification of Cyrus the Great as Israel's liberator, the servant of Yahweh whose reign did not even commence until 150 years after Isaiah's proclamation (Isa. 44:28–45:1). The most persuasive evidence of all that the God of Israel knows the future as the logical corollary to his omniscience was that not only could he foretell the coming of a ruler who would emancipate his people from Babylonian exile but he could name him. Skeptical criticism attempts to vitiate this foundational argument of the prophet (and of the Lord himself) by assuming that the reference to Cyrus was not from the pen of Isaiah of Jerusalem in 700 BC but from an anonymous prophet known popularly as Second Isaiah who wrote not predictive prophecy but a historical note of what had already happened. Nevertheless, the text as it stands is making the claim for Yahweh's foreknowledge based on his ability not only to see into the future but also to arrange future events according to a program of redemption of his own choosing.[22] In fact, to deny this kind of prescience is to undercut the prophet's foundational point that only his God is capable of such knowledge of the future.

The Eternality of God

A final insight into the character of God gained from the creation narratives is that he is eternal and infinite; that is, he had no beginning

[22] For a powerful rejoinder to the view that the name Cyrus is a *post eventu* redaction and an anticipation of the fallacy of "open theism," see O. T. Allis, *The Unity of Isaiah* (Philadelphia: Presbyterian and Reformed, 1950), 62–80.

and will have no end. The terse way in which the account begins—"in the beginning God"—presupposes that God and the beginning are not coterminous but that God preexisted the beginning. Before there was heaven and earth, there was God. The reference to the tree of life also suggests his everlastingness (Gen. 2:9). After Adam and Eve sinned, the Lord said, "Since man has become like one of Us, knowing good and evil, he must not reach out, and also take from the tree of life, and eat, and live forever" (Gen. 3:22). Clearly implicit is the idea that part of what it means to be like God is to be immortal.

These suggestive hints are fully developed in the remainder of the Old Testament revelation that touches on the matter of God's eternality. Tracing the theme canonically, we first address a number of passages where this aspect of his nature is expressed epithetically. He is eternal, the record testifies from beginning to end.

Abraham is said to have worshipped "the LORD, the Everlasting God," at Beersheba (Gen. 21:33). The adjective here is *ʿōlam,* by far the most common term to speak of God's everlastingness. Deuteronomy 33:27, on the other hand, employs the synonym *qedem* to describe the Lord as "the God of old." Psalm 90:2 states it in the phrase "from eternity to eternity, You are God," using *ʿōlam* again. The psalmist noted in this connection that God preceded all the things he made at creation. Speaking of the enduring nature of Yahweh's throne, Psalm 93:2 acclaims, "You are from eternity," a sentiment shared by the writer of Psalm 106 who spoke of the Lord as the One "from everlasting to everlasting" (v. 48).

Isaiah described the messianic figure to come as *ʾăbîʿad,* "Eternal Father" (Isa. 9:6), in some sense One who shares God's eternal nature. The same prophet extolled the Lord as "the everlasting God, the Creator of the whole earth" (Isa. 40:28). This is in the context of polemic in which the transitoriness of the pagan gods is contrasted with the permanence of the God of Israel (cf. vv. 18–20). Habakkuk spoke of the Lord as the eternal *(qedem)* one (Hab. 1:12) whereas Jeremiah in his Lamentations emphasized his unchangeableness from one generation to another (Lam. 5:19). The postexilic literature also testifies to this aspect of God's nature. Having assembled the Jewish community at the time of the fall festivals, the leaders of the Levites spoke to the people of the Lord as he who is "from everlasting to everlasting" (Neh. 9:5). The Chronicler employed the same formula in his account of David's song of praise on the occasion of the moving of the ark into Jerusalem (1 Chron. 16:36).

Akin to the use of these predications is the assertion that Yahweh lives forever. This is particularly seen in so-called oath formulas where he makes promises based on his eternal existence—"as surely as I live," etc. (cf. Deut. 32:40).[23] Otherwise he is said to live "from everlasting to everlasting" (Ps. 41:13) and is addressed as the One who continues forever (Ps. 92:8). Alongside such direct confessions are predications that describe the Lord as the eternal *(ʿōlam)* Rock (Isa. 26:4), the One who inhabits eternity *(ʿad)* (Isa. 57:15), the everlasting *(ʿōlam)* light (Isa. 60:20), and the eternal *(ʿōlam)* Redeemer (Isa. 63:16).

In line with his role as Sovereign over all things, Yahweh is king forever (Ps. 55:19), whose kingdom is everlasting (Ps. 145:13). Jeremiah spoke of him as "the true God; He is the living God and eternal *(ʿōlam)* King" (Jer. 10:10). As such, he reigns forever, a point explicitly made in Psalms 9:7; 29:10; and 66:7. The poet declared in Psalm 102:12 that "You, LORD, are enthroned forever; Your fame endures to all generations." Even more emphatic is the testimony of Psalm 146:10: "The LORD reigns forever; Zion, your God reigns for all generations." Even the pagan king Nebuchadnezzar was forced to conclude that "His [God's] kingdom is an eternal *(ʿōlam)* kingdom, and His dominion is from generation to generation" (Dan. 4:3; cf. v. 34).

Other features of the divine essence—God's omnipresence, immutability, and perfection—find expression more subtly than these whose roots are found already embedded in the creation narratives. They do appear elsewhere in the sacred record, however, and will be treated at the point where they occur in connection with God's relationships with his people and his works on their behalf. To this point we have focused on God's nature—who he is. We turn now to examine his character—what he does—as revealed in the Old Testament canonically and progressively. To use standard theological terminology, we will consider his attributes, the sum total of which present us with the biblical portrait in all its beauty.

---

[23] For the idea of God's eternality as the basis for his reliability in Old Testament oath formulae, see M. R. Lehmann, "Biblical Oaths," *ZAW* 81 (1969): 74–92.

The Character of God

The Holiness of God

In agreement with many theologians we propose that the fundamental truth about the character of God of the Bible is that he is holy.[24] Nearly everything else that may be said of him springs from this conviction. By *holy* at least two things are meant: (1) that God is separate from all else that exists (thus the semantic field of *qdš)*[25] and (2) that his holiness is translated into moral and ethical perfection. A plethora of passages make this clear and taken together form a framework in which this essential quality takes a central place.

The two key relevant terms are *holiness (qōdeš)* and *holy (qādôš)*, a noun and adjective respectively. The first place that either is used of God is in the Song of Moses where the lyricist describes him as being "glorious in holiness," incomparably so in contrast to all other gods (Exod. 15:11). David used the combination "splendor of His holiness" suggesting, with Moses, that holiness emits an aura (Ps. 29:2). It is not just an abstraction, but it produces a tangible effect on all who come in contact with it. More of the ethical aspect of holiness is seen in the avowal by Yahweh that "I have sworn an oath by My holiness; I will not lie to David" (Ps. 89:35).

The prophet Isaiah contributed to the understanding of God's holiness by his observation that in the day of his redemption his people will be overcome by his saving grace and will "honor the Holy One of Jacob and stand in awe of the God of Israel" (Isa. 29:23). A similar sentiment was expressed by Ezekiel who said that when Israel is faithful to bear witness to God's holiness before the nations, then "the nations will know that I am Yahweh" (Ezek. 36:23; cf. 38:23). God's holiness, then, sets him apart and compels men to acknowledge him and him only as Lord.

The formulaic declaration that God is holy is first articulated in the book of Leviticus, a book more preoccupied than any other with holiness in general. Here the Lord commanded his people, "You must consecrate yourselves and be holy because I am holy" (Lev. 11:44; cf. v. 45; 19:2;

---

[24] Eichrodt proposes that "of all the qualities attributed to the divine nature there is one which, in virtue both of the frequency and the emphasis with which it is used, occupies a position of unique importance—namely, that of holiness," *Theology of the Old Testament,* vol. 1, 270.

[25] Jackie A. Naudé, קדשׁ, *NIDOTTE* 3:877–87.

21:8). A formal definition of what this means is seen in Leviticus 20:26 where the Lord said, after enjoining his people to be holy, "I have set you apart from the nations to be Mine." This, at least in part, is what it means to be holy. Another facet of this truth is in the command "You must not profane My holy name; I must be treated as holy among the Israelites" (Lev. 22:32; cf. Exod. 20:7; Deut. 5:11).

Yahweh's incomparable holiness, though hinted at in the Song of Hannah (1 Sam. 2:2), is most greatly elaborated in the Psalter and in Isaiah. David plainly asserted that God is holy, therefore worthy of worship (Ps. 22:3); and an unnamed poet added to this connection of praise and holiness by referring to the Lord as the Holy One of Israel (Ps. 71:22; cf. 2 Kings 19:22), an epithet fully developed by Isaiah. Psalm 89:18 ties in human kingship as a gift of the Holy One of Israel. But no psalm features this attribute more than Psalm 99, which declares that God's name is holy (v. 3), He should be worshipped precisely because he is holy (v. 5), and he is to be exalted above all, again because "the LORD our God is holy" (v. 9).

Isaiah, who had seen the Lord enthroned in the temple and had heard the accolades of the seraphim who called out "holy, holy, holy," was most impressed of all prophets by the holiness of God. As a result of this beatific vision, he saw clearly his own sinfulness (i.e., unholiness) and confessed his need for a touch from God (Isa. 6:1–7). But he was not alone. Sinful Israel had turned away from Yahweh, despising the Holy One of Israel (1:4). This epithet captures Isaiah's most immediate and powerful impression of the Lord: He is the Holy One. And it became almost a refrain throughout his book, one that unified his thinking about the fundamental nature of his God (cf. 5:19, 24; 10:20; 12:6; 17:7; 29:19, 23; 30:11, 12, 15; 31:1; 37:23; 40:25; 41:14, 16, 20; 43:3, 14–15; 45:11; 47:4; 48:17; 49:7; 54:5; 55:5; 60:9, 14).

Isaiah nuanced the idea of God's holiness in various ways in these and other texts. He linked it with God's righteousness (5:16), his word (5:24), and his glory (6:3). He viewed God's holiness through the metaphor of light (10:17) and associated it with power (12:6), especially power in creation (17:7). As the Holy One he cares for the poor and oppressed (29:19) and is the only One who can save (30:15; cf. 31:1). But God as the Holy One is most apparent by contrast to the earthly, reprehensible, indeed, filthy gods of popular pagan imagination. "Who will you compare Me to?" the Holy One asks (Isa. 40:25). He will dispose of these phantom deities (41:16); and when he does, everyone will understand that "it is the LORD, the Holy One of Israel, who did it" (41:20 NLT).

The holiness of God was also associated by Isaiah with his creation of Israel as a people (43:15) and with his redeeming them from Egyptian bondage (43:14, 16–17). What he did in the past he will do in the future in another exodus deliverance, this time from Babylon (45:11; cf. 47:4; 48:17; 49:7; 54:5). And the time will come when the nations, attracted to the holiness of Israel's God, will come willingly to submit to his sovereignty (55:5; cf. Zech. 14:16–19). They will honor him with their wealth (60:9) and will describe their erstwhile captives as "the City of the LORD" (60:14).

The holiness of God as exemplified in his people was clearly articulated by Ezekiel who, with reference to the return of the Jews from Babylonian exile, said of them, "I will demonstrate My holiness through you in the sight of the nations" (Ezek. 20:41). That is, an Israel chastened by the discipline of exile would return the better for it, a people more like the LORD who desires that they be holy as he is holy. The purpose is that "the nations may know Me, when I show Myself holy through you in their sight" (Ezek. 38:16; cf. 39:7, 27). When God's holiness is recognized and displayed, it has the effect of silencing the prideful claims of arrogant and rebellious men.

The Righteousness of God

Concomitant with God's holiness and a practical ethical expression of it is his righteousness, his adherence to principles and norms of integrity that provide further evidence of his moral perfection. The basic idea of the root *ṣdq* is that of a standard to which one must aspire if he is to be considered in conformity with agreed upon moral and ethical conventions.[26] To speak of the righteousness of God, who is absolutely holy, is to speak of the achievement of perfect compliance to his own impeccable standards. In a remarkable passage Isaiah made the linkage

---

[26] David J. Reimer, צדק, *NIDOTTE* 3:744–69.

between God's holiness and his righteousness by affirming that "the holy God is distinguished by righteousness" (Isa. 5:16).

In a great many cases in which *ṣaddîq (righteous)* and *ṣedeq* / *ṣĕdāqâ (righteousness)* occur, they are merely predicative, that is, they describe the Lord, often without reference to how he is righteous or does righteously (thus Pss. 4:1; 7:9; 116:5; 129:4; 145:17; Prov. 21:12; Isa. 24:16; 45:21; Lam. 1:18; Dan. 9:14; Zech. 8:8; Ezra 9:15). Usually, however, he is called righteous because his ways and deeds are righteous. Moses asked whether any other nation had a body of law as righteous as that given by the Lord, thus attributing to him a standard of righteousness unknown to other nations and their gods (Deut. 4:8; cf. Ps. 119:137).

The Song of Deborah celebrates "the righteous acts of the LORD," in this context his leadership in Israel's battles (Judg. 5:11). Samuel, too, in his valedictory rehearsed all the righteous deeds the Lord had brought to pass in Israel's history (1 Sam. 12:7). Other individuals also called to attention God's righteous acts on their personal behalf (Ps. 71:24). It is in the realm of justice, however, that God's righteousness comes most to the fore, disclosing thereby an indissoluble linkage between righteousness and justice. He is called a righteous judge (Ps. 7:11), one who loves justice (Ps. 11:7). Jeremiah testified that whenever he pled a case before him, the Lord was always righteous (Jer. 12:1). Zephaniah, speaking of Jerusalem, said, "The righteous LORD is in her; He does no wrong. He applies His justice morning by morning; He does not fail at dawn, yet the one who does wrong knows no shame" (Zeph. 3:5).

By virtue of being righteous the Lord does righteously, both in and of himself and through those who serve him. His righteousness deters him from being oppressive (Job 37:23) and ensures that he will rule with justice (Ps. 9:8) and vindicate the innocent of wrongdoing (Pss. 35:24; 96:13; 98:9; 103:6). Indeed, all that he does is righteous. As a psalmist put it, "Your right hand is filled with justice" (Ps. 48:10; cf. Ps. 65:5). He brings salvation as an expression of his righteousness (Ps. 71:2), and David testified that by God's righteousness he had been delivered from trouble (Ps. 143:11). Isaiah drew a parallel between the righteousness, of the Lord and his salvation (Isa. 46:13). To him salvation is a product of

God's righteousness, for it is a sign of the vindication of the people of the Lord who rest in that aspect of God's character. Best of all, that kind of righteousness is not fleeting or time bound; rather, because it is inherent in the nature of God, it is everlasting (Pss. 111:3; 112:3, 9; 119:142).

All this leads God's people to praise him for his righteousness (Ps. 35:28) and to proclaim it to all who will hear. David declared that he did not hide God's righteousness within but spoke of it publicly (Ps. 40:10). Having pleaded with the Lord for forgiveness for his murder and adultery, he pledged that once that had been done "my tongue will sing of Your righteousness" (Ps. 51:14). God was righteous in condemning that sin, but he is also righteous in providing a way of atonement for it. Such acts of grace, founded as they are on righteousness and not mere pity, evoke praises from those who have experienced them (Ps. 89:16).

The Justice of God

Justice is the application of righteousness, especially in situations of legal disposition. Where law is interpreted in a righteous manner, justice will prevail. It is therefore not surprising that one of the important attributes of God in the Old Testament is that he is just. It is likewise not surprising that the key words for justice *(mišpāṭ)* and righteousness (*ṣedeq, ṣĕdāqâ*) occur commonly together, usually in parallel, at least in poetic texts.[27] In fact, they sometimes share common translation in the various English versions. It is further worth noting that the notion of God's justice is rarely found outside poetic passages. This no doubt is to be explained by its synonymity to righteousness and other more common terms to which it is conceptually linked.

The earliest of these texts is Deuteronomy 32, the Song of Moses, where the great lawgiver declares that the Lord's "work is perfect; all His ways are entirely just" (v. 4; *mišpaṭ)*. The following couplet calls him "faithful" *(ĕmûnâ)*, "righteous" *(ṣaddiq)*, and "true" *(yāšār)*, all of which are in the same semantic domain. What this means in practical application is spelled out in a legal text in Deuteronomy: "He executes justice for the fatherless and the widow, and loves the foreign resident" (10:18).

[27] See, respectively, Peter Enns, מִשְׁפָּט, *NIDOTTE* 2:1142–44; David J. Reimer, צדק, *NIDOTTE* 3:744–69.

Not unexpectedly in a book whose major theme has to do with the righteousness and fairness of the Lord, the issue of his justice occurs a number of times in Job. Bildad asked, "Does God pervert justice?" (Job 8:3), expecting, of course, a negative response. Job was convinced of God's integrity in this respect and asked whether anyone can call him to account (9:19 LXX). Elihu, like Bildad, found it unimaginable for God to be anything but just (34:12) and, combining the ideas of righteousness and justice, asserted that it is impossible for God to misuse his unlimited power (37:23).

Psalm 9 places the righteousness *(ṣedeq)* of God in parallelism with his justice (here *mēšārîm)*, proclaiming that he judges and rules according to these standards (v. 8). On the other hand, David set *ṣĕdāqâ* and *mišpāṭ* in synonymous parallelism, comparing the one to the heights of great mountains and the other to the depths of the deepest sea, so inexhaustible are they (Ps. 36:6). Psalm 89:14 joins together a collection of terms that shed light on God's role as Sovereign and the attributes essential to it: "Righteousness *(ṣedeq)* and justice *(mišpāṭ)* are the foundation of Your throne; faithful love *(ḥesed)* and truth *(ʾemet)* go before You." The last two of these terms, though found occasionally in reference to God's justice, are more at home in other settings to be explored later.

In a song attributed to Solomon, the king (or someone speaking on his behalf) pleaded for God to "give . . . justice *(mišpāṭ)*" to the king and "Your righteousness *(sĕdāqâ)* to the king's son" (Ps. 72:1). That is, the qualities that characterize the Lord as ruler are necessary also to kings and others who rule on his behalf. In the eschatological day in particular, the Lord "will judge the world righteously *(ṣedeq)* and the peoples fairly *(mēšārîm)*" (Ps. 98:9; cf. 96:13). Justice will prevail because it is founded on God's impeccable righteousness. "The mighty King loves justice," says another poet, and has "established fairness" (Ps. 99:4). Because of these traits and truths David could pledge, "I will sing of faithful love *(ḥesed)* and justice *(mišpāṭ)*; I will sing praise to You, LORD" (Ps. 101:1).

Next to the Psalter, Isaiah has most to say about God's justice. Describing terrible days of judgment that will fall upon Israel, the prophet made the ironic declaration that "the LORD of Hosts is exalted by His justice *(mišpāṭ)*, and the holy God is distinguished by righteousness *(ṣĕdāqâ)*" (Isa. 5:16). Even the condemned will have to concede the fairness of their judgment. The first of the Servant Songs lays great emphasis on God's eschatological justice. The Servant, empowered by God's Sprit, "will bring justice *(mišpāṭ)* to the nations" (Isa. 42:1) and "will faithfully bring justice" (v. 3). Nor will he flag in his efforts to do so "until He has established justice on earth" (v. 4).

The Love of God

The God of justice and judgment is also the God of love, the attribute of God that prompts him to seek a remedy for sin and thus to be able to avert his wrath. Several terms are commonly translated *love*; one of these *(ḥesed)*, because it has an especially highly nuanced and important usage in its own right, will be treated later. For now the root *ʾhb* and its variations will occupy our attention.

Though this lexeme has its ordinary meaning of strong affection, with other similar emotional overtones, recent study has indicated that in covenant contexts especially it is virtually synonymous with *bḥr*, "to choose."[28] That is, God chooses because he loves, and for him to love is in many cases tantamount to choosing (cf. Mal. 1:2). This is clear first of all in that it was because the Lord loved *(ʾāhab)* their patriarchal ancestors and chose *(bāḥar)* their offspring that he delivered Israel from Egypt (Deut. 4:37; cf. 7:8; 10:15). Clearly the love of God here is elective, not emotive, though an emotional element may certainly lie behind it. This idea that God also displays love in its ordinary sense is in view in Deuteronomy 7:13 where his love results in blessing and in Deuteronomy 23:5 where the curse of Balaam was changed into a blessing of Israel purely and simply because of God's strong affection for his people.

Both kinds of divine love are attested to throughout the Old Testament record. The elective nuance is implicit in God's love for Jacob whose inheritance the Lord chose (Ps. 47:4) and in his love for Mount Zion, that is, Judah, whom he also chose (Ps. 78:68). Israel was the special object of his love however that love is to be understood. Isaiah asserted that the

---

[28] William L. Moran, "The Ancient Near Eastern Background of the Love of God in Deuteronomy," *CBQ* 25 (1963): 77–87.

Lord will exchange the nations for Israel because of his love for her (Isa. 43:4); and Jeremiah, at the outset of describing the new covenant, spoke even more forcefully of God's love for his people: "I have loved you with an everlasting love; therefore, I have continued to extend faithful love *(ḥesed)* to you" (Jer. 31:3). This was also Hosea's message, one particularly poignant in light of the prophet's own unrequited love. The Lord declared, "When Israel was a child, I loved (i.e., chose) him, and out of Egypt I called My son" (Hos. 11:1). And then, despite Israel's "adultery" he could say, "I will heal their apostasy; I will freely love them" (Hos. 14:4).

More generally, God loves the just (Ps. 37:28), the righteous (Ps. 146:8), and his holy sanctuary (Mal. 2:11). He loved Solomon specifically (2 Sam. 12:24–25) and even Cyrus (Isa. 48:14) whom he had selected to be Israel's deliverer (Isa. 44:28–45:1). Finally God loves the principles and attributes that make up his own person and which he expects his people to embody, abstractions such as justice (Ps. 11:7; Isa. 61:8) and righteousness (Ps. 33:5; 45:7). He loves them for their inherent worth and because they testify to him.

The Pity of God

God's love often moved him to pity when he beheld the desperate and miserable condition of his people. Though pity, love, compassion, and mercy overlap in some ways, there are clear semantic and theological distinctions that can and ought to be drawn. The two key terms most commonly translated "pity," *ḥamal* / *ḥemlâ* and *ḥûs,* are synonymous and quite evenly distributed throughout the Hebrew Bible though generally the later literature favors *ḥûs.*[29]

God is said to pity those in distress, almost exclusively the people of Israel in the Old Testament. Psalm 72, speaking obliquely of the messianic king, says that "He will have pity on the poor and helpless and save the lives of the poor" (v. 13). Joel also predicted that in the Day of the Lord he "will be jealous for his land and take pity on his people," this time providing for their material needs and relieving them of the scorn of the nations (Joel 2:18–19 NIV). Ezekiel recalled that the Lord had pitied

[29] S. Wagner, חוּס, *TDOT* 4:271–77.

Israel in the desert despite their sin, but this abeyance of his judgment should not engender false comfort (Ezek. 20:17; cf. 2 Chron. 36:15).

More often than not, in fact, the Lord withheld his pity; and because he did, the consequences of sin were allowed to take their course. Job complained that God showed him no pity but instead attacked him severely (Job 16:13). Jeremiah prophesied that the Lord would smash wicked Judah, allowing no pity *(ḥāmāl)*, no mercy *(ḥûs)*, and no compassion *(rāḥām)*. And in his Lamentations he reported after the fact and with great sadness that the Lord indeed had shown none of these things (Lam. 2:2, 17, 21; 3:43). Ezekiel, if anything more passionately, predicted the same for exilic Israel. Their idolatry would force a withdrawal of God's pity (Ezek. 5:11; cf. 7:4, 9; 8:18) as would their murderous deeds and acts of injustice (Ezek. 9:10). He would, without relenting, pour out his dreadful wrath (Ezek. 24:14). Zechariah, too, spoke of a day when the Lord would no longer cast an eye of pity on his people but would "turn everyone over to his neighbor and his king" (Zech. 11:6). It is thus not always just the display of his attributes that constitutes a theological understanding of God but their withdrawal as well.

The Grace of God

Closely associated with God's pity is his grace, the bestowment of his unmerited favor on sinners and saints alike. The principal term used to speak of this feature of God's character is *ḥēn* ("grace") and its cognate adjective *ḥannûn* ("gracious") and verb *ḥnn* ("to be gracious"). They are commonly found in synonymous parallelism with other terms such as pity and compassion so it is clear that they share a larger semantic field generally having to do with God's loving favor.[30]

Many texts describe the Lord as gracious or as bestowing grace. As early as in the book of the covenant, the Lord commanded that garments taken as security for loans to the poor be returned to them at night lest when they cried out the Lord should hear, for he is gracious (Exod. 22:27). Men may lack that quality but not the Lord. The Psalter is especially rich in its description of God as gracious. David referred to him as "a compassionate *(raḥûm)* and gracious *(ḥanûn)* God, slow to anger and abundant in faithful love *(ḥesed)* and truth *(ʾemet)*" (Ps. 86:15). The same is said in Psalm 103:8

---

[30] Terence E. Fretheim, חנן, *NIDOTTE* 2:203–6.

and partly repeated in Psalm 111:4 *(ḥannûn* plus *raḥûm)*. Psalm 116:5 calls him gracious *(ḥannûn)* but also righteous *(ṣaddîq)* and full of compassion *(raḥûm)*. The *ḥannûn / raḥûm* combination occurs also in Psalm 145:8. Apart from the Psalms, Nehemiah alone speaks of the Lord with this epithet. "You are a forgiving God," he says, "gracious *(ḥannûn)* and compassionate *(raḥûm)*, slow to anger and rich in faithful love *(ḥesed)*" (Neh. 9:17). The dependence on Psalm 86:15 is obvious (cf. Neh. 9:31).

More commonly, God shows or effects grace. He had grace *(ḥēn)* on Noah, sparing him from the flood (Gen. 6:8). It is true that Noah is described as a righteous and blameless man (v. 9), but it is not this evaluation that qualified him for salvation. Rather, it was his arbitrary selection by the LORD.[31] Such a notion of grace ought to be clear from the testimony of Jacob who attributed all his success to the grace of God despite his devious behavior toward his brother Esau (Gen. 33:11). In his encounter with the Lord on Sinai, Moses reminded the Lord that he had previously told him that he had found grace *(ḥēn)* with him. If that be so, he went on, he wanted that grace to continue so that he would know the Lord and his ways even better (Exod. 33:12–13). In response the Lord made the remarkable declaration, which really clarifies the monergistic nature of grace: "I will be gracious *(ḥannûn)* to whom I will be gracious, and I will have compassion *(raḥûm)* on whom I will have compassion" (Exod. 33:19; cf. 34:6). How and why God bestows grace remains in the realm of mystery so far as the biblical witness is concerned.

Gideon made a request similar to that of Moses in that he too pleaded for an act of God based on his grace (Judg. 6:17). David, on the other hand, hoped for God's grace in sparing his illegitimate son, but it was not forthcoming (2 Sam. 12:22). Jonah knew that God would not in the final analysis destroy Nineveh, for, as he put it, "I knew that You are a merciful and compassionate God, slow to become angry, rich in faithful love" (Jon. 4:2; cf. Ps. 86:15; Neh. 9:17). There clearly is no hint here of Nineveh's worthiness to be spared, a fact that contributed all the more to Jonah's frustration with the ways of God.

---

[31] Mathews notes that "there is no antecedent act of righteousness by Noah that would explain his favored place before God. This points theologically to the elective purposes of God for Noah, showing that the patriarch already enjoyed a relationship with the Lord before his recorded acts of obedience." Kenneth A. Mathews, *Genesis 1–11:26,* NAC 1A (Nashville: Broadman & Holman, 1996), 356–57.

Isaiah made the important observation that the Lord desires to be gracious and compassionate; therefore, when his people cry out to him, he will respond in grace (Isa. 30:18–19). He himself pleaded for God's grace (Isa. 33:2) as did many others. The great priestly blessing implores the Lord to "make His face shine on you and be gracious to you" (Num. 6:25). The psalmists repeatedly made this appeal (e.g., Pss. 25:16; 67:1; 119:29, 58), and Malachi urged his countrymen to pray with him that God would be gracious (Mal. 1:9). Occasionally it seems as though grace is contingent. Psalm 84:11 links grace and honor with a blameless walk. However, the grammar here suggests that godly living is not the prerequisite to grace but its fruit.[32] It is true that God gives grace to the humble (Prov. 3:34), but it is not because they are humble. He is gracious because of his great love and mercy. On the other hand, if grace is not contingent on human worthiness, it is at least based on God's character and promises. As for the latter, the historian observed that King Jehoahaz's and Israel's preservation in the face of enemy oppression was because "the LORD was gracious to them and had compassion on them and turned toward them because of His covenant with Abraham, Isaac, and Jacob" (2 Kings 13:23). God is gracious by nature, almost by definition; but his grace, at times at least, is bound up with his solemn pledges. Even so, he takes the initiative in effecting it and not those who are its beneficiaries.

The Compassion of God

God's love, pity, grace, and compassion are intricately connected; and, in fact, the terms for each are commonly interchanged. By etymology and usage, however, a case can be made that compassion *(raḥămîm)* has a stronger emotive quality, one more at home in a human context. As for God's compassion, it is expressed often as the feeling a parent has for a helpless child.

In numerous instances the Lord is said to be compassionate (Exod. 34:6; Deut. 4:31; Pss. 86:15; 103:8; 111:4; 145:8; Jon. 4:2; Joel 2:13; Neh. 9:31; 2 Chron. 30:9) or to have compassion (Pss. 25:6; 116:5; 119:156; 145:9; Isa. 49:10; 54:10; 63:7; Lam. 3:22). It was because of his compassion in the past that he called, guided, and delivered his people

---

[32] Artur Weiser, *The Psalms* (Philadelphia: Westminster, 1962), 569.

(Ps. 78:38; 2 Kings 13:23; Neh. 9:19, 27–28), and it will be because of his compassion that he will save them in the future, even in eschatological times (Deut. 30:3; Ps. 102:13; Isa. 14:1; 49:13; 54:7–8; 55:7; 60:10; Hos. 1:7; 2:19, 23; Mic. 7:19; Jer. 12:15; 30:18; 33:26; 42:12; Ezek. 39:25; Zech. 1:16). Sometimes he withdraws his compassion with disastrous results (Isa. 63:15; Jer. 16:5), and there is always the fear that he might do so (Pss. 40:11; 77:9; Isa. 9:17; 27:11; Hos. 1:6; 2:4; Jer. 13:14; Zech. 1:12). Often, therefore, there was urgent petition that he would not follow through with that possibility but instead extend grace (Pss. 79:8; 119:77; Hab. 3:2).

Sometimes there appear to be contingencies to the extending of God's compassion. In discussing the possibility of idolatry arising in Israel's midst, Moses pointed out that God's wrath could be averted and his compassion displayed if his people put away from themselves those who practiced idolatry (Deut. 13:17–18). Psalm 103:13 compares the Lord's compassion to that of a human father and says that he has compassion "on those who fear Him," that is, those who are totally submissive. On the other hand, compassion may be prevenient, providing the grounds for forgiveness. In his great prayer of repentance, David implored the Lord, "according to Your abundant compassion, blot out my rebellion" (Ps. 51:1). Clearly David was aware that only through God's compassionate love for him could he be restored.

The Covenant Fidelity of God

The term *ḥesed,* one of the richest theological words of the Old Testament, is found commonly parallel to or juxtaposed with *ʾhb, ḥnn, rḥm,* and other terms in the semantic field of love or compassion. However, it is a highly specialized synonym, one closely connected to the idea of covenant and found frequently in company with *ʾemet / ʾemûnâ, faithfulness / faithful.* It is the love of God that commits him to a relationship or course of action to which he has pledged himself by covenant.[33]

One of the most frequent descriptions of the Lord is that he "abounds in *ḥesed*" (Num. 14:18; Jon. 4:2; Joel 2:13; Neh. 9:17) and even more

---

[33] A fundamental study of this rich term is K. D. Sakenfeld, *The Meaning of* hesed *in the Hebrew Bible: A New Inquiry,* HSM 17 (Chico, Calif.: Scholars, 1978).

commonly it is said of him that his "*ḥesed* endures forever" (Ps. 106:1; cf. Pss. 107:1; 118:1–4, 29; 2 Chron. 5:13; 7:3, 6; 20:21). The second lines in the couplets that make up all twenty-six verses of Psalm 136 consist of this refrain. But his *ḥesed* has specific objectives—purposes and goals for which it is exercised. Abraham and Joseph were among the individuals who benefited from divine *ḥesed* (Gen. 24:27; 39:21), and they were only typical of the experiences of God's people who were joined to him in a special relationship.

Sometimes the notions of *ḥesed* and salvation or deliverance are conjoined in a cause-and-effect connection. The psalmists pleaded that the Lord would save them by his *ḥesed* (Pss. 6:5; 31:16; cf. 69:13; 85:7; 109:21; 119:41) and otherwise prayed for its presence (Ps. 33:22) or recognized their need for it (Pss. 13:6; 25:7; 44:27; 51:1; 64:3). Among the blessings of God's *ḥesed* were the leading of his people (Exod. 15:13), their sense of forgiveness based upon it (Num. 14:19), and its presence all the days of their life (Ps. 23:6). Though there may appear to be conditions attached to its bestowal such as loving God (Exod. 20:6; cf. Deut. 7:9), fearing him (Pss. 103:11, 17; 147:11), and trusting him (Ps. 32:10), in truth God, who cannot lie, has sworn that his *ḥesed* will never depart from those he has called into covenant with himself (2 Sam. 7:15; cf. 22:51; Ps. 18:50). He was called by Solomon in his temple prayer the One "keeping the gracious covenant" (1 Kings 8:23). To unfaithful Israel who had committed spiritual whoredom against him, the Lord pledged, following her repentance and restoration, "I will take you to be My wife forever. I will take you to be My wife in righteousness, justice, love *(ḥesed)*, and compassion *(raḥămîm)*" (Hos. 2:19). Isaiah spoke the promise that though the Lord had for a time punished his recalcitrant people, he "will have compassion on you with everlasting love *(ḥesed)*" (Isa. 54:8; cf. Lam. 3:32).

The most theologically potent use of the term *ḥesed* was in connection with God's initiation and maintenance of the several covenants by which he committed himself to the patriarchal fathers and then to their offspring, the nation Israel. The word occurs in a number of places in parallel to *bĕrît, covenant,* or in juxtaposition to it, thus cementing the idea that *ḥesed* is particularly at home in covenant contexts. David, for example, testified that "all the Lord's ways show faithful love *(ḥesed)* and truth to those who keep his covenant *(bĕrît)* and decrees" (Ps. 25:10). In an even tighter parallelism, Psalm 89:28 reads, "I will always preserve My faithful love *(ḥesed)* for him, and My covenant with him will endure." The reference here is to David and the Davidic covenant through which the Lord promised David and his dynasty an unending reign (vv. 20–29; cf. 2 Sam. 7:12–16).

Isaiah, clearly dependent on both the original word to David and its reiteration in the psalm, spoke the message of the Lord who said, "I will make an everlasting covenant with you, the promises *(ḥesed)* assured to David" (Isa. 55:3). Micah reached even further back in sacred history, recollecting the ancient promises to the patriarchs with which the Davidic covenant had such vital linkage: "You will show loyalty to Jacob and faithful love *(ḥesed)* to Abraham, as You swore to our fathers from days long ago" (Mic. 7:20). Daniel connected *ḥesed* and *covenant* even more closely, making them virtual synonyms. In his great prayer he prayed, literally, "Ah, LORD—the great and awe-inspiring God who keeps His gracious covenant *(ḥesed)*" (Dan. 9:4). The construction is a hendiadys to be translated "covenant of *hesed*" or the like, but the equivalence of *ḥesed* and covenant is not to be ignored. Nehemiah used exactly the same construction to make this connection (Neh. 1:5; 9:32).

We have already noted that the Lord's *ḥesed,* as an element of his character, is unending. This idea is reinforced by the great number of texts in which *ḥesed* is linked in some manner with terms that suggest the reliability of the Lord and his *ḥesed,* terms such as *ʾemet* and its related noun *ʾĕmûnâ,* both to be rendered *loyalty* or *faithfulness* (e.g., Pss. 36:5; 40:10–11; 57:3, 10; 61:7). God and his covenant promises are to be relied upon forever because he himself is irrevocably committed to the promises he has made.

The Dependability of God

This leads to a consideration of God's faithfulness more generically, quite apart from its special connection to *ḥesed* and covenant. The cluster of terms favored by the Old Testament derive from the verb *ʾmn,* the fundamental idea of which is to be firm, trustworthy, faithful.[34] As just pointed out, the derivative nouns *ʾemet* and *ʾĕmûnâ* commonly occur with *ḥesed* in covenant contexts; and these are best translated *reliability* or

[34] R. W. L. Moberly, אמן, *NIDOTTE* 1:427–33.

trustworthiness. An adjective, *ʾāmôn,* occurs a few times but by far the most prevalent way of speaking of God's faithfulness is with the nominal forms and/or the use of the verb.

To begin with the predicative or epithetical uses of these terms, both within and outside covenant contexts, the Lord is called the God of faithfulness (Ps. 31:5), the One, in fact, whose faithfulness surrounds him like a garment (Ps. 89:5). All that he does is a reflection of his dependability (Ps. 33:4; Neh. 9:33). He is faithful to save (Ps. 69:13; cf. 143:1) but also to destroy those deserving of his judgment (Ps. 54:5; 96:13). His faithfulness is seen in the justness and uprightness with which he relates to mankind, especially to his own chosen ones (Pss. 40:11; 85:11; 111:7–8; Isa. 11:5). His faithfulness is like a glorious light (Ps. 43:3) or a protective shield (Ps. 91:4).

As God's faithfulness relates to his covenant requirements and promises, the psalmist declared that his commands and statutes are characterized by integrity and reliability (Ps. 119:86, 138). For his part, God keeps faith with his covenant forever (Ps. 146:6; cf. 119:90). The dead, of course, "cannot hope for Your faithfulness" (Isa. 38:18). On the other hand, as the prophet declared, "The living, only the living can thank You, as I do today; a father will make Your faithfulness known to children" (Isa. 38:19). The covenant overtones here found expression also in the Lord's promise in Hosea to his repentant and restored people: "I will take you to be My wife in faithfulness, and you will know the Lord" (Hos. 2:20).

A more concrete assertion of God's faithfulness as covenant keeper may be seen in the linkage between the verbs *ʾmn* and *bḥr* (to choose) in Isaiah 49:7: "Kings will see and stand up, and princes will bow down, because of the Lord, who is faithful *(neʾĕmān)*, the Holy One of Israel—and He has chosen *(wayyibḥārekā)* you" (Isa. 49:7). The verb *chosen* occurs regularly as a technical term for covenant election (cf. Deut. 14:2; Pss. 78:70; 105:26; 1 Kings 3:8).[35] God's choice of Israel was an expression of his faithfulness in keeping the promises to the patriarchs; and his faithfulness was also a guarantee of the ongoing, permanent nature of the covenant. Isaiah 61:8 makes the same point: "I will faithfully *(ʾemet)* reward them [Israel] and make an everlasting covenant with them." What

[35] Horst Seebass, בחר, *TDOT* 2:82–86.

makes it everlasting is the dependability of Israel's God. Jeremiah could with good cause exclaim, "Because of the LORD's faithful love *(ḥesed)* we do not perish, for His mercies *(raḥămîm)* never end. They are new every morning; great is Your faithfulness!" *(ʾĕmûnâ)* (Lam. 3:22–23).

The Patience of God

God's *hesed* and faithfulness presuppose to a great extent that He is patient, long-suffering, not quick to exercise his awesome judgment. The absence of any technical term in the Old Testament for patience, especially as applied to God, bears this out. In fact, a circumlocution must suffice—*ʾerek appayîm*—literally, "slow in anger." This does not suggest that he is never an angry God. The section to follow will, in fact, make clear that anger is an important aspect of God's holy and righteous character. But his anger comes into play only when his patience has been exhausted.

The patience of the Lord is expressed in a recurring, almost formulaic refrain first found in Exodus. Following the golden calf debacle, the Lord appeared to Moses with this elaborate self-predication: "Yahweh—Yahweh is a compassionate and gracious God, slow to anger and rich in faithful love and truth" (Exod. 34:6). In the next verse Moses went on to say, however, that "He will not leave the guilty unpunished" (v. 7). His patience may be long, but it is not inexhaustible. In another scene of rebellion, this time prompted by the negative report of the ten Israelite spies, Moses invoked the wrath of God and yet tempered his request with the reminder that "the LORD is slow to anger and in faithful love, forgiving wrongdoing and rebellion" (Num. 14:18). The cliché continues in virtually the same wording throughout the Old Testament (Pss. 86:15; 103:8; 145:8; Jon. 4:2; Nah. 1:3), capped off by Nehemiah's résumé of Israel's rebellious history. Though his ancestors deserved the awesome judgment of God, even to the point of being abandoned by him, the Lord was slow to anger and therefore would not forsake them (Neh. 9:17).

The Anger/Wrath of God

God may restrain his anger for a time; but at last, in the face of incorrigible disobedience, he must bring it to bear. The view that anger somehow is a negative feature unworthy of a God of love and compassion must be examined more deeply against the backdrop of his ineffable holiness, righteousness, and justice. For God never to be angry would be a denial of his full-orbed character in that it would allow him a tolerance of evil diametrically opposed to that which is central to his essence—absolute holiness.[36]

In nearly every case in the Old Testament the Lord was angry not at mankind in general but at his own people. His anger burned against Moses for his excuse-making when called to lead Israel out of Egypt (Exod. 4:14) and again in the incident of the ill-advised smiting of the rock in the desert (Deut. 1:37; cf. 4:21). He was also angry at Solomon because of his toleration of foreign cults and drift toward syncretism (1 Kings 11:9). But God's anger was directed most at Israel as a nation, first and perhaps most vehemently because of the worship of the golden calf. In his fury the Lord instructed Moses to step aside so that he might destroy his people and make of Moses the founder of another. Moses interceded, however, pleading with God to protect his own reputation from the inevitable calumny of the Egyptians and to remember the covenant promises he had made to the fathers. With strong urging Moses begged the Lord to "turn from your great anger and change Your mind about this disaster planned for Your people" (Exod. 32:10–13; cf. Deut. 9:8, 19–20).

A few years later, in the Moabite plains, Israel entered into blatant immorality and idolatry at the shrine dedicated to Baal-Peor. The result was God's burning anger, a rage that could be ameliorated only by the slaughter of the leaders of the rebellion (Num. 25:4). This act of covenant violation was the kind of thing Isaiah had in mind when he spoke of the Lord's anger against his people because they had "rejected the instruction of the LORD of Hosts, and have despised the word of the Holy One of Israel" (Isa. 5:24). Failure to repent of that spirit brought inevitable judgment in the form of exile, under both the Assyrians and the Babylonians. Of the latter the historian notes that "because of the LORD's anger, it came to the point in Jerusalem and Judah that He finally banished them from His presence" (2 Kings 24:20; cf. 2 Chron. 6:36).

---

[36] For helpful insights, see Bruce E. Baloian, *Anger in the Old Testament* (New York: Peter Lang, 1992).

Solomon had anticipated such a result and in his prayer of temple dedication said, "When [not if] they sin against You . . . and You are angry with them and hand them over to the enemy" (1 Kings 8:46). But even this could have been avoided had the conditions of confession and repentance been met. The psalmist asked, "Will You be angry forever?" (Pss. 79:5; 85:6), and the prophet Isaiah answered on behalf of the people in anticipation of the day of their future redemption, "I will praise You, LORD, although You were angry with me. Your anger has turned away, and You have had compassion on me" (Isa. 12:1).

The Forgiveness of God

Wrath and judgment need not be the end of the matter, for God also forgives. This too is a work of grace, but the forgiveness of God is at the same time contingent on the confession and repentance of the guilty. That forgiveness is inherent in the character of the Lord is clear from a number of passages that describe him as One who forgives as a matter of course (Exod. 34:7; Num. 14:18; Pss. 99:8; 103:3; Mic. 7:18). Yet the appeal is made over and over again for him to do so in specific circumstances. Abraham asked whether the Lord would forgive Sodom if a few righteous persons could be found there (Gen. 18:24), and the Lord said he would if the quota was found (v. 26). Moses begged the Lord to forgive idolatrous Israel (Exod. 32:32; 34:9) and after acknowledging him as a forgiving God, pleaded with him to forgive the rebels in the desert (Num. 14:19), a prayer God answered without delay (v. 20).

In his temple prayer Solomon, anticipating Israel's sins in the future, prayed that the Lord would forgive them (1 Kings 8:30, 34, 36, 39, 50). Amos did the same, basing his appeal on God's own reputation as well as his mercy in seeking forgiveness for his people who were living in such ruinous conditions (Dan. 9:19). This is the grounds for the petition of the psalmist as well: "Because of Your name, LORD, forgive my sin, for it is great" (Ps. 25:11).

On the other hand, Job asked, "Why not forgive my sin and pardon my transgression?" (Job 7:21), the answer to which, in another place and time, was, "Why should I forgive you?" (Jer. 5:7). Moses went so far as to say that the Lord would never forgive those who persisted in idolatry (Deut. 29:20; cf. Exod. 23:21), a point that Joshua reiterated with regard to rebellion against God (Josh. 24:19). Isaiah prayed that God would not forgive the wicked generation of his day (Isa. 2:9), and the Lord himself said of adulterous Israel, "I will no longer have compassion on the house of Israel. I will certainly take them away" (Hos. 1:6). The historian, summarizing the events that had led up to Judah's destruction and deportation at Babylonian hands, stated laconically that "the LORD would not forgive" (2 Kings 24:4).

More positive, on the other hand, is the good news that he does and will forgive under other circumstances. David exulted that the Lord "took away the guilt of my sin" (Ps. 32:5), as a result of which he could joyfully proclaim, "How happy is the one whose transgression is forgiven, whose sin is covered" (v. 1). Isaiah promised that the time would come when Zion's sins would be forgiven (Isa. 33:24) and when those who forsook sin and turned to the Lord would be freely pardoned (Isa. 55:7). There are therefore conditions that must be met. The Lord through Jeremiah made clear that he would forgive Judah's sins when "each of one of them will turn from his evil way" (Jer. 36:3). Perhaps the Chronicler records it most fully and clearly in the vision of Solomon: "[If] My people who are called by My name humble themselves, pray and seek My face, and turn from their evil ways, then I will hear from heaven, forgive their sin, and heal their land" (2 Chron. 7:14). God the forgiver forgives freely but only as those in need of it come in true contrition before him and seek his mercy and grace.

Chapter Three

The Revelation of God

The Judeo-Christian tradition holds tenaciously to the idea that God has revealed himself to mankind in a variety of ways but most especially in communication preserved in sacred texts considered authoritative and thus canonical. Without that revelation God could not be known in any meaningful way; in fact, he could not be known at all in propositional terms. God's self-initiated self-disclosure is therefore central to any sensible definition of biblical theology. How and why he revealed himself are questions crucial to the working out of that theology, for it is the corpus of texts understood to be revelation that constitutes the raw material of theological discourse.

In line with the thesis already argued that Genesis is the fountainhead of all subsequent theological reflection, it is striking to observe that the two standard ways of thinking of God's revelation in classical theology—general (or natural) revelation and special revelation—appear at the beginning of the creation narratives. "In the beginning God created the heavens and the earth" (that is, all things) reflects revelation by God's mighty works, that is, natural revelation. "And God said" (Gen. 1:3; cf. 5–7, 9–11, 14, 20, 22, 24, 26, 28–29) suggests revelation by word. The two, the spoken word and the created work, testify to God's existence and ultimately to his character, purposes, and objectives.

Revelation by Word

The record of what God did and said is in the texts that claim for themselves and are claimed by ancient Jewish and Christian tradition to be the Word of God. These claims are not fully articulated at the outset but only gradually and will be examined as they occur. For now it must suffice to look only at the creation narratives themselves for clues to God's self-presentation in the two ways described above. After naming various phenomena such as *day, night,* and *sky,* God turned to the means by which they reveal. Thus, of the heavenly bodies he said, "They will serve as signs for festivals and for days and years" (Gen. 1:14) and "to dominate the day and the night" (v. 18). All generations of mankind that look upon these things draw theological conclusions about them for good or ill, for in some sense they are declarative of God (Ps. 19:1–6; cf. Rom. 1:18–23). With man's creation and consciousness, however, there is not only a being who can "read" the silent revelation of the divine works but who can hear the Creator himself, first in audible tones or other sensory media and then in written texts.[1]

The first recorded utterance is the so-called creation mandate delivered by God to mankind, his image. And it is a word of blessing: "Be fruitful, multiply, fill the earth, and subdue it" (Gen. 1:28). How that word was transmitted is impossible to know—perhaps by dream or vision or even by spoken utterance. Subsequent conversation scenes certainly support the latter possibility (cf. Gen. 2:16–17; 3:3, 9–19, 22). What man learned of God is not presented as some kind of theological insight or deduction based on empirical evidence but as words in ordinary, comprehensible speech.

Revelation by normal conversation or by divine speech uncharacterized as to mode or medium continued throughout the period of primeval history (Gen. 1–11). Cain (4:6) and Noah (6:13) among others appear to have been addressed directly and immediately by the Lord. In the absence of any qualification as to the mode, there is no reason *a priori* to suppose that it was in any way other then verbal. Such occurrences are, indeed, noted elsewhere in much later Old Testament and even New

---

[1] For an early but still useful discussion of the phenomena of revelation, see H. Wheeler Robinson, "The Philosophy of Revelation," *Record and Revelation,* ed. H. Wheeler Robinson (Oxford: Clarendon Press, 1938), 303–20.

Testament literature (Exod. 3:4; Josh. 7:10; 1 Sam. 3:1–18; Matt. 3:17; Acts 9:4–6). With the passing of time, however, spoken revelation was communicated increasingly through secondary channels such as visions and dreams and then eventually by means of prophets.

Revelation by Visions and Dreams

Some hint of this may be seen already in the call of Abram. After the Lord had commanded him to leave Ur and then Haran for a land that he would show him, he appeared to Abram, first at Shechem (Gen. 12:7). The *niphal* stem of the verb here *(rā'āh)* suggests literally that God made himself to be seen. How he was seen is not stated, and perhaps to see means only that he spoke as in former times. Against this, however, is the occurrence of the same verb form in Genesis 18:1 where the Lord's appearance is in tangible form in the person of the angel of the Lord who, in fact, is equated with the Lord himself (Gen. 18:10, 13, 17, 20, etc.). In this instance, at least, the revelation of God is by means of a heavenly agent.

The same verb is used again with reference to the Lord's appearances to Isaac (Gen. 26:2, 24), the second of which was at night, a hint, perhaps, that Isaac saw a dream. Jacob, too, experienced an appearance of God at night while he was anticipating with dread his encounter with his alienated brother Esau (Gen. 35:1; cf. 32:21). Like Abraham, he witnessed a human form of divine manifestation, one with whom he wrestled throughout the night (Gen. 32:22–32). Though the nocturnal setting of the encounter might suggest that this was a dream, Jacob's physical injury as a result of this mismatch testifies otherwise.[2] Clearly God had revealed himself in word and act. Upon his return to Bethel, Jacob had a second experience of God's revelation. He appeared to the patriarch and blessed him, changing his name to Israel (Gen. 35:9–10). From his later conversation with Joseph in which he reiterated the blessing God had pronounced upon him and his descendants, Jacob was aware that he had in some manner or other encountered God Almighty (Gen. 48:3–4).

---

[2] As Gunkel long ago pointed out, "One's hip does not become disjointed in a prayer struggle." Hermann Gunkel, *Genesis,* trans. by Mark E. Biddle (Macon, Ga.: Mercer University Press, 1997) (repr. of German edition of 1901), 349.

Though the revelation of God described as his appearance is attested to a number of times later in the Old Testament, almost always it is in conjunction with some other factor or feature such as the burning bush (Exod. 3:2), the *shekinah* glory (Lev. 9:23; Num. 14:10; 16:19, 42; 20:6; Deut. 31:15), the angel of Yahweh (Judg. 6:12; 13:3, 10), dreams (1 Kings 3:5; 9:2; 11:9), or visions (Ezek. 1:1, 16; etc.). There is an obviously discernible trend from direct, unimpeded revelation by word to revelation mediated through various secondary channels.

Ironically enough, the first account of dream revelation features the pagan ruler of Gerar, Abimelech, who in a dream was informed by the Lord that the woman he was about to take into his harem was the wife of Abraham (Gen. 20:3–7). That such a means of communication by the gods was thought to be possible was, of course, a common belief in the religions of the ancient Near East so Abimelech need not be particularly surprised.[3] For the Lord God of the Hebrews to reveal himself to the heathen is perhaps unexpected, but it is by no means unique. The baker and butler of Egypt had dreams initiated by the Lord (Gen. 40) as did Pharaoh (Gen. 41), an unnamed Midianite soldier (Judg. 7:13), and, most famously, the Babylonian king Nebuchadnezzar (Dan. 2; 4). What this shows, among other things, is that the Lord is sovereign beyond the narrow confines of Israel, acting and revealing himself as he chooses. This, in fact, is precisely the lesson Nebuchadnezzar learned as a result of his dreams (Dan. 4:34–37).

Jacob was the first of the biblical patriarchs who is specifically asserted to have had revelation from God by a dream (Gen. 28:10–15). His reaction upon awaking is worth noting, for he said, in effect, that he had no idea that he was in a place where the revelation of God might be expected. He therefore called the place Bethel, for, as he observed, "This is none other than the house of God. This is the gate of heaven" (Gen. 28:17). Though one should not read too much into this declaration, the reference to a special place of revelation might lend support to the notion that God was felt to be particularly associated with certain holy sites where he was most likely to appear (cf. Gen. 32:30; 35:7, 14; Exod.

---

[3] James C. Vanderkam, "Prophecy and Apocalyptics in the Ancient Near East," *Civilizations of the Ancient Near East,* vol. 3, ed. Jack M. Sasson (New York: Charles Scribner's Sons, 1995) 2083–86; Martti Nissinen, ed. *Prophecy in Its Ancient Near Eastern Context: Mesopotamian, Biblical, and Arabian Perspectives* (Atlanta: Society of Biblical Literature, 2000).

3:5; Deut. 12:5, 14).[4] On the other hand, Jacob told of another dream whose location is undisclosed except that it was somewhere in or about his home in Paddan Aram, far from the land of promise (Gen. 31:10–11). Even here, however, he was told in the dream to return to Canaan, to the place where God had revealed himself at Bethel (v. 13).

Of all the dreams of the patriarchs, Joseph's is most famous. His age at the time of his first dream, only seventeen, is instructive in suggesting that dream revelation was not limited to Israelites or even to patriarchs, prophets, or other persons of recognized leadership. God bestowed his gift of self-disclosure to whomever he would at his own pleasure. Needless to say, Joseph's dreams were not well received by his brothers or even by his father, but their fulfillment in time validated their authenticity as divine revelation.

In later times dreams gradually fell out of use as legitimate modes of revelation, partly because they were increasingly associated with pagan practices and partly because of the rise of prophetism. As early as the time of Moses, there is at least the slightest hint that visions and dreams could not stand on the same plane as the revelation the Lord accorded Moses (Num. 12:6–8). Isaiah derisively described the prophets of his day as blind and mute. They are dogs, he said, who "dream, lie down, and love to sleep" (Isa. 56:10). This, of course, was not a blanket indictment of Israelite prophetism; but it does anticipate Jeremiah's even more scathing assessment of dream revelation as it was manifest by at least some of the prophets he knew:

> I have heard what the prophets who prophesy a lie in My name have said: I had a dream! I had a dream! How long will this continue in the minds of the prophets prophesying lies, prophets of the deceit of their own minds? Through their dreams that they tell one another, they make plans to cause My people to forget My name as their fathers forgot My name through Baal worship. The prophet who has only a dream should recount the dream, but the one who has My word should speak My word truthfully, for what is straw compared to grain?—the LORD's declaration (Jer. 23:25–28).

[4] The notion of sacred space will occupy our attention at length later on. For now see William Dyrness, *Themes in Old Testament Theology* (Downers Grove, Ill.: InterVarsity, 1979), 146–48.

The contrast between worthless straw and precious grain highlights well the deterioration of dream revelation by the seventh century, perhaps because of its openness to fraud and deception.[5]

Akin to the dream is the vision, the main differences between them being that (1) the dream was obviously a phenomenon connected with sleep whereas the vision could and often did occur in waking moments; and (2) the vision is "conceived of as presented to the physical eye."[6] Abram had a vision about a promised heir (Gen. 15:1), and Jacob was told by the Lord in a vision that he should not fear to go down into Egypt (Gen. 46:1–4). Visions, like dreams, were not restricted to God's own people, as the example of the heathen prophet Balaam clearly shows. He saw a vision with his eyes wide open (Num. 24:4), a message that he knew came from "the Almighty" (v. 16). But visions were rare in the cultures outside the circles of Israel.[7] In addition to Balaam, they are linked in the Old Testament only to false prophets cited by Jeremiah (Jer. 14:14; 23:16), Ezekiel (Ezek. 13:6–9, 23; 22:28), and Zechariah (Zech. 10:2). Samuel had a vision of God's call when visions were still rare (1 Sam. 3:15; cf. v. 1). At the same time the text equates the "word of the LORD" with visions, implying that hitherto God's revelation was at least on occasion communicated in that manner. With Samuel's role as founder of the prophetic school visions became much more prolific; in fact, they appear to have become the principal means of divine revelation through the prophets. Few of the canonical prophets fail to attribute their oracles to visions even to the end of the Old Testament era when visions, like dreams, were becoming somewhat suspect as reliable means of communicating truth (Jer. 14:14; 23:16; Ezek. 12:24; 13:6–9, 16, 23; 21:29; 22:28; cf. Isa. 1:1; Ezek. 1:1; 8:3; 40:2; 43:3; Mic. 1:1; Neh. 1:1; Dan. 1:17; 4:5, 10, 13; Zech. 1:8).

Revelation through the Angel of Yahweh

In a number of passages, primarily narrative accounts, a mysterious figure known as the angel (or messenger) of Yahweh appears, either

[5] Robert P. Carroll, *The Book of Jeremiah* (Philadelphia: Westminster, 1986), 474.

[6] Willis Judson Beecher, *The Prophets and the Promise* (Grand Rapids: Baker, 1963), 118.

[7] Herbert B. Huffman, "Prophecy in the Mari Letters," *The Biblical Archaeologist Reader*, vol. 3, ed. Edward F. Campbell Jr. and David Noel Freedman (Garden City, N.Y.: Doubleday, 1970), 200–2.

as a representative of the Lord or, in a few instances, as his surrogate. Though some Christian theologians have proposed that this being was the preincarnate Christ,[8] nothing in the Old Testament alone gives support to such a notion. Nor is it proper to think of any kind of divine incarnation. The angel was just that—a superhuman spokesman for the Lord himself. The occurrences of this angelic person throughout the Old Testament record makes this most apparent.[9]

He first appeared not to Abram or one of the other patriarchs but to Sarah's despised slave girl Hagar. Hagar had been expelled from Abram's camp and driven out into the Negev desert where she found herself in dire straits along with her young son Ishmael (Gen. 16:1–6). With no introduction as to his identity and nature, the angel encouraged Hagar to return to Abram and then promised her, "I will greatly multiply your offspring, and they will be too many to count" (v. 10). The first-person pronoun thus in some sense equates the angel with the Lord, who alone can make such promises. Hagar must have understood this to some degree because the story goes on to say of her that she called him "the God Who sees" (v. 13). Some years later Hagar was banished again, and again the angel came to succor her, this time "from heaven" (Gen. 21:17). He spoke for God, and then the narrator says, "God opened her eyes" (v. 19). Though the angel is not explicitly called God, the juxtaposition of angel and God shows at least a close connection.

Abraham next encountered the angel of Yahweh. Having been commanded by God to offer his son Isaac as a sacrifice, Abraham was about to plunge his dagger into the boy's body when the angel spoke from heaven (as he had to Hagar) and interdicted him (Gen. 22:11). He then spoke a second time from heaven with these remarkable words: "By Myself I have sworn, says the LORD: Because you have done this . . . , I will indeed bless you" (vv. 15–17). Here the angel is virtually equated

---

[8] Thus J. Barton Payne, *Theology of the Older Testament* (Grand Rapids: Zondervan, 1962), 170.

[9] As Eichrodt put it, the angel of Yahweh is a "form of Yahweh's self-manifestation which expressly safeguards his transcendent nature, and associates with this immediate but concealed form of his presence only those special activities which he undertakes among men for the accomplishment of his saving will. In the quasi-human form of the messenger he can temporarily incarnate himself in order to assure his own that he is indeed immediately at hand." Walther Eichrodt, *Theology of the Old Testament,* vol. 2, trans. by J. A. Baker (Philadelphia: Westminster, 1967), 27. We will address further aspects of this figure at a later point.

with the Lord. In a later incident Jacob spoke of him as "the Angel of God" (Gen. 31:11), and again he was at the same time called "the God of Bethel" (v. 13; cf. 48:15–16).

The same theology continues with the story of the burning bush of Moses. The angel of Yahweh appeared to him (Exod. 3:2); and then the narrator says, "When the LORD saw that he [Moses] had gone over to look [at the bush], God called out to him from the bush, 'Moses, Moses'" (v. 4)! Here the "Angel," "the LORD," and "God" appear to be used interchangeably. The angel disclosed himself again in connection with the exodus, leading the hosts of Israel across the sea (Exod. 14:19). At the resumption of the journey from Sinai to Canaan, "an angel" was promised by the Lord to lead the way. He is said to bear the name of the Lord ("My name is in him"), thus associating the angel with the Lord but at the same time making a distinction between them (Exod. 23:21). This same angel would command Israel's armies in the conquest, expelling the Canaanite nations from the land (Exod. 33:2).

The militaristic character of the angel of Yahweh is apparent in the story of the prophet Balaam who, while on his way to curse Israel in Moab, kindled God's anger and then encountered the angel in the pathway (Num. 22:22). The angel stood with drawn sword as the captain of the Lord's hosts, forbidding the mercenary prophet from carrying out his intended objective. The Lord then opened Balaam's eyes; he saw the angel and then prostrated himself in worship. The coalescence of the angel and the Lord, only implicit here, seems complete in the warning of the angel to Balaam: "Go with the men [of Moab], but you are to say only what I tell you" (v. 35). The angel was therefore the Lord, or at the very least, his spokesman.

Only twice more does the angel of the Lord appear in any kind of extended narration, both times in the days of the judges. Overrun by the numerically superior Midianites, Israel, under Gideon's leadership, appeared doomed until the angel of the Lord intervened by offering Gideon words of encouragement (Judg. 6:11–24). Introduced first as the angel (vv. 11–12), he then is called "the LORD" (vv. 14, 16, 18) except by Gideon who took him to be but human and spoke to him as "Lord" (*ʾādôn*) (v. 15). When commanded to offer a sacrifice in place of his intended hospitality meal, Gideon began to understand that his guest was no ordinary man. In fact, once the food has been consumed on the altar,

Gideon exclaimed, "Oh no, Lord God! I have seen the Angel of the Lord face to face" (v. 22)! Not in a mood to quibble over fine theological distinctions, Gideon identified the angel as God himself.

In a final pericope, one recounting the circumstances of Samson's birth, the angel of the Lord once more figured prominently. Bereft of children, Samson's mother encountered the angel who assured her that she would have a son, albeit one who must serve the Lord as a Nazirite (Judg. 13:1–5). She took him to be a prophet ("a man of God," v. 6) who looked like an angel. How this was so she declined to relate, except that he was "awe-inspiring." Manoah, her husband, took her word for what she had seen and prayed to the Lord to send once more the man of God. When the angel returned, the couple offered him a meal (as Gideon had done); but the angel declined with the caveat, "If you want to prepare a burnt offering, offer it to the Lord," not realizing the angel was "the Angel of the Lord" (v. 16). Suspicious, Manoah asked about his name to which the angel replied, "It is wonderful" (v. 18). Manoah then ignited the sacrifice and with amazement watched the angel ascend into heaven in the flames. They then knew he was the angel of the Lord; and falling on his face in worship, Manoah said, "We have seen God!" (v. 22). In his view there was no distinction to be made between the Lord and his angel.

The apparent ambiguity in the biblical witness as to the nature and role of the angel of the Lord as a revelatory agent exists because of a general lack of appreciation of the concept of a representative who stands in for another person in such close relationship as to be virtually identical to him. Such a concept is well understood in diplomatic affairs where, for example, the ambassador of a nation personifies that nation itself to the extent that an act of violence against him could be considered an act of violence against the state he serves. At the same time, of course, the envoy is not in essence the same as his government.

We have dealt already with the matter of God's essence and nature and have observed that the Old Testament testimony unambiguously points to his transcendent invisibility. While communicating with his creation, he is totally different and distant from it. Only by intermediation can that chasm be bridged, and that intermediation is what we are describing as revelation in all its forms. The angel of the Lord, while representing God almost to the point of identifying with him, is not God but only his agent, albeit one with supernatural power and a typological role that for Christians, at least, finds antitypical fulfillment in Jesus Christ.[10]

Revelation through the Divine Names

The names and epithets *Elohim* and *Yahweh* have already been introduced in previous discussions of God as Creator and will receive attention again in the unfolding narrative of his dealings with mankind and especially Israel. The ensuing consideration of the divine names will therefore treat only some of the lesser known and less frequently occurring ones.

A year before his son Isaac's birth, Abram, despairing of ever having a covenant son, was visited by the Lord, who said to him, "I am God Almighty. Live in My presence and be devout. I will establish My covenant between Me and you, and I will multiply you greatly" (Gen. 17:1). This is the first occurrence of a self-designation whereby God revealed something of his character. The other names encountered so far—Elohim (God) and Yahweh (the LORD)—are simply asserted in the text and are never pronounced by the Lord in any revelatory sense. As we have just suggested, these names will receive treatment in due course in other, more revelatory settings. As for the name with which Hagar described God in the desert, it, though theologically pregnant, was her own reaction to the One who had seen her and ministered to her in her time of need. Thus, she called him, indirectly at least, El Lahai Roi, "the Living One Who Sees" (Gen. 16:14).

El Shaddai, translated in Genesis 17:1 as "God Almighty," is of dubious etymology but by usage conveys the idea of the all-abundant One who steps up in times of special urgency and by his power meets human need.[11] In its first occurrence the name is associated with covenant blessing, particularly in the multiplication of offspring (cf. Gen. 12:2; 15:5). Isaac, invoking the name *El Shaddai,* reiterated the blessing to his

---

[10] For a helpful discussion of the theology inherent in the angel as a prototype of Christ, see Geerhardus Vos, *Biblical Theology* (Grand Rapids: Eerdmans, 1954), 85–89.

[11] For a technical lexical study of the name, see Frank M. Cross, *Canaanite Myth and Hebrew Epic* (Cambridge, Mass.: Harvard University Press, 1973), 52–60; a more theological approach is that of U. Cassuto, *A Commentary on the Book of Exodus,* trans. by Israel Abrahams (Jerusalem: The Magnes Press, 1967), 77–79.

son Jacob, praying that he would "make you fruitful and multiply you" (Gen. 28:3). Upon Jacob's return from Aram, God Himself appeared to him, again identifying himself as El Shaddai and promising that "a nation, indeed an assembly of nations, will come from you, and kings will descend from you" (Gen. 35:11). Finally, on his deathbed Jacob blessed Joseph's sons Ephraim and Manasseh, wishing for them the same things that El Shaddai had promised to him (Gen. 48:3–4; cf. 49:25). The common theme permeating these uses of the epithet *El Shaddai* is most apparent; it is in and by this name that the Lord will bless his people Israel in ages to come.

Exodus 6:2–5 is a crucial passage to the use of the name El Shaddai *vis-à-vis* God's more common designation Yahweh (LORD). On the eve of Moses' appearance before Pharaoh, God said to Moses, "I am Yahweh. I appeared to Abraham, Isaac, and Jacob as God Almighty, but I did not make My name Yahweh known to them" (vv. 2–3). Critical questions aside,[12] there remains the conundrum of God's suggestion that he was first being revealed then as Yahweh when, in fact, that name occurs scores of times in the patriarchal narratives and even on the lips of the patriarchs themselves. In fact, Genesis 4:26 states explicitly, "At that time [prior to the Flood] people began to call on the name of the LORD [i.e., Yahweh]."

The most satisfying theological resolution is that God never invoked his name *Yahweh* when making covenant promises to the patriarchs though that name occurs regularly in covenant contexts (e.g., 12:1; 15:1; 22:15). Rather, he revealed himself as El Shaddai in those situations. Something new and momentous was now about to take place in Israel's life under Moses. No longer was the issue immediately one of lands, goods, and offspring but one of exodus redemption and the anticipation of a covenant in which Israel would pledge itself in fealty to the great King whose name *Yahweh* best captures all that these things imply.[13] El Shaddai would now give way to Yahweh as the name by which God would direct the course of sacred history.

---

[12] For these see, e.g., Brevard S. Childs, *The Book of Exodus* (Philadelphia: Westminster, 1974), 111–14.

[13] Christoph Barth, *God with Us: A Theological Introduction to the Old Testament* (Grand Rapids: Eerdmans, 1991), 66–67; Benno Jacob, *The Second Book of the Bible: Exodus*, trans. Walter Jacob (Hoboken, N.J.: KTAV, 1992), 146–47.

Subsequent revelation makes this clear. Almost always where the epithet *El Shaddai* (or *Shaddai* alone) occurs, it is in poetic texts as a parallel to either Yahweh or Elohim (e.g., Num. 24:4, 16; Job 5:17; 6:4, 14; 8:3, 5; 11:7; 13:3; *passim* in Job; Ps. 91:1; Isa. 13:6). Its other uses carry little or no special theological import (Ruth 1:20–21; Ps. 68:14; Ezek. 1:24; 10:5; Joel 1:15).

Revelation through the Prophets

By far the most common medium of divine revelation in the Old Testament was through the prophets. They wrote most of the canonical books and are featured in those books as well as others as being the channels of God's communication. The office of prophet as such first emerged with Samuel and his school in the eleventh century and was moved forward by Elijah and Elisha two centuries later in an institution popularly called "the sons of the prophets." Before these are addressed, however, it may be useful to look at earlier references to prophets to see what information they yield and also to see what, in the pre-Samuel era, prompted a whole new prophetic movement.

The first mention of a prophet is by the Lord to Abimelech of Gerar with reference to Abraham. The patriarch had passed his wife Sarah off as his sister; and just as Abimelech was about to take her into his household, the Lord intervened and said, "Return the man's wife, for he is a prophet" (Gen. 20:7). The evidence of his status as such was that "he will pray for you and you will live." To be a prophet, therefore, was to be an intercessor between God and men.

The term used here is *nābîʾ*, by far the most common Old Testament word to speak of prophets. Etymologically it likely relates to Akkadian *nabû*, "to proclaim, announce," and this meaning fits well with the use of *nābîʾ* throughout the canon.[14] More particularly it suggests speaking on behalf of another, that other almost invariably being the Lord when speaking of the true prophets of Israel. The Greek translation *prophētes* ("speak for") captures the meaning well. A clear instance of this nuance is in the narrative of Exodus 7 where the Lord made the amazing declaration to Moses, "I have made you like God to Pharaoh, and Aaron

[14] P. A. Verhoef, "Prophecy," *NIDOTTE* 4:1067–78.

your brother will be your prophet" (v. 1). That is, Moses would be God in the sense that he would be the channel of revelation and Aaron would be a prophet by proclaiming it. Earlier, in fact, the Lord, speaking to Moses of Aaron, had said, "He will speak to the people for you. He will be your spokesman, and you will serve as God to him" (Exod. 4:16). A prophet, then, was the mouthpiece of God.

Moses eventually submitted to God's call to be a prophetic spokesman and, in fact, became the prophet *par excellence* against whom all others were measured. While still in the desert, he exercised the prophetic gift, one he shared with seventy elders whom he appointed to serve the people with him. To empower them the Lord placed his Spirit on them, and they began to prophesy (Num. 11:16–17, 25). The Hebrew verb form here does not connote the idea of proclamation but rather of behavior; they began to act like prophets.[15] That is, they were overwhelmed by the Spirit and in some form of ecstasy demonstrated to the community that God had indeed invested them with unusual power and authority. Such displays of emotion, however, never characterized the canonical prophets of later times.

Shortly after this incident Moses' siblings Miriam and Aaron challenged his authority as the sole spokesman for the Lord (Num. 12:2). In response the Lord made a most enlightening observation about prophetism in general and that invested in Moses in particular: "If there is a prophet among you from the LORD, I make Myself known to him in a vision; I speak with him in a dream. Not so with my servant Moses; he is faithful in all My household. I speak with him directly, openly, and not in riddles; he sees the form of the LORD" (vv. 6–8). There are two truths to be observed here: (1) God ordinarily revealed himself in visions and dreams; (2) Moses was the only exception. Mosaic prophetism therefore cannot be viewed as the paradigm to which Israelite prophetism was to conform and against which it was to be compared.

The uniqueness of Moses in this respect is elaborated in Deuteronomy 18. The Lord said to Moses with regard to the whole prophetic movement that was to follow, "I will raise up for [Israel] a prophet like you from among their brothers. I will put My words in his mouth, and he will tell them everything I command him" (v. 18). The singular pronoun

---

[15] *HALOT* 1:659.

is used here perhaps to single out one person who would establish an order of prophets that would in turn pave the way for the great canonical prophets of Israel. That man was Samuel who, after a virtual hiatus of three hundred years of prophetic proclamation, introduced a whole new phase of prophetism (1 Sam. 3:1, 19–21).

Before that new phase is explored, it is important to give some attention to the perversion or misappropriation of the prophetic office. Prophetism was a phenomenon abundantly attested to in the ancient Near Eastern world and in a variety of cultures and forms.[16] Based as it was on systems of religious thought and practice greatly at variance with biblical models, its alleged spokesmen for the gods were to be avoided in Israel and their techniques disavowed. Unfortunately, such was not always the case, and thus the Old Testament is replete with guidelines as to how to recognize false prophetism and mandates as to its elimination from Israelite life.

The first example is that of Balaam who, though not described by the term *nābîʾ,* was clearly a soothsayer or seer of some kind, a pagan hired by the king of Moab to curse the people of Israel (Num. 22–24). He came from Pethor (Akkadian Pitru), near Mari on the Euphrates, a place where scores of prophetic texts have been found detailing the divination and incantation techniques displayed by Balaam.[17] Most of the other non-Israelite false prophets mentioned in the Old Testament sprang from Canaanite sources and were continually the target of Israel's true prophets who warned the nation over and over to avoid them and not to be taken in by them (cf. 1 Kings 18:16–40).

The greatest danger came not from outside Israel, however, but from within. Moses warned about prophets who would arise from among God's people and who would either prophesy in the name of other gods or prophesy lies in the Lord's name. Two principal passages, both in Deuteronomy, address this grave threat. In Deuteronomy 13 Moses says that even if a dream prophet were able to perform signs and wonders to authenticate his message, if that message was designed to lead to the worship of other gods, the prophet must be judged false. In other words,

---

[16] James C. Vanderkam, "Prophecy and Apocalyptics in the Ancient Near East," *Civilizations of the Ancient Near East,* vol. 3, ed. Jack M. Sasson (New York: Charles Scribner's Sons, 1995), 2083–94.

[17] A. Malamat, "Prophetic Revelations in New Documents from Mari and the Bible," *Vetus Testamentum* Supp. 15 (Leiden: Brill, 1966), 207–27.

authenticating signs were such only if they were in line with the truth that the Lord is God and only he is to be worshipped. In fact, the Lord himself would allow these charlatans the ability to work such wonders in order that he might know (more correctly, that they might know) the depth of Israel's love for him (vv. 1–4). For an Israelite prophet to apostatize so egregiously was an unthinkable act of treasonous rebellion, one that required nothing less than the death penalty (v. 5). No mercy could be showed, even if the false prophet were a member of one's own family, for the well-being of the whole community outweighed any other consideration of kinship or natural familial affection (vv. 6–11). Furthermore, any town that harbored false prophets and refused to turn them over to Israel's leaders must be placed under *ḥērem,* that is, devoted to the Lord in an act of total annihilation (vv. 12–18). There could be no mistake here as to the heinousness of the sin of prophets who, despite all signs to the contrary, were set on leading God's people astray.

In the other passage, Deuteronomy 18, Moses first cautioned the people of Israel against imitating the abominable practices of the Canaanites, especially in terms of their prophetic devices, and then spoke of an order of prophets to come from within Israel. As to the former, God's people must be on guard because "no one among you is to make his son or daughter pass through the fire, practice divination, tell fortunes, interpret omens, practice sorcery, cast spells, consult a medium or a familiar spirit, or inquire of the dead" (Deut. 18:10–11). Again, the issue was not so much the Canaanite prophets *per se* but Israel's tendency to emulate them as, indeed, they tended to do in every aspect of life.

By stark contrast they were to recall how God had revealed himself to Moses at Sinai, a direct revelation requiring none of the manipulative devices typical of heathen prophetism. And when Moses passed from the scene, that kind of Mosaic prophetism would continue in the form of a prophet like him, that is, an order of prophets who, like Moses, would receive a word from the Lord that was free of human machination and ambiguity. It would be verbal revelation, received in words and to be communicated by words (Deut. 18:14–19). Should such a prophet ever speak from his own heart, however, and not as the spokesman of God, or should he ever speak in the name of other gods, he must be put to death (v. 20). The gravity of the prophetic office was beyond any dispute.

The question still remained: How could a prophet be tested as to his credibility as a true spokesman for the Lord? According to Deuteronomy 13, he would prove fraudulent were he to preach a message advocating the worship of other gods (vv. 1–5). Here the test was whether what he prophesied came to pass (v. 22). One could therefore prophesy in the Lord's name and even urge compliance with his covenant requirements and still prove to be false. In this second test there was also the element of prediction, an element that had to this point been of little interest in defining the prophetic ministry. Now the ability or inability to predict future events would have a bearing on genuine prophetism.

How this test could be applied in all situations is problematic. In short-term cases, that is, within the lifetime of the prophet himself, predictions that he made and that he said would come to pass in his own time could easily be assessed—they were either fulfilled or not. The prophet Hananiah was a case in point (Jer. 28:1–17). He maintained, contrary to Jeremiah, that the Babylonian exile that was already underway would be over within two years and all the looted furnishings of the temple would be returned (vv. 1–5). Jeremiah had already predicted a seventy-year exile (Jer. 25:11–12), a prediction he repeated after Hananiah's two years had already elapsed (29:10). As it turned out, Hananiah died, thus fulfilling a prediction of Jeremiah (28:16–17), but Jeremiah's seventy years still remained unfulfilled at the time of his death. There was no way, then, to validate Jeremiah's prophetic claims for the distant future other than to see him vindicated in the near future, as he was with Hananiah's predicted demise.[18] Daniel later on had no qualms about Jeremiah's reputation; for near the end of the seventy-year epoch, he "understood from the books according to the word of the LORD to Jeremiah the prophet that the number of years for the desolation of Jerusalem would be 70" (Dan. 9:2).

The next move forward in understanding revelation through the prophets revolved around Samuel, the apparent founder of an order of the prophets. Having been devoted by his mother to the service of the Lord, Samuel was in priestly training when God called him to be a prophet (1 Sam. 3:1–21). Up till then, prophets lived and ministered singly, stepping into situations as the need required. Now under Samuel prophetism took on a decidedly different character, one that might rightly

[18] Theo Laetsch, *Bible Commentary: Jeremiah* (Saint Louis: Concordia, 1965), 229.

be described as a movement. Very early on, despite the infrequency of prophetic revelation in the past, Samuel came to be recognized throughout Israel as a true prophet of the Lord. He passed the test of authenticity—the Lord "let nothing he said prove false" (literally, "none of his words fell to the ground")—and it became obvious to all that he was the recipient and dispenser of verbal revelation (vv. 19–20).

That a subtle shift had occurred with the inauguration of Samuel's ministry is hinted at in the historian's observation that "formerly in Israel, a man who was going to inquire of God would say, 'Come let's go to the seer,' because the prophet of today was formerly called the seer" (1 Sam. 9:9). This is not so much a fundamental sea change in the institution itself as it is a change in emphasis or focus, for some persons were called both prophet and seer (e.g., "the prophet Gad, David's seer," 2 Sam. 24:11). The word *seer* is a translation of the participial forms of either *ḥāzāh* or *rā'āh,* both of which mean literally "to see," usually in a normal, mundane sense. When used technically in prophetism, they underscore the receptive side of revelation whereas *nābî',* far more common, emphasizes the proclamatory function.[19] Clearly both aspects were essential to the full-orbed ministry of a true prophet of the Lord.

The first reference to what might be called "institutionalized" or organized prophetism comes from Samuel himself, who told Saul that one of the signs God has called him to be king was that he would meet a band (Heb. *ḥebel)* of prophets descending from a high place, playing instruments and prophesying (1 Sam. 10:1–7). The Spirit would come upon him; and he too would begin to prophesy, thus assuring him that he had been endowed with gifts requisite to kingship. The prophesying here has nothing to do with prediction or even proclamation but, as the verb form suggests, with ecstatic utterance inspired by God's Spirit (cf. Num. 11:25).[20] The same verb form occurs later to describe Saul's henchmen and Saul himself as they sought to apprehend a beleaguered David who was under Samuel's protective custody at Ramah (1 Sam. 19:18–24). In this instance they were overwhelmed by God's Spirit and lay prostrate in convulsive fits of ecstatic prophesying.

---

[19] Eugene H. Merrill, "Name Terms of the Old Testament Prophet of God," *JETS* 14/4 (1971): 239–48.

[20] *HALOT* 1:659.

What Saul and his men saw at Ramah was a group of prophets prophesying, "with Samuel leading them" (v. 20). This group (here *lahăqâ*) is the same as the band mentioned in 1 Samuel 10:5. How Samuel first gathered them and why, what constituted their training (perhaps music, at least; cf. 1 Sam. 10:5), how they functioned under Samuel's headship, and what led to their apparent demise as a band of prophets—such questions cannot be answered.[21] It is possible that they continued in some form or other until they reemerged as "the sons of the prophets" in the days of Elijah and Elisha.

In the interim certain individuals known as prophets or seers undertook public ministry, especially in the court of David. Among these were Nathan (2 Sam. 7:2; 12:25; 24:11; 1 Kings 1:8–10, 22–24, 32–40, 45), Gad (1 Sam. 22:5; 2 Sam. 24:11), and Heman (1 Chron. 25:5). The latter was devoted to prophesying in connection with music whereas Gad served primarily as David's counselor (1 Sam. 22:5), one through whom God spoke directly. Gad advised David of the three options available to him when the Lord was about to punish him for his ill-advised census, and he instructed the king to build an altar on Araunah's threshing-floor "as the LORD had commanded" (2 Sam. 24:18–19).

Nathan's role as close confidant of the king was to inform him of the covenant by which David's royal ancestry would continue forever—a massive and detailed prediction stretching into the eschaton (2 Sam. 7:5–16)—and also to chide him for his adultery and murder (2 Sam. 12:7–12). This dual ministry of the prophets as predictors and proclaimers continued throughout the era of the monarchies and beyond, even to the close of the Old Testament canon. They were spokesmen of the Lord with an eye to the future as well as to their own times. In either case the true prophet was a vehicle of divine revelation, one who declared not his own word but also that of God.

The sudden and mysterious appearance of the prophet Elijah ushered in a whole new phase of prophetic ministry. The first statement by and about this enigmatic character was confrontational, and from that point on his mission was essentially one of standing against the evils of the nation from the king on his throne to the lowliest citizen. Yet all this was

[21] For suggestions, see Verhoef, "Prophecy," *NIDOTTE* 4:1072–74.

clearly done in the name of the Lord and as his mouthpiece (1 Kings 17:14; 19:9, 15; 21:19, 28; 2 Kings 1:16).

The first hint of a continuing institutional order of prophets occurs with reference to the reign of King Ahab of Israel (874–853). His wicked queen Jezebel had initiated a slaughter of many of them, a massacre in the making that prompted one of Ahab's officials, Obadiah, to save those prophets who had managed to escape (1 Kings 18:3–4). Elijah, the head of the "sons of the prophets" as they were now called, lamented that he was the only prophet of the Lord left standing (v. 22), somewhat an exaggeration as the Lord himself made clear later on (19:18; cf. 20:13, 22, 28, 36; 22:8). The already existing company of the prophets at Bethel in Elijah's last days confirms the fact that such a movement was still in place since the days of Samuel 150 years earlier or had been revived from dormancy (2 Kings 2:3).

The sons of the prophets ministered primarily in and around two different sites—Bethel and Jericho. Following Elijah's disappearance into the heavens, they gathered about Elisha, calling him lord even as Elisha had called Elijah father (2 Kings 2:19; 2:12). Both were terms of respect and conveyed the idea that the two great prophets were regarded as the heads of their respective communities. As was the case with Samuel's band of prophetic disciples, however, little is known of the ministry of these sons of the prophets. They lived communally (2 Kings 2:3, 5, 19; 6:1–6) but were not monastic or at least not celibate (4:1). At least one incident suggests that these young men acted on behalf of their masters, carrying out assignments as important as the anointing of Jehu as the future king of Israel, delivering to him a message that the prophet involved said was the word of God transmitted through him (2 Kings 9:1–10).

Beyond that the only reference to the sons (or son) of the prophets is in Amos 7:14 where Amos disclaimed any connection to vocational prophetism: "I was not a prophet or the son of a prophet; rather, I was a herdsman, and I took care of sycamore figs." Since Amos lived a half century or so past Elisha, however, this may not be an allusion to the Elisha school at all but rather just a way of denying any association with professional prophetism.[22]

---

[22] C. Hassell Bullock, *An Introduction to the Old Testament Prophetic Books* (Chicago: Moody, 1986), 74.

Since Amos is generally regarded as the earliest of the canonical prophets, that is, those whose writings were recognized by their contemporaries as Scripture and incorporated into the canonical collection, this leads to a consideration of this next phase of the prophetic tradition. From Amos's time (ca. 760 BC) to the last of the prophets, Malachi (ca. 460 BC)—a period of only three centuries—the sixteen writing prophets spoke and wrote the word of God with full awareness and explicit testimony of doing so. Hundreds of times they introduced their oracles with the formula, "thus says the LORD," and the like, leaving no doubt to those willing to hear them that they had indeed received revelation from him and that they were conveying it in the actual words impressed upon them.

Jeremiah is one example of the awareness of these prophets that they were indeed communicating not just some hazy recollection of a divine encounter but the authentic word(s) of God. Having been incarcerated by wicked King Jehoiakim for his allegedly treasonous advice to surrender to the Babylonians, the prophet took advantage of his leisure to pen the words of what eventually came down to us as the book that bears his name. The original composition, however, was confiscated by the king's officials who took the scroll to Jehoiakim. Sitting by the fire on a cold winter day, the king, enraged by what he read, cut the scroll into pieces and cast them into the fire. Undeterred by this destruction of the autograph of God's written word, Jeremiah set about to do the work all over again, this time adding other writing besides (Jer. 36).

Take careful note of how this narrative reads. The Lord commanded Jeremiah to write on a scroll "all the words" he had spoken from the commencement of Jeremiah's ministry until the present (v. 2). This presupposes Jeremiah's ability (1) to recognize the word of God when impressed by it and (2) to distinguish between what was truly the word of God and what was merely some religious conviction or emotional response to a gracious act of God toward him. Moreover, the text is insistent that "words" (plural, not word or idea in the abstract) were at stake. The record declares that "Jeremiah summoned Baruch son of Neriah. At Jeremiah's dictation, Baruch wrote on a scroll all the words the LORD had spoken to Jeremiah" (v. 4).

After the traumatic and apparently decisive act of the destruction of the scroll, Jeremiah, prompted by the Lord, took another scroll, having been told: "Take another scroll, and once again write on it the very words that were on the original scroll that Jehoiakim king of Judah burned" (v. 28). Handing the scroll to Baruch, Jeremiah began at the beginning; and as he dictated, "Baruch . . . wrote on it at Jeremiah's dictation all the words of the scroll that Jehoiakim, Judah's king, had burned in the fire" (v. 32). The intent of the narrative is beyond dispute: The word of God to the prophets was verbal; and what they spoke and wrote, therefore, was also verbal.[23] The means by which the verbalizing was effected is never disclosed, nor is it necessary to know. The point is that the prophetic word, the highest form of divine revelation, was recognized at the time to be the words of God, a view maintained by virtually unanimous consensus in Jewish and Christian tradition until the inroads of modern criticism.

Revelation through Signs

In addition to revelation by dream, vision, and word, the Lord, active in and through events, also revealed himself by signs and deeds. When the great flood was over, God made a covenant with Noah that included the promise never again to destroy the earth with a flood. Then, as a reminder to himself—and surely to mankind—he placed a rainbow in the sky to be "a sign of the covenant between me and the earth" (Gen. 9:13). The rainbow spoke (and speaks), therefore, of an aspect of the character of God, namely, his covenant loyalty.

The terms most commonly employed to speak of the communicative signs and wonders of the Lord are *ʾôt* and *môpēt,* both of which are found frequently in the same contexts and used interchangeably.[24] They function most often to indicate God's presence in any given place or situation or to serve as pledges of events that lay still in the future. In either case they were revelatory though obviously in not such an unambiguous manner as the prophetic word. This is why many of the signs were accompanied by an interpretive word uttered by a prophet or other trustworthy spokesman.

Many of these signs were clustered around the exodus event because of the enormous historical and theological significance of that period. When Moses questioned whether God had called him to lead the people,

---

[23] Laetsch, *Bible Commentary: Jeremiah,* 287.

[24] Paul A. Kruger, אות, *NIDOTTE* 1:331–33.

the Lord told him that when he arrived back at Sinai after the exodus, that arrival itself would constitute a sign of his divine call (Exod. 3:12). As for the people of Israel, their skepticism about God's presence, especially with Moses, would be allayed by such signs as the turning of his rod into a snake and the healing of his leprous hand (Exod. 4:1–8). If those signs failed, perhaps they would believe when water turned to blood (v. 9).

Pharaoh also would witness miraculous signs and wonders designed to reveal Israel's God and his power. These were first performed in part exclusively in the presence of the Israelites to convince them that the Lord was with them and also to persuade them that the signs would be effective before Pharaoh (Exod. 4:17, 21, 28, 30). In this hope they would be disappointed, however, for over and over again Pharaoh hardened his heart against the overwhelming evidence of God's presence (Exod. 7:3; 8:19; 10:1–2; 11:9–10). Nor were the Israelites much more sensitive to God's disclosure of himself and his purposes through these supernatural works. Inquiring of Moses the Lord asked, "How long will these people despise Me? How long will they not trust in Me despite all the signs I have performed among them?" (Num. 14:11; cf. v. 22).

Such remarkable demonstrations on their behalf ought to have persuaded the Israelites that Yahweh is God (Deut. 4:34; 6:22) and that he was able to deliver them from whatever they might face in the future (Deut. 7:19; 11:2–9). Sadly, even these clear revelations were unable to penetrate their hardened hearts and darkened minds (Deut. 29:2–6).

Central to the epitaph of Moses was the tribute that "He was unparalleled for all the signs and wonders the LORD sent him to do against the land of Egypt—to Pharaoh, to all his officials, and to all his land, and for all the mighty acts of power and terrifying deeds that Moses performed in the sight of all Israel" (Deut. 34:11–12). Joshua, in his farewell address, recollected this series of events; and his audience, mindful of them, pledged their undying loyalty to the Lord, a loyalty questioned, however, by a dubious Joshua (Josh. 24:16–20). Long afterward the works of the Lord were celebrated by the poets of Israel but often with reminders that their ancestors had not properly appreciated them or seen God in them (Ps. 78:40–56; cf. 105:27; 135:8–12). They exhorted their own hearers, on the other hand, not to forget these signs that testified to the power and glory of their God (Ps. 105:5).

Signs occurred sporadically in Israel's later history to attest to God's presence and/or to provide witness to what he would do in the future. Gideon asked for a sign confirming his call to leadership (Judg. 6:17); Eli was given a sign that his priestly line would end (1 Sam. 2:34), and Saul was promised and given signs that God had indeed called him to be Israel's king (1 Sam. 10:7, 9). Years later an unnamed prophet made his way to the illicit shrine established by Jeroboam I of Israel and declared that King Josiah would some day destroy that evil place. As a sign thereof, the altar was split apart and its ashes strewn about (1 Kings 13:1–5). In due course the prophecy came to pass in accordance with the predictive sign (2 Kings 23:15–16).

One of the most famous signs occurred in relation to the message of Isaiah to King Hezekiah that the king had contracted an illness from which he would not recover (2 Kings 20:1–11; cf. Isa. 38:1–8; 2 Chron. 32:24). The Lord, moved by Hezekiah's prayer, relented and promised him fifteen more years of life. Heartened by this good news, Hezekiah nevertheless asked what sign he might have to certify that the message of the prophet would, indeed, come to pass. God, altering the whole rhythm of the universe, made the shadow of the sun retreat on the sundial of Ahaz by ten steps.[25] This stupendous act, though in no way a word from God as such, confirmed that word and thus was as much a revelation in its own way as was the oracle of the prophet.

The same prophet had announced a sign to rebellious and reluctant King Ahaz confirming the fact that the Lord would bring upon him and the nation an awesome judgment at the hands of Assyria (Isa. 7:3–17). That sign would be the birth of a baby boy to a young woman who hitherto had never conceived, and his name would be Immanuel (v. 14). The child presumably was born shortly thereafter (Isa. 8:3–4); and before much time had elapsed, the Assyrians came and wreaked havoc on both Israel and Judah. The New Testament elevated this sign to a new and more glorious dimension, seeing in it a prediction of the virgin birth of Jesus Christ (Matt. 1:22–23).

---

[25] Though post-Enlightenment rationalism cannot accept the literal reality of such a sign, nothing in the text itself affords an alternative interpretation. See Paul R. House, *1, 2 Kings*, NAC, vol. 8 (Nashville: Broadman & Holman, 1995), 373.

Sometimes the prophets themselves were signs, either by some work they performed or merely by their presence. Isaiah declared himself and his children to be signs (Isa. 8:18; cf. 20:1–5), and Ezekiel in particular is singled out as being in his life and labors a metaphor communicating divine revelation. He drew a map of Jerusalem and pretended to lay siege to the city, thus providing a sign of its imminent destruction (Ezek. 4:1–3). Then, dressed like a prisoner of war, he appeared in public as a portent of the exile that was already underway and that would intensify (12:3–6). Finally, the prophet, bereft of his beloved wife, was told by the Lord not to weep or mourn but rather to serve as an example of the futility, indeed, the impropriety of national lament over the forthcoming devastation of the Babylonian conquest (Ezek. 24:15–27). "You will be a sign for them," the Lord told the prophet, "and they will know that I am the LORD" (v. 27).

Nonverbal signs like these, though lacking in precision and suffering from the likelihood of misinterpretation without a clarifying word, were nonetheless means of revelation. They, like God's works in creation and his mighty acts in history, certified who he is and offered pledges as to what he would do in the future.

Revelation through Lots

The discussion of revelation in the Old Testament would be incomplete without some attention to manipulable devices such as lots and their special category, the priestly Urim and Thummim. Resort to the techniques typical of ancient Near Eastern divination; and incantation was, as we have noted above, strictly forbidden. The casting of lots as a divinely sanctioned means of decision making was, however, not only permitted under certain circumstances but actually commanded. Though not verbal in the strict sense, the information yielded by such means did provide access to the mind of the Lord in response to verbal questions.

The lot (Heb. *gôrāl)* was employed almost exclusively for the division of the land among the tribes and clans of Israel following the conquest and the allocation of Levitical and priestly assignments in the tabernacle and temple. Its use is first attested to in Numbers 26 where the question of equitable apportionment of the promised land became an issue. It must be divided in proportion to the population of the clans (vv. 53–54), but the parts of the tribal inheritances in which they would settle would be determined by casting lots (vv. 55–56). The nature of these devices and how they were employed can no longer be known, but they were likely similar to the dice used in modern times.[26]

Once the conquest was over, lots were cast as Moses had stipulated and the various entities received their rightful inheritances (Josh. 14:1–2; 15:1; 16:1; 17:1, 14, 17; etc.). The Levites were a special case since they had no geographic allotment but only certain cities where they were to minister to the surrounding peoples. But these cities, like the distributions to the tribes and clans, also were determined by lot. Thus the Kohathites (Num. 21:11–26), the Gershonites (vv. 27–33), and the Merarites (vv. 34–40) occupied forty-eight towns throughout the land as the Lord made clear to them through the casting of lots.

Once David had built his house of worship on Mount Zion and installed the ark there, he took charge of the recruitment of temple personnel, assigning them their places of residence in line with Torah prescription (1 Chron. 6:54–81) and then defining for them by lot their various duties in and about the temple (1 Chron. 24:5, 7, 31). The same was done for the Levitical musicians whose ministry was also associated with the temple. Their particular duties, organization, and schedules were all determined by lot (25:8–9). The gatekeepers likewise followed procedures determined by lot (26:13–14).

A special use of the lot was associated with Yom Kippur, the Day of Atonement, when, as an important part of the ritual, two goats were selected as sin offerings. One of these would be slain; but the other, the scapegoat, could remain alive and secure atonement for the people by being driven off into the desert. This second animal was chosen by lot and not arbitrarily or according to some criterion (Lev. 16:7–10). But the other goat also was chosen in this manner. It was "the goat chosen by lot for the Lord" (v. 9) and that must therefore be offered upon the altar. Two lots were used in the process and not just one. One must have pointed out the scapegoat and the other the sacrificial goat but in what manner or means is unclear.[27] What is clear is that all this was done under God's own direction (Lev. 16:1–2).

---

[26] Cf. Joh. Lindblom, "Lot-casting in the OT," *VT* 12 (1962): 164–78.

[27] Jacob Milgrom, *Leviticus 1–16,* AB 3 (New York: Doubleday, 1991), 1019–22.

The Urim and Thummim were akin to the lots just described and yet the differences are also worth noting.[28] First, their origin, description, and even the meaning of the terms ("lights" and "uprightness"?) are shrouded in mystery. They are first mentioned in connection with the apparel of the chief priest who was to place them in the breastpiece of his ephod (Exod. 28:29–30; cf. Lev. 8:8), perhaps in a pocket or pouch of some kind. Their purpose, if not their mode of function, is quite clear: The chief priest could use them to elicit revelation from the LORD, probably in a simple binary or yes and no manner (Num. 27:21). When King Saul in desperation sought a revelation from the Lord, "the LORD did not answer him in dreams or by the Urim or by the prophets" (1 Sam. 28:6). That is, he had no private word from God, nor could he access one through either priests or prophets.

Lots—including the Urim and Thummim—provided infallible revelation when properly administered, but such revelation was obviously rather *ad hoc* and very much bound to special and limited situations. Only the word mediated through prophets and eventually written and canonized provided first Israel and then the church an unambiguous and everlastingly relevant divine disclosure.

---

[28] Cornelis Van Dam, *The Urim and Thummim* (Winona Lake, Ind.: Eisenbrauns, 1997).

Chapter Four

The Works of God

In prefacing the previous section on God's revelation, we observed that it was communicated in the Old Testament through either his words (by a variety of channels) or his works. It is to the latter that we now turn, not just as an extension of God's revelatory design but as a means of becoming conversant with his purposes for mankind from another angle. His works do, indeed, reveal much about his nature and character, but they also—and perhaps more importantly—constitute those turning points that make sense of history and point to eschatological fulfillment. In line with the method already established in this work, we begin at the beginning of the canonical record with the act of creation.

Creation

The second word of the Hebrew Bible is *bārāʾ,* a verb almost universally translated *created.*[1] It occurs only about fifty times with this meaning and always with God as subject. The lexical evidence suggests, therefore, that only God can and does create, the creative endeavors of human beings being expressed by other verbs, some of which do, indeed,

---

[1] Raymond C. Van Leeuwen, ברא, *NIDOTTE* 1:730.

appear in synonymous parallelism with *bārā'*. Some scholars argue on the basis of its exclusively divine subject that *bārā'* means to create out of nothing *(creatio ex nihilo)*. There is nothing inherent in the lexeme itself, however, nor in its usage to prove that point conclusively though the creation narratives of Genesis 1 and 2 clearly favor that view.[2]

Two major passages in the Old Testament focus on God's work of creation, namely, Genesis 1–2 and Isaiah 40–55, and a number of the Psalms provide helpful comment. These occur where they do (1) in order to instruct Israel as to her origins as a nation among nations and as to her role in the kingdom purposes of God that precipitated his work of creation; and (2) to enable exilic Israel to understand that a re-creation is about to take place, one with both historical (return from exile) and eschatological (restoration and reconstitution of the nation to its intended perfection) dimensions. Thus, in a sense history begins and ends with creation.

The object of the creation in Genesis 1 is the heavens and the earth, that is, all things that exist. The narrative admits of no precreation matter out of which everything was made, nor does it bother to provide a detailed description as to how it was done. The account is theological and not cosmological; and though scientific inquiry into processes is not illegitimate, it misses the point and can never recover the intent of the text. That God preexisted his creation and by fiat declaration brought it to pass is the central message.

The details that appear contribute to the theology intended by the narrative. What God made was "formless and empty" *(tōhû wābōhû)*, that is, without discernible structure or design (cf. Jer. 4:23). Moreover, the "great deep" *(tēhôm)* or primeval oceans were overlaid with darkness with God's Spirit hovering over the whole (Gen. 1:2). "Formless and empty" and "darkness" may appear to be foreboding, but they simply are ways of describing reality that has not yet been touched by the shaping and enlightening presence of God.[3] There is no hint of imperfection or fallenness but only of the anticipation of the difference he makes when he engages in the oversight of nature and history. The Spirit is to be

---

[2] Alexander Heidel, *The Babylonian Genesis,* 2nd ed. (Chicago: The University of Chicago Press, 1963), 89–96.

[3] Weston W. Fields, *Unformed and Unfilled* (Nutley, N.J.: Presbyterian and Reformed, 1976), 129–30.

understood here as an effect of God and not yet, as in New Testament and Christian theology, the third Person of the triune Godhead.[4]

The hovering of the Spirit suggests loving care on God's part for what he is about to do, and that is to speak order out of chaos and light out of darkness. Two motifs come to the fore at this point: (1) the contrast between light and darkness and (2) the division of things from one another. Light and darkness are common biblical antitheses with clear spiritual overtones. God is light and evil is dark, and those who know God walk in light whereas those who do not know him walk in darkness (Pss. 18:28; 82:5; 89:15; Prov. 4:18–19; 13:9; Isa. 5:20; Lam. 3:2). The light that comes with the spoken word is, in some sense, a metaphor for the holiness and glory of God. It dispels the darkness and prepares the way for living things.

The second motif—separation—appears in the division between light and darkness (v. 4), the earthly and atmospheric waters (vv. 6–7), the earth and the seas (v. 9), and the day and the night (v. 14). Order emerges out of chaos by the separation of the constituent and often contradictory elements of creation. The days of creation that follow the initial act can be seen as complementary according to some rhetorical structures.[5] Thus the light and darkness of day one corresponds to day and night of day four; the separation of the waters of day two matches the creation of the marine and aerial creatures of day five; and the dry land with its vegetation of day three finds a counterpart in the creation of land animals and man himself in day six. The separation of contrasting entities is balanced by the complementary pairing of the separated parts into a harmonious, almost symbiotic pattern. Day seven is the culmination of the whole, its distinctiveness lying in the fact of its uniqueness.

Throughout the narrative the Lord renders a verdict about what he has done; it was good (vv. 4, 10, 12, 18, 21, 25) or, in the case of the creation of man, very good (v. 31). This assessment not only speaks to the physical and moral perfection of creation but draws attention to the aesthetic as well. God's creation serves not only a practical function but is designed

---

[4] Eugene H. Merrill and Alan J. Hauser, "Is the Doctrine of the Trinity Implied in the Genesis Creation Account?" *The Genesis Debate,* ed. Ronald Youngblood (Nashville: Thomas Nelson, 1986), 110–29.

[5] Kenneth Mathews, *Genesis 1–11:26,* NAC 1A (Nashville: Broadman & Holman, 1996), 113–16.

to give pleasure to those who witness it and participate in it. This aspect of his creative genius appears over and over again in the biblical record in God's insistence that what is done for him by mankind be of exquisite beauty of workmanship, for such an aesthetic endeavor is a reflection of his own beauty. The later construction of the tabernacle and temple makes this point most clearly (Exod. 25:1–9; 28:1–5; 1 Chron. 29:1–5).

The crowning work of creation was the appearance of mankind on the sixth day (Gen. 1:26–28). He is said to be in the image and likeness of God, but the grammar permits and theology favors the idea that he was created *as* his image and likeness, that is, as God's representative on earth.[6] The "us" of the optative verb form "let us" (v. 26) should be construed not as hinting of a plurality of divine persons or even as God's consultation with angelic beings but merely as a literary convention (plural of deliberation) common in the ancient as well as modern world.[7] God alone initiated the idea and carried out the work of bringing into existence a creature who would serve him as his agent of dominion over all the created order.

The purpose and function of mankind will be addressed in greater detail at a later point; for now only some general and preliminary observations need be made. First, it is clear that man was created for a specific task, to rule under God's hegemony. In the first address to man and the first statement as to his role in creation God said, "Be fruitful, multiply, fill the earth, and subdue it. Rule the fish of the sea, the birds of the sky, and every creature that crawls on the earth" (v. 28). The need for population increase was to enable mankind to exist in sufficient numbers as to cover the whole expanse of God's dominion.

The cosmological account of creation in which mankind is merely introduced, though in clearly a climactic and central way, yields to a second narrative whose focus is exclusively on him and his God-given responsibility. Between the two accounts, however, a hiatus is introduced and concluded by the observation that all things were completed and that the record of the creation of the heavens and the earth was at an end (2:1, 4). That hiatus is punctuated by the introduction of the seventh day,

---

[6] See the more full discussion of this on pp. 168–169.

[7] Claus Westermann, *Genesis 1–11: A Commentary* (Minneapolis: Augsburg, 1984), 145; cf. Genesis 11:7; 2 Samuel 24:14; Isaiah 6:8.

the Sabbath,[8] a day on which God did no work and which thereafter was to be a reminder both of God's creation and of his cessation from labor (Exod. 20:8–11). The placement of the injunction to observe the Sabbath was well conceived for man as a worker was about to be introduced. He, like his Maker, must at regular intervals pause to reflect upon his work with appreciation and renewed vigor.

The story of mankind's creation—the anthropologic account—is introduced by the need for someone to "work the ground" on God's behalf (Gen. 2:5). No vegetation had yet appeared and no rain had fallen; only artesian springs provided life-giving nourishment to the soil. Everything was in suspension until God brought man upon the scene to carry out the creation mandate that had already been declared (Gen. 1:28). Now filling in the details of man's creation, described only in broad brush strokes before, the text reveals that "the LORD God formed *(yāṣar)* the man out of the dust from the ground and breathed the breath of life *(nišmat ḥayyîm)* into his nostrils, and the man became a living being *(nepeš ḥayyâ)*" (Gen. 2:7).[9]

The highly figurative language of the text is designed to emphasize the intimate involvement of the Lord (Yahweh) in this version of human creation as opposed to the more distant, almost impersonal noninvolvement of God (Elohim) in Genesis 1. For God to form, breathe, plant, and place is to put in human terms activities that clearly required no effort or labor on his part but simply the spoken word as the Genesis 1 narrative presents it. But the theology of the immanence of God is important to help mere mankind have at least some grasp of his nearness and participation in human affairs.

The creation of man is distinct from and clearly superior to the creation of the animals in both its result (man is the image of God) and its process. God breathed the breath of life, thus imparting into man something of his own essence. This is not said of other creatures who are merely formed out of the ground (Gen. 2:19; cf. 1:20–25). Whatever the breath of life might be, the manner of its impartation is unique to the human race.[10]

---

[8] From *šābat,* "to rest" or "cease"; *HALOT* 2:1407.

[9] For the various technical terms used here and elsewhere in the Old Testament to describe the nature of the human being, see Hans Walter Wolff, *Anthropology of the Old Testament* (Philadelphia: Fortress, 1974), esp. 10–60.

[10] Gordon J. Wenham, *Genesis 1–15,* WBC 1 (Waco, Tex.: Word, 1987), 60–61.

Perhaps it is the sum of the human characteristics and attributes such as rationality, introspection, creativity, and God-consciousness that separate man from the rest of creation.

The breathing of God into the body of the man produced a *nepeš,* that is, a living being. This result by itself is not distinctly human, however, for even animals are said to be living beings *(nepeš ḥayyîm)* (Gen. 2:19; 9:10–16; Lev. 11:10–46; Ezek. 47:9). It is thus the process of the creation and not its result that makes man different and superior. Not to be overlooked is the fact that man is not said to have *gotten* a *nepeš* (commonly translated *soul*) but to have *become* one. Classical trichotomy, even if it be theologically accurate in light of later (New Testament) revelation, cannot find its basis in Old Testament anthropology.

The creation of woman in the Genesis 1 account is subsumed under "man" in the generic sense (v. 26). She, like the male, was entrusted with the creation mandate of exercising lordship as the image of God. The text is clear in this regard: "So God created man in His own image; He created him in the image of God; He created them male and female" (v. 27). The anthropomorphic picture of God creating the woman from Adam's rib must therefore be seen as a functional distinction of the woman from the man and not an essential one (Gen. 2:21). They are both the image of God, they are both to have dominion, and it follows that they are both to work the garden and otherwise serve the Lord their God. In fact, Adam's inability to care for all these things prompted the creation of woman, a companion described literally as "a helper who is like him" (2:18). The term *helper (ʿēzer)* suggests that the woman, far from being a mere assistant or even servant to the man, was his complement, his other half without which he would be incomplete and incapacitated.[11]

Just as the formation of man from the dust of the ground is best understood as the language of accommodation to human cognitive limitation, so the woman's origins as a rib of Adam must be similarly understood. The point is not that Eve was a physical part of Adam that became separated from him but rather that the relationship between them was so intimate that they could be said to have had a common physical source.[12] The opposite of that idea is expressed in the union of the two:

---

[11] The same term occurs frequently to describe God, who clearly is not thereby inferior to mankind; cf. Exod. 18:4; Deut. 33:7; Pss. 115:9, 11; 121:2; 124:8, *HALOT* 1:811–12.

[12] Mathews, *Genesis 1–11:26,* 216.

"This is why [her being "bone of my bone"] a man leaves his father and mother and bonds with his wife, and they become one flesh" (Gen. 2:24). They do not literally become one flesh nor was Eve literally fashioned from Adam's rib. The picture of intimacy created by this imagery transcends anything that could be said by a flat theological assertion and for that reason is so much the more beautiful and communicative.

Isaiah's preoccupation with creation is much more theologically oriented, not in its inherent theological content but in its interpretive thrust.[13] The prophet, making use of the ancient Torah traditions, expands upon them in both a polemical and an eschatological manner. He speaks from the vantage point of a prophet who, witnessing the calamitous days of Jewish exile, declares that that era will end with a glorious return to the homeland, one both in historical times and at the end of the age. His special appeal is to the God of creation who, having created all things in the beginning, is well able to re-create, to make all things new, as it were. And this ability is unique to him, the true God of Israel, a theological point made crucially important by the fact that the exiles were living in a Babylonian culture rife with pagan creation mythologies. The questions to be addressed were: Is the Lord truly God, and is he able to subdue all other gods and bring his people back to the land of their fathers?

The polemic begins in Isaiah 40:26 with the rhetorical question, "Who created these?" (with reference to the starry hosts). The answer, of course, is that the Lord did, the One to whom nothing can be compared (v. 25). He, as Creator, will also transform the deserts into lush garden land through which his exiled people can make their journey back to their homeland (Isa. 41:20). His power as Creator will furthermore be evident in history. He will empower his chosen servant by his Spirit, enabling him to bring forth justice in the earth. And as the one "who created the heavens and stretched them out, who spread out the earth and what comes from it, who gives breath to the people on it and life to those who walk on it" (Isa. 42:5), he will lead his servant to the successful completion of his mission (cf. vv. 1–7).

---

[13] Philip B. Harner, "Creation Faith in Deutero-Isaiah," VT 17 (1967): 298–306; Theodore M. Ludwig, "The Traditions of the Establishing of the Earth in Deutero-Isaiah," *JBL* 92 (1973): 345–57.

Israel can take comfort in the Lord despite the oppression of exile for "the One who created" them and "the One who formed" them will also redeem them (Isa. 43:1). In fact, he had created them at the beginning for his glory, a reference no doubt to God's choice of Abraham as the father of the covenant nation (v. 7; cf. v. 15).[14] The juxtaposition of creation and redemption is an important theological idea, one whose roots go back implicitly to the exodus at least. Israel was regarded by the Lord as his firstborn son, created such, as it were, by God's elective grace (Exod. 4:22; cf. Gen. 18:19; Deut. 7:7–8; Isa. 63:16). That son was in bondage to another lord, mighty Egypt, and must be delivered and brought to the land promised to the ancestors so that he might there live out his covenant commission.

Isaiah 45 is especially rich in allusions to creation. The chapter begins with an assurance to the Persian king Cyrus that the Lord will use him, pagan though he is, to effect the return of Israel from exile to their own land. He reminds him at the same time that only he is God and there is no other, not even in Persia. With perhaps an overt reference to the state cult of Persia that was emerging at the time—one based on the teachings of Zoroaster—Isaiah, speaking for the Lord, says, "I form the light and create darkness, I make success and create disaster; I, the LORD, do all these things" (v. 7). At the heart of the Zoroastrian mythology is the idea of a dualism of light and darkness, a ceaseless struggle between them for dominance.[15] The Lord dismisses this notion by asserting that these phenomena are nothing but products of his own creation and therefore serve his creation purposes.

Any lingering questions doubting Israel might have about God's ability to choose Cyrus and use him as an instrument of redemption should be muffled in light of the fact that "I made the earth, and created man on it," (v. 12) he says, and therefore "I will raise up Cyrus in my righteousness" (v. 13 NIV). Then, when the redemptive work has been accomplished, those who make and worship idols and attribute success to them will be forced to conclude that there is no other God than the Lord (v. 14). Creation as a basis for such acknowledgment is clear from the participial predications of verse 18: "For this is what the LORD says—God is the

---

[14] Franz Delitzsch, *Biblical Commentary on the Prophecies of Isaiah,* vol. 2 (Grand Rapids: Eerdmans, n. d.), 189–90.

[15] John B. Noss, *Man's Religions,* 3rd ed. (New York: Macmillan, 1963), 471–74.

Creator of the heavens, He formed the earth and made it; He established it; He did not create it to be empty, [but] formed it to be inhabited." Israel's hopes for redemption in the future lay in the God who created all things in the past.

Isaiah's final word on the matter of creation addresses the eschatological transformation that will usher in the kingdom of God in all its fullness and perfection. The Lord promises that he will create two new things—a new heaven and a new earth, and a new Jerusalem (Isa. 65:17–18). The implications of that for Old Testament theology will be the subject of a later treatment. For now it suffices to say that the new creation will repristinate the old but with the impossibility of its tragic fall and dissolution and with even more heightened dimensions.

Judgment

The fall of mankind into sin and alienation from God engendered far-reaching consequences that could never have been imagined by the first couple: exile from paradise, family strife, murder, rebellion, and death. The race had become infected with an incurable disease and without divine intervention would have utterly perished. As the narrative puts it, "The earth was corrupt in God's sight, and the earth was filled with violence [and] all flesh had corrupted its way on the earth" (Gen. 6:11–12). The verdict was "I [the Lord] have decided to put an end to all flesh, for the earth is filled with violence because of them; therefore I am going to destroy them along with the earth" (v. 13). This first threat of judgment was tempered by the fact that "Noah . . . found favor in the eyes of the Lord" (v. 8), but the judgment nonetheless came in the universal flood, an act of devastation that required nothing less than a virtual re-creation for its recovery. Judgment is thus also an act of God, a response to the violation of his holy and righteous standards, principles that in turn are reflective of his character.

Judgment in the Old Testament ranged from such cataclysmic and universal examples as the flood to instances affecting just one or a few individuals. In no case, however, was it forthcoming in a whimsical manner or as merely an expression of God's sovereign prerogative to act as he pleases regardless of circumstantial considerations. His judgment was always prompted by a failure on the part of the parties who suffered it to conform to expected norms of attitude and behavior.

The narrative of the tower of Babel (Gen. 11:1–9), like the flood story, is another example of widespread judgment, this time the confusion of speech and dispersion of the human race because of a failure to obey the mandate to increase in number, fill the earth, and subdue it (Gen. 1:28; cf. 9:7). Judgment may therefore not always result in death or destruction, but in the altering of a course of events to bring people into line with the purposes of God.

By way of another example, God's judgment on the cities of the plain was narrowly focused both geographically and in terms of its rationale (Gen. 18:16–19:26). All that is said is that their sin was "extremely serious" (18:20), so much so that their reputation had reached all the way to heaven. God's intention was to destroy them at once; but because of Abraham's intercession, God relented little by little until his justice required that judgment come if only one sinner remained. Abraham's query as to whether the just should perish with the unjust, couched in the almost accusatory interrogation, "Won't the Judge of all the earth do what is just?" (18:25), highlights both Abraham's role as a prophet and also his inability to fathom the mystery of God's righteousness in light of the fact that he was about to annihilate a whole population of men, women, and children. This dilemma persists throughout the Old Testament record and poses one of the most perplexing of all theological conundrums. For now it will suffice to point out that the kind of total, unexceptional destruction envisioned here is characteristic of holy war, an issue to be addressed at length at a more appropriate place. It resulted in a "sweeping away" (Heb. *sāpāh*; v. 23), a removal of not only living beings but also material structures and, in this case, even the vegetation itself (19:25).

The judgment of the Lord upon Egypt much later was precipitated by the pharaoh's truculent and stubborn resistance to the demand of the Lord through Moses that the people of Israel be freed to leave the land and worship him (Exod. 5:1–2). Behind this demand, of course, was the concern of the Lord for the suffering of his people and his commitment to honor his covenant with their patriarchal ancestors (Exod. 3:7–10, 16–17). When Moses' pleas went unanswered, God sent the plagues, a series of judgments that culminated in the death of Egypt's firstborn sons (cf. 6:6; 7:4; 12:12). Such acts of divine wrath were performed not only to punish Pharaoh for his intransigence but to open his eyes to the reality that only the Lord of Israel is God and to induce him to avert even worse disaster by allowing the Hebrews to leave the land. The latter was ineffective as it turned out so the Lord levied his judgment, a response celebrated in the Song of the Sea: "LORD, Your right hand is glorious in power. LORD, Your right hand shattered the enemy" (Exod. 15:6; cf. Ps. 76:6–9).

The exodus story drives home the point that judgment inevitably falls upon those resistant to the redemptive purposes of the Lord. Moreover, judgment is applied whenever mere men, kings or not, refuse to recognize and submit to his sovereignty as Lord over all. Even Pharaoh's magicians were forced to concede, in light of the evidence, that "this is the finger of God" (Exod. 8:19), referring to the mighty works that they could not replicate. But Pharaoh lacked even that degree of spiritual sensitivity until at last he personally encountered God's judgment with the loss of his own firstborn son and heir to the throne (Exod. 12:29).

Being Israelite did not of itself exempt the disobedient from judgment. The narratives of the desert sojourn document this over and over (Lev. 10:1–3; 24:10–23; Num. 11:1–3, 31–34; 12:10; 16:28–35; 25:6–9), and the Old Testament record throughout is a sorry saga of disobedience that provoked God's judgment against individuals, families, and eventually the whole nation. We will address this latter aspect of the Lord's retributive justice in a more appropriate setting.

Before that is done, we should turn our attention to what is perhaps the most ethically and theologically perplexing issue of all relative to the judgment of the Lord and that is the policy of *ḥērem,* sometimes called "holy war," perhaps more accurately, "Yahweh war."[16] Its disclosure as a theological principle in the ensuing pages will be illustrated at a later point by its historical application. As noted already, the overthrow of the cities of the plain has overtones of Yahweh war, but the technical terminology does not appear until the account of the destruction of certain cities in Numbers 21:1–3 and the anticipation of such conflict

---

[16] See especially, Gerhard von Rad, *Holy War in Ancient Israel,* ed. and trans. Marva Dawn (Grand Rapids: Eerdmans, 1991); Daniel G. Reid and Tremper Longman III, *God Is a Warrior* (Grand Rapids: Zondervan, 1995); Stanley N. Gundry, ed., *Show Them No Mercy* (Grand Rapids: Zondervan, 2003).

in the book of Deuteronomy (7:1–5, 26; 20:17). The verb *ḥrm* occurs almost exclusively in the causative stem and carries the basic meaning of "put under a ban" or "dedicate" (usually to the Lord). The idea is that persons or things that come under *ḥērem* (the noun form) are either destroyed totally or surrendered over to the Lord for his own use.[17] Full consideration of the implementation of Yahweh war as a special aspect of *ḥērem* will be deferred to a later point, but its theological rationale should receive at least brief attention here. Nowhere is it set forth in such clarity as in Deuteronomy, so to those texts we now briefly direct our attention.

First and foremost is Deuteronomy 7:1–6, 25–26, a passage that not only identifies who or what should be the object of *ḥērem* but spells out its theological justification. The Lord had promised the patriarchs that their descendants would someday occupy the land that Abraham first settled, a land then populated by various Canaanite nations as well as others such as the Hittites and Amorites (Gen. 15:19–21). The patriarchs appear to have lived peaceably among these nations, but eventually it became clear that when their descendants arrived in the land following their four hundred years in Egypt, the inhabitants of Canaan would prove to be hostile to them (Gen. 22:17). The only way the land could be taken from them would be through military action.

From the human standpoint such an action would appear totally without warrant, for the Canaanites had lived in the Levant for at least a millennium before Abraham ever arrived. Did they not, therefore, have legal claim to it on the basis of prior possession? On what grounds could Abraham and his family settle there, to say nothing of his descendants who had left it and were not to return for hundreds of years? Even Abraham seems not to have assumed any territorial rights, for when his wife Sarah died, he felt constrained to purchase a burial plot for her, not having any land of his own it seems (Gen. 23:1–4). In fact, he called himself "a resident alien among you [the Hittites]" (v. 4). Years later Jacob, having arrived at Shechem from his twenty-year sojourn in Aram, bought a property there where he could pitch his tent and build an altar (Gen. 19–20). There is not the slightest hint that he considered the land his even though God had promised it to Abraham, his grandfather (Gen. 15:18).

[17] N. Lohfink, חרם, *TDOT* 5:180–99.

The answer to these perplexing questions lies in the sovereign and providential plan of God who, as the Lord of the nations, allocated to them their spheres of occupation and dominion. This is both a theological deduction based on the nature of God and a truth spelled out in biblical texts as well. Following the Lord's judgment on Babel, "the LORD scattered [the people] over the face of the whole earth" (Gen. 11:9). This resulted in their settlement throughout the entire world, a dispersion reflected in the "Table of Nations" of Genesis 10. Of special interest here is the disposition of the Canaanites whose clans, it is said, scattered and whose borders eventually included the Mediterranean coastal lands from Sidon in the north to Gaza in the south (Gen. 10:18–19).

All of this was prophesied in the curse of Noah who condemned Canaan for his father Ham's filial disrespect and declared that Canaan would be enslaved by his brothers, in particular by Shem (Gen. 9:25–26). Shem, of course, was the ancestor of the Eberites (that is, the Hebrews) of whom Abraham was the culminating and most important individual (Gen. 10:21; 11:14–26). The land to which the Lord called Abraham was the land of Canaan, already destined to be the land of promise long before the Canaanites or Hebrews ever dwelled there.

The Song of Moses confirms the idea of God's sovereign allocation of the lands to the nations: "When the Most High gave the nations their inheritance, and divided the human race, He set the boundaries of the peoples according to the number of the people of Israel. But the LORD's portion is his people, Jacob, His own inheritance" (Deut. 32:8–9).

While certain textual difficulties plague this passage, the central message is clear: God has exercised lordship over the nations and has determined where they should and should not live. Paul made precisely this point in his Mars Hill address. Speaking of Adam, he said, "From one man he has made every nation of men to live all over the earth and has determined their appointed times and the boundaries of where they live" (Acts 17:26). He did this, the apostle went on to say, "so that they might seek God, and perhaps they might reach out and find him" (v. 27).

Sadly, this was not the case, and particularly as illustrated here by the Canaanites. Not only were they under a curse for their moral turpitude and therefore subject to bondage, but their national character was incorrigibly evil so as to be beyond repentance and redemption. Like Pharaoh, they were hardened and incapable of responding to God's gracious overtures (cf. Deut. 2:30). Because of this unresponsiveness, they were subject to *ḥērem,* the judgment of God applicable to them not only because of this but also because they occupied the land that God had promised to his chosen people Israel. Moreover, to allow them to live would perpetuate an environment in which Israel would be inclined to fall away from the LORD into Canaanite polytheism with all its lascivious practices.

For Israel to undertake *ḥērem* against the Canaanites was therefore not an option. In line with its prosecution, the Lord would lead the way, gain the victory, and direct the subsequent occupation of the land. Israel must do the fighting and leave none alive, men, women, and children. Failing that, they must make no treaties with them including covenants of marriage, lest their ungodly spouses lead them into idolatry. Finally, they must eradicate all vestiges of Canaanite worship including altars, sacred pillars, Asherim, and idols. The reason for such drastic measures is clear. Israel was God's chosen people, a holy nation called to serve him; and because of that call, Israel must live before him in purity and faithfulness (Deut. 7:1–6).

The justification for holy war lies in the nature of God as the holy one who cannot countenance sin and as the just one who must punish it when it goes unrepented. It is also explicable in view of his omniscience. God knows how people will respond to his dealings with them; and by knowing that, he has not only the capacity but the right to act preemptively when it is clear that they are hopelessly beyond the pale of retrieval and restoration. But it is important to note that only God has such knowledge and only he can authorize and initiate holy war. This is why all the legitimate instances of this policy in the Old Testament are commanded by the Lord, led by him alone, and brought by him to a successful conclusion. When the Lord was in it, there were no "innocents"; for even infants, incapable as they were of making moral decisions, had the potential for evil and idolatry against which the Lord desired to preserve his people.

Salvation and Deliverance

The judgment of the world by flood was mitigated by God's gracious act of salvation and deliverance, at least of Noah and his family. God had created all things not for destruction but to provide a venue in which he might exercise his everlasting sovereign rule. Judgment therefore cannot be the last word. There must always be either the averting of it or deliverance through and from it if the creation design is to come to fruition.[18] This is seen already in the promise to Eve that her seed would ultimately triumph over evil though pain and death would be the common human lot until the day of perfect rectification (Gen. 3:16). The darker shades of curse and alienation notwithstanding, God will save and deliver as an act and aspect of his gracious pleasure (cf. Gen. 4:15).

Having resolved to destroy the earth by a flood, the Lord interposed his favor (Heb. *ḥēn*) and spared righteous Noah along with his wife, his three sons, and their wives (Gen. 6:8–10). Grace is thus the *sine qua non* of salvation, and grace comes not in response to man's just deserts but as an expression of God's undeserved love. It is true that Noah is called "righteous" *(ṣaddîq)* and "upright" *(tammîm)*, but nothing in the text suggests that these qualities were prerequisite to Noah's salvation.[19] He found favor "in God's eyes"; he did not earn it; that is, God looked favorably upon him and in an act of sovereign will preserved him from calamity.

The flood narrative illustrates well the concept of salvation in the Old Testament, namely, deliverance from a real or perceived danger into a place or position of security. The most common set of terms used to describe this work of the Lord *(yšʿ, yĕšûʿâ)* carries the fundamental idea of being released from a confining, narrow place or situation.[20] Thus, anytime one felt constricted—whether by fear, enemies, disease, frustration, or even death—he could call on the Lord and find in him a Savior, one willing and able to grant him freedom. Salvation in the full New Testament sense as a once-for-all forensic transaction is unknown in the Old Testament, at least insofar as the use of these technical terms is concerned. Redemption is a more accurate description; but, as we shall see, even this cannot capture the fullness of what it means to be eternally saved from sin and death.

We have noted repeatedly that the exodus event was of central importance to Israel's self-understanding as the elect and treasured people

---

[18] Claus Westermann, *Elements of Old Testament Theology,* trans. Douglas W. Stott (Atlanta: John Knox, 1982), 36–40.

[19] Victor P. Hamilton, *The Book of Genesis: Chapters 1–17,* NICOT (Grand Rapids: Eerdmans, 1990), 276.

[20] Robert L. Hubbard Jr., ישׁע, *NIDOTTE* 2:556–62.

of the Lord. And nowhere is the theme of salvation and deliverance more paradigmatically presented than in narratives descriptive of that event. Israel's greatest need after four hundred years of bondage in Egypt was for the Lord to rescue them and set them on their way to the land of promise. To do this would put in play a contest of will and strength between a weak and disorganized colony of slaves on the one hand and the mightiest kingdom on earth on the other hand. If ever salvation was dependent on some outside source, for Israel it was then. And it was precisely at that critical moment that the Lord stepped in, enabling Moses to assert, "Don't be afraid. Stand firm and see the LORD's salvation He will provide for you today. . . . The LORD will fight for you; you must be quiet" (Exod. 14:13; cf. v. 30).

This introduction of the Lord as Savior in battle is tangential to his role as divine warrior, to which some attention has already been paid. At this point, however, the focus has been narrowed to the salvation that resulted from his engagement of hostile forces bent on doing harm to his weak and defenseless people. Immediately after the crossing of the sea, Moses proclaimed that "the LORD . . . has become my salvation" (Exod. 15:2) and "[He] is a warrior" (v. 3). This set the stage for a number of texts in which the Lord's deliverance of his people militarily was one of the key indicators of his work of salvation.

Deuteronomy 20, the "Manual of War," celebrates the fact that "the LORD your God is the One who goes with you to fight for you against your enemies to give you victory" (lit., "salvation"; v. 4). Many years later Gideon, called to deliver his people from the Midianites, was told to go and save them for the Lord had sent him (Judg. 6:14). Gideon objected at first but, having subjected the Lord to a test, was finally convinced that the Lord would save Israel by Gideon's own weak hand (vv. 36–37). Then, lest Israel should think that victory was achieved by its own prowess, the Lord commanded Gideon to pare down the number of troops, assuring him that despite (or because of) those reduced numbers he would grant salvation (Judg. 7:2, 7).

Unfortunately, the role of the Lord in holy war came to be confused with or even replaced by some of its cultic aspects, in particular the use of the ark of the covenant as a symbol of the divine presence. For example, in one instance the Israelite army, having suffered defeat at the hands of the Philistines, resorted to the ark so that it may "go with us and save us" (1 Sam. 4:3). Saul's son Jonathan, in a later incident, had a better understanding of such matters, recognizing that it was the Lord who saved (1 Sam. 14:6; cf. v. 23). At times he did so directly and at other times through human instruments such as Jeroboam II (2 Kings 14:27). King Hezekiah knew that only God could deliver Jerusalem from the Assyrians, and he prayed that he would do so for the sake of his own great name (2 Kings 19:19), a prayer God promised to answer (v. 34).

God's power to save gave rise to a number of epithets such as "*Savior,*" "deliverer," or "warrior." He is first called Savior in the Song of Moses as an aftermath of the exodus (Deut. 32:15), and Samuel harked back to that event in describing the Lord as the one "who saves you from all your troubles and afflictions" (1 Sam. 10:19; cf. 17:47; 2 Sam. 22:3; 1 Chron. 16:35; Pss. 35:3; 68:19; 88:1; 89:26; Isa. 63:1). He also was the one who brought salvation as a function of his person and his purposes for his people (Pss. 3:8; 55:16; 57:3; 62:1; 74:12; 119:166). In fact, he had become salvation itself so that the Lord and his saving work became synonymous (Ps. 118:14, 21). Zephaniah summed it up well with the declaration that the Lord "is mighty to save" (Zeph. 3:17 NIV).

All these descriptions of the Lord's capacity to save are predications based on some experience of an individual or group that had witnessed or benefited from God's gracious acts. He is a Savior, but he saves in concrete ways that testify to his character. David, in a situation of discouragement bordering on despair, was able to affirm that "the LORD is near the brokenhearted; He saves those crushed in spirit" (Ps. 34:18). Others, in an unknown set of similar circumstances, "cried out to the LORD in their trouble; He saved them from their distress" (Ps. 107:13). Eliphaz recognized that the Lord saves the needy who are in peril (Job 5:15) and will deliver the downcast (Job 22:29). Salvation in such instances consists of freedom from feelings of constraint as much as from literal, actual bondage.

Not only was the Lord portrayed as a Savior; there was no other. This truth was advanced most especially by Isaiah and Jeremiah who, in their own times and situations, faced competing claims from Babylonian quarters that the gods of the nations could also deliver. Such propaganda was making serious inroads in Judah and had to be challenged with great persuasive power. With scathing polemic Isaiah, speaking on the Lord's behalf, asserted, "I, I, am the LORD, and there is no Savior but Me. I alone declared, saved, and proclaimed—and not some foreign god among you" (Isa. 43:11–12; cf. 45:20). He singled out the man-made idols for ridicule, charging that "they cry out to it but it doesn't answer; it saves no one from his trouble" (Isa. 46:7). The Babylonian diviners were no more effective—"no one can save you" (Isa. 47:15; cf. v. 13).

Jeremiah took up the same cudgel. Idolaters, he said, cry out, "Rise up and save us!" when they are in trouble, but their false gods were totally inept. "Let them rise up and save you in the time of your disaster if they can," he teased (Jer. 2:27–28). When the disaster of Babylonian exile loomed on the near horizon, the Jews would cry out to the gods whom they had been worshipping but to no avail, for such nonentities could not save (Jer. 11:12).

Since only the Lord saves and since mankind is so in need of salvation from all kinds of difficulties, the Old Testament is replete with wishes and petitions by God's people that he might deliver them. When Israel was under attack by the Philistines at Mizpah, they demanded that Samuel beg the Lord to save them (1 Sam. 7:8). The psalms, to be expected, are especially rich in such prayers. David, under severe duress, cried out, "Save me, my God!" (Ps. 3:7), and then yearned for the salvation of Israel, that is, the restoration of the blessings they had lost (Ps. 14:7; cf. 53:6). He even prayed that the Lord would save him, the king, as head of the covenant people (Ps. 20:9; cf. 86:16). The community prayed similarly, especially in pleading for deliverance from exile (Ps. 106:47; cf. Pss. 108:6; 118:25). With that in mind, the prophet Jeremiah interceded for his people with urgent appeal: "LORD, save Your people, the remnant of Israel" (Jer. 31:7). From another angle, Habakkuk, frustrated at the Lord's apparent indifference to the plight of his nation, demanded, "How long, LORD, must I call for help and You do not listen, or cry out to You about violence and You do not save?" (Hab. 1:2).

But God is never depicted as indifferent or unmoved by appeals for salvation. He assured Samuel that he would save Israel through Saul (1 Sam. 9:16) and promised David that he would use him to save the nation from the Philistines and other enemies (2 Sam. 3:18). The psalmist was confident that the Lord would save Zion (Ps. 69:35); and the prophets, too, held out such hope (Isa. 33:22; 35:4; Hos. 1:7). Salvation extended also to individuals, and they as well could claim the promises of God's deliverance from their various predicaments (Ps. 72:13; Prov.

20:22). Jeremiah was personally assured that he, as the representative of the Lord, would be assailed by wicked Judah; but he had no need to fear because, as the Lord said, "I am with you to save you and deliver you" (Jer. 15:20).

The question that arises at this point is whether God's salvation was conditioned upon some act or disposition on the part of those who sought or actually received it. In Psalm 7 David pleaded for the Lord's saving intervention (v. 1) and went on to say that he saved "the upright in heart" (v. 10). Elsewhere he concluded that it is the humble who benefit from God's deliverance (Ps. 18:27), a point made also in Psalm 149:4 which declares that he "adorns the humble with salvation." Psalm 91 appears to stress the need for one to love the Lord if he is to expect his salvation: "Because he is lovingly devoted to Me," says the LORD, "I will deliver him" (v. 14). Psalm 145:19 intimates that the fear of the Lord is necessary. Isaiah seemed to imply that salvation comes to those who trust God (Isa. 25:9) but stated unequivocally as well that though the Lord's arm is not too short to save, he cannot or will not do so as long as those who need it persist in their sin (Isa. 59:1–2).

This reading of Old Testament salvation—even on just the level of deliverance from physical and psychological peril—must be balanced by the equally clear evidence that salvation was (and is) based on grace and grace alone.[21] David prayed, "Turn, LORD! Rescue *[nṣl]* me; save *[yšʿ]* me because of Your faithful love *[ḥesed]*" (Ps. 6:4). He understood fully that any hope he had of rescue from life's predicaments must issue from God's covenant commitment to him. God's *ḥesed* is also the grounds of his salvation in Psalm 31:16 and in Psalm 109:26: "Help *[ʿzr]* me, LORD my God; save me according to Your faithful love *[hesed]*." The grammar in these passages makes clear that God's gracious interposition of *ḥesed* is the very basis for any human hope of salvation. A similar sentiment is associated with the Lord's name. We have noted already that God's name is a virtual synonym for God himself so that what he does in his name or for his name's sake is merely a circumlocution for his own acts. Thus David urged upon the LORD, "God, save me by [lit. "in"] Your name, and vindicate me by Your might" (Ps. 54:1). The author of Psalm 106,

---

[21] Edmond Jacob, *Theology of the Old Testament*, trans. Arthur W. Heathcote and Philip J. Allcock (New York: Harper & Row, 1958), 101.

reflecting back on the events of the exodus deliverance, observed that the Lord "saved them because of His name *[lēmaʿan šēmô]*, to make His power known" (v. 8). This puts to rest any idea that Israel, by its own wisdom and strength, was able to bring about its salvation from Egypt. If the Lord does not save at his own initiative and for his own sake alone, then salvation cannot and will not take place.

When God's people experience salvation, it is to be expected that they respond to his gracious overtures on their behalf with delight and joy. Hannah, having given birth to a son against all odds and in defiance of her mocking rival Peninnah, described her success as "salvation" (1 Sam. 2:1). That is, she was delivered from bondage to her barrenness and in this she delighted *(śmḥ)*. David, too, prayed for deliverance from his enemies and pledged that once that had taken place he would "rejoice *(gyl)* in [the Lord's] salvation" (Ps. 9:14). In a particularly enlightening passage, God's *ḥesed* is linked with his salvation and in that linkage David found cause for great joy (Ps. 13:5). The delight and joy expressed by these recipients of salvation derived not from satisfaction with their own efforts but reflect their awareness that salvation was of the Lord alone.

God's greatest work of deliverance from the Old Testament perspective lay in the eschaton, the great Day of the Lord at the end of history. Isaiah and the later prophets addressed this cataclysmic series of events with special emphasis in light of their own milieu in which the great nations of the earth were rising in opposition to God's kingdom purposes. For now, only the terms and texts relative to salvation as a work of God will receive attention. At a later point, the whole matter of Old Testament eschatology as a theological topos will be addressed in detail.

In the second servant song and its subsequent proclamation of salvation (Isa. 49:1–6, 24–26), Isaiah looked to the restoration of dispersed Israel who, he says, will be saved from those who have taken them captive (Isa. 49:25). In this instance salvation has to do with military success. Jeremiah, in the throes of the Babylonian exile, spoke of God's promise that he will "without fail save you from far away, your descendants, from the land of their captivity!" This will come at the cost of the destruction of all the nations that are foolish enough to imprison God's people (Jer. 30:10–11). The result of salvation for Israel is that he "will return and have calm and quiet with no one to frighten him" (Jer. 46:27).

Ezekiel employed the language of salvation to describe the gathering of God's flock, Israel, in the day of his restoration (Ezek. 34:22), and he also spoke in this way of Israel's deliverance from their sinful backsliding (Ezek. 37:23). Here salvation enters the realm of relationship, the forgiveness of sin that enables fellowship with a holy God to be possible. In the postexilic period the prophet Zechariah had an even clearer perspective on God's work of salvation in the last days. The LORD, he said, will save his people from the east and the west, regathering them back to their beloved Jerusalem (Zech. 8:7). He will then convert them from being an object of cursing to being a vehicle of blessing, thus restoring them to their original mission (Zech. 8:13; cf. 10:6). Eschatological salvation, at least from the Old Testament viewpoint, is tantamount to Israel's return from exilic bondage and restoration to covenant service in the kingdom of the Lord.

Redemption

Two virtually synonymous word clusters occur in the Old Testament with the common translation "redeem, redeemer, redemption," and the like, namely, *g'l* and *pdh*. Both basically connote the underlying idea of buying back, recovering, reclaiming, releasing, or even avenging.[22] Though human subjects are attested with both, the focus here is on the Lord as Redeemer. His role as judge and hence, as avenger, has already been treated in at least a broad and general manner.[23]

There are two great redemptive moments in the Old Testament purview: (1) the redemption of Israel in connection with the exodus and (2) the eschatological redemption that will bring God's people back from the ends of the earth to take up their task as his kingdom citizens. But individual, personal redemption is also a matter of interest, usually in the context of deliverance from peril or difficulty. In that sense, to be redeemed is synonymous with being saved. God can be called upon to redeem and be praised for having done so. So much does He act redemptively on behalf of those who cry out to Him for deliverance that the epithet *Redeemer* is one of the more common titles by which he is

---

[22] Robert L. Hubbard Jr., גאל, *NIDOTTE* 1:789–94; פדה, *NIDOTTE* 3:578–82, respectively.

[23] See pp. 109-14.

known (cf. Job 19:25; Pss. 19:14; 78:35; Isa. 41:14; 43:14; *et passim* in Isaiah).

The Lord is never directly said to be a Redeemer from sin. That is a New Testament concept which, though finding Old Testament roots in such theological ideas as sacrifice and atonement, may not legitimately be traced back to the Old Testament notion of redemption. For that reason the issue of sin and its remedy will be treated later in consideration with worship and the cult. At the same time, however, there are a few hints to the effect that one can be redeemed from death. When applied to the nation Israel, this idea, in fact, becomes a major eschatological motif.

One thing the Old Testament teaching makes clear is that redemption was an act of God limited to his own people and not one designed to convert people to that status. That is, the Lord redeemed his own from whatever situations or circumstances warranted this gracious intervention. Nowhere is this more evident than in the exodus itself, for as we have already been careful to emphasize, the exodus did not make Israel the people of the Lord; rather, it delivered them because they were his people (Exod. 4:22–23). In the first reference to the exodus as a redemptive act on behalf of Israel, the Lord said, "I will deliver you from the forced labor of the Egyptians and free you from slavery to them. I will redeem you with an outstretched arm and great acts of judgment" (Exod. 6:6). Once this had been done, Moses reflected back on it and, with great confidence for the future, sang, "You will lead the people You have redeemed with Your faithful love *[ḥesed]*" (Exod. 15:13).

In Deuteronomy Moses capitalized on the Lord's work of exodus redemption, drawing upon it over and over again for inspiration and encouragement. He reminded Israel that because they were descendants of the patriarchs to whom the Lord swore an oath of covenant faithfulness he redeemed them from Egyptian bondage (Deut. 7:8). It was incumbent on them also, therefore, to be obedient to him and specifically on the grounds that he had redeemed them (Deut. 13:5). They must, for example, free their bond-slaves in the seventh year since God had graciously freed them as a nation when he redeemed them from onerous Egyptian slavery (Deut. 15:15; cf. 21:8; 24:18).

Many years later David, in extolling the Lord for making a covenant of everlasting kingship with him, praised him for having redeemed Israel from Egypt and thus making Israel unique among the nations of the earth

(2 Sam. 7:23). By this redemptive work the Lord had established Israel to be his own people forever, and he had become their God—not for the first time, of course, but in the context of mutual covenant pledges that sprang from the exodus redemption (1 Chron. 17:21). Nehemiah added to this the idea that the Jews were the servants of the Lord, a status granted them as a redeemed people (Neh. 1:10).

Rich theological insight into Old Testament redemption is gained from Psalm 74:2, where the poet implored the Lord to "remember Your congregation, which You purchased long ago and redeemed as the tribe for Your possession." Redemption was costly. In terms of Christian theology, one is reminded that the redemption of sinners demanded the life of the Savior, an ultimate and unfathomable payment (1 Pet. 1:18–19). As for the exodus redemption, though it took place without condition or qualification on Israel's part, it required the lives of the firstborn of Egypt, a tit-for-tat payment by which an Egyptian life would stand in place of an Israelite. More apropos, however, was the price demanded by the Lord in consequence of the exodus, namely, the firstborn male of every Israelite family (Exod. 13:1). Yet this was not so much a payment to the Lord for having secured redemption as it was a symbolic reminder of the cost he incurred in the exercise of his grace, a cost reflected in his awesome judgment on the wicked nation of Egypt (cf. Isa. 43:3). By rights the firstborn of Israel should also have been slain as the price of redemption, but in lieu of their death an animal sacrifice could be made instead, thus illustrating clearly the fact that redemption indeed is never truly free (Exod. 13:14–16).

Despite that truth the Old Testament still insists that the Lord's acts of redemption sprang not out of a given or anticipated compensation but from the wellsprings of his grace. Isaiah, harking back to the exodus, exclaimed that "He redeemed them because of His love *('ahăbâ)* and compassion *(ḥemel)*; He lifted them [Israel] up and carried them all the days of the past" (Isa. 63:9). These strong terms of divine preemption suggest unmistakably that the exodus deliverance was not carried out in response to some great act of merit on Israel's part but purely and simply as a display of God's undeserved and unexpected favor. The psalmist appealed to the Lord for redemption on this same basis—"redeem us because of Your faithful love *(used)*" (Ps. 44:26). Only as the Lord acts according to his own plan and purpose will redemption come to pass.

God's redemption of Israel at the Red Sea gave rise, as we have seen, to the common participial description of the Lord as Redeemer (he who redeems). Job knew him as such (though in the sense of vindicator), affirming that his Redeemer lives and will someday stand upon the earth to declare Job innocent (Job 19:25). David appealed to the Lord as his Redeemer and Rock before whom he wanted to live with integrity (Ps. 19:14). Isaiah employed this descriptor by far the most frequently and did so, not surprisingly, in making a comparison of the return of Israel from Babylonian exile to the exodus from Egypt under Moses. The exodus motif permeates Isaiah's prophecy about the return and restoration of Israel from captivity. Its themes and imagery therefore pervade Isaiah's account of God's deliverance that lay just ahead.

The return from Babylon would be eased by the "Redeemer [who] is the Holy One of Israel," he who would overcome all adversaries to effect it (Isa. 41:14). As he had overthrown the Egyptians in the sea, the Lord would overthrow the Babylonians, again as the Redeemer (43:14). Also as Redeemer he would assert his sovereignty over all pretender gods (44:6) and bring to pass the redemption that he had long promised through his prophets (44:24). Speaking of the servant of the Lord, Isaiah said of him that the "Redeemer of Israel, his Holy One" would exalt him and cause the kings and princes of the earth to bow in submission to him (49:7).

Israel itself would be enlarged and blessed, and like a wife who for a time is rejected by her husband, she would be brought back by her Redeemer out of his deep kindness and compassion (54:5–8). Israel would then know beyond any shadow of a doubt that the Lord is Redeemer (60:16; cf. 49:26).

The Old Testament emphasis on the Lord as Redeemer of the nation should not obscure the fact that individuals also could know him as such. David, in almost a cliché, spoke of him as the one "who has redeemed my life from every distress" (2 Sam. 4:9; cf. 1 Kings 1:29). When in danger, he prayed that the Lord would redeem him (Pss. 26:11; 31:5; 69:18; cf. 44:26); and the author of Psalm 107, in gratitude for the deliverance he had experienced, urged all who had experienced similar blessings from God to "give thanks to the LORD, for he is good; his faithful love endures forever. Let the redeemed of the LORD proclaim that He has redeemed them from the hand of the foe" (Ps. 107:1–2).

Isaiah made the remarkable observation that the Lord had redeemed Abraham, and because of that Israel could have confidence that they too would be redeemed (Isa. 29:22–24; cf. 44:22; 48:20; 52:9). In what sense Abraham was redeemed is not clear, though most likely the reference is to his having an heir when the prospects of doing so seemed bleak indeed.[24] Jeremiah, in the depths of despair and on the verge of abandoning his prophetic ministry, received a word of encouragement from the Lord who promised, "I will deliver you from the power of evil people and redeem you from the control of the ruthless" (Jer. 15:21). Redemption here, as the parallelism suggests, is identical with salvation from trouble.

Of special interest are the few passages that speak of redemption from death. Job 5:20 is probably not to be included because the statement "in famine He [God] will redeem you from death" seems to imply that famine will not result in death. That is, the Lord will intervene and thus spare Job from starvation. David, however, is confident that the Lord "redeems [his] life from the Pit; He crowns [him] with faithful love and compassion" (Ps. 103:4). Though there is no doubt a reference here also to escape from death, the language prepares the way for a full-blown conviction that God can and will indeed deliver from the grave itself in a mighty work of redemption.

The classic text that joins death and redemption together is Hosea 13:14: "I will ransom them from the power of Sheol. I will redeem them from death." There is no question here that death has taken its dreadful toll and that the only hope of delivery from it is the gracious redemption afforded by the Lord. The grave and death here in context are metaphorical, referring to Israel's spiritual condition; but metaphor is based on reality, in this case the belief that God can and does deliver from death (cf. 1 Cor. 15:55). How clearly Hosea's audience may have understood the ramifications of the prophet's word of hope about life out of death cannot be known, for the doctrine of bodily resurrection was far from full development in Old Testament times. That some glimpse of this truth was already seen in some circles, at least, is clear from the unambiguous testimony of the psalmist who triumphantly declared, "God will redeem my life from the power of Sheol, for He will take me"

---

[24] For various views see Edward J. Young, *The Book of Isaiah,* vol. 2, NICOT (Grand Rapids: Eerdmans, 1969), 330.

(Ps. 49:15). This glimpse of immortality lends a dimension to the idea of redemption that had far-reaching implications, a signification that found full revelation and accomplishment in Christ.

Attention to such future possibilities leads to a brief consideration here of redemption as an eschatological theme. David hinted at this early in his plea for God to redeem Israel "from all its distresses" (Ps. 25:22), a plea that merged into the hope of Psalm 130 that "He will redeem Israel from all its sins" (v. 8). Isaiah, in more heavily freighted eschatological terms, asserted that "Zion will be redeemed by justice" (Isa. 1:27); and in the day of the future regathering, only "the redeemed will walk" on the sacred soil of restored Israel (Isa. 35:9). He elaborated on that restoration by drawing analogies to the exodus in which the redeemed crossed through the sea and then declared that "the ransomed of the Lord will return and come to Zion with singing, crowned with unending joy" (Isa. 51:11). Micah, also with an eye to the last days, saw Israel in the future as a dispersed people in bondage to Babylon. But from there the Lord would deliver them in a work of redemptive grace (Mic. 4:10). Jeremiah assured his beleaguered hearers that "the Lord has [already] ransomed (*pdh*) Jacob and redeemed *(gʾl)* him from the power of one stronger than he" (Jer. 31:11). Zechariah, from the postexilic perspective, offered the promise of the Lord that "I will whistle and gather them because I have redeemed them; they will be as numerous as they once were" (Zech. 10:8).

God's works are indicative of who he is. They reveal the outworking of his nature and provide an embodiment of his character as the Almighty One who, with wisdom and purpose, has created all things for his glory and praise. Those works outlined here—creation, judgment, salvation, and redemption—are not exhaustive but are only illustrative of God's ways in the world. These will be revisited in subsequent portions of this work, along with others of his mighty deeds that clarify the overarching theological message of the Old Testament.

Chapter Five

The Purposes of God

Throughout our treatment of theology proper to this point, we have made constant if only incidental reference to the purposes of God, either as inherently associated with his nature and character or as expressed in his works. It is important now to consider those purposes more intentionally and synthetically in order to allow them to take their place as an essential element of Old Testament theology. To think of God as having no purpose for creation and history is, of course, an absurdity on the face of it, for random incoherence—the opposite of entelically driven views of divine activity—is inconsistent with the concept of an intelligent deity. But even apart from such philosophical necessities or even theological deductions is the clear witness of Old Testament texts to the effect that the God of Israel is a God of clear-cut objectives. He has a plan and has not been slow to make it known.

Israel and the Purposes of God

We have argued that the theology of the Old Testament was first revealed to Israel through Moses at Moab precisely to disclose who God is, how and why Israel existed, and what God had in mind for them. In revealing this he at least partially unfolded his purposes, particularly in the crucial text in which he challenged Israel to make covenant with him, namely, Exodus 19:4–6. True to the method we have adopted, it will be best to turn to that programmatic passage first in order to lay the foundation for a fuller understanding of God's intentions, first for Israel and then for the whole world.

The setting of the text is the foot of Mount Sinai from whose summit the Lord spoke to Moses regarding the stupendous offer he was about to make to Israel. He had delivered them from Egyptian bondage according to his promises (Gen. 15:13–14; 46:4; Exod. 3:8; 6:6) and now brought them to himself in an unprecedented encounter (Exod. 19:4). This way of putting it is anticipatory of some special relationship that the Lord was prepared to enter into with them, one different from anything they had ever known before. Israel had already been identified as the Lord's son (Exod. 4:22–23), a sovereign work of familial association; but now they would become his servant, a sovereign work of privileged responsibility. By becoming servant as well as son, Israel would take its place within the grand purpose of God to reconcile the nations to himself. In this way the seed of Abraham would fulfill the promise God made to the patriarch that "all the peoples on earth will be blessed through you" (Gen. 12:3).

The terms of the covenant of servanthood are clear: If Israel would faithfully adhere to the agreement about to be promulgated, then it would become the Lord's treasured possession (Heb. *sĕgullâ*)[1] out of all the options available to him. The role of that treasured people—the only one selected out of the vast family of nations—would be an active one, a role requiring service based on status. The status was that of holiness, meant here as a uniqueness among the nations brought about by the Lord's sovereign choice. By the way they lived, they must communicate something of the holiness of God himself and thus be a magnet to attract the nations to him. The service would be one of mediation between the holy One and the peoples of the earth. Like a priest who represented his community before God and who carried out whatever ritual was necessary to a harmonious relationship, so Israel must be a priestly

[1] *HALOT* 1:742; cf. E. Lipínski, סְגֻלָּה, *TDOT* 10:144–48; Deut. 7:6; 14:2; 26:18; Ps. 135:4; Mal. 3:17.

nation that could bridge the chasm between the Lord and the peoples of all other nations.

Imbedded in this set of conditions was the clear note of sovereignty and servanthood, a theme first articulated in the creation narratives and repeated throughout the Genesis and early Exodus narratives. It was a note Israel had to hear in order to understand its relationship to all other peoples. But the meaning of that relationship would in turn depend on the reality of the fact that the nations had alienated themselves from the sovereign rule of God who had created them in the first place to serve and praise him as Lord. The call to covenant at Sinai thus provided an entrée to the comprehensive purposes of God first disclosed to Adam and now brought up-to-date for the nation that needed to hear afresh, if not for the first time, what God would have them do as part of his plan. Exodus 19:4–6 was to provide the answer to Genesis 1–3.

The Reigning of God

At a later point the argument will be made that the core, unifying theme of Old Testament theology is the reigning of God, not so much in its concrete form as kingdom but in the process itself. The Bible presents him as independently sovereign, answerable to no one and in need of nothing or no one outside himself. But it also presents him as in vital contact with all he has made, especially with mankind, that part of his creation made uniquely as his own image. At the risk of oversimplification, the following discussion of God's reigning will be considered under the rubrics of his dominion over (1) all things, (2) the nations, and (3) individuals. Israel's particular place in that scheme will become apparent in due course.

Creation and Divine Sovereignty

We proposed earlier that the purpose of the creation narratives was not so much to answer for Israel the question as to *how* the worlds came into existence but *why*. In other words, it was (and is) not the satisfaction of the scientific mind that was at stake but a response to other, more profound theological questions. The scientific side of the matter surely causes one to stand in awe at the wisdom and power of God, but it can never disclose his ultimate purposes. God created the universe not as an object of academic scrutiny but as an arena in which he can display something of his nature and intentions.

Of the two creation narratives (Gen. 1:1–2:3; 2:4–25), the purpose of the first was to provide a cosmic look at the vastness, order, and beauty of what God has done. In a sense it provided the setting of the stage for a drama that would unfold upon it. The scenery was all in place; the features necessary to the action were there, and the principal actors were at least introduced in the program. But everything was static, almost lifeless in this rendition, which is as it should be. Until the audience of theatergoers had time to admire and assimilate the environment in which the action would take place, it could not fully appreciate the outworking of the drama as evidence in itself of the genius of the playwright, the artists, and the director who had labored long and hard to prepare for the production.

Dropping the analogy for now, we should conceive of the narrative as a springboard from which all of God's purposes for the cosmos would be launched and then observed in the remainder of the Old Testament. To do this will result in some inevitable overlap with previous discussion relative to God's work as Creator and with things yet to be said about man as the image of God and the world as the arena of the outworking of God's royal designs. Yet these aspects depend for their fullest interpretation on the purposes of the narrative at hand itself as it speaks both implicitly by the actions of God unaccompanied by commentary as well as by the explicit word.

The structure of the passage is most plain, but in its simplicity it connotes a powerful theological message and that is that God does all things in an orderly, logical, and aesthetically effective way. The story revolves around six days of creation (Gen. 1:1–31) and a summary in which the seventh day is accorded special recognition (2:1–3). The sixth day stands out because of the length of its description (vv. 24–31) and, more important, because it is the only day in which the Lord gives any clue as to what he has done and why. This is because man was created on that day as the climactic act of creation, and man is featured in the second narrative (Gen. 2:4–25) and thereafter as the central focus of God's great plan.

The tensions between light and darkness and the waters and dry land, while not in themselves and as natural phenomena indicative of any imperfections in the work of the Creator, play their role metaphorically in later revelation and are suggestive of the basic cosmic struggle between good and evil that will become apparent in the postfall world. The imagery is carefully chosen in that the story, written long after the event, functions polemically against pagan mythological ideas of creation in which darkness and the deep are major elements, but also as a useful way of speaking of the life and death conflict between good and evil, which is a major theme in Scripture.[2]

The narrative opens with the scene of a chaotic cosmos in which the earth is unformed and unfilled *(tōhû wābōhû)*,[3] and the ocean depths are covered over with stygian darkness *(ḥōšek)*. Then God speaks light *(ʾôr)* into existence, declaring it to be good, and draws a line of distinction between it and darkness (Gen. 1:1–5). The antithesis is thus clearly established between the two, an antithesis that provides imagery for Israel's poets and prophets who use it heuristically to make the distinction between the natural man's ignorance of God and the enlightenment he gives, on the one hand, and between righteousness and wickedness, on the other. Job spoke of the nobles of the earth who "grope around in darkness without light," a testimony to their foolishness (Job 12:25), and he himself yearned for the days when the Lord was close to him, when "I walked through darkness by His light" (29:3). The psalmist made the connection between light and darkness and good and evil even more apparent when he observed that "light shines in the darkness for the upright" (Ps. 112:4). And Qohelet added that "there is an advantage to wisdom over folly, like the advantage of light over darkness" (Eccl. 2:13).

Isaiah contrasted light and darkness in his famous denunciation of those "who call evil good and good evil, who substitute darkness for light and light for darkness, who substitute bitter for sweet and sweet for bitter" (Isa. 5:20). Darkness, thus, is evil and bitter. The same prophet,

---

[2] Allen P. Ross, *Creation & Blessing* (Grand Rapids: Baker, 1988), 108–10; Richard E. Averbeck, "Ancient Near Eastern Mythography as It Relates to Historiography in the Hebrew Bible: Genesis 3 and the Cosmic Battle," *The Future of Biblical Archaeology,* ed. James K. Hoffmeier and Alan Millard (Grand Rapids: Eerdmans, 2004), 328–56.

[3] For the term and its ramifications for the creation narrative, see Weston W. Fields, *Unformed and Unfilled* (Nutley, N.J.: Presbyterian and Reformed, 1975), 113–30; cf. Mark M. Rooker, *Studies in Hebrew Language, Intertextuality, and Theology* (Lewiston, N.Y.: Edwin Mellen, 2003), 143–49.

speaking on behalf of the Lord, said, "I form light and create darkness, I make success and create disaster" (Isa. 45:7). In God's eyes, darkness also symbolized trouble and difficulty. Jeremiah put it plainly: "He has driven me away and forced me to walk in darkness instead of light" (Lam. 3:2).

God's eschatological day of judgment is also presented as a time of darkness. Amos asked, "Won't the Day of the LORD be darkness rather than light, even gloom without any brightness in it?" (Amos 5:20). Even so, the righteous have hope and Israel can say, "Though I sit in darkness, the LORD will be my light" and "He will bring me into the light" (Mic. 7:8–9).

The second great division in the Genesis 1 creation story is that between the waters on the earth and the waters above the earth, a separation that prepared the way for the emergence of the dry land (Gen. 1:6–10). This, too, is called "good" (v. 10). At the beginning water covered everything, so massive in its extent that it was known as the "deep" *(tĕhōm),* a term cognate to the Akkadian word *tiamtu,* the name of the primordial goddess of the oceans. According to Sumerian and Babylonian mythology, Marduk, a champion of the gods, did fatal battle with Tiamat and, having slain her, divided her body with half forming the sky and half the earth.[4] There is no myth in the Genesis record, to be sure, but the author of the account almost certainly knew of such pagan cosmologies and cast his version in Genesis in direct antithesis to those. It was not Marduk who could claim sovereignty over the world by battle but the Lord who, by a mere word, tamed the chaotic waters and made the dry land appear.

These waters provided their own apt fund of imagery to later theologians who saw in them a metaphor for the hostile forces of heaven and earth that posed a constant threat to the Lord's sovereignty and to the well-being of his people. Nearly all of the allusions to the sea as metaphor are grouped around (1) the creation, (2) the exodus, and (3) the eschaton. In each of these the sea is seen in negative terms, as something resistant to the Lord but that cannot in the end prevail.

God's mighty power was celebrated by the psalmist who sang of the Lord that "He gathers the waters of the sea into a heap; He puts the

[4] For the "Epic of Creation" see Benjamin R. Foster, *The Context of Scripture,* vol. 1, ed. William W. Hallo and K. Lawson Younger Jr. (Leiden: Brill, 1997), 390–402.

depths *(tĕhōm)* into storehouses" (Ps. 33:7). This poetic way of putting it describes the gathering of the seas so that the dry land could emerge. Psalm 74 employs stronger, even militaristic language. Referring to the Lord as "king . . . from ancient times," the poet says, "You divided the sea with Your strength; You smashed the heads of the sea monsters in the waters" (vv. 12–13). Verse 14 names the monster as Leviathan, a mythical being associated with the sea as an angry beast that must constantly be subdued.[5] The poet did not ascribe reality to this creature, of course, but made use of mythopoetic language to aggrandize the power and sovereignty of the Lord (cf. Job 3:8; 41:1; Ps. 104:26; Isa. 27:1). Job did the same but employed the name Rahab instead, equating this fictional monster with Tiamat of Mesopotamian mythology. This is clear from his statement concerning the Lord that "by His power He stirred the sea, and by His understanding He crushed Rahab" (Job 26:12). This, of course, was the same fate Tiamat suffered at the hands of Marduk in Sumero-Babylonian epic tradition. Psalm 89:10 also puts it in terms of the Lord crushing Rahab, that is, placing the beast under his feet as a show of triumph.

The Lord's victory over the sea is expressed elsewhere in terms of treading on its waves (Job 9:8), or putting boundaries around it as though it were a wild animal to be restrained (Jer. 5:22). He need only to speak to it to bend it to his will (Amos 5:8; cf. 9:6), failing which he can rebuke it and cause its waters to dry up (Nah. 1:4). The laconic prose of the creation narrative that speaks simply of God's separation of the waters contains within it the seeds of his sovereignty that will be exercised not only over the seas but over all creation whether compliantly or by force.

Much of the imagery associated with the Lord's reigning over creation is carried over into the exodus narrative where, again, the sea becomes symbolic of resistance to the will of God and therefore must be domesticated by being split asunder. As is well-known, there are two exodus accounts, the prose rendition (Exod. 14) and the poetic (Exod. 15:1–21). The former is rather straightforward, content to state the facts of the matter without a great deal of theologizing. Moses stretched out his staff, the Red Sea parted, the Israelites crossed over dry land between

---

[5] For the Ugaritic equivalent Lotan, see Dennis Pardee, "The Baʿlu Myth," *COS,* vol. 1, 265–66.

walls of water, and the Egyptians drowned when the waters collapsed and the sea returned to its bed. In the Song of the Sea (Exod. 15) Moses saw in the exodus event more than just a crossing, however, as miraculous as it was. He saw a victory over the sea which poetically reflected a victory over mighty Egypt and, by extension, over all powers resistant to his regnant will.[6]

The Lord, says Moses, is highly exalted because he has confronted and destroyed the hosts of Egypt. But the way he has done this is by demonstrating his mastery of the elements, specifically the Red Sea. He hurled Israel's enemies into the waters, covered them with it, and they sank like lead into its depths. "The waters heaped up at the blast of Your nostrils; the currents stood firm like a dam. The watery depths congealed in the heart of the sea" (Exod. 15:8). Psalm 66:6 declares that the Lord "turned the sea into dry land," thus permitting Israel to pass through unencumbered. Psalm 77 personifies the sea, saying that "the waters saw You, God. The waters saw You; they trembled. Even the depths shook" (v. 16). And just as the Lord had rebuked the primeval oceans, so he rebuked the Red Sea, "and it dried up" as though it were a desert (Ps. 106:9). In a certain sense, then, the sea was as much an antagonist of the Lord as it was his means of inflicting judgment on the Egyptians. Habakkuk captured that truth when, referring to the exodus, he spoke to the Lord as "You [who] tread the sea with Your horses, stirring up the great waters" (Hab. 3:15). The word rendered "tread" *(drk)* occurs commonly as a term for conquest and dominion, thus adding to the idea of God's sovereignty over his creation (cf. Deut. 1:36; 11:24–25; Josh. 1:3–5).[7] The eschatological day of the Lord will also feature a struggle against the sea or the denizens that inhabit it. Isaiah declared that "on that day the Lord with His harsh, great, and strong sword, will bring judgment on Leviathan, the fleeing serpent—Leviathan the twisting serpent. He will slay the monster that is in the sea" (Isa. 27:1). Whether to be identified with the Canaanite sea dragon Lotan or not, this personification of the sea represents first the tensions inherent in the dividing of the waters at creation and second, and more important, any hostile entity or movement

---

[6] For the view that this piece is a "song of triumph" and for a careful analysis of it as early Hebrew poetry, see Frank M. Cross Jr. and David Noel Freedman, *Studies in Ancient Yahwistic Poetry,* SBL Diss. Series 21 (Missoula, Mont.: Scholars, 1975), 45–65.

[7] Eugene H. Merrill, דרך, *NIDOTTE* 1:989–93.

that would seek to subvert the kingship of the Lord.[8] No doubt such imagery also underlies the New Testament concept of Satan, who is likewise described in terms of a serpent or dragon (Rev. 12:9, 15; 13:1, 2, 4, 11; 16:13; 20:2). Zechariah likens that day to the exodus and says of the Lord's leading of restored Israel that "He will pass through the sea of distress and strike the waves of the sea; all the depths of the Nile will dry up" (Zech. 10:11).

The divisions of light from darkness and of the waters from each other in the creation narrative anticipate already an aspect of the sovereignty of God, not just in the events of creation but historically and eschatologically as well. But the utterances of God in the creation stories are also suggestive of his dominion there and throughout the course of biblical revelation. He merely says the word, and it is done. A dozen times he speaks in the Genesis 1 story, and each time there is a response reflective of his power and majesty. This is more than the so-called effective word common to ancient Near Eastern ideology. God's word is an extension of himself and when uttered comes loaded with all the magisterial authority inherent in his nature.[9]

The word spoken to human beings is somewhat different, of course, in that they have the God-given capacity to disregard and disobey whatever he has to say. In this case the word is still evidential of God's omnipotence; but the consequences of ignoring it are usually not immediately forthcoming since He is patient and long-suffering, willing to endure human insubordination at least for a time. But the word of creation also becomes the word of judgment so that just as all things came into being at the spoken word, so they come to an end at the word of his wrath (Ps. 105:31).

The climax of the narrative of Genesis 1 is the creation of mankind which in this context is also the clearest expression of the divine purpose in creation. After all things else had been made and put into their several positions of function and interrelationship, the Lord said, "Let Us make man [as] Our image, according to Our likeness. They will rule" (Gen.

---

[8] John N. Oswalt, *The Book of Isaiah Chapters 1–39,* NICOT (Grand Rapids: Eerdmans, 1986), 490–91.

[9] Frederick C. Moriarty, "Word as Power in the Ancient Near East," H. N. Bream, R. D. Heim, Carey Moore, ed., *A Light unto My Path* (Philadelphia: Temple University Press, 1974), 345–62.

1:26). The significance of this for communicating a (if not *the)* major theme of Old Testament theology cannot be overstated, and the fact that it is the first divinely articulated expression of the reason for man's existence makes it doubly significant. What is lacking apparently after the whole cosmos has been spoken into existence is its management, a caretaker as it were who will govern it all according to the will of the Creator. He could have done it himself without mediation, but for reasons never revealed in the sacred record, God elected to reign through a subordinate, a surrogate king responsible only to him.

This is fundamentally what it means to be created in (or as) the image of God. The anthropological implications of this must await a later treatment; for now it must suffice only to see what man as the image is to be and do on God's behalf. The whole thrust of the narrative to this point has been to assert the sovereign rule of God over the entire cosmos so it is not surprising that dominion is in view in the creation of mankind. Man was commissioned to rule over all the creatures of the earth (Gen. 1:26); and by multiplying in sufficient number, he was to fill the earth and subdue it (v. 28). The technical terms employed are not to be hastily dismissed. The verb *to rule (rdh)* bears overtones of oppression in some instances and even here suggests dominion of a dictatorial nature. There is to be no question as to who is in charge! This is supported by the companion verb, *subdue (kbš),* the meaning of which elsewhere is to subjugate (by force) or even to humiliate.[10] Inasmuch as the earth was not yet in rebellion against its Maker, the harshness implicit in these verbs anticipated a time when the creatures of the earth would be recalcitrant and must be controlled by sheer force (cf. Gen. 3:17–19; 5:29).

The implementation of the creation mandate is the subject of part 2 of this work. There the history of man's successes and failures to carry it out will receive much fuller attention. For now it is necessary only to make the point that the purpose of God in creation was channeled largely through the human race so that its effectiveness was directly proportional to man's faithfulness in bringing it to pass. This is not to say, of course, that the kingdom program is of necessity synergistic but only that God has chosen to work in partnership with mankind. The wonder of all this not only astounds the modern mind but baffled David as well, who, in a

---

[10] S. Wagner, כָּבַשׁ, *TDOT* 7:53–54.

commentary on the creation mandate, asked the question, "What is man that You remember him, the son of man that You look after him? You made him little less than God and crowned him with glory and honor. You made him lord over the works of Your hands; You put everything under his feet" (Ps. 8:4–6).

History and Divine Sovereignty

Man's role notwithstanding, God is still King, a role recognized and celebrated throughout the Old Testament. David declared him to be the King of glory (or, perhaps, the glorious King) to whom belongs the whole earth (Ps. 24:7, 1).[11] He invited him into the temple where he could be praised as the one "mighty in battle" (v. 8), "the LORD of Hosts" (v. 10). In his temple vision Isaiah saw the LORD as the exalted King, lamenting that because of his sinfulness he was not worthy to have looked upon "the King, the LORD of Hosts" (Isa. 6:5). The same epithets occur in Jeremiah. The Lord refers to himself there as the King: "The LORD of Hosts is his name" (Jer. 46:18; cf. 48:15; 51:57), thus attaching omnipotence to His ruling. Finally, the Lord spoke through Malachi the self-attestation, "I am a great King . . . and My name will be feared among the nations" (Mal. 1:14).

Beyond his role as Sovereign over the universe in general, the rule of the Lord over the nations is expressly affirmed in Psalm 47:8: "God reigns over the nations; God is seated on His holy throne." As the "great King over all the earth" (v. 2), he has a right to their praises (v. 6). Indeed, all earthly rulers not only must submit to him but must also recognize that they belong to him and exercise rule at his pleasure (v. 9). Jeremiah questioned why the nations would not worship the Lord in any event. "Who should not fear You, King of the nations?" he asked. "It is what You deserve" (Jer. 10:7). After all, he went on to say, "The LORD is the true God; He is the living God and eternal King" (v. 10). Zechariah looked to the day when the Lord will, in fact and practice, be king over the whole earth (Zech. 14:9). Then his erstwhile enemies "will go up year after year to worship the King, the Lord of Hosts, and to celebrate the Festival

---

[11] For sovereignty as the foundational aspect of the nature of God, see the earlier discussion of his attributes on pp. 42-44.

of Booths" (Zech. 14:16). On the other hand, failure to recognize and submit to his rule will result in the plagues of Egypt, the fate of the pharaoh who also rebelled against the God of all the earth (v. 17).

With God's choice of Abraham as the founder of a nation that would be his vehicle of redemptive grace, the Lord's kingship became increasingly focused on that nation although never to the exclusion of his claims to universal sovereignty. The first explicit reference to his rule over Israel as king occurs in Moses' blessing of the tribes where he is said to be "king in Jeshurun," a term of endearment for his covenant people (Deut. 33:5). Surprisingly little is made of that role of the Lord, however, until the people of Israel began to conceive of the possibility of a human monarchy that would coexist with the rule of the Lord or perhaps even supplant it. As we shall see at a later point, such a conception was not alien to God's overall purpose; indeed, he had promised Abraham that he and Sarah would generate a line of kings (Gen. 17:6, 16); and Jacob, with prophetic insight, spoke of a ruler who would issue from the tribe of Judah (Gen. 49:10; cf. Num. 24:17–19). However, that development must take place at a time and under circumstances of God's own choosing.

The first human challenge to divine kingship was in connection with Gideon's triumph over Midian, an exploit so remarkable and so much appreciated by his Israelite countrymen that they wanted to make him king and even founder of a dynasty. "Rule over us, you as well as your sons and your grandsons," they urged (Judg. 8:22). But Gideon, sensitive to the fact that the demand was historically and theologically premature, responded, "I will not rule over you, and my son will not rule over you; the Lord will rule over you" (v. 23). Sadly, however, his son Abimelech, frustrated by his father's rejection of such a heady offer, proclaimed himself king, a pathetic self-promotion that brought him and his followers to a disastrous end (Judg. 9).

The second movement toward the usurpation of the Lord's regency took place nearly two centuries later. Having come under severe threat from the Philistines early in the eleventh century, the people of Israel petitioned Samuel to "appoint a king to judge us the same as all the other nations have," referring to the city-states that surrounded Israel at the time (1 Sam. 8:5). Samuel was greatly displeased by this request, interpreting it correctly as a denial of the Lord's just claims to sole rulership or at least as a lack of faith in his ability to save them. He had little time to ponder the matter, however, for the Lord put his finger on the heart of the matter: "They have not rejected you; they have rejected Me as their king" (v. 7; cf. 12:12).

Ironically, it was after the legitimate human kingship of David and his royal house was brought to pass that the theologians of Israel returned to the notion of God's overarching sovereignty of which David's rule was merely a physical and political expression. Psalm 48, celebrating Zion as the dwelling place of the Lord, refers to it as "the city of the great King" (v. 1; cf. 149:2). Isaiah confessed that "the LORD is our King. He will save us" (Isa. 33:22), and this at a time when Hezekiah and other monarchs were firmly in place. The Lord himself declared, "I am the LORD, your Holy One, the Creator of Israel, your King" (Isa. 43:15). Here he linked his election of Israel with his lordship over it just as, in Isaiah 44:6, he linked his redemption of the nation from bondage with his sovereign rule.

Zephaniah, with an eye to the day of the Lord, assured his contemporaries that they could rejoice because "the King of Israel, the LORD, is among you" and He is "a warrior who saves" (Zeph. 3:15, 17). He who has dominion over all things as their Creator will never relinquish his claims to sovereignty but will forever exercise it over the faithful of Israel and the nations.

God's rule, as expansive and universal as it is, is not unmindful of the individual man or woman, for inherent in his nature is his understanding of his creation and his care for every part of it. The psalms are especially replete with the testimonies of those who confessed the Lord's sovereignty and who rejoiced in it. David, in a moment of need, begged the Lord to "pay attention to the sound of my cry, my King and my God" (Ps. 5:2). Here he as king recognized both the reality of God's rule and his dependence on it for his own salvation. The anonymous author of Psalm 44 also acknowledged God's lordship, calling him "my King, my God" (v. 4). Psalm 74 presents the Lord as not only the Ruler of the individual for the present but as the "king [who] is from ancient times" (v. 12). Finally, David praised the Lord for all the riches of his grace, addressing him again as "my God the King" (Ps. 145:1).

The most potent expressions of God's sovereignty are collected most clearly and conveniently in the so-called "psalms of Yahweh's kingship" (Pss. 47, 93, 95–99). The precise setting of none of these can be determined, but inasmuch as the overall theme and style of this collection are similar to many of the Davidic psalms, there is in principle no reason to doubt their antiquity, perhaps even their Davidic provenience.[12] They celebrate Yahweh's kingship and may have accompanied some kind of temple ritual, though there is no objective basis to the view of Sigmund Mowinckel and other scholars of the "Myth and Ritual School" that they were composed to memorialize Yahweh's enthronement annually, perhaps as part of a New Year's festival.[13]

Psalm 47 boldly declares that Yahweh, the awesome One, is "a great King over all the earth" (v. 2; cf. v. 7; Zech. 14:9; Mal. 1:14). He manifests his kingship by bringing all nations under Israel's ultimate control, a theme reminiscent of the creation mandate (Gen. 1:28). This presupposes that he is King also of the nations (v. 8; cf. Ps. 22:28; 1 Chron. 16:11) who, if they do not recognize his sovereignty now, will surely do so in the ages to come (v. 9; cf. Pss. 72:11; 102:22; Isa. 49:7, 23; Phil. 2:11; Rev. 19:15–16).

Psalm 93 (and also Pss. 97 and 99) commences with the powerful expostulation, "The LORD reigns!"[14] The poet goes on to explain how that looks and what it means. The Lord, he says, has for his royal robes majesty and strength (v. 1). He is everlasting and with powerful voice, more powerful than anything he has created, he exercises his dominion (v. 4). Moreover, his decrees cannot be overturned and his reign is characterized by the attribute of holiness (v. 5).

The contrast between the power of Yahweh and the impotence of the so-called gods of the nations is a major motif of Psalm 96. The psalmist issues a universal appeal to all people to recognize and pay homage to Yahweh in light of the fact that "the gods of the peoples are idols, but the LORD made the heavens" (v. 5). They should come (as Ps. 47 also urges upon them), for he is worthy of their praises and worship (v. 9). Appealing to his role as Creator, the poet enjoins his fellows to proclaim to all the world that Yahweh is King and that some day he will come also as Judge (v. 13; cf. Ps. 98:9).

---

[12] C. Hassell Bullock, *Encountering the Book of Psalms* (Grand Rapids: Baker, 2001), 62–64.

[13] Ibid., 188–90.

[14] See A. Gelston, "A Note on *Yhwh melek,*" VT 16 (1966): 507–12; contra Roy A. Rosenberg, "Yahweh Becomes King," *JBL* 85 (1966): 297–307.

Like Psalm 93, Psalm 97 pictures the transcendent God as clothed with garments, this time with the impenetrable robes of cloud and darkness. This view of the Lord as *deus absconditus* lends an aura of mystery and majesty to his person. But though he himself cannot be seen, his displays in nature give evidence that he is there (vv. 3–4; cf. Ps. 18:8; 50:3; Dan. 7:10). So powerful is his presence that idolators must abandon their pursuit of such vanities (v. 7) and acknowledge, with the Lord's own people, that "You, LORD, are the Most High over all the earth; You are exalted above all the gods" (v. 9).

Psalm 98 begins with a call to praise Yahweh because of all he has done for Israel, works of salvation that have been visible to all the nations (vv. 2–3). With appropriate fanfare he is proclaimed King and not just of Israel but of the whole earth (v. 6). Again picking up the creation motif, the psalmist anticipates the coming of the Lord in judgment, a fitting function of God as Sovereign (v. 9).

Finally, Psalm 99 also utters the majestic exordium "The LORD reigns" (cf. Ps. 93:1; 97:1) and depicts him doing so "enthroned above the cherubim" (v. 1). This links his kingship with the temple, a connection observed also by Isaiah who, in a vision, saw the LORD "seated on a high and lofty throne, and His robe filled the temple" (Isa. 6:1). The cherubim first appear as guards of the holiness of Yahweh who prevented fallen humanity from entering the garden and illicitly partaking of the tree of life (Gen. 3:24). Their more prominent role, however, was that of hovering over the ark of the covenant in the tabernacle and temple, for the ark symbolized the throne of Yahweh who sat invisibly among his people as king over them (Exod. 25:10–22; 1 Kings 8:6–11). In a sense the temple was Yahweh's royal palace, the place he chose to locate his name, that is, his very presence (Deut. 12:5, 11).[15]

The psalmist continues with this in mind, asserting that "the LORD is great in Zion; He is exalted above all the peoples" (Ps. 99:2). Filled with profound adulation, he speaks of the Lord's awesome name (picked up from Deuteronomy 12) but focuses especially upon his holiness. Twice he exclaims "He is holy" (vv. 3, 5), and he concludes with the glorious affirmation that "the LORD our God is holy" (v. 9). The sovereignty of

---

[15] For this psalm and so-called "temple theology," see Erhard S. Gerstenberger, *Psalms, Part 2, and Lamentations,* FOTL XV (Grand Rapids: Eerdmans, 2001), 200.

God thus undergirds his attributes which all together contribute to the biblical picture of how he is to be understood as King.

Every area and aspect of life is thus under the dominion of Almighty God and is answerable to him. His purpose in bringing it all into being was that he might display his wisdom and power in both its origination and in its maintenance. But his sovereignty is not an abstraction, a mere theological datum. It takes place in time and space, in both history and geography. The former of these will be a subject of more detailed study in part 3 of this work, but some attention should now be directed to the arena in which the reigning purposes of the Lord found and continue to find actualization.

The Territory of Divine Sovereignty

The creation narrative of Genesis 1:1–2:3, while speaking generally of "the heavens and the earth" as the finished product of God's creative work, quickly gets to the point that his interest is not fundamentally universal in scope but intensely geocentric. Contrary to the heliocentric structure of our solar system as determined by astronomy, the theology of the Old Testament (and the New Testament, we might add) places the earth at the center of the universe. There man was placed, where Israel lived out its history, where the church carries out its mission, and where, at the end, the kingdom of God will take up everlasting residence (Rev. 21:1–2, 22–27).

The geocentric focus is clear from the transition between Genesis 1:1 and 1:2. After speaking of the creation of the heavens and the earth, the text drops all consideration of the heavens to give undivided attention to the earth. References to the upper waters and the sun, moon, and stars of the sky make clear that they exist not for the benefit of the heavens but for life on the earth. The upper waters became the repository of life-giving rain (Gen. 7:11), and the celestial bodies became signs "for festivals and for days and years" and to provide illumination on the earth (Gen. 1:14–15).

The second creation narrative (Gen. 2:4–25), moreover, is exclusively earthbound. In fact, it is geographically limited to just a part of the earth, to a garden somewhere in Eden from which flowed four rivers. It is fruitless to speculate as to the precise location of that spot, and it is theologically unnecessary to do so.[16] The point is that the locus of God's sovereignty over his creation by means of humankind was but a tiny speck in the universe. From there the kingdom would grow until it covered all the earth.

The thrust of the story is that man was placed in that limited area—perfect in all its setting and features—to exercise his God-given hegemony over what, it seems, was a microcosm of the universe. How he functioned in the manageable and idyllic surroundings of that environment would determine his suitability for larger things. That is, the garden was a probationary setting, the proper governance of which would lead to the fullness of dominion for which man was created: "Be fruitful, multiply, fill the earth, and subdue it" (Gen. 1:28).

The pristine earth, pregnant with life, lay nonetheless devoid of vegetation and though well watered was unproductive because there was no man to work it (Gen. 2:4–6). Surely the Creator could have worked it, but his plan was otherwise. He therefore created man and placed him in a paradisal setting rife with foliage of every variety. His task was clear. He was to work *(ʿbd)* the garden and take care *(šmr)* of it (2:15). To *work* ground, in the first place, is to till it and otherwise to prepare it for crop production. It is the kind of labor to which Cain put himself as a dirt farmer (Gen. 4:2, 12). However, this seems not to exhaust the meaning here for man was the servant *(ʿebed)* of God and as such must serve *(ʿbd)* him through his management of the earth.[17] The second verb, *šmr,* conveys the idea of watching over something so as to guard or preserve it against harm. Man's task was to serve God by caring for what he had created and entrusted to him. In other words, man's dominion consisted, in part at least, of the stewardship of God's estate. More than a hireling, he is the image of God and as such has the authority, at least potentially, to act on his behalf and with his full backing.

---

[16] For a full treatment of the possibilities, see Claus Westermann, *Genesis 1–11,* trans. by John J. Scullion (Minneapolis: Augsburg, 1984), 208–10.

[17] The verb *ʿbd* also occurs frequently with the meaning to worship or otherwise serve God in the cultus (Exod. 3:12; 4:23; Deut. 6:13; Judg. 2:7; etc.); cf. *HALOT* 1:774. The present context cannot sustain that meaning here, however, especially in view of the parallelism of the verb with the one that follows.

The Hierarchy of Divine Sovereignty

We will treat the implications of mankind as the surrogate king more fully at a later point. It might be useful here, however, to touch briefly on the matter of God's purposes as King as they are mediated through the layers of sphere privilege and responsibility as disclosed in the creation texts. These, too, will be more fully elaborated at the appropriate place; but they find their point of origin here.

The narrative leaves no doubt that God is absolutely sovereign. He preexisted his creation and had no need for it. Only his inscrutable design called it forth; but once it was in place, the creation became the physical realm over which he displayed his dominion. But was he alone at the beginning? What about the angelic hosts and their role vis-à-vis both God and mankind? The answers to these questions are not easily forthcoming because the sacred record is frustratingly deficient in its treatment of angelology. One thing is clear, however: Angels are not divine and therefore played no part in the work of creation.

The "Us" of "let Us make man in Our image" (Gen. 1:26) has been thought by some interpreters to be a reference to angels,[18] but the majority of scholars correctly observe that mankind is not the product of angelic creativity or in any sense either the image of angels or in the image of angels.[19] The major support for the notion that the "Us" includes angelic beings is based on such terms as "the sons of God (or the gods)," "the assembly of the gods," or "the host of heaven." The last of these occurs only in 1 Kings 22:19 (and the parallel 2 Chron. 18:18) with this nuance, but the phrase is clearly identical to the "sons of the gods" in Psalm 29:1 and the "divine assembly" of Psalm 82:1 (cf. v. 6). In no case is any of these in creation contexts.

The "sons of God" of Genesis 6:2 and 4 are certainly angels, though demonic and not in any way associated with God's rule (cf. 2 Pet. 2:4; Jude 6).[20] As for Job 38:7, though they witnessed in some way God's work of creation, these "sons of God" played no part in it except to rejoice at what they saw. Two other references to the sons of God in Job

---

[18] Thus, e. g., Franz Delitzsch, *A New Commentary on Genesis,* trans. by Sophia Taylor (Edinburgh: T. & T. Clark, 1888; repr. Minneapolis: Klock & Klock, 1978), 98–99.

[19] Westermann, following W. H. Schmidt, describes the formula as a "plural of deliberation in the cohortative"; Westermann, *Genesis 1–11,* 145; cf. *GKC* ¶ 124g N.

[20] Gordon J. Wenham, *Genesis 1–15,* WBC 1 (Waco, Tex.: Word, 1987), 139–41.

(1:6; 2:1) place them in Job's historical setting and therefore outside any participation in creation.

Apart from the angel of the Lord, already dealt with in connection with God's revelation, there are numerous references to other angels, none of whom has any ruling function. The first of these references is Genesis 19 where two angels are said to have gone to Sodom to warn Lot and his family of the impending destruction of the cities of the plain. Here their role is to serve as messengers of the Lord on behalf of human beings. Jacob later saw angels ascending and descending a stairway between earth and heaven (Gen. 28:10–15) and en route to his fateful encounter with Esau was met by "God's angels" who apparently were there to encourage him (Gen. 32:1).

In time the favorable comparison "as an angel of God" became a common cliché with no clear theological content except to show an awareness of these heavenly beings (1 Sam. 29:9; 2 Sam. 14:17, 20; 19:27). At least once angels are portrayed as instruments of divine revelation (1 Kings 13:18), and the angel who spoke on numerous occasions to the prophet Zechariah either spoke the word of God to him or interpreted for him what he saw in vision (Zech. 1:9, 13–14, 19; 2:3; 4:1, 4–5; 5:5, 10; 6:4–5). Angels, with men, are to praise God (Ps. 148:2). Psalm 103 urges this upon them and goes on to describe angels as beings "of great strength, who do His word, obedient to His command" (v. 20). Psalm 104:4, speaking of the Lord, says he is "making the winds His messengers [or angels], flames of fire His servants."

All was not well in the angelic world at the beginning, however. Aside from the "sons of God" who had cohabited with mortals (Gen. 6:2, 4), there were others whom God charged with error (Job 4:18). Chief among them, of course, was the accuser (Heb. *haśśāṭān)* known in the New Testament as the devil. He is the only angel who professed any kind of sovereignty and in the prologue to Job is seen as the adversary of the Lord. How he came to be such and thus to be evil and destined to judgment cannot be known.[21] He simply appears in the narrative as one among other angels who reported their doings to the Lord (showing, incidentally, that the Lord's sovereignty was still recognized even by Satan). When he tried to attack Job, he could do so only by God's permission (Job 1:12; 7:6), for

[21] For various options and the literature, see K. Nielsen, שָׂטָן, *TDOT* 14:73–78.

in the final analysis even he must submit to the Lord's dominion. In later Old Testament texts, Satan incited David to take an ill-advised census of his armies (1 Chron. 21:1) and in postexilic times stood before Joshua the high priest to accuse him in the Lord's presence. Instead, the Lord rebuked Satan on that occasion, scolding him for having slandered a man whom God himself had vindicated (Zech. 3:1–2).

To return to the primordial history, Satan made his earliest appearance in the guise of the serpent that successfully tempted Eve and then Adam to sin (Gen. 3:1–15). At the purely exegetical level, there is no hint, of course, that the serpent was a manifestation of Satan, but subsequent Old Testament imagery (Job 26:13; Isa. 27:1) and explicit New Testament testimony (Rev. 12:9, 15; 20:2) put the identification beyond question. Moreover, the adversarial stance taken by the serpent comports well with the idea already advanced that Satan, by definition, is the great antagonist to the purposes of God.

This rather lengthy discourse on angels precisely at this point can be justified on at least two grounds: (1) Angelology is in itself a theological topos that cannot be ignored in a full treatment of Old Testament theology; and (2) in a section dealing with the purposes of God as King whose rule is a mediated one, the mediation is one of descending order in which he is the great King who assigns royal responsibilities to layers of his servants, including angels, who do his bidding. The case has been made that God created man precisely so that man could function as a vice-regent. But the role of angels, who are presented as superhuman beings if not divine, cannot be overlooked. All evidence suggests that despite their exalted status angels do not enjoy a role superior to that of mankind; but, in fact, they were created to serve the human race in ways both known and unknown. This is seen in the narrative texts surveyed above, and it is explicitly affirmed in the fullness of God's revelation (Ps. 91:11; cf. Ps. 34:7; Isa. 37:36; Acts 5:19; 12:8). Paul asked the question, "Do you not know that we will judge angels?" (1 Cor. 6:3), and the author of the Epistle to the Hebrews also posed a query regarding angels: "Are they not all ministering spirits sent out to serve those who are going to inherit salvation?" (Heb. 1:14).

The hierarchy that emerges from the biblical witness, therefore, is (1) God, then (2) mankind, then (3) angels, and finally, (4) all other beings. This is not just a matter of disinterested pigeonholing. To the contrary, man's sin and fall and their repercussions cannot be fully understood until these levels of authority are seen in their proper relationship. We turn now to the matter of human dominion in a preliminary and idealistic way; the fall, its aftermath, and the resulting radical alteration of God's rule through the human race must be deferred to a more appropriate setting.

As we have already noted, man exercised dominion by working and overseeing the garden. But it is also evident in his naming of the various animals that the Lord brought before him "to see what he would call [them]" (Gen. 2:19). That is, God was already delegating responsibility to man, but it was not mere drudge work. In the world of the ancient Near East, he who named another manifested by that act a form of headship, a point already made previously.[22] God named man (Gen. 1:26), and man named the animals. To underscore the authority implicit in these acts, the text asserts that "whatever the man called a living creature, that was its name" (2:19). Once pronounced, there was no room for debate or alteration. But man also named woman, a naming that itself has ramifications for spheres of rulership (2:23).

The intrusion of sin and the resultant fall of the human race cannot be disconnected from the structure of governance established by the Lord whereby he was pleased to administer the affairs of his kingdom. Because of a violation of the interrelationships included in that governance, the fall was precipitated; and subsequent human history is a record of man's failure to recognize and abide by these divine principles of societal structure. The narrative of Genesis 3 is constructed in such a way as to drive these points home.

The story of the fall is like a mini-drama, the *personae dramatis* of which are the man, the woman, and the serpent, listed this way because they appear in this order in the events leading up to the drama. This is also the order of headship, for God had created the male and female to have dominion over all other things (Gen. 1:26–28) and then had sanctioned man's naming of the woman (2:23). But the play begins with the serpent in scene 1—the temptation and fall (3:1–8)—and then the woman and man make their appearance in that order. This is clearly an inversion of the intended sequence; for in scene 2 (3:9–13), the interrogation, the Lord confronts man first as head; but man assigns responsibility for disobedience

---

[22] See p. 45; cf Gerhard von Rad, *Genesis,* trans. John H. Marks (London: SCM, 1961), 81.

to the woman who in turn lays her culpability at the feet of the serpent. In scene 3, the judgment (3:14–19), the order of scene 1 is repeated: the serpent, the woman, and the man.[23] Since insubordination was the issue in the sin, it is appropriate that the punishment reflect that fact by beginning with the serpent and climaxing with the man. The animal world had attempted to dominate woman, woman usurped authority over man, and man failed to carry out his responsibility under God as his image.

The fundamental issue was one of authority and its disposition. The animal world (that is, the demonic world in disguise) refused to submit to the dominion of mankind, and man refused to submit to the dominion of the Lord. Therein lay the seeds and the fruit of the great sin, the results of which make up the stuff of history, both biblical and otherwise. The remedy for this state of affairs was the reestablishment of relationship with God through the forgiveness of sins, and thereby a renewal of the apparatus within which all parts of God's creation could find their rightful place under his sovereign sway. The prophet Isaiah foresaw a time when harmony will prevail in the kingdom of God, a harmony that will restore the proper balance of his rule to the extent that "the wolf will live with the lamb, and the leopard will lie down with the goat. The calf, the young lion, and the fatling will be together; and a child will lead them" (Isa. 11:6). The same prophet went on to make the astounding observation that "an infant will play beside the cobra's pit, and a toddler will put his hand into a snake's den," all without harm (Isa. 11:8). It is no coincidence that the youngster will need no longer to fear the wiles and terror of the serpent, the creature that led his first parents into sin, for it will be defanged and brought under the authority of redeemed humanity.

God's Fellowship with Mankind

Fellowship as a Creation Motif

God's purpose in creation was not limited to his establishment of a realm over which he could reign. Were this the case, it need not have involved sentient beings. Seas and mountains, forests and fauna would

---

[23] For a similar, more expanded analysis of the pericope, see David A. Dorsey, *The Literary Structure of the Old Testament* (Grand Rapids: Baker, 1999), 49–50.

have been enough. The fact that he created man (and perhaps angels as well) suggests, rather anthropopathically, that God was lonely and desired relationship with beings that, as his image, could communicate with him. These rationales are, of course, purely speculative, for the text is silent as to such things. But their being speculative does not rule out their plausibility; and, in fact, the pervasive process of Old Testament revelation on the one hand and man's response in praise, petition, and even lament on the other hand strongly suggest that God delights in fellowship.

To say such things is assuredly to speak in intensely human terms, for it is manifestly obvious that a God who existed for all time in solitary independence needs no one or no thing to make him complete or to meet some other need. But the Bible speaks of God in such human terms so we must live and work only with the language of the sacred narrative itself.

The first recorded conversation—the one detailing the terms of the so-called creation mandate in which God informed Adam directly as to what he was to do as God's image (Gen. 1:28–30)—is one-sided, at least so far as the record goes. The next occasion was also without human response and consisted of instructions regarding the trees of the garden (2:15–17). Ironically, true conversation is recorded only after the fall. The Lord spoke to Adam and he replied (3:9–12) and then to the woman who also responded (3:13). Following this the Lord spoke to the serpent, the woman, and the man in that order but without response from any of them (3:14–19).

The Lord's direct address continued thereafter throughout the biblical account in ways already described as special revelation. There is a tendency, however, to overlook the fellowship aspect of revelation and to view it only as a one-way self-disclosure entirely devoid of passion or mutual communication. To understand revelation in this limited way is to discount the desire of the Lord not merely to inform mankind of truth but to engage them in meaningful dialogue. The prayers and praises that make up such a large portion of the biblical corpus should be seen as at least part of the other side of the conversation. The theological significance of this human input into revelation will receive lengthy treatment later; but it is worth noting now that while it is inspired and canonical in the fullest sense of these terms, the response of God's people to him is also an act of fellowship, one in which he greatly delights.

Fellowship in the Wake of the Fall

Perhaps the most tragic consequence of the fall was the rupture of the fellowship that man had enjoyed with God, certainly in the open and free manner hinted at in the early chapters of Genesis. The intimacy of association suggested in the second creation narrative (the Lord formed man and breathed into him the breath of life; 2:7), God's placement of man in the garden (2:8), the freedom he gave him to eat of everything but the fruit of the tree of the knowledge of good and evil (2:17), his response to man's loneliness and need for a partner (2:18), and his presenting all the animals before him to scc what he would name them (2:19)—all of this testifies to God's desire to know man and to bring him into his confidence as a partner in kingdom dominion. Even after the fall God continued what seems to have been his habit of walking "in the garden at the time of the evening breeze" (3:8). But things were different now. Fellowship had been broken, a fact of which man and woman were keenly aware; and they sought to avoid the intimacy with God they had once known by hiding from him. The Lord made man to fellowship with him, however; so despite the rupture brought by man's rebellion, the Lord sought him out, clothing him with animal skins as a portent of the atonement that would restore all that had been lost through sin (Gen. 3:21).[24] In the interim, however, though fellowship continued at a certain level, it was greatly hindered and, in fact, was far short of the ideal. Man was barred from the tree of life lest he become sinfully immortal and was banished from the garden, the microcosm of the universe, having failed to discharge the reigning privileges and responsibilities granted him by a generous and loving God (3:22–24).

The reigning purposes of God may appear to have been irreparably damaged, but the eschatological picture is far from pessimistic. The kingdom will emerge in all its glory, a repristinating of what God had intended in his initial creation and even more. The full description and dimensions of this aspect of the kingdom will be addressed in a more appropriate place, but hints of God's ongoing dominion continue even in the immediate aftermath of the fall. We have already noted a great

---

[24] As Hamilton puts it, "Adam and Eve are in need of a salvation that comes from without. God needs to do for them what they are unable to do for themselves." Victor P. Hamilton, *The Book of Genesis Chapter 1–17,* NICOT (Grand Rapids: Eerdmans, 1990), 207.

number of texts in which the Lord is extolled as King and which narrate the exercise of that kingship throughout the history of Old Testament Israel.[25] These are reflective of not mere wishful thinking or some effort retrojectively to appropriate eschatological idealism. The theologians of Israel were convinced that, despite all evidences to the contrary, their God was King and those whom he appointed as his earthly surrogates ruled over an extension of the kingdom of heaven. The earthly kingdom was imperfect, to be sure, and was even destined to judgment. But it would reemerge and become the realm over which the Lord himself would rule.

A foreshadowing of the eschatological realm is seen in the account of the flood which destroyed the earth but from which came a new earth and a new opportunity at kingdom building. Noah, like Adam, was "a man of the soil" (the Hebrew *ʾîš hāʾădāmâ* makes the connection even clearer) (Gen. 9:20) whose first act after the flood was to plant a vineyard. This he did in obedience to the reiteration of the original creation mandate to "be fruitful and multiply and fill the earth" (Gen. 9:1). There is now no explicit command to subdue and rule, but it is implicit in the statement that all the creatures of land, water, and air "are placed under your authority" (v. 2). This constitutes a delegation of dominion over creation just as God had done in the precurse world (Gen. 1:28).

The crippling effect of the fall is seen nevertheless in the qualifying clause of the mandate that the creatures over which Noah and his descendants were to rule would now submit only involuntarily. They would yield to mankind out of a sense of fear and dread (9:2) and not as a natural response to their subsidiary role in the divine scheme of sphere sovereignty. Just as the serpent had inverted the God-man-animal relationship, animals now would live in incorrigible rebellion against humankind just as humankind would oppose the lordship of God. Only by sheer superiority of intelligence and skill would the human race prevail over lower orders. So severe would the imposition of that dominion be and so alienated the creature from the man that man would from thenceforth be allowed to slay animals for food (Gen. 9:3), a concession to the altered conditions brought about by sin, conditions that fostered

---

[25] See pp. 43–44.

antipathy where there had been harmony and death where there had been nothing but life.

Fellowship through Human Government

The roots and tendrils of human government also grew out of the postflood soil. Not only did the issue of interspecies sovereignty arise, but so did that of horizontal interpersonal relationships. How were sinners to relate to one another under the umbrella of God's ultimate rule? The answer lay in an attitude and system of mutual respect in which human beings lived life with a constant awareness of their being, without exception, the image of God. Though animal blood could now be shed, even for food, man's blood—the very essence of his life—could not be shed lest the murderer encounter the wrath of God to whom he was accountable (Gen. 9:5–6).[26] It is this fact, that man is the image of God, that must dictate how one person should treat another. To violate that image is, in effect, to violate the person and authority of God himself. The penalty for such egregious disregard of the sanctity of human life could be nothing less than the application of *lex talionis*: "Whoever sheds the blood of man, by man shall his blood be shed" (Gen. 9:6 NIV).

This ideal undergirds all human government in the Old Testament, even (or especially) that of Israel. As the model people of the Lord, Israel must exemplify, for all others to see, what it meant to exercise divine hegemony in a just and fair manner; for Israel was a microcosm, ideally at least, of the kingdom of heaven. Its rulers and citizens must seek to achieve the kind of society that would attract the nations to their God. When Israel succeeded, the nations were blessed; when it failed, the nations suffered. This is what it meant to be a kingdom of priests and a holy nation.

The prophetic blessing and curse of Noah directed to his three sons and their offspring provided the nucleus of the composition of the nations and their geographical distribution that found fulfillment in Moses' day in the "Table of Nations" (Gen. 9:18–27; cf. 10:1–32). Though the principle of separation and even its geographical rationale may be

[26] Kenneth Mulzac, "Genesis 9:1–7: Its Theological Connections with the Creation Motif," *JATS* 12/1 (2001): 73–76; James E. Priest, "Gen. 9:6: A Comparative Study of Bloodshed in Bible and Talmud," *JETS* 31 (1988): 145–51.

difficult to determine, the truth that it was done by divine intervention and according to divine purpose is clear.[27] Human government had determined to declare its anticovenant independence of the Lord and, rather than be fruitful and have dominion over all things (Gen. 1:28), had decided to entrench itself in one place where it could make a name for itself (Gen. 11:1–4). This hubris was an unthinkable challenge to the dominion of the Lord, one diametrically opposed to the function he had ordained for mankind: to rule over all things under his aegis.

The peoples thus found their several places of habitation where they established social and political apparatuses in line with a design which, even if they could not see it or would not willingly comply with it, nonetheless contributed to God's sovereign plan. Within that structure an inner purpose was being formulated, one hardly discernible without the benefit of later hindsight. By this we mean the pattern of the dispersion of the nations following the Babel debacle. Contrary to the order of the birth of Noah's sons, they are first listed as Shem, Ham, and Japheth (Gen. 9:18), setting the stage for Shem's theological priority. Only he is specifically linked with the name *Yahweh* (9:26), and it is his descent that occupies the climactic place at the end of the table (10:21–31). Of particular importance is the truncated genealogy of Genesis 10:21 which states simply: "Shem was the father of all the children of Eber." This brief summary serves as a caption for what follows, that is, the Shemite genealogy which finds its central focus in Eber[28] and his son Peleg (10:24–25). The line then splits, with Peleg's brother Joktan being identified as the ancestor of the various Arabian tribes whereas Peleg, according to the genealogy of Genesis 11, produced the line that culminated in Abram (v. 26). And Abram, as it turns out, would sire a line of descendants that would constitute the nation Israel. The function of the table is unmistakable: it is to prepare the groundwork for a theocratic people by tracing them back to their roots in Shem, the blessed son of Noah.

---

[27] Eugene H. Merrill, "The Peoples of the Old Testament according to Genesis 10," *BSac* 154 (1997): 3–22.

[28] The Old Testament clearly traces the term *ʿibri* (Hebrew) to this patronym. For full discussion see D. N. Freedman, B. E. Willoughby, and H.-J. Fabry, עֵבֶר, *TDOT* 10:430–45.

Fellowship through a Chosen People

Long before the people Israel consolidated into a nation, God was working through their patriarchal forebears to provide a glimpse into his strategy of ruling through human instrumentality. The Lord had told Abram that he would make him into a great nation (Gen. 12:2; cf. 17:4–5; 18:18); but even before that happened, he and his offspring would be the means by which "all the peoples on earth will be blessed" (12:3). It is inaccurate, of course, to conceive of Abram, even with all his entourage, as a government. He had no land, except by promise, and no structure of governance apart from that naturally associated with his being a tribal sheik. But nonetheless, he, like Adam and Noah, represented and was in fact a conduit of the divine rule transmitted condescendingly from the Lord of heaven to his creation on earth. A few examples must suffice.

When Abram went to Egypt because of a famine, his beautiful wife Sarai, as she was then called, caught the eye of the pharaoh, ruler of the mightiest nation on earth. He took her into his harem in exchange for an enormous payment of all kinds of commodities, and she would have become his wife had the Lord not disclosed to him Sarai's true identity. Abram's role here was anything but a channel of blessing, but from the experience the pharaoh at least was exposed to the God of the patriarch and submitted to him (Gen. 12:16–20).

The invasion of the cities of the Dead Sea plains by the kings of the East is a clearer example of God's rule through a man, in this case Abram once again (Gen. 14:1–24). Having defeated these cities, the foreign kings returned to their homelands taking Abram's nephew Lot among other captives. Though Abram was hopelessly outnumbered, he pursued the invaders as far north as Hobah, triumphed over them in battle, and retrieved the stolen goods and persons. Of greatest interest and theological significance is the encounter Abram had with a priest of El Elyon, Melchizedek by name. This man of God proceeded to utter a blessing upon Abram, one that singled out Abram as a special servant of God and that drew attention to the Most High as Creator of all and Ruler of the nations: "Abram is blessed by God Most High, Creator of heaven and earth, and give praise to God Most High, who has handed over your enemies to you" (Gen. 14:19–20). The connection between the kingship of the Lord and its exercise through Abram could not be clearer.

The turmoil of the nations was largely brought to resolution through the offices of one man who, as God's image, asserted God's dominion.

The anticipation of God's rule through Abram (now Abraham) and the nation that existed already in his loins is set forth in Genesis 17. Here Abraham is called "the father of many nations" from whom kings would descend (vv. 5–6). They would inherit the land of Canaan "as an eternal possession" (v. 8), thus providing a realm for governance; and his descendants would be numerous, constituting a citizenry for such a kingdom (v. 2). The same promise was reiterated following Abraham's obedience in the matter of Isaac's sacrifice (Gen. 22:17–18) with the added proviso that "your offspring will possess the gates of their enemies," a strong hint of Israelite domination in the future. Isaac himself received this promise (Gen. 26:3–4) as did Jacob (27:27–29). Of special interest was Isaac's hope for Jacob that nations might serve him and peoples bow down to him (v. 29). These verbs are redolent of the imagery of divine rule through appointed administrators, especially in a world of sinful rebellion (cf. 28:3–4).

Jacob furthermore received a promise by direct revelation that his descendants would inherit the land and become the means of blessing the nations (Gen. 28:13–15). Then, after Jacob's successful encounter with God in the nocturnal wrestling match, the Lord changed his name to Israel in recognition of his triumph over both God and men (Gen. 32:22–28). This might have been a harbinger of things to come when the nation of Israel would assert its dominion over the nations of the world. Such an idea is supported by the repetition of the terms of the Abrahamic covenant: "Be fruitful and multiply. A nation, indeed an assembly of nations, will come from you, and kings will descend from you. The land that I gave to Abraham and Isaac I will give to you. And I will give the land to your descendants after you" (Gen. 35:11–12). The command to "be fruitful and multiply" recalls the original mandate to humankind as a crucial element to the universal sovereignty of God (Gen. 1:26–28). There can be no mistaking the significance of its repetition to Jacob, the father of the chosen nation. That nation, Israel, will become the expression of the kingdom of God on earth. Jacob himself understood this as is clear from his patriarchal blessing of the tribes, in particular the blessing of Judah: "The scepter will not depart from Judah, or the staff from between his feet, until He whose right it is comes and the obedience of the peoples belongs to Him" (Gen. 49:10). Jewish and Christian tradition is in general agreement in understanding this promise messianically, the former as fulfilled in David and his descent and the latter in the greater Son of David, Jesus the Christ.[29] In either case the focus is on the glorious reign of the Lord God through a nation, then a tribe, then a solitary King.

Messiah as King and his messianic reign is a separate topic yet to be explored, so we shall desist from pursuing that avenue of the reigning purpose of God at this point. But Israel as the embodiment of that intention must be considered, at least in its formative stages. The full historical course of the nation's role with respect to the implementation of the creation mandate cannot be traced for now beyond its foundational layer; for this concept, like that of the Messiah, is also best reserved for a more appropriate place.

The book of Exodus opens with a contest of sovereignties, that of the pharaoh and his government on the one hand and that of Israel's God on the other. Egypt at this time (the Late Bronze Age) enjoyed undisputed preeminence among the nations of the earth. One might say it represented the sum and substance of human military and political power, the crystallization of the anti-God forces of a world in rebellion against the Lord of the universe. This is not a far-fetched analysis as the narrative of the plagues and exodus make abundantly clear. Like the Babel community Egypt symbolized everything resistant to the rule of God and to the creation mandate that humankind should have dominion under his and not its own sovereignty.

Moses was forced to choose sides in the matter of kingdom loyalties, and in the final analysis chose to align himself with the Lord and his downtrodden slave people (Exod. 2:15; cf. Heb. 11:24–26). He understood the fundamental question at stake: Who really is God and how could he and his people, having settled the matter, begin to live out the implications of their identity in light of the ancient promises to the patriarchs? While Moses languished in exile, the cry of his people because of their onerous bondage to Pharaoh, the anti-God, rose up to heaven, thus setting the stage for a showdown that would resolve the issue of ultimate authority.

[29] Eugene H. Merrill, "Rashi, Nicholas de Lyra, and Christian Exegesis," *WTJ* 38/1 (1975): 66–79.

In response, the Lord heard their cry and "remembered His covenant with Abraham, Isaac, and Jacob" (Exod. 2:24).

The impending contest is put in starkly clear terms with the Lord's instruction to Moses to perform signs and wonders attesting to his power but with the added note that Pharaoh would give no heed because the Lord would harden his heart so as to leave no room for negotiation or compromise (Exod. 4:21). With the matter of sovereignty hanging in the balance, there could be no equivocation: The contest must settle once and for all who it was that deserved the allegiance of the nations, God who created them or Pharaoh who, like the serpent, arrogated to himself a competing dominion. Thus Pharaoh stood in the tradition of those who opposed the regnant purposes of God from the beginning and who will do so in the ages to come until the day of final consummation when the Lord's sovereignty will stand unchallenged. Every age has had its pharaohs, for the cosmic struggle for dominion is one that will not go away.

Moses' first appeal to Pharaoh was met with a statement encapsulating the challenge of unregenerate mankind to God's right to rule: "Who is the LORD that I should obey Him by letting Israel go? I do not know the LORD, and what's more, I will not let Israel go" (Exod. 5:2). This is not the naïve question of an earnest seeker but a blatant denial of the LORD's right to rule. As a quasi-divine being himself (at least in Egyptian theology), Pharaoh correctly understood the transcendent nature of the contest in which he was engaged. It was not just a struggle between God and men but between God and the gods.[30] Moses seems not to have grasped the full significance of this; and in Moses' moment of discouragement and loss of nerve, the Lord made the remarkable declaration that he would make Moses like God to Pharaoh (Exod. 7:1). Clearly, then, the fight was not Moses' but the Lord's and ultimately not Pharaoh's but Satan's. The battle must be fought in a wholly new, unworldly dimension, one elaborated well in the prologue to Job among other places (Job 1–2).

Once the plagues had begun to take their toll, the Egyptians "will know that I am the LORD," said he (Exod. 7:5). The issue for them would be settled in the white-hot crucible of conflict. The Lord's triumph would provide irrefutable evidence of his mastery over all things including

[30] Ronald E. Clements, "History and Theology in Biblical Narrative," *HBT* 4 (1982): 47–48.

mighty Pharaoh and his nation. It is important to observe that the works the Lord performed were all in the realm of nature, either as a kind of replication of creation or a display of mastery over it that in any case would link him with the origins of all that exists and therefore as the only one with just claim to have dominion over it.[31] At last the magicians of Egypt had to concede that they could not replicate the creative power of Israel's God and in a moment of theological clarity confessed that "this is the finger of God" (Exod. 8:19). Pharaoh resisted to the end, however, and finally had to hear the humbling word from God that all his posturings and reputation notwithstanding, he was but a pawn in the Lord's hand, one raised up by God, as the Lord said to him, "to show you My power and to make My name known in all the earth" (Exod. 9:16). The truth was out, then. The reigning purposes of God, though challenged by the evil forces of heaven and earth, could not in the end be stymied. Indeed, they will prevail until the whole world confesses him as King of kings and Lord of lords.

The event of the exodus weaves together many theological strands not least of which is the one under consideration here, the recognition of the Lord as King and an understanding of his reigning purposes mediated through human instruments. God's mastery over Pharaoh and Egypt in itself testified to his lordship (Exod. 14:4, 18), but his victory over the Red Sea removed any lingering doubt, for the sea brought to mind the work of the Creator who at the beginning spoke to the chaotic primeval oceans and brought them under his dominion. Just as those oceans were divided so that dry land appeared (Gen. 1:9–10), so he split the Red Sea, enabling Israel to cross over on dry ground (Exod. 14:21).

In another context we noted that the Song of the Sea (Exod. 15:1–21) is especially instructive in its celebration of these motifs and others as well.[32] In it Moses spoke of the Lord as "highly exalted," a clear allusion to royalty (v. 1), and described his power and greatness as being majestic (vv. 6–7). Then, as Master of the sea, he returned its parted waters, sealing the Egyptian army in a watery tomb (v. 4). Moses could only marvel at this display of sovereignty. "LORD," he asked, "who is like You among the gods? Who is like You, glorious in holiness, revered with praises,

[31] Greta Hort, "The Plagues of Egypt," *ZAW* 69 (1957): 84–103; 70 (1958): 48–59.

[32] See p. 49.

performing wonders?" (Exod. 15:11). The answer, of course, is no one; for only the Lord sits in such regal splendor and acts in such sovereign ways. The astounding dominion exhibited by his deliverance of his people from the hostile forces of men and nature would terrify the nations who heard of it (vv. 14–16), a tacit admission of their acknowledgment of his kingship over them.

The poem closes with a reference to the land of Canaan as the arena of the Lord's rule, the place he had prepared for his dwelling (v. 17). His people Israel would populate the kingdom and from his holy sanctuary, says Moses, "The LORD will reign forever and ever!" (v. 18). The Lord's encounter with Pharaoh and Egypt and his deliverance of Israel through the Red Sea were therefore inextricably linked to his kingship over both human and cosmic forces. His royal purposes, inherent in his person and in his creation work, as frustrated as they are by the inroads of human sin, will nevertheless prevail until they are universally fulfilled.

The final text to be considered now with respect to the Lord's design to rule over the works of his hands is the one we have already singled out as a key to the understanding of Old Testament theology as a whole, namely, Exodus 19:4–6: "You have seen what I did to the Egyptians and how I carried you on eagles' wings and brought you to Me. Now if you will listen to Me and carefully keep My covenant, you will be My own possession out of all the peoples, although all the earth is Mine, and you will be My kingdom of priests and My holy nation."

We shall revisit this passage many more times at appropriate places, but its theological centrality demands rather extensive consideration at this point of the discussion of God's reign. The occasion was the offer of a covenant relationship by the Lord to Israel, an offer implicitly made even prior to the exodus but not in the clear language about to be uttered (cf. Exod. 3:5, 12; 6:6–7). The Lord had promised the patriarchs that the nation they sired would be his means of blessing all the peoples of the earth (Gen. 12:3; 22:18; etc.), but how that would be effected had never been spelled out. One thing was clear: It was not just that they were the people of the Lord that would suffice. Rather, it was the mission to which they were called as a people that had true significance, a mission paradoxically of both servanthood and sovereignty. As God's servant nation they would become the channel through which human redemption would be proclaimed and even brought to pass. As God's kingdom they would model what it means to have dominion over all things as an extension of his sovereignty.

The sovereignty aspect was already evident in Israel's miraculous deliverance from Egypt. The Lord had wreaked judgment on that nation that epitomized human rebellion against him and had brought his people out "on eagles' wings," that is, with speed and ease. Then, in terms of conditionality the Lord pledged to make Israel his "own possession" (Heb. *sĕgullâ)*[33] *if* they were faithful to keep the covenant with him that he was about to disclose. We must constantly bear in mind that this was not a covenant to make Israel the Lord's people, for they were already that (Exod. 4:22–23).[34] Rather, it was a covenant to bring the already chosen nation into a place of divine service. Their being the elect people was never a matter of being obedient to a set of stipulations; indeed, they were elect before such legislation ever came into existence. It was their function as a servant nation that depended upon unswerving obedience to covenant demands, and that was at the heart of the present offer.

Precisely what the offer entailed was left to the end of the covenant presentation. Israel had experienced the mighty exodus deliverance; they had been told that they could become a treasured possession of the Lord if they would commit to obedience, and now they learned what they had been chosen to do: to be a kingdom of priests and a holy nation.[35] This startling declaration went beyond the mere assertion that they would be a kingdom and a nation; this had been hinted at already in the promises to the fathers. The important advancement here was the use of the adjectives *priestly* and *holy,* for they respectively spell out the function and nature of the people of Israel.

"Kingdom of priests" is, indeed, better understood as "priestly kingdom" as the parallel to the more grammatically precise "holy nation" makes clear.[36] What it suggests is that just as a priest serves his people

---

[33] For this important term suggesting Israel's special relationship to the LORD, see pp. 128–29, and Eugene Carpenter, סגלה, *NIDOTTE* 3:224.

[34] W. J. Dumbrell, *Covenant and Creation* (Nashville: Thomas Nelson, 1984), 98–99.

[35] The use of *goy* here rather than *ʿam* (people) is not surprising inasmuch as the emphasis here and elsewhere (cf. Gen. 12:2; 17:4–6; 18:18; 46:3; etc.) is on Israel in its role as a political entity among other nations, the parallelism to *kingdom* here also making the same point. See Ronald E. Clements, גוֹי, *goy, TDOT* 2:429–30.

[36] For other options as well as this, see John I. Durham, *Exodus,* WBC 3 (Waco, Tex.: Word, 1987), 263.

as both a cultic mediator and, in the case of the Old Testament, a teacher of Torah (Lev. 10:11; Deut. 17:10–11; 33:10), so Israel must stand in ministry between the Lord and the nations of the earth that needed to be reconciled to him and learn of him. But the functional term *priestly* should, at the same time, not overshadow the nominal *kingdom,* the term reminiscent of Israel's royal character. Israel would mediate; but it would also embody the reigning purposes of the Lord and, moreover, would rule on his behalf, at least in the eschatological age when the frustrations of historical realities at last give way to the unfettered expressions of God's eternal plan (Deut. 26:16–19; 28:1, 13; Isa. 14:2; cf. 11:14).

As for "holy nation," this expression suggests both the moral character of Israel and its distinction from all other nations. Part of the attractiveness of Israel as a servant of the Lord must be its likeness to him. When the nations looked upon Israel, their impulse ought to be a desire to know the God who could mold and make such a people. At the same time, for Israel to be holy was for it to be set aside exclusively for the Lord's use. Such a desirable trait lies at the heart of the Lord's demand that his people not contaminate themselves with the abominations of the nations but rather maintain their aloofness from influences that would make them no different from all other people.

Israel's acceptance of the terms of the covenant was unequivocal: "We will do all that the LORD has spoken" (Exod. 19:8). The millennium of history that followed that confident assertion would become a record of abysmal failure, however, so much so that the nation would go into exile never to recover its potential for kingdom service. Only the eschatological hope founded on the faithfulness of the sovereign Lord remained to them, a hope certain and secure because of the irrefragable nature of his commitment to them. These themes—Israel's inability to live out its pledge of covenant fidelity and the Lord's assurance that he would provide future enablement—receive full attention in part 3 of this work.

In summary, the creation purposes of God can be adumbrated in just a brief statement: he created all things in order to display his glory and majesty over a kingdom of time and space. Concomitant with that work was his desire for fellowship with sentient beings with whom he could share the responsibilities of universal dominion. These beings—the human race—were created as his image and placed in a paradisiacal setting, a microcosm of the heavens and earth, to provide them an arena in which to exercise their derivative lordship. Dissatisfied with their role of subordination, man and woman yielded to the enticements of the serpent, Satan in the guise of an animal, and ate of the forbidden fruit of the garden, thus crippling their ability to live out God's mandate for them to have dominion and rule over all things. But God devised a plan by which the curse could be overcome, and which, through the selection of chosen vessels, would result in the restoration of his rule, if not in history then certainly in the eschaton. To that human instrument we now turn, a channel first revealed in Adam and Eve, then through a nation, and finally through the single scion of that nation, the messianic descendant of David who by life and by death would bring God's plan into perfect consummation.

PART TWO

MANKIND: THE IMAGE OF GOD

Chapter Six

The Creation of Mankind

The methodology adopted for this work inevitably necessitates a certain degree of repetition or overlap of subject matter since we must frequently view the same topoi from different angles and with different emphases. This will be immediately apparent from the outset of part 2, which addresses mankind as a discrete theological entity. The nature, character, and purposes of God—all of which were the subject of part 1—must obviously come to the fore again since man's creation and role finds its roots in God's essence and design. Part 1 did indeed briefly contemplate the subject of man's creation but almost in passing, as only somewhat adjunctive to the larger concern there of identifying the God of the Old Testament as the matter of central interest. The task here will be to address more comprehensively and in a more focused manner mankind's theological significance—his creation, nature, fall, redemption, and restoration. This requires some retracing of issues already raised and also forces some intrusion into matters more thoroughly and properly reserved for part 3.

The Creation and Purpose of Mankind

We have already proposed that Exodus 19:4–6 is central in addressing the question as to the origins and role of the nation Israel, a question that must certainly have dominated the thinking of its theologians and to which Moses felt impelled to seek satisfying answers. Assembled as they were in Moab and at a critical historical juncture, they needed to understand their historical roots, their present situation, and, in view of Moses' impending demise, what the future held for them. In other words they needed someone to recite their narrative, the story that would identify them as a people among but distinct from all other nations. Moses, the servant of God whom they knew to be his spokesman, was the obvious candidate for the job. Prompted by the Spirit, he stepped forward and declared in both speech and sacred text that God had indeed selected them to be his people by patriarchal promise and that he had redeemed them from Egypt to make of them a servant nation with a special task—to instruct the nations as to his unique existence and to inform them of the grace by which he desired to be reconciled to them.

Israel's role would be worked out in the framework of a covenant, the introduction to which makes clear that though Israel was but one nation among many, it was the special object of God's concern, his "treasured possession" (Exod. 19:5 NIV).[1] Then, from all the choices available to him, the Lord sanctified Israel to himself and charged it with the privileged responsibility of mediating his gracious plan of salvation to the whole world (v. 6). This stunning revelation would certainly have led thoughtful persons to ask how it was that the nations needed redemption and reconciliation and what set of circumstances led to God's choice of Israel as his means of bringing it about.

Moses therefore needed to provide a "brief history of the world," one adequate at least to trace the origins of the nations within Israel's purview. Of special importance would be the discovery of Israel's roots and how they intertwined around those of all the other peoples. But for Israel to know these things without knowing why they in particular existed would leave the story incomplete. The more fundamental question, therefore, was the question of ultimate beginnings. Who is God, what has he done, how and why did the nations originate, and what was the cause of the moral and spiritual crises that testified to their alienation from God and that only he could redress?

---

[1] See pp. 128–29.

The beginning of Israel's narrative lies, therefore, at the beginning, that is, at creation. Israel obviously consisted of people; and in the biblical scheme all peoples, including Israel, were offspring of the first couple, Adam and Eve. The genealogy of 1 Chronicles 1 consists of an unbroken line between Adam and Israel. Its purpose was to make the connection for which we are arguing here, that is, that Israel could arrive at an accurate self-perception only by understanding its place in relationship to the first parents and, indeed, to creation itself.[2] A theology that ignores this connection is one that is likely either to underplay the significance of Israel by viewing it as just another nation, albeit a privileged one, or to focus so much on that nation in its historical context that its subservience to higher divine ends is obfuscated. Israel could be the servant of God to the nations precisely because it, like all nations, sprang from a common creation and by its commonality could make a sincere claim to identification with them.

The Creation Narratives

The approach to be taken here is (1) to look carefully at the creation narratives and learn from them what it means to be human in the individual sense and (2) to consider how humanity grew beyond such narrow particularity to form interpersonal and community relationships such as marriage, family, clan, tribe, and nation. The temptation to engage overmuch in sociological and political aspects of these strata must be strenuously avoided, at least at this point. Every effort must be bent toward gaining most of all a theological perspective on these categories of social delineation.

We have noted repeatedly that Genesis presents two creation narratives, one in Genesis 1:1–2:3 and the other in Genesis 2:4–25. The former is sometimes described as the cosmocentric account because of its all-embracing view of the origins of all things in heaven and earth, whereas the latter is the anthropocentric, so-called because its focus is on the creation of man. Within each of these, however, only a few verses relate directly to man's creation. In the case of Genesis 1, verses 26–30 contain the whole record. In Genesis 2, the creation in the strict sense

[2] Roddy Braun, *1 Chronicles,* WBC 14 (Waco, Tex.: Word), 14.

encompasses only verses 7, 21–22. Despite their brevity, each of these demands careful exegesis, for each is rich with theological potential.

After having created everything else in five days, on day six the Lord made *(ʿśh)* both wild and domesticated land animals and then created *(brʾ)* man. Though one should not make too much distinction between these two verbs since they are sometimes used interchangeably (e.g., Gen. 1:26–27), it is nonetheless a fact that *brʾ* occurs in the Hebrew Bible as a verb of creation with only God as subject (thirty-three times in all).[3] Furthermore, in many of these instances *brʾ* (as opposed to other verbs such as *ʿśh* or *yṣr)* connotes the idea of creation out of nothing *(creatio ex nihilo)*. This is clearly the case in Genesis 1:1 since there is no hint whatsoever in the text of material preexistent to the heavens and the earth from which they were made. A straightforward reading suggests that apart from God himself nothing existed until he spoke it into being. The second use of *brʾ* in the narrative appears in verse 21, which marks a major distinction between the fourth and fifth day. Up until day five no living creatures whatsoever had come into being. Light, darkness, the skies, the seas, vegetation, and the sun, moon, and stars—all of these had appeared but nothing yet called a "living thing" *(nepeš ḥayyâ)* had emerged. Their creation therefore marked a significant step forward, creatures "according to the kinds" that were totally unrelated to anything that had preceded them. What set them apart was the fact that they were alive, possessing in some sense the "breath of life" *(nišmaḥ rûaḥ ḥayyîm)* (Gen. 7:22 NIV), an impartation from God hitherto unknown.

The third occurrence of *brʾ* is in reference to the creation of man (Gen. 1:27). God had said, "Let Us make *(naʿăśeh)* man" (v. 26), and the result is that he "created" *(wayyibrāʾ)* him (v. 27). The making is generic; the creating is specific. That is, man was made, like everything else, but only he, along with the heavens and earth and living creatures, is said to have been created. The uniqueness of the heavens and the earth needs no comment. As for the living creatures, their distinction from all that preceded them lay in their possessing the breath of life. What then was there about man that set him apart from both the heavens and the earth and all other living beings? The answer lies not in the fact that he had the breath of life, though that distinguished him from the inanimate

---

[3] Raymond C. Van Leeuwen, ברא, *NIDOTTE* 1:732.

universe, but that that breath was communicated by divine inbreathing and not merely through the spoken word (Gen. 2:7).[4] We shall address the ramifications of this presently.

To return to Genesis 1:26–28, it is instructive to observe the literary structure:[5]

A God's description of man's nature (26a)
    B God's description of man's purpose (26b)
A´ God's creation of man (27)
    B´ God's commission to man (28)

A and A´ have to do with what man is; B and B' concern what man is to do. Two terms are employed to convey the idea of man's identity, *viz, image (ṣelem)* and *likeness (dĕmût).* In creation contexts they are essentially synonymous (cf. Gen. 5:1, 3), though elsewhere *image* commonly refers to idols or other man-made objects of worship whereas *likeness* is just a term of comparison by which something is said to resemble something else (cf. Isa. 40:18; Ezek. 1:5, 10, 13, 16; etc.). As we shall see, the nuances of both nouns may be implicit here in that man is a representation of God and thus is, in some respect, like God.[6]

The Image of God

Traditional interpretations of the doctrine of the *imago Dei* propose that man is *in* God's image in the sense that he shares much of what God is. That is, man, like God, has personality, intelligence, feeling, and will.[7] To be in God's image is indeed to be godlike though obviously in a highly nuanced and restricted sense. A case can in fact be made for justifying this point of view through a careful study of Old Testament theology proper (the doctrine of God) and anthropology (the study of man) which discloses many apparently common attributes and capacities.

---

[4] See pp. 105–6.

[5] For a similar scheme, see Gordon J. Wenham, *Genesis 1–15,* WBC 1 (Waco, Tex.: Word, 1987), 27.

[6] Wolff understands *image* to refer to a relationship of domination, i.e., of man over creation, and *likeness* as a relationship of correspondence, i.e., of man's nearness to God. Hans Walter Wolff, *Anthropology of the Old Testament* (Philadelphia: Fortress, 1974), 160–61.

[7] Strong defines "image of God" as "1. Natural likeness to God, or personality; 2. Moral likeness to God, or holiness." Augustus Hopkins Strong, *Systematic Theology* (Philadelphia: Judson, 1907, repr. 1958), 514.

The differences between the transcendent God and mere mortals are so vast, however, as to require a better explanation of the *imago Dei,* one that focuses not so much on ontological equivalence as on functional comparisons.

A number of scholars in recent years have drawn attention to the ancient Near Eastern (especially Mesopotamian) practice by conquering kings of erecting images (Akkadian *ṣalmu* = Heb. *ṣelem)* of themselves in lands they had brought under their control.[8] These statues were not identical to the kings themselves, of course, but they represented them and therefore were to be treated with the same respect the king himself would demand. To deface or remove the image would be interpreted as an act of rebellion against the sovereign, and the perpetrator could expect severe repercussions.

The application of this analogy to our text in Genesis 1:26–27 demands a different way of understanding the preposition ordinarily translated *in* (the image). The Hebrew particle *bĕ* admittedly bears the locative nuance most of the time, but its use as an adverb of comparison is also well attested.[9] If viewed this way, the phrase in question would read "as our image" and not "in our image." The difference may be minute grammatically, but it is profound theologically, for the point being made is no longer one of ontological identification but functional representation. That is, to *be* the image of God is radically different from being *in* his image. In the one case man stands in the place of God; in the other case he is much like God.

Besides alleviating the tension inherent in comparing the ineffable God to his creation, no matter how noble, to understand man's relationship to God in terms of role and not essence is much more in line with the purpose and commission of mankind outlined in the statement concerning his creation. Having determined to "make man in[/as] Our image, [in/as] our likeness," God says of that image, "let them rule" (Gen. 1:26 NIV). It is obvious that the nature of man (his being an image) was closely connected to his task (to rule). Just as the statue of a king was taken to be the king himself in terms of its representation, so mankind was to be

---

[8] See especially Gerhard von Rad, *Old Testament Theology,* vol. 1, trans. D. M. G. Stalker (New York: Harper & Row, 1962), 146–47; for the Akkadian evidence, see CAD 16:80–81.

[9] For other examples see Bruce K. Waltke and M. O'Connor, *Biblical Hebrew Syntax* (Winona Lake, Ind.: Eisenbrauns, 1990), 198.

understood as God insofar as he stands in the place of God. God's rule over the earth and its subjugation to his dominion would be exercised through his image according to his good plan and pleasure. This radical notion that man could be God, as it were, finds indirect support in the statement of the Lord to Moses that "I have made you God [not "*as* God" as in most translations] to Pharaoh, and Aaron your brother will be your prophet" (Exod. 7:1). There is no claim here, of course, that Moses had been made divine; the point is that he had been commissioned to represent God in the Egyptian court.

Contrary to God's sovereignty, man's role in this capacity was not unlimited, for the boundaries of his authority are clearly defined as the fish, the birds, the livestock, and all other land animals. This is the order in which these creatures were created, an order that speaks perhaps of increasing complexity of life form. All share in common the breath of life, but all in common are also relegated to a position far below the dignity of man. Man is to them as God is to man; and just as God has dominion over man, so man is to dominate the animal world. This presumably was a matter of little effort at the beginning before the fall. The record states that the Lord brought before the man all the creatures of earth to see what he would name them (Gen. 2:19–20). The docility with which they came suggests a harmony of relationship both within the realm of nature and between it and mankind. And man's naming of the animals, a sign of his lordship over them, testifies to the recognition by all creation of the chain of command established by the Lord as the theocratic ideal.

With his fall into sin, man surrendered much—but not all—of his capacity to be the image of God. His reigning became now not one of willing compliance on the part of creation under his charge but an obedience predicated on man's superior intelligence and resourcefulness. In the repetition of the creation mandate to Noah, the Lord reminded him that his rule, unlike Adam's, would require coercion and domestication. Rather than submitting by a mere word of command, animals in the post-diluvian world would come to heel only because of the terror that man would engender within them (Gen. 9:2). Man's role as suzerain remained intact, but his ability to enforce it was profoundly inhibited.

Human history attests to the implacable distrust and fear that men and beasts mutually experience. Animals may be tamed and even put to human service, but the harmonious relationship indigenous to the creation purposes of God has been undermined, and only by patient and ingenious training can mankind bring about even a superficial semblance of dominion. The historical exception to this dismal scene of creaturely recalcitrance relies on texts outside the Old Testament, but these texts cannot for that reason alone be ignored in the present discussion since they have bearing on Old Testament eschatological perspectives concerning human rule. We refer to the life and ministry of Jesus Christ. What we propose in the following comments is done with a great deal of tentativeness since, as far as we can determine, we are virtually alone in making the case that Jesus, in his earthly ministry, frequently performed miraculous works to demonstrate not just his full deity but also his role as *Urmensch,* the second Adam who came to display in character and life what God had intended as the ideal for the whole human race.

Without pursuing the biblical arguments for a full-blown Christology that is sensitive to both his divine and human natures, let it be said that there is universal consensus that the New Testament presents Jesus not only as God but also as perfect man. He often referred to himself as "the son of man," an epithet that describes both his lowliness as a man among men and also his identity as the man *par excellence,* the embodiment of what God created all of us to be (cf. Matt. 8:20; 9:6; 10:23; 11:19; and especially many references in Luke).

Miracles performed by Jesus were commonly done to attest to his claims to Deity (John 20:20–31), but some were clearly for the purpose of manifesting his perfect humanity, to model what sinless man was created to do by virtue of his role as the image of God. In order to remain within the boundaries of man's dominion as revealed in Genesis—that is, his reign over all living beings—we will consider only those incidents in which Jesus exercised authority in this realm. And even here we proceed with a good measure of caution, for the line between the works of Jesus as evidence of his deity and those attesting to his nature and character as the second Adam is fine indeed.

The first of these is the miraculous catch of fish after the disciples had labored all night in vain (Luke 5:1–11). It is possible, of course, that Jesus acted here as the Son of God, not as perfect man, but his assembling of the fish at the precise place and the precise moment could just as well reflect the dominion over the fish of the sea promised to Adam at the beginning (cf. John 21:1–6).[10] A second example also has to do with fish, this time a single fish with a coin in its mouth with which the disciples could pay their taxes (Matt. 11:24–27). The intent of the story is to display Jesus' power to meet needs, but the lack of any suggestion that he was attempting to validate his deity supports the notion that this miracle was evidence of his authority as perfect man. The final incident is the story of Jesus' triumphant entrance into Jerusalem on the back of a colt "on which no one has ever sat" (Mark 11:2). Scholars have advanced many suggestions as to why the animal must be one never before broken; but one obvious answer is that this was the King who, in demonstration of his sovereignty over people, chose first to manifest it over the world of nature. Jesus thus came not only as the second David but as the second Adam to show what loss man incurred in the fall and also what hope awaits him in the eschaton when his sovereignty will be fully restored.

Whether these examples offer persuasive evidence of Jesus' functioning as perfect man and thus as a portrayal of what God intended for man as his image, what he did is not out of line with what one might expect of prefall humanity in light of the creation mandate. Beyond dispute, however, are Old Testament texts that offer glimpses into eschatological times, exhibiting, among other things, the return of nature to its proper balance and to conditions in which the sovereignty of God is once more free to operate through human instruments who rule on his behalf. A few examples must suffice.

Isaiah, describing the messianic age, sees a time when wolves will live at peace with lambs, leopards will lie down with goats, calves and lions will graze together, and—most amazing of all—a young child will have the authority (thus the participle) to lead them (Isa. 11:6). This is clearly an undoing of the interspecies hostility brought about by the fall of man and its ensuing curse. Even more remarkable will be the scene of the infant entertaining itself by a cobra's den or even sticking its hand into the nest of a poisonous viper, all without harm (Isa. 11:9–10).[11] If paradise was lost at the fall, it will be regained at the re-creation, not least in the restoration of man's glory as the vice-regent of the King of kings.

---

[10] Darrell L. Bock, *Luke 1:1–9:50,* BECNT 3A (Grand Rapids: Baker, 1994), 459.

[11] Edward J. Young, *The Book of Isaiah,* vol. 1, NICOT (Grand Rapids: Eerdmans, 1965), 387–92.

The Fashioning of Man

Having digressed to a consideration of the undoing of the curse incurred by sin in both history and the eschaton, we revert now to the larger subject immediately at hand—the creation of man and all that it intimated. Turning again to Genesis 1:26–28, we shall give brief attention to a final matter of interest and that is the introduction of the female who, with the male, was likewise created as the image of God. The two together were assigned sovereignty over all other creatures, a point made explicitly in verse 28 as opposed to verse 26 which, though framing the mandate in a grammatical plural, gives no hint as to feminine gender. The command in verse 28, on the other hand, to "be fruitful and increase in number" (NIV), obviously presupposes the role of woman not only as mother but also as coregent over the created order. God told *them* to subdue, and the plural imperatives undergird the cooperative nature of what they were to do.

The account of creation in Genesis 2—the so-called anthropocentric version—elaborates on the creation of man and woman, viewing it not just as the last of God's creative acts, as in Genesis 1, but as his central concern. Moreover, there is an intimacy here, a relationship between the Lord and mankind so precious that man is said to have come into being not merely through the spoken word but by God's hands-on molding and shaping and inbreathing. As we intimated earlier, the name of God in this narrative, "the LORD God," is indicative of the emphasis on the fellowship of the Creator with mankind, those created as his image and likeness.

As the account puts it, when all was ready for someone to manage the earth that God had made, he "formed the man out of the dust from the ground and breathed the breath of life into his nostrils, and the man became a living being" (Gen. 2:7). This text, brief as it is, adumbrates the most crucial elements of Old Testament anthropology. It therefore deserves careful exegetical as well as theological consideration. First, it is the "LORD God" who is the subject of the sentence and not "Elohim," his epithet in the Genesis 1 account. This does not suggest at all that two gods are involved or even that the narratives existed independent of each other before they were joined in a final redaction of the book. The introduction of the name *Yahweh* (LORD) at this point is a deliberate move by the author to link this version of man's creation with the divine name that most clearly speaks of God's immanence, particularly in covenant contexts. The name is thus a clue to the proper reading of this text, a reading whose intent is to drive home the idea that God desires to fellowship with and work through those whom he created as his image.

The combination "LORD God" (Yahweh Elohim) is the only way the Deity describes himself in this narrative (11 times in 21 verses). This clearly is a deliberate theological strategy designed to make the point that the great Creator God of Genesis 1 is the covenant making "LORD" of Genesis 2 and pervasively throughout the Old Testament (cf. Gen. 15:1–21; 17:1–3; 22:15–18; Exod. 19:3–6; Deut. 5:1–5; etc.). The name change also signals a shift in emphasis that has a direct bearing on how man's creation is perceived and described in the present pericope.

The verb *br'* ("create") never occurs in this passage, perhaps because man's creation *ex nihilo* has already been sufficiently addressed in Genesis 1 and is presupposed here. Rather, the Lord God "formed" man from material already at hand, the dust *(ʿāpār)* of the ground *(ʾădāmâ)*. The verb *formed* translates a Hebrew verb *(yṣr)* most at home in the context of pottery manufacture. As a potter takes moistened clay, puts it on the potter's wheel, and then carefully and skillfully shapes it into the vessel of his choice, so the Lord scooped up earth *(ʾădāmâ)* and with deliberate care molded it into a man *(ʾādām)*. Man was no accident, then, but the product of an omniscient Potter who crafted him into precisely the being he wanted him to be (cf. Isa. 64:8; Jer. 18:1–6; Rom. 9:21).

As a material entity the result is called "man" (or better, "mankind" so as not to import gender into the meaning), so called because of the association with the ground from which he was taken. But this materialistic understanding of mankind, as though he were nothing but minerals and chemicals, falls far short of a full-orbed biblical view. Indeed, the present text is sensitive to this and though the physical aspect is called *man* even before he receives the divine inbreathing, he is not fully so until he becomes a "living being." The act of inbreathing, like that of the forming, is couched in highly anthropomorphic terms. What the Lord God did in imparting life might be seen as analogous to a CPR procedure in which the breath of a donor is forced into the lungs of an injury victim until he can breathe on his own.

The means of the forming of the body and the impartation of life is not the central concern here, however, despite the attention paid to it.

The importance of the process lies in its result, that "the man became a living being." He became such because he was activated by the "breath of life." That breath, coming in contact with his body, made man a living thing. "Breath of life" renders the Hebrew phrase *nišmat ḥayyîm.* The noun *nĕšāmâ* refers at base to any movement of air (2 Sam. 22:16), particularly breathing (1 Kings 17:17; Isa. 2:22).[12] It is used frequently as a synonym for a person or persons ("anyone who breathes"; cf. Deut. 20:16; 1 Kings 15:29; Ps. 150:6). Here (Gen. 2:7) and in Genesis 7:22, however, it bears the technical meaning of a life-giving infusion from God himself, a process and result unique to mankind.[13]

As to that result—man became a "living being"—the phrase is *nepeš ḥayyâ.* Unfortunately, *nepeš* (or *nephesh)* has been so universally and traditionally translated *soul* that it is difficult to think of it otherwise. Popular theology, influenced no doubt by later Hellenistic anthropology, thus thinks in terms of mankind *having* a soul, but the text (here and elsewhere) declares that he *is* a soul. Whether the New Testament conceives of man as a three-part entity (trichotomous) (and we think not), the Old Testament knows nothing of such a concept but rather views man monistically. He does not *have* a body, soul, and spirit but *is* all of these and lacking any part of it ceases to be a human being. The dust of the ground plus the divine inbreathing equals a living being.[14] Not only are people called living beings *(nepeš ḥayyâ),* but so are animals (cf. Gen. 1:20, 24; 2:19; 9:10, 12, 15–16; Lev. 11:10; Ezek. 47:9). That is, they do not possess souls but are souls, living things brought about by the God of life. They (and human beings as well) are also described as those that have the "breath of life," this time the term being *rûaḥ ḥayyîm,* usually rendered "spirit of life" (Gen. 6:17; 7:15; cf. Job 12:10; Ps. 143:6; Isa. 26:9; Zech. 12:1). There is no discernible difference between *nišmat ḥayyim* and *rûaḥ ḥayyîm* except that only the former is imparted to man by the divine inbreathing.[15]

[12] H. Lamberty-Zielinski, נְשָׁמָה, *TDOT* 10:65–70.

[13] Wolff, *Anthropology,* pp. 22, 60.

[14] For a helpful overview of the matter, see Edmond Jacob, *Theology of the Old Testament,* trans. Arthur W. Heathcote and Philip J. Allcock (New York: Harper & Row, 1958), 158–61.

[15] John Skinner, *Genesis,* ICC (New York: Charles Scribner's Sons, 1910). Skinner remarks that "the fact that God imparts his own breath to man, marks the dignity of man above the animals" (p. 57).

Death occurs when the *ruaḥ* departs the body and "returns to God who gave it" (Eccl. 12:7; cf. Ps. 31:5; Eccl. 3:21). This again should not be understood in terms of some kind of physical or even psychical bifurcation but as an empirical way of describing the reality of death. When one stops breathing, he dies; therefore, when he dies, his breath has left him and has returned to wherever it originated from, namely, from the Creator. A clinical Old Testament psychology or anthropology cannot legitimately be built on the fragmentary texts that exist. On the other hand, it is possible to speak of mankind as a holistic being brought about by the breath of God imparted to a physical form. As such a composite yet unified entity, man is the image of God uniquely qualified to carry out his creation purposes.

Man's maleness and femaleness are already presupposed in Genesis 1:26–28, but the account of woman's creation as such appears only in Genesis 2:21–23. The setting is the realization on Adam's part that of all the creatures on earth none was a "suitable helper" for him (v. 20). The Lord had already observed that man's loneliness was not good and he resolved to remedy that deficiency by making such a "helper" (v. 18).

The common idea of a helper as some kind of subordinate whose task is to wait on another, usually in a menial manner, is not in view here. The word for helper *(ʿēzer)* can indeed bear that idea (e.g., Ezek. 12:14; Neh. 4:22), but more often it is used to describe God, for example, as one who comes alongside to do for one what he cannot do for himself (cf. Exod. 18:4; Deut. 33:29; Pss. 10:14; 27:9; 118:7; Hos. 13:9). Woman is to be such a helper, one suitable to man *(kĕnegdô),* that is, one who complements him so that together they are what neither one alone can be.[16] Nothing else in the created order filled the bill, so God made a special creature to match the man and thus made possible the filling of the earth with progeny as well as the filling of man's empty life with one who could in other respects also implement the divine mandate with him.

Having been taken from his physical being, Adam could say of Eve that she was "bone of my bone, and flesh of my flesh" and therefore was to be called "woman" *(ʾiššâ),* the female counterpart to "man" *(ʾîš)* (v. 23). The generic *ʾādām* gave way to gender distinctions that were

[16] Allen P. Ross, *Creation & Blessing* (Grand Rapids: Baker, 1988), 126–27.

intended not to fracture the concept of mankind but to enrich it with a sense of companionship and collaboration that would enable the image of God to function in his finest and fullest capacity.

The Nature of Mankind

Long ago David asked, "What is man that You remember him, the son of man that You look after him?" (Ps. 8:4). The thrust of the question was oriented toward man's position and role more than to his ontological reality, but David also could not have helped wondering about what man was really like in all the aspects of his being. The Old Testament has much to say about all this but not in technical anthropological, sociological, or psychological terms. Its theology is much more concerned with functionality, with man's relationship to God and the carrying out of his God-given mission. What may be learned must therefore be discovered inductively by observing mankind in the various contexts of life and history in which he found himself. For convenience's sake we will address the topic according to Old Testament categories, which may or may not occur in historical or even canonical sequence. They begin with the individual and then follow the family, the clan or tribe, the nation or people, and finally mankind as a whole. Every attempt will be made to resist merely anthropological, sociological, and political analyses; rather the focus will be on the theological significance of man as man and man in relationship to family and community.

The Theology of the Individual

Of necessity we have already addressed much of this topic in connection with man's creation. The emphasis there was on the physical aspect with the spiritual side of his makeup also receiving some attention. These will be reinvestigated now more fully and consistently along with other features of human existence such as the intellectual, emotional, psychological, and social. The Bible presents man as a complex being who must live out life in an equally complex interpersonal, social environment. What all that means and how it contributes to a theology of the Old Testament requires attention to a great many issues, not least of which is the incalculable negative impact of sin and the fall. What man (and men) is both *sui generis* and in his various relationships must be understood against both God's creation intentions and the failure of the human race to conform to them. The theology of mankind, in sum, is a theology largely of what is rather than what could have been.

The Old Testament text first speaks of the individual in terms of the physical, his bodily form and composition (Gen. 2:7). He is said to be made of dust *(ʿāpār)* and thus of the ground. This rather poetic way of putting it does not, of course, pretend to be biologically precise; and, indeed, it is not long before the record speaks of Adam's flesh which the Lord used to seal up the place from whence Eve was extracted (Gen. 2:21). Man then is flesh *(bāśār),* a term used hundreds of times to refer to the body (e.g., Ps. 63:2; Prov. 5:11; 14:30; Job 4:15; Ezek. 11:19; 36:26; Dan. 1:15) as well as to parts of the body (2 Kings 5:14), to meat (1 Sam. 2:13–15), to kinfolk (Gen. 37:27), and, in a general sense, to all mankind (Num. 16:22; Isa. 40:5).[17] Unlike the New Testament, the Old Testament never uses the term metaphorically to describe man's sinful condition and propensities (cf. Rom. 7:5, 18; 8:1, 3–5; 1 Cor. 5:5; 2 Cor. 10:2; etc.), though it does distinguish mankind from God as being weak and temporary (Pss. 56:4; 78:39; Job 10:4; Isa. 10:18; 31:3).

As we have noted already, God breathed into man's body the breath of life, and man became a living being. From the Hebraic point of view, this was not something added to the body as a separate entity (thus forming a dichotomy), but the *nišmat ḥayyîm* coalesced with the body to form a unitary being, that is, a *nepeš ḥayyâ.* At the same time there was a clear recognition that the individual had an internal element, a life in the body that was subject to a range of emotions and feelings. But so much were these inextricably linked to the body that they are usually described as affecting the person's physical being and not some indefinable and separate psychical element. The person as person rejoiced, lamented, enjoyed, regretted, was thankful, despaired, and experienced a host of other reactions to life. He or she never thought in terms of only the person within who ran this gamut of emotions.

For this reason the Old Testament, perhaps in response to psychosomatic impulses, emphasizes various internal organs such as the heart, the kidneys, the liver—and more generally, the bowels—as being impacted

[17] For the wide range of meaning see *HALOT* 1:164; cf. Robert B. Chisholm, בשר, *NIDOTTE* 1:777–79.

by the various pleasant and unpleasant experiences of life. The heart is especially singled out and associated with a wide variety of functions.[18] It is the seat of the intellect (Gen. 8:21; 17:17; Exod. 7:23; 2 Sam. 13:33; Jer. 7:24), the part of man that reasons and gives consideration to the issues that confront him (Gen. 31:20; Prov. 10:8; 1 Sam. 4:20; Job 7:17; Isa. 42:25). Man's basic disposition is centered there (Gen. 6:5; Exod. 4:11; 1 Kings 8:23; Jer. 3:16; 7:31) along with such virtues as courage (1 Sam. 17:32; 2 Sam. 17:10; Ps. 40:12; Ezek. 22:14). With the heart man makes plans and reveals his intentions (Exod. 35:34; Pss. 7:11; 37:4; Prov. 22:17; Isa. 63:4). His conscience also speaks to and from his heart (1 Sam. 24:6; 2 Sam. 24:10; Isa. 59:13).

The kidneys (*kilyôt*—always plural in the OT) are viewed in Old Testament physiology and psychology as being at the center of human emotion and feeling. At the same time the term is either parallel to heart or is taken to be synonymous with it, suggesting in many places that it conveys cognitive or intellectual nuances. For example, David praises the Lord who counsels him and says "even at night my kidneys instruct me" (Ps. 16:7). Jeremiah, speaking of wicked Judah, says to the Lord, "You are ever on their lips, but far from their conscience [lit. 'kidneys']" (Jer. 12:2), that is, far from their minds. Their religious exercise is merely *pro forma,* lacking any thoughtful performance.

More generally, the kidneys are perceived as being at the core of one's being, almost in the sense of a metaphor for the person himself. David observes of the Lord that "You . . . created my inward parts [lit. kidneys]; You knit me together in my mother's womb" (Ps. 139:13). Here "kidneys" and "me" are synonymously parallel. In other instances the kidneys are (sometimes with the heart) the seat of intense emotional feeling. The psalmist says, "When I became embittered and my innermost being [lit. kidneys] was wounded, I was a fool and didn't understand; I was an unthinking animal toward You" (Ps. 73:21–22). Proverbs 23:15–16 says, "My son, if your heart is wise, my heart will indeed rejoice. My innermost being [lit. kidneys] will cheer when your lips say what is right." Job, longing to see God, said of him, "I will see Him myself; my eyes will look at Him, and not as a stranger. My heart [lit. kidneys] longs within me" (Job 19:27). Finally, Jeremiah laments following Jerusalem's

[18] Wolff, *Anthropology of the Old Testament,* 40–44.

destruction that the Lord "pierced my kidneys with His arrows" (Lam. 3:13). He obviously was speaking in metaphorical language.

In a number of texts, the Lord is said to test or examine (Heb. *bḥn)* the kidneys (usually with the heart as well). David pleads, "Test me, LORD, and try me; examine my heart [lit. kidneys] and mind [lit. heart]" (Ps. 26:2). The context here focuses on the intellectual aspect. David was thus asking the Lord to assess his motives. The same idea was expressed by Jeremiah who described the Lord as the one who tests (*bōḥēn;* a participle suggesting a characteristic practice) the kidneys and the heart (Jer. 11:20). The same prophet quoted the Lord who testified, "I, the LORD, examine the mind [lit. heart], I test the heart [lit. kidneys]" (Jer. 17:10), and also said of the Lord that he is the one "testing the righteous and seeing the heart [lit. kidneys] and mind [lit. heart]" (Jer. 20:12). In all these instances the kidneys and heart are juxtaposed and convey the basic idea of motive, intention, or thought. The translation here (the HCSB)—with many others—reflects the interchangeable nature of the various organs used metaphorically to describe human emotion.

Another, less commonly employed organ descriptive of human emotion is the liver. The term for liver (Heb. *kābēd)* is cognate to the term for honor or glory (Heb. *kābôd)*, with the result that both function as ways of looking at the inner person.[19] David pledged that if he is guilty of sin he would wish for his enemy to "trample me to the ground and leave my honor in the dust" (Ps. 7:5). Here *honor* and *me* are identical. In Psalm 16 he declared, "My heart is glad, and my spirit [lit. glory] rejoices" (v. 9), and in Psalm 30 he extolled the Lord for having delivered him so that "I [lit. my glory] can sing to You and not be silent" (v. 12). David's glory is figurative for David himself.[20]

The same poet encouraged his "glory" to awaken so as to praise the Lord (Ps. 57:8) and then pledged to "sing praises with the whole of my being [lit. glory]" (Ps. 108:1). In his warning about the adulteress, the sage instructed that she leads the naïve youth astray "till an arrow pierces his liver" (Prov. 7:23 NIV). Here the imagery shifts from *kābôd* (honor) to *kābēd* (liver), but the import is the same. To flirt with the adulteress is to

---

[19] Thus *HALOT,* 456.

[20] Willem A. VanGemeren, "Psalms," *The Expositor's Bible Commentary,* vol. 5, ed. Frank E. Gaebelein (Grand Rapids: Zondervan, 1991), 262.

bring one's honor and his life (his liver) into mortal danger. Jeremiah, the "weeping prophet," employed the metaphor of the liver as the strongest possible figure for unspeakable sorrow. Having viewed Jerusalem's ruin at the hands of the Babylonians, he cried out, "My eyes are worn out from weeping; I am churning within. My heart [lit. liver] is poured out in grief because of the destruction of my dear people" (Lam. 2:11). What he was saying is that he was emotionally drained!

The clause translated here "I am churning within" reads literally, "My intestines [Heb. *mēʿîm]* are in torment," thus juxtaposing livers and intestines and viewing them as synonymous metaphorically speaking. Of all the internal organs associated with emotion in Old Testament psychology, this is the most graphic and intense. To turn first to human subjects, Job, in the face of God's silence, cried out: "I [lit. my intestines] am churning within and cannot rest" (Job 30:27). At the polar opposite of emotion, Solomon's lover, anticipating his coming to make love, exclaimed, literally, "My intestines were stirred for him" (Song of Sol. 5:4). One could say she was lovesick. No one experienced a greater range of emotions than Jeremiah, and no one felt them as painfully and powerfully as he. Already sensing the imminent destruction of his people, he wailed, again literally, "My intestines, my intestines! I writhe in agony" (Jer. 4:19); and once it had become a *fait accompli,* he reflected upon it: "I [lit. my intestines] am churning within; my heart is broken" (Lam. 1:20; cf. 2:11).

The references to intestines with God as subject are even more shocking. Though extremely anthropopathic, they nonetheless communicate something of God's great compassion and distress. Isaiah spoke for the Lord who said concerning Moab, "I [lit. My intestines] moan like the sound of a lyre for Moab, as does My innermost being (Heb. *qereb*) for Kir-heres" (Isa. 16:11). But the prophet himself later lamented that the agitation of God's intestines was withheld from his people; that is, he seemed no longer to have compassion for them (Isa. 63:15). Jeremiah, however, proclaimed God's reassuring promise that "My inner being [lit. intestines] yearns for him [Ephraim]; I will truly have compassion on him" (Jer. 31:20). In the ultimate day God would hear the repentant prayers of his people and be moved by them.

Even such a brief survey of the matter makes clear the intense interest on the part of the Old Testament in the inner person and not merely the physical and in what motivates human action and response as well as an account of those actions. Lacking insight into modern behavioral science with its neurological and psychological analyses and explanations of how human beings act and how they manifest inner compulsions driving those acts, the Old Testament links such phenomena with the physical, specifically with the internal organs that seem to *sense* or *feel* in times of stress or danger, on the one hand, or joy and love, on the other. In other words, the empirical science with which it is at home does not and could not dissociate the emotions of the person from the physical person himself. This underscores the notion already argued (and patently clear from the Old Testament) that man is a unitary being, not to be dichotomized (to say nothing of trichotomized) into various compartments in line with postbiblical Greek philosophical notions.

The Bible begins with the individual person—his creation, his commission, and his encounter and fellowship with God. He is a rational being to whom God can speak (Gen. 1:28–30; 2:16–17) and one who can make choices; that is, he has a will and is not a mere automaton. The fact that the Lord presented options to Adam and Eve as regards the eating of the tree of the knowledge of good and evil establishes this beyond doubt. Moreover, the terms *good (ṭôb)* and *evil (raʿ),* besides connoting the full compass of knowledge, proleptically anticipate a moral, ethical capacity, the ability to know the essence of these values and the differences between them. He was also a creature with social needs. It was "not good" for him to be alone, so God created from him a companion who was complementary, one who exactly matched him and met his needs. Finally, he was capable of exercising intelligence, both of a scientific, observational kind and of a logical kind. The Lord brought before him all the living creatures, of which there must have been thousands of species; and he assigned names to them all, presumably according to whatever taxonomical categories were meaningful at the time (Gen. 2:19–20). And as we have already seen, whatever name was given was the name that stuck, for by the very naming Adam was claiming the lordship with which he had been endowed at his creation. As for logical thinking, this is evident in the simple syllogism of Genesis 2:23: Woman is the same as man in physical essence; she was taken from man; therefore, she shall be called woman (that is, the feminine form of the word for *man* by popular etymology).

The Theology of the Community

The shift in biblical anthropology from exclusive attention to the individual toward more of a social realm comes slowly and subtly with the creation of woman. Now there are two—a matching pair—from whom the first family and then all the human race emerged. This is implicit in the original mandate—"let Us make man . . . they will rule"—and in the summary statement, "He created them male and female" (Gen. 1:26–27). Once woman was made and presented to the man, the narrator records the institution of the family by observing that "this is why a man leaves his father and mother and bonds with his wife, and they become one flesh" (Gen. 2:24).

The creation of the family, while not obliterating the significance of the individual, not only made possible the filling and subjugation of the earth but also created an environment of fellowship and kinship inherent in God's original creation design. It is noteworthy that childbearing is unmentioned specifically in the record until after the fall though it certainly is implicit in the command to "be fruitful, multiply, fill the earth" (Gen. 1:28). When it is expressly noted, it is in connection with the curse that woman must experience because of her disobedience, a curse that will be manifest in her pain at childbearing as well as in a forced subservience to her husband that had previously not been her lot (Gen. 3:16). Nonetheless, family was in the offing, one that would entail the begetting of offspring who would eventually issue in the populating of the whole earth. In recognition of both his family headship and the fact that his wife would now produce a progeny, "Adam named his wife Eve *(ḥawwâ)* because she was the mother of all the living" (Gen. 3:20).

It is impossible, of course, to trace the development of families or even the concept of family throughout the Old Testament, nor is it theologically necessary. Such a study could become sidetracked in the direction of sociology as a community phenomenon thereby losing its importance as a theological datum. However, it may be well to consider the concept of family in the abstract and from that to determine the essence of family structure and how it is necessary to the outworking of the divine purpose.

The basic unit of the ideal Old Testament (Hebrew or Israelite) family was the father and mother and their immediate children. The technical term for this tightly circumscribed unit is *bêt ʾāb,* literally "house of the father" (cf. Gen. 24:38; 46:3; 47:12; Num. 1:2; Judg. 6:15; etc.).[21] The earliest example is the family of Adam who, when his wife gave birth to a son, formed a *bêt ʾāb,* a family by biblical definition (Gen. 4:1). The family grew with the birth of Abel (4:2), then Seth (4:25), and finally other "sons and daughters" (5:4). The third generation commenced with Cain's wife's delivery of a son, a development that gave rise to the later nomenclature of extended family (Gen. 4:17). The extended family itself evolved into the unit of clan unit, a term appropriate to an extended family of multiple generations and a sizable population.

Quite clearly the husband and father of a family was expected to be monogamous, that is, married to only one wife at a time ("*a* man leaves his father and mother and bonds with *his wife,* and they become *one* flesh" [Gen. 2:24; cf. Matt. 19:5; Mark 10:7–8; 1 Cor. 6:16]). This was the pattern until Lamech, the seventh generation from Adam through Cain, "took two wives for himself, one named Adah and the other named Zillah" (Gen. 4:19). The fact that polygamy was practiced commonly in Old Testament times therefore gives no sanction to it, and in fact it was the occasion for a serious breakdown of Israelite family, social, and religious life.

In line with the "sphere of sovereignty" model we have been proposing, God created mankind to reign on his behalf and then charged the father with the responsibility of headship in the family, a custom usually called "patriarchy." The family thus was viewed somewhat as a microcosm of humanity, a tiny subdivision to be governed by the father much as the garden of Eden was a microcosm of the earth under Adam's watch care. Patriarchy was the most prevalent form of family governance in the ancient Near Eastern world, but Old Testament patriarchy was not just an imitation of that universal custom; rather, it is more accurate to suppose that ancient Near Eastern custom was the legacy of a long forgotten institution ordained by God himself.[22]

In any event, the father (and the mother) held undisputed headship in the immediate family and, in fact, in the extended family so long as that

---

[21] Roland de Vaux, *Ancient Israel,* vol. 1 (New York: McGraw-Hill, 1965), 7–8.

[22] Samuel Greengus, "Legal and Social Institutions of Ancient Mesopotamia," *Civilizations of the Ancient Near East,* vol. 1, ed. Jack M. Sasson (New York: Charles Scribner's Sons, 1995), 478–81; Marten Stol, "Private Life in Ancient Mesopotamia," *Civilizations of the Ancient Near East,* vol. 1, 488.

family remained nuclear, that is, in close spatial and communal proximity. For example, Terah, father of Abram, moved from Ur to Haran, taking with him two of his three grown sons and all their offspring, and they remained with him until his death (Gen. 11:27–32). Abram was by then seventy-five years old; and though he had no children of his own, he had incorporated a great number of people into his "family" and became their undisputed "father" (Gen. 12:4–5, 16; 14:14). His patriarchal authority continued well into the middle age of his son Isaac who was at least forty years old before he married Rebekah, the bride chosen for him by his father (Gen. 24:1–4). Isaac (Gen. 26:34–35; 27:46–28:5) and Jacob (Gen. 46:5–7, 26–27; 47:12; 48:5–6), too, were regarded as heads of their families long after their children were grown.

The Sinaitic Covenant contains many commands and stipulations directly relevant to the family and its interrelationships. The fifth commandment is unambiguous: "Honor your father and your mother so that you may have a long life in the land that the Lord your God is giving you" (Exod. 20:12; cf. Deut. 5:16 where there is further elaboration). To honor means literally to "consider heavy," that is, to esteem them as having great worth and to recognize them as authoritative figures. The opposite of honoring is cursing, that is, considering light or unimportant (Heb. *qll*). The book of the covenant (Exod. 21–23) specifies that the person who views his parents in this way is worthy of death (Exod. 21:17; cf. Deut. 27:16). Leviticus 19:3 puts it in terms of fearing (that is, holding in reverence) one's parents, placing that command on the level of keeping the Sabbath.

Deuteronomy permits parents who have a "stubborn and rebellious son" to hail him before the town elders; and if they determine that he is indeed incorrigible, he may be stoned to death (Deut. 21:18–21). Such harsh punishment (cf. also Exod. 21:15) cannot be explained apart from the overarching theological principle that the parent (and especially the father) is the vice-regent of God responsible specifically for his family, his share of the vast universal domain over which the Lord exercises ultimate rule. To dishonor or attack one's parents in any way is tantamount to an assault on the sovereignty of God himself.

The Theology of the Clan

The point at which the family merged into an entity known technically as a clan *(mišpāḥâ)* is not easy to discern since the Old Testament provides no explicit information.[23] With the continuing increase in family size, to speak of them as families when they numbered in the hundreds and even thousands would be imprecise. Furthermore, fathers of such families could no longer be expected to exercise the governance associated with households of more manageable size. It seems therefore that families began to merge into consanguineous communities with the leading "father" among them assuming the role of sheik or chieftain of the clan.

A clear example of the family/clan relationship appears in the narrative of Abraham's servant who was sent by his master to Aram Naharaim to obtain a wife for Abraham's son Isaac. Abraham's concern was that Isaac might take a wife from among the Canaanites and thus pollute the line of descent (Gen. 24:1–4). This fear anticipated what would become enshrined in the law as a clear-cut prohibition against Israelite intermarriage with pagans, specifically the Canaanite nations (Exod. 34:15–16; cf. Deut. 7:3–4). Abraham had come to Canaan by way of Haran, and his brother Nahor had settled in that region. By then his family had grown as had Abraham's until each extended family no doubt was counted in the hundreds. The two families, though separated territorially, constituted the makings of a clan, perhaps the clan of Terah their father.

When the servant disclosed his identity to Laban, Nahor's son, he revealed also the purpose of his visit. He had been solemnly charged to get Isaac a wife from (as Abraham put it) "my father's family" *(bêt ʾābî)* and from "my own clan" *(mišpaḥtî)* (Gen. 24:38). Twice more the clan is mentioned (vv. 40–41) emphasizing how important it was that the marriage be undertaken within that framework.

The Mosaic law also speaks to the significance of the clan as an extension of the immediate family. In the event an Israelite should have to become a bond servant to a foreigner, for example, he could be redeemed from that situation by a "brother" (that is, a member of his own family)

---

[23] Robert H. O'Connell, משפחה, *NIDOTTE* 2:1139–42; for a full discussion of the family-clan-tribe nexus, see James D. Martin, "Israel as a Tribal Society," *The World of Ancient Israel,* ed. R. E. Clements (Cambridge: Cambridge University Press, 1991), 95–117.

or by a relative from his clan (Lev. 25:49). Or if a man had no sons or daughters to whom he could leave his inheritance, he could bestow it upon "the nearest relative in his clan" (Num. 27:11). As for daughters who stood to inherit their father's estate because they had no brothers, they must marry within their clan so that family land would not be lost to one tribe and given over to another by inheritance (Num. 36:6). The clan was thus the family at its greatest extent.

The Theology of the Tribe

Most nomadic or seminomadic cultures are tribal in identification and affiliation.[24] That is, they consist of families and clans that claim blood relationship because of a common eponymous ancestry. In the unfolding of the prepatriarchal narratives of Genesis, there is no reference to tribes or tribalism. The transition is abrupt—from family to city or nation, suggesting that nomadism was not the common mode of life. Cain, we're told, built a city and named it after his son Enoch (Gen. 4:17). One of Lamech's wives, on the other hand, gave birth to Jabal, "the father of the nomadic herdsmen" (v. 20), a description that seems to set him off from other folk. Noah was a farmer and, indeed, lived in a tent, but this hardly suggests nomadism, for in the immediate postflood world one would hardly expect otherwise than to be in temporary shelter and a nonurban setting.

The descendants of Noah were distributed "by their clans, in their nations" (Gen. 10:5), and thus appeared kingdoms and cities and territories (vv. 10–11, 20), "the clans of Noah's sons, according to their family records, in their nations" (v. 32). The impetus for this distribution was the Lord's interdiction of the tower of Babel project which itself was concentrated around a city with no hint of a tribal society (Gen. 11:4; cf. v. 9). Abram also was the product of a city, Ur, and en route with his family to Canaan he lived in the great city of Haran (Gen. 11:27–31). As to whether the Terah family considered itself to be part of a tribal affiliation, the biblical record is silent on the matter.

---

[24] George E. Mendenhall, *The Tenth Generation* (Baltimore: The Johns Hopkins University Press, 1973), 184–88; Victor H. Matthews, "Pastoralists and the Patriarchs," *BA* 44 (1981): 215–18; for the dangers of comparison with modern social structures, however, see Allan S. Gilbert, "Modern Nomads and Prehistoric Pastoralists: The Limits of Analogy," *JANES* 7 (1975): 53–71.

The principal terms for *tribe* in the Old Testament *(maṭṭeh* and *šēbeṭ)* do not occur in Genesis to describe the sociological lifestyle of the patriarchs. They are in families and clans, as we have seen, but their numbers were insufficiently large to be called tribes in any meaningful sense. Tribalism existed elsewhere, as in the case of Ishmael and his bedouin offspring (Gen. 25:16), and Abraham's descendants too would be structured by tribes in the future. In Jacob's blessing of his sons, he refers to Dan as "one of the tribes of Israel" (Gen. 49:16), and at the end the narrator says of Jacob that "these are the tribes of Israel, 12 in all, and this was what their father said to them. He blessed them, and he blessed each one with a suitable blessing" (v. 28).

The theological significance of the tribal unit is not immediately apparent, but the fact that tribal identity was maintained not only throughout Old Testament history but into eschatological times suggests that it was not just a temporary measure designed for a nomadic ancient Near Eastern lifestyle (cf. Isa. 49:6; 63:17; Ezek. 37:19; 45:8; 47:13; 48:1–35; Matt. 19:28; Rev. 7:4; 21:12). Moreover, the insistence that there be twelve tribes is worthy of note. Apart from the discredited idea that Israel was constituted along the lines of so-called amphictyonic societies frequently consisting of twelve tribes,[25] the best solution seems to be the most evident: Jacob had twelve sons, no fewer, no more, and as the eponymous patriarch the wholeness of his descent depended upon the retention of each tribe.

Already in the Old Testament the tribe of Judah was singled out as the one through which God would accomplish his salvific intentions, and this despite the less than admirable behavior of its namesake (Gen. 38:1–26). Yet Judah showed evidence of a desire to mediate and, if necessary, to place himself in harm's way for others (Gen. 37:26–27; 43:8–9; 44:14–20; 46:28). The key text in Genesis that points up the singular privilege of Judah as covenant vehicle is Genesis 49:10, to which frequent attention will be paid in subsequent discussion: "The scepter will not depart from Judah, or the staff from between his feet, until He whose right it is comes and the obedience of the peoples belongs to Him." This promise came increasingly to fruition until it found its historical fulfillment in

---

[25] Thus especially Martin Noth; see his *Das System der zwölf Stämme Israels* (Darmstadt: Wissenschaftliche Buchgesellschaft, 1966; repr. of 1930 ed.).

David and his dynasty (1 Sam. 13:13; 16:1, 12–13; 2 Sam. 7:8–16). The eschatological fulfillment awaits the coming of Jesus of Nazareth, the Son of David who eclipsed his namesake in power and glory and who will sit on David's throne forever (Matt. 1:1; 20:30–31; 21:9; 2 Tim. 2:8; Rev. 5:5; 22:16). Further consideration of Judah as the progenitor of both David and the Messiah must be deferred to a more appropriate point.

The Theology of the Nations

Tribes do not inevitably evolve into nations, nor do nations necessarily spring from tribes. Before this observation is carried forward, it will be helpful to consider such terms as *peoples* and *nations*. Two key Hebrew terms, *gôy* and *ʿam,* lie behind these translations; and despite the attempts by some scholars to distinguish between them, the two are frequently interchangeable; and both refer to Israel and the nations in general alike. In Genesis, however, *gôy* is to be understood for the most part as a nation in the normal political sense whereas *ʿam* has to do with ethnicity, the recognition of blood relationship. For that reason the translation *people* seems generally preferable.[26]

In line with our purpose to proceed from the specific (the individual) to the universal (humanity as a whole), we will first consider Israel as a nation or people and then the nations of the earth, the Gentiles. In what sense is Israel a theological topos, to say nothing of the nations and peoples as a whole? The full answer to that question must be explored at a later point, but even the early chapters of Genesis provide some entrée to the matter. In any case, Genesis, as in all other matters, provides the background against which the people Israel could understand themselves and find their place in the program of redemption to which God had called them by exodus and covenant.

The prospective descendants of Abraham are first designated as a nation in the pivotal text in which he receives his call to leave his land and people (Gen. 12:1–3). The Lord said to him at the time, "I will make you into a great nation *(gôy gādôl),* I will bless you." Here *gôy* connotes nationhood and not ethnicity, and the implication is that Abraham's seed will some day become a distinct political entity among all the nations of the earth. The promise is reiterated, especially in Genesis 17, where the

[26] Daniel I. Block, "Nations/Nationality," *NIDOTTE* 4:970–72.

Lord said to Abraham, "You will become the father of many nations" (v. 4). The plurality accommodates the idea that Abraham was to have descendants by Hagar (Gen. 16:10) and Keturah (25:1–4) as well as by Sarah, but it is the offspring of Sarah that is especially in view. This is clearly the focus as verses 6 and 16 show. Abraham will not only be the progenitor of nations (*goyyîm*; vv. 5–6) but the ancestor of kings (v. 6). And they will descend through Sarah of whom the Lord said, "She will produce nations; kings of peoples will come from her" (Gen. 17:16). The nation to come will be a monarchy, a fact that is particularly pertinent in light of the theological truth that God created everything and invited mankind to reign over it in a kingly manner.

Jacob received a similar revelation at Bethel where the Lord informed him that "a nation *(gôy)*, indeed an assembly of nations *(qĕhal gôyyîm)*, will come from you, and kings will descend from you" (Gen. 35:11). Like Abraham (Gen. 18:18; 22:18), Jacob would sire nations, but in Jacob's case there is a distinction between a nation (singular) and nations (plural). Whatever the latter means (a divided Israel?), the former refers to Jacob's immediate family that would descend into Egypt and there be made into a great nation (Gen. 46:3).

Jacob's domination as a nation was predicted already at his birth when the Lord revealed to Rebecca the following startling announcement: "Two nations *(gôyyîm)* are in your womb; two people *(lĕʾummîm)* will come from you and be separated. One people will be stronger than the other, and the older will serve the younger" (Gen. 25:23). Besides introducing another ethnic term *(lĕʾom)* that commonly occurs as a poetic synonym for *gôy*, this text paves the way for the conflict between Jacob (i.e., Israel) and his twin brother Esau (i.e., Edom), a contest that would eventuate in Israel's domination. Mindful of this, perhaps, Jacob on his dying bed also blessed his grandsons Ephraim and Manasseh, offspring of his favored son Joseph, and in the same unexpected way. Joseph was insistent that Manasseh, the elder of the two boys, should receive the primary blessing in line with standard custom. Jacob was not to be denied; and though he blessed Manasseh with the promise that "he too will become a people (*ʿam*)," his brother Ephraim will be greater "and his descendants will become a group of nations" *(mĕlōʾ haggoyîm)*.

Manasseh will become an *ʿam* and Ephraim a *gôy*, but here the terms function only in poetic parallelism. Invariably elsewhere the patriarchs are associated with the term *gôy* except in the well-known euphemism that when certain individuals died they were said to be "gathered to their people," that is, to their ancestors (Gen. 25:8; 35:29; 49:29). On the other hand, *ʿam* occurs, along with *gôy,* with reference to the nations of the earth.

The Theology of Mankind

We turn now to a consideration of the nations and of their place in God's grand design. It goes without saying that for the earth to be filled and dominated there must be human beings to do so. Thus, at the beginning when the Lord says, "Let us make man" and "they will rule," he is alluding not just to a single person or even a chosen nation but to mankind, the human race. Corporate mankind was created to carry out God's kingdom program. But mankind began as man and woman, solitary beings from whom eventually the families, clans, tribes, and nations of the earth emerged.

The earliest reference to the origin of nations is in the Table of Nations of Genesis 10.[27] But as we have already noted, the nations as such sprang out of the dispersion of the human race on the occasion of God's interruption of man's arrogant claims at the tower of Babel. Here the Lord calls them a people *(ʿam),* folks all speaking the same language, that is, exhibiting a cohesion and homogeneity in the face of God's command to fill the earth (Gen. 11:6). After they were scattered (Gen. 9:19; note the passive), they formed themselves into nations, social orders based presumably on language as much as anything else or even more so (Gen. 10:5; cf. vv. 20, 31).

It is futile to speculate on whether nations were part of God's original plan or came into being as a result of mankind's stubborn refusal to implement the creation mandate. Had signs of rebellion such as the tower of Babel never taken place, would God have accomplished his objectives without the need to fracture the race into national entities? If so, would Israel have become a nation, or would God have worked redemptively through the seed of Abraham in some other way?

---

[27] Eugene H. Merrill, "The Peoples of the Old Testament According to Genesis 10," *BSAC* 154 (1997): 3–22.

All such questions are moot because God did, in any event, not only create an environment in which discrete nations and peoples were inevitable, but he promised the patriarchs that they would sire nations that would in turn bless other nations. The list of nations in Genesis 10 (all of which are described by the term *gôy)* reflects sociopolitical realities in the time of Moses; and since his world was relatively narrow in scope, one should not look there for an exhaustive list of the nations in patriarchal times (to say nothing of modern times!). Only those in the purview of Late Bronze Israel come in for attention so only those need to be considered here in order to discover what if any theological content they yield.

Though one could make a case for some theological significance in the distribution of the nations as a whole and perhaps even in their names, the greatest theological potential lies in the narrative interludes of the table. The first of these features Nimrod, the founder of (or at least dominant figure in) the Mesopotamian nations that lay to Israel's east (Gen. 10:8–12). He is called "a powerful hunter *(gibbôr ṣayid)* in the sight of the LORD," a proverb that suggests intense hostility to the Lord and his will as the reference to Babel (v. 9) implies given the following story of the tower built there (Gen. 11:9). To Nimrod may thus be attributed a subversion of God's kingdom plan, and as such he became the prototype of persons and nations that refuse to acknowledge the Lord's sovereignty.[28]

From that time onward Babylon (= Babel) epitomized the refusal of the nations to submit to God's rule and to rule on his behalf. The full ramifications of this antitheocratic spirit will receive attention in due course. For now it is worth observing that though the Assyrian and Babylonian exiles of Israel and Judah respectively did not take place until hundreds of years after Moses' time (722 and 586 BC respectively), the two great powers used by the Lord to discipline his people in that way are featured in the Nimrod narrative. The intent clearly is to anticipate that course of events.

The second interruption of the lists of the nations explains the scattering of the Canaanites, descendants of Ham through Mizraim (Gen.

---

[28] Kenneth A. Mathews, *Genesis 1–11:26,* NAC 1A (Nashville: Broadman & Holman, 1996), 450–51.

10:18–19). Canaan had been cursed by Noah because of Ham's lack of filial respect toward him and had been told that he (i.e., his offspring) would become the slave of Shem (Gen. 9:25–26). By Shem obviously is meant Israel in the Mosaic context of the exodus and impending conquest of Canaan.[29] The result of Canaan's scattering was the occupation of the Palestinian littoral from Sidon in the north to Gaza in the south and eastward to the great Rift Valley. This is the land that had been promised to Abraham and his seed (Gen. 13:14–15; 15:18–20); but as long as it was dominated by the Canaanite nations, the promise of God would be stymied. This explains Moses' insistence that Israel under Joshua must remove them to provide the appointed arena for the exercise of the Lord's hegemony through his chosen people (Deut. 7:1–6; Josh. 1:1–5; 24:8–13). Canaan thus symbolizes the wicked nations that seek to suppress the implementation of God's creation purpose to bring the whole world into compliance with his sovereignty.

The third, much briefer interlude focuses on Shem who "was the father of all the children of Eber" (Gen. 10:21). Eber appears in the following list of Shemites as the father of Peleg, so named because "during his days the earth was divided" (*niplēgâ,* from *plg,* "divide") (Gen. 10:25). Most likely the division refers to the dispersion of the human race following the tower of Babel episode. In any event Eber is singled out from all the names in the genealogy because his name *(ʿēber)* is most likely the etymon for the term *Hebrew (ʿibrî).*[30] In this way the Hebrew people are introduced, albeit in a most subtle manner. The genealogy of Shem in Genesis 11 bears out this contention by placing the name *Eber* about halfway between Shem and Abram, providing a linkage between the father of the Shemites and the first man to be called a Hebrew (Gen. 14:13).

Thus three nations or peoples are proleptically introduced in the table of nations. Two of these—Babylon and Canaan—represent the hostility of the nations in general to the Lord and his purposes for them. The third, the Hebrews, will in God's own time become Israel, the chosen nation, the instrument of redemption whereby the wayward and rebellious peoples of the earth can be brought into harmony with the divine will.

---

[29] Thus Claus Westermann, *Genesis 1–11,* trans. John J. Scullion (Minneapolis: Augsburg, 1984), 493.

[30] Merrill, "The Peoples of the Old Testament according to Genesis 10," 18–19; cf. Wenham, *Genesis 1–15,* 228.

Examples of the complex interrelationships between the Hebrews and the surrounding nations abound in the Genesis narratives and must receive at least brief notice here. The first of these is the contact with Egypt, the mightiest nation on earth in the Middle Bronze age of the patriarchs (ca. 2000–1550 BC).[31] Abram traveled there with some considerable apprehension at a time of famine, beseeching his wife Sarah to pass herself off as his sister "so it will go well for me because of you, and my life will be spared on your account" (Gen. 12:13). His fear was that the Egyptians would kill him in order to take his wife. But the Lord visited disease upon Pharaoh, which alerted the king to the fact that he was up against a force more powerful than he, and so he sent Abram away without further ado.

Abram later had a dream in which the Lord told him that his descendants would be "strangers in a land that does not belong to them; they will be enslaved and oppressed 400 years" (Gen. 15:13). That country of course was Egypt, and the picture here is one of persecution of God's people that would end only with a miraculous deliverance. The dream came to pass with the descent of Jacob and his sons to Egypt, preceded by Joseph's generally favorable treatment there. The final assessment of their sojourn in Egypt was much less bleak, however:

> So the Egyptians assigned taskmasters over the Israelites to oppress them with forced labor. They built Pithom and Rameses as supply cities for Pharaoh. But the more they oppressed them, the more they multiplied and spread so that the Egyptians came to dread the Israelites. They worked the Israelites ruthlessly and made their lives bitter with difficult labor in brick and mortar, and in all kinds of fieldwork. They ruthlessly imposed all this work on them (Exod. 1:11–14).

The Old Testament presents an ambivalent view of Egypt on the whole, but one motif comes through loud and clear, and that is the employment of Egypt as a paradigm of the oppression of God's people from which he must deliver them by his great initiative and power. This motif will demand considerable attention at a later, more appropriate

---

[31] For justification of this setting and chronology, see Eugene H. Merrill, *Kingdom of Priests: A History of Old Testament Israel* (Grand Rapids: Baker, 1987), 78–79.

place. Something of this ambivalence is seen already in Genesis, however, where Egypt provided both a haven for the Hebrews in times of physical need and yet bondage and suffering when God's people appeared to be a threat.

The episode of Genesis 14, a narrative subject to enormous scholarly discussion because of its interruptive nature and the elusiveness of its historical context, refers to four kings who invaded the region of the Dead Sea, bringing five small states there under their control.[32] After a time they rebelled, prompting the four kings to return and to ravage a number of surrounding territories before bringing the cities of the plain to heel. They looted these cities and took many prisoners including Lot, nephew of Abram. This brought the patriarch and his allies into the fray, thus setting the stage for another of the conflicts between God's people and the nations.

Having pursued the enemy kings and defeated them, Abram returned to his home but en route was met by Melchizedek, king of Salem and priest of God Most High (v. 18). Melchizedek then blessed him, praising God Most High "who has handed over your enemies to you" (v. 20). These enemies, one of whom was from Shinar (i.e., Babylon) (v. 1), once more clearly represented the nations of the earth that refuse to concede the sovereignty of the Lord and instead act out their rebellion against the Lord's chosen people. Their defeat was not by Abram's hand in the final analysis but by the hand of the Lord who rose in defense of Abram and his family.

The last of the nations or peoples with whom the patriarchs had dealings according to Genesis were the Philistines of Gerar under their king(s) Abimelech.[33] The situation this time is different from the others in that the Philistines were an immediately neighboring people, if not, indeed, cohabitants of the same land. Their contact with the Hebrews thus anticipated the struggles that would take place in Israel's history with the later Philistines as well as with various Canaanite nations. Abraham's first contact with the little principality of Gerar came about for undisclosed

---

[32] See K. A. Kitchen, *On the Reliability of the Old Testament* (Grand Rapids: Eerdmans, 2003), 319–23.

[33] For the complex issue of these early Philistines as opposed to those of the much later Iron Age, see David M. Howard Jr., "Philistines," *Peoples of the Old Testament World,* ed. Alfred J. Hoerth, Gerald L. Mattingly, and Edwin M. Yamauchi (Grand Rapids: Baker, 1994), 231–32.

reasons; but having arrived in Gerarite territory, he feared that his life was in jeopardy for the same reason it had been in Egypt: His beautiful wife Sarah would be taken by force at his expense (Gen. 20:2). Abraham's rationale for his deception was, as he said to King Abimelech, that "there is absolutely no fear of God in this place. They will kill me because of my wife" (v. 11). Abraham was obviously scrambling for an excuse for his duplicity, but he put his finger nevertheless on the fundamental issue between himself and these pagans; there really was no fear of God among them. Like all the nations in rebellion against him, Gerar too was hostile to his lordship over them.

Though Abimelech allowed Abraham to escape with his life, their troubles with each other were not at an end. Abimelech's men had taken over a well belonging to the Hebrews, and only a treaty of peace between the two parties prevented an outbreak of violence (Gen. 21:22–34). Isaac experienced a similar confrontation with the Philistines many years later. Threatened by a famine, Isaac moved into the Negev where his wife, like his mother before him, became a topic of conversation among the men of the place (Gen. 26:1–7). Like father, like son, Isaac passed off Rebekah as his sister, and only the Lord's intervention averted what surely would have been Isaac's swift and sure death. But conflict nonetheless ensued between the Hebrews and the Philistines, again, as before, over water rights (vv. 17–22). Abimelech and some of his officers came to Isaac about the matter, a cause of concern to Isaac since, as he said, "You hated me and sent me away from you" (v. 27). Nonetheless, things were finally patched up, and further conflict was avoided by the drawing up of treaties of mutual forbearance and respect (vv. 30–31).

This brief survey of the nations of the Genesis lists and narratives reveals that for the most part they stand in opposition to the Lord and to his servants chosen to minister to them on his behalf. This is not surprising in light of the fall of the first couple into sin, a fall that, as it turns out, included all their descendants as members of the human race. But even within this pessimistic view of things, God could be seen working out his program of redemption and reconciliation whereby his creation design for the nations can be fully realized. This brings us to the account of the fall, the single event of disobedience that explains all subsequent human behavior and despair as well as the measures put in place by God to provide sufficient remedy.

Chapter Seven

The Fall of Mankind

The word *fall* never occurs in the Bible to describe mankind's act of rebellion against God that precipitated his alienation from him and gave rise to the impairment of his capacity to represent and serve him. However, the term is most apposite, for it communicates clearly the fundamental idea that mankind has indeed fallen away from his original state of perfection and now lies far below that blessed condition in helpless and hopeless despair absent some great work of God on his behalf.

The following discussion adheres to the message disclosed by the Old Testament itself, focusing, as we have done to this point, on the book of Genesis as the wellspring from which Moses drew to prepare Israel to understand itself and its mission. The topic in view consists of two major parts, the fall itself and its aftermath, though ancillary ideas will come to the fore as inevitable by-products or adjuncts to the principal themes.

The Narrative of the Fall

The biblical record clearly asserts that man was a perfect being at creation, one of whom the Creator could say that "it was very good" (Gen. 1:31). While this may be taken as an assessment as to the aesthetic value of what God had done, it certainly includes also a moral evaluation of mankind, the only creature possessing such a faculty. In fact, that man was the image of God in the pristine world before he sinned presupposes his perfection, for God could hardly have been well represented by a flawed being. Man continued (and continues) to be the image of God even in the wake of the fall (cf. Gen. 5:1–3; 9:6), but the sorry history of the race following that tragic turn of events attests to the radically altered and weakened form that image bears.

The Possibility of a Fall

The possibility that the human race could fall from its state of perfection existed already in the prohibition by the Lord God's forbidding man to eat of the tree of the knowledge of good and evil (Gen. 2:17 NIV). Should Adam eat of it, he would "surely die" *(môt tāmût).* The narrative goes so far as to imply that the fall was inherent in man's creation—certainly as a possibility if not a necessity. This inevitably raises the question as to the purpose of a probationary tree in the first place. If God knew that man could—indeed, would—sin, why allow a set of conditions that encouraged that to take place? Anterior to that question is why God created man with the capacity to sin at all. Could he not have made him incapable of falling; and, if so, why didn't he?

Since the Bible nowhere provides even a hint toward resolving these conundrums, either here or anywhere else in the sacred record, one can only conclude that the issue in the end must remain in the secret counsels of God himself.[1] That said, one might well speculate that the solution is bound up with the idea of man as God's image with all that implies. If our previously developed understanding of image is correct—that man stands in the place of God and therefore shares something of the nature and character of God—it follows that he is a creature with free will, one able to choose among various options. To the extent that he is denied such choices, to that extent he is robot-like—unable to think independently and forced to act only as he is programmed to do—a being deficient in reflecting the fullness of God. In short, the probationary tree or some other such device was essential in order for man to demonstrate his capacity to choose and, ideally, to choose aright.[2]

---

[1] Gustave Friedrich Oehler, *Theology of the Old Testament,* trans. George E. Day (Grand Rapids: Zondervan, repr. of 1883 edition), 52–53.

[2] Thus Geerhardus Vos, *Biblical Theology* (Grand Rapids: Eerdmans, 1954), 42–43.

The probation was not so God could determine what kind of creature he had made; his omniscience precluded that need. Rather, it was designed that man might be able to see for himself that he could make genuinely independent decisions and thus demonstrate his "imageness" to his own satisfaction. The fact that he chose wrongly and plunged himself and the race into a fallen state reveals just how legitimate the choice was and how tragic were its consequences.

The knowledge of good and evil associated with the tree has been the subject of intense investigation yielding a bewildering variety of proposals.[3] We offer here our own interpretation, one based first of all on the meaning of the opposites *good* and *evil.* The word for *good (ṭôb)* occurs in a number of places in the immediate context to describe God's assessment of his creation (Gen. 1:4, 10, 12, 18, 21, 25, 31). It is used also to speak of all the trees of the garden that were "pleasing in appearance and good for food" (Gen. 2:9). Immediately following that sentence is the introduction of the tree of the knowledge of good and evil. It is apparent that the term *good* thus far has no moral or ethical content; rather, it bears its most normal meaning, describing what is pleasant, desirable, beautiful, and the like.

As for *raʿ,* the opposite of *good,* it is best rendered here not *evil* in the moral sense but *bad,* that is, harmful or undesirable.[4] The antonyms of *raʿ (evil)* are ordinarily *ṣedeq (righteousness)*, *ḥesed (kindness)*, and *mēšārîm (integrity)*. The adjective *ṭôb* can admittedly serve as the opposite of *raʿ (evil)*, but as we have noted the usage of *ṭôb* to this point in the narrative seriously weakens that possibility here. Beyond this, the notion that man, should he sin, would then *know* evil, that is, would know it by becoming evil, is difficult to square with the Lord's observation following Adam's fall that "man has become like one of Us, knowing good and evil" (Gen. 3:22). Adam, having sinned, came to know evil—whatever it is—just as God knows evil. One could argue perhaps that this knowledge, if it describes moral lapse, was in the purely cognitive, abstract sense. In this case Adam had become informed as to what moral

[3] G. W. Buchanon, "The Old Testament Meaning of the Knowledge of Good and Evil," *JBL* 75 (1956): 114–20; H. S. Stern, "The Knowledge of Good and Evil," *VT* 8 (1958): 405–18; Nahum Waldman, "What Was the Effect of the Tree of Knowledge?" *Dor le Dor* 19 (1990/91): 105–13.

[4] For this meaning of the antonyms in this context, see I. Höver-Johag, טוֹב, *TDOT* 5:309.

evil is without experiencing it, exactly as God understands it; but if that is the way he knew it, his subsequent fall becomes inexplicable. The answer, it seems, lies not in the essence of the knowledge thus achieved, for whatever *raʿ* is, Adam came to know it as God does, thus usurping the divine prerogative. He acquired it in a manner that greatly displeased the Lord.

The preferred solution is to view the combination *good* and *bad* as a merism, as polar opposites encompassing everything between but having no reference to experiential evil. Since one way of looking at life is in terms of the extremes of the best and the worst, this figure of speech is a way of expressing the totality of knowledge.[5] All man knew before his sin was the good. Now he would know the bad as well, as the Lord's judgments on him would shortly disclose. God as the omniscient one also knows the bad as well as the good; and to at least a limited extent man became like him, knowing, conceptually at least, the gamut from the good things of life to the bad.

It is true, of course, that Adam also came to know evil when he yielded to temptation and became evil, but this becomes apparent only by his subsequent words and actions. He made garments to hide his nakedness (Gen. 3:7); he hid himself in the garden (v. 10); he blamed the woman, and indirectly the Lord himself, for the temptation (v. 12)—all of which testifies to his self-awareness as a sinner. He had come to know both bad and evil by actual experience.

The Result of the Fall

What bad would Adam and Eve begin to know? It is epitomized in the punishments they would suffer because of their disobedience. The woman would have to endure pain in childbearing, and her relationship with her husband would from then on be forever altered. "Your desire will be for your husband, yet he will dominate you," was the Lord's verdict (Gen. 3:16). The word for *desire* (Heb. *tĕšûqâ)* occurs also in Genesis 4:7 where the Lord said to Cain the murderer, "If you do not do what is right, sin is crouching at the door. Its desire is for you, but you must master it." In both cases ruling is the issue, and in the latter passage Cain was told that either he must rule over sin or sin would rule over him.

---

[5] Gerhard von Rad, *Genesis,* trans. John H. Marks (London: SCM, 1961).

This clarifies the judgment on the woman. Her initiative in first taking the forbidden fruit and then giving some to her husband suggests already an attitude of headship for which she had no warrant.[6] That attitude was now exacerbated by the fall itself, so the woman would want unrestrained domination. This would not be possible to her, however, for her husband would rule over her.

The verb *rule (mšl)* ordinarily bears overtones of an autocratic exercise of power (cf. Gen. 45:8; 2 Sam. 23:3; Ps. 105:20; Prov. 28:15; Eccl. 10:4; Isa. 52:5; Dan. 11:4). Nothing in the creation accounts suggests, however, that this kind of rule was to be in the hands of either man or woman vis-à-vis their relationship to each other.[7] They were created to share dominion over the earth (Gen. 1:26–28), and their essential equality in doing this is evident from the fact that it was not good for the man to be alone; he needed a partner who corresponded to him and made him complete (Gen. 2:20–23). The two in mutual forbearance were called to be the image of God in implementing the exercise of his sovereignty.

This is not to deny an innate functional male headship, however, a point made clear in later (New Testament) revelation (1 Cor. 11:1–10; 1 Tim. 2:11–15).[8] In a sense, what Eve did in offering the fruit to Adam was an act of usurpation, but what he did in taking it was an act of abdication. Both misunderstood the spheres of sovereignty in which they were placed or, having understood them, willfully rebelled against them. In any event, whatever headship may have existed was not of the dictatorial kind that sin wished to have over Cain or that Eve desired to impose upon Adam. Sadly, however, the fall brought about an alienation between mankind and God and between husband and wife that issued in the kind of dominance of man over woman that was never intended in the creation mandate.

Eve thus would come to know the pain of bringing a new generation into the world and the frustration of an often unfeeling and even abusive male domination. But what would Adam experience now that his "eyes . . . were opened" (Gen. 3:7)? He had been placed in the garden to work

---

[6] For an excellent presentation of this view, cf. Susan Foh, "What Is the Woman's Desire?" *WTJ* 37 (1974–75), 376–83.

[7] J. Alberto Soggin, "The equality of humankind from the perspective of the creation stories in Genesis 1:26–30 and 2:9, 15, 18–24," *JNSL* 23/2 (1997): 21–33.

[8] Gordon J. Wenham, *Genesis 1–15, WBC* 1 (Waco, Tex.: Word, 1987), 81.

it and watch over it as the custodian of God that he was intended to be by divine decree (Gen. 2:8, 15). Now the ground *(hā'ădāmâ)* over which he, Adam *('ādām),* was to have dominion and, indeed, from which he was taken (Gen. 3:19), would be cursed because of him (v. 17). Rather than producing its fruit by springing up (cf. Gen. 2:5), the soil would resist man's every effort to cultivate it. Nature, it seems, would be in rebellion against its lord and only man's arduous labor would be able to tame it into submission. Rather than the trees "that were pleasing in appearance and good for food" (Gen. 2:9), the ground would yield ugly and worthless "thorns and thistles" (Gen. 3:18).

Worst of all, the end of man's ceaseless struggle just to survive would be a return, ironically, to the ground from which he had been made (v. 19; cf. 2:7). He who was to have dominion over the earth would now become its prisoner, consigned to its depths and to an unknown fate. The serpent was right after all. Adam and Eve did come to know good and bad just as God himself knows all that life can teach. But they knew it by bitter experience whereas he knows it only in the abstract by virtue of his omniscience.

At the heart of these judgments by God was the issue of dominion. Woman would want to rule man, and man would be unable to rule the earth with the ease that God intended. But there is one more facet to this problem of sphere sovereignty; and that is the one involving the serpent, the creature that lay behind the entire tragic reversal of roles. What (or who) was he? How did it fit into God's program of kingdom rule? What is the meaning and what are the implications of its being cursed?

Let us address the last question first. For a second time in the narrative the word *'arûr (cursed)* occurs, the other being in reference to the cursing of the ground (Gen. 3:17). Before its meaning is further explored, note that the term is not used to communicate God's intentions toward woman and man; they were not to be cursed. Eve might suffer pain, and Adam might have to coax a living from the soil by backbreaking labor, but only the ground would be cursed. The serpent itself was cursed, however, and therein lies a most significant difference between it and mankind. At the same time, note that the serpent would be cursed "more than any livestock and more than any wild animal" (v. 14). That is, they all would suffer that fate, but the serpent more than all the rest. The serpent clearly played the role of representative of the animal world. It spoke for them;

and, conversely, they would share with it the curse resulting from its unbridled hubris (cf. Rom. 8:18–21).

The verb translated *curse* (*ʾrr,* here in the qal passive participle) functions as both a deterrent and a judgment, the latter being the case here.[9] In the world of the Old Testament, it was thought that the utterance of a curse had the power to bring it about; and with God as the subject that was certainly the case. With the speaking of the words of judgment, the curse was immediately in effect. The question naturally arises as to the nature of the beast in view in Genesis 3. It is called a serpent *(nāḥāš)* (Gen. 3:1–2, 4, 13–14), but it speaks; and as some suggest, before it was cursed, it may have stood erect.[10] But the curse consigned it to everlasting degradation, to the eating of dust (from which man was formed, Gen. 2:7), and to incessant enmity with the human race (3:15). At some future time it would strike the heel of the woman's seed (singular), but it itself would be mortally crushed.

The Identity of the Tempter

We have already had occasion to consider the identity of the serpent and have argued for its being the guise under which Satan revealed himself to Adam and Eve.[11] One could almost speak of its being the incarnation of that adversary of God or, better still, his image, representing him just as mankind was created to represent God. Therefore, the issue as to whether snakes could talk is irrelevant, for the animal was only a channel through which Satan spoke.

One can hardly make an exegetical case alone for a personal devil being in view here. The text says simply that "the serpent" made an appearance, engaged the woman in conversation, tempted her to sin, and suffered God's curse for its wickedness. A full biblical theology, from both the Old Testament and the New, makes clear that the serpent was the manifestation not only of "the satan" (as a generic term meaning *adversary*) but, in the later development of the concept, of Satan (the proper noun) or the devil (cf. 1 Chron. 21:1; Job 1–2; Zech. 3:1–2; Rev.

---

[9] Robert P. Gordon, ארר, *NIDOTTE* 1:525.

[10] More likely this is figurative for abject lowliness and humility. Thus Victor P. Hamilton, *The Book of Genesis Chapters 1–17,* NICOT (Grand Rapids: Eerdmans, 1990), 196–97.

[11] See pp. 145–46; cf. *Baker Encyclopedia of the Bible,* Vol 2, ed. Walter A. Elwell (Grand Rapids: Baker, 1988), s. v. "Satan," 1907–8; K. Nielsen, שָׂטָן, *TDOT* 14: 73–78.

12:9; 20:2). His origins as the adversary are not disclosed in the sacred text; but as a creature apart from God, he obviously had a beginning in time. And as for when and why he fell from the state of perfection in which he was created, such musings must also remain a mystery. The best that can be done is to understand the relevant texts here and elsewhere that are pertinent to the matter and draw from them appropriate theological conclusions.

Whatever might be said of Job—its authorship, date, and literary genre—it professes to provide the account of a historical person whose life was profoundly affected by a supernatural being who, though under the ultimate authority of God, was free to exercise his baneful influence upon the human race. Job himself apparently had no idea of this evil one; for he was not privy to the goings on described in the first two chapters of the book, the "prologue." Those chapters are indispensable to the understanding of sin and the fall, however, and must be given detailed consideration.

It seems that angelic beings in general exist at the pleasure of God and carry out his bidding as the sovereign One. This includes not only those who were created perfect and remain so but also those that have rebelled and fallen away, becoming thereby the enemies of God and accusers of the human race. Chief among them is one who is called simply "the accuser" (thus Heb. *haśśāṭān)*. Eventually the article was dropped, and "the satan" became known by the proper name Satan (1 Chron. 21:1; Zech. 3:1–2).

On one occasion the accuser came before the Lord to report his whereabouts and, when questioned about them, said that he had been "roaming through the earth" and "walking around on it" (Job 1:7; cf. 2:2). The verb rendered "walking around" (Heb. *mĕhithallēk)* is of considerable interest and importance, for in this stem it conveys the idea not just of a leisurely stroll but of claiming dominion over the territory being traversed.[12] The same form occurs, for example, in Genesis 3:8 where God's sovereignty is suggested by his walking throughout the garden. Ezekiel 28 speaks of the king of Tyre in mythopoetic language as a "guardian cherub" who "walked among the fiery stones" of God's holy mountain (v. 14). The imagery is reminiscent of Satan's walking about

[12] Eugene H. Merrill, הלך, *NIDOTTE* 1:1034–35.

upon the earth. Finally, the prophet Zechariah used the verb to describe divine sovereignty in a number of places (1:10–11; 6:7; 10:12). To cite just one of these, Zechariah, in a vision, asked an angel as to the identity of certain horses and their riders and was told, "They are the ones the LORD has sent to patrol the earth" (1:10). He then heard them report to the Lord that "we have patrolled the earth, and right now the whole earth is calm and quiet" (v. 11). The overtones of dominion here are unmistakable.[13] To Satan's claims of dominical authority over the earth, the Lord replied, "Have you considered My servant Job? No one else on earth is like him" (Job 1:8). That is, the Lord may have conceded to Satan that he did, indeed, have some control but not over Job at least. To this Satan retorted that Job was off limits only because the Lord would not allow him to be victimized by the evil one. One may infer from this that in all other areas Satan had had free rein precisely because God had permitted it. And this is a most critical point in coming to grips with Satan's freedom to do harm (and to tempt) in the context of God's absolute sovereignty. For reasons known only to God, he has granted temporary hegemony to Satan but one that is never outside God's own ultimate and overarching kingship.

To return to the story of the fall, it is possible now to see that behind the machinations of the serpent was the insidious figure of the accuser who, for the first time in human history, was exercising his God-given freedom to tempt mankind into an act of rebellion against the Creator. Bearing in mind what we have just said—that Satan can proceed only as far as the Lord will permit—we can only conclude that the tempting was part of a divine plan already hinted at in the prohibition to abstain from the tree of the knowledge of good and evil. Just as God had allowed Satan to touch his otherwise invulnerable servant Job, so he allowed him to provide the means by which his servants Adam and Eve could demonstrate their absolute fidelity to him and to the mandate for which he had created them as his image. Thus Satan, in his own way, turned out to be the servant of God albeit in ways he never suspected and for purposes to which he could hardly have subscribed. His testing of Job turned Job ever closer to God. His tempting of Adam and Eve, though it was the immediate

[13] For further development of these nuances, see Eugene H. Merrill, *Haggai, Zechariah, Malachi* (Chicago: Moody, 1994), 104, 189, 282.

occasion of their sin, turned out to be the means by which the human race could clearly see its own need for complete dependence on God as well as on his grace which restored it to the position of privilege for which it had been created.

Satan might well have come in some other form, perhaps even human, so his choice of an animal form must be significant. That significance, we suggest, has a direct bearing on the matter of the spheres of sovereignty to which we have repeatedly referred. By way of review, by this we mean that God created the universe with built-in gradations of authority and responsibility and those assigned to their own strata must stay within them and not attempt to serve at a lower or a higher level. God, of course, is the Sovereign over all. Next follows mankind, the image of God. Below him is the angelic world which, as we have proposed earlier, was created to render service to mankind, its superhuman nature notwithstanding. The animal world comes next, a world of living beings but lacking the attributes that qualify them for any kind of dominion. At the bottom is the world of lifeless matter, the spatial arena in which God's kingdom program can be acted out. The following diagram may clarify these relationships:

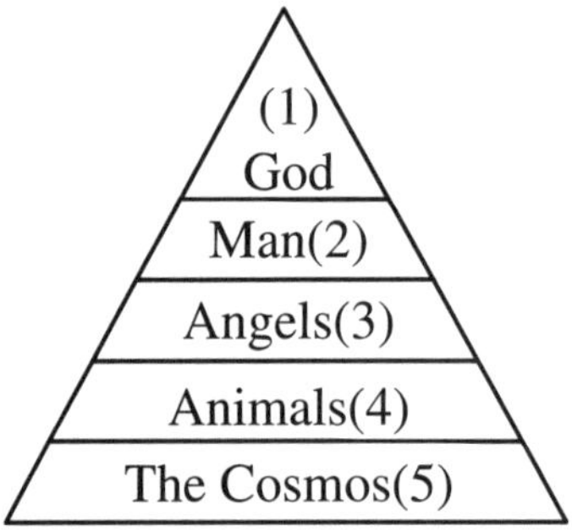

(1)
God
Man(2)
Angels(3)
Animals(4)
The Cosmos(5)

The narrative states that God (1) created man (2) from the dust of the ground (5) (Gen. 2:7). But it also goes on to say that because of man's (2) sin he would return to the ground (5) at death (3:19). There is thus an ironic reversal in that man originated in the ground and will return to the ground, his life as a sinner being conceived of as a cycle. The cause of the fall was the unwillingness of Satan (3) in the garb of a serpent (4) to be content with his divinely appointed role. Rather, he competed with God (1) for earthly dominion (Job 1:7) and, frustrated with his inability to usurp the heavenly throne attacked the image of God (2), next lower than God in the royal echelon. That is, number (3) tried to be equal to number (1) and to dominate number (2). To heighten his arrogance (if that were possible), Satan employed an animal (4), thus seeking to make man no longer dominant over himself (3) but over the even lower realm of animal life (4).

This scenario, though presented rather simplistically, finds strong support in the biblical texts when viewed synthetically across the biblical testimony. The issue therefore is who is truly God and how has God ordained to manage the universe he called into being? With these questions the entire Old Testament theology is preoccupied. Their ramifications in the postfall world of Genesis must now receive attention along with some hints as to how they impacted the rest of sacred history.

Death and the Hereafter

Some of the results of the fall have already been addressed in God's threatened judgments against the serpent, the woman, and the man. Not to be overlooked is the Lord's solemn warning about the tree of the knowledge of good and evil: "On the day you eat from it, you will certainly die" (*môt tāmût,* an emphatic form; Gen. 2:17). Death and the hereafter are among the most mysterious concepts in Old Testament theology.[14] This passage alone tells little except that man's life will end and he will return to the ground. To preclude any idea that he could bypass that process he was exiled from the garden and barred access to the tree of life (Gen. 3:22–24). The Lord denied him this access lest man "reach out, and also take from the tree of life, and eat, and live forever" (v. 22).

One gathers from the narrative that eternal human life (a qualitative concept) was not necessarily inherent in man's creation though it was certainly God's ultimate desire and plan for his image. Otherwise the purpose of the probationary tree of the knowledge of good and evil lacks substantive meaning as does the tree of life which presumably was

---

[14] Nicholas J. Tromp, *Primitive Conceptions of Death and the Nether World in the Old Testament,* BO 21 (Rome: Pontifical Biblical Institute, 1969); more theologically informed is Alexander Heidel, *The Gilgamesh Epic and Old Testament Parallels* (Chicago: The University of Chicago Press, 1963), especially chapter 3, 137–223.

available for human consumption before the temptation but which had no life-giving efficacy until afterward. The tree of life before the fall symbolized the quality of life that man would experience were he to pass the probation. That same tree after the fall possessed the properties of immortality (everlastingness) absent the quality possible only through forgiveness and restoration. Unable to eat of that tree, Adam and Eve died, lacking life in both its qualitative and physically quantitative sense.[15]

The sorry tale of human mortality dominates the Genesis narrative from Adam to Joseph. Abel died at his brother's hand (Gen. 4:8), Lamech boasted of his murderous deeds (4:23), and all the patriarchs thereafter till Noah died (Gen. 5:5, 8, 11, 14, 17, 20, 27, 31), Enoch excepted (v. 24). Of him it is said simply that "he was not there, because God took him" (v. 24). This laconic observation tells little about death, but it does provide intimations of immortality. Death reached nearly universal proportions as a result of the flood (Gen. 6:7, 17; 7:21–23) and continued thereafter as part of the normal course of life.

Fear and uncertainty surrounding death were somewhat ameliorated by viewing death euphemistically as being gathered to one's fathers. This is said of Abraham first (Gen. 25:8) and then of Ishmael (25:17), Isaac (35:29), Jacob (49:29, 33), and, later in the Pentateuch, of Aaron (Num. 20:24–26) and Moses (Num. 31:2; Deut. 32:50). The formula occurs only twice more in the Old Testament, once in reference to the generation of Israelites contemporary with Joshua (Judg. 2:10) and once to speak of good King Josiah's peaceful death (2 Kings 22:30 = 2 Chron. 34:28).

An even more assuring way of putting it was to say that the deceased *lay* or *rested* with his ancestors. There was hope of being with loved ones who had gone before and the image is one of peaceful repose. Jacob asked of his son Joseph, "Do not bury me in Egypt. When I lie down with my fathers, carry me away from Egypt and bury me in their burial place" (Gen. 47:29–30). David was convinced that his "body also rests securely," because "You will not abandon me to Sheol" (Ps. 16:9–10). Thus there was hope beyond the grave, a matter to be more fully considered presently.[16] Job's feelings on the matter were at best

[15] Vos, *Biblical Theology,* 37–39.

[16] Franz Delitzsch, *A New Commentary on Genesis,* vol. 2, trans. Sophia Taylor (Minneapolis: Klock & Klock, 1978; repr. 1888 ed.), 121.

ambivalent. In one of his more pessimistic moments he complained to the Lord, "Soon I will lie down in the grave. You will eagerly seek me, but I will be gone" (Job 7:21). Later that despair gave way to the joyful prospect of life beyond the grave (19:25–27).

The formula used almost exclusively to speak of the death and burial of kings—"X rested with his fathers and was buried in Y"—is first anticipated in the Lord's word to David, "When your time comes and you rest with your fathers" (2 Sam. 7:12). When the moment finally came, the historian notes that "David rested with his fathers and was buried in the city of David" (1 Kings 2:10). He speaks of Solomon's death in a similar manner: "Solomon rested with his fathers and was buried in the city of his father David" (1 Kings 11:43). Other examples, with slight variations in wording, are the death notices of Jeroboam I (1 Kings 14:20), Rehoboam (14:31), Abijah (15:8), Asa (15:24), Baasha (16:6), Omri (16:28), Ahab (22:40), and Jehoshaphat (22:50). The records of the northern kings obviously lack the reference to being buried in Jerusalem.

What does it mean, however, to be *gathered* to one's fathers or to *rest* or *lie* with them? David viewed the journey of the dead to the hereafter as a one-way street. When his first son by Bathsheba died, he resigned himself to the finality of death in his plaintive response to his friends as to why he no longer fasted and wept for him. "Now that he is dead," he asked, "why should I fast? Can I bring him back again? I'll go to him [that is, I will die], but he will never return to me" (2 Sam. 12:23). Psalm 88 in its entirety reflects not only on the irreversibility of death but also paints a most dreary and hopeless picture of those who reside in the grave. The poet says that the dead are no more remembered by the Lord (v. 5) in the dark pit in which they are confined (v. 6). They cannot escape (v. 8) from that place of despair. It is impossible for the dead to praise God and his loving favor *(ḥesed),* and faithfulness *(ʾĕmûnâ)* cannot be found there (v. 11).

Before moving on to other texts, it will be helpful to look briefly at the various technical terms found in Psalm 88 to designate the place of the dead. It is called Sheol (v. 3), the pit (*bôr,* v. 4), the grave (*qeber,* vv. 5, 11), the lowest pit (*bôr taḥtîyyôt,* v. 6), the darkest depths (*maḥăšakkîm mĕṣōlôt,* v. 6; cf. v. 18), destruction (*ʾăbaddôn,* v. 11), place of darkness (*ḥōšek,* v. 12), and land of oblivion (*ʾereṣ nĕšiyyâ,* v. 12). The characteristics that stand out are those of unbridgeable distance, impenetrable darkness, and hopelessness of restoration.[17] No wonder the Old Testament Israelite's view of the state of the dead was so gloomy, at least from the empirical or logically deductive standpoint.

Job's testimony is not so foreboding. He thought of the grave as the place where "the wicked cease from turmoil" and "the weary are at rest" (Job 3:17). Given his sufferings in life, he supposed that things could not be any worse in death; in fact, they might be better. On the other hand, to Job death was the great common denominator. The wicked and the righteous both die. "Side by side they lie in the dust, and worms cover them both" (Job 21:26 NIV).

In a passage generally conceded to be heavy with mythopoetic imagery and overtones, Isaiah described the abode of the dead in most graphic terms (Isa. 14:4b–20).[18] The prophet here predicted the calamitous fall of mighty Babylon, a nation which, though at a point of weakness in his own day (ca. 700 BC), would soon rise to a position of nearly universal domination. The Lord, in fact, would use Babylon as his own instrument of judgment against wicked Judah but then would punish Babylon in turn for its prideful arrogance (vv. 4–6). As a result, the king of Babylon would be broken in the Lord's hands and would be consigned to Sheol, the netherworld home of all human rulers who seek to elevate themselves to a position of equality with God.

These departed ones will rise up to meet the Babylonian king and will taunt him with the reminder that he now has become as weak as they (vv. 9–10). Instead of lying between sheets of silk, he finds himself in a bed of maggots (v. 11). He who was the brightest star in the firmament of nations has been cast down now to the lowest parts of the earth (v. 12). He had aspired to be like God; but rather than occupying a heavenly throne, he sits in abject humiliation in the grave *(šĕʾôl),* in the depths of

[17] As Delitzsch put it, "[Psalm 88] is all one pouring forth of deep lament in the midst of the severest conflict of temptation in the presence of death, the gloom of melancholy does not brighten up to become a hope, the Psalm dies away in Job-like lamentation." Franz Delitzsch, *Biblical Commentary on the Psalms,* vol. 3, trans. Francis Bolton (Grand Rapids: Eerdmans, n. d.), 23.

[18] Scholars are generally agreed that the imagery reflects ancient Near Eastern or classical mythology in which the sovereignty of the great god is threatened by the Day Star, whether Venus, Ishtar, or Ugaritic Helel. See Brevard S. Childs, *Isaiah,* OTL (Louisville: Westminster John Knox, 2001), 126–27. In any case the imagery is used for illustrative or even polemical purposes to highlight the superiority of Yahweh to the gods of the nations.

the pit *(bôr)* (vv. 13–15). Ordinarily kings lie in state in their own private tombs, but the king of Babylon will lie in a jumble of corpses, bereft of any dignity and never again to be remembered (vv. 18–20).

Ezekiel envisioned a similar fate for other evil nations. Egypt, like Babylon, will be consigned to the pit and will be ridiculed by the leaders of nations that are already there (Ezek. 32:17–21). These include Assyria (vv. 22–25), Elam (vv. 24–25), Meshech and Tubal (vv. 26–27), Edom (v. 29), and the "princes of the north," including Sidon (v. 30). All together they will experience the awesome wrath of God because of their unbridled pride.

The poetic nature of these texts notwithstanding, the picture of the hereafter that emerges from them and others is that the place of the dead is one to be feared and dreaded. At the best it is mysterious; at its worst it is a realm of unimaginable distress, a world from which escape seems utterly impossible.

But that is not the end of the story, at least in the expectation of the poets and sages and in the clear words of the prophets. In the same psalm in which David spoke of his body's rest in the grave, he also affirmed that he would not be left there. In unshakable faith in the Lord, he declared his gladness to him: "You will not abandon (Heb. *'zb*) me to Sheol; You will not allow Your Faithful One to see the Pit" (*šahaṭ,* a common parallel to *Sheol)* (Ps. 16:10). That life beyond the grave was in David's purview is clear from his following confident assertion that the Lord had already revealed to him the "path of life" and would in the future fill him with joy in God's own presence, with "eternal pleasures" at his right hand (v. 11). The ways and means by which this glorious translation from the grave to glory would be accomplished are not disclosed, for David no doubt lacked revelatory insight as to such matters. But his understanding of God's justice and fairness left him no other conclusion than that God would overcome death and the grave, at least for him.

Job's profound need for vindication, coupled with his sense of God's fundamental integrity, led him to even greater heights of confidence in a life hereafter. He posed the age-old question, "When a man dies, will he come back to life again?" and answered affirmatively that though life for him had been grueling and painful, if there does indeed exist a hereafter "I would wait all the days of my struggle until my relief comes" (Job

14:14). Surely, he reasoned, if wrongs are not made right in this world, there must be a world to come when justice is done.

Job 19 is one of the clearest presentations of hope of life beyond the grave in the Old Testament and not merely in respect to immortality but full-blown resurrection. Job boldly affirmed, "I know my living Redeemer (thus *go'ēl)*, and He will [afterward] stand on the dust" (Job 19:25). This, of course, asserts that God is everlasting, a point not up for consideration here in Job's confession. But he went on to say, "Even after my skin has been destroyed, yet I will see God in my flesh. I will see Him; my eyes will look at Him, and not as a stranger" (vv. 26–27).

At the very least Job was certain that he would see God in some manner whether literally or by the eye of faith. That it is the latter is put beyond question by the adding of "my eyes" to the verb "I will see," a needless redundancy unless Job intended to speak of the physical eye. The major crux in the passage pertains to the words "in my flesh" (Heb. *mibbēśārî*). The form is a noun with a pronominal suffix *(my)* and the prefixed preposition *min.* The preposition most commonly bears the ablative/locative meaning "from," the most likely meaning here as well. Job declared that he would see God from within his body, obviously a resurrection body in light of the fact that he had already posited the destruction of his present body (v. 26). If the phrase is to be interpreted "apart from," Job was merely asserting that he would see God, even if only in a disembodied state.

The evidence clearly favors the idea that Job believed that he would see God while clothed in a physical body, the corollary of which is that Job would experience resurrection.[19] Most scholars are troubled by the possibility that the Old Testament reveals the doctrine of bodily resurrection so they either reinterpret texts like this which appear to teach it, they date them to a late postexilic period so as to account for them by contact with later apocalyptic ideas,[20] or they attribute it to wishful thinking on the part of desperate people like Job who need some kind of psychological crutch to lean on.[21]

---

[19] For a host of opinions, see E. Dhorme, *A Commentary on the Book of Job,* trans. Harold Knight (Nashville: Thomas Nelson, 1984), 282–86.

[20] Horst Dietrich Preuss, *Old Testament Theology,* vol. 2, trans. Leo G. Perdue (Louisville: Westminster John Knox, 1996), 151–53.

[21] David J. A. Clines, *Job 1–20,* WBC 17 (Dallas: Word, 1989), 457–66.

While some might suppose that the poetic and wisdom literature is largely a reflection of human hopes and dreams in the midst of irresolvable human moral and theological dilemmas, the same cannot be said of the prophets unless one is willing to concede that they, too, spoke only out of their own hearts and minds. The Old Testament testimony is that they were spokesmen for the Lord and therefore their utterances were not of their own making but were in fact a reflection of the divine message.

Hosea was the earliest of the prophets to bear witness not only to an immortal existence but also to a transition from the grave to life in another dimension. The Lord made the glorious declaration through the prophet that "I will ransom them from the power of Sheol. I will redeem them from death." He then asked rhetorically, "Death, where are your barbs? Sheol, where is your sting?" (Hos. 13:14). It is evident from the context that those being rescued from death were the nation Israel and not isolated individuals (vv. 9–13). Nonetheless, the concept being expressed—that life can continue after death—arose from the belief that such a thing was possible, indeed, that it was a foregone conclusion. Hosea had already alluded to the fact that after the Lord had torn his people to pieces he would bind up their wounds and then, speaking on behalf of Israel, said, "He will revive us after two days, and on the third day He will raise us up so we can live in His presence" (Hos. 6:1–2). Ezekiel also spoke of Israel's restoration as a resurrection (Ezek. 37:1–14); and, of course, the New Testament quotes Hosea 13:14 to argue for the resurrection of the saints made possible by the resurrection of Jesus Christ (1 Cor. 15:55).

Isaiah is even more explicit on the matter. Looking toward the eschatological day of the Lord, the prophet said to Israel, "Your dead will live; their bodies will rise. Awake and sing, you who dwell in the dust! For you will be covered with the morning dew, and the earth will bring forth the departed spirits" (Isa. 26:19). Again, though it is the restoration of national Israel that is in view, the language of resurrection provides solid evidence that a resurrection theology was already extant and understood by the eighth century BC. Figurative language of this kind always finds its source in reality.[22]

The most famous text in the Old Testament regarding the possibility of life after death is Daniel 12:2, a passage that not only asserts the reality

---

[22] Geoffrey W. Grogan, *Isaiah,* EBC 6 (Grand Rapids: Zondervan, 1986), 167.

of resurrection but distinguishes between the righteous and the wicked and their respective destinies: "Many of those who sleep in the dust of the earth will awake, some to eternal life, and some to shame and eternal contempt" (Dan. 12:2). The New Testament concept of heaven and hell is lacking here and, in fact, is nowhere to be found in the Old Testament. However, the eternal outcome of those raised up from the bowels of death is clearly affirmed here and elaborated in later Jewish and Christian literature.[23] And so we come full circle. Because of mankind's primordial sin, he was told that he would return to the dust in death (Gen. 3:19). But in the day of God's restoration of his creation program, those who have lain buried in the dust will rise again. Death will have been defeated, and everlasting life will become a reality (1 Cor. 15:50–57).

The Fall and Human Sinfulness

Man's disobedience of God's command to abstain from eating of the tree of the knowledge of good and evil was an act of sin, an act that transformed him from at least a neutral moral being into a sinner. As a sinner, he must suffer death, the penalty already stipulated before the disobedience took place (Gen. 2:17). Chronologically the sin preceded the actual deed of disobedience, for the decision to partake of the fruit was, in fact, an insubordination leading to the deed. Theologically, however, the issue of the fall and its consequences was articulated in the narrative before the event of disobedience occurred, and therefore it seemed best to deal with that first, as we have done in the previous section. Here we give attention to sin as both an act and an attitude and to its repercussions upon mankind and his ability to fulfill the creation mandate.

The Alienation of Sin

First, when Adam and Eve sinned, they were keenly aware of what they had done. Their eyes were opened, as the serpent had said they would be (Gen. 3:5), and they took note that they were naked (v. 7). The nakedness here is more than physical nudity—they surely had observed

---

[23] *Auferstehung=Resurrection: the Fourth Durham-Tübingen Research Symposium: Resurrection, transfiguration and exaltation in Old Testament, ancient Judaism and early Christianity* (Tübingen, September 1999), WUNT 135 (Tübingen: Mohr Siebeck, 2001).

that before—but a sense of shame and vulnerability before God. The physical nakedness betokened a loss of innocence, a stripping away of the glory that partly accounted for their being the image of God. They had known the good, and now they knew the bad, and beyond that they knew evil. Desperate to cover their bodies and the act of rebellion that had enlightened them as to their nakedness, Adam and Eve made themselves loincloths of fig leaves (v. 7). This futile resort to a human remedy for sin is the first evidence in the Old Testament of a man-made religion based on works and not on grace.

This first effort of man and woman to distance themselves from the gaze of a holy God was followed by their naïve decision to hide themselves from him as he walked about in the garden as was his wont (v. 8). When discovered, the man revealed the reason for his reluctance to show himself to the Lord: He was afraid because of his nakedness (v. 10), a state of existence he could know only because he had eaten of the tree of knowledge (v. 11). Put briefly, the couple were not afraid of the Lord because of their nakedness but because they correctly understood that their awareness of nakedness was an index of their loss of innocence before God and the rupture of their fellowship with him. As a portent to the reclamation of what had been lost, the Lord made garments of skins for them, pointing to the fact that any restoration of pristine innocence must be initiated by God and God alone (v. 21).[24]

There still remained, however, a distantiation suggested by the fig leaves and the seclusion in the garden, one followed by an act of even greater alienation between the Lord and mankind—their complete and permanent expulsion from the garden (v. 23). This time the Lord was the one who, in a sense, did the hiding, for sin is like a firewall that cannot be penetrated until it finally collapses under the weight of grace. And a hint of grace is visible still in the narrative. The Lord banished the man from the garden but permitted him to continue to "work the ground from which he was taken" (v. 23). The image had been distorted but not broken, and man must continue to undertake the mandate for which he had been created (cf. Gen. 3:17–19), albeit now with profound difficulty.

---

[24] Von Rad, *Genesis,* 94. Von Rad, quoting Bonhoeffer, says that the incident shows that God "accepts men as those who are fallen."

Sin in the first place is disobedience. But disobedience is deeper than an action; it is an attitude or spirit that may or may not issue in a deed. This is clear from the woman's response to the serpent's question as to whether it was permissible to eat of the tree. She reported that God had said, "You must not eat it or *touch it,* or you will die" (Gen. 3:3). This gross misquotation adds the emphasized words to God's original prohibition (Gen. 2:17). The rebellion was thus already in place, for the misrepresentation of God's edict cast aspersions upon the character of God himself. He was made to be seen as unduly repressive, as lacking in even a small measure of expansiveness of spirit. Was the lie the sin, or was it the eating the fruit? Was Adam present; and if so, was he complicit in the misquotation of the Lord and therefore as guilty as the woman? If he was not there, could he have refused the later offer of the fruit and thereby remained in his innocence while his wife alone sinned and fell? Such questions and many others raise provocative possibilities but have little to do with the intent of the narrative itself, namely, to recount how the human race finds itself in its present predicament.

The eating of the fruit and the decision that lay behind it were expressions of sin though none of the technical terms for sin appear yet in the record. They are not long in coming, however; and in line with our stated method of proceeding diachronically and according to the progressive revelation of key theological ideas, we will deal with the terms as they occur in the unfolding course of their disclosure.

The fall of the human race and the alienation from God that ensued required that some means of restoring the relationship be found. That means involved the sacrifice of animals whose blood (i.e., life) would be spilled in substitutionary atonement. Other offerings of grain and the like were necessary expressions of thanksgiving, signs of peace or wholeness between God and the worshipper. The concept of atonement was already hinted at—if only dimly—in the death of the animal whose skin was made into a garment covering the first couple's nakedness (Gen. 3:21). This paved the way to an elaborate system of cult and ritual, the full description of which must be deferred to a later, more appropriate place.

Adam and Eve had two sons, Cain and Abel, who respectively cultivated the land and kept flocks (Gen. 4:2; cf. 3:23). Each brought the tokens of his labor to the Lord; and though Abel's gifts were pleasing to him, the Lord was dissatisfied with Cain and his offering. As a result, Cain became angry, a response that set the stage for his great sin (vv. 3–5). The anger alone was sin enough, but the Lord warned Cain that there was still hope for him (lit., "a carrying away" or forgiveness) if he did what is right; but if he failed to do so, sin, like a ferocious beast, was crouching at the door (v. 7). Here sin zoomorphically is likened to a wild beast and by metonymy refers to the result of temptation. Should Cain respond with continuing anger and fail to act in faith as he should have done at the first (cf. Heb. 11:4), he would be devoured by sin. It would master him as a serpent had mastered his parents (Gen. 3:13), but he still had time to prevail. Sadly, he did not overcome and in a premeditated act of violence took his brother's life (v. 8). He was now no longer worthy to work the ground, for it had become soaked with his brother's blood. Cain thus was sentenced to be a vagabond, constantly in fear for his life (vv. 10–12).

The Technical Terms for Sin

Etymologically, the word for sin *(ḥaṭṭā't)* in verse 7 has to do with missing a target or losing one's way.[25] The verb occurs about 240 times in the Old Testament and its cognate noun some 220 times, making the lexeme in its various forms one of the most common terms to describe wrong done against the Lord or against another human being. The central idea is that God has a standard or a goal to which he expects conformity, and any deviation from that standard whatsoever constitutes failure and thus God's disapprobation.[26] Cain, for reasons not entirely clear, had displeased the Lord by his offering. This itself was a missing of the mark, but his murder of Abel fell incalculably short of God's standard of behavior, for it struck at the image of God himself (cf. Gen. 1:26; 9:6). Cain seems intuitively to have known that what he did was so offensive that he too should die (Gen. 4:14). Only God's grace intervened to prevent that from happening in an untimely manner (vv. 15–16).

Other occurrences of *ḥaṭṭā't* in Genesis shed little additional light on its meaning. The Lord regarded the sin of Sodom and Gomorrah as grievous (18:20), He informed Abimelech that he had prevented him

[25] *HALOT,* 305.

[26] Richard E. Averbeck, חטאת, *NIDOTTE* 2:93–103.

from sinning against him (20:6), and Abimelech asked Abraham how he had sinned against him to bring such guilt of sin upon himself (20:9). After Laban overtook Jacob, Jacob asked, "What is my sin, that you have pursued me?" (31:36). When tempted by Potiphar's wife to have an affair with her, young Joseph asked, "How could I do such a great evil *(hārāʿâ)* and sin against God?" (39:9). To miss the standard, then, is to do something greatly displeasing to God. Reuben understood that what he and his brothers had done in selling Joseph into slavery had been sinful (42:22), but Jacob, according to the brothers, had pleaded with Joseph to forgive that sin, something he was all too willing to do (50:17–21).

The fall of Adam and Eve, exhibited by the sin of their first son, eventually reached such universal proportions that the narrator noted with dismay that "the LORD saw that man's wickedness was widespread on the earth and that every scheme his mind thought of was nothing but evil all the time" (Gen. 6:5). The words translated *wickedness* and *evil* spring from the same root *(raʿ),* a word also associated with the forbidden tree in the garden. There (Gen. 2:9) we argued that it should be rendered *bad*; here, however, it clearly is a synonym for sin. Things had come to such a pass that the Lord determined to destroy the earth and every living thing on it and to undertake a work of re-creation.

Besides introducing the term *raʿ* and its cognates, the flood account describes well the human condition as being not merely adversely affected by the fall but totally corrupted by it. The language could not be more emphatic. Man's wickedness *(rāʿâ)* was "great," and every tendency *(yēṣer)* of his deep-seated intentions *(maḥšēbôt)* was only evil *(raʿ)* all the time. There could scarcely be a more powerful statement of human depravity. This assessment is not allayed in any way by the destruction brought by the flood, for even after Noah's sacrifice the Lord continued to speak of the fact that "man's inclination is evil *(raʿ)* from his youth" (Gen. 8:21). These two texts come close to the later theological formulation of the doctrine of original sin. Man is not a sinner because he sins; he sins because he is a sinner.

In later Genesis narratives, all elements of the Joseph story, *raʿ* became a favorite term to describe evil or wicked deeds. Joseph told Potiphar's wife that what she wanted him to do would be a "great evil" *(hārāʿâ haggēdôlâ)* (Gen. 39:9), the same phrase used of the predeluge world with all its depravity (Gen. 6:5). Joseph spoke also of his brothers' theft of his divining cup as a "wicked thing" (44:5 NIV), underscoring the gravity of the crime they had committed against him. Finally, what the brothers did to Joseph in selling him into slavery was acknowledged by them to be an evil thing, a deed so heinous that they had good cause to fear Joseph's retribution (Gen. 50:15, 17).

Another term for sin found in the early Genesis narratives is iniquity (Heb. *ʿāwôn*), with which *ḥaṭṭāʾt* is often synonymously parallel (e.g., Hos. 4:8; 8:13; 9:9; 13:12), though iniquity has more the idea of the guilt incurred because of sin. Its first occurrence is in Genesis 4:13 where Cain laments that his *ʿăwôn* "is too great to bear." True to its meaning as both sin and its result, i.e., punishment, Cain appeals to God's protective grace.[27] Genesis 15:16 says of the Amorites that their iniquity "has not yet reached its full measure," that is, they had not come to the point where the Lord would step in with his fearsome judgment (cf. Deut. 7:1–2). Sodom and Gomorrah were also characterized as being hopelessly condemned to judgment. The angels who came to warn Lot about their imminent destruction urged him and his family to flee "or you will be swept away in the punishment [lit. iniquity] of the city" (Gen. 19:15), that is, the iniquity of Sodom was so great that the only recourse was for it to be destroyed. We noted before that Sodom and Gomorrah had been singled out for their sinfulness, thus equating sin and iniquity (Gen. 18:20). Genesis 13:13 describes the men of Sodom as "wicked, sinning greatly," again displaying the virtual synonymity of these terms.

Finally, to return to the Joseph narrative, we recall that Joseph said that the theft of his cup was wicked (*rāʿâ*; Gen. 44:5), to which his brothers replied when caught red-handed, "God has exposed your servants' iniquity" (v. 16). Once more it is clear that the various terms for sin encountered so far are interchangeable, conveying perhaps only fine nuances of distinction here and there.

The fourth common term for sin, to trespass or transgress *(pšʿ, pešaʿ)* occurs only twice in Genesis, once in the confrontation between Jacob and Laban (31:36) and once with reference to Joseph's treatment by his brothers (50:17). We have had occasion to examine each passage and need only to draw attention here to the fact that in each case *pešaʿ* is juxtaposed to *ḥaṭṭāʾt (sin)* and has essentially the same meaning. Elsewhere in the

---

[27] K. Koch, עון, *TDOT* 10:551.

Torah the term in question has to do with illegal possession of goods (Exod. 22:9) or, more commonly, with a spirit of rebellion in which one oversteps the boundaries of behavior mandated by covenant law. This, in fact, is at the heart of the term's significance.[28] To be guilty of it was to go against the guidelines that God himself had instituted as appropriate for a holy people.

Exodus 23:21 presents a warning by the Lord to Israel not to rebel *(mrr)* against his guiding angel, for if they did, "He will not forgive your acts of rebellion." On the other hand, Moses described the Lord as the "compassionate and gracious God, slow to anger and rich in faithful love and truth, maintaining faithful love to a thousand generations, forgiving wrongdoing *(ʿāwôn),* rebellion *(pešaʿ),* and sin *(ḥaṭṭāʾt)*" (Exod. 34:6–7). This collocation of technical terms presupposes a certain equation among them while allowing each to communicate some unique facet of affront to a holy God. Leviticus 16:16, 21 and Numbers 14:18—the only other occurrences of *pešaʿ*—support this contention.

These terms and others like them (e.g., *ʾašam, guilt)* will be accorded fuller treatment in the next major section where the matter of the resolution of sin and restoration of the sinner will occupy our attention. With the revelation of the Mosaic Law, finer distinctions are drawn between the various kinds of sins along with sacrifice and ritual appropriate to each. One thing, however, is clear at this point: Mankind's sin and resultant fall so altered the course of the kingdom of God in its historical expression that only his intervention could salvage anything worthwhile at all. But as we shall see, that history was interlaced with evidence of his sovereignty and gracious direction at every turn.

Sin and Competing Dominions

The final aftereffect of sin and the fall with which Genesis is concerned was the desire of mankind to conceive of and establish a world system hostile and antithetical to the one God intended at creation. There are subtle overtones of this in many places, but only the most blatant examples can be adduced here. At the same time, we must be careful not to misread all human ambition and attainment as arrogant rebellion against the Lord, for surely the creation mandate authorized all such

---

[28] Thus Eugene Carpenter/Michael A. Grisanti, פשע, *NIDOTTE* 3:708–9.

things that were done in line with his sovereign purposes. It will take skill to recognize the differences in some cases.

The building of cities and other sedentary centers has often been cited as an example of man's stubborn resistance to the agricultural or nomadic ideal associated with the pristine world.[29] That notion cannot be sustained, however, especially in light of eschatological (and even historical) texts in which the kingdom of God takes on undeniably urban features (Isa. 60:14; 62:12; Ezek. 48:15–35; Zech. 2:4; 8:3, 21). On the other hand, the account of city life in Genesis is anything but favorable. And the same can be said of the nations of the earth. Without exception they are viewed there as implacably antagonistic to the sovereignty of God and the outworking of his own earthly dominion.

There are suggestions of this in the city Cain built and named for his son Enoch (Gen. 4:17). Cain had been consigned to a life of nomadism because of his sin (vv. 10–12), but tiring of that, he presumptuously turned to a sedentary life. The seventh in his line, Lamech sired three sons, two of whom took up pursuits most at home in an urbanized setting, a musical culture associated with leisure and metallurgical industries appropriate to settlement in fixed places (vv. 19–22).

The classic example, of course, is the relocation of hitherto scattered—and presumably rural—people from their original areas to Shinar, a central location where they decided to build a city (Gen. 11:1–9). The hubris that inspired this project is evident even in the language of the builders. No fewer than four times they say "let's," "we," "ourselves," and the like. Even more telling are the motivations, one positive and one negative: Let us "make a name for ourselves," and let us not "be scattered over the face of the whole earth." The "making a name" suggests establishing a reputation, in this case a reputation in competition with that of the Lord. In the only other reference so far to the term *name* in this sense, we are told that "people began to call on the name of the LORD" (Gen. 4:26). The refusal to be scattered is obviously in direct defiance of the creation mandate to "fill the earth, and subdue it" (Gen. 1:28). There can be no mistake in concluding that the two expressed motives for building the tower reveal a calculated determination to create a human

---

[29] See (without endorsement of this idea) Roland de Vaux, *Ancient Israel,* vol. 1, *Social Institutions* (New York: McGraw-Hill, 1965), 13–14.

kingdom structure to rival that of the Lord.[30] This is clear from the Lord's observation that "nothing they plan to do will be impossible for them" (Gen. 11:6) and his forced scattering of them "over the face of the whole earth" (v. 9). They "stopped building the city," so reads the text (v. 8), for the city they envisioned was anything but the city of heaven.

Reference to cities continues in the table of nations of Genesis 10 with a list of major urban centers founded by the rebel hunter Nimrod (vv. 10–12). As we noted earlier, two of these—Babylon and Nineveh—became capitals of empires that deported Israel and Judah into cruel captivity. The notice that Babylon was in Shinar (v. 10) is a deliberate literary device linking the tower of Babel narrative to the table. What Nimrod did, then, was to provide leadership in a movement to sidetrack the kingdom program of the Lord in favor of one of human creation. The Babel (Babylon) kingdom of God antithesis marks the pages of the sacred text not only throughout the Old Testament but the New Testament as well (Isa. 47:1–15; 48:14–15; Jer. 50–51; Dan. 2, 4; Rev. 17–18). Babylon epitomizes all the cities and nations of the world that challenge the City of God and his dominion.

The wickedness of cities is virtually the theme of the story of Lot and the cities of the Jordan plain (Gen. 13:1–18). When it was apparent that Abram and Lot could not share the same space because of population growth, they decided to separate, with Lot choosing the well-watered Jordan valley and Abram being left with the hill country. Two ominous notes are struck, both portending the foolishness of Lot's choice: (1) "This was before the LORD destroyed Sodom and Gomorrah" (v. 10 NIV) and (2) "the men of Sodom were evil *(raʿ)*, sinning *(ḥaṭṭāt)* greatly against the LORD" (v. 13). The narrative resumes with the Lord's decision to destroy these cities because "the outcry against Sodom and Gomorrah is immense, and their sin *(ḥaṭṭāt)* is extremely serious" (Gen. 18:20). Despite Abraham's urgent intercessions on behalf of the cities because of his nephew Lot who by then lived in Sodom, the Lord would not relent in the face of the people's wickedness *(rāšāʿ)*. That wickedness manifested itself specifically in the attempted homosexual rape of Lot's angelic visitors by a mob of Sodomite ruffians (Gen. 19:4–9). This breach of

[30] Mathews sees the city as a sign of human autonomy. Kenneth Mathews, *Genesis 1–11:26*, NAC 1A (Nashville: Broadman & Holman, 1996), 481–82.

hospitality and decency was so egregious that it became paradigmatic of deviant sexuality, both literal and figurative, from that time forth (Deut. 32:32; Isa. 3:8–9; Jer. 23:14; Ezek. 16:46–48; 2 Pet. 2:6; Jude 7; Rev. 11:8).

Clearly cities and city life in Genesis enjoy little approbation. The reasons for their origination, the character of their culture and inhabitants, and the inevitable divine judgment that befell them testify to a spirit of antitheocratic rebellion. The Lord had placed man in a paradisiacal environment where he was to work the soil; but in his fierce independence of God, he rejected the God-given mandate and gathered himself into self-sufficient communities that saw themselves as having no need of God. In effect, they created the kingdom of man as a defiant alternative to the kingdom of God.[31]

We must hasten to affirm again, however, that the concept of the city is not alien to the purposes of God *per se*. In his own time he will permit—indeed, will sanction—the creation of cities, particularly Zion, the city of the Lord (Ps. 102:12–17; Isa. 60:14; Zech. 8:3). Abraham pressed forward to that city, as the author of Hebrews declares: "By faith he stayed as a foreigner in the land of promise, living in tents with Isaac and Jacob, co-heirs of the same promise. For he was looking forward to the city that has foundations, whose architect and builder is God" (Heb. 11:9—10). We shall return to this theme at a later point.

In conclusion, the temptation, sin, and fall of mankind plunged the race into a state of alienation from God that seriously jeopardized the carrying out of his great creation design, namely, to reign through his human image over all that he had made. But to imagine that all was over, that no hope remained to achieve the divine purpose, would be grossly to underestimate all that is inherent in God's sovereignty and to sell short the remedial love and grace that provides forgiveness and restoration. We turn now to that aspect of God's kingdom work.

---

[31] As Otto puts it, "Once the protective security of paradise was lost (Gen. 2:4b–3:34), creative labor became a necessity to secure the necessities of life; humankind, having fallen from the security of Yahweh's protection into a yearning for autonomy, turns on its head every vital cultural achievement, abusing urban civilization (4:17) as a triumphal attempt to take heaven by storm (11:1–9)." E. Otto, עִיר, *TDOT* 11:63.

Chapter Eight

The Redemption of Mankind

Given the nature and attributes of the God of the Old Testament, it is inconceivable that he, having determined a course of action, could fail to achieve it under any circumstances. It is conceivable, however, that his purposes could now and then be couched in contingent or conditional terms that must be met as a prerequisite to his realization of them. Having said that, nothing in the Genesis record—or elsewhere in the Old Testament, for that matter—suggests that God's plan for human redemption rests on anything other than his sovereign will and enabling grace. This assertion must, of course, be supported from the text itself and not merely affirmed as dogma.

Our strategy here is to confine the discussion of Old Testament soteriology to God's program of redemption in general, exempting for now the issue of Israel's special relationship to the Lord with its particular covenant and cultic ramifications.[1] The reason is that Israel was a unique case, a people set apart for the purpose effecting the Lord's gracious provisions on behalf of all the nations. He therefore dealt with Israel in unique ways—not insofar as individual salvation is concerned, to be sure, but in respect to their corporate identity as his servant people. In other words, individual Israelites, like all other people, must be accorded the benefits of God's gracious provision for

[1] We address that aspect thoroughly in part 3, pp. 325–82.

forgiveness; as a nation, however, he treated them as a people endowed with a special mission and related to him in a singular manner.

The need for redemption and its early expressions followed hard on the heels of man's fall into sin. We have noted already that man and woman were conscious of their lostness immediately upon their eating of the forbidden fruit, for "the eyes of both of them were opened, and they knew they were naked" (Gen. 3:7). Their feeble efforts to cover themselves failed precisely because they themselves attempted to improvise the means of their own reconciliation to an offended God. The man and woman could no more effect their re-creation than they could their creation. Unless the Lord provided the covering, they would forever remain in their spiritual nakedness before him. He therefore made them garments of skin and clothed them (Gen. 3:21). This obviously presupposes the slaughter of an animal, the first reference to animal death thus far in the account

The Principle and Practice of Sacrifice

One must be careful not to infer too much of the notion of substitutionary atonement from this rather cryptic account, though it will become clear at a later point that atonement for sin did indeed call for animal sacrifice which involved, among other things, a covering or a "smearing" (Heb. *kpr*) of a victim's blood on an altar. This presumably placed a barrier between the repentant sinner and God's holy gaze so that he no longer saw the sinner but saw only the substitutionary animal. It therefore is not unreasonable to see hints in our passage that the Lord was pleased with the garments of skin because (1) he had made them and (2) they accomplished what the fig leaves could not—they covered the nakedness of the couple, laying the predicate thereby for a system of atonement that would remedy the problem of their alienation.[2] In order to pursue the theme of animal sacrifice without interruption, we will return at the end to the "proto-evangelium" of Genesis 3:15. For now we observe

[2] John S. Feinberg, "Salvation in the Old Testament," *Tradition & Testament: Essays in Honor of Charles Lee Feinberg,* ed. John S. Feinberg and Paul D. Feinberg (Chicago: Moody, 1981), 59. One must insist, however, that just a hint at best is there, for the technical language of atonement is missing, and the verb *clothe* never applies to the application of blood in sacrifice. See Claus Westermann, *Genesis 1–11,* trans. John J. Scullion (Minneapolis: Augsburg, 1984), 270.

that not only did animal slaughter become understood as a religious obligation by the second generation, but with it had emerged at least a primitive cultus. The record states that "in the course of time [lit., "at the end of days," perhaps a reference to sabbath-keeping, Gen. 2:2–3] Cain presented some of the land's produce as an offering to the LORD" (Gen. 4:3). This is not surprising since Cain "cultivated the land" (v. 2). But what prompted him to make such an offering, and why did it prove to be displeasing to the Lord?

In the first place, what Cain brought was not intended for atonement, for it was a gift *(minḥâ),* the first time this term appears in the Old Testament and the only time it has the technical meaning of an offering made to God (cf. Gen. 32:14, 19; 43:11). It would become a symbol of homage in later revelation, and there is no reason to think of it otherwise here.[3] It is a serious misreading of the text and of Cain's intentions to assume that he offered produce rather than an animal to achieve atonement, thereby scouting God's own appointed way of effecting it. Purely and simply, he was offering tribute to his God. Were he seeking atonement, nothing would have prevented his purchase of an animal for this purpose.

Then why is there a negative cast to the story? The answer is suggested by the deliberate inclusion of the words "but for Cain and for his offering" the Lord had no regard (Gen. 4:5 NASB). The placement of "for Cain" before "his offering" must not be ignored, for the narrator wants to make the point that the Lord rejected not so much the gift as the giver. Something about Cain made his offering of no value to the Lord. It is ill-advised to be dogmatic about what that was in such a succinct account, though the passage goes on to say that Cain would be acceptable if he did right, that is, if he were to be righteous as Abel was (v. 7). The New Testament appears to link Cain's rejection to his lack of faith (Heb. 11:4),[4] and Cain's reaction to the Lord's rebuke seems to bear this out: "Cain was furious, and he was downcast" (v. 5). Something about Cain's prior attitude—his lack of faith, his pride, his grudging presentation of something precious to him—must have been at work. In the end, however,

---

[3] Richard E. Averbeck, שלם, *NIDOTTE* 2:980–81.

[4] Bruce associates Abel's faith with his righteousness as did Jesus in Matthew 23:35. See F. F. Bruce, *The Epistle to the Hebrews,* NICOT (Grand Rapids: Eerdmans, 1964), 283–86.

there is one important lesson, and that is that offerings made apart from righteousness and a proper spirit have no efficacy.[5]

Abel, on the other hand, brought "some of the firstborn of his flock and their fat portions" (v. 4). At first blush one might assume that his offering was acceptable because it was a bloody sacrifice, but the same caveat must obtain here as in the case with Cain. The text insists that "the LORD had regard for Abel and his offering" (v. 4). What he presented was an expression of his own righteousness before God, and therefore the Lord was pleased with it. It is true that Abel was a shepherd and should reasonably present a token of his labor in that industry, but the "fat portions" (Heb. *ḥălābîm*) imply a gift (again, *minḥâ,* v. 4) suitable only to the Lord alone. The combination of *blood* and *fat* elsewhere (Lev. 4:18–19; 7:2–3, 33; Num. 18:17) underscores the sanctity of the use of fat in sacrifice and its strict prohibition for human consumption. It may be that Abel was making atonement here, but the mere mention of "fat portions" cannot establish that since those portions could be offered for other kinds of sacrifices as well.

The principal value of the passage, it seems, is to connect acceptable offering with proper attitude and to reveal the nascent development of an apparatus of worship. Such worship could include a plea for atonement or (as here) the proffering of tribute to the Lord to whom all mankind is in debt and is to be subservient.

Worship in the postdiluvian world found its earliest expression in the story of Noah, an account that introduces several technical terms and concepts lacking to this point. Immediately after the flood Noah built an altar and offered sacrifices of clean animals and birds, an offering that satisfied the Lord and prompted him to swear that he would never again curse the ground and destroy all living creatures (Gen. 8:20–21). The preparation for the ceremony is suggested in the command the Lord gave to Noah that he should take on the ark "seven pairs, male and female, of all the clean animals" (7:3). The purpose was to preserve these creatures in particular, for they would be essential to sacrifice.

Altars as places of sacrifice appear here first, though certainly they are implied in the offerings of Cain and Abel, especially the latter. The word

---

[5] Bruce K. Waltke, "Cain and His Offering," *WTJ* 48 (1986): 363–72. For various other explanations see Gordon J. Wenham, *Genesis 1–15,* WBC 1 (Waco, Tex.: Word, 1987), 104.

translated *altar (mizbēaᶜ)* occurs about four hundred times in the Old Testament, but fewer than a dozen times in Genesis. It is a derivative of the verb *zbḥ, sacrifice,* and connotes the place where sacrifice is made.

All attested religions of the ancient Near East practiced sacrifice and therefore included altars and other cultic paraphernalia. Archaeological evidence reveals that the Canaanite nations built their altars of quarried stone and on high places, a custom strictly forbidden in later Mosaic law (Exod. 20:24–26).[6] The altars of Israel, on the other hand, must be constructed of field stone lest they be confused with those of pagan manufacture. No such stricture existed in patriarchal times, so it seems that the forefathers were free to make their altars in any form or fashion they wished. The Noah pericope leaves no clue except to say that Noah "built" an altar, implying that it was not a solid block of stone. Its surface was commodious enough to allow the sacrifice of large animals, a fact that also supports the idea of a manufactured altar whether of cut or rough stones.

Later, Abram, having entered Canaan, "built" an altar to the Lord at Shechem (Gen. 12:7). The narrative fails to speak of his making a sacrifice there; in fact, the inspiration for building the altar is that the Lord "appeared to [him]." This may suggest that *mizbēaḥ* here refers not so much to an altar of sacrifice as to some kind of stele or monument marking God's presence there. As we shall see, this was not an uncommon thing even among the Israelites (e.g., Judg. 6:24; Josh. 22:21–34; 2 Kings 16:15b). Future generations of Abram's offspring would see the altar at Shechem and remember the promises the Lord had made to their ancestor and to them. The same was true at Bethel (v. 8), and though there is no reference to the appearance of the Lord at that place, there is likewise no record of a sacrifice being made there. Abram himself returned to Bethel; and seeing the altar still there, he "called on the name of the LORD" (Gen. 13:4 NIV). The altar clearly served the purpose of a sacred memorial.

The situation is altogether different at the mountain of Moriah where the Lord commanded Abraham to sacrifice his only (covenant) son Isaac as a burnt offering (Gen. 22:2). To do this he "built" an altar there and, placing his son on the fuel, would have slain him had not the Lord intervened by providing an animal in his stead (vv. 9–13). The

---

[6] "Altar," *Baker Encyclopedia of the Bible,* vol. 1, ed. Walter A. Elwell (Grand Rapids: Baker, 1988), 62–63.

theological difficulties inherent in this command of the Lord will be addressed presently.

On his return to Mamre from Paddan Aram, Jacob stopped off at Bethel, the place he had visited on his way to Paddan Aram and where, in a dream, he had seen the stairway leading from earth to heaven (Gen. 28:12). He now took the stone he had used for a pillow and set it up *(śym)* as a pillar *(maṣṣēbâ),* a monument, like the altar, celebrating the presence of the Lord (v. 18). He then poured oil on the pillar, not as part of a sacrifice ritual but as an anointing to set the stele apart as a commemorative device. So taken was Jacob by God's appearance to him, that he vowed to make the pillar the nucleus of a temple, thus naming the place Bethel, "God's house" (v. 22).

Back at Bethel Jacob built an altar, this time modifying the name of the place to El Bethel, "God of Bethel" (Gen. 35:7), because God had revealed himself there. Scholars debate whether the pillar and the altar were one and the same or whether the altar replaced the pillar (or even whether the narrative consists of two complementary or contradictory sources); but in any case the altar as a memorial finds continuing reinforcement.[7] This time God had commanded him to build an altar (v. 1); but Jacob himself, having embraced to some extent the paganism of Aram, saw in the erection of the altar a way of affirming his commitment to the Lord. Whenever he looked upon it, he would be reminded of God's gracious self-manifestation there on his behalf.

The Material of Sacrifice

In the brief account of Genesis 4, we learn only that Cain brought "the land's produce" as an offering and that Abel brought "some of the firstborn of his flock and their fat portions" (vv. 3–4). This bifurcation between animal and nonanimal offerings foreshadows the consistent Old Testament practice from then on. Both are called an "offering" here (Heb. *minḥâ*), a rather generic term to describe any kind of a gift whether secular or sacred. Therefore, nothing can be learned from this text about the intended purpose for the offerings, the best guess being that they

[7] E. A. Speiser, *Genesis,* AB 1 (Garden City, N.Y.: Doubleday, 1964), 271.

were expressions of homage or tribute to the Lord, an offering known later as a thank, peace, or fellowship offering *(šĕlāmîm).*[8]

Noah's offering is qualified by the descriptions "clean" and "burnt offerings" (Gen. 8:20). How the clean animals and birds were distinguished from one another is not clarified here, but the Torah has a later detailed list of the criteria to be followed in making such decisions (Lev. 11; Deut. 14:1–22). Many scholars argue that the Noahic allusion to clean animals and birds is a late gloss from post-Mosaic (or even postexilic) times since no definition of *clean (ṭāhôr)* occurs in the Genesis passage.[9] It can be equally well argued that the distinction between clean and unclean was so well-known in ancient times that there was no need to define the term here. In any case, Noah was sensitive to what in the animal world was satisfactory as a burnt offering to the Lord. That it must be "clean" is anticipatory of further theological development relative to holiness and separation, especially of God's chosen people Israel. They must be clean in that sense so what they presented to the Lord must also be clean.

The burnt offering *(ʿōlâ),* as the term suggests, must be totally consumed by the flames of the altar, that is, wholly given over to God. It was associated with atonement in the Mosaic legislation (Lev. 1; 9:7; 12:8; 14:19–20; 15:15; etc.), as well as with the so-called peace offerings (Lev. 4:10; 6:12; 9:22; 23:18–19; Num. 6:14; Deut. 27:6–7). In the context of God's goodness in preserving Noah and his family from the waters of the flood, the sacrifice he made was primarily an expression of thanksgiving to the Lord. He had built an altar "to the LORD" (that is, as an act of devotion to him) and now took the clean animals he had saved for just this occasion (cf. 7:2–3, 8) and offered them up as an act of gratitude.

The verb cognate to the noun *ʿōlâ* has the basic meaning of "rise up, ascend," suggesting that the burnt offering in some sense made its way to the heavens where the Lord received it as a token of the worshipper's praise. The ascending smoke of the sacrifice visually communicated that idea. The anthropomorphism implied here continues with the observation that "when the LORD smelled the pleasing aroma, He said to Himself, 'I

---

[8] See p. 273. Cf. Victor P. Hamilton, *The Book of Genesis Chapters 1–17,* NICOT (Grand Rapids: Eerdmans), 223.

[9] Westermann, citing Dillmann; cf. Westermann, *Genesis 1–11,* 428. Westermann himself allows that the Yahwist assumes that knowledge of such distinctions existed already in the ancient world and universally.

will never again curse the ground because of man, even though man's inclination is evil from his youth'" (Gen. 8:21). The adjective describing the aroma *(hannîḥōaḥ)* contains the idea of appeasement. It seems that Noah, by his offering, beseeched the Lord to put his wrath behind him and never again repeat the judgment that he had wreaked upon the earth. It was an appeal to the Lord to renew the fellowship that had been broken between himself and mankind, and it served also as an act of atonement. Noah functioned as a priestly mediator between God and the postdiluvian world.[10] If that reading is correct, the burnt offering both effected atonement and celebrated salvation and the confidence that the Lord had not given up on the human race but was ready to begin again.

The Lord's satisfaction with Noah's overtures is evident from his pledge never again to curse *(qll,* not the verb of Gen. 3:17, *ʾrr)* the ground because of mankind even though the flood brought about no fundamental change in the human disposition. Man, he acknowledged, was still inexorably inclined to do evil from his birth (cf. Gen. 6:5). Despite this, Noah's priestly intercession moved the Lord not only to swear that such a cataclysm as the flood would never be repeated but to repeat and amplify the creation mandate originally given to Adam and Eve (Gen. 9:1–17; cf. 1:26–28), an issue to be elaborated at a later point.

The burnt offering next appears in the account of Abraham's near sacrifice of Isaac (Gen. 22). The Lord had commanded the patriarch to go to Moriah and there offer up *(haʿălēhû)* his son as a burnt offering *(ʿōlâ).* Human sacrifice was not unknown in the ancient Near Eastern world of Abraham's day, but everything Abraham knew of his God was antithetical to this demand. Furthermore, God had promised him that this son, Isaac, would be the one through whom all the nations would be blessed (Gen. 17:19). For now the covenant implications of Abraham's testing must be held in abeyance so that the nature of the sacrifice as a burnt offering can be the focal point. What was required, of course, was an altar, wood, fire, a knife, and a sacrifice. The last of these is the most problematic here and not just because it called for Isaac as the covenant heir to be the victim. As we saw in the case of Noah's burnt offering, it

[10] Kenneth A. Mathews, *Genesis 1–11,* NAC 1A (Nashville: Broadman & Holman, 1996), 373.

required the use of clean animals; and in terms of later Mosaic legislation, at least, that would clearly rule out a human being.

As it turns out, these considerations are moot since the sacrifice was never carried out. And the very fact that the call for such a sacrifice was to test Abraham's faith also rules out the possibility that burnt offerings of this kind were in any way normative. Had he been asked to offer a "normal" sacrifice, there would have been no challenge to his faith. In short, the Moriah episode cannot be used to shed light on pre-Mosaic concepts of sacrifice. At the same time, there are advancements here in our own understanding of what constituted burnt offerings and some new insight into their theological significance.

Isaac himself raised the question "Where is the lamb?" (Gen. 22:7). For the first time a particular species appears to be singled out and coming as the question did from a boy presumably unschooled in fine distinctions as to proper sacrificial protocol, the reference to a lamb may be laden with special theological meaning. That is, what his father was about to do seemed to Isaac to require a lamb as opposed to some other animal. The term used here, however, is not the usual one for *lamb (kebeś)* but one usually employed to describe any small livestock such as a sheep or goat *(śeh).* It is the same term found in Exodus 12 to speak of the Passover lamb (vv. 3–5) and in Isaiah 53:7, the famous messianic text that says of the suffering servant that "like a lamb *(śeh)* led to the slaughter and like a sheep *(rāḥēl)* silent before her shearers, He did not open His mouth." This is also the animal that could be offered as a redeemer in the stead of a firstborn donkey, an animal of great value to the ancient Israelite economy (Exod. 13:13; 34:20).[11]

Isaac's choice of the term *śeh* might therefore have ramifications beyond the boundaries of the narrative itself. At the risk of reading later Old Testament revelation into the passage, or worse still, New Testament Christology, we still must observe the peculiarities of the text before us and be prepared to explain them in light of an intertextual hermeneutic. After all, we are looking at a canon of sacred literature—one, we submit, that must be read holistically and with an eye to those themes and motifs that unify it as divine revelation. Without pushing the matter beyond

[11] Cf. E. J. Waschke, שֶׂה, *TDOT* 14:46–49.

proper hermeneutical boundaries, let us look at some of the features of the narrative that seem to have a forward thrust.[12]

First, we note that when questioned about the missing lamb, Abraham said that God himself will provide it. The verb means literally that God will see it for himself, that is, will choose it (cf. Gen. 41:33; Deut. 12:13; 33:21; 1 Sam. 16:1). There is no human initiative here. God himself will move on behalf of human need and will provide what is necessary to meet it. This was true of the covering of animal skins that concealed man's nakedness as a sinner and, as we shall see, of the provision of the seed of the woman that would crush the head of the serpent.

In the second place, God provided for Abraham a ram, an animal in place of his son whose death appeared so imminent. This instead became the burnt offering that God had requested at the beginning, for in a sense Isaac did indeed die. His "death," however, was enacted through a substitute, an animal whose literal death provided full satisfaction to God's demands. Moved by such a display of grace, Abraham named the place "The LORD Will Provide" (*yireh,* Gen. 22:14; cf. v. 8), giving rise to a proverbial saying, "It will be provided *(yērā'eh)* on the LORD's mountain" (v. 14). The Christian cannot help but recall a hill two thousand years later on which God provided a substitute for all humanity so that he, not they, might take on himself the just wrath of God for human sin.

The question remains as to the significance of the burnt offering in the Moriah incident. The answer must be sought in the Lord's response to it. First, we have already seen that the command to sacrifice Isaac was a test by God to Abraham to see if he could believe the promises about a covenant heir that had already been given. Having passed the test, the Lord said to him, "Now I know that you fear God" (v. 12). It was not so much that God needed proof but that Abraham himself needed the assurance that God would provide no matter the need. Second, the Lord promised, "Because you have done this thing and have not withheld your only son, I will indeed bless you" (vv. 16–17). There follows then the statement of the covenant promise that through Abraham all nations would be blessed, "because you have obeyed My command" (vv. 17–18). From these two points we gather that the only valid test of Abraham's faith was the total,

[12] For a most balanced, insightful assessment of the hermeneutical and theological issues here, see Gordon J. Wenham, *Genesis 16–50,* WBC 2 (Dallas: Word, 1994), 112–18.

irrecoverable loss of his only son Isaac. And the only apt mechanism to accomplish this was to offer him to the Lord as a burnt offering, one that consumed its victim in its entirety, leaving nothing but ashes and smoke. Such sacrifice alone could be a "pleasing aroma" to the Lord.[13]

The remaining instance of sacrifice in Genesis adds little to the pre-Mosaic theological significance of this religious act. It is of interest for other reasons, however, and should be given at least cursory attention. After Jacob had fled from his father-in-law Laban, the latter caught up with him; and after prolonged, mutual recriminations, the two hammered out a treaty stipulating their common boundary line, thus prohibiting trespass from either side (Gen. 31:22–50). The ceremony was capped off by a sacrifice followed by a meal to which all parties were invited (v. 54). There can be no doubt that the sacrifice here was what later texts call the fellowship or peace offering (*šĕlāmîm,* always plural, with one exception) (cf. Exod. 20:24; 24:5; 29:28; etc.). It was designed either to establish a peaceful relationship or to celebrate the fact that such a relationship already existed. The meal consisted of parts of the slain animals devoted to human consumption, the rest having been offered up to the Lord. Sharing with each other and with the Lord bespoke a harmonious state of affairs sanctioned by the shedding of blood. The warm good-byes the next morning suggest that peace had indeed been achieved and that fellowship was now possible.

We have proposed that Noah's sacrifice was also of this kind though it is called a burnt offering and had overtones of atonement. The common juxtaposition of the terms for each leads to the conclusion that they were either interchangeable or, more likely, that the fellowship offering was based on and followed the burnt offering (cf. Exod. 20:24; 24:5; 32:6; Lev. 4:10; etc.).[14] Noah thus presented a burnt offering to the Lord as a tribute to his gracious deliverance, but the offering also spoke of a renewal of relationship between the Lord and mankind that had seemed threatened by man's sin and God's response of judgment.

---

[13] As Ross puts it, "Here Abraham demonstrated what it meant to fear God; here readers learn what is at the heart of true worship." Allen P. Ross, *Creation & Blessing* (Grand Rapids: Baker, 1996), 401–2.

[14] Richard E. Averbeck, שלם, *NIDOTTE* 4:140.

Covenant and Redemption

The estrangement of mankind from his Creator because of sin and the fall was so drastic and irreparable from the human side that only an act initiated by God himself could overcome it. We have seen this initiative at work already and have given attention to the means by which the chasm of alienation could be bridged. But behind and beyond the means lay the principle by which God and man were related in the first place and which, in various forms, made possible their reconciliation and the renewal of the relationship. That principle is covenant, a concept so pervasive in the Old Testament that many theologians see it as central to Old Testament theology, so much so that one can speak of "covenant theology."[15]

Our intention is to define the notion of covenant in Genesis and then trace it through the book in preparation for its highly specialized application to the people Israel. Because it takes on a different shape there and on into the New Testament, our treatment here can only be suggestive of the trajectory it will take in subsequent revelation. We must at this point be cautious about the full ramifications of the Genesis texts lest we prematurely presuppose what can be understood only by examination of later texts, but at the same time we must not be reticent about going beyond mere exegesis. To leave it at that is a denial of the holistic nature of Old Testament theology which lies at the heart of our stated methodology.

The technical term for covenant *(bĕrît)* occurs more than 250 times in the Old Testament, with 10 percent of those occurrences in Genesis. The etymology of the term is a matter of some dispute (most likely cognate to Akkadian *birūtu,* "link, clasp, fetter"), but there is consensus that in the Old Testament it is to be rendered *covenant* with secondary meanings of "treaty," "pact," or the like.[16] In most instances it refers to an agreement between God and people, one always initiated by him.

Studies of covenant in the Old Testament and in the ancient Near East over the past century have yielded a number of insights important to Old Testament interpretation and theology, especially in terms of form-critical

---

[15] For this term in a nontechnical sense, see J. Barton Payne, *The Theology of the Older Testament* (Grand Rapids: Zondervan, 1962), 73.

[16] J. Gordon McConville, בְּרִית, *NIDOTTE* 1:747–55.

distinction among the various covenants to be found there.[17] For example, it is now agreed that the Old Testament gives evidence of the "royal grant" model based on ancient Assyrian prototypes and the "suzerain-vassal" model analogous to Late Bronze Hittite and Neo-Assyrian exemplars. The Abrahamic covenant is akin to the royal grant model in that it is unilateral and unconditional in form and intent and consists of the awarding of a boon or blessing by a superior to an inferior merely on the basis of the benefactor's good will and the loyalty of the beneficiary. The Mosaic covenant, on the other hand, is bilateral and conditional. The Great King invites (or imposes upon) his vassal to participate with him in an agreement whereby he will protect and reward the vassal in return for his service and loyal obedience. This is the kind of arrangement the Lord made with Israel at Sinai, the stipulations of which are outlined throughout much of the Torah. As we shall see, the law was in effect the body of covenant requirements essential to a covenant of this kind.

Covenant in Genesis is of the royal grant genre as far as the evidence allows a judgment to be made. This is indubitably the case with the covenants made with the patriarchs, and there is every reason to believe that it is true of the others as well. The first occurrence of the term *bĕrît* is in the flood narrative where the Lord said to Noah, "I am bringing a deluge—floodwaters on the earth to destroy all flesh under heaven with the breath of life in it. Everything on earth will die. But I will establish My covenant with you" (Gen. 6:17–18). The "but" is extremely significant, for it indicates that Noah will be the exception to this blanket warning of judgment, an exception made possible by the Lord's invoking of a covenant.

This was not an entirely new covenant, however, for it is called "My" covenant, suggesting that it was one already known to the Lord and thus to be recalled and reimplemented.[18] If this reading of the "My" is correct, the only possible candidate for a prior covenant is the creation mandate of Genesis 1:26–28. That passage has all the essentials of a royal grant—a superior (God), an inferior (mankind), and a blessing (man as the image of God). There were no conditions or qualifications to be met in achieving

---

[17] See conveniently G. E. Mendenhall, "Covenant Forms in Israelite Tradition," *BA* 17 (1954): 50–76; Meredith G. Kline, *Treaty of the Great King* (Grand Rapids: Eerdmans, 1963); *By Oath Consigned* (Grand Rapids: Eerdmans, 1968); Moshe Weinfeld, "The Covenant of Grant in the Old Testament and in the Ancient Near East," *JAOS* 90 (1970): 184–203.

[18] Thus W. J. Dumbrell, *Covenant and Creation* (Nashville: Nelson, 1984), 26.

this status. It was initiated by God unilaterally as an act of his free grace with no prior merit on man's part necessary to bring it about. All that was needed was for man to exercise the privileges of the relationship, namely, to "be fruitful, multiply, fill the earth, and subdue it" (v. 28).

The idea that "My" covenant harks back to the creation mandate finds support in the actual wording of the covenant as outlined to Noah following the flood. He and his sons (i.e., the new human race) were told to "be fruitful and multiply and fill the earth" (Gen. 9:1), the very wording of Genesis 1:28a. At this point the text goes in a different direction, however, for the postflood world was radically different from the prefall one; and so, in line with covenant restatements necessary to changed conditions and relationships, the old privileges and responsibilities could no longer be expected. Thus, rather than reading "fill the earth and subdue it," the Noah version reads, "The fear and terror of you will be in every living creature on the earth, every bird of the sky, every creature that crawls on the ground, and all the fish of the sea. They are placed under your authority" (v. 2).

The last clause is fraught with ominous overtones, for the next verse goes on to say that being "under your authority" includes human consumption of animals, "every living creature" (v. 3). How different this is from the original charge to "rule the fish of the sea, the birds of the sky, and every creature that crawls on the earth" (Gen. 1:28b). The dominion is still there, but it is a dominion that will permit mankind to be carnivorous at the expense of the creatures over which he was created to rule. Thus ensue the dreadful alterations of relationship occasioned by the fall.

Life was still sacred, however, whether that of men or animals, so animal blood could not be eaten. The idea that blood is virtually synonymous with life, first hinted at here, is fully articulated in the Mosaic Law (Lev. 17:11). And if animal blood is taboo, what about human blood? The passage goes on to assert that human life is of inestimable value; for man, depraved as he is, remains the image of God. Therefore, whoever sheds human blood as though it were no more precious than the blood of an animal must himself be slain; for an assault on the image of God is tantamount to an assault on God Himself (vv. 4–6).[19]

Thus far, the old Adamic covenant was reiterated but with the modifications necessary to a different time and circumstance. God now

[19] Geerhardus Vos, *Biblical Theology* (Grand Rapids: Eerdmans, 1954), 65.

began to address new features that went beyond the foundational premises of the earlier arrangement. For the first time after the flood, he referred again to his covenant, pledging by it that he would never again destroy the earth and all life by a flood (vv. 8–11). As a sign of his commitment to that promise, he invited attention to the rainbow which, whenever it appeared, would be a visible reminder to both himself and mankind that he would be true to his word (vv. 12–17). A confirming sign from then on would be a standard feature of covenant agreements (cf. Gen. 17:9–14; Exod. 31:13).

The Noahic covenant clearly was universal in scope. Like the creation mandate, of which it was a reiteration with necessary amendment, it spelled out the central features of God's relationship to mankind in general as well as the privileges and responsibilities that still remained despite the fall. The covenant with Abraham was altogether different in that respect; for though, like the Noahic, it was in the form of a royal grant, its focus and purpose were more narrowly defined. The Noahic covenant held out the hope of human redemption; the Abrahamic revealed the means by which that would be done.

The first reference to God's covenant with Abraham is Genesis 15:18, but it is presupposed in the call narrative of Genesis 12 where Abraham was singled out as its recipient. The way had been prepared for his selection in the preceding record, in particular in the genealogy of Shem which culminated in Abram, a descendant of Eber (the Eberite or Hebrew) (Gen. 11:10–26; cf. 10:21). With no hint of any basis on which Abraham was qualified, he was simply directed by the Lord to leave his homeland and go to a country the Lord would reveal to him (Gen. 12:1). He would become a great nation and the source of blessing for all other nations. In turn, those that blessed him would be blessed, but those that cursed him would be cursed (Gen. 12:2–3; cf. 22:18; 27:29).

As we have just noted, this was not the setting or text of a covenant in itself but the announcement to Abraham of a covenant to which he would be a party should he agree to the requirement to leave Ur and go to a land where the covenant could be lived out. In other words, the only conditionality to the covenant was Abraham's willingness to accept it.[20] Nothing in the promise here or elsewhere demanded of the patriarch any prerequisite behavior or

---

[20] John Goldingay, *Old Testament Theology,* vol. 1 (Downers Grove, Ill.: InterVarsity, 2003), 198–99.

even enduring commitment in order for the agreement to stand. It was in every respect a royal grant, a gift given by the Great King to an individual whom he had chosen out of the bounty of his grace.[21]

When the covenant was addressed *per se* (Gen. 15), its terms were disclosed to Abraham in a dream. He was concerned, of course, about his lack of offspring since the promise was that his seed would bless all nations. The Lord therefore showed him the numberless stars and said that his descendants would also be uncountable. Moreover, he would possess the land of Canaan as a permanent inheritance. The Lord then commanded Abraham to slaughter sacrificial animals and to divide their carcasses into two rows. Following this, the Lord, symbolized by a blazing torch, walked between the piles of carcasses. By this act he invoked upon himself a curse should he fail to keep covenant with Abraham (v. 18). The boldness of this metaphor is almost incomprehensible, but it conveys the strength of the commitment of the God who cannot lie.

The revelation of the covenant to Abraham was not yet complete, nor was there yet any hint of Abraham's agreement to it. So far only the Lord had sworn his fealty, but this only confirms the nature of the covenant as a grant whose only obligations were on the bestower. The clarification of these matters is advanced in Genesis 17, where we find Abraham, many years later, still without an heir. Introducing himself as El Shaddai, the all abundant one, the Lord then enjoined upon Abraham that he be blameless (*tāmîm*; cf. 6:9 where the word describes Noah). The next sentence begins, "I will establish My covenant between Me and you" (v. 2). Some interpreters understand this to be the apodosis of a conditional clause, thus: "If you walk before me and are blameless, *then* I will confirm my covenant," etc. The grammar does not demand this view, however.[22] The imperative is followed by a (pseudo-) cohortative, yielding the sequence: "Be blameless and I will confirm." Thus, even here the promise of God to confirm the covenant has no strings attached. The command to be blameless is not a condition for blessing, but it is expected of one who is so privileged as to be blessed by the Lord.

---

[21] For the ancient Near Eastern background to this type of covenant, see especially Moshe Weinfeld, "The Covenant of Grant in the Old Testament and in the Ancient Near East," *JAOS* 90 (1970): 184–203.

[22] Bruce K. Waltke and M. O'Connor, *Biblical Hebrew Syntax* (Winona Lake, Ind.: Eisenbrauns, 1990), 34.6.

The Lord's confirmation of the covenant to Abraham brought about a change of his name from Abram (elevated father) to Abraham (father of a multitude), the promise that nations (not just an amorphous seed) would descend from him, and the prediction that he would be the progenitor of kings (vv. 5–6). There is here already the shadowy glimpse of a day when Abraham's seed would be more than an abstraction. It would take the form of a nation *(gôy)* among nations with a king administering its affairs. As for a territory, the land in which Abraham sojourned would be his forever. And as for Abraham's concern about a son through whom all these promises must come to pass, the Lord assured him in no uncertain terms that his wife Sarai (now named Sarah, princess), though ninety years of age, would bear a son within the year (cf. 18:14). That son would also be blessed with the covenant promises, the first in the line of countless generations through which God would effect the reconciliation of fallen humanity to himself.

One thing remained and that was the sign of the covenant (here, by metonymy, called the covenant itself, v. 9). As Noah would see the rainbow and remember God's faithfulness in preserving him and his promise never to destroy all life again, so Abraham and his descendants must have a sign that would bear witness to their status as the special people of the Lord. That sign was circumcision, a rite not unique to the Hebrew people but that to them had unique significance (vv. 10–14). Its theological import is a matter of much disagreement, but those scholars who view it as a sign to the Hebrews themselves and not to outsiders or even to the Lord seem to have the better case.[23] Every time a male engaged in sexual intercourse, he would be reminded of his inclusion in the covenant race and of his responsibility to propagate that race in line with the creation mandate to "be fruitful and multiply" and to do so in keeping with the promise to Abraham of an innumerable seed.

The term *bĕrît* does not occur elsewhere in Genesis (except to speak of treaties and contracts: 21:17, 32; 26:28; 31:44), but the reaffirmation of the covenant to Abraham and his descendants continues in a number of places. After Abraham had entertained his angelic guests, including the angel of the Lord, the Lord informed him of his plans to destroy the

---

[23] Walther Zimmerli, *Old Testament Theology in Outline* (Atlanta: John Knox, 1978), 132–33.

cities of the plain on the grounds that all the nations of the earth would be blessed through him (Gen. 18:16–19). One cannot escape the irony that the one who would become God's means of blessing nations must shortly witness the destruction of nations that were beyond redemption despite his fervent intercessions on their behalf.

Abraham's descent must be different, however, for, as the Lord said of him, "I have chosen him so that he will command his children and his house after him to keep the way of the LORD by doing what is right and just. This is how the LORD will fulfill to Abraham what He promised him" (v. 19). In the present context, what God promised was that Abraham's descendants would be the instruments of universal blessing, but their effectiveness in doing so would obviously depend on their own integrity. This by no means infused the covenant itself with conditionality, but it did (here and elsewhere; cf. Gen. 26:5) underscore the need for the covenant bearers to present themselves before the world in such a manner that they would qualify to transmit the blessing of God to them. That is, the covenant was unconditional; but its effectiveness and the blessings that accrued to those included in it depended on their faithfulness to obey it.

A test of unbelievable magnitude was not long in coming, one we have already observed from another angle.[24] God had commanded Abraham to sacrifice his one and only son and thereby demonstrate his confidence in the Lord and his willingness to obey no matter how unreasonable and illogical the command might be (Gen. 22). A certain degree of conditionality is implicit in the Lord's response to Abraham's compliance with this incomprehensible demand: "Now I know that you fear God" (v. 12). Because he now "knew," the Lord was able to reward Abraham's faith by reiterating the promises of the covenant (vv. 16–18). Had Abraham failed to comply (a moot point, of course), the covenant would still be in place; but how his descendants might have carried it out cannot be known.

Isaac, too, received the Lord's promise of multifold blessing as an heir of the covenant made with Abraham. The Lord would give him the land of Canaan, confirming by this act the oath he had sworn to his father. His seed, like Abraham's, would be innumerable, and all the nations would be blessed by them. The reason is that "Abraham listened to My voice

---

[24] See pp. 81–82.

and kept My mandate *(mišmeret),* My commands *(miṣwôt),* My statutes *(ḥuqqôt),* and My instructions *(tôrôt)*" (Gen. 26:5). These technical terms presuppose the covenant stipulations that would become central to the Mosaic covenant law later revealed in detail. Once more there are conditional aspects to the unconditional covenant that God made with the patriarchs. Its terms must be kept if blessing were to ensue, but never once in the Genesis record (or elsewhere) is there a threat by the Lord to annul the covenant or to revoke from Abraham and his descendants the privilege of implementing it. This is not precisely the case with the Mosaic covenant as we shall see (cf., e.g., Exod. 32:9–10; Deut. 9:14).

The covenant privilege devolved upon Jacob in a somewhat truncated statement with the central blessing consisting of a wish that those who cursed Jacob (i.e., Israel) might be cursed and those who blessed him might be blessed (Gen. 27:29). Later elements appear such as the promise of the land and a multitude of descendants (28:13–14) and, in particular, the pledge that Jacob would found a nation over which kings would rule (35:11–12). This promise, already shared with Abraham in a more embryonic form (Gen. 17:6, 16), holds special significance in the progressive outworking of God's covenant program for, as we shall demonstrate later, the nation and its kings would evolve from an entirely different covenant matrix, one nonetheless subsidiary to the royal grant made to Abraham, Isaac, and Jacob. The relationship between the Abrahamic and Mosaic covenants will turn out to be of critical importance to a comprehensive Old Testament theology.

The final assertion of covenant to the fathers occurred on the eve of Jacob's departure for Egypt at the behest of his son Joseph, a departure that would eventuate in a four hundred-year sojourn there. But the Lord told the patriarch not to fear going to Egypt, for he would make him a great nation there and then, in time, would deliver that nation back to Canaan (Gen. 46:3–4). Little by little the covenant plan of God to and through the patriarchs was disclosed until it is clear that it would be worked out through a chosen nation. Moses would reveal that the nation was Israel, a point that needed to be stressed in preparation for the conquest about to take place. Thus we find ourselves with Moses at Moab once again, hopefully with a better understanding of why the covenant history of Genesis was so crucial to Israel's self-understanding.

The *Protevangelium*

We return finally to Genesis 3, where the narrative of the fall, which explains the human condition and the need for a redemptive work by God himself, has embedded within it the dim outline of how that redemption will finally come to pass. We refer to Genesis 3:15, a text often described by Christian theologians as the *protevangelium,* the "first Gospel," because it hints so strongly of the messianic atonement that lies at the heart of the Christian faith. At this point, however, we are obliged to issue a strong caveat for at least two reasons: (1) In following consistently the method adopted for this work, we make a sharp (but not necessarily contradictory) distinction between the exegesis of a text and the theology inherent in it or derivative from it. (2) This is a theology of the Old Testament, not of the whole Bible; and though we confess the unitary and unified nature of the whole, we must allow Old Testament texts to disclose their theological messages first without input from the New Testament or even from later Old Testament testimony.

Having said this, Old Testament texts, including this one, are part of the warp and woof of a total biblical revelation, one that derives ultimately not from prophets, poets, and sages but from the Spirit of God himself. What human authors might not or could not see even in their own writings is nevertheless latent there, ready to be mined theologically by later writers and modern readers. What David, Isaiah, or Zechariah might have made of our text we cannot know since there are no allusions to it in later Old Testament literature. The New Testament, on the other hand, though not quoting Genesis 3:15, certainly shows that the Christian student can hardly avoid the messianic tone of the passage, nor should he, for the theological (if not the exegetical) intent of its message is clear.[25]

Ironically, the word of hope in the midst of divine threat of judgment appears not in the word of the Lord to Adam or even to Eve but to the serpent. Only he was cursed, and the epitome of that curse was his mortal wound at the hand (or the foot) of the woman's seed. The Lord declared that he would establish a state of hostility (Heb. *ʾēbâ*) between the serpent and the woman. The word *hostility* is used elsewhere to speak of the Philistines' age-old hatred of Judah (Ezek. 25:15) and

[25] For a concise history of the interpretation of the text, see Jack P. Lewis, "The Woman's Seed (Gen. 3:15)," *JETS* 34 (1991): 299–319.

Edom's implacable abhorrence of Israel (Ezek. 35:5). From then on the descendants of the serpent and the offspring of the woman would be locked in mortal combat until one or the other was vanquished and destroyed. The seed of the serpent is mentioned first in the confrontation; but by a chiastic arrangement of the poetic lines, the woman's seed first acts by crushing the serpent's head; and then the serpent will crush the heel of the woman's seed. In actual and logical fact, of course, the attack by the serpent must precede that of the woman's seed since that seed will rise up to slay the serpent.

The verb describing these blows *(šwp)* is the same in both cases though some translations, perhaps under the influence of messianic theology, distinguish them by translating the second occurrence as "strike at" (NIV) or the like. This is understandable since in the one event the blow is mortal whereas in the other it is painful but hardly lethal. The more important observation to be made is that the serpent's attempt to administer a fatal blow is unsuccessful because he can only try to avert the crushing heel as it drives against his head. With futility he lashes out, but all he can do is bruise the heel of the one who is placing him underfoot.

Not to be overlooked is the fact that the final showdown will not be between the woman and the serpent or even between their respective descendants. Rather, the seed of the woman will crush the head of the serpent himself. The serpent and his seed are thus one and the same, an embodiment of evil that will plague the course of history only to be annihilated at the end. The seed of the woman is separate and discrete from her, however. He will spring from her but as a "seed," a being that biologically can originate only with a male; the woman's offspring will have a more complicated genetic makeup and history than meets the eye immediately. Our text leaves us with no answers, but a theology informed by New Testament revelation cannot help but see, at least in dim outline, a supernatural paternity to be understood in Christian theology as the incarnation, the birth of a child apart from human intercourse.[26]

One further point remains to complete the discussion for now and that is the use of the heel to crush the head. The imagery is one of conquest, a metaphor found commonly in the Old Testament (Josh. 10:24; 2 Sam. 22:39; 1 Kings 5:3; Ps. 47:3; Lam. 3:34). The creation mandate itself

---

[26] Goldingay, *Old Testament Theology,* 141, n. 14.

decreed that as God's image mankind was to rule over *(rdh)* and subdue *(kbš)* all of creation, including the animal world. Both verbs have the idea of bringing under control by force, even by treading down. The woman's seed will finally vanquish the foe by violence, crushing his head and thereby manifesting his dominion over him. The openness of this idea to the triumph of Jesus Christ over the devil is too clear to need proof. In his work of redemption he was wounded on the cross; but by his triumphant resurrection he crushed the head of wickedness, rendering it toothless and powerless until its day of ultimate destruction.

Conclusion

Genesis provides the record of God's creation of man, of man's sinful rebellion and fall, and (in nascent form at least) of God's strategy for undoing the effects of sin and bringing mankind back into fellowship with himself. It describes a primitive cultus with its holy places, altars, and sacrifices, and, most important, it introduces the covenants, the instruments signifying God's interest in establishing a relationship with those chosen to be its recipients as well as the terms by which the relationship can be maintained and achieve its intended objectives. There are, thus, two goals to the redemptive program of the Lord: (1) to restore the broken fellowship between himself and his creation; and (2) to accomplish this by a soteriological method initiated by him and worked out through a progressive series of atoning measures that will culminate at last in his triumph over the antitheocratic forces of this world.

The covenants addressed thus far we have conveniently labeled "royal grant" for, like those of the secular ancient Near Eastern world, they originated with God, they were bestowed unilaterally by him upon those whom he sovereignly chose, and they were unconditional in their bestowment and in their durability. Only the blessings of which they spoke were contingent on the obedience and faithfulness of the grantees. They might—indeed, did—fail, and more than once, but the covenant itself remained intact because the God who cannot lie had sworn himself to its everlastingness.

The covenant concept, tacitly expressed in the so-called creation mandate, took on a formal character in its application to Noah. In both cases it was a covenant made with all the world, an outline of what it meant for mankind to be God's image and to have the dominion for which it was created. The intrusion of sin and the fall crippled the divine intention, however, so covenant must now allow for human alienation from God and provide within it a means of restoration of his original purposes. This found expression in the call of Abram, a solitary man who would father a nation that would inherit a land, multiply in number, and be the means of blessing the whole earth. In Abram we see the fountainhead of a line of descendants who would in time be God's means of reestablishing the perfections consonant with his own character and expectations.

The next section of our work will focus on the promised nation Israel and the peculiar covenant relationship that set that nation apart and gifted it to undertake all that God had promised to the patriarchs.

Chapter Nine

The Creation of a Nation

The Promise of a Special People

Along with many other promises the Lord made to the patriarchs was the pledge that they would sire nations and one in particular that would become the touchstone of blessing for all nations that blessed it (Gen. 12:2–3; 18:18). Moreover, this nation would be a monarchy complete with human rulers to administer its affairs (Gen. 35:11; cf. 17:6, 16). The fulfillment of the promise of a nation was obviously most apparent to Moses and the assembly of Israelites in Moab, for they embodied it. The family of Jacob that had entered Egypt more than 450 years earlier had emerged from their bondage there to become a people vast in number and rich in resources if not yet a nation. As for a king, none existed except for the Lord himself. Ideally, he ruled the tribes of Israel, hence the commonly used term *theocracy* to describe this phase of Israel's history. Human kingship, the kind promised to Abraham, would have to wait for more than three hundred years.

Besides the intimations of nationhood and kingship resident in the patriarchal covenant, Jacob in his farewell blessing on his sons singled out one of them, Judah, in a special way, predicting that Judah, like a lion, would dominate his enemies and, perhaps as a consequence, his brothers would praise him (Gen. 49:8). Jacob went on to say that "the scepter will not depart from Judah, or the staff from between his feet, until He whose right it is comes and the obedience of the peoples belongs to Him" (v. 10). Though this text has already commanded our attention, it must be viewed again from a different vantage point, one particularly pertinent to Israel's emergence as a national entity.

The scepter *(šēbeṭ)* and staff *(mĕḥōqēq)* are clearly metaphors for royalty. In fact, the latter term in some contexts can be translated *ruler* or *commander* (Judg. 5:14; Isa. 33:22, referring to the LORD).[1] According to this promise, kingship will never leave Judah but will be a constituent element of that tribe's identity. The reference to the staff coming from "between his [Judah's] feet" no doubt pertains to his royal progeny who will come "from his loins," that is, who will be his descendants. There will not be just one king but a dynasty of them until "He whose right it is comes" (Gen. 49:10). This phrase is sometimes rendered "until Shiloh comes" (NASB), but besides the obfuscation caused by the reference to Shiloh (otherwise a place-name; cf. Josh. 18:1; Judg. 18:31; 1 Sam. 1:3; etc.), nowhere else does a messianic figure bear this designation. A slight revocalization of the Hebrew text yields the sense we have adopted here, one that provides good parallelism to the line that follows.[2]

Judah's royal descent will continue uninterrupted until finally a scion of his line will appear whose claims on sovereignty will be final, full, and indisputable. All the nations will concede his kingship and will submit to him. Jewish and Christian theology is in agreement that the promise here includes a fulfillment in David but that David does not exhaust it. Its implications of universal sovereignty outstrip the regal claims and accomplishments of David as grand as they were. The text must therefore have an eschatological dimension, one understood by Christian interpretation as messianic, specifically, as Christological.[3] It is Jesus, the Son of David, who will, in the eschaton, meet all the requirements of the passage.

Obviously, Moses could not have known all this, to say nothing of Jacob. On the other hand, he clearly grasped the truth that out of all the

---

[1] *HALOT,* 1:347; H. Ringgren, חקק, *TDOT* 5:141.

[2] Eugene H. Merrill, "Rashi, Nicholas de Lyra, and Christian Exegesis," *WTJ* 38 (1975): 73–76.

[3] Christoph Barth, *God with Us* (Grand Rapids: Eerdmans, 1991), 221–22.

tribes Judah would be the one through which the Lord would exercise his rule. We see unmistakable hints of this in the course of the exodus and wilderness sojourn where Judah seems already to occupy a place of special prominence.

The Founding of the Nation

We turn now to the narrative of the birth of the nation after a gestation period of four hundred years. The book of Exodus opens with a bridging between the descent into Egypt by Jacob and his family (1:1–5) and the situation of his descendants there that would shortly necessitate their departure to the land of promise. True to the covenant blessing spoken to Abraham, the Lord had so worked on their behalf that "the Israelites were fruitful, increased rapidly, multiplied, and became extremely numerous" (Exod. 1:7; cf. Gen. 15:5; 17:2; 46:3). Such an obvious fulfillment of God's promises suggested to anyone of a spiritually sensitive nature that more such blessing was yet to come, including that of land.

One of the major elements of the Abrahamic covenant was the promise that the Lord would bless those nations that blessed Abraham's descendants and curse those that cursed them. On the other hand, all the nations on earth would be blessed through Abraham's offspring (Gen. 12:3). This was clearly the case in Egypt during the lifetimes of Jacob and Joseph. As soon as the latter had become head of Potiphar's household, "the Lord blessed the Egyptian's house because of Joseph. The Lord's blessing was on all that he owned, in his house and in his fields" (Gen. 39:5). Following his appointment as Pharaoh's minister of agriculture (or the like), Joseph devised a plan for storing up food supplies in the years of abundance and distributing them in the following period of famine, thus saving Egypt from starvation (Gen. 41:46–57). Once more, Joseph became God's means of blessing Egypt.

When Jacob arrived in Egypt, he appeared before Pharaoh and immediately pronounced a blessing on him, a verbal affirmation of what God had already done for Pharaoh and Egypt (Gen. 47:7). And Pharaoh, meeting the condition that God would bless the nation that blessed Abraham's seed, bequeathed to Jacob and his family "property in the best part of the land, the land of Rameses" (Gen. 47:11).

But the good times were not to continue always. Sometime after Joseph's death there came to power a new king "who had not known Joseph" (Exod. 1:8). That is, he did not reflect back on Joseph with favor and certainly did not intend to treat the Hebrew people with the kindnesses extended by earlier dynasties of kings. Egypt would no longer bless the people of the Lord and therefore would forfeit the blessings that otherwise could be expected. The result of this new policy was an increasing oppression of the Hebrews and, after many judgments by the Lord upon Egypt, his mighty deliverance of his people in the exodus redemption. None of this should have surprised Moses and his generation, for the Lord had foretold to Abraham that his descendants would be strangers and slaves in a foreign land for four hundred years but that he would punish that wicked nation and bring his own people out with great possessions (Gen. 15:13–14). As long as Egypt blessed the Hebrews, it was blessed; but when it mistreated them, it set itself up for divine judgment.

The tension between Egypt and the Hebrews both illustrates the repercussions of the covenant curses in that particular situation and serves paradigmatically to anticipate Israel's relationship with nations yet to come in Old Testament times and even till the present day. Those that bless Israel will be blessed whereas those that do not will be cursed. Despite all else, the truth remains that through God's chosen people all the nations of the earth will be blessed. This finds messianic fulfillment as well as eschatological realization, points to be fully developed later.

The sociopolitical and theological significance of Israel's transition from a people to a nation is a matter of great importance. The Abrahamic covenant consistently describes the descendants of the patriarch as a nation *(gôy)* rather than a people *(ʿam)* (Gen. 12:2; 17:4–6, 16; 18:18; 25:23; 35:11; 46:3) whereas Israel in Exodus is called a people scores of times and a nation only three times and then never prior to the establishment of Israel as the covenant nation (Exod. 19:6; 32:10; 33:13). We noted earlier that *gôy* and *ʿam* occasionally occur as synonyms and in fact are sometimes used interchangeably.[4] However, the distinction between them in the accounts of the Abrahamic and Mosaic covenants respectively

[4] See pp. 190–92.

cannot be ignored. Israel as a people was a temporary phase on the way to nationhood, and only as a nation could the full extent of the kingdom promises made to the fathers be realized.[5] The semantic thrust therefore is not so much ethnic as it is sociopolitical. Israel as a nation would be the channel of world blessing and not Israel as a (Jewish) people. The eschatological implications of this truth are indeed profound.

At the same time the people Israel were already recognized prior to the exodus as not only a people but as "God's people," that is, a people already chosen by him even before the inauguration of the Mosaic covenant. That covenant, we have repeatedly argued, was not initiated to make Israel the people of the Lord but to validate that status and to clarify for Israel what its role was to be as a nation. The first time Israel was identified as the Lord's people was immediately after the theophany of the burning bush where the Lord said to Moses, "I have observed the misery of My people in Egypt . . . and I know about their sufferings" (Exod. 3:7; cf. v. 10). The plea thereafter to Pharaoh is that he "let My people go" (5:1; 7:16; 8:21; 9:1, 13; 10:3).

When this did not happen soon enough to satisfy Moses, he chided the Lord by pointing out that despite Moses' incessant appeals to Pharaoh to release Israel, "he has caused trouble for this people, and You haven't delivered Your people at all" (Exod. 5:23). The Lord responded and promised that "I will put My hand on Egypt and bring out the ranks of My people the Israelites, out of the land of Egypt by great acts of judgment" (Exod. 7:4). The Lord's identification of Israel as "My people" continues in the pericope of the plague of flies where he threatened, "If you will not let My people go, then I will send swarms of flies" (Exod. 8:21). Then, in a most remarkable statement of differentiation, he asserted that where his people lived there would be no flies; and by this means the Lord "will make a distinction between My people and your people" (v. 23). This principle of demarcation between Israel as the people of the Lord and the nations at large would become a major theme in the Mosaic covenant whose fundamental purpose was to set Israel apart as God's own special possession (cf. Exod. 19:5; Deut. 7:6; 14:2).

Sadly, shortly after the covenant was made, the people violated its foundational principle—that the Lord alone is God and only he is to be

[5] Ronald E. Clements, גּוֹי, *TDOT* 2:429–30.

worshipped—by making a golden calf and bowing down before it (Exod. 32:1–6). This precipitated a crisis of faith and identity, for it seemed that Israel had rejected the Lord in favor of another god and had by this act become no longer his people. The Lord in fact instructed Moses to descend from the holy mountain "for your people you brought up from the land of Egypt have acted corruptly" (v. 7). Moses was quick to disavow any such connection with Israel and turned the question around: "Why does Your anger burn against Your people You brought out of the land of Egypt with great power and a strong hand?" (v. 11). "Turn from Your great anger," he prayed, "and change Your mind about this disaster planned for Your people" (v. 12).

The issue of who would lay reluctant claim to Israel was resolved at last in Moses' favor: Israel was the people of the Lord despite their terrible act of covenant infidelity. Lest he forget, Moses pleaded with the Lord to "consider that this nation *(gôy)* is Your people *('am)*" (Exod. 33:13). And he further urged that the Lord go with them to the promised land. "How will it be known that I and Your people have found favor in Your sight unless You go with us?" he asked. And then he asserted, "I and Your people will be distinguished by this from all the other people on the face of the earth" (v. 16). The world would know that Israel was unique among the nations by witnessing God's presence with them. And that presence would come in fulfillment of the ancient patriarchal promises of a nation to come, with which he would have a special relationship (cf. Gen. 17:8).

Before we address the Mosaic covenant, one more epithet for Israel should come to the fore; and that is the term *son,* a term which, if anything, evokes a sense of even more intimacy than either *people* or *nation.* Even before Moses returned to Egypt to deliver his people, the Lord instructed him to say to Pharaoh, "This is what the LORD says: Israel is My firstborn son. . . . Let My son go so that he may worship Me" (Exod. 4:22–23). It was a foregone conclusion that Pharaoh would not comply so the Lord went on to say, "Now I will kill your firstborn son!" (v. 23).

The firstborn son *(ben bēkôr)* enjoyed a place of special privilege as the one who carried on the family name and who inherited the bulk of the father's estate (cf. Gen. 48:14, 18; Deut. 21:15–17).[6] The firstborn of Pharaoh would be in line to succeed him on Egypt's throne; so with his death at the hands of the Lord, the well-being of the kingdom was at stake (Exod. 11:5; 12:12, 29). The reciprocal price that Israel must pay for the Lord's gracious deliverance was the firstborn of each of its households, not in death, of course, but in dedication to the Lord (Exod. 13:2). The death of the human firstborn would be circumvented by the offering up of a sacrificial animal that thus redeemed the human son from such a fate (Exod. 13:15 cf. 22:29; 34:20).

The most poignant example is one we have already looked at in a different context: the Lord's command to Abraham to offer up his only son Isaac (Gen. 22). Ishmael had already been born, to be sure, but Isaac was the only *(yāḥîd)* son in that he was uniquely the heir of the covenant promises (Gen. 17:18–19). Therefore, to sacrifice him would nullify the promises that God had made and thus bring to naught the hope of human redemption. The repeated references to Isaac as the "only son" underscores the seriousness of the threat as well as the bond of love that melded the hearts of father and son (vv. 2, 12, 16).

The same pathos is suggested in the Lord's demand that Pharaoh release his son from cruel bondage and allow him to go and worship (that is, serve) him. Israel was the Lord's firstborn and as such enjoyed not only the intimacy presupposed by such a relationship but also the status of heir of all the good things that a God of unlimited resources could provide. Chief among these was the privilege of being the conduit through which the redemptive plan of God would be channeled to all the nations.

We must again and emphatically make the point that Israel's sonship was established not by the exodus redemption—in fact, sonship was the basis for that redemption—but by virtue of Israel's descent from the patriarchs, the heir of all that God had promised to them. The language of family connotes a kinship that transcends the normal relationship of a god and his nation. For Israel to be the Lord's firstborn son was to share consanguinity, if not in a literal or physical sense then at least in a profoundly theological sense. The same idea appears later in David's

---

[6] Roland de Vaux, *Ancient Israel,* vol. 1, *Social Insitutions* (New York: McGraw-Hill, 1965), 41–42.

designation as the Lord's son (Ps. 2:6, 12), and in the New Testament believers are known as God's sons and daughters (Matt. 5:9, 45; John 1:12; Rom. 8:16; 1 John 3:2).

Studies of ancient Near Eastern treaty texts have disclosed that on a few occasions royal superiors referred to lesser kings with whom they made covenant as their sons.[7] This suggests both a relatively inferior status and an atmosphere of mutual trust. The superior king, as father, was willing and able to attend to the needs of his subordinate partner; but at the same time he expected compliance to his sovereignty and a willingness to adhere to all the terms of the covenant to which he had pledged himself. His sonship was thus a mark of privilege, but privilege heavily freighted with responsibility.

The deliverance of God's "son-people" Israel from Egypt was in a sense a prison break instigated by the Lord and brought by him to a successful conclusion. As we shall see, the purpose of the Mosaic covenant was to present Israel with an offer of servanthood, an opportunity for engagement in the Lord's salvific design of world redemption. But before Israel could become the Lord's servant, it had to be emancipated from slavery to Egypt, the antithesis of the kingdom of God. This major motif of the exodus became, in fact, a paradigm event to provide a model of deliverance from oppression of every kind, and in contemporary times it is employed frequently in liberation theology with little or no attention to its historical and theological matrix. We will find it enlightening to trace in an ongoing manner this idea of competing sovereignties up through and beyond the exodus, a notion as ancient as the Eden temptation itself.

The Deliverance of the Nation

The Significance of the Plagues

After nearly three hundred years of favor in Egypt, Israel arrived at the historical point where a king of Egypt arose who did not know about Joseph and who, with his successors, instituted a regime of oppressive slavery and even genocide. This had been predicted (Gen. 15:13), but

[7] *CAD* 10:314; cf. Hans Walter Wolff, *Hosea,* trans. Gary Stansell (Philadelphia: Fortress, 1974), 198.

foreknowledge of it hardly sufficed to make it more bearable. The only remedy was for Israel to be freed of its manacles of bondage and to be set in a place where it could enter into a new relationship with the Lord, one, indeed, of service but a service sweetened by his gracious enablement. In other words, one master must be defeated so that another Master could come into his rightful place as Sovereign. Added to this is the fact that the one to be freed was not just a people randomly chosen but God's Son.

The struggle of the competing masters is everywhere to be seen. The more the Egyptians oppressed the Israelites, the more the latter multiplied and prospered (Exod. 1:13). When the edict went out for Hebrew baby boys to be slaughtered, the midwives disobeyed and once more "the people multiplied and became very numerous" (v. 20). In defiance of Pharaoh, the Lord's kingdom moved forward reminiscent of the ancient covenant mandate to be fruitful and increase in number (Gen. 1:28). For every attempt to suppress the outworking of the divine purpose, there was a counterreaction that only enhanced it.

The exodus deliverance was foreshadowed largely by Moses' own private exodus, a hasty departure from the land precipitated by his slaying of an Egyptian taskmaster (Exod. 2:11–15). This encounter crystallized at the personal level the conflict between Israel and Egypt and beyond even that the cosmic struggle between the Lord and the forces of evil that compete with him for universal dominion. The battle is thus not ultimately on the human plane but in the heavens. What occurs in history is merely a visible outworking of that which goes on behind the scenes where the sovereignty of God is challenged and assailed (cf. Ezek. 28:11–19; Eph. 6:10–18).

Through all the years of Moses' absence, the oppression of his people intensified until "God heard their groaning, and He remembered His covenant with Abraham, Isaac, and Jacob. God saw the Israelites, and He took notice" (Exod. 2:24–25). Two factors now moved the Lord to action: (1) his covenant promises to the fathers to deliver their descendants from bondage (Gen. 15:14); and (2) his loving concern for their well-being. The reason for Moses' long sojourn in the desert now became clear. He was being prepared to lead his people through that same harsh environment and for the same length of time.

The plagues narratives recount in dramatic form the essence of the struggle for dominion, for while it seems at first glance that its protagonists were on the one hand the mightiest nation on earth and on the other hand an intimidated, powerless community of slaves, we do not read far before we begin to understand that Egypt acted as it did at the behest or in the name of its gods. The whole contest, in fact, is summarized by the Lord's announcement on the night of the Passover that "I will pass through the land of Egypt on that night and strike every firstborn male in the land of Egypt, both man and beast. I am the LORD; I will execute judgments against all the gods of Egypt" (Exod. 12:12). The Lord God of Israel would do battle against the (imaginary) gods of Egypt. The outcome would make plain who is sovereign.

Reinforced by God's promise to be with him, Moses returned to Egypt to assume the leadership role to which God had called him (Exod. 3:11–12). But he was warned from the beginning that Pharaoh would not let the people go unless "he is forced by a strong hand" (v. 19). At that point the Lord would step in with that mighty hand and would, with great signs and wonders, prove beyond dispute his omnipotent power to save.

The first encounter with Pharaoh immediately forced the underlying theological issue: "Who is the LORD," he asked, "that I should obey Him by letting Israel go? I do not know the LORD, and what's more, I will not let Israel go" (Exod. 5:2). This does not mean that Pharaoh had never heard of Israel's God but only that he refused to recognize that such a God had any claim on his life. He represented another divine authority—in fact, according to Egyptian thought he himself was a god—and therefore he refused to acknowledge any competing deity, especially on his own home soil.[8] Rather than free the Israelites and thereby allow them to serve their God, he increased the severity of their labors, thus demonstrating that he and he alone was lord over them.

When Moses laid the matter before the Lord, he repeated to Moses once again the grounds upon which he would deliver his people: (1) he remembered his covenant promises to the patriarchs, and (2) he was moved by their cries for salvation (Exod. 6:4–5). This time, however, he would respond not just as God Almighty (Heb. *El Shaddai*) but as

---

[8] John A. Wilson, "Egypt: The Function of the State," *Before Philosophy,* ed. Henri Frankfort, et al. (New York: Penguin Books, 1949), 81–96.

the Lord (Heb. *Yahweh)*. We have already considered the significance of these names[9] and in this context. The all-powerful One would now manifest himself as the covenant God who is willing and able to save (v. 3). He would free his people from being slaves and by acts of redemption and judgment will "take you as My people, and I will be your God" (v. 7). This remarkable pledge incorporates both his work of salvation and his desire to be linked with a people whom he could call his own and who would reciprocate by acknowledging his lordship (cf. Lev. 26:12).

As the encounter between Moses and Pharaoh unfolded, the Lord revealed to Moses that the transcendent nature of the conflict would be clarified by the amazing role that Moses would play from thenceforth. "I have made you like God to Pharaoh," he said, "and Aaron your brother will be your prophet" (Exod. 7:1). The king of Egypt would not be dealing with a mere man but with Israel's God. When at last the deliverance took place, "the Egyptians will know that [He is] the LORD" (v. 5).

The evidentiary value of God's signs and wonders in establishing his sovereignty over Pharaoh, Egypt, and the whole world is a major leitmotif in the plagues stories. The Lord declared to Pharaoh that when the river turned to blood "you will know that I am the LORD" (Exod. 7:17) and likewise, when the frogs disappeared from the land, it would be done so that "you may know there is no one like the LORD our God" (Exod. 8:10). When the plague of flies came, it would affect only the Egyptians, not the land of Goshen where the Israelites lived. This would be done, the Lord continued, so that "you [Pharaoh] will know that I, the LORD, am in the land" (v. 22). This audacious assertion must have been galling to the extreme, for it was commonly believed in the ancient Near Eastern world that a deity's power never extended beyond its own territorial borders.[10] The Lord was asserting that he is not bound by such constrictions; for wherever his people are, there he is Lord.

The plague of hail was designed to teach Pharaoh something else about Israel's God, namely, that he is incomparable. He would send the disaster so "you will know there is no one like Me in all the earth" (Exod. 9:14). Then in a statement of absolute supremacy, he informed Pharaoh,

---

[9] See pp. 84–86.

[10] For Egyptian thought in particular, see J. H. Breasted, *Development of Religion and Thought in Ancient Egypt* (New York: Harper & Brothers, 1959), 312–15.

"I have let you live for this purpose: to show you My power and to make My name known in all the earth" (v. 16). Thus at Pharaoh's expense the Lord would be seen as not only superior to him but also as one worthy to be praised by all nations. Moses added to this exaltation of his God when, at the conclusion of the hailstorm, he promised Pharaoh that he would pray that it might cease "so that you may know the earth is the LORD's" (v. 29). No longer touted as the Lord of Goshen alone, he must now be seen as the sovereign over all creation.

Israel, too, must be instructed by the plagues, for it was all too easy for them to lose sight of the power and majesty of their God. When his signs and wonders became a thing of the past, his redeemed people must teach about them to their children and grandchildren so that "you will know that I am the LORD" (Exod. 10:2). The greatest sign of all would be the sparing of Israel's firstborn from the tenth plague while those of Egypt perished. This gracious, miraculous event would take place so that "you may know that the LORD makes a distinction between Egypt and Israel" (Exod. 11:7). At the same time Israel would come to understand that their God must also be distinguished from all the so-called gods of the nations. His triumph over Egypt and all its gods offered sufficient proof of his incomparability and universal dominion.

One of the most persuasive signs of the Lord's sovereignty over Egypt and its rulers and gods was the hardening of Pharaoh's heart, a condition brought upon him by the Lord so that he would carry out his nefarious designs against Israel and thus, by his judgment, bring glory to God alone. The most common verb translated *harden* in this narrative *(ḥzq)* has (in the stem used here) the idea of making the heart stubborn or obstinate so that it refuses to comply with God's will. The question of the fairness of such an act by God must be tempered by the recognition that Pharaoh also hardened his own heart, thus sealing by his own decision what God had ordained.[11] Moreover, the clear biblical teaching is that the sovereignty of God permits him to undertake courses of action that to the human perspective seem unjust but that, in consideration of his omniscience and ultimate objectives, prove to be altogether appropriate. Paul, citing the hardening of Pharaoh's heart, made the observation that God "shows mercy to whom He wills, and He hardens whom He wills"

---

[11] Robert B. Chisholm Jr., "Divine Hardening in the Old Testament," *BSac* 153 (1996): 428–29.

(Rom. 9:18). Then, appealing to the analogy of pottery manufacture, he asked, "Has the potter no right over his clay, to make from the same lump one piece of pottery for honor and another for dishonor?" (v. 21).

Regardless of the question of fairness, the point in the plagues narratives is that God hardened Pharaoh's heart and Pharaoh hardened his own heart so that God's sovereign nature and purposes might be displayed. Before Moses ever appeared before the king of Egypt, the Lord told him that the king would not let his people go because the Lord would stiffen his resolve not to do so (Exod. 4:21). The reason, as it turns out, was that the display of God's sovereignty in the face of such resistance might bring him great glory and praise (cf. Exod. 14:4, 17).

On a number of occasions, the Lord threatened to harden Pharaoh's heart (besides Exod. 4:21; cf. 7:3; 14:4, 17), and the record states that he did so (9:12; 10:1, 20, 27; 11:10; 14:8). Equally common, Pharaoh hardened his own heart. Even before the first plague Pharaoh steeled himself against the words of Moses and Aaron, stubbornly refusing to listen to them (Exod. 7:13). He was encouraged in his intransigence by the ability of his magicians to replicate the miracle of changing the water into blood (v. 22). And when the Lord brought relief from the plague of frogs, Pharaoh, perhaps sensing weakness on the Lord's part, hardened himself again (Exod. 8:15). At last Pharaoh's magicians ran out of tricks and were forced to concede of the plague of gnats that "this is the finger of God" (v. 19). By then, however, Pharaoh had become so recalcitrant that it was impossible for him to acknowledge the Lord's superiority (v. 32). The last time the term is used with Pharaoh as subject describes him as sinning, his sin being a hardness of heart that by then had infected his royal officials as well (Exod. 9:34). He had become hopelessly obstinate against the will of God, something the Lord had told Moses would happen (v. 35).

The end result of Pharaoh's obstinacy was God's judgment upon him, a clear-cut signal to him, his nation, Israel, and the whole world that the Lord is king and that his kingly objectives will, in the end, be achieved to his glory. The sequence of plagues led step-by-step to the climactic event of the death of Pharaoh's firstborn, a fitting response to Egypt's enslavement of Israel, the Lord's firstborn son. To commemorate this victory and demonstrate appropriate gratitude for the sparing of Israel's firstborn, the people were commanded thenceforth to observe the festival of Passover. To the question as to why this would be done, the answer would be, "When Pharaoh stubbornly refused to let us go, the LORD killed every firstborn male in the land of Egypt, from the firstborn of man to the firstborn of livestock. That is why I sacrifice to the LORD all the firstborn of the womb that are males, but I redeem all the firstborn of my sons" (Exod. 13:15).

The exodus event itself, however, best encapsulated the triumph of the Lord over the forces of evil represented by Pharaoh and his hosts. The telling of this most significant narrative of Israel's sacred history exists in two forms, a prose account in which the facts are laid bare and a poetic version rich in interpretive and theological value. The story line is straightforward. After leaving Succoth, just east of Rameses, the Israelites arrived at the western shore of the Red (or Reed) Sea where they found themselves hemmed in by the desert on all sides except to the east where the impassable waters of the sea prevented any further forward progress (Exod. 13:20–14:4). The stage was thus set for a confrontation that would result either in Israel's extermination at the hands of a vastly superior military force or a miraculous deliverance by the LORD that would forever settle the question of who truly is lord. With great faith Moses urged his people to be calm for, as he said, "you will see the LORD's salvation He will provide for you today" (Exod. 14:13). The LORD then spoke and assured the people that He would prevail on their behalf, and once He had the Egyptians "will know that I am the LORD" (v. 18).

In a mighty act reminiscent of the separation of the primordial waters at creation (Gen. 1:9–10), the Lord parted the waters of the Red Sea, and the hosts of Israel crossed to the other side on dry land. Too late the Egyptians found themselves in the midst of the sea when its waters returned in a chaotic cataclysm that drowned every last man (vv. 21–28). The victory thus achieved was not over just the armies of a powerful nation but over the sea itself. The God of creation had reenacted the scene of his earliest triumphs in nature by displaying now his sovereignty over human forces hostile to his creation design.

The poetic version even more clearly makes the point that the battle is the Lord's and that the conquest of Egypt was to be viewed proleptically as the conquest of all opposition to him both historically and eschatologically. What he did for his people in redeeming them from bondage to a competing sovereign he will do over and over again until all evil dominions are overthrown and the kingdom of God remains alone and supreme.

The poem, commonly titled "The Song of Moses" (Exod. 15:1–18), commences with a celebration of the crushing defeat of Pharaoh and his hosts in the waters of the Red Sea (vv. 1–5).[12] Israel had nothing to do with the success of the campaign except to witness it and praise God for it. The exalted LORD won the battle, the God of Israel who was also the God of the fathers. Appropriately enough, Moses speaks of him as a warrior, that is, a leader in battle who single-handedly drowned the armies of Egypt in the watery depths (v. 3). The term used here, literally "man of war" (Heb. *ʾîš milḥāmâ*), occurs only here with reference to the Lord, but an equivalent term, *gibbôr* (military hero), provides further insight into its range of meaning. Deuteronomy 10:17 speaks of the Lord as "God of gods and Lord of lords, the great God *(hāʾēl haggādōl haggibbōr),* mighty and awesome" (NIV). Psalm 24, in more militaristic terms in line with Exodus 15, asks, "Who is this King of glory?" and the answer is, "The LORD, strong and mighty *(gibbôr),* the LORD, mighty *(gibbôr)* in battle" (v. 8). Finally, Zephaniah links God's heroic deeds with his ability to save (Zeph. 3:17).

The designation of the Lord as warrior recalls again the question of holy war, an act of military conquest initiated by the Lord, undertaken by him, led by him, and brought by him to a successful conclusion.[13] In addition to earlier discussion of holy war[14] and to later, more thorough consideration, its prominence in the Song of Moses requires that it receive at least some attention here as well.

The poem opens with the note of triumph that the Lord has "thrown the horse and its rider into the sea" (v. 1). He did this as one engaged in battle and without assistance from Israel or anyone else. In the second section of the song (vv. 6–8), Moses speaks of the Lord's right hand with

---

[12] For a useful literary analysis, see Frank Moore Cross Jr., and David Noel Freedman, *Studies in Ancient Yahwistic Poetry,* SBL Diss. Series 21 (Missoula, Mont.: Scholars, 1975), 45–65. They title it "The Song of Miriam."

[13] For the "divine warrior" motif associated with this text, see especially Millard C. Lind, *Yahweh Is a Warrior* (Scottdale, Penn.: Herald, 1977); and P. D. Miller, *The Divine Warrior in Ancient Israel,* HSM 5 (Cambridge, Mass.: Harvard University Press, 1973).

[14] See pp. 111–14.

which he shattered the enemy. The right hand is elsewhere associated with strength for war (cf. v. 12; Pss. 17:7; 60:5; 89:13; 98:1; 108:6; 118:15–16) as is the powerful (right) arm (v. 16: cf. Deut. 4:34; 5:15; 7:19; 9:29; 2 Kings 17:36; Ps. 44:3; Jer. 27:5; etc.). Other weapons at his disposal are the heat of his anger (v. 7) and "the blast of [his] nostrils" (v. 8), what the prose account identifies as "a powerful east wind" (14:21). The same idea is expressed by the breath of the Lord (v. 10) which caused the sea to return to its bed and thereby to overwhelm the hapless Egyptians.

The purpose of the song is not to praise the heroic exploits of the Lord for their own sake but to see beyond them to the victory achieved by him. His success put beyond any question his incomparability. As Moses put it, "Who among the gods is like you, O LORD? Who is like you—majestic in holiness, awesome in glory, working wonders?" (Exod. 15:11 NIV). Hearing of these things the nations would tremble and be terrified. The Canaanites in particular would "melt away; terror and dread will fall upon them" (vv. 15–16 NIV), thus preparing the way for Israel's conquest. Their residence in the land of promise will be everlasting and over them "the LORD will reign for ever and ever!" (v. 18).

Before we leave the song, it will be helpful to give some attention to the sea motif that weaves itself throughout, for Moses' intention clearly was to link the exodus deliverance with God's work of creation. We have already dealt with the creation narrative of Genesis 1 and noted that the scene as described on day one was that of a formless chaos. The earth was without shape and was empty of life and structure, covered over by the waters of the great deep (Gen. 1:2). The Spirit of God hovered over the whole scene until God gathered all the waters into one place, and the dry land appeared (vv. 2, 9–10). The idea clearly is one of taming the unruly sea and bringing it into submission so that life could originate and fill the earth. While one should not read into this any notion of an imperfect creation (to say nothing of the sea as the personification of evil resistance to the will of God), God's restraint of the sea and its division and separation from the dry land set the stage for the employment of imagery in later texts in which the sea represents antagonism to the Lord which he must constantly subdue (cf. Job 9:8; 38:8; Ps. 33:7; 74:13; 89:9–10; Isa. 27:1; Jer. 5:22).[15]

This imagery occurs in the Song of Moses and is applied both to Egypt and, by extension, to all forces that rise up to oppose the Lord and his people. In the case of Egypt, the sea was the Lord's agent of the destruction of its armies, having been brought under his dominion for that purpose. They were hurled into the sea (v. 1) and drowned (v. 4). The depths covered them (v. 5) after the Lord had piled up the waters like a wall on both sides (v. 8) and then permitted the sea to return to its bed (v. 10). The Psalter, reflecting on the exodus redemption, also presents the sea as an instrument of judgment against the enemies of the Lord (Ps. 106:11) and, at the same time, as his servant effecting the deliverance of his chosen people (Ps. 66:6; 106:9). In the latter text the Lord is said to have "rebuked the Red Sea, and it dried up" (Ps. 106:9). The verb translated *rebuke* (Heb. *gʿr*) invariably has a ring of authority to it, the sense of putting someone or something in its place (cf. Zech. 3:2; Mal. 3:11). The same verb occurs in Nahum 1:4, which says of the LORD that "He rebukes the sea so that it dries up, and He makes all the rivers run dry."

Psalm 77 recounts the exodus crossing in terms that view the Red Sea waters as an adversary that must be bent to God's will. The poet declares, "The waters saw You, God. The waters saw You; they trembled. Even the depths shook" (v. 16). Then, speaking of the Lord, he continues, "Your way went through the sea, and Your path through the great waters, but Your footprints were unseen" (v. 19). The docile sea had first to be tamed, and then it could provide a pathway for Israel's redemption.

Isaiah, however, made the clearest case for the sea as a hostile power that must be overcome if Israel was to find safe passage. In a strong appeal that God will act on Israel's behalf in the present and in the eschaton, the prophet harked back to the exodus, God's redemptive act *par excellence*:

> Wake up, Wake up!
> Put on the strength of the LORD's power.
> Wake up as in days past,
> As in generations of long ago.

---

[15] Gerhard Hasel, "The Polemic Nature of the Genesis Cosmology," *EvQ* 46 (1974): 81–102.

Wasn't it You who hacked Rahab to pieces,
who pierced the sea monster?
Wasn't it You who dried up the sea,
The waters of the great deep,
Who made the sea-bed into a road
for the redeemed to pass over? (Isa. 51:9–10).

Like some mythical monster Rahab personified the Red Sea and only its total subjugation by the Lord could make Israel's deliverance possible.[16] At the same time Rahab refers at least obliquely to Egypt, a point suggested in Psalm 89 which, referring to the exodus, says, "You [the LORD] crushed Rahab like one who is slain; You scattered Your enemies with Your powerful arm" (v. 10). Israel's redemption was therefore not without opposition. Mighty Egypt, the epitome of human political power, tried to thwart it as did the sea, the metaphor of all powers, seen and unseen, that stand in implacable resistance to God's saving purposes.

The experience of the exodus was instrumental in forming the people Israel into the nation Israel because it revealed in unmistakable terms that God was about to do something significant for and through them that would advance the kingdom program. Moreover, it taught the people that their God was true to his promises to the fathers and that he had the capacity to overcome all obstacles to bring them to fruition. At the same time, their incessant complaints in the immediate aftermath of their deliverance, complaints that reached the point of outright rebellion against the Lord and his spokesman Moses (cf. Exod. 16:8; 17:1–4), appeared to imperil the relationship the exodus was intended to facilitate. Would the community disintegrate even before it reached the appointed place and time God had set in which to encounter them with the next stage of kingdom development? The answer obviously is no, for the Lord had assured Moses that once the exodus deliverance had been accomplished he would meet them at the sacred mountain and they would worship him there (Exod. 3:12). Moreover, his promises to the fathers were inviolable; and based on them the people Israel were guaranteed safe passage to the promised land, the arena in which they would accomplish the mission of being a blessing to all the nations (3:16–17; 6:6–8).

[16] For this kind of imagery in the Old Testament, see Mary K. Wakeman, *God's Battle with the Monster: A Study in Biblical Imagery* (Leiden: Brill, 1973).

The Covenant at Sinai

The arrival of Israel at Sinai and the events that occurred there were as momentous as the exodus itself, for there the people became a nation founded on a covenant that both constituted them as such and provided the mechanism by which they could live out the privileges and responsibilities inherent in a new relationship with the Lord. The nature and function of this covenant will receive full attention in section 3, but we must treat it to some extent now as an element in the creation of Israel as a national entity.

At the outset we must stress again that Israel's encounter with the Lord at Sinai was not to make them the people of the Lord by sovereign choice. That had been done by anticipation in the framework of the Abrahamic covenant and in reality by the emergence of Jacob and his family as a discrete ethnic and social entity in Egypt if not before. The Sinai event was designed to bring this people into the awesome presence of the Lord at the site already sanctified by his appearance to Moses forty years earlier. There they were to be presented with the offer of serving the Lord God as his servant nation, the nation descended from Abraham that would be a blessing and the means of blessing all the peoples of the earth (Gen. 12:2–3; 22:18; 26:4).

The presentation of the offer is clear and concise (Exod. 19:3–6). Moses must remind his people that the Lord had afflicted and defeated Egypt and by a mighty act of redemption had brought them to himself, that is, to the holy mountain (v. 4). The reference to eagles' wings makes clear that Israel had nothing to do with its own salvation; rather, the Lord had picked them up and by his own power and grace had saved them from onerous Egyptian bondage. What followed next was the condition that must be met if Israel was to be the Lord's "treasured possession," that is, "a kingdom of priests and a holy nation" (vv. 5–6 NIV). Close examination of the text reveals that it was not Israel's status as a people or even its relationship with the Lord that was at stake. They were his people and had been since the Lord foresaw them by promise. What was conditional was the nation's privilege of being a treasured possession with its corollary responsibilities. And that condition was complete obedience to the Lord and faithful compliance with the covenant he was about to offer to them.

The phrase "treasured possession" (Heb. *sĕgullâ*) refers in general to personal property but when used of Israel describes that nation as the most precious of all the assets claimed by God.[17] Deuteronomy uses this imagery to speak of Israel's unique relationship to the Lord (Deut. 7:6), in one case linking it to the idea of Israel's holiness, that is, its radical distinction and separation from all other nations (Deut. 14:2). Psalm 135:4 declares that "the LORD has chosen *(bāḥar)* Jacob for Himself, Israel as His treasured possession." Finally, speaking of eschatological Israel, the Lord asserts that "they will be Mine, . . . a special possession on the day I am preparing" (Mal. 3:17). When this happens, "you will again see the difference between the righteous and the wicked, between one who serves God and one who does not serve Him" (Mal. 3:18). To be God's treasured possession means that Israel must be separate and distinct from all other nations.

Though the verb *choose* does not appear in Exodus 19:4–6, it is clearly implied in the Lord's disclosure that "although all the earth is Mine, . . . you will be My kingdom of priests and My holy nation" (vv. 5–6). Out of all the options available to him, the Lord chose Israel, here, of course, for special service to the kingdom. But the choice was not purely random or arbitrary, either, for as Deuteronomy puts it, "The LORD was devoted to you and chose you, not because you were more numerous than all peoples, for you were the fewest of all peoples. But because the LORD loved you and kept the oath He swore to your fathers, He brought you out with a strong hand and redeemed you from the place of slavery" (Deut. 7:7–8). To put it another way, the Lord chose Israel because of a love for them based on the promises to the patriarchs. Nothing in or about Israel commended them to him except his faithfulness to the covenant he had made with their ancestors.

If the conditions of full obedience to the Lord and to the terms of the impending covenant were to be met, Israel could serve him as a "kingdom of priests" *(mamleket kōhănîm)* and a "holy nation" *(gôy qādôš)*. These two terms have occasioned a great deal of discussion; but in the context of the Mosaic covenant, one commonly described as a suzerain-

---

[17] E. Lipinski, סגלה, *TDOT* 10:144–48; M. Greenberg, "Hebrew *sᵉgullā*: Akkadian *sikiltu*," *JAOS* 71 (1971): 172–74.

vassal treaty text, they should be understood as functional terms.[18] That is, they explain not so much what Israel was to be but what Israel was to do, namely, to function in a mediatorial role between the Lord and all other nations.

The first of these descriptors, "kingdom of priests," is not intended to mean that all Israelites were to be priests in the technical sense but that the nation as a whole and collectively would serve the Lord in the role of priest.[19] Israel's later priests in general had many responsibilities including the communication of divine revelation, the offering of sacrifices on behalf of the community, and the teaching of Torah. These were among the duties to which the Lord was calling Israel at this critical juncture. By fulfilling them, they, as the seed of Abraham, would become the means of blessing all the peoples of the earth. Just as the priest in any religious system stands between God and the people and the people and God, so Israel's ministry would be one of intercession and intermediation between the God of all creation and the peoples of earth whom he desired to restore to perfect fellowship with himself.

The term *holy nation,* on the other hand, suggests not so much an intermediary activity as a state of being. For the first time Israel would be called no longer just a people *(ʿam)* but a nation *(gôy),* that is, a discrete and ethnically identifiable political entity that would take its place among all the other nations of the world. As such it would serve a priestly function, indeed; but it would be especially marked by its status as a people set apart by God to be his uniquely and one exhibiting, by its laws and conduct, a model of morality and righteousness to which all nations should aspire. This understanding is in line with the fundamental idea of the root *qdš,* which means "be cut off from" in the sense of being distinctly different.[20] As an adjective (as here), it carries various nuances such as commanding respect, being consecrated for, or exhibiting moral and ethical purity. The last of these may be especially clarified by the commonly adduced epithet of the Lord that he is holy (cf. Lev. 11:44–45; 19:2; 1 Sam. 6:20; Ps. 22:3; Isa. 1:4; 6:3; 10:20; Hos. 11:9; etc.). For Israel to be a holy nation called for a deportment that would cause the

[18] George E. Mendenhall, "Covenant Forms in Israelite Tradition," *BA* 17 (1954): 50–76.

[19] Umberto Cassuto, *A Commentary on the Book of Exodus,* trans. Israel Abrahams (Jerusalem: Magnes Press, 1967), 227.

[20] *HALOT* 2:1072–73.

peoples of the earth to see in Israel's behavior a reflection of the God they professed to serve.

This was the challenge to Israel at Sinai if they chose to enter into covenant with the Lord. Theirs would be an inestimable privilege, but at the same time the commitment they made would entail enormous responsibility. Should they refuse God's gracious overtures, he surely would work out his redemptive program by some other means, the nature of which defies human imagination. In fact, even though Israel agreed to the covenant terms, their subsequent history displayed an abysmal failure to keep them; yet God worked out a plan of redemption, Israel's historical failure notwithstanding. We shall see the outworking of this alternative course of action in due course.

To continue speculating, one might ask what would have happened had Israel refused the offer of a covenant, a matter that is obviously moot since the record informs us of their ready acceptance of whatever obligations it might lay upon them: "We will do all that the LORD has spoken" (Exod. 19:8). The faith (or rashness) of this avowal is impressive indeed, for the Lord had not yet outlined the terms of the agreement, not even to Moses it seems. Then, by a service of consecration, Moses prepared the people for an encounter with their God, one so awesome in its potential that they must keep at a safe distance from the mountain where the Lord would manifest his presence (Exod. 19:14–19). Meanwhile, the Lord's response to the people's acceptance of the covenant was the display of his theophanic glory on the mountain summit. By thunder, lightning, and cloud, he announced his intentions to enter into covenant with Israel. As the narrative describes it, "Moses brought the people out of the camp to meet with God, and they stood at the foot of the mountain" (v. 17).

The book of the covenant (Exod. 20:1–23:33) contains the covenant text to which both the Lord and Israel committed themselves. Since we shall fully develop the historical and theological significance of this text at a more appropriate place, it will suffice for now to bring to a conclusion the discussion of Israel's emergence as a covenant nation by giving only brief attention to the ceremony that solidified that development and testified to the new reality of Israel's life and role before God.

It was customary for parties to a covenant or treaty in the ancient Near Eastern world to celebrate their newly established relationship by sharing in a common meal. Exodus 24 describes this very thing, making clear the idea that the Lord and Israel were now linked in a partnership of mutual obligation that would forever alter the course of human history. First, Moses, Aaron and his sons, and seventy elders—all representing the people as a whole—were invited to meet God at the sacred mountain, though only Moses was permitted to ascend to its top (vv. 1–2). Moses then returned to the people with the revelation of the covenant terms; and when he read them out, the people gladly assented to keep them (v. 3). To symbolize the mutual pledges of the Lord and the people, Moses erected an altar surrounded by twelve stone pillars, the altar representing the Lord, and the pillars the twelve tribes of Israel. Priests then offered up fellowship offerings *(šĕlāmîm),* sacrifices appropriate to the occasion of bringing contracting parties together into a common bond.[21] The sprinkling of the blood on the altar and stones portrayed the binding nature of the relationship that was being effected. Once more the people, on cue, affirmed their intention to be wholly obedient to what the covenant required (v. 7). Next, Moses and his close associates ascended the mountain again and there, on behalf of the community, partook of a meal in the presence of the Lord who appeared in indescribable splendor (vv. 10–11). Finally, the Lord revealed his pleasure at the commitment of the people by displaying his glory for six days on the top of Sinai and then inviting Moses to remain there while he disclosed further information relative to Israel's new status as the nation called to serve him (vv. 13–18).

This brief review of the historical circumstances of Israel's development from a seed to a people to a nation has approached the subject primarily from the external standpoint with little attention to the theology that called the nation into existence and located it within the larger redemptive program of God. This will be done at a more appropriate point. We have thus far attempted to provide the foundation for the kingdom theology to be fully articulated in the next section of our work, a foundation which, in our view, must give consideration to the person and nature of God and then to humanity in all its aspects and development. Upon this foundational understanding it will be possible to explore the meaning and outworking of the kingdom of God, the concept which, to our mind, is the proper integrating theme of a consistent biblical theology. We will therefore address that concept in the remainder of this work.

---

[21] Richard E. Averbeck, שלם, *NIDOTTE* 4:139–40.

PART THREE

THE KINGDOM OF GOD

Chapter Ten

God and the World

The controlling thesis of the present work is that God, who has existed from eternity past, interrupted the endless eons by a mighty work of creation in which he brought about an arena over which he might display his glory and power as the sovereign Lord. His immanence in doing so is balanced, however, by his transcendence, a distancing from the material universe that underscores his separateness from it as an aspect of his holiness. The bridging of the chasm between God, the ineffable one, and his creation in general was accomplished by the creation of mankind as God's image and likeness. To this privileged creature was assigned the responsibility of stewardship over all else that God had made. God the Great King thus deigned to administer his kingdom through a surrogate ruler, not as an afterthought but as the central feature of his grand design for history and eternity.

We turn now to the kingdom theme in three stages: God and the world, God and Israel, and God and the future, each as a major section of our work. There must of necessity be some overlap with ground already covered because by its nature biblical theology cannot be neatly categorized by discrete, mutually exclusive compartments. In parts 1 and 2 we have focused on God and mankind as theological concepts necessary to the development of the idea of kingdom, which, in the Old Testament, is the expression of God's rule through those made as his image. These twin concepts must inevitably emerge over and over again in any discussion of the kingdom, for the kingdom obviously does not exist in the abstract. With these considerations in mind, we now address the kingdom theme with all its variegated richness.

The Concept of the Kingdom

The word *kingdom* (Heb. *mamlākâ*) occurs only twice in Genesis (Gen. 10:10; 20:9) and in each case refers to a human realm. In fact, the phrase "kingdom of God" (or "of the Lord") occurs only once in the entire Old Testament (2 Chron. 13:8). In addition, Psalm 103:19 speaks of "His [the Lord's] kingdom" that "rules over all," and David says of the saints of God that "they will speak of the glory of Your kingdom" and its "glorious splendor," for "Your kingdom is an everlasting kingdom; Your rule *(memšālâ)* is for all generations" (Ps. 145:11–13).

Absence of the technical terms by no means suggests absence of the idea of God's kingdom, however, whether in Genesis or pervasively throughout the Old Testament. In our view it is the dominant theological motif, a proposal that must, of course, be supported by the evidence. Even the biblical witness of the Lord as supremely independent, self-sufficient, and wholly apart from whatever exists besides him presupposes his kingship, at least when kingship is understood in terms of a status superior to that of anyone or anything else. By definition a king must have a realm and subjects if he is to have any legitimate claim to the title. In the Old Testament view, God the King reigns over heaven and earth, a dominion populated by the heavenly hosts and earthly inhabitants created to praise him and serve him world without end.

The kingdom story begins with the first sentence of the Bible: "In the beginning God created the heavens and the earth" (Gen. 1:1). By this simple but majestic affirmation, both king and realm are introduced; and in the six days that follow, the citizens of the kingdom, inanimate and animate, appear in their course until mankind, the crowning glory of the Creator, takes center stage. The sequence of the subjects of creation demonstrates a line of progress that leads unmistakably to a structure of hierarchy in which the higher orders are to dominate the lower, mankind itself resting at the apex. Formlessness and emptiness give way to order, darkness succumbs to light, and land emerges from the great deep. From the ground vegetation sprouts and then marine and aerial life comes into being. The higher orders of mammals and other land creatures follow and then, at last, the human race. The stage has been set, the players are ready, and the drama may now begin.

The principal player, of course, is the Lord. His kingly role is apparent in his merely speaking the powerful word that brings into existence things that had never before been (Gen. 1:3, 6, 9, 11, 14, 20, 24, 26). The command "let there be" is imperious, not hesitant or doubtful. The whole narrative shows design, purpose, direction, order, and significance. An end is clearly rooted in divine omniscience and backed by divine omnipotence. A secondary role is acted out by mankind, one in an order of ascending sovereignty already implicit in the unfolding of the account. Light overcomes darkness, land prevails over sea, life dominates the inanimate, land animals are superior to all other beasts, and man, we see clearly, is master over all in nature, position, and authority.

What is implicit up till the creation of man becomes explicit from that point onward. We have already dealt with mankind's creation and attributes[1] so it suffices here to concentrate on his function within the context of God's universal rule. This is articulated in what may be described as a creation or dominion mandate (Gen. 1:26–28), the first statement in the Bible that delineates who and what man is and what he is to do within the framework of God's creation design. The whole can be compressed into the two action verbs of the text, namely, to *rule (rdh)* and to *subdue (kbš)*. The former verb has overtones of treading and thus describes rule by force or even oppression.[2] For example, it occurs in Leviticus 25 where the Israelites are forbidden to rule ruthlessly over fellow Israelites who have become bond servants (vv. 45–46, 53). On the other hand, when Israel goes into exile for its sins, its enemies will rule over them oppressively (Lev. 26:17). More positively, Balaam states, "One who comes from Jacob will rule; he will destroy the city's survivors" (Num. 24:19), a clear messianic reference (cf. v. 17). That

---

[1] See pp. 104–7.

[2] *HALOT* 2:1190.

same figure will "rule from sea to sea" and "his enemies [will] lick the dust" (Ps. 72:8–9). Finally, of David and his messianic descendant it is said, "The LORD will extend Your mighty scepter from Zion. Rule (here the imperative) over Your surrounding enemies" (Ps. 110:2).

The mandate to Adam and Eve thus anticipates a rule by coercion, looking proleptically as it does to the fall and curse that will alienate God from his creation, a creation always in rebellion against him. The second verb in the pair *(kbš)*, much less commonly used, reinforces this understanding because it too occurs regularly with the idea of overbearing rule.[3] Moses, for example, told the eastern tribes that they could settle down in the Transjordan only after Canaan "is subdued before the LORD" (Num. 32:22), a reference to the conquest. Joshua used the verb to speak of that conquest once it had come to pass (Josh. 18:1), and it also summarized David's defeat of his various enemies (2 Sam. 8:11). Amos employed *kbš* as he excoriated the oppressors of Israel "who trample on the needy" (Amos 8:4). Jeremiah rebuked his fellow citizens for having brought back their freed bond slaves to place them in subjection once again (Jer. 34:11, 16). David referred to all Israel as having gained control of the land (1 Chron. 22:18); but as late as the postexilic period, Nehemiah had to address the problem of Jews putting their own children into slavery *(kbš)* in order to pay off their debts (Neh. 5:5).

Thus, man's assignment was clear. He was to exercise mastery over all creation—and in the order of their creation and level of sovereignty: fish, birds, land animals. This is what it meant to be God's image and to represent him on the earth. But mankind's dominion was not to be one of iron-fisted subjugation only. In fact, we have already proposed that the mandate as worded in Genesis 1:26–28 foresaw a time when such rule would be necessary only because of the negative consequences of the fall. A different emphasis appears in Genesis 2 where the pristine conditions of the paradisiacal world are in view. No plant life had sprouted from the ground at the beginning because "there was no man to work the ground" (Gen. 2:5). Work, then, was also part of the mandate, the part that authorized man to eat of the produce of the soil to sustain himself and his descendants (Gen. 1:29–30).

[3] *HALOT* 1:460.

The notion that work is a necessary evil bereft of any pleasure or nobility is far short of the biblical idea. Even the curse on the human race that made work onerous has not altered the fact that work has value in itself, and all the more when it is done in pursuit of kingdom values. The verb *work (ʿbd)* occurs first, in fact, with a divine subject. God "completed His work that He had done, and He rested on the seventh day from all His work that He had done" (Gen. 2:2; cf. v. 3). For man to work is to function as the image of God.

The arena of man's work was the garden, a microcosm, we will argue, of the whole universe. If he could rule there, he might be fit to rule a greater realm (cf. Matt. 25:21, 23). The whole garden—not just the tree of the knowledge of good and evil—was a place of probation where man and woman could demonstrate their capacity to serve the Lord as he had created them to do. Along with working the garden man was to take care of it (v. 15). The distinction between the two verbs (*ʿbd* and *šmr*) is not great, but the latter carries with it a sense of responsibility for what had been entrusted. Adam and Eve must not only initiate the process of serving God by work, but they must carry it forward as a permanent assignment.[4] At least part of that assignment was the care of the animal world over which man had been placed. His naming of them demonstrated not only his sovereignty, a point noted earlier, but also his personal interest in them (vv. 19–20). He was not to be a cruel and heartless despot but a beneficent provider for all the creatures that were so dependent on him.

The Concept of Sacred Space

The Garden of Eden

We refer to the garden as a microcosm of the universe, a sacred space where man and woman first encountered the Lord according to

[4] Mathews draws attention to the use of the verb in covenant-keeping contexts, a most appropriate use here. See Kenneth A. Mathews, *Genesis 1–11:26,* NAC 1A (Nashville: Broadman & Holman, 1996), 210.

the record.[5] It was sacred precisely because it was invested with God's presence. The concept of sacred space unfolds with the progress of revelation, manifesting itself in altars, shrines, tabernacles, and temples, until in eschatological times the whole world becomes holy ground. At a later point we will consider Israel's understanding of the matter, but for now we will attend to the notion of sacred space in general terms and in pre-Israelite times.

The garden in Eden was a perfect environment. God himself had planted it with flora of all kinds that were both beautiful ("pleasing in appearance," Gen. 2:9) and good for food. A river ran through it to provide irrigation; and from it the river flowed in four directions, carrying something of the blessing of Paradise to the rest of the world.[6] Then God placed man there (vv. 8, 15). And God named Adam as the ruler and caretaker, delegating to him the authority to name the animals and later even his wife (vv. 19–20; 3:20). As we noted earlier, even the act of naming was indicative of rulership. God could have named the animals himself; but in line with his purpose for mankind as his image, he "brought each to the man to see what he would call it. And whatever the man called a living creature, that was its name" (v. 19). The line of command is clear: God the sovereign reigns over his kingdom through the human race which he created and placed in the garden for that purpose.

Eviction from Sacred Space

The perfection of the Edenic sacred space was soon shattered, however, by the devastating consequences of man's premeditated rebellion against the Lord. What was at stake in man's temptation and fall was the very thing under consideration here, namely, the question of kingdom hierarchical authority. To portray it in any other way is to lose sight of the central issue of the Bible, *viz,* who indeed is God and how does everything else relate to him? The serpent (i.e., Satan) usurped the role of the man—who

---

[5] For the notion of sacred space in general, see Mircea Eliade, *Cosmos and History,* trans. Willard R. Trask (New York: Harper & Row, 1959), 6–21; for a more theological view, see Walther Eichrodt, *Theology of the Old Testament,* vol. 1, trans. J. A. Baker (Philadelphia: Westminster, 1961), 102–7.

[6] For the configuration of the rivers and their relationship to the garden, see E. A. Speiser, "The Rivers of Paradise," *Oriental and Biblical Studies,* ed. J. J. Finkelstein and M. Greenberg (Philadelphia: University of Pennsylvania, 1967), 23–34.

after all had named him!—and man, having succumbed, usurped the role of God. The serpent had said to the woman, "God knows that when you eat it [the tree] your eyes will be opened and you will be like God" (Gen. 3:5). Even the Lord conceded after the fact that "man has become like one of Us, knowing good and evil" (Gen. 3:22).

The first challenge to divine sovereignty came about through a scheme designed to rearrange the spheres of authority and responsibility established by the Lord at creation. Though Satan was behind the scheme, he presented himself as a mere animal in order that the subordinate (the animal realm) might subvert the position of the superior (mankind), thus leading the superior to challenge the headship of him who is Most Superior (the Lord). The success of the strategy is clear from both the immediate biblical narrative and the sorry course of human history ever since. It is not too much off the mark to interpret history as the account of a crippled kingdom that God is healing and repairing and that he will someday bring back to perfect wholeness.

To focus now on the immediate aftermath of the fall and its impact on the kingdom, we must take note of a number of matters. First is the series of warnings and curses that the Lord directed to the animal, the woman, and the man, in that order. The animal's status, represented by its crawling on its belly and "eating" dust, would henceforth be more servile than ever. Moreover, there would be incessant hostility between the animal world and that of mankind until human dominion was enforced by crushing the life out of the vicious contender for illegitimate privilege. The text is speaking ultimately, of course, of the victory of the seed of the woman over Satan, here in the garb of a snake; but the enmity between man and beast is also in view and finds elaboration in our narrative and those immediately following.

The death of an animal implicit in the garments of skin the Lord made for Adam and Eve suggests not only a substitutionary atonement in germinal form but the permissibility of animal slaughter for this purpose and for other purposes as well, including for human consumption. Abel was a herdsman, an occupation that clearly presupposes domestication, exploitation, and even death of the animal for which he cared. Cain's descendant Jabal was "the father of the nomadic herdsmen" (Gen. 4:20), again with all this suggests for animal subordination. Noah's ability to gather every kind of animal into the ark seems to suggest a kind of natural domination on his part, though, of course, the Lord himself may have tamed them with a supernatural docility for the purpose of saving them. But Noah's selection of seven of every species of clean animal (Gen. 7:2) was ominous, for it anticipated a time when these animals would be offered up as a tribute to the Lord (Gen. 8:20).

Most significant, however, was the radically altered relationship between mankind and the animal world spelled out in the details of the Noahic covenant (Gen. 9:1–7). The old Edenic mandate to "be fruitful, multiply, fill the earth" was followed now not with "subdue it" and "rule the fish of the sea, the birds of the sky, and every creature that crawls on the earth" (Gen. 1:28). Rather, Noah learned that all of these creatures, once so harmoniously compliant to man's every directive, would be terrified of him and, moreover, would be "placed under your authority" (Gen. 9:2). This last statement bears heavy overtones of threat and warning. Man the vegetarian could now become man the carnivore for the mutual trust and recognition of levels of sovereignty that were inherent in creation were no longer operative—at least unimpededly—in a world alienated from God and already judged by him in a cataclysmic flood.

Eschatological Renewal of Sacred Space

The disruption of the kingdom in this respect continues to this day. Man has continued his domination of the animal world, even going so far as to domesticate some to his service, but the domination is achieved only by force and superior intellect and not by the willing subservience intended by the creation mandate. Only eschatological texts speak of a time of the peaceable kingdom when all of God's creatures will live in perfect harmony and bliss. Paul anticipated it in light of the present situation in which "the creation eagerly waits with anticipation for God's sons to be revealed. For the creation was subjected to futility—not willingly, but because of Him who subjected it—in the hope that the creation itself will also be set free from the bondage of corruption into the glorious freedom of God's children" (Rom. 8:19–21). This certainly includes the animal world. In the same epistle the apostle drew attention to another consequence of the inversion of the human and animal relationship. Speaking of the pagans he commented that "claiming to be wise, they became fools and exchanged the glory of the immortal God for images resembling mortal man, birds, four-footed animals, and reptiles" (Rom.

1:22–23). No longer did man have dominion over all things; instead, he abdicated his role as sovereign and worshipped what he should have ruled.

What Paul yearned for the prophets had already foreseen. Isaiah anticipated a day when the spheres of sovereignty would once more be properly aligned and peace among them would become a reality:

> The wolf will live with the lamb,
> And the leopard will lie down with the goat.
> The calf, the young lion, and the fatling
> will be together,
> and a child will lead them.
> The cow and the bear will graze,
> their young ones will lie down together,
> and the lion will eat straw like an ox.
> An infant will play beside the cobra's pit,
> And a toddler will put his hand
> into a snake's den.
> No one will harm or destroy
> on My entire holy mountain,
> for the land will be as full
> of the knowledge of the LORD
> As the sea is filled with water (Isa. 11:6–9).

The same prophet, emphasizing in a different passage the Lord's conquest over evil, described that day of kingdom blessing as one in which "the serpent's food will be dust" (Isa. 65:25), clearly referring to the curse on the serpent (Gen. 3:14).[7]

Ezekiel, speaking of the Davidic kingdom of the last days, prophesied that the Lord "will make a covenant of peace with [Israel] and eliminate dangerous animals in the land, so that they may live securely in the wilderness and sleep in the forest" (Ezek. 34:25). Hosea went so far as to include the animals in a reconciliation with human kind: "On that day I will make a covenant for them with the wild animals, the birds of the sky, and the creatures that crawl on the ground" (Hos. 2:18). The curse of the fall will be undone, and God's creatures—man and animal alike—will

---

[7] Walter Brueggemann, *Isaiah 40–66* (Louisville: Westminster John Knox, 1998), 250.

resume the roles *vis-à-vis* each other that God purposed for them from the beginning.

We have already suggested ways Jesus may have demonstrated on a few occasions the dominion of the animal world foretold by the prophets, providing thereby a glimpse into the norm that will characterize the kingdom to come.[8] If the mandate that empowered mankind to rule over the animal realm (Gen. 1:26) had any literal reality at all, then one should expect that such power would extend to Jesus' mastery of brute beasts, enabling them to serve him and man in unimaginable ways. What he did in those instances may well, indeed, have been a display of his deity. But could they not equally as well be reflective of his regal authority as the second Adam (1 Cor. 15:22; cf. 15:45)?

Some may challenge these assertions of Jesus' earthly dominion and perhaps even question that mankind's dominion over creation extended to such practical, mundane extremes. In response we can only ask what form man's dominion ought to take in light of the authority granted him in Genesis. If we, as fallen beings, can train and bend to our use the animal world around us, what capacity did sinless Adam and Eve possess to rule over all other creatures that themselves had not become corrupted by the fall? Only the eschatological texts already cited provide any kind of certain answer, but the examples of Jesus may also provide some glimpse into what that dominion may have entailed.

If one effect of the fall on the kingdom concept was the hostility between mankind and other creatures because of the inversion of sphere sovereignties, the second was the exclusion of man and woman from the sacred space where untrammeled access to the presence of God was possible. At first all seemed well, for as Adam and Eve moved about the garden, they sensed the presence of the Lord as before (Gen. 3:8a). However, they now were physically naked and spiritually vulnerable, keenly aware that they could no longer encounter the God with whom they had enjoyed fellowship. For his part, the Lord consigned them to a life of pain and struggle, clothed them with a garment of his own making, and banned them from the garden, from his own holy presence (Gen. 3:23–24). They had tried to be like God just as the animal had tried to be like man. Now both man and animal found themselves restricted to their

---

[8] See pp. 172–173.

proper roles but lacking the freedom to exploit the potentialities with which they had been created.

Altars and Shrines as Sacred Space

The abandonment of Eden as sacred space did not foreclose the notion that God touched earth and dwelled among mankind in certain places. His omnipresence notwithstanding, he chose to appear in special locales whose boundaries were clearly circumscribed and where he could be approached by individuals and communities committed to clearly defined protocols. These latter were associated with cultus, that is, with certain rites and liturgies that paved the way to audience with the Holy One. Only as they were adhered to could the worshipper gain access to him. The link between sacred space and access to it is intimated early on in the Old Testament but only with the revelation of the Torah law at Sinai were its full ramifications clarified. Until that matter can be broached, we must for the moment restrict ourselves to the development of this complex of ideas in the pre-Mosaic era.

The first narrative about worship relates the respective offerings by Cain and Abel of their produce to the Lord (Gen. 4:1–5). Sacred space plays no role here—not even an altar is mentioned—but the two worshippers clearly understood that access to the Lord demanded certain procedures. We have considered the outcome already, and there is no need to rehearse it here.[9] What matters at this point is the fact that access to the Holy One was no longer automatic as it was in the garden. Encounter with him would henceforth necessitate prescribed form and ritual. However, Cain's failure did consign him to a distance from the Lord, a distance, he said, that came about because he "must hide [himself] from [God's] presence" (Gen. 4:14). Just as his parents were banished from the garden and thus excluded from God's nearness, so Cain was exiled even more from sacred space, left to be a "restless wanderer on the earth" (v. 12; cf. v. 16).

Sacred space thereafter became associated with altars and their immediate environs. Yet, as limited as they were, they represented a divine claim on the earth, a stake as it were that signified that kingdom claims had not been abandoned. Mankind may have been banished from

---

[9] See p. 219.

the garden, but God had not been exiled from the world. He was still King, and he could still be approached but only at times and places of his own choosing.

Noah's altar was such a place, its acceptability ratified by the fact that the Lord was pleased with the aroma of sacrifice and promised Noah then and there never again to destroy the earth in a flood (Gen. 8:20–22). On the other hand, the tower of Babel symbolized the antithesis of God's presence. Man was at home there (Gen. 11:4), but God had to come down from heaven to see what was going on (v. 5).[10] Beginning with Abraham, God's presence was usually manifested by an appearance called *theophany,* a disclosure at a certain place that transformed it into sacred space.[11] When he first arrived in Canaan, the patriarch built an altar at Shechem "to the LORD who had appeared to him" (Gen. 12:7). The altar marked the place as holy ground, and from that time forward Shechem enjoyed that status.[12] Jacob, Abraham's grandson, made Shechem his first stop upon his return from Paddan Aram and there bought a piece of land upon which to build an altar (Gen. 33:18–20). He did this without doubt because of Shechem's association with Abraham to whom the Lord had appeared at that place. More than half a millennium later Joshua gathered the Israelite tribes at Shechem. Harking back to the days of Abraham and the patriarchs, Joshua led the community in a ceremony of covenant renewal before the Lord, a most appropriate place in light of the Lord's appearance to Abraham there (Josh. 24:1–27). When Rehoboam centuries later attempted to consolidate all twelve tribes under his monarchy, he went to Shechem, the place of divine presence and covenant-making, sensing with the people the need for God's sanction.

Abraham's next stop, Bethel, also became a sacred site by virtue of the altar he built there, presumably (though not stated) because of an

---

[10] The Lord's "coming down" does not at all suggest a limitation to his omniscience; rather, as Cassuto observed, "There is a satiric allusion here: they imagined that the top of their tower would reach the heavens, but in God's sight their gigantic structure was only the work of pygmies, a terrestrial not a celestial enterprise, and if He that dwells in heaven wished to look at it, He had to descend from heaven to earth." U. Cassuto, *A Commentary on the Book of Genesis,* trans. Israel Abrahams (Jerusalem: Magnes, 1964), 244–45.

[11] Samuel Terrien, *The Elusive Presence* (New York: Harper & Row, 1978). Terrien prefers the term "epiphanic visitation" (p. 68).

[12] For the history of Shechem and its political and religious significance, see Bernhard W. Anderson, "The Place of Shechem in the Bible," *BA* 20/1 (1957): 10–19.

appearance by the Lord (Gen. 12:8). He revisited Bethel upon his return from Egypt; and as he had done before, he "worshiped the LORD there" (Gen. 13:3–4). It was Bethel's association with Jacob, however, that most clearly defined its significance as sacred space. On his way to Haran, Jacob rested at Bethel and in a dream saw the Lord who reminded him of the covenant promise that his descendants would fill the land and become the means of blessing the whole earth (Gen. 28:10–14). Awaking, Jacob in astonishment blurted out, "Surely the LORD is in this place, and I did not know it" (v. 16). He then observed, "This is none other than the house of God. This is the gate of heaven" (v. 17). Impressed by what had transpired, Jacob called the place Bethel, that is, "the house of God" (v. 17). Finally, to memorialize the site as a place of holy presence, Jacob erected a pillar (Heb. *maṣṣēbâ*) there, calling it, too, the house of God (v. 22).

The Lord's pleasure with Jacob on this occasion is evident from his own self-ascription as "the God of Bethel" (Gen. 31:13). That is, he ratified Jacob's (and Abraham's) selection of the site by identifying himself with it. When Jacob returned from Haran, he stopped once more at Bethel (Gen. 35:1–7), this time to build an altar and to reaffirm the name in recognition of the fact that God had revealed himself there (vv. 7, 15). The Lord then changed Jacob's name to Israel (cf. Gen. 32:28) and reiterated to him that he would sire a nation and give rise to kings (vv. 10–11). In response Jacob (re)erected a stone pillar at Bethel and consecrated it by a drink offering and an anointing of oil (v. 14). The anointing set the pillar and the place apart as a holy shrine (cf. Exod. 40:10).

Bethel's reputation as a holy place continued to the time of Samuel (1 Sam. 10:3), but after that it became the site of syncretistic worship at best and perhaps outright paganism. Upon the split of Solomon's kingdom, Jeroboam I selected Bethel as a cult site where he erected a golden calf, most likely as a pedestal upon which stood the invisible Lord (1 Kings 12:28–29). Moreover, he appointed an order of illicit priests and established his own liturgical calendar of festivals (vv. 32–33). As a result, a prophet from Judah predicted that Jeroboam's shrine would be demolished and its priests slaughtered, a prophecy that came to pass under the leadership of good King Josiah three hundred years later (1 Kings 13:1–3; cf. 2 Kings 23:15–16). Meanwhile, Bethel continued to enjoy pride of place among the holy places of the Northern Kingdom, first as a shrine favored by King Jehu

(841–814 BC) (2 Kings 10:29) and then as the chief cult center under King Jeroboam II (793–753 BC). Amos railed against the latter, prophesying that Israel's wicked ways would be terminated and the nation itself would go into exile (Amos 7:7–11).

Amos had previously condemned the paganism of Bethel (3:14; 4:4; 5:5–6) as did Hosea somewhat later (Hos. 10:15). The place continued to thrive as a place of worship, however, even into postexilic times. By then some degree of legitimacy may have returned to Bethel, and once more it may have become the house of God (cf. Zech. 7:1–3). Whether this was the case or not, Bethel is instructive in demonstrating that sacred space once made such by the presence of the Lord could become corrupted and put to the use of apostate cults. Those who converted such sites in this manner did so, however, because they recognized the sanctity of the site in the first place. That is, holy places were not created *ex nihilo* but came into being through a common recognition that they had at one time been visited by Deity.

The Temple as Sacred Space

The concept of sacred space would find its most glorious expression (although only in seed form) in the command of the Lord to Abraham to take his beloved son Isaac to "one of the mountains I will tell you about" and there offer him as a sacrifice (Gen. 22:2). Upon his arrival, Abraham proceeded to carry out God's edict, but God himself intervened and provided a substitute animal in Isaac's place (v. 13). Recognizing then that this was a special place, one hallowed by the Lord's presence, Abraham called it *YHWH Yireh,* "The Lord Will Provide" (v. 14), a name, the narrator says, that remained to his very day.

The mountain on which this took place was called simply "one of the mountains" of the "land of Moriah." The Chronicler (as well as Jewish extra-biblical tradition) identified the place as Mount Moriah, probably the most prominent peak of the area and the place where the Lord had appeared to David (2 Chron. 3:1).[13] It was there, on what today is known as the Temple Mount, that Solomon constructed the first temple, the holy place of the Lord *par excellence.* While the full implications of this holy

---

[13] For references, see Sara Japhet, *I & II Chronicles* (Louisville: Westminster/John Knox, 1993), 551–52.

site must await a later discussion, it will be useful here to provide some background to the choice of the place for the location of the temple.

Following David's capture of the city of Jerusalem, he brought the ark of the covenant into the city and placed it in a tent he had pitched for it on Mount Zion (2 Sam. 6:17; cf. Pss. 2:6; 9:11). Though the rationale for the selection of this particular place is not disclosed by the historian, various psalms make clear that the choice was appropriate because the Lord sanctified it by his presence and declared it to be the place of his dwelling (Pss. 74:2; 76:2; 132:13). But Zion was not Moriah, and the connection of Moriah to Abraham and the patriarchs was so strong and meaningful that only Moriah would suffice as the place for the Solomonic temple, a structure that by its very beauty, massiveness, and durability seemed much more suitable to the everlasting God and his presence among his people than the temporality suggested by a mere tent. David may or may not have sensed that, though he confessed how troubled he was that he was "living in a cedar house while the ark of God sits inside in tent curtains" (2 Sam. 7:2). But even if David lamented the comparative inadequacy of the tent structure and wanted to build something grander for the Lord, the question of its location remained. It must be built not just anywhere but at a place where the presence of the Lord was apparent and which had become sacred space by virtue of that fact.

The revelation of that place came about in a most unexpected manner indeed. David, having foolishly undertaken a census of his military force, thus bringing God's judgment on the nation, encountered the angel of the Lord at the threshing floor of Araunah the Jebusite and there confessed his sin of leading the people astray (2 Sam. 24:1–17). The prophet Gad then instructed David to build an altar on that spot and to offer up burnt offerings in order that the Lord might bring to an end the plague he had inflicted on them (vv. 18, 21). This altar likely became the focal point of the sanctuary that later occupied the site. The Chronicler adds the information that David was convinced by the Lord's acceptance of the sacrifice that "this is the house of the LORD God, and this is the altar of burnt offering for Israel" (1 Chron. 22:1), the latter at that time still being at the high place at Gibeon (1 Chron. 21:29). By both accounts the threshing floor of Araunah, that is, Mount Moriah, was deemed to be sacred space because the Lord had answered David there by fire, an awesome sign of his presence (1 Chron. 21:26; cf. 2 Sam. 24:25).

Further consideration of the tabernacle and temple as sacred space must be deferred for now since they related uniquely to Israel, at least insofar as the Old Testament is concerned. It should be clear by now, however, that though man and woman were expelled from the garden, the primordial and microcosmic arena of God's earthly kingdom, the Lord did not abandon either the world or its inhabitants. Indeed, he established special points of contact, other realms of holy ground sanctified by his presence where mankind could approach him and enjoy fellowship with him. These have been traced through Genesis and will be coming to our attention again, especially with refcrence to the theocratic community of Israel.

To this point we have proposed that the kingdom of God as it relates to the world of humanity in general requires kingdom participants and a realm in which it can be exercised. These participants relate to one another in clearly defined spheres or strata of authority, an arrangement implicit in the order of the creation events and placed in bold relief precisely at the point of its threatened breakdown and dissolution. God, of course, is King, a self-evident fact in view of his eternal existence, his creative power, and his delegation of regal authority to mankind. Mankind, the image of God, is his vice-regent, his servant empowered to reign in his name over all creation. As for that creation, it—in its entirety, animate and inanimate—is placed under the hegemony of the Lord mediated through the human race. As such, it is to be used but not exploited, worked but not exhausted.

The realm of God's rule is without spatial limit—the heavens and the earth—but the Old Testament views the earth as the special place where he displays his glory and grace. Here the Almighty has deigned to come among his people in a unique manner, and here mankind was to "be fruitful and multiply" and "to fill the earth, and subdue it." The proving ground was the garden, a slice of the kingdom that was to be worked and supervised until the whole world could be managed. But this realm was forfeited because of the fall so that man now reigns only with great toil and struggle. Yet God has not abdicated his throne. He still reigns and through those made in his image, but the sacred space of special communion is no longer the garden but wherever he manifests his presence, be that altar, shrine, tabernacle, or temple.

The Mediation of the Kingdom

The exercise of God's sovereignty must now be addressed. How can the Transcendent One carry out his royal purposes and yet maintain the distance inherent in his nature as God? The answer by now has become apparent—he reigns through those whom he created for that purpose, the race of beings known as mankind. The mechanism by which this authority is channeled from God to man and which governs its exercise is, in biblical terms, the covenant, an arrangement that takes on many forms according to its different functions.

The Concept of Covenant

We have already introduced the subject of the Old Testament covenants but only briefly and not in direct relationship to the kingdom motif now under consideration. We turn to that now, especially in its ramifications for humanity in general. The special covenant with Israel must await treatment later on.

The technical term for covenant (Heb. *bĕrît)* occurs first in Genesis 6:18 on the eve of the universal flood. As previously noted, the first person pronominal suffix on the noun ("My covenant") implies that it was not just then being revealed for the first time but that the term was referring to a covenant already known.[14] That covenant can only be the one intimated in the Genesis creation account, particularly in Genesis 1:26–28. This is clear for a number of reasons. First, the Lord said he would "wipe off the face of the earth: man, whom I created, together with the animals, creatures that crawl, and birds of the sky" (Gen. 6:7). The language is clearly reminiscent of Genesis 1:26 and 30. Second, the reference to "all flesh under heaven with the breath of life in it" (Gen. 6:17) harks back to Genesis 1:30. Third, and most important, the statement of "My covenant" expressed to Noah after the flood was virtually identical to the creation mandate of Genesis 1:26–28 in its central thrust (Gen. 9:1–7). The two will be more carefully scrutinized presently.

If Genesis 1:26–28 is indeed a covenant text, what is its form and function? We have already noted that two basic kinds appear in the Old Testament, one unconditional and the other conditional. Those with

[14] See pp. 239–40.

theological content are called technically either covenants by royal grant or suzerain-vassal treaties. Only the latter are by definition conditional, but it is an oversimplification to view them as mutually exclusive. The royal grant had certain conditional elements at times, and in certain respects the most famous suzerain-vassal treaty text of the Old Testament (the so-called Mosaic covenant), though apparently conditional, was articulated ultimately in terms of unconditionality.

Having drawn these formal distinctions, we must hasten to add that the biblical examples of covenants, though based on well-documented analogues from the ancient Near East, were adapted to the special needs and concerns of the Old Testament theological agenda.[15] Elements found in the secular models may be missing here, and others in the biblical texts may be unique to them alone. And it goes without saying that the contents of the Old Testament material and the wording in which it is expressed are vastly different from the ancient Near Eastern examples. All the same, careful study of the Old Testament covenants in light of those of the cultural context of the Old Testament has yielded profound exegetical and even theological insight into the biblical texts.

With these considerations in mind, we conclude that Genesis 1:26–28 is at least a truncated example of a royal grant document. The bare essentials of such a form are (1) a royal grantor, (2) a beneficiary, and (3) the elements of the grant, all of which appear here.[16] What is lacking is any statement of the background or context of the grant. What if anything had mankind done to warrant God's attention or to deserve his gracious favor? The answer obviously is nothing, since the grant was conceived of and articulated before mankind was even created. There were no conditions to be met in order for the grant to be given, nor are any stated in order for the benefits of the grant to be ongoing. Not until the prohibition against eating from the tree of the knowledge of good and evil, in fact, was there any hint of conditionality permitting man to remain in good standing with the Great King.

There is no need here to repeat what has been said already about the "creation mandate" (another term for the royal grant under consideration)

---

[15] See the helpful comments of Delbert R. Hillers, *Covenant: The History of a Biblical Idea* (Baltimore: The Johns Hopkins University Press, 1969), esp. 1–7.

[16] Moshe Weinfeld, "The Covenant of Grant in the Old Testament and in the Ancient Near East," *JAOS* 90 (1970): 184–203.

except to summarize its central element, its provisions of privilege and responsibility: mankind, the image of God, was granted the authority to reign on God's behalf and at his behest over all that he had created. This is, pure and simple, the statement to which the Lord referred when he spoke to Noah of "My covenant."

Inasmuch as the Lord promised to establish (Heb. *hăqîmōtî,* from *qwm,* a standard verb for making a covenant)[17] his covenant with Noah, it was not a new one. Noah, like Adam, was granted an undeserved privilege. Yet the elements of the grant were different because the circumstances of the covenant renewal had also become greatly different. The injunction to increase in number and fill the earth was still there, but the command to rule over all the creatures was lacking, at least in explicit terms (Gen. 9:1, 7). Instead, animals would be terrified of human beings, no longer trusting them and obeying as a matter of natural course. The only way they would continue to be subservient was by being "under your authority" (lit., "given into your hands") (v. 2), that is, by a submission forced upon them by intuitive impulses and by man's superior capacity to bend them to his will. On the other hand, so great was the disruption of the creation order and harmony occasioned by the fall that animals could now be slaughtered for human consumption (v. 3). Though nothing in the creation account had explicitly mandated that mankind should be vegetarian, the effects of the fall that now permitted the eating of meat strongly points in that direction (cf. Gen. 1:29–30).[18]

The permission to eat meat came with many strict caveats, however, restrictions that had great bearing on kingdom life and relationships. Chief among them was the principle of the sanctity of life symbolized by the disposition of blood whether animal or human. Long before the circulatory system was understood, it was most apparent that when a body was drained of its blood death was the inevitable consequence. Thus Leviticus 17:11 can say with astounding scientific accuracy that "the life of a creature is in the blood" (or as the LXX has it, "in its blood"). This is why the Old Testament (as well as modern Judaism) considers the eating

---

[17] Elmer A. Martens, קום, *NIDOTTE* 3:903–4.

[18] Victor P. Hamilton, *The Book of Genesis Chapters 1–17,* NICOT (Grand Rapids: Eerdmans, 1990), 313–14.

of blood to be taboo. Our text is clear: "You must not eat meat with its lifeblood in it" (Gen. 9:4).

The corollary to this is the termination of human life by violent means, namely, by the shedding of blood. By the logical principle of "light and heavy" (or *a fortiori*) comparison, the text makes the case that if the life of animals is sacrosanct, how much more so is the life of human beings? Moving from the prohibition to eat animal blood, the passage makes the analogous (and theological) transition to the matter of shedding human blood, not even for human consumption but simply as an act of violence resulting in the termination of life. Those who perpetrate such a heinous deed will be held accountable to God for it whether the instigator be an animal or a fellow human being (Gen. 9:5). It goes without saying that an animal that committed such a usurpatious act as to kill a man or woman would suffer the same fate. But how should homicide be treated, the killing of a human being by an equal?

The answer is clear and to the point: "Whoever sheds man's blood, his blood will be shed by man, for God made man in His image" (Gen. 9:6). The reference to man (Heb. *hāʾādām,* "the man") is not just to an individual but to mankind in general. Its use in the second line of the stanza is particularly noteworthy, for it suggests mankind collectively or, to put it in other terms, to human government. For the first time in the sacred record, mankind is viewed corporately, as an abstract entity acting in concert. Whoever murders a fellow human being must be prepared for mankind to exact vengeance. What in later texts is called *lex talionis,* the application of punishment in direct measure to the crime (Exod. 21:24; Deut. 19:21), is called for in cases like this. Otherwise, the gravity of what has been done and the underlying principle of the worth of human life is eroded and devalued.

The value of a human being resides in the fact that he or she is the image of God (v. 6). Once more the Noahic covenant reveals its continuity with the so-called Adamic, for man's *raison d'être* is to serve God as his representative on earth, reigning under and for him over all creation. To murder a human being is thus to disregard not only his inherent worth as an individual but (and perhaps more serious) to do violence to the kingdom of God itself by attacking its authorized representative. In a sense, an assault on the image of God is an assault on the one whom he serves, that is, the sovereign Lord of heaven and earth.[19]

The full implications of this for the church and the modern world, especially with regards to the sanctity of life and capital punishment, will be addressed at a later point. Long before the existence of Mosaic law, a system of universal law and government was in place that, as an arm of the Lord God, was designed to regulate and, if need be, punish human behavior.[20] It will not do, then, to ignore or sidestep such moral or even legal principles as capital punishment on the grounds that they were all "under the law." They anticipated the law of Moses, provided its foundation, and remain in place as the expression of the mind and will of a just and holy God.

This first allusion to human government is within the framework of God's kingdom, but it must not be construed as synonymous with it. Until the kingdoms of the world are fully redeemed and brought into perfect compliance with the dominion of the Lord, there will always be not only a distantiation between the two realms but a fundamental antagonism. All the same, human social and political apparatuses exist and carry out their various functions within the purview of the Great King and, indeed, under his ultimate control whether or not they themselves recognize that fact (cf. Rom. 12:19; 13:1–5).

The justification for the flood, in fact, was that "the LORD saw that man's wickedness was widespread on the earth and that every scheme his mind thought of was nothing but evil all the time" (Gen. 6:5). Though it is inaccurate perhaps to refer to man here as government or as kingdom, the term does represent a social and political structure governed by invisible spiritual forces locked in mortal combat with the Lord. Its destruction by the flood did not eradicate those underlying motivators; indeed, Noah himself predicted the rise of internecine conflict that would eventuate in the proliferation of nations hostile to one another and, as we shall see, hostile to the sovereignty of God (Gen. 9:24–27; cf. 8:21).

---

[19] William J. Dumbrell, *Covenant and Creation* (Nashville: Thomas Nelson, 1984), 28.

[20] Mathews, *Genesis 1–11:26,* 404.

Resistance to the Kingdom by the Nations

The Kingdoms of the World

The episode of the tower of Babel reveals with utmost clarity the ineradicable inclination (thus Heb. *yēṣer*; Gen. 8:21; Deut. 31:21; 1 Chron. 28:9) of mankind to assert his independence of God and to form kingdom structures inimical to God's own (Gen. 11:1–9).[21] Possessing a common speech, the "whole world" decided to solidify its unity by building a city whose tower would reach to the heavens. This represented not only competition with the kingdom of heaven but a kind of invasion, a crossing of boundary lines that said, in effect, that the kingdom of man was a threat to the kingdom of God. The motive for the project—"Let us make a name for ourselves; otherwise we will be scattered over the face of the whole earth" (v. 4)—reinforces this interpretation, for it was a blatant refusal to submit to the name of the Lord and to fulfill the creation mandate. But the Lord's sovereignty could not be so easily challenged. He therefore interrupted the work, confused the speech of the builders, and scattered those rebels all over the earth (v. 9).

The theme of the collision of kingdoms surfaces over and over in the biblical record. We have already described it with reference to Egypt where clearly the contest was not just between Pharaoh and Moses or even Egypt and Israel but between wicked spirits in high places (Egypt's gods) and the God of creation.[22] Beyond this were the nations of Canaan that illegally occupied the land God had promised to the fathers and that therefore had to be defeated and expelled or even put to the sword. The evil impulses that characterized and motivated these peoples were fundamentally spiritual in nature. They were outposts of a kingdom that transcended mere territorial boundaries, a kingdom impelled by the spirit of Babel that was eager to make a name for itself rather than concede anything to the Creator.

The prophets of Israel came to understand the antithesis between the kingdom of heaven and the kingdoms of the earth, all without exception hostile to God's saving purposes, especially as they were transmitted

---

[21] Allen P. Ross, *Creation & Blessing* (Grand Rapids: Baker, 1988), 233–34.

[22] See pp. 258–68.

through God's servant nation Israel. Again and again the nations were addressed, sometimes collectively as a world system but more often singled out for special attention. Hardly a prophet failed to include oracles against the nations so significant is this theme in the development of Israel's theology. We must therefore take careful note of how and when the nations appear in the sequence of their predicted judgment. Then we can learn from the cumulative testimony of the prophets the intensity of the nations' rebellion against the sovereignty of the Lord and the measures he took and will take to affirm his lordship in the face of human resistance. We will look first at some general or blanket assessments of the kingdoms of the earth and then turn to a consideration of the dozen or so whose history intersected with that of Israel in significant ways.

The prophet Joel, in the context of his description of the "Day of the Lord" (Joel 2:28–32), foresaw a day when all nations will be gathered at the Valley of Jehoshaphat so that the Lord might judge them there. The issue would be their mistreatment of Israel, the seed of Abraham, abuse of which was certain to bring about God's displeasure as even the Abrahamic covenant had made plain (Joel 3:1–3; cf. Gen. 12:3). The scene at Jehoshaphat would be one not only of adjudication of charges against the nations but of the application of divine punishment. The Lord would be on the bench, as it were, and would authorize the destruction of the nations as though they were crops ready to be cut down and harvested (Joel 3:12–13). So awful would that day be, it is called a time of darkness. The Lord will roar like thunder in his rage, causing nature itself to tremble (vv. 14–16). Because of their sins the nations would be depopulated, never again to be a threat to God's people. Israel, on the other hand, would come to fear the Lord and "will know that I am the LORD your God, who dwells in Zion, My holy mountain" (v. 17). Israel, at the expense of the nations, would enjoy God's blessings of abundant and fruitful life. As the earthly expression of his kingdom, they would, by his victory, reveal something of the glories of the kingdom yet to come in its fullness.

Isaiah 24, a passage with strong apocalyptic overtones, paints in graphic color the destiny of the nations that have rebelled against the Lord and his kingdom without remorse and repentance. The prophet employs the imagery of creation but in reverse—the Lord is going to undo creation, laying waste the earth and scattering its inhabitants (v. 1). The judgments of the flood and of Babel come immediately to mind. However, rather than being overwhelmed by water, the earth will be desiccated, unable to bear the fruit for which it had been created (v. 4). The reason is that the earth's peoples have defiled *(ḥnp)* it by disobeying God's laws *(tôrōt)* and statutes *(ḥōq)* and have broken *(prr)* "the everlasting covenant" (v. 5). The technical terms used here are much at home in covenant contexts, especially the Mosaic covenant, but that is not the covenant in view here. Rather, the reference is to the creation mandate and the pre-Mosaic covenants that issued from it.[23] The same verb *(prr)* is employed by Zechariah who describes the Lord as having taken a staff in his hand and broken it, thus "annulling the covenant I had made with all the peoples" (Zech. 11:10), this time referring to Israel and Judah. On the one hand, the nations break their covenant with the Lord; and on the other hand, he breaks his covenant with them. The failure of mankind to fulfill the divine design will result in their utter ruin.

In even stronger language Isaiah predicted that the earth would be rent asunder, reverting back almost to the chaotic conditions that preceded God's ordering of all things at creation (24:18b–20a). Again, the cause is human rebellion, a spirit of insubordination so grievous that the earth will fall, never to rise again (v. 20b). In a remarkable theological contribution the prophet linked the unseen demonic powers of the heavens with the kings of the earth, proclaiming that together they will be consigned to God's prison house of judgment (vv. 21–22). Isaiah leaves no doubt that the affairs of human rulers are governed by principalities and powers in a higher realm so that the struggle between kingdoms is ultimately one between the kingdom of the Lord and the kingdom of Satan, the one already identified as the protagonist in the Genesis temptation account. This will become clearer in Daniel (Dan. 10:13, 20) and fully developed in New Testament revelation (cf. John 12:19; Eph. 2:2; 3:10; 6:12). But the kings of the earth, pawns though they may be, can find no exoneration because of their role as relative subordinates. They and the nations they rule have consciously and deliberately broken God's covenant and can therefore expect nothing less than his severest reprisal.

---

[23] John N. Oswalt, *The Book of Isaiah Chapters 1–39,* NICOT (Grand Rapids: Eerdmans, 1986), 446.

Isaiah addressed the same theme in chapter 34. In a so-called *ʿrîb* setting,[24] the Lord convened an assembly and then, seated on a judge's bench, laid out his allegations against the nations, charging them point by point with crimes and misdemeanors against himself and his people Israel and outlining what their punishment must be. He was angry with them, he said, and would place them under *ḥērem,* the annihilation reserved for those for whom there is no hope of redemption (v. 2). Once more turning to creation imagery, the prophet saw a day when the stars would no longer give their light and the sky, like a scroll, would be rolled up (v. 4). Edom in particular, as a *pars pro toto,* would suffer the divine wrath. So severe will be its judgment that it will look like the chaotic earth before its formation: the Lord "will stretch out a measuring line [over Edom] and a plumb line over her for her destruction *(tōhû)* and chaos *(bōhû)*" (v. 11), the very terms used to describe the preformed earth (Gen. 1:2). Clearly the intention is to hark back to creation and to the creation mandate, the violation of which will inevitably lead to a de-creation, a reduction of the earth and its kingdoms to nothingness. The prophet, in fact, declared that "no nobles will be left to proclaim a king, and all her princes will come to nothing" (Isa. 34:12).

Zechariah envisioned all the nations of the earth gathering against Jerusalem at the end of the age, but before their nefarious plans can be effected, the Lord will intervene. He will do battle against them "as He fights on a day of battle," that is, in line with the principles and practices of Holy War (Zech. 14:3). Having defeated them, the Lord will emerge triumphant. As the prophet puts it, "On that day Yahweh will become king over all the earth.—Yahweh alone, and His name alone" (v. 9). Once and for all the question of sovereignty will be settled. The nations, mere surrogates of the wicked spirits in the heavens, will come to utter ruin, signifying by their defeat the overthrow of all powers that stand in opposition to the Lord.

---

[24] For the term and its use by the prophets, see Marvin A. Sweeney, *Isaiah 1–39 with an Introduction to Prophetic Literature,* FOTL 16 (Grand Rapids: Eerdmans, 1996), 541–42.

The Prophets and the Nations

Amos

Individual nations came in for considerable attention by the prophets who viewed them, without exception, as enemies of the heavenly kingdom that must and will be put down. It will be best to consider the prophets in their historical sequence one by one rather than attempting to deal with each of the nations in its turn. This, we believe, is more consistent with our general method that places a high premium on progressive revelation (though, of necessity, we must allude to the same nations over and over as the prophets dealt with them sequentially). Thus, we begin with Amos, early in the eighth century, a time of great ferment in Israel and of increasing threat against Israel from outside nations, especially Assyria. Amos was more concerned about Israel's nearer neighbors than he was Assyria, however, for he perceived their pernicious influence as having a devastating effect on Israel's moral and spiritual life.

Amos 1:1–2:3 is a catalog of warnings against six different nations, the last three of which were closely related to Israel by consanguinity. Damascus (that is, Aram or Syria) comes to the fore first because of her transgressions *(pešaʿ)* against Gilead, which, from ancient times, was the Transjordanian territory of Israel. Damascus is said to have "threshed Gilead with iron sledges" (1:3) and whether this is to be taken literally, the result is the same. In some way undocumented in the historical record, the Arameans had shamefully mistreated Israel and for that reason alone were deserving of God's judgment. The Philistines likewise come in for condemnation (Amos 1:6–8), for they had collaborated with Edom in taking whole populations of Israel captive (v. 6). For this they would suffer destruction to the point of annihilation.

Having addressed his enemies to the northeast and southwest, the Lord now spoke through the prophet about Tyre, to the northwest (Amos 1:9–10). Their sin was in violating a covenant made with Israel (the details of which are unknown) and, like the Philistines, delivering Israel over to Edom. As for Edom (Amos 1:11–12), its judgment will come because, as a people related to Israel by virtue of the brotherhood of Jacob and Esau, Edom should have done all it could to protect Israel rather than cooperate in its destruction (cf. Obadiah, whose message is the same). Ammon was also connected ethnically to Israel by virtue of a common descent from Terah, father of Abraham (see Gen. 11:31). Furthermore, like Edom, Ammon also owed Israel special fraternal consideration but, to the contrary, had slaughtered the Israelite settlers of Gilead in pursuit of territorial enlargement (vv. 13–14). For this the Ammonites could expect the Lord's judgment of exile from their land (v. 15). Finally, Moab, half brother of Ammon, would suffer divine wrath because of its mistreatment of Edom which, though not the people of the covenant, were nonetheless objects of God's special covenant blessing (cf. Gen. 27:39–40).

Isaiah

Isaiah spoke at length about a number of human kingdoms destined for God's wrath because of their antitheocratic hubris. First among them were the Assyrians, a nation God had raised up as an instrument of discipline against his own people (Isa. 10:5–6) but that took personal credit for its success (vv. 13–14). For this arrogance the Lord would consume mighty Assyria, reducing its population to a mere remnant (vv. 16–19). Isaiah saw Assyria as a paradigm against which to measure all nations, its judgment reflecting universal judgment. "This is the plan prepared for the whole earth," Isaiah said, "and this is the hand stretched out against all the nations. The Lord of Hosts Himself has planned it; therefore, who can stand in its way? It is His hand that is outstretched, so who can turn it back?" (Isa. 14:26–27).

By prophetic foresight Isaiah also included Babylon in his purview. In a great apocalyptic oracle he foresaw a day when Babylon, the archetype of human rebellion against God's kingdom since the days of the tower of Babel, would suffer terrible devastation at God's hand (Isa. 13:1–14:23). In martial imagery Isaiah described the Lord coming against Babylon with a great host that would destroy not only Babylon (Isa. 13:5) but also the whole world and all its wicked inhabitants (vv. 9–13). Like Sodom and Gomorrah, the epitome of evil culture in patriarchal times, Babylon would be overthrown (v. 19). Her kings will descend into Sheol where they will be met by earthly rulers who have preceded them. "Sheol below is eager to greet your coming," proclaimed Isaiah. "He stirs up the spirits of the departed for you—all the rulers of the earth. He makes all the kings of the nations rise from their thrones" (14:9).

Most striking is the association of the king of Babylon and the Babylonian state with the "shining morning star" *(hēlāl ben-šāḥar)* (v. 12).[25] Drawing upon mythopoetic imagery, the prophet understood the human ruler to be the lackey or even incarnation of a superhuman being who aspired to ascend to heaven and even to dethrone the Lord God and sit in his place. While the immediate reference was clearly to a king of Babylon in Isaiah's near future, he portrayed this king against the backdrop of a more transcendent struggle for supremacy, one reflected in common mythical motifs but, beyond that, one acted out in primeval times between the Creator and the fallen angel. This archenemy of God first appeared as the being incarnated in or represented by the snake of the temptation story, identified in later revelation as Satan or the devil (cf. Job 1:6–7; 2:1–2; 1 Chron. 21:1). Jesus likely had the Isaiah passage in mind when he said, "I watched Satan fall from heaven like a lightning flash," in the context a reference to the Lord's conquest over demonic spirits (Luke 10:18).[26] And that same pretender to the throne of God will someday be bound and cast into the Abyss, much as the "shining morning star" is consigned to the depths of Sheol (Rev. 20:2).

Like all other evil rulers who oppose the sovereignty of God and resist his kingdom principles, the king of Babylon will lie in abject humiliation, "covered by those slain with the sword and dumped into a rocky pit like a trampled corpse" (Isa. 14:19). His realm will be turned into "a swampland and a region for wild animals" (v. 23). In another oracle the prophet viewed Babylon as a shameful daughter no longer worthy to be called "queen of the kingdoms" (Isa. 47:5 NIV). Her children would be taken away (v. 9), her sorcerers shown to be false, and her idols exposed for the vanities they really are (vv. 12–15).

Casting his eyes now on a nearer nation, Isaiah exhorted the Philistines not to become overly joyous at the ruin of Assyria for the Babylonians would take Assyria's place as God's instrument of judgment (Isa. 14:29). This he would do in order to provide security for his own people Israel (v.

---

[25] For an earlier discussion of this passage, see pp. 205–7.

[26] Thus Darrel L. Bock, *Luke 9:51–24:53,* BECNT 3B (Grand Rapids: Baker, 1996), 1006–7.

32). Moab, though kinsfolk of Israel, would come in for punishment as well because of her pride (Isa. 16:6) and, implicitly, her idolatry (v. 12). Damascus (Isa. 17:1–3), Cush (18:1–7), Edom (21:11–12), and Arabia (21:13–17) would taste of God's retributive justice. The same is true of Tyre whose destruction the Lord had planned long ago "to desecrate all its glorious beauty, to disgrace all the honored ones of the earth" (23:9). The issue again was clear-cut: the nations of the earth, seeking to assert their independence of the Lord, would inevitably be humbled and made subservient to him.

As for mighty Egypt, Isaiah foresaw a time when the Lord "will deliver Egypt into the hands of harsh masters, and a strong king [Assyria and/or Persia] will rule it" (Isa. 19:4). In Egypt's case, however, the judgment of God would bring about a spirit of repentance and a realization that he, and only he, is Lord of all. As a sign of their conversion to this point of view, the Egyptians "will return to the LORD and He will hear their prayers and heal them" (v. 22). This points to the eschatological day when the people of the Lord will be comprised of men and women "from every tribe and language and people and nation" who will be made to be "a kingdom and priests to our God, and they will reign on the earth" (Rev. 5:9–10). The idea of God's universal reign in the church will receive detailed attention at a later point.

Nahum

The prophet Nahum, late in the seventh century, devoted virtually his entire message to Nineveh and the judgment of the Lord that would befall that arrogant nation. He began with a general statement of the Lord's stance toward all his enemies, the Assyrians being the epitome of all these: "The LORD is a jealous and avenging God; the LORD takes vengeance and is fierce in wrath. . . . The LORD is slow to anger but great in power; The LORD will never leave the guilty unpunished" (Nah. 1:2–3). The Assyrians would be left without descendants, and the images of their gods would be destroyed, testifying to their powerlessness (1:14). Their fall would be at the hands of a fierce invading army—Babylon as it turns out—that would strip Nineveh bare and leave the city and nation an object of pitiless scorn (2:5–7). The final outcome, said the prophet, would be that Assyria, like Thebes, would disappear from the face of the earth (3:8, 17). Addressing Assyria's hopeless state, the prophet declared the impotence of human government in a final epitaph: "King of Assyria, your shepherds slumber; your officers sleep. Your people are scattered across the mountains with no one to gather them together" (Nah. 3:18).

Jeremiah

No prophet spoke more forcefully or at greater length about the conflict between the kingdom of God and those of mankind than Jeremiah. Living at the time of transition between Assyria and the newly emergent Neo-Babylonian Empire, Jeremiah could not help but be impressed with the wealth and power of the great nations around him. At the same time he was in contact with the smaller states that surrounded him; for they, like his own nation Judah, were inexorably caught up in the vortex of international struggle and, moreover, were themselves antagonistic to the sovereignty of the Lord of all the earth and therefore deserving of his judgment.

For obvious reasons Jeremiah devoted most of his attention to Babylon. With his own eyes he had witnessed the invasion of his land by the irresistible foe from the east, an invasion that resulted in the deportation of many of his fellow citizens, the exile and death of Judah's kings, and, most tragic of all, the destruction of Jerusalem and looting and destruction of its holy temple. But he saw more than this. With eyes of faith, he was able to understand that the contest was not merely at a human level—nation against nation—but was fundamentally spiritual in nature. It was only a new appearance of the age-old conflict with roots in the temptation and fall of mankind at the dawn of history. Babylon was Babel again, the embodiment of unbridled human pride and disobedience of the creation mandate.

Jeremiah anticipated the day when Babylon would fall and be laid waste (Jer. 50:1–3). Having been the greatest of the nations, she would become least (v. 12). The Lord, warned the prophet, will have "opened His armory and brought out His weapons of wrath, because it is a task of the LORD God of Hosts in the land of the Chaldeans" (v. 25). The reason for the Lord's wrath is obvious: Babylon "has acted arrogantly against the LORD, against the Holy One of Israel" (v. 29) and so the day for the "arrogant one" (v. 31) to fall has come to pass. "I will chase Babylon away from her land in a flash," says the LORD. "Who is like Me?

Who will summon Me?" he asks (v. 44). The issue therefore is, who is supreme? And the answer will be self-evident.

The tool in God's hands to bring about Babylon's demise was not unknown. As he had used both Assyria and Babylon as his instruments of judgment in the past, so he would raise up another nation now. Jeremiah thus announced that "the LORD has put it into the mind of the kings of the Medes because His plan is aimed at Babylon to destroy her" (Jer. 51:11). He will have "both planned and accomplished what He has threatened against those who live in Babylon" (v. 12). He, the Creator, will also do away with Babylon's worthless idols demonstrating that only he, indeed, is Lord (vv. 15–19).

The reason for such drastic measures, in part at least, was Babylon's mistreatment of God's people Israel (v. 49). Harking back to the story of the tower of Babel upon whose ruins the city of Jeremiah's day was built, the Lord vowed that "even if Babylon should ascend to the heavens and fortify her tall fortresses, destroyers will come against her from Me" (v. 53). The conflict begun at Babel will culminate at Babylon with the triumph of the Lord. And the nation that cursed the seed of Abraham, as Babylon had done, will fall under the curse of the Lord.

Egypt, successor to the pharaohs of the plagues and exodus, must also once again experience the wrath of Israel's God because in Jeremiah's day it continued to stand in opposition to his dominion. Sending against Egypt the armies of Babylon and then Persia, the Lord would bring to pass a day of vengeance on his foes (Jer. 46:10). Though human forces would be involved, the battle would be the Lord's. He will lead the attack and will thrust Egypt down (v. 15). And the enemy was not really Egypt *per se* but the gods of Egypt, the unseen demonic powers that ultimately motivate all human resistance to the kingdom of the Lord. This is put beyond question by the Lord's assertion as the "LORD of Hosts, the God of Israel": "I am about to punish Amon, god of Thebes, along with Pharaoh, Egypt, her gods, and her kings—Pharaoh and those trusting in him" (v. 25). Just as the real conflict in the days of the exodus was against the gods of Egypt and not those who worshipped them (Exod. 12:12), so in the day of God's judgment in history and in the eschaton it is the wicked spirits in high places that will be brought low before the kingdom of God.

Like Isaiah, Jeremiah also had a condemnatory word about the Philistines (Jer. 47:1–7), Ammon (49:1–6), Damascus (49:23–27), and Edom (49:7–22). In words reminiscent of the prophet Obadiah, he announced the utter destruction of Edom, but unlike Obadiah he omitted reference to Edom's mistreatment of Israel as its cause. Rather, Edom's pride and self-sufficiency were offensive (v. 16). Asserting his claims to sole regency, the Lord asked concerning his threats against Edom, "Who is like Me? Who will summon Me? Who is the shepherd [that is, king] who can stand against Me?" (v. 19). The answer obviously is that no one can for he alone is king.

Moab came in for special consideration by Jeremiah; for at the time of the Babylonian conquest of Judah and its aftermath, an element in the Transjordan attempted to overthrow the interim government of Judah appointed by the Babylonians. The Ammonites were heavily involved in this conspiracy, and perhaps the Moabites were as well (cf. Jer. 41:10–15). Whether this supposition is correct, it is clear that Moab had offended the Lord in some manner serious enough to warrant severe condemnation.

The land would be overrun and utterly laid waste (Jer. 48:1–9). The gods of Moab would be discredited (v. 13); and because Moab served them in defiance of the Lord, she would be brought low (v. 26). At the root of Moab's rebellion was her pride and arrogance (v. 29), a spirit, as we have seen, that was characteristic of all the nations that stood in opposition to the Lord's creation design. What made Moab's sins in this respect so grievous was the fact that Moab (with Ammon) was related to Israel and Judah by common descent. For Moab thus to ignore the Lord in favor of their god Chemosh was an act of betrayal so serious as to invite his severe displeasure.

Zephaniah

Zephaniah, a contemporary of Jeremiah, uttered a series of oracles against the Philistines (Zeph. 2:4–7), Assyria (2:13–15), Cush (2:12), and Moab and Ammon (2:8–11). The message concerning the latter states that the judgment of these two "brother" nations was largely precipitated by their maltreatment of God's people Israel (v. 8), a familiar theme by now. This, like the other instances, was an act calculated to bring the Lord's curse upon them (Gen. 12:3). Recollections of the Genesis context in which these covenant curses were first enunciated can be seen also in the threat that Moab and Ammon would become like Sodom and Gomorrah respectively so complete would their judgment be (v. 9). The fact that these two peoples could trace their lineage back to Lot's two daughters who had escaped with him from the cities of the plain adds all the more poignancy to the connection (see also Isa. 13:9; Jer. 49:18; 50:40; Amos 4:11).

Ezekiel

Finally, Ezekiel, a prophet living in exile, addressed a number of nations that had incurred God's displeasure and therefore were in line for his judgment. Missing, of course, are Assyria and Babylon, for by Ezekiel's time the Assyrians had passed off the world scene, and the fate of the Babylonians was a foregone conclusion. All that needed to be said about them, even from the eschatological perspective, had already been said by the prophets who preceded him. As for the rest, Ammon, first on Ezekiel's list, must be punished because they had rejoiced in the destruction of the temple and the exile of their Israelite kinsmen (Ezek. 25:3). Once they had suffered at the Lord's hands, they would come to know that he is the Lord (vv. 4, 7). Moab likewise would experience divine justice and likewise would at long last recognize that only the Lord is God (vv. 10–11). As for Edom, Israel's "brother," it will be laid waste because of its treachery against the chosen people (v. 12). The Philistines also "acted in vengeance and took revenge with deep contempt, destroying because of their ancient hatred" (Ezek. 25:15), and therefore they must be cut off. Even they would learn from God's harsh punishment that he is the Lord (v. 17).

In a second oracle against Edom (Ezek. 35:1–15), that nation too is said to have harbored "an ancient hatred" against Israel, going so far as to deliver them over to their enemies (v. 5). Edom's hostility was in actuality an animosity toward the Lord, Israel's God. As the Lord reveals here, "You boasted against Me with your mouth, and spoke many words against Me. I heard it Myself" (v. 13)! This points up again the truth that the central struggle in the universe is between the nations of the world that are inspired by the invisible forces of evil on the one hand and the kingdom of God on the other.

Ezekiel's principal targets were Egypt and Tyre, the former addressed in his tenth year (ca. 582 BC) and the latter in his eleventh year (ca.

581 BC). In the oracle against Egypt (Ezek. 29:1–32:32), Pharaoh is described as a great sea monster who takes credit for the creation of the Nile and, by implication, the whole earth (v. 3). The imagery is in line with the mythical language associated with the exodus in the Song of Moses (Exod. 15) thus connecting the work of historical redemption with God's eschatological salvation. But Pharaoh was not the creator; it is the Lord. And because Pharaoh took credit for what God himself had done, Egypt must be decimated and its population exiled (vv. 10–12). Even when it returned to its own land, it would never again be a powerful nation (vv. 15–16).

Comparing Egypt's fate to that of Assyria, the prophet predicted that Egypt too would be hewed down like a giant tree of the forest, lying not only on the surface of the earth but with the wicked rulers who inhabit the chambers of the netherworld (Ezek. 31:18). Egypt's connection to the trees of Eden forms another linkage to the creation narratives, one that reminds the nations that they too are but God's planting and that they have no independent existence of their own. The kingdoms of the world, like trees, were set in the earth by him and in their day of judgment will be cut down by Him.

Employing another simile, the Lord spoke of Egypt again as "a lion of the nations" and "a monster in the seas" (Ezek. 32:2). But with all its fearsome power, Egypt would be ensnared in the net of God's retributive justice (vv. 3–4). Because Egypt was universally recognized as the greatest of the nations, its fall would be particularly astonishing and unexpected. The kings of the other nations "will shudder with fear because of you," says the Lord, and "on the day of your downfall each of them will tremble every moment for his life" (v. 10). Among the rulers that would join Egypt in its collapse and consignment to Sheol were the kings of Assyria, Elam, Meshech and Tubal, Edom, and Sidon. All of them are described as the uncircumcised, that is, nations outside the covenant fellowship and blessing of God.

One more nation would also come to its final destruction in Sheol, and that was Tyre, the proud Phoenician city-state that had rarely known defeat. Ezekiel devoted three chapters to Tyre (chs. 26–28), suggesting something of its importance politically but more so as a model of anti-God arrogance. Tyre's character and its final outcome provide a striking lesson as to what happens to the nations of the earth that arrogate to themselves the glory that belongs only to the Lord.

The instrument of Tyre's judgment would be Babylon. Though Tyre took comfort in its inaccessibility as an island fortress, Nebuchadnezzar's armies would breach her walls and dismantle her buildings, scraping the rock on which she was built until it lacked any sign of human habitation (Ezek. 26:7–14). Hearing of Tyre's fate, the surrounding nations would be terror stricken, dumbfounded that such a mighty city should come to such a ruinous end. As for its citizens, they, with their king, would take their final rest in the depths of the earth (v. 20).

The reason for this unusually calamitous turn of events lay in Tyre's sense of independent self-sufficiency and prosperity (Ezek. 27:1–36) and, more to the point, her assertion of her equality with the Lord and his kingdom, an attitude typical of mankind in general but expressed most blatantly in this oracle (Ezek. 28:1–19). The first part of the prophet's message is a lament over the impending destruction of Tyre, an act of divine judgment all the more noteworthy because of Tyre's (self-perceived) superiority to all other nations. From all over the world raw materials and artisans came who created from them a city whose beauty and riches were without peer.[27] If ever a human kingdom could compare to that of heaven, this was it. But the glory of the place was only ephemeral, for a day of reckoning was coming when all that made Tyre great would pass away in a great convulsion of God's wrath.

Following the lament, Ezekiel addressed the king of Tyre as perhaps the personification of his kingdom. As in Isaiah's apostrophe to the king of Babylon (Isa. 14:3–23), Ezekiel employed mythological language and imagery in order to raise the issue of the king's hubris to a supernatural level, one that made clear that the opposition to the sovereignty of God was not humanly originated but derivative of unseen spiritual powers.[28] A holistic biblical theology identifies these powers as demonic, angelic beings beholden to Satan and acting on his behalf.

---

[27] H. Jacob Katzenstein, *The History of Tyre* (Jerusalem: The Schocken Institute for Jewish Research, 1973), 15–17.

[28] Daniel I. Block, *The Book of Ezekiel Chapters 25–48,* NICOT (Grand Rapids: Eerdmans, 1998), 117–21. Though conceding that the prophet made use of mythological imagery, Block correctly concludes that the major motifs were drawn from Old Testament creation and paradise settings.

This is clear from the outset where the king of Tyre says, "I am a god; I sit in the seat of gods in the heart of the sea" (Ezek. 28:2). The response of the Lord is not slow in coming: "You are a man and not a god, though you have regarded your heart as that of a god" (v. 2b). Such an attitude would bring severe judgment in the form of foreigners who would come and drag the proud ruler of Tyre off his throne and into the pit (vv. 7–8). This word of imminent judgment was followed by another lament, this one addressed to the king personally and not his nation (Ezek. 28:11–19). Here, in obviously mythopoetic language, he is described as "the seal of perfection, full of wisdom and perfect in beauty" (v. 12). His residence in Eden, "the garden of God" (v. 13), can leave no doubt that the king of Tyre is being compared either to Adam or to the serpent (i.e., Satan). The following description of his setting and office strongly suggests the latter.[29] He is depicted as covered with precious stones and metals, a fit adornment for a creature described as a "guardian cherub" (vv. 14, 16).

Before wickedness was found in him, this noble being had access to the "holy mountain of God" (v. 14), that is, to God's presence. The prelude to Job makes the same assertion, declaring that "one day the sons of God came to present themselves before the LORD, and Satan also came with them" (Job 1:6). The guardian cherub without doubt is identical to Satan, an angelic being who at one time enjoyed unfettered access to the Lord in heaven. But wickedness was found in him; and the one who said, "I am a god" (Ezek. 28:2) was expelled from his privileged position and cast down to the earth in disgrace (vv. 16–17). Thus the attempt to usurp the power and glory that belongs to God alone was averted and the king of Tyre, symbolic of all sinful human rulers, was forced to concede that the Lord alone is king and his kingdom alone will prevail.

Daniel

Nowhere in the Old Testament is the issue of the conflict of the kingdoms more prominent than in Daniel. In fact, a strong case can be

[29] Lamar Eugene Cooper Sr., *Ezekiel,* NAC 17 (Nashville: Broadman & Holman, 1994), 266–69.

made that this issue is the main theme of the book.[30] The setting of Daniel was sixth-century Babylon and in the court of King Nebuchadnezzar. In the first of three major campaigns against the Mediterranean littoral, Nebuchadnezzar had taken certain Jewish prisoners from Jerusalem including young Daniel. Because of his obvious potential as a sage and public servant, Daniel was schooled in the arts and sciences of Babylon, eventually rising to a position of prominence in the royal entourage. A loyal citizen of Babylon, Daniel gained a reputation for his ability to recount and interpret dreams, so much so that he performed these services for the king himself. Thus ingratiating himself with the king, Daniel continued to be a man of influence and increasingly so as the king became more and more dependent on him. At the same time Daniel was a devoted citizen and servant of the kingdom of heaven. He refused to break its dietary laws (Dan. 1:8) or to make other concessions or compromises out of keeping with his Jewish traditions. His stance was so unyielding that Nebuchadnezzar took note of it and was even willing to acknowledge Daniel's God as a powerful deity worthy of recognition among his own (cf. Dan. 2:47; 3:28–29; 4:34–35, 37).

The time came at last when Daniel had to choose between sovereigns and kingdoms. Though Nebuchadnezzar had given lip service to the existence of Daniel's God and had even confessed his greatness, he and the kingdom over which he ruled stood diametrically in opposition to the kingdom of heaven in both its ideology and its practice. Daniel pointed up the difference subtly but unmistakably when asked to interpret Nebuchadnezzar's dream. With proper deference to human authority, he addressed the king as "king of kings" but then went on to testify that "the God of heaven has given you sovereignty, power, strength, and glory. Wherever people live—or wild animals, or birds of the air—He has handed them over to you and made you ruler over them all" (Dan. 2:37–38). In a manner of speaking, Nebuchadnezzar had been authorized by the Lord to fulfill the terms of the creation mandate (Gen. 1:26–28), though, of course, he could not have known that he was providing a model of what that might involve. Moreover, his kingdom was not synonymous

---

[30] See Eugene H. Merrill, "Daniel as a Contribution to Kingdom Theology," in *Essays in Honor of J. Dwight Pentecost,* ed. Stanley D. Toussaint and Charles H. Dyer (Chicago: Moody, 1986), 211–25; "A Theology of Ezekiel and Daniel," in *A Biblical Theology of the Old Testament,* ed. Roy B. Zuck (Chicago: Moody, 1991), 365–95.

with God's; in fact, it was to be subservient to it. When the dream's message was revealed, Daniel went on to inform the king that all the kingdoms of the world—including his own—would one day be crushed and replaced by the kingdom of heaven (2:44–45).

Kingdom conflict occurs also in the account of Daniel's three young Jewish friends who, when commanded to bow before an image of the king, refused to do so and were thrown into the furnace for their obduracy (Dan. 3). Their remarkable deliverance forced Nebuchadnezzar to praise their God and to be amazed that the three trusted in him and "violated the king's command and risked their lives rather than serve or worship any god except their own God" (v. 28). Nebuchadnezzar's dream of a tree brought the same matter to the fore. Acknowledged by Daniel to be great and strong, Nebuchadnezzar's power, he said, "has grown and even reaches the sky, and your dominion extends to the ends of the earth" (Dan. 4:22). But like a tree he would be cut down "until you acknowledge that the Most High is ruler over the kingdom of men, and He gives it to anyone He wants" (v. 25). His kingdom would be restored to him, Daniel went on to say, "as soon as you acknowledge that Heaven rules" (v. 26). This the king did, at least superficially, when his sanity returned. In a remarkable confession he proclaimed, "Now I, Nebuchadnezzar, praise, exalt, and glorify the King of heaven" (v. 37). Similarly, Nebuchadnezzar, anxious about Daniel's well-being in the den of lions, asked whether Daniel's God had been able to rescue him, to which Daniel replied, "My God sent His angel and shut the lions' mouths" (Dan. 6:22).

Daniel's experience in the lion's den followed the one time on record when he himself was forced to declare his kingdom allegiance. He served both his God and Nebuchadnezzar faithfully and well until he was called upon to make a choice between them. At this moment of crisis, the conflict of kingdoms became for Daniel more than just a theological abstraction; for to choose the one could cost him his life, but to choose the other could cost him the favor of the King of heaven. The setting was Darius the Mede's ill-advised command that all people of his realm must pray to him and him alone lest they surrender their very lives (Dan. 6:7). The king's henchmen had put their finger squarely on the theological issue of the whole book: "We will never find any charge against this Daniel unless we find something against him concerning the law of his God" (v. 5).

Meanwhile, Daniel prayed to God as always despite the decree and did so with open windows as though to force the issue (v. 10). Caught by his own devices, Darius was compelled to enforce his decree, but Daniel's God prevailed, and Daniel was delivered, prompting Darius's confession that "He is the living God, and He endures forever" (v. 26).

All these narrative incidents share in common a situation in which human rulers were brought face-to-face with the Lord God of heaven and without exception were shown to be wholly inept and inadequate. Moreover, they acknowledged this disparity and confessed that Daniel's God is indeed the God of heaven and earth. It logically followed that the kingdoms over which they ruled—mighty as they might be in their international context—were insignificant, powerless to contend with the dominion of the Lord. But the most informative presentation of the conflict of kingdoms occurs not in the narratives but in Daniel's dreams and visions. Here we find texts whose sole purpose was to declare the sovereignty of God and his kingdom over and against all human pretenders.

In the first of these (Dan. 7:1–28), Daniel saw a lion, a bear, a leopard, and an unidentifiable fourth animal rising up out of the sea. The fourth had ten horns, but three of these were uprooted by another horn with human-like eyes and a boastful mouth. Next the prophet saw the "Ancient of Days" sitting on a throne, his clothing as white as snow and his throne aflame with fire. Myriads of attendants surrounded him as he sat in judgment before open books, records, it seems, of words and deeds. Then the fourth beast was slain and cast into a blazing fire. Finally, "one like a son of man" (v. 13) appeared and was granted by the Ancient of Days "authority to rule, and glory, and a kingdom; so that those of every people, nation, and language should serve Him" (v. 14). The kingdom over which he reigns "is an everlasting dominion that will not pass away, and His kingdom is one that will not be destroyed" (v. 14b).

An interpreter enlightened Daniel as to the meaning of his dream: "These huge beasts, four in number, are four kings who would rise from the earth. But the holy ones of the Most High will receive the kingdom and will possess it forever, yes, forever and ever" (v. 17). Troubled especially about the identity of the fourth beast, Daniel inquired and learned that the fourth represented a kingdom of universal extent. From it would emerge ten kings, three of whom would be subdued by a fourth. This one, Daniel was told, "will speak words against the Most High and oppress the holy ones of the Most High. He will intend to change religious festivals and laws" (v. 25). He will prevail over the saints for awhile, but then the judge of all the earth will strip him of his power and put him to death. Then, the interpreter says, "the kingdom, dominion, and greatness of the kingdoms under all of heaven will be given to the people, the holy ones of the Most High. His kingdom will be an everlasting kingdom, and all rulers will serve and obey Him" (vv. 26–27).

Daniel's vision recorded in chapter 8 expands on the dream just described. This time he saw a ram with two horns, one longer than the other, and a goat with a horn between its eyes. The goat attacked the ram, broke its two horns, and trampled it into the ground. The goat became powerful; but at its peak of power, it too lost its horn; and in its place four more horns emerged. From one of them still another grew, one so powerful that it reached heaven itself. From there it cast down some of the starry host and then presumed to take the place of the Prince of the host, going so far as to dominate the sanctuary and its worship. In conclusion, Daniel noted that the great horn "will throw truth to the ground and will be successful in whatever it does" (v. 12).

For obvious reasons Daniel needed an interpretation of what he had just seen; so Gabriel the archangel came forth to provide one. The ram, he said, was Media and Persia, and the goat was Greece with the horn representing its first king. Four kings would replace him and from them another of whom Gabriel said, "His power will be great, but it will not be his own," strongly hinting of a supernatural being behind the scenes (v. 24). "He will make himself great," the angel continued, and "he will destroy many; he will even stand against the Prince of princes. But he will be shattered, not by human hands" (v. 25).

Reference to Gabriel, an emissary of the Lord (8:16; cf. 9:21), leads to the notion of superhuman beings that serve him in a variety of ways.[31] Though a full-blown angelology is not achieved in the Old Testament, enough exists—especially in late literature such as Daniel—to suggest

[31] See, *inter alia,* Gustave Friedrich Oehler, *Theology of the Old Testament,* trans. George E. Day (Grand Rapids: Zondervan, repr. of 1883 ed.), 441–51; Edward Langton, *The Ministries of the Angelic Powers According to the Old Testament and Later Jewish Literature* (London: J. Clarke, 1936); Walther Eichrodt, *Theology of the Old Testament,* vol. 1, trans. J. A. Baker (Philadelphia: Westminster, 1967), 194–202.

that Gabriel and others were part of a heavenly court that convened to praise God and to attend to his bidding. Satan was such a being until his fall from God's favor, an angel *par excellence* who enjoyed special privileges as God's servant (Job 1:6; 2:1; cf. Ezek. 28:12–15). The Old Testament also hints at (and the New Testament confirms) a hierarchy of fallen angels as well as those who refused to join in the heavenly rebellion (Exod. 23:20, 23; Num. 20:16; Luke 1:19, 26; 2 Cor. 11:14; Jude 6; Rev. 12:7–9). Among their functions, it seems, is the administration and even control of the affairs of the nations, a notion underlying the struggle in Daniel's vision of the man dressed in linen (Dan. 10).

This man, whose appearance and demeanor were so glorious as to leave Daniel prostrate before him, spoke to him of an errand he had intended to undertake on Daniel's behalf, "But," he said, "the prince of the kingdom of Persia opposed me for 21 days" (v. 13a). The man speaking to Daniel is not further identified, but the fact that he was sent by someone else rules out his being deity. On the other hand, his splendor precluded his being a mere man. Most likely he was one of the angelic beings that Ezekiel had encountered, less than God but more than man (Ezek. 1:4–25). In any event, he was restrained by a person more powerful than he, called here the prince of Persia.

He too was not a human king as is clear from the fact that the man speaking to Daniel was rescued from him by another prince, Michael by name (v. 13). Michael, it seems, was assigned by the Lord to be the special protector of God's people Israel (Dan. 12:1) and thus occupied the same role *vis-à-vis* Israel as the prince of Persia did with reference to that nation. The New Testament identifies Michael, like Gabriel, as an archangel (Jude 9; Rev. 12:7), that is, a ruler of angels serving the Lord at the highest level. As such, he was invested with the power and authority of Almighty God and was able to deliver the kingdom of God and its citizens from all powers, heavenly and earthly, that would seek to do them harm. The prince of Persia and the prince of Greece (whose coming was also prophesied, v. 20) must also be archangels but fallen ones. Under the dominion of Satan, they and many others governed the nations of the earth in an attempt to frustrate the Lord's kingdom purposes. But the angel of Israel prevailed, and the kingdom of heaven stood no matter the resistance to it.

Daniel brought to a close the most important prophetic texts concerning God's kingdom, and the machinations of the hostile powers of heaven and earth are arrayed against it. He with all the others spoke with a united voice to declare that at the end of history the kingdom of the Lord will be triumphant. His creation plan that he should reign over all things through those created as his image cannot be frustrated and will, through his redemptive grace, come to full fruition.

Reinstitution of the Kingdom

The Psalms of Yahweh's Kingship

Israel's poets also testified to the Lord as King, not only of Israel but of all nations, and to his kingdom, not only heavenly but, in the ages to come, earthly as well. Their witness is communicated primarily through the "psalms of Yahweh's kingship" (Pss. 47, 93, 96–99), but other texts convey the theme as well, especially the royal psalms in which the rule of Israel's kings is celebrated.[32] These will be addressed at length at a later point; but where they treat the theme of God's universal dominion, we must give them at least brief consideration here.

Psalm 47, the first of the psalms of Yahweh's kingship, opens with an invitation to the nations to acclaim God's rule with joy and describes him as "a great King over all the earth" (v. 2). Repeating this epithet of God's universal rule, the poet goes on to specify that he "reigns over the nations" (v. 8) just as he does over Israel ("the people of the God of Abraham," v. 9a), and that "the leaders of the earth belong to God" (v. 9b). All this does not come easily or naturally, however, for the nations and their rulers are at enmity with God. Their submission to God's sovereignty comes by force, as the inspired author makes clear: "He subdues peoples under us and nations under our feet" (v. 3). Though this brings to mind God's victories of the past, specifically the conquest of Canaan, his role as "King over all the earth" (v. 2) presupposes his future conquest of all nations, for the Old Testament witness to the nations'

[32] For helpful introductions to this genre, see C. Hassell Bullock, *Encountering the Book of Psalms* (Grand Rapids: Baker, 2001), 187–97; Hans-Joachim Kraus, *Psalms 1–59,* trans. Hilton C. Oswald (Minneapolis: Fortress, 1993), 45–46.

unremitting hostility to the Lord is abundantly clear (e.g., Ps. 2:1–2; 9:5; 45:5; 59:5; etc.).

Psalm 93 opens with the declaration, "The LORD reigns," a hallmark of psalms of this genre (cf. 47:8; 96:10; 97:1; 99:1).[33] Though some scholars have understood it to mean that the Lord has begun to reign, linking it with a hypothetical enthronement festival,[34] it seems best to take it as a gnomic form of the verb that makes the point that it is in the nature of the Lord to reign. This he does by virtue of who he is. The poet sets the beginning of the Lord's reign in eternity past, that is, even before creation. Then, picking up the motif of the sea as an unruly opponent that must be tamed, he compares to it the mighty power of God and declares God the victor (v. 4).[35] He concludes then that the Lord's testimonies are unassailable and will remain in force forever (v. 5). The term translated *testimonies* (or *statutes*) here *(ʿēdût)* is associated with covenant stipulations. In the context of the Lord's work of creation, those stipulations could be understood as the creation mandate of Genesis 1:26–28, the only statutes recorded in the creation accounts. The mandate, then, is founded on the Lord's sovereign claim to authority, one enhanced by his triumph over the chaotic waters.

Most scholars identify Psalm 95 as one of the psalms celebrating Yahweh's kingship, a position that we believe has a good form-critical and theological basis.[36] Almost at the outset the claim is made that "the LORD is a great God, a great King above all gods" (v. 3), an assertion that leaves little doubt as to his incomparability. Immediately after the establishment of his credentials follows their grounds, namely, his work as Creator: "The depths of the earth are in His hand, and the mountain peaks are His. The sea is His; He made it. His hands formed the dry land" (vv. 4–5). The response to this recognition of the Lord as Creator and King is to worship Him, "our Maker" (v. 6), because "we are the people of His pasture, the sheep under His care" (v. 7). The connection between

[33] Roy A. Rosenberg, "Yahweh Becomes King," *JBL* 85 (1966): 297–307.

[34] Thus notably Sigmund Mowinckel in *The Psalms in Israel's Worship,* 2 vols. (Nashville: Abingdon, 1962).

[35] A. H. W. Curtis, "The 'Subjugation of the Waters' Motif in the Psalms: Imagery or Polemic," *JSS* 23 (1978): 245–56.

[36] Bullock, *Encountering the Book of Psalms,* 189. For a contrary view, see Erhard S. Gerstenberger, *Psalms, Part 2, and Lamentations,* FOTL 15 (Grand Rapids: Eerdmans, 2001), 184–85. Gerstenberger prefers the label *sermon.*

God's creation and his kingship could not be clearer, nor could the role of mankind. He, like a shepherd, is sovereignly working out his purposes through those whom he made as his own image.

Psalm 96 continues the theme of the Lord's incomparability. The poet avers that "He is feared above all gods. For the gods of the peoples are idols, but the LORD made the heavens" (vv. 4–5). Here again the Lord's exclusive right to rule is based on his work as Creator. Moreover, the gods of the nations have no ontological reality; they are merely products of the craftsman's shop! In light of this, the nations of the earth are exhorted to lay aside their idolatry and "ascribe to the LORD glory and strength" and to "tremble before Him, all the earth" (vv. 7, 9). The message the nations need to hear is, "The LORD reigns," a confession, once more, founded on his creation of all things (v. 10). Failure to acknowledge his lordship, the psalmist implies, will result in the fearsome coming of the Lord who "will judge the world with righteousness and the peoples with His faithfulness" (v. 13). The Israelite poet sees clearly that his God is the God of all mankind and that his realm is all of creation.

The exordium "The LORD reigns" also introduces Psalm 97. Its universal scope appears in the appeal for all the earth to be glad, and all the distant shores rejoice in the fact of his sovereignty (v. 1). His awesomeness is seen in his hiddenness (v. 2) as well as in his blazing glory (vv. 3–4), a manifestation of his kingship that is so compelling that even the gods should worship him (v. 7). This, of course, is no more an admission that gods exist than the affirmation of verse 9 that "you, LORD, are the Most High over all the earth; You are exalted above all the gods." Gods did exist in the superstitious imaginations of the pagans, but Israel's theology most certainly would perceive them at most as manifestations of the demonic powers that oppose the Lord's kingdom purposes.

Psalm 98 urges all the earth (that is, its peoples) to "shout to the LORD" and "be jubilant, shout for joy, and sing" (v. 4), for he is "the LORD, our King" (v. 6). The connection between the Lord's sovereign rule and creation, a theme common in this type of psalm, is clear from the appeal to the sea, the world, the rivers, and the mountains to join the nations in their expressions of praise and worship of the Lord (vv. 7–8). That he is over all is seen in the promise (and threat) that he is coming to judge the earth and its peoples in righteousness and equity (v. 9). Only one who is duly accredited with absolute and universal authority can exercise such a function. Thus, from creation at the beginning to judgment at the end, the Lord is supreme and his kingdom all-encompassing.

The last of the psalms of Yahweh's kingship, Psalm 99, commences with the now familiar "The LORD reigns!" and describes him as the one who "is enthroned above the cherubim" (v. 1). This is an allusion to the ark of the covenant of the tabernacle and temple, the cover of which served as a throne upon which the invisible Lord sat as the Great King of Israel (1 Sam. 4:4; 2 Sam. 6:2; 2 Kings 19:15). But though he localizes his rule on the earth in the sacred shrines of Israel, "He is exalted above all the peoples" (v. 2). All nations therefore should praise his "great and awe-inspiring name" (v. 3).

The fundamental message communicated by this category of psalms is that though the Lord has become the God of Israel by virtue of a special covenant relationship, his dominion extends beyond Israel to embrace the whole world. A secondary but highly significant theme is that the Lord's claims to sovereignty rest upon and are validated by his work of creation. He is King because all that exists has come to pass through him and has been designed by him to be an arena in which he can display his dominion. The nations of the world, as well as Israel, must acknowledge that dominion and desist from their own claims of sovereignty lest the judge of all the earth come and call them to account for their sinful insubordination.

The Royal Psalms

The second major genre of psalms that address the rule of the Lord and opposition to it—the so-called royal psalms—focuses on the rule of the kings of Israel, specifically of the Davidic dynasty, but touches also on God's universal kingship. The theological relevance of these compositions for Israel in particular will be the subject of later discussion so our treatment of them here will be selective, viewing them from the broader perspective of whatever light they might shed on God's relationship to the nations at large.

The first of these, Psalm 2, asks why it is that the nations rage against the Lord and his Anointed One (that is, the Davidic king). They chafe under his rule and desire independence of his authority. However, they will someday become subservient to Israel (and thus to Israel's God) who will rule them with an iron scepter (vv. 8–9). Their kings are therefore advised to be wise and to give attention to the Lord's warnings to worship him and him alone lest he come to destroy them in his wrath (vv. 11–12). Why they rage and are resistant to the Lord finds answer in the alienation between the Lord and humanity that issued from mankind's sin in the garden. Once he refused to let God be God and tried to arrogate to himself the divine status and privileges, man has assumed a posture of hostility that can be overcome only by "kissing the Son" (v. 12), a symbolic act of repentance and submission that makes possible his reconciliation to the Creator.[37]

Psalm 89, while concerned primarily with God's covenant with David, celebrates the Lord of the covenant in a broader context as Creator and sovereign over all the heavens and the earth. The poet asks concerning him, "Who in the skies can compare with the Lord? Who among the heavenly beings is like the Lord?" (v. 6). The answer is self-evident and, as always, is grounded in God's works, in particular in creation. The sea, the symbol of chaotic resistance to the Lord, cannot stand before Him (v. 9). Portrayed as Rahab, the monster of the deep (cf. Job 26:12; Isa. 51:4), it was crushed and forced to scatter like a defeated foe (v. 10). The allusion is to the parting of the waters on the third day of creation (Gen. 1:9–10), a separation that allowed the dry land of earth to appear (v. 11).[38] It is on the basis of such sovereignty of God over all the universe that David is able to have confidence in his own ability to rule on God's behalf (vv. 19–29).

Finally, Psalm 110, a poem celebrating the reign of David and his dynasty in strongly messianic terms, undergirds Davidic regency with an appeal to the majestic sovereignty of David's God. Seated at the Lord's right hand as his agent of rulership, David is told to have confidence in the Lord, for David's enemies are his enemies as well, and they will be reduced to abject humiliation before him (v. 1). By God's power David will succeed because the Lord "will crush kings on the day of His anger. He will judge the nations, heaping up corpses; He will crush leaders over the entire world" (vv. 5–6). The psalm clearly has a historical setting applicable to David's own time and situation, but the thrust of it is overwhelmingly eschatological. At the end of the age, the Lord will

[37] The messianic implications of Psalm 2 will be fully developed on p. 578.

[38] Artur Weiser, *The Psalms* (Philadelphia: Westminster, 1962), 592.

gain victory through the scion of David and will assert his rightful role as sovereign over all things.

Conclusion

We have at some length given attention to the rule of God over creation as a whole and the opposition to that rule occasioned by mankind's sin and fall. That opposition, we have argued, originated in the heavens, instigated by Satan who, in the guise of a snake, tempted mankind to join him in a course of action disruptive and even destructive of the spheres of sovereignty inherent in God's creation design. Thus, animals became resistant to the authority of man, and man rebelled against the authority of God in both an individual and a collective sense. No longer willing to fulfill the creation mandate as God had presented it, mankind chose to go its own way, asserting its independence of God and carving out rival kingdoms to his own. These kingdoms—the nations of the world—remain implacably hostile to the Lord's rightful claims of dominion over them and at the same time stand in dire need of redemption and restoration by him. This is where God's covenant with Israel comes to bear. The ancient covenants with the fathers that held out hope for the reconciliation of mankind with the Lord through Abraham's seed will now find clearer definition in the nation embodying that seed, the nation the Lord himself describes as a "kingdom of priests" and a "holy nation" (Exod. 19:6). We must now give our attention to the affairs of that nation with an eye toward its function as God's channel of redemptive grace.

Chapter Eleven

God and Israel

The Mosaic Covenant

In our study thus far, we have noted repeatedly that God promised Abraham that he would have innumerable descendants who would occupy the land of Canaan and who would give rise to kings. All of this would result in blessing for the nations of the earth that blessed Abraham's seed but cursing on the nations that cursed them (Gen. 12:1–3; 15:5–7, 18–19; 17:3–8; 22:15–18). This seed would eventually make the transition from a loosely affiliated nomadic society bound only by ties of common ancestry to a nation among the nations of the earth. Yet the sense of consanguinity and ethnic solidarity would not be lost whatever political form the nation might take. To the end of the Old Testament historical record, the theologians of Israel never lost sight of the Abrahamic roots of their identity as a people (Neh. 9:7–8; 2 Chron. 20:6–9; 30:6), and the prophets invariably linked the nation's destiny to the ancient covenant promises made to Abraham, Isaac, and Jacob (Isa. 29:22–23; 41:8–9; 51:1–3; Jer. 33:23–26).

The rise of the nation Israel was no aberration or historical accident; to the contrary, it was the centerpiece of God's program of world redemption. The human race, comprised of all the nations, was hopelessly alienated from the Lord because of the fall; hence, God by his own sovereign and gracious initiative called Abraham to father a nation that would be God's appointed means of effecting his salvific design. Already his people from their inception, Israel became a nation by virtue of a special covenant arrangement, one that spelled out this functional role and that provided the social, political, and religious structures necessary to its effective implementation. That arrangement is best described as the Mosaic covenant (rather than the Sinaitic, for example) since it appears in two different forms and on two different occasions, one immediately following the exodus and the other some thirty-eight years later in Moab on the eve of the conquest of Canaan.

We have already traced the historical circumstances that brought the people Israel to the threshold of nationhood.[1] It is our intention now to address the nature of the covenant that transformed Israel from being merely a people who shared a common patriarchal ancestry to a theocratic community with a sense of divine calling and mission. Hints of that mission occur already in the Genesis accounts. The nation would be a source of blessing, said the Lord (Gen. 12:3; 18:18; 22:18; 26:4), and even in its infantile stage it proved to be such as its members encountered individuals and nations long before the Mosaic covenant had formalized its privileged status (Gen. 20:17; 21:22–27; 26:26–31; 30:27; 39:2–5; 47:13–27). Standing between the Lord and the nations, Israel was to assume a mediatorial role that would transmit the Lord's blessings to them, thus the challenge to Israel to be "My kingdom of priests and My holy nation" (Exod. 19:6).

The Abrahamic covenant, described form-critically as a "royal grant," was unconditional in both its offer and its durability. That is, God initiated it with Abraham unilaterally, Abraham's only responsibility being to accept it; and its promises likewise were guaranteed of fulfillment no matter how faithful Abraham might be to its terms.[2] The blessings were to be derived from faithful obedience to its various stipulations. "Live in My presence and be devout" the Lord had said to Abraham (Gen. 17:1), but nowhere is this injunction said to be the basis for the covenant

---

[1] See pp. 251–58.

[2] Jakob Jocz, *The Covenant: A Theology of Human Destiny* (Grand Rapids: Eerdmans, 1968), 22–23.

relationship itself. However, the blessing of land, numerous descendants, and the enrichment of the nations would be directly related to how Abraham (and the others) "listened to My voice and kept My mandate, My commands, My statutes, and My instructions" (Gen. 26:4–5; cf. 22:15–18). That is, the covenant remained unconditional, but the extent to which each of its recipients became the instrument of its benefaction was dependent on their personal fidelity to its requirements.[3]

The Mosaic covenant is another matter. At the outset it is clear that Israel was being granted the privilege of being a kingdom of priests and a holy nation, but on the condition that "you listen to Me and carefully keep my covenant" (Exod. 19:5). It was Israel's vocation, its ministry, that was the issue here and not its existence as a people. As we have argued at length already, Israel was God's "son," the people he redeemed from Egypt in fulfillment of the promises to the fathers. Now the son would be given a task, a position of trust that would demand nothing less than total and unreserved obedience to the Father. This point cannot be stressed too much because there are those who suggest that the Mosaic covenant was in direct succession to the Abrahamic in both form and content when, in fact, they are vastly different in both respects. The Mosaic is subsidiary to the Abrahamic, a special arrangement with Abraham's seed to put it in a position to become the means of blessing which the Lord had promised to his descendants.[4]

This leads to a consideration of the nature of the Mosaic covenant from both a formal and a functional point of view, a matter we have already addressed in passing.[5] Since the mid-twentieth century scholars have recognized that this covenant was analogous to suzerain-vassal treaty texts recovered from the world of the ancient Near East, in particular from Hittite and Neo-Assyrian sources.[6] Both the Hittite of

[3] Victor Hamilton states the matter as follows: "Although the emphasis is on the unilaterality of God's covenant with Abraham, any covenant relationship, if it is to be healthy, needs accountability by both partners." *The Book of Genesis Chapters 1–17,* NICOT (Grand Rapids: Eerdmans, 1990), 461.

[4] William J. Dumbrell, *Covenant and Creation* (Nashville: Thomas Nelson, 1984), 89–90.

[5] See pp. 268–73.

[6] For the former see George E. Mendenhall, "Covenant Forms in Israelite Tradition," *BA* 17 (1954): 50–76, based on V. Korošec, *Hethitische Staatsverträge* (Leipzig: J. C. Hinrichs'sche, 1931); and for the latter see D. J. Wiseman, *The Vassal-Treaties of Esarhaddon* (London: The British School of Archaeology, 1958).

the Late Bronze period (ca. 1400–1200 BC) and the Assyrian (seventh century BC) examples contain standard elements of treaty form that also appear in the Old Testament, especially in the "book of the covenant" (Exod. 20–23) and the book of Deuteronomy as a whole. Advocates of the Mosaic (or at least early) date of these texts naturally draw attention to their similarity to the Hittite models whereas those scholars who locate Deuteronomy, especially, in the late monarchy period favor the comparisons between it and the Assyrian documents. Objective analysis leaves no room for doubt that the proponents of the earlier date have far better arguments in light of current evidence.[7] The structure of these secular texts and a careful comparison of them to the book of the covenant and Deuteronomy respectively is even more important than their dates. While no two of them are exactly identical, the following elements are generally accepted as *sina qua nons,* especially for the Hittite texts:[8]

Title
Historical Prologue
Stipulations
Deposit and Reading
Witnesses
Curses and Blessings

The book of the covenant (Exod. 20–23) and its additions can be viewed in the following manner:[9]

Title/Preamble (20:1)
Historical Prologue (20:2)
Stipulations (20:3–17, 22–26; 21–23; 25–31)
Depositing Text (25:16)
Reading Out (24:7)
Witnesses (Exod. 24:1–4)
Blessings (not in Exod.; cf. Lev. 26:3–13)
Curses (Lev. 26:14–43)

[7] K. A. Kitchen, *On the Reliability of the Old Testament* (Grand Rapids: Eerdmans, 2003), 283–94.

[8] Ibid., 288.

[9] Ibid., 284.

Deuteronomy[10]

Title/Preamble (1:1–5)
Historical Prologue (1:6–3:29)
Stipulations (Intro. 4; Basic 5; Detail 6–11, 12–26)
Depositing Text (31:9, 24–26)
Reading Out (31:9–13)
Witnesses (31:19–22, 26; 32)
Blessings (28:1–14)
Curses (28:15–68)

At a later point we shall address Deuteronomy at length in light of its own setting, purpose, and content since it is quite different in these respects from the version revealed at Sinai.

After the people had agreed to become covenant partners with the Lord and had undergone appropriate purification ceremonies (Exod. 19:8, 14–15), the Lord revealed to Moses the terms of the covenant to which the people had already pledged themselves. He introduced himself in the Preamble to the text as "the LORD your God" (Exod. 20:2a), a disclosure disarming in its verbal simplicity but overwhelming in its theological implications. He is not just deity but a personal God, the Lord of Israel. We have already drawn attention to the theological significance of the names and epithets of God. As Elohim he is the transcendent, all-powerful Creator and Sustainer of the universe. As Lord (Yahweh) he is the immanent one, God who discloses himself to mankind and who delights in their fellowship. As Lord of Israel, he had chosen that people out of all the nations of the earth for a special covenant relationship oriented around a mission, namely, to be a servant nation modeling the kingdom of God and mediating his redemption grace to all other nations.

Compared to the elaborate and expansive titularies and self-serving accolades typical of the kings of the secular treaty texts, this introduction of the King of kings and Lord of Israel by its brevity reveals the inadequacy of human speech to communicate who and what he is. He is God and Lord, each term inexhaustible in its potentiality. The historical prologue to this covenant text (Exod. 20:2b) helps with the identification of Israel's God by moving beyond metaphysical assertions to speak of how he had

---

[10] Ibid.

revealed himself in action, especially on Israel's behalf. Once again in the briefest of declarations, he described himself as he "who brought you out of the land of Egypt, out of the place of slavery." Encapsulated in these six words of Hebrew text was the essence of Israel's *Heilsgeschichte* to that point. All that had happened to Israel since Jacob's descent to Egypt 430 years earlier—their multiplication, their oppressive bondage, their miraculous deliverance—is wrapped up in this summation of their history. God is and he did. He is their Lord, and he rescued them from slavery to another master. Their rescue was not from subservience to independence, however, but from obligation to one lord to subservience to another, the Lord of heaven and earth. The nation had committed itself to this when it said, "We will do all that the LORD has spoken" (Exod. 19:8; cf. 24:3).

THE TEN COMMANDMENTS

The central unit of the General Stipulation section of the Sinai covenant (Exod. 20:3–17) consists of ten statutes or commands (Heb. "ten words," Deut. 10:4) that comprise the legal, moral, and spiritual foundation of the nation's life. Everything else in the law is an interpretation and application of these basic principles. And even these are distilled in the Deuteronomic rendition to just one central confession and injunction: "Listen, Israel: The LORD our God, the LORD is One. Love the LORD your God with all your heart, with all your soul, and with all your strength" (Deut. 6:4–5). Jesus added to this a command with horizontal dimensions: "Love your neighbor as yourself," quoting Leviticus 19:18. He went on to observe that "there is no other commandment greater than these" (Mark 12:31), or, as Matthew put it, "All the Law and the Prophets depend on these two commandments" (Matt. 22:40).

The order of the Ten Commandments is theologically significant. Of the ten, the first two, which have to do with God's uniqueness and incomparability, are most important; for unless and until these are observed, all the rest have no true significance. The third deals with an aspect or representation of God and forms a link with Sabbath-keeping, a time of introspection and celebration by which God's people reflect upon him and his works. The last six commandments are more interpersonal in nature, commencing with proper recognition of parental status and authority and then increasingly transitioning from the overt and objective violation of other human beings to a purely internalized or subjective attitude toward them in the last of the ten, coveting and lusting after what one does not or cannot have.

The basis of God's redemptive work at the exodus was his sovereign grace and power; and, conversely, the exodus and the signs and wonders that preceded it bore eloquent testimony to the fact that he is God and, more specifically, the Lord of Israel. He had already demonstrated that his victory in Egypt was not just over Pharaoh and his armies but, in fact, was over their gods (Exod. 12:12). Even Pharaoh's magicians were forced to concede that the terrible signs and wonders that had befallen Egypt and that they could neither replicate nor avert were nothing more or less than "the finger of God" (Exod. 8:19). By his mighty acts he had made clear that if he was not indeed the only God, he was at least a God without compare.

The First Commandment

Against this backdrop and all that Moses had recounted of primeval and patriarchal times, the first command, "Do not have other gods besides Me" (Exod. 20:3), had special potency. This was not so much (or even primarily) an argument for monotheism as it was for the Lord's exclusive claims on Israel as Israel's only God.[11] To be sure, monotheistic faith was part of normative Hebrew dogma even this early (cf. Exod. 9:14; Deut. 4:35, 39; 32:12, 39), but the intent of the prohibition here was to ensure that Israel would give undivided allegiance to the Lord as opposed to all other deities, real or imaginary. Literally the text reads, "Let there not be *to you* other gods in my place." If the nations of the world wished to believe in and worship other deities, so be it, but as for Israel, they must recognize only the Lord as their God.

One might think that such a command was unnecessary for Israel at that decisive moment of redemption and covenant bestowal, but that would be to misread her (and our) congenital predilection to seek out and worship gods of human contrivance. The patriarchal ancestors had struggled with this issue (Gen. 31:34; 35:2–5), and Israel would no sooner commit herself to the covenant in view here than set about constructing

[11] John I. Durham, *Exodus,* WBC 3 (Waco, Tex.: Word, 1987), 284–85.

a golden calf and attributing to it the marvelous exodus deliverance (Exod. 32:4). From that time forward—at least until the return from Babylonian exile—Israel and Judah almost incessantly succumbed to the blandishments of pagan idolatry, a matter we will document in detail.

Without making excuses for Israel, it is important to understand something of the cultural and religious milieu in which the nation came to birth. Without exception the great civilizations of the ancient Near Eastern world were steeped in a worldview that accounted for all phenomena, natural and supernatural, as expressions of random acts by innumerable gods and goddesses, all of whom had to be placated lest they wreak vengeance on mankind or who must be induced by various means to bring fortune and well-being.[12] Abundance or want, health or illness, peace or war, life or death—all were at the whim of powerful beings that must somehow be invoked or tamed if life was to have any satisfaction. Israel lived in such a world, having come to any sense of a true and living God only by his grace in calling Abraham out of Sumerian paganism and placing him and his descendants in the relative incubation of a largely uninhabited Canaan and an isolated part of Egypt in which to mature. But total removal from that world was impossible, and Israel found itself caught up in the crosscurrents of cultural and religious life that time and again brought it to the brink of spiritual disaster until, in fact, it at last went into Assyrian exile precisely because of its covenant infidelity in going after other gods (2 Kings 17:7–22).

Israel's experience of God's provision of protection and exodus redemption notwithstanding, the temptation in a world governed largely by a cause-and-effect nexus to attribute blessing to the gods of nature would be enormous. The command to have no other gods was therefore not a theological principle articulated in the safe confines of academic abstraction but one affecting everyday thought and life. To hold fast to it would demand resources beyond the mere human; to disobey it, on the other hand, would invite the severest retribution; for to have a god other than the Lord would be an act of malfeasance and covenant disloyalty of the highest magnitude.

---

[12] For an incisive analysis of this environment, see Henri Frankfort, Mrs. H. A. Frankfort, John A. Wilson, and Thorkild Jacobsen, *Before Philosophy: The Intellectual Adventure of Ancient Man* (New York: Penguin, 1946).

The Second Commandment

The second commandment (Exod. 20:4–6) logically follows the first since to the pagan mind the notion of the invisibility of the gods with no means of representing them in some material or physical form was difficult if not impossible to grasp. Yet it is probably incorrect to suppose that the worshippers of these gods, or at least the deeper thinkers among them, actually saw no difference between the deities per se and the plastic forms they assumed as aids to their worship. To put it another way, idols and images in all likelihood were merely representations of invisible beings whose reality could be fully appreciated only by their being seen.[13] At the same time, to many, perhaps most, of the ordinary devotees of these gods, there was no practical distinction between the visible and invisible so that the wood or stone or metal objects themselves were thought to possess a divine numinosity and were worshipped as such.

Whether this was an accurate construal of Israel's concept of images, the fact remains that such visible representations of perceived invisible powers were strictly forbidden. And if this was the case with false gods, how much more heinous to attempt to capture the eternal God of heaven and earth in some object made by human hands! First, to do this was to worship a product of human creation or at least an object adequate to capture the essence of the being it represented. How small a god must be that could be portrayed in any form conceived by the human mind. Beyond this, the attempt to iconicize the invisible God suggested that he could be localized, reduced in scope to something that could be manipulated.[14] In effect, God became a prisoner of the artisan's skill, the substance and qualities of his raw materials, and the incapacity of the worshipper to imagine him beyond what he could see with his own eyes and handle with his own hands.

The prophets later expounded on the evil and folly of idol worship in highly sarcastic and even humorous ways. Isaiah asked, "Who will you compare God with? What likeness will you compare Him to?" (Isa. 40:18). He then pointed out that images were man-made. They were cast in molds and dressed in finery of gold and silver. If a person was too poor

---

[13] A. Leo Oppenheim, *Ancient Mesopotamia* (Chicago: The University of Chicago Press, 1964), 183–96.

[14] Dale Patrick, *Old Testament Law* (Atlanta: John Knox, 1985), 44–47.

for such an elaborate idol, he could have one made of wood, employing a carpenter who must fashion it in such a way that it would not topple over (vv. 19–20)! This calls to mind the image of Dagon, the god of the Philistines, which fell from its pedestal and lost both its head and its hands in the presence of the ark of the covenant (1 Sam. 5:1–5). Thus it proved to be without knowledge or power. Isaiah, carrying on with the idea of the impotence of idols, said of the craftsman who was fearful of the humiliating of the god he had made, "He fastens it with nails so that it will not fall over" (Isa. 41:7). The foolishness of idolatry reflects the foolishness of those who practice it. Isaiah observed of them that they "are nothing, and what they treasure does not profit. Their witnesses do not see or know anything, so they will be put to shame. Who makes a god or casts a metal image for no profit? Look, all its worshipers will be put to shame, and the craftsmen are humans" (Isa. 44:9–11). Then with undisguised mockery the prophet addressed the process of idol manufacture.[15] The various skilled artisans exhaust themselves in their labor to produce a god before whom they can prostrate themselves. In the course of their project, they must cook their meals over fires fueled with the same wood from which their images are carved, not understanding that the block before which they bow is as fragile and combustible as the scraps from it that have provided fuel for the flames. The prophet summarized on a note of scathing ridicule: "He [the idolater] feeds on ashes. His deceived mind has led him astray, and he cannot deliver himself, or say, 'Isn't there a lie in my right hand?'" (Isa. 44:20).

Jeremiah added to Isaiah's description of idolatry and, if anything, in even more caustic terms. Like Isaiah, he depicted the futile process of idol manufacture (Jer. 10:3–9) but then went on to draw the theologically important conclusion that "the gods that did not make the heavens and the earth will perish from the earth and from under these heavens" (Jer. 10:11). Their makers, he continued, are "stupid and ignorant. Every goldsmith is put to shame by his carved image" (v. 14a). As for the idols, they "are a lie; there is no breath in them. They are worthless, a work to be mocked. At the time of their punishment they will be destroyed"

---

[15] "Temple Program for the New Year Festival at Babylon," *Readings from the Ancient Near East,* ed. Bill T. Arnold and Bryan E. Beyer (Grand Rapids: Baker, 2002), 129–30; S. Parpola, "Letters from Assyrian Scholars to the Kings Esarhaddon and Assurbanipal," *AOAT* 5/1 (Neukirchen-Vluyn: Verlag Butzon und Bercker Kevelaer, 1970), #277.

(vv. 14b–15). By contrast, Jeremiah said, "Jacob's Portion is not like these because He is the One who formed all things. Israel is the tribe of His inheritance" (v. 16). That is precisely the point of the first two commandments. There was no God but the Lord of Israel and the idols and images that represented other deities were human creations that stood for nonentities. For Israel to worship them was to commit abominable sacrilege.

The Decalogue states in unambiguous terms why Israel must reject idolatry: The Lord is a "jealous God" (Exod. 20:5). This, of course, has nothing to do with the petty envy that human beings experience toward others who outdo them in some way or other. Rather, the Hebrew term *(qannā')* has the idea, when describing the "feelings" or "emotion" of the Lord, that he is insistent on establishing and maintaining his uniqueness in the face of all competing claims.[16] For him to be jealous in the usual sense of the term would be a tacit admission that other gods existed, something, we have seen, already soundly refuted. But if they existed even in the perception of those who worshipped them, such a false assumption by itself was a challenge to the sovereignty and sole existence of the Lord. Therefore, images must not be made, for they symbolized a competing claim to the Lord's revelation to his people Israel that he and he alone was their God.

The sin of idolatry—and, hence, of the repudiation of the Lord's sole dominion over his covenant people—would have most serious repercussions. It would bring his punishment not only upon the generation that was guilty of it but upon "the third and fourth generations of those who hate Me" (Exod. 20:5). This did not mean that the descendants of sinners were culpable for their parents' misdeeds since other contemporary (Deut. 24:16) as well as later texts (Jer. 31:29–30; Ezek. 18:1–4) rule this out. The answer lay in the idea of corporate solidarity, the concept that families—and, indeed, larger communities—shared in common both blessing and curse, especially in a covenant context. What one member did or failed to do had repercussions for all the members affiliated with him (cf. Num. 16:25–33; Josh. 7:24–26). Thus, whereas the sins of the fathers were the specific acts that would invoke God's judgment, the bond of family relationships would tend to galvanize succeeding generations

---

[16] H. G. L. Peels, קנא, *NIDOTTE* 3:939.

to the same propensities and behaviors as their parents' and thus lead to the same consequences.[17] We should also note that the third and fourth generations are described as "those who hate Me." These descendants therefore must be subject to God's wrath not only because they were likely to imitate their fathers' idolatry but because, in fact, they would do so. The sins of the fathers, by their example, would so have affected their offspring that they too would inevitably commit the same sins.

The converse was also true. The descendants of the ones who loved and obeyed the Lord would be recipients of his *ḥesed* (his covenant loyalty) after thousands of generations (v. 6). Just as idolatry breeds idolatry in a family, so obedience to the Lord as Israel's only God breeds faithfulness to him generation after generation. These promises must, of course, be understood as general principles in line with proverbial wisdom that elsewhere speaks in blanket categories while allowing for exceptions. Observation of life in both biblical texts and everyday experience shows clearly enough that evil parents may produce God-fearing descendants and the righteous all too often generate evildoers. However, this does not by any means vitiate the overriding truth of the second commandment, that parental influence has enormous potential for good or ill.

The terms *hate* and *love* need special attention here because of their technical connotations in covenant contexts such as this. Though they bear their ordinary meaning here in some respects, their major thrust is to communicate covenant disobedience and obedience respectively. That is, to hate God is to violate his covenant, and to love him is to submit to its requirements.[18] Usually the Lord is the subject of the verbs, which describe his acts of either choosing or not choosing the objects of his grace. Deuteronomy 7:7–8 provides a clear example of love as election: "The LORD was devoted to you and chose you, not because you were more numerous than all peoples, for you were the fewest of all peoples. But because the LORD loved you and kept the oath He swore to your fathers, He brought you out with a strong hand and redeemed you from the place of slavery, from the power of Pharaoh king of Egypt." Moses then went on to speak of the Lord as the faithful God who keeps "His

---

[17] Benno Jacob, *The Second Book of the Bible: Exodus,* trans. Walter Jacob (Hoboken, N.J.: KTAV, 1992), 554–55.

[18] P. J. J. S. Els, אהב, *NIDOTTE* 1:279–83; W. L. Moran, "The Ancient Near Eastern Background of the Love of God in Deuteronomy," *CBQ* 25 (1963): 77–87.

gracious covenant loyalty for a thousand generations with those who love Him and keep His commands" (v. 9). "But He directly pays back and destroys those who hate Him. He will not hesitate to directly pay back the one who hates Him" (v. 10).

Quite clearly God's choice of Israel as a covenant recipient was based on his love, but his love was at the same time not merely an emotional reflex but was itself an act of choice. In other words, God loved Israel because he loved them, a verbal tautology, indeed, but a theological proposition that lies at the heart of covenant grace.[19] Beyond his initiative in choosing Israel, he also pledged to keep his covenant of love (i.e., his loyal commitment to it) with those who in turn loved him and kept his commands. That is, the covenant relationship demanded reciprocity. Israel must show its covenant fidelity to the LORD by obedience to its terms, and the Lord would continue to affirm his covenant choice of Israel in response. Those who hated (i.e., rejected and disobeyed) the Lord would be punished, but those who loved (i.e., submitted to and obeyed) him would be beneficiaries of his covenant loyalty (his *ḥesed)* for ages to come (Exod. 20:6).

The Third Commandment

The third commandment (Exod. 20:7), while not in any way contravening the second in its concept and intent, opens up the important Old Testament theological idea that God can and does manifest or represent himself by means that guard his awesome and remote transcendence while making it possible for mankind to encounter him in meaningful ways. In this case, the name of the Lord becomes almost his alter ego, another way of speaking of him and his nearness. We shall explore "name theology" at a later point and in greater detail, but we cannot utterly ignore it in this critical text (Exod. 20:7; cf. Deut. 5:11). The command reads literally, "You shall not take up the name of the LORD for an unworthy purpose." That is, the Lord's name, like the Lord himself, cannot be manipulated to secure some personal gain or advantage for oneself.[20] This degrades his

[19] Eugene H. Merrill, *Deuteronomy,* NAC 4 (Nashville: Broadman & Holman, 1994), 180–81.

[20] Gerhard von Rad, *Old Testament Theology,* vol. 1, trans. D. M. G. Stalker (New York: Harper & Row, 1962), 182–84.

name to the level of a shibboleth or an open sesame that makes him who pronounces it master over it, thus upending the role of sovereign and servant which undergirds the covenant relationship.

We have already observed that names in the world of the ancient Near East and in the Old Testament were indicative of the circumstances of the birth of the person named, some character trait that later manifested itself, or some radical change in life's circumstances that warranted a change of name.[21] One's name was therefore precious and charged with meaning and was not to be given or bandied about without thought. What was true on the human plane was infinitely more the case at the divine level. The various names and epithets of God were revelatory of his nature and indicative of what he had done or would do in the future. They were powerful, and when invoked in fear and reverence by those who knew him, his names could provide solace, joy, deliverance, redemption, and whatever else was necessary to meet human need. But to view the name of God as merely a device, a means of *ex opere operato,* and to use it crassly to advance a personal agenda, was to violate the covenant and render one guilty before him.

On the other hand, the text is careful not to say that the name of the Lord could never be used at all for any reason. As early as Genesis 4, "people began to call on the name of the LORD" (v. 26). In a real sense there was already an awareness that the name was a surrogate for the person of the Lord himself. Abraham later called on him by name (Gen. 12:8; 13:4; 21:33) as did Isaac (26:25) and Jacob (31:53). In an interesting encounter between Jacob and an anonymous nocturnal stranger, the latter asked Jacob to reveal his name, and when he did, the stranger renamed him Israel because, as he said, "you have struggled with God and with men and have prevailed" (Gen. 32:28). Jacob then asked the stranger his name, but he refused to disclose it, pronouncing upon Jacob a blessing instead. But Jacob now understood by the power of the stranger and his authority to bless that he was none other than a manifestation of God (cf. Hos. 12:3–4). He therefore called the name of the place Peniel ("face of God"), for, said he, "I saw God face to face, and yet my life was spared" (Gen. 32:30 NIV). He did not in fact see God, of course, but

[21] Allen P. Ross, שֵׁם, *NIDOTTE* 4:147–48.

came to recognize his antagonist as a manifestation of God despite his unwillingness to disclose his name.

Prior to the articulation of the third commandment, Moses' engagement with the Lord at the burning bush and later in Egypt provides the most helpful data for theological reflection on the names of God. Seeing the bush that burned but was not consumed and then hearing the command that he was to lead his people out of Egypt, Moses had an overpowering urge to know the name that could effect such phenomena and evoke such authority. The people would want to know that name, said Moses, so what should he tell them? The epithet *God* was not enough, for it was too ontologically freighted and, at the same time, too nondescript to communicate what it was he was about to do. Only a name with precise theological content could provide insight and assurance to the people in their particular time and circumstances. That name was Yahweh (Lord), the same name as that of the Creator of mankind (Gen. 2) and the one upon whom the patriarchs called. They had known him especially by the name *El Shaddai* (Exod. 6:3); but Yahweh, according to the biblical testimony, was also familiar to them (cf. Gen. 9:26; 14:22; 15:2, 8; 16:2; 21:33; 22:14; 24:12; etc.).[22] But they had never needed him for what he was about to do now for Israel, namely, for redemption and deliverance. Thus, it was important for Moses to know and use the name appropriate to the historical situation.

The Fourth Commandment

The fourth commandment (Exod. 20:8–11), while clearly an integral element of the first four—those pertaining to the person, nature, and worship of the Lord—is transitional to the remaining six in that it has to do with the treatment of fellow human beings, especially in their relationship to a day of rest. It is anticipated in the creation narrative, which states that "by the seventh day, God completed His work that He had done, and He rested on the seventh day from all His work that He had done. God blessed the seventh day and declared it holy, for on it He rested from His work of creation" (Gen. 2:2–3). For God to rest did not (and cannot) mean for him to recover from the exhaustion of labor but

---

[22] U. Cassuto, *A Commentary on the Book of Exodus,* trans. Israel Abrahams (Jerusalem: Magnes, 1967), 77–79.

simply to cease what he had been doing (thus Heb. *šbt)*. By blessing the day, he celebrated the finished work of creating, adding to it, as it were, his amen of approval.

The Mosaic covenant, though made with Israel alone and not with the world at large, nonetheless emphasized Israel's need to recollect God as Creator and to celebrate with him the perfection of his finished work. He had declared holy the seventh day *(yĕqaddēš)* and now Israel must do the same by remembering what he had done (Exod. 20:8). But the remembering was not merely a calling to mind; it required reenactment.[23] Just as God had ceased his labor, so must Israel; and in so doing they could reflect at least once a week on the wonder of creation and the magnificent way that God provided for them through its bounties. Then, as the God-appointed regent over all creatures, man (and especially the Israelite) must permit them also to rest whether they be family members, slaves, foreigners, or even lowly animals (Exod. 20:10).

As we shall observe more carefully later, the motive clause for the observance of the Sabbath (the reason for it to be done) differs in the Deuteronomy version and, indeed, the day of the week would change in the observance of the New Testament church. The point remains, however, that a day must be set apart whereupon the people of the Lord could give deep thought and worshipful attention to his great creative and salvific work. Not to be ignored was the connection this command made between the Mosaic covenant and the work of divine creation. Israel was called to serve the Lord as a kingdom of priests and a holy nation, but that commission did not disconnect Israel from the world of nations that shared in common an origin in God's creation design. Indeed, as we have stressed repeatedly, Israel's dual role was, first, to model a paradigm of how the nations should live before God and, second, to be a conduit through which the means of world redemption would come to pass.

Many scholars suggest that the first four commandments—those with a vertical, God-directed orientation—were written on one side of a stone tablet while the other six—with a horizontal, societal orientation—were written on the other side (Exod. 32:15). Though this is possible, nothing in the narrative accounts would lead to this conclusion. As for there being

---

[23] Eugene H. Merrill, "Remembering: A Central Theme in Biblical Worship," *JETS* 43/1 (2000): 27–36.

two tablets, some interpreters take this to mean that four commandments were written on one tablet and six on the other and that, in each case, the inscriptions covered both the obverse and reverse sides. Again, there is no objective basis for such a view. In fact, as we shall argue later, the two tablets were likely identical, with one to be given to Israel and the other to the Lord as covenant partners.

The Fifth Commandment

The first of the last six commandments touches directly upon a profoundly significant theological point around which much of our approach revolves, and that is the interrelationships inherent in the creation and in the creation mandate (Exod. 20:12). God as Creator is sovereign, but he has chosen to mediate his rule through mankind. Within mankind, however, there are spheres of sovereignty, persons or institutions that by nature or appointment are designated to exercise beneficent lordship over others. This begins at the level of marriage and the family, a matter we have briefly addressed in passing. The Old Testament model is clearly patriarchal but not patridictatorial. As we shall see, many of the covenant stipulations regulating the behavior of children required them to act toward the father and the mother in exactly the same way. In fact, this commandment itself reads, "Honor your father and your mother" (Exod. 20:12). The verb *honor* (Heb. *kabbēd)* means literally "to regard as heavy, that is, heavy with authority and responsibility and thus worthy of utmost respect."[24] One's attitude toward his parents was therefore not to be one of cavalier indifference to say nothing of ridicule and insubordination. In the creation hierarchy they represented divine authority and so must be revered even as the Lord is to be esteemed. How this was to be fleshed out in everyday life remains to be seen as are its implications for contemporary life apart from the framework of Old Testament theocracy.

The Sixth Commandment

The remaining commandments appear to be graded from the most blatantly and obviously heinous to the least evidently and ostensibly

---

[24] C. John Collins, כבד, *NIDOTTE* 2:578–79.

violent. Commandment six states succinctly but forcefully, "Do not murder" (Exod. 20:13), a rendering of the verb accepted by most modern versions and correctly so since the intent clearly was not to rule out homicide in war, revenge, and other cases sanctioned by law. Nor did it cover cases of manslaughter or accidental homicide inasmuch as these are by definition unintentional and therefore could not be forbidden.

Like every other commandment thus far, this too found its roots in ancient soil, long before the emergence of Israel as a covenant-bearing people. It, like them, is therefore of universal scope and has never been rescinded. However one chooses to view the Israel-church relationship is irrelevant to the fact that the Ten Commandments, though revealed in their present form to Israel, are transhistorical and transdispensational. We have already treated the text of the so-called Noahic covenant that warns that "whoever sheds man's blood, his blood will be shed by man, for God made man in His image" (Gen. 9:6). We noted there that the special egregiousness of premeditated murder lies in its extinguishing of the life of one who has been created as the image of God. The only fitting punishment, then, is for government, on God's behalf, to administer the ultimate penalty of capital punishment (cf. Rom. 13:4).

Man as God's image lies at the center of the prohibition of murder because man does not just bear the image of God as though he in some way resembles God. He *is* in fact that image, the surrogate or vice-regent through whom God exercises his sovereignty over all creation. One might thus view mankind as the ambassador of the kingdom of heaven sent by the King of that realm to represent him on kingdom business. As such, he bears all the magisterial authority of that King and is to be treated as though he were the King. To slay him therefore is to attack God, at least symbolically, an act of sedition so severe that only the application of *lex talionis* is suitable as punishment. This is true whether the assailant or the victim is an Israelite or not; for, as we have already argued, the law is global in its intent, covering the full range of human interrelationships.

The Seventh Commandment

The command to abstain from adultery (Exod. 20:14) has at heart the protection of the marriage relationship and the family it entails; but because human sexual relationships also served metaphorically to describe Israel's relationship to the Lord, it had ramifications beyond the merely interpersonal. At the human level this injunction, like that mandating proper respect for parents, was crucial because of the role of the family in the implementation of God's kingdom design. A man or woman who betrayed his or her partner—the one without whom neither was complete—contributed to the breakdown of the hierarchical model of kingdom dominion for which they had been created as complementary beings (cf. Gen. 2:18). Adultery was therefore not just an isolated, private act; it had profound effect upon the immediate and even universal community of those who constituted the kingdom of God on earth. If a man or woman could not live in marital fidelity, what hope could there be for other kingdom commitments, including commitments to the Great King himself?

Because God's covenant with Israel is sometimes described as a marriage (cf. Isa. 54:5–6; Jer. 3:14, 20; 31:32; Ezek. 16:32; Hos. 2:16), infidelity in that relationship by Israel was nothing short of adultery (cf. Hos. 4:15; 7:4; Jer. 3:8; 5:7; 9:2; 13:27; Ezek. 6:9; 16:32; 23:37–45).[25] The other partner in such a case were the idols and gods of the nations with which Israel flirted and to which she succumbed over and over throughout her history. Jeremiah recorded the plaintive lament of the Lord who asked, "Have you seen what unfaithful Israel has done? She has ascended every high hill and gone under every green tree to prostitute herself there" (Jer. 3:6). But Judah was no better, and having seen her sister's adulterous behavior, she "also went and prostituted herself. Indifferent to her prostitution, she defiled the land and committed adultery with stone and tree" (vv. 8–9).

The command to avoid adultery was designed not just to keep intact the human family and its role in displaying kingdom principles. It also had direct relevance to the role of Israel among the nations as the seed through which God would bless them. An unfaithful Israel could no more carry out its mission as a kingdom of priests than could an unfaithful wife discharge hers as the vessel without whom her husband is incomplete.

The Eighth Commandment

The scope of the next commandment, "Do not steal" (Exod. 20:15), is broader and yet less damaging to the kingdom since it centers more

[25] Durham, *Exodus,* 294.

on property than on persons (though some scholars propose that it may include kidnapping).[26] Nevertheless, it was a serious matter for one to take by force or by stealth what belonged to a fellow citizen because what he possessed came to him by the gracious hand of God who, as Sovereign, bestowed upon his people what was most necessary and best for them. Ultimately, all that people have is theirs on loan from God, and theirs is the responsibility to administer it on his behalf as stewards. Servants in the Master's household had no right to steal from one another because in such a case they were actually stealing from the Master himself and in so doing were communicating their dissatisfaction with what he had already entrusted to them.

This kind of spirit was directly counter to the creation design which assigned to mankind jurisdiction over all that God has made.[27] Within the structures of government and society, some exercise one kind of authority and some another. Some appear to be more privileged than others and to enjoy greater realms of stewardship than others. But the Sovereign, who is all-wise, dispenses his gifts and favors as he sees fit; and within that framework of kingdom organization, each element must function as he alone determines to be best. The thief—whether he should steal material things or aspire to a position not allotted to him—proves to be an unprofitable servant, unworthy of discharging whatever stewardship has been granted to him.

The Ninth Commandment

Akin to the abuse of a brother by theft was to violate him by bearing false witness against him (Exod. 20:16). Though the prohibition might legitimately be applied to lying in general, the technical wording ("false testimony," Heb. *ʿed šāqer)* suggests a legal or court setting in which a case concerning a crime or misdemeanor is being adjudicated.[28] Witnesses were (and are) essential in determining guilt or innocence (cf. Deut. 17:6–7; 19:15), but persons called to testify must tell the truth about what

---

[26] Thus Albrecht Alt, cited by Brevard Childs, *The Book of Exodus* (Philadelphia: Westminster, 1974), 423.

[27] William Dyrness, *Themes in Old Testament Theology* (Downers Grove, Ill.: InterVarsity, 1979), 178–79.

[28] Martin Noth and most modern scholars. Martin Noth, *Exodus* (Philadelphia: Westminster, 1962).

they had seen or heard. To do less and thus to inculpate an innocent party and subject him to a miscarriage of justice would infringe grievously on his freedom, his possessions, and possibly even his life. Again, the repercussions on a well-ordered structure of kingdom administration are obvious and detrimental.

The Tenth Commandment

The last of the commandments (Exod. 20:17) is somewhat a summary of the others, and at the same time it is vastly different from them in terms of the perceptibility of the offense in view. It has to do with an interior disposition or inclination that could, indeed, be manifest in behavior if left unchecked, but that might never be detected by an outward sign. However, whether visible or not, to covet for oneself what belonged to another was to sin against both God, the giver of all things, and the person who was the recipient of his gracious bestowment. Coveting a brother's property was tantamount to stealing it; for if, indeed, the urge to have it was strong enough, it might well lead to theft, the overt violation of the eighth commandment. Likewise, the man who coveted his brother's wife already had adulterous designs on her and, if not restrained, was likely to break the seventh commandment and have an illicit affair with her. If prevented from doing so by the woman's husband, the coveter might go so far as to commit murder in order to satisfy his lustful impulses.

Seen in this way, coveting appears far less benign than at first glance; for it is an index of a sinful attitude that need not find active expression in order to be injurious to the covenant and the covenant community. In some respects this last of the commandments is the most theologically suggestive because it locates the wellspring of sinful human behavior exactly where it belongs, deep within the heart and mind. Jesus understood this well when he said, "You have heard that it was said, 'Do not commit adultery.' But I tell you, everyone who looks at a woman to lust for her has already committed adultery with her in his heart" (Matt. 5:27–28).

The Book of the Covenant

The Decalogue (Exod. 20:1–17) is the first part of the book of the covenant (Exod. 20:18–23:33). The remainder consists of covenant principles that expound upon and apply the principles articulated in the

Commandments. There is no need here to examine in detail all the case law that constitutes the specific stipulations of the Sinai covenant. It will suffice to consider only those examples that contribute most to the overall theological message being espoused here.

The Altar Law

The revelation of the Ten Commandments is followed by a brief narrative interlude (Exod. 20:18–21) and then an altar law closely linked to the first two commandments (vv. 22–26). The reiteration of these, albeit in summary form, underscores the fact that the truth of God's sole existence and incomparability and the absolute prohibition of idolatry formed the bedrock of Israel's covenant faith. All else in the law was supplemental and elucidatory. The connection between this fundamental tenet and instruction concerning the erection of altars is also edifying because it makes the point that this solitary God, invisible as he is, must be addressed by means of cult and ritual. Where this point of contact is made, there he will come to meet his people and bless them (v. 24). We have already traced the history of Old Testament sacred places and have noted that at these sites the Lord chose to manifest himself in special ways.[29] It was in such venues, he said, that "I cause My name to be remembered." Deuteronomy greatly expands upon this matter of "name theology" and on the need for the community to meet the Lord at designated places. In fact, Deuteronomy specifies that in the land of Canaan toward which they were headed, there could be only one such place, the central sanctuary to which all Israel must repair (Deut. 12:5–7).

The Deuteronomic legislation, however, was to be a renewal of the Sinaitic covenant specially redacted and expanded to suit the conditions of a sedentary lifestyle in the land of Canaan. The one propounded here in Exodus dealt with Israel's situation at Sinai and en route to Canaan, a mode of existence characterized by transitory pastoralism. A permanent central sanctuary would be impossible under these circumstances so the Lord informed his people that "I will come to you and bless you in every place where I cause My name to be remembered" (Exod. 20:24). This presupposes a community on the move and one that would continue to lack

[29] See pp. 287–90.

strong central cohesion even in Canaan until long after the conquest. In fact, the Deuteronomic code is clear that even forty years after the giving of the law at Sinai there would be no certain place where community worship would be centered: "You are not to do as we are doing here today; everyone is doing whatever seems right in his own eyes. Indeed, you have not yet come into the resting place and the inheritance the LORD your God is giving you. When you cross the Jordan and live in the land the LORD your God is giving you to inherit, and He gives you rest from all the enemies around you and you live in security, then the LORD your God will choose the place to have His name dwell. Bring there everything I command you" (Deut. 12:8–11).

This did not come to pass until the reign of Solomon four centuries later. Only then did consolidation of the kingdom and peace with the nations make possible the erection of the temple, the central sanctuary prescribed by the covenant stipulations (1 Chron. 22:6–10).

In the interim, and especially following the conquest, local shrines with their altars sprouted up all over the land alongside the Mosaic tabernacle in its various fixed locations. We shall take note of this fact in due course and learn how the continued existence of local worship centers proved to be increasingly problematic to Israel's spiritual well-being, especially after the location of the temple at the permanent central site at Jerusalem.

One more point must be made regarding the altar law of the book of the covenant and that has to do with altar construction itself (Exod. 20:25–26). In what is clearly an anti-Canaanite polemic, the Lord specified that the altars the Israelites constructed must not be built of quarried stones, as was the Canaanite practice, but rather of earth or rough fieldstones, much as their patriarchal ancestors had done (cf. Gen. 22:9; 31:51–54).[30] The reference to the use of a tool suggests that only what is natural; i.e., made by God and not dressed by human hands, was suitable. What man makes, i.e., a nicely fashioned stone, smacks too much of human improvisation and therefore of human participation in his own atonement and fellowship with God. Also unlike pagan custom, the Israelites must not build steps by which to ascend to the altar lest they

---

[30] Childs, *The Book of Exodus,* 466.

immodestly expose themselves and thus bring shame to themselves and to their holy God.

The structure of the present passage (Exod. 20) yields one overriding message and that is that the God of Israel was the only God and that he must be worshipped in a way that honored him and at the same time set him apart from the imaginary gods of the pagans who approached their deities according to their own inventiveness. Upon this platform the following covenant stipulations found a basis and from it derived their ultimate theological significance.

Other Laws

The remaining laws of the book of the covenant address such matters as the treatment of Hebrew bond servants (Exod. 21:2–11), personal injuries (21:12–36), property rights (22:1–15), social responsibility (22:16–31), and justice and mercy (23:1–9). Of more obvious theological consequence are those at the end that deal with the observance of the Sabbath and the annual festivals (23:10–19). The fourth commandment had already stated the reason for Sabbath keeping and stressed the idea that the seventh day was to be a day of cessation of labor for both human beings and the work animals of Israel. Added to that, here is the remarkable declaration that even the soil must be allowed to rest and to remain unharvested except by the poor of the people and the wild animals that could eat what grew up by itself (Exod. 23:11). Sabbath therefore was not just prohibitive of activity, but it provided an occasion for blessing those whose dire straits made them utterly dependent on others.

The thrice annual festivals as described in Exodus (with the exception of the Feast of Unleavened Bread) were exclusively agricultural in significance. Moreover, they were mandatory only for the men of Israel, who must make pilgrimage to the earthly dwelling place of the Lord in order to pay tribute to him there. All this is in line with the premise argued earlier that the Mosaic covenant was modeled after the suzerain-vassal treaty texts of the Hittite Empire, which demanded that the rulers of secondary states pay homage regularly to the great Hittite king at his capital city.[31] By doing this they acknowledged his sovereignty and pledged anew their covenant fidelity. Thus Israel, the vassal of the King

---

[31] M. G. Kline, *Treaty of the Great King* (Grand Rapids: Eerdmans, 1963), 92.

of heaven and earth, could do no less than to proffer him the fruit of their labor and thereby demonstrate both their commitment to him and the covenant but also their continued need for his gracious largess.

The Feast of Unleavened Bread (mentioned here without reference to Passover, which introduced it) had already been commanded on the eve of the exodus departure (Exod. 13:3–10). There, as here, the focus was on the avoidance of yeast because of the delay necessitated by the time for it to rise in the dough. Both places also link the festival with the exodus deliverance and therefore with a historical moment as well as with an agricultural harvest. The latter is still clearly in view in the reminder that "no one is to appear before Me empty-handed" (Exod. 23:15).

The Feast of Harvest *(qāṣîr),* mentioned here for the first time, was associated with the completion of the grain harvest fifty days after the Feast of Unleavened Bread, hence its alternative names Feast of Weeks (Exod. 34:22) or Feast of Pentecost (Acts 2:1). The third, the Feast of Ingathering *(ʾāsip),* otherwise known as the Feast of Tabernacles (or Sukkot), is also first alluded to here. It occurred in the seventh month to celebrate the harvesting of the fall crops (Exod. 23:16). The later association of these feasts with great redemptive events in Israel's sacred history will require extensive comment when that connection is made.

The Covenant Ceremony

Treaties and covenants between contracting parties were usually formalized by a ceremony consisting of sacrifices of animals whose blood was applied to the participants and by a common meal which they equally shared.[32] Moses, in line with these protocols, built an altar at the foot of the mountain and near or around the altar erected twelve stone pillars *(maṣṣēbôt)* representing the twelve tribes of Israel (Exod. 24:4). The altar obviously symbolized the presence of the Lord. Then Moses ordered that burnt offerings and fellowship offerings be made and that some of the blood of the latter be collected in bowls and the rest sprinkled on the altar, binding the Lord to a commitment to covenant loyalty (v. 6). Following this, Moses read to the assembly the words of the book of the covenant, and the people responded, "We will do and obey everything

[32] D. J. McCarthy, *Old Testament Covenant* (Atlanta: John Knox, 1972), 30–31; Ernst Kutsch, "Das sog. 'Bundesblut' in Ex XXIV 8 und Sach IX 11," *VT* 23 (1973): 25–30.

that the LORD has commanded" (v. 7). These are the words they affirmed even before the terms of the covenant were known to them (Exod. 19:8), so by this double pledge the nation swore itself to faithful compliance to all that God demanded. Moses then sprinkled the blood of the bowls upon the people (i.e., upon the pillars) as a sign that they too had entered into covenant fellowship with the Lord, the blood binding both parties into an indissoluble union (v. 8; cf. Gen. 15:9–21; Jer. 34:18).

Finally, Moses, Aaron, and other leaders of the community ascended part way up the mountain where they encountered the God of Israel and this time without terror or danger, for the offerings of fellowship had paved the way for a face-to-face meeting otherwise impossible. The Great King had ushered his servant people into his august presence and made them feel at home. Then all together the Lord and the representatives of the people "ate and drank" (Exod. 24:11), celebrating the oneness brought about by the mutual pledges of fealty made by the one to the other (vv. 9–11).

Israel as a Cultic Community

The remainder of Exodus and all of Leviticus and Numbers contain additions, amplifications, interpretations, and applications of the covenant precepts just elaborated in the book of the covenant of Exodus 20–23. As we shall see, Deuteronomy must be considered as a case unto itself, for it was not essentially an addendum to the book of the covenant but a restatement of it in terms appropriate to the covenant renewal the nation must undergo upon entering and conquering the land of Canaan. The Sinai version of the covenant was designed to lay out prescriptions for the civil and religious life of a community in transition. The Moab version, on the other hand, speaks to and about a community becoming an urbanized monarchic state with all the complexities that the Sinaitic covenant did not and could not address. At the same time, the fundamental principles and practices of covenant life spelled out in the book of the covenant and the chapters in Exodus that follow were never abrogated or significantly altered later on. They were either appropriated into the Deuteronomic rendition without comment or were further elucidated by the Deuteronomic need to reapply them to the new conditions that Deuteronomy presupposes.

We turn now to those elements of the Sinai covenant that were a natural and necessary outgrowth of the principles and stipulations articulated there. Fundamentally these were limited to Israel's cultus, the organization of her mode of worship and the constituent aspects of it that gave it a framework within which to function. Their theological overtones are rich, indeed, and must be elicited carefully from the complexity of details that make up their description in the sacred text. These elements include especially (1) sacred space, (2) sacred persons, (3) sacred times and seasons, and (4) sacred acts. Each will be dealt with here in order and then traced throughout Leviticus, Numbers, and even beyond as seems appropriate.

Sacred Space

We have already come to understand that the notion of sacred space or holy ground arose as early as the times described by the creation narratives themselves.[33] The garden of Eden was its earliest expression; but then whenever and wherever the Lord manifested himself in special ways, there was a sense that such sites were uniquely invested with divine presence and power and were therefore to be marked and memorialized for that reason.

With the selection of Israel as a covenant people and the covenant commitments that formally bound that people to its God, a whole new understanding of sacred space came to the fore. Moses had already encountered the Lord at Sinai forty years before the covenant was initiated and had heard God's own words on the matter: "Do not come closer," God said. "Take your sandals off your feet, for the place where you are standing is holy ground" (Exod. 3:5). The same sense of the awesomeness of God associated with special places pervades the narrative of the Sinai covenant as a whole. God was on the mountaintop concealed by cloud and yet revealed epiphanically by the flash of lightning and the sound of thunder and trumpet (Exod. 19:16–19). When Moses and his companions later ascended Sinai to obtain the stone tablets of the law, they "saw the God of Israel. Beneath His feet was something like a pavement made of sapphire stone, as clear as the sky itself" (Exod.

[33] See pp. 281–84.

24:10; cf. Isa. 6:1–3; Ezek. 1:22–28). Thus Moses attempted with feeble words to paint a picture of the presence of God.

But the situation now would change. Moses would no longer go up a mountain to encounter the Lord in a realm of holiness too glorious to describe; rather, the Lord would come down and dwell among his people, the nation Israel that he had graciously deigned to bring into special fellowship with himself. Heaven would be on earth, housed first in a tabernacle and then in a temple, both of which were so imbued with God's holiness as to be fatally dangerous to those foolish enough to mishandle them or underestimate their significance.

The Lord initiated this new arrangement with the remarkable words, "They [the Israelites] are to make a sanctuary for Me so that I may dwell among them" (Exod. 25:8). And this sanctuary must not be designed and built according to human specifications, but it and its furnishings must be made "according to all that I show you" (v. 9). There was no room for human creativity or mere guesswork here because every part of the structure was laden with meaning, as much a revelation as God's own words. The same care extended later to the building of the great Jerusalem temple. When David, unable to build the temple himself, sent for Solomon, he "gave him the plans of all that the Spirit had put in his mind for the courts of the temple of the LORD and all the surrounding rooms, for the treasuries of the temple of God and for the treasuries for the dedicated things" (1 Chron. 28:12 NIV). David had received these specifications from the Lord himself and, as he went on to say, "By the LORD's hand on me, He enabled me to understand everything in writing, all the details of the plan" (v. 19).

The technical term for the Mosaic tabernacle is *miškān,* a noun derived from a verb meaning "to dwell."[34] This is an important idea because it provides a note of intimacy or immediacy in the larger context of God's overwhelming power and glory. The great Sovereign of heaven—the wholly inconceivable and unapproachable One—would, in some sense at least, dwell in an earthly structure among fallen mankind. Christian theology sees in this condescension a type of the incarnation in which "the Word became flesh and took up residence [lit., pitched His tent] among us" (John 1:14). This language of anthropomorphism concerning

[34] Richard E. Averbeck, מִשְׁכָּן, *NIDOTTE* 2:1130–34.

the tabernacle must not, however, obscure the fact that God's dwelling was not in any way to be seen as physical or comprehensive. He was there, at home, in the sense that the tabernacle (and the later temple) was the focal point of his glory, the sacred space where that glory touched the earth in a uniquely revelatory manner. Solomon well understood this in his dedicatory prayer where he asked, "But will God indeed live on earth? Even heaven, the highest heaven, cannot contain you, much less this temple I have built" (1 Kings 8:27)! And yet he was aware that God was there in a way he could not be found anywhere else on earth (vv. 44–45).

Like any other house, the tabernacle of the Lord must have its furnishings. Furthermore, each piece must conform to precise specifications, for the furniture, like the structure itself, had symbolic value, typifying great theological realities whose full significance could not be understood at the time except in dim outline. Chief among these was the ark of the testimony, so called because it contained the stone tablets of the Decalogue which served as a witness to the community of the covenant the Lord had made with them (cf. Exod. 32:15; 34:29). The lid of this richly decorated chest was called the *kappōret* (a substantive derived from the verb *kpr,* "to cover," with the greatly expanded technical meaning, "to make atonement" [cf. Exod. 32:30; Lev. 4:20, 26, 31; etc.]).[35] The cover served also as a throne upon which the invisible God sat in regal splendor. Overshadowed by two cherubim, angelic beings that served to shield the glory of God from profane eyes (cf. Gen. 3:24), the *kappōret* marked the spot where, the LORD said, "I will meet with you" and "speak with you from there about all that I command you regarding the Israelites" (Exod. 25:22).

The two ideas conjoined here—the ark as a place of atonement and as the throne of the Lord—cannot be separated because the only way the Holy One of Israel could be approached as Israel's King was by an act of atonement requiring sacrifices that satisfied his justice and effected the cleansing of those who would come to pay homage to him. The text that pulls these ideas together is Leviticus 16, a ritualistic formula that deals with the issue of national, collective sin and the annual ceremony designed to address it. On this Day of Atonement *(yôm hakkippurîm),*

[35] *HALOT* 493–94.

the tenth day of the seventh month (Lev. 25:27), Aaron (and every chief priest thereafter) must appear before the Lord to offer atonement on behalf of the whole nation.[36] He must not do so on any other day for, said the Lord, "he will die, because I appear in the cloud above the mercy seat" (Lev. 16:2). That is, to enter the throne room without invitation was to violate the sacred space reserved only for a holy God. Only on that day and only after proper sacrifices had been made could the priest presume to enter the holy place. He must first offer a bull for a sin offering on his own behalf (v. 6), and then he would be qualified to approach the Lord on behalf of others. The nation would be atoned for by the offering of one goat and the dispatching of another to the wilderness, symbolically carrying away the peoples' collective guilt.

After burning incense whose smoke provided concealment of the ark and the *kapporet,* the priest could enter the Most Holy Place and there sprinkle on the *kapporet* the blood of the bull as an atonement for his own sin and then the blood of the goat on behalf of the people. The great bronze altar in front of the tabernacle must be cleansed in a similar way with the mixture of the blood of the bull and the goat (vv. 18–19). Finally, the living goat would be chased away, bearing on its head the sins of the nation that the priest had confessed (vv. 20–22).

The point to be made by this digression describing ritual is that the ark of the testimony and its environs represented the most sacred area of Israel's encampment, for it was there that the Lord chose to meet with them. Moreover, they must meet him on his terms, not theirs, and approach his holy presence according to proper protocol and preconditions. He was, after all, the Great King; and it was only by his gracious overtures toward those who knew and served him that they could draw near to him. But come near they could, for God had created not just Israel but all humanity to have fellowship with him and despite their sin and rebellion had provided means of atonement so that even the holy of holies could become accessible.

The ark of the covenant was located in the part of the tabernacle called the holy of holies (or *debir*). That area was sectioned off from the larger

[36] For a helpful description of the ritual of the Day of Atonement and its theological significance, see Allen P. Ross, *Holiness to the Lord: A Guide to the Expositon of the Book of Leviticus* (Grand Rapids: Baker, 2002), 313–25.

room, the holy place *(mishkan)*, by a thick curtain, sometimes known as the veil. The holy place contained three items—the table containing the bread of the Presence, the lampstand, and the altar of incense. Each of these played an important role in the worship ritual, and each has profound symbolical or typological significance. Exodus 25:23–30 addresses the table first, describing its dimensions, its various decorative and functional features, and the vessels associated with it in the carrying out of priestly ministry. Its principal purpose was to hold the "bread of the Presence" which, the Lord said, was to be "on the table before Me at all times" (v. 30). The table itself was to be placed on the north side of the holy place opposite the lampstand (Exod. 26:35).

The priests and Levites were responsible for placing twelve loaves of bread on the table in two rows of six each. Along with the bread was incense which, when burned, represented the offering of the bread up to the Lord. The bread is always said to "be set out before the LORD" (Lev. 24:8), hence its description as the "bread of the presence [of God]." In actual fact, it was eaten by the priests as part of the fellowship offerings that were made to the Lord (v. 9). Thus the table was, in the truest sense, a place where the Lord and his people, represented by the priests, symbolically broke bread together. This was done "every Sabbath day as a perpetual covenant obligation on the part of the Israelites" (Lev. 24:8). Its connection with the Sabbath suggests that the covenant in view here was the Mosaic covenant in its entirety since Sabbath keeping, as we shall see, served as a sign of that covenant (Exod. 31:12–13, 16).[37] When the Lord presented the terms of the covenant to Moses and his associates on Mount Sinai, "they ate and drank" (Exod. 24:11), that is, the Lord and Israel's representatives shared a common meal. The bread of the Presence was therefore a perpetual reminder of the covenant that God had made with Israel.

Directly opposite the table, on the south side of the holy place, stood a solid gold lampstand (Heb. *mĕnōrâ*) with a central shaft and six branches, three on each side (Exod. 25:31–40). Since the interior of the tabernacle was dark because of the lack of windows, the lampstand obviously served the practical function of providing light. However, there was meaning far

---

[37] Gordon J. Wenham, *The Book of Leviticus,* NICOT (Grand Rapids: Eerdmans, 1979), 310.

beyond mere practicality, a fact true of the tabernacle as a whole and all its furnishings.[38] Like the tabernacle the lampstand must be made "according to the model of them you have been shown on the mountain" (Exod. 25:40; cf. v. 9). That is, the materials, form, use, and meaning of the lampstand were of heavenly origination and were intended to communicate something of the nature of the Lord and reveal something of Israel's role in his kingdom design. The priests must keep the lamps burning before the Lord from evening till morning every day, and in so doing they would be observing a "permanent statute for the Israelites throughout their generations" (Exod. 27:21).

Like the bread of the Presence, the lamps were to burn "before the LORD," i.e., they must direct their light to him almost as an offering. Furthermore, they must burn through the night even when no human being was in the holy place. The light, then, was as much for his benefit or pleasure as for the people's. King Abijah of Judah, hundreds of years later, described the ministry of the priests as follows: "They offer a burnt offering and fragrant incense to the LORD every morning and every evening, and they set the rows of the bread of the Presence on the ceremonially clean table. They light the lamps of the gold lampstand every evening. We are carrying out the requirements of the LORD our God" (2 Chron. 13:11). Here the bread and the lamps with their illumination are linked to the offering of incense and burnt offerings as vital parts of the worship of the Lord.

The Old Testament nowhere elaborates on the meaning intended by the menorah but the association of the light with the Lord himself suggests anything from the light at creation which dispelled the darkness with its ominous overtones, to the tree of life in the garden, to the idea of the Lord's provision of fertility and blessing. The fact that the lampstand had treelike features (Exod. 25:31–36) might tend to favor the second option. In any case, God is consistently portrayed in the Old Testament as a glorious, transcendent being whose splendor is best manifested in fire and light. It is fitting that the tabernacle and temple provide a setting where this symbolic means of representing his presence among his people could be strikingly evident.

---

[38] Rachel Hachlili, *The Menorah, the Ancient Seven-Armed Candelabrum: Origin, Form, and Significance* (Leiden: Brill, 2001).

The command to Israel to make a sanctuary for the Lord so that he might "dwell among them" (Exod. 25:1–9) was followed with precise instructions as to how it must be done. Like sanctuaries known elsewhere in the ancient Near Eastern world, this one consisted of three main parts: the tent structure itself with two chambers and an outer court surrounding the tabernacle.[39] This implies a gradation of accessibility or holiness that will be elaborated upon at a later point. For now we simply observe that the outer court was accessible to the people at large (provided they were ritually pure), the holy place was open to the priests and Levites when they ministered there from time to time, and the most holy place was permitted only to the chief priest and then only once a year, on the Day of Atonement. The Lord symbolically occupied the most holy place, seated upon the *kapporet* of the ark of the covenant and overshadowed by the cherubim.

The outer court measured approximately 150 feet long by 75 feet wide. The tabernacle was about 45 feet long, 15 feet wide, and 15 feet high. The holy place was 30 by 15 by 15 feet, and the most holy place a perfect cube, 15 by 15 by 15 feet, thus one-half the size of the holy place. The sides of the building were made of acacia wood covered over by curtains, and the roof consisted of a covering of several layers of animal hides. The entrance was concealed by curtains, and a curtain (the veil) also separated the holy place from the most holy place. The whole effect was stunningly beautiful, a fitting tribute to the Lord who evidenced his presence there. Most important, it was made "according to the plan for it that you have been shown on the mountain" (Exod. 26:30). The building and all its decorations and furnishings embodied divine revelation, a theological message which, though still unclear and debatable in its particulars, testifies with profound clarity to the glory and majesty of the God of Israel who condescended to dwell within.

This is not the place to trace the history of the tabernacle and subsequent holy places that took its place. This will be done in the course of exploring Israel's history in general up to the time of the Davidic monarchy and the erection of the temple that formed such an important element of the Davidic covenant. For now we return to the remaining furnishings of

---

[39] John Monson, "The New 'Ain Dara Temple: Closest Solomonic Parallel," *BAR* 26 (2000): 20–35, 67.

the tabernacle in order to view in its entirety the theological message it intends to convey.

In addition to the table of the bread of the Presence and the golden lampstand, the holy place housed the altar of incense (Exod. 30:1–10). It stood immediately in front of the curtain separating the holy place and the most holy place and served a twofold purpose: (1) to offer up to the Lord a continuous sweet aroma and (2) to pave the way for the chief priest to enter the most holy place once a year to make atonement for the people. This was done by applying the blood of a sin offering on its horns before it was sprinkled on the ark of the covenant within the most holy place. Incense is associated with prayer at least once in the Old Testament (Ps. 141:2), and the New Testament even more explicitly affirms the connection: "Another angel, with a gold incense burner, came and stood at the altar. He was given a large amount of incense to offer with the prayers of all the saints on the gold altar in front of the throne. The smoke of the incense, with the prayers of the saints, went up in the presence of God from the angel's hand" (Rev. 8:3–4; cf. 5:8). At the least, incense served the purpose of disposing the Lord to look favorably upon his people and to act graciously on their behalf.[40]

The altar of burnt offering stood in the tabernacle courtyard just in front of the entrance to the holy place. Like altars in general—apart from the incense altar—its function was to provide a means of making sacrifice of animals and agricultural produce according to particular occasions and needs. Unlike all others so far known, however, it was made not of stone but of a wooden framework overlaid with bronze and fitted with corner rings and carrying poles for easy transportation (Exod. 27:1–8). This, of course, was for the practical considerations of movement in the desert sojourn until the nation could find permanent rest in Canaan under the leadership of David and Solomon. The great bronze altar of the Solomonic temple was obviously not portable, though details of its manufacture are lacking (2 Chron. 4:1; cf. the eschatological altar of Ezekiel's temple, Ezek. 43:13–17). To preclude human inventiveness once more, Moses was told to make the altar "just as it was shown to you on the mountain" (Exod. 27:8).

---

[40] Richard Averbeck links incense with the idea of protection against the holiness of the Lord. See אוּרִים, *NIDOTTE* 3:914–15.

The final sacred object was a bronze basin placed at the eastern end of the courtyard between the tabernacle and the great bronze altar (Exod. 30:17–21). It was to contain water for the priests to undertake ritual purification of their hands and feet preparatory to entering the tabernacle for ministry and also before they offered sacrifice at the altar of burnt offering. This last item in the list of objects pertaining to the tabernacle most appropriately summarizes and underscores the nature of the structure and its accoutrements—it was sacred space dedicated to God's dwelling on the earth and especially among his chosen people Israel. It was only fitting that those called to minister in such a place should be pure in the eyes of the Lord.

Sacred Persons

Every "high religion" has an order of priestly or clerical personnel who represent the community in its approach to its god (or gods) and who function on behalf of deity vis-à-vis the community. To this point priests by this term have appeared only rarely in the Old Testament and almost always as officiants in pagan or, at least, non-Israelite cultuses such as those of Egypt (Gen. 41:45, 50; 46:20; 47:22, 26) and Midian (Exod. 2:16; 3:1; 18:1). Melchizedek, as we saw, was a priest of "God Most High" (El Elyon; Gen. 14:18), a reference certainly to the true God. His origins, functions, and relationship otherwise to the fathers of Israel are shrouded in mystery. The first time a priest is mentioned with regard to Israel is in the covenant declaration that Israel would become "My kingdom of priests and My holy nation" (Exod. 19:6). Moses and his people surely understood what that meant, for despite the fact that a priesthood was yet to be established in a formal way in Israel, it is inconceivable that they, as a theocratic community living in Egypt for over four centuries, would not have given rise to an order of persons recognized as priestly leaders among them. In fact, the Lord warned Moses at Sinai to command the people to keep at a safe distance from the mountain when he manifested his glory and went on to specify that "even the priests who come near the Lord must purify themselves or the Lord will break out in anger against them" (Exod. 19:22). Some scholars suggest that the mention of priests here is anachronistic since the Aaronic priesthood had not yet been instituted. However, Aaron's role in the present narrative anticipates a formal installation of him and his sons at a later point (chs. 28–29).[41]

One or two observations can be made about priests as sacred persons prior to the appointment of a more formal and permanent order. First, their ministry is most comprehensively described as those "who approach the LORD." The verb employed here *(ngš)* is used elsewhere as a technical term to speak of priests in their official capacity as ministers of the sanctuary (Ezek. 44:13). Such an office clearly existed in Israel prior to its formation as a covenant nation. Second, these priests must "consecrate themselves" in anticipation of the Lord's imminent self-disclosure. This presupposes knowledge of a ritual of cleansing that would qualify a priest (or anyone else) to approach God in his dangerous holiness. That is, not only must a priesthood have existed at this precovenant period, but there must also have been at least a preliminary structure of ritual and worship within which Israel's religious life and traditions were carried out.

The instructions to build a sanctuary and to furnish it in an appropriate manner would obviously have communicated to Israel the need for specially called religious personnel to staff it, particularly now that they had become a covenant nation quite distinct from their status prior to that critical event. The old order would not do, including whatever priestly apparatus might have existed. The new concept of a tabernacle as sacred space in which dwelt a holy God called for a corresponding body of priests, sacred persons suitable for such an environment.

The introduction of this new regime is startling in its lack of preparatory information as to the criteria by which the priests should be chosen and as to what their responsibilities would entail. We are told simply that Moses was to have his brother Aaron brought to him along with his sons Nadab, Abihu, Eleazar, and Ithamar "to serve Me as priest" (Exod. 28:1). Inasmuch as Moses and Aaron were of the tribe of Levi (Exod. 6:16–25), it is clear that that tribe was divinely elected as custodian of this holy office. Nothing in the history of the patriarchs or in the blessing of Jacob on his sons, however, provides a hint as to the place the Levites would occupy in God's unfolding design of redemption. The only clues in the book of Exodus itself up to this point are the inclusion of the genealogy of Levi, by far the longest (and nearly the only) record of this type in

[41] Cf. Durham, *Exodus,* 273.

the book (Exod. 6:16–25), and the role of Aaron and his sons in the ceremony of covenant inauguration (Exod. 24:1; 9–11).

The early Moses narrative does, of course, introduce him as a son of a Levite man and woman (Exod. 2:1–2) and the younger brother of Aaron (Exod. 4:14; cf. 7:7; Num. 33:39). As for Aaron, he is called "Aaron the Levite" on our first meeting him (4:14), a proleptic announcement of the role he would later play. His close association with Moses thereafter also suggests that Aaron would figure prominently in the leadership of the nation, though in what capacity could hardly have been guessed. As the story progressed, Aaron's involvement in leadership became even more pronounced. He met with Jethro, Moses' father-in-law and a priest of Midian, in a cultic setting (Exod. 18:12) and, as we have just pointed out, ascended Mount Sinai with Moses to receive the covenant (19:24) and, with two of his sons, to participate in the covenant sacrifices and ceremonies (24:1, 9–11). Finally, a definitive word occurs in the text as to how Aaron would function in the theocracy: "In the tent of meeting, outside the curtain that is in front of the testimony, Aaron and his sons are to tend the lamp from evening until morning before the LORD. This is to be a permanent statute for the Israelites throughout their generations" (Exod. 27:21).

Aaron's call to priestly service involved two sets of procedures that testified to his vocation both outwardly and inwardly. The first called for special attire, a set of clothing every part of which, like the parts of the tabernacle, conveyed some aspect of truth, in this case the nature of the priestly office (Exod. 28). The second was an elaborate ritual of consecration setting aside Aaron and his descendants to the high and holy privilege for which he had already been chosen by the Lord (Exod. 29). We shall address these in turn.

The garments of Aaron and his sons are called "sacred" *(qōdeš),* an apt description in light of their call to be sacred servants of the LORD.[42] Moreover, the clothing was designed and fashioned not just to serve the practical function of dress but for "dignity" (*kābôd,* "glory") and "honor" (*tipʾeret,* "beauty"). Again, nothing is left to human artifice or creativity,

[42] Cornelis Van Dam, "Priestly Clothing," *Dictionary of the Old Testament: Pentateuch,* ed. T. Desmond Alexander and David W. Baker (Downers Grove, Ill.: InterVarsity, 2003), 643–46.

for those who serve God must, as his image, do so in such a way that even in their appearance his majesty and glory shine through.

But serve him they did, and the various elements of the priests' wardrobe make clear what that service was all about. The ephod, an apron-like garment with shoulder straps, is a prominent example. Two onyx stones engraved with the names of the twelve tribes of Israel must be mounted on the shoulder straps "as memorial stones for the Israelites" (Exod. 28:12). That is, the priests must shoulder the responsibility of remembering on whose behalf they discharged their sacred trust. Their care for the covenant nation must weigh heavy upon them. This was the essence of priestly duty.

The front of the ephod was adorned with a breastpiece folded double. Embedded in it were four rows of three stones each, each one again representing a tribe of Israel. This time the stones were over the heart, not on the shoulders. But the weight of priestly duty was still there for "whenever he enters the sanctuary, Aaron is to carry the names of Israel's sons over his heart on the breastpiece for decisions, as a continual reminder before the LORD" (Exod. 28:29). The decision in mind involved two more precious stones, the Urim and Thummim, which presumably were carried in the pouch of the breastpiece. By carrying and making use of these devices, "Aaron, will continually carry the means of decisions for the Israelites over his heart before the LORD" (v. 30).

The nature and function of the Urim and Thummim have been a matter of intense discussion and little consensus.[43] The words themselves appear to mean "lights" and "uprightness" respectively, but what this has to do with their use in determining the will of God in any given matter is to this point most unclear. Moreover, the texts where these stones or dies are mentioned (Exod. 28:30; Lev. 8:8; Num. 27:21; Deut. 33:8; 1 Sam. 28:6; Ezra 2:63; Neh. 7:65) provide little information as to how they were manipulated. What is clear is that they are always associated with the priestly office and they were means of communicating the divine intention in mutually exclusive, unambiguous ways, perhaps as a binary or yes or no response to any given question.

The high priestly wardrobe was completed by a blue robe with pomegranates and bells attached to its lower hem, a gold plate with the

[43] Cornelis Van Dam, אוּרִים, *NIDOTTE* 1:329–31.

inscription "Holy to the LORD" which was worn on the front of a turban, a tunic, and undergarments of linen. All of these were to adorn the priests with dignity and honor (Exod. 28:40; cf. v. 2), and without them they could not approach the holy place to minister there lest they die (v. 43). Theologically, these beautiful garments and the precise instructions as to how they were to be made suggest the importance of the aesthetic in the worship of the Lord. He had created all things to be perfect and glorious, for he himself is characterized by these attributes. It is fitting, then, that the sacred space devoted to his earthly presence and worship be a reflection of his glory and the glory of his works. This would be no less true of his servants the priests who ministered in these celestial precincts.

Having described the clothing of the priests, Moses was told to consecrate Aaron and his sons to the priesthood, thus making them worthy to wear these symbols of their honor (Exod. 28:41). This led to the ceremony of consecration, the details of which are also theologically pregnant and worthy therefore of careful attention. The root idea of the verb to consecrate *(qdš)* is to set someone or something apart from the mundane in order to use it for a specially designated purpose. This is clearly the case here, for Aaron and his sons were to be set apart, said the Lord, "to serve Me as priests" (Exod. 29:1). That is, they would become holy or sacred persons qualified to minister in sacred space.

The candidates must first be washed with waters of purification and then attired in the garments described above. Then a sin offering consisting of a bull must be made, with its blood applied to the great bronze altar and its choice parts burned on the altar as an offering to the Lord. Aaron and his sons must place their hands on the head of the animal before its slaughter, indicating by this act the transfer of their sin to the innocent animal and thus their innocence by identification with it.

Once declared free of the impediments of sin, Aaron and his sons could be sanctified to service. This required the slaughter of a ram as a burnt offering to the Lord. Again, the hands of the candidates were placed on the animal's head, this time suggesting that they were presenting themselves to the Lord for him to use them in any way he chose. They became, with the ram, "a pleasing aroma" (Exod. 29:18). A second ram was then slain, and its blood was applied to the right ears, thumbs, and big toes of Aaron and his sons, symbolically setting off these parts of the body for special service. The ear was dedicated to the hearing of the word and will of God, the thumb (or hand) to its accomplishment, and the toe (or foot) to walking in accordance with its requirements. By another symbolical act, the priests presented the choice parts of this ram plus loaves of bread and cakes and wafers and waved them before the Lord as a wave offering. They then burned them on the altar as a sacrifice to the Lord except for the breast, which was waved before the Lord but then retained by the participants as a fellowship offering. The waving was a movement of the hands in a gesture of presentation to the Lord, a way of surrendering what the offerer had, including himself. From that time forward the breast and thigh of a sacrificial animal would be devoted to Israel's priests as a contribution to their livelihood (Exod. 29:27–28).

This ritual must be repeated for seven days before the ordination to priesthood was complete. And then forever after the tabernacle and its priests were to be similarly set aside for service by sacrifices and offerings. Generations would come and go, but the Lord would remain in this sacred place. Each generation must therefore come to its own realization of the holiness of God and prepare to meet him there. When the conditions were met, "I will meet you to speak with you," the Lord promised the priests, "I will also meet with the Israelites there, and that place will be consecrated by My glory" (vv. 42–43). He went on to declare that "I will dwell among the Israelites and be their God. And they will know that I am the LORD their God, who brought them out of the land of Egypt, so that I might dwell among them" (vv. 45–46).

No question should remain therefore as to the purpose of the tabernacle and its priestly ministers. It became sacred space, an extension of heaven on earth, and its officiants were his special servants, his representatives who made possible a vital and living contact between a holy God and his people who came to proffer him adoration and praise at this sacred place.

Of the principal institutions of the Old Testament theocracy—the priesthood, the monarchy, prophetism, and wisdom—only the priesthood was set apart permanently with such rituals of consecration. Kings were anointed to their office, indeed, and the Lord made with David an eternal covenant of rulership through his dynastic successors, but the priesthood enjoyed a special status as the servants of God ordained to mediate his gracious work of forgiveness and reconciliation. The changing vicissitudes of Israel's history impacted the history of the priesthood as well but not in its core function within Israel's cultus. How it underwent adjustment from time to time will be a matter of discussion at a later point. For the Mosaic period and the premonarchic era that followed, we shall give further attention to the priestly role when we consider the sacred seasons and acts with which they were so vitally involved.

Sacred Times

The carrying out of Old Testament worship was strictly governed by a sacred calendar that dictated the times when certain religious activities were to be observed.[44] This was no more left to the discretion of the community—even its priestly and royal leaders—than was the conception and use of the tabernacle and the selection of consecrated persons employed in its ministry. The creation narrative itself exhibits a calendrical regularity when it speaks of day and night, the six days of creation, and the heavenly lights that were to serve as signs to mark seasons and days and years (Gen. 1:3–14). God clearly intended for mankind to be sensitive to the orderly progression of time and to take note of special events that must be recalled and celebrated at set times.

The Sabbath

The first of these was the seventh day of the creation week, the day by which creation was completed and on which God rested (Gen. 2:2). He therefore consecrated *(qdš)* that day, the celebration of which came to be known as the Sabbath (from *šbt,* "to rest"). The antiquity of a Sabbath tradition is apparent from its linkage to the creation story. Its pre-Sinaitic observance as a matter so well-known to the community as to require no explanation attests also to its long-standing practice among the people of Israel (Exod. 16:21–26). The fourth commandment merely codified the practice and underscored its significance as a fundamental principle of the Sinaitic covenant.

The first time the Sabbath is mentioned following the revelation of the book of the covenant to Moses, the need to keep it was reinforced, but to that was added the information that it "is a sign between Me and you throughout your generations, so that you will know that I am the

[44] J. van Goudever, *Biblical Calendars* (Leiden: Brill, 1961).

Lord who sets you apart" (Exod. 31:13). So holy was the Sabbath that the one who desecrated it must be put to death (v. 14; cf. Num. 15:32–36, where a Sabbath breaker is said to have suffered that fate). It was to be celebrated not just because the Lord created all things in six days and rested on the seventh (v. 17) but also as a sign of a "perpetual covenant" (v. 16). In context that covenant is best understood as the covenant implied in the creation account, the creation mandate that otherwise has no sign such as the covenants with Noah (Gen. 9:17) and Abraham (Gen. 17:11) had.[45] The importance of Sabbath observance is clear elsewhere in Torah as well (Lev. 19:3, 30). Leviticus 23 lists it as the first in a series of holy days in the calendar (v. 1), specifying that it was to be not only a day of rest but also a day of sacred assembly as well (v. 3). Numbers 28:9–10 prescribes the offerings to be made on the Sabbath, suggesting its integral significance in the practice of the cultus. As for the Deuteronomic covenant renewal text, its version of the Decalogue insists on the observance of the Sabbath but bases the observance not on creation rest but on Israel's miraculous redemption and deliverance from Egypt (Deut. 5:12–15). We shall examine the historical and theological implications of this change in due course. For now it is sufficient to note that the Old Testament requirement to observe the Sabbath was not affected one way or the other by the reasons for doing so.

The Psalms and Wisdom literature have virtually nothing to say about the Sabbath (or other festivals, for that matter), but the prophets viewed it as a matter of the greatest importance. Isaiah spoke of a special blessing for him who "keeps the Sabbath without desecrating it" (Isa. 56:2) and linked Sabbath keeping with fidelity to the Lord's covenant (vv. 4, 6). Jeremiah was commanded by the Lord to stand at Jerusalem's gates and to warn its citizens against violating the Sabbath day by their pursuit of financial gain (Jer. 17:19–22). Should they fail to mend their ways, they could expect the unquenchable fires of God's judgment (v. 27). Ezekiel, reviewing Israel's long history of disobedience, reminded the people of the exile that the Lord had given them the Sabbaths "as a sign between Me and them, so they will know that I am the Lord who sets them apart as holy" (Ezek. 20:12). But they utterly desecrated his Sabbaths in their pursuit of idols and would have perished had the Lord not pitied them.

---

[45] Cassuto, *A Commentary on the Book of Exodus,* 404.

In his grace he had turned to them again and again, pleading, "Keep My Sabbaths holy, and they will be a sign between Me and you, so you may know that I am the LORD your God" (v. 20). Sadly, such exhortation was in vain, and for their Sabbath desecration they at last were destined to exile among the nations (vv. 21–24).

The other sacred times listed in connection with the book of the covenant—the Feast of Unleavened Bread, the Feast of Harvest, and the Feast of Ingathering—find but bare mention there but are fully developed in the books of Leviticus, Numbers, and Deuteronomy. For the sake of convenience, we will address them and the others not included in Exodus feast by feast and not book by book. In line with our oft-stated method, we will pay careful attention to what if any development occurs in their description and in their unfolding enactment.

The Passover and Unleavened Bread

In line with precedent set in the narrative of Israel's exodus from Egypt, Leviticus sets the time of the Passover celebration at twilight on the fourteenth day of the first month (Lev. 23:5; cf. Exod. 12:2, 6). The Feast of Unleavened Bread commenced the next day, the fifteenth, thus linking the two so closely that the book of the covenant called both together the feast of Unleavened Bread (Exod. 23:15). The feast continued for seven full days and was marked especially by abstinence from bread with yeast (cf. Exod. 13:3–10). The week as a whole was to be bracketed by sacred assemblies and by Sabbath days on which no work could be done (Lev. 23:7–8).

The Passover and Unleavened Bread rituals appear already in the narrative accounts of the events that gave rise to these festivals. In each case they were nonagricultural in origin, designed, rather, to commemorate the greatest event in Israel's sacred history, namely, the deliverance from Egyptian bondage in the exodus.[46] The first hint of such a deliverance occurs in Genesis where the Lord promised Abraham that after four hundred years in a foreign land his descendants would "go out with many possessions" (Gen. 15:14). Their mistreatment, which intensified in the days of Moses, gave rise at the end of that time to

---

[46] This assessment opposes what is almost a consensus among critical scholars. See, e. g., Roland de Vaux, *Ancient Israel,* vol. 2, *Religious Institutions* (New York: McGraw-Hill, 1965), 488–93.

increased promises of a mighty redemption (cf. Exod. 3:7–10; 6:1–8), culminating in the threat of one last plague on Egypt that would result in Israel's miraculous escape (Exod. 11:1–10). So momentous would that event be that the month in which it occurred—the seventh according to the secular calendar—would become the first month in the festival calendar (Exod. 12:2; cf. 13:3–4).

On the tenth of that month, each family of Israel must select a lamb (or kid) without defect, give it special care until the fourteenth day, and then slaughter it at twilight of that day. Its blood must be applied to the doorway of their house and its meat, with herbs and unleavened bread, entirely consumed. Moreover, they must dress as though in a hurry to leave; for when the judgment of the Lord fell, there would be no time for further preparation. Then, in recognition of the Lord's bypassing his own people who had marked their houses with blood, the name Passover[47] would forever be attached to this mighty work of divine salvation (Exod. 12:1–11). The blood, not atoning in this case, signified that an innocent victim had become a substitute for a family whose eldest son would otherwise have to perish in the Lord's judgment on Egypt (vv. 12–13, 21–23).

Immediately following the Passover meal, the families of Israel would observe seven days of abstinence from leavened bread, the absence of leaven testifying to the haste with which the people must leave Egypt (Exod. 12:14–20; cf. vv. 11, 39). The whole complex—Passover and Unleavened Bread—would end on the evening of the twenty-first day of the month, encompassing parts of eight days in all. The purpose for the festival was to celebrate God's redemptive grace on behalf of his people (Exod. 13:3). Fathers must recite to their sons for all generations to come a creedal summation of the meaning of the celebration so they would never forget what God had done for them: "In the future, when your son asks you, 'What does this mean?' say to him, 'By the strength of His hand the LORD brought us out of Egypt, out of the place of slavery. When Pharaoh stubbornly refused to let us go, the Lord killed every firstborn male in the land of Egypt, from the firstborn of man to the firstborn of livestock. That is why I sacrifice to the LORD all the firstborn of the

[47] Heb. *pesaḥ*, "pass by, spare"; *HALOT* 947.

womb that are males, but I redeem all the firstborn of my sons'" (Exod. 13:14–15).

Exodus 23:14–15 and Leviticus 23:4–8 add little to our understanding of Passover and Unleavened Bread, but the account in Numbers 28 provides a detailed prescription of the sacrifices and offerings to be made daily as part of the festival ritual, all of which were designed to create "a pleasing aroma to the Lord" (Lev. 23:18). Like the sacrifices Noah made which also pleased the Lord by their scent and led to his promise never again to curse the ground (Gen. 8:21), so his judgment on wicked Egypt would never again be manifest as it was in the event of the exodus.

The version of the Passover and Unleavened Bread festival in Deuteronomy 16:1–8, typical of the theology of that book with its forward look to postconquest Israel, makes several modifications of the earlier model. Chief among them is the insistence that the festival be celebrated "in the place where the Lord chooses to have His name dwell" (vv. 2, 6). As long as Israel was confined to the Sinai deserts, there was no need to speak of a central location to which the community would gather for festival. But in the days ahead when the nation would be scattered across the length and breadth of Canaan and even beyond, the need for a central focal point where the nation could meet the Lord as a nation would be most apparent. That place would be wherever the Lord chose to dwell, eventually, of course, the Jerusalem temple. To reinforce this point, Moses specified, "You are not to sacrifice the Passover animal in any of the towns the Lord your God is giving you. You must only sacrifice the Passover animal at the place where the Lord your God chooses to have His name dwell" (vv. 5–6).

In addition to centralizing the observance of the festival, this amended protocol removed the Passover from a family observance in the home to a national assembly to which at least the men of Israel were required to gather (Deut. 16:16). The rationale, of course, was the fact that the Lord would localize himself within the community, and, even more important, he would do so as the Great King to whom his vassal subjects must pay homage and tribute.[48] The collective community—Israel as a nation—would come to supersede even the family as God's servant people and

---

[48] Merrill, *Deuteronomy,* 252.

thus must appear before him *en masse* on stipulated occasions, the Passover being one of them.

The Festival of Harvest

Exodus 23:16 refers to this occasion in the briefest of terms: "Observe the Festival of Harvest with the firstfruits of your produce from what you sow in the field." This description distinguishes it from the last of the festivals of the year, the Festival of Ingathering, when the last of the harvest was brought in. Only here is the term *harvest* used of this festival *(ḥag haqqāṣîr);* otherwise it is known as the Festival of Weeks *(ḥag šābuʿōt)* since it was to be celebrated exactly seven weeks after the conclusion of Passover-Unleavened Bread (Lev. 23:11, 15–16). The "firstfruits of the produce" was the earliest of the ripening wheat (Exod. 34:22). Leviticus describes this ingathering of wheat as the "new grain" (Lev. 23:16). Unlike Passover and Unleavened Bread, the Festival of Weeks commemorated no historical event in Old Testament times but was for the purpose of celebrating the bounties of grain harvest and providing in some manner for the needs of the priests (Lev. 23:20).

Numbers explicitly connects the Festival of Weeks with "the day of firstfruits," but apart from some incidental details relative to the sacrificial ritual to be carried out, it provides no further elaboration (Num. 28:26–31). Deuteronomy, however, commands that a freewill offering be made on the day of the Festival of Weeks, offering "in proportion to how the LORD your God has blessed you" (Deut. 16:10). Like the other festivals, it too must be celebrated "in the place where He chooses to have His name dwell" (v. 11), becoming thus a pilgrimage festival in the sedentary life of Canaan. Moreover, Deuteronomy enjoins the Israelites to include in their observance of the Festival of Weeks not only their immediate families but also their servants, the Levites, foreigners, and dependents such as orphans and widows (vv. 11–12). The festival therefore took on the character of a welfare mechanism, a means of providing for elements of Israelite society that were most in need. The impetus, Moses reminded them, was that "you were slaves in Egypt" (v. 12). Those who had been delivered from dire circumstances should be first to attend to the sorrowful plight of others.

The Festival of Ingathering

The last of the pilgrimage festivals, called the Festival of Ingathering *(ḥag hāʾāsîp)* in Exodus 23:16, is otherwise (and more commonly) known as the Festival of Tabernacles or Booths *(ḥag hassukkôt)*. These alternative designations reflect clearly the dual functions of the festival, i.e., to celebrate the harvesting of the crops at the end of the year and to commemorate the desert sojourn when the tribes of Israel dwelled in rude tents or huts. This celebration, like Passover-Unleavened Bread, lasted for seven days, from the fifteenth to the twenty-second day of the seventh month, and was highlighted by sacred assemblies on the first and eighth days (Lev. 23:33–36). The observance consisted of the presentation of burnt offerings and other gifts to the Lord as well as the erection of temporary shelters in which the pilgrims should reside for the duration of the festivities. The reason for this deprivation was "so that your generations may know that I made the Israelites live in booths when I brought them out of the land of Egypt" (Lev. 23:43).

The Numbers version consists once more of a lengthy but repetitive rehearsal of the ritual to be followed in observing the feast, including the sacrifices and offerings appropriate for each of the eight days (Num. 28:12–38). As for Deuteronomy, it underscores the need to include the disenfranchised of Israel in the bounties of the harvest and to assemble for the festival only in the place the Lord would choose (Deut. 16:13–15).

Before turning to the remaining sacred times addressed by Torah, it will be useful to make a few concluding observations about the three pilgrimage festivals—Passover-Unleavened Bread, Weeks, and Tabernacles. (1) Of all the festivals, only these three required mandatory attendance by the men of Israel (Exod. 23:17; 34:23; Deut. 16:16). (2) The objective of the pilgrimages was primarily to appear before the sovereign Lord (Exod. 23:17; 34:23). (3) The journey to the place where the Lord would cause his name to dwell was, in effect, undertaken by the nation in recognition of its need regularly to report to the Lord, give account to him, and offer tribute to him as the great King (Exod. 23:15; 34:20; Deut. 16:16–17). In this way one of the requirements of suzerain-vassal treaty texts of this kind could be met. As for the theological import, the concept of a servant nation answerable to its God as Lord is commensurate in every way with a major emphasis of Old Testament theology on the God of the universe who, having chosen a people through whom to mediate his saving grace to the nations, created a means by which they could fellowship with him and carry out his redemptive program.

Exodus treats only the Sabbath and the three pilgrimage festivals as sacred times, but the remainder of the Pentateuch adds more, all of which now occupy our attention in the order of their disclosure.

The Festival of Trumpets

Having dealt with the Festival of Weeks and anticipating the Festival of Tabernacles, which occurred in the seventh month, Leviticus draws attention to the first day of the seventh month as a day of special significance (Lev. 23:23–25). Though it has no name as such in this early tradition, eventually the festival came to be known as Rosh Hashanah, literally, “the first of the year,” but only in postbiblical times. It was to be a day of rest on which a (nonmandatory) assembly convened to present offerings to the Lord. Numbers 29:1–6 repeats the same information, adding, as usual, instructions about sacrifices and offerings. Deuteronomy, perhaps somewhat surprisingly, has nothing to say about such a festival.

The Day of Atonement

Ten days after the Festival of Trumpets the nation must assemble (perhaps in connection with the Festival of Tabernacles four days later) to make atonement for its collective sins. The day thus became known as the Day of Atonement *(yôm hakkippurîm)*. We have already had occasion to pay some attention to the elaborate ritual of that most holy day as disclosed in Leviticus 16:1–34. Here we will take note of the meaning of the day for the people as opposed to the liturgical role of the chief priest revealed there. The day was a Sabbath on which no work could be done on pain of death (Lev. 23:28, 30). It was also a day of fasting so strictly to be observed that infraction of that prohibition would result in the excommunication of the offender from the community. Numbers adds to this its usual information about the material and presentation of appropriate sacrifices (Num. 29:7–11). Deuteronomy, once more, is silent regarding the day.

The Sabbatical and Jubilee Years

Two remaining periods or times of special sanctity will complete our survey of sacred seasons. Each of these was celebrated apart from annual schedules, the first, the Sabbatical Year, once every seven years; and the other, the Year of Jubilee, once every fifty years. In each case the celebration or commemoration lasted for an entire year. Exodus briefly introduces the Sabbatical Year (Exod. 23:10–11) but ignores the Year of Jubilee. What the Sabbatical Year observance required was merely to leave the farmland uncultivated and unharvested except by the poor and by wild animals that could help themselves to whatever grew up by itself. This gave rest and revitalization to the soil and at the same time provided some modicum of relief to those who otherwise might go hungry. Leviticus describes the seventh year as "a Sabbath to the LORD" (Lev. 25:2), suggesting that another dimension to its significance was the fact that the year must be devoted to the Lord as a kind of offering to him. As for the Year of Jubilee (*šĕnat hayyôbēl,* "year of remission"), only Leviticus provides any detailed instruction (Lev. 25:8–55).

Every seventh year was a Sabbatical Year, and every seventh sabbatical year the (forty-ninth) was followed by the year of remission (the fiftieth). The blowing of trumpets on the Day of Atonement would announce the arrival of the Year of Jubilee, a proclamation, fittingly, that informed the people of a blanket release from all their encumbrances and a freedom for all to return to their ancestral homes and families (vv. 8–10). As the Lord had pardoned them on the Day of Atonement, so the powerful of Israel must pardon their countrymen who were in financial bondage to them. Even the land must be freed from exploitation on that year which means that for two straight years, the forty-ninth and fiftieth, neither plowing nor reaping was permissible.

A major theme coursing throughout these instructions is the fact that God owns the land and his people are but aliens and tenants who temporarily live on it and care for it on his behalf. They therefore cannot buy or sell it permanently since, in fact, it is not theirs to begin with (vv. 23–24). Likewise, should an Israelite indenture himself to a fellow citizen because of financial constraints, that relationship must end at the Year of Jubilee with no obligations outstanding by either party (vv. 39–43). Foreign slaves and non-Israelite debtors forced into bondage must also be treated with special consideration, especially with respect to the Year of Jubilee (vv. 44–53). The mercy to be expected in releasing all such persons should spring from the recognition and remembrance that "the Israelites are My slaves. They are My slaves I brought out of the land of Egypt. I am the Lord your God" (v. 55). No clearer statement could be found to affirm the role of Israel as the blessed, if undeserving, vassal whom God had graciously brought into covenant fellowship with himself.

Sacred Acts

The fourth element of Israel's life as a theocratic covenant community pertains to the ways in which the nation approached and related to the Lord in view of the sacred space, persons, and times and seasons just described. That is, now that a framework for Israel's religious expression had been formed, how was Israel to function within that framework in order to worship God and serve him with genuine devotion? The answer lay in the concept of cultus, a term we have used on several occasions but have yet to define. First, it is important to dissociate cultus from cult, at least in the pejorative sense in which the latter word is understood in modern times. Though both derive from a common etymology (Lat. *cultus,* pertaining to the soil as in agriculture), *cult* has come to denote an aberrational or heterodox religious movement whereas *cultus,* as a technical religious or theological term, describes any system of religious beliefs and ritual as well as its adherents. By this definition, Israel was, in a certain sense, a cultus; and the sum total of its religious beliefs and performance was a cultus as well.[49]

Ritual and Liturgy

The doctrine or body of truth that constituted Israel's normative faith is the subject of this theology and need not be given separate consideration here. As for cultic practice—the ritual and liturgy that governed its exercise—much of that is presupposed in the pre-Mosaic narratives where such matters as prayer, offerings, sacrifices, and the like have already been noted. Furthermore, our study of sacred sites, the priesthood, and special festival and sabbath occasions has necessarily touched upon matters of cultus in the nature of the interweaving of all of these elements into the fabric of Israel's religious and national life.

To look briefly at the more immediate past, the Lord had told Moses to lead Israel out of Egypt so that they might worship him at Sinai, the

---

[49] De Vaux, *Ancient Israel,* 271.

holy mountain (Exod. 3:12). Worship presupposes a cultus of some kind, but it is hardly definable here. Things become somewhat clearer when Moses first addressed Pharaoh and entreated him to let the people go into the desert "so that we may sacrifice to the LORD our God" (Exod. 5:3). Their worship thus included at least the making of sacrifices. But they must not worship in Egypt–though Pharaoh appeared to permit this—for, as Moses protested, "What we will sacrifice to the Lord our God is detestable to the Egyptians" (Exod. 8:26). Whatever form Israel's cultus was to take, it would differ greatly from Egypt's and would cause offense. When Pharaoh at last permitted the men of Israel to worship the Lord in the desert, Moses declined and said that in light of the festival to be celebrated there, the women and children, as well as the livestock, must be allowed to leave as well (Exod. 10:9). Worship was therefore more than sacrifice; it was assembly before God as a community. Finally, Moses demanded that all of Israel's flocks and herds go with them so that Israel could have "sacrifices and burnt offerings to prepare for the LORD our God" (Exod. 10:25). The variety of possible expressions of worship is revealed in Moses' argument that all kinds of animals must be taken because "we will not know what we will use to worship the LORD until we get there" (v. 26).

The first account of religious ritual was the instruction about the offering of Passover animals, a passage we have already addressed in a different context (Exod. 12:1–11). This text is particularly instructive because it is almost paradigmatic of what was to be expected in the performance of Israel's worship in general. It set forth the time of the service (v. 3), the kind of animal to be offered (v. 3), the quality of that animal (v. 5), its preparation for slaughter (v. 6), and the disposition of the blood and other parts of the animal (vv. 7–10). A secondary passage explains that the Passover ritual in the future would include a liturgy in which fathers would instruct their children as to its meaning as they gathered around the Passover table (Exod. 13:14–16).

The next instance was the service of covenant confirmation that followed the Lord's revelation of the book of the covenant (Exod. 24:4–8). This required an altar, the sacrifice of bulls, and the application of blood in an appropriate manner. Unlike the Passover service, which is unnamed in terms of formal category (*ordinance* is the Bible's own term, Exod. 12:14), the covenant ceremony is described as a fellowship (or peace, *šĕlāmîm)* offering because it affirmed the fellowship between the Lord and Israel inherent in the covenant (v. 5).[50] The covenant must be reaffirmed regularly thereafter; and though no other passages contain the ritual outlined here, such a service most likely took place and with a similar set of procedures (cf. Deut. 31:9–13; Josh. 8:30–35; 24:25–27).[51]

Finally, we have also already dealt with the ritual of the consecration of the priests, a service of dedication or ordination (Exod. 29:1–43). Fundamentally, it featured a burnt offering, that is, one that was consumed totally as an offering to the Lord (v. 18). However, it also included a sin offering, the blood of which made atonement (v. 14), and a fellowship offering to be shared between the Lord and Aaron and his sons as a sign of the oneness of their relationship and their common purpose (v. 28).

The acts of worship discussed thus far contribute little to an understanding of the cultus as a whole because they were by and large ad hoc responses to special and peculiar situations. Exodus makes no attempt to deal with sacred acts in a comprehensive and systematic manner, being content to deal with these few isolated cases and with the setting forth in detail of the sacred settings and personnel within and by which the cultus would ordinarily be carried out. The books of Leviticus and Numbers, on the other hand, address these matters in particular and must, therefore, receive at least brief attention.

As the name *Leviticus* suggests, the book is concerned primarily with the priests and Levites and their role in Israel's religious life. There is no need in a theology of the Old Testament to examine in minute detail every facet of their ministry or every technicality of ritual and liturgy encompassed by it. The attempt here will be to focus on the cultus as acts of worship that contain unusual theological relevance to both Old Testament Israel and the New Testament church.

---

[50] John W. Hilber, "Theology of Worship in Exodus 24," *JETS* 39 (1996): 177–89.

[51] The fact that the reading of Torah was part of the observance of the Festival of Tabernacles almost certainly presupposes some kind of sacrificial ritual. McConville speaks of a "ceremonial reading of the law." J. G. McConville, *Deuteronomy,* AOTC 5 (Downers Grove, Ill.: InterVarsity, 2002), 439.

Liturgy and Holiness

The dominant theme of Leviticus is holiness, that of God and of the people whom he chose to reflect that aspect of his nature (cf. Lev. 10:3; 11:44; 19:2; 20:7–8, 26; 22:32; etc.).[52] Everything required in the worship of God must be undertaken to the end that his holiness might be recognized and respected and that those who desired to have fellowship with him and worship him might realize their need for some means of achieving the holiness requisite to that privilege. These sacred acts were primarily twofold in nature: (1) those that provided forgiveness for sin so that unbroken fellowship with the Lord can be achieved; and (2) those that expressed the reality of that fellowship with heartfelt thanks and a desire to please and serve him as his image on the earth. In addition, there were laws regarding ritual purification necessitated by contact with such impure things as childbirth, skin diseases, mildew, and certain bodily discharges. These were not necessarily unclean in and of themselves but symbolized the human condition spiritually as a result of the fall and of willful choices to sin.

The first seven chapters of Leviticus provide instructions to the priests regarding the sacrifices appropriate to various situations and the ritual to be followed in each case.[53] Those that pertained to atonement for unintentional sins followed the presentation of a burnt offering *(ʿōlâ),* an animal or bird consumed in its entirety on the altar as "a pleasing aroma to the Lord" (Lev. 1:9, 13, 17). The idea is that the Lord had accepted the sacrifice as an act of genuine contrition and would therefore forgive the offense. The sinner's identification with the sacrificial animal was dramatized by placing his hand on its head and slaying it, thus transferring his guilt to the animal and, at the same time, receiving the innocence of the animal (v. 4).

The Categories of Sacrifice

The sin offering *(ḥaṭṭ'āt)*—the sacrifice for a violation of covenant law—depended for its substance on the identity of the sinner, whether priest, the community as a whole, a leader, or an ordinary member of

---

[52] Thus the aptly named study of Leviticus by Allen P. Ross, *Holiness to the Lord: A Guide to the Exposition of the Book of Leviticus.* Cf. note 36 above.

[53] For a helpful analysis of these chapters, see Ross, *Holiness to the Lord,* 85–193.

the community.[54] If the sinner were a priest or the whole community, the guilty person(s) placed his hand on the head of the animal and slaughtered it "before the Lord" (Lev. 4:4). The priest officiating at the time would take some of the blood and sprinkle it toward the veil and apply it to the horns of the incense altar, then pour out the rest at the base of the altar of burnt offerings in the outer courtyard. The choice parts would be burned on the altar of burnt offerings as an offering to the Lord with the rest taken outside the camp to be burned up as refuse. The ritual for the sin of a leader or an ordinary citizen differed somewhat from the preceding. The blood this time was limited to the altar of burnt offerings and thus was not directed to the Lord in the inner sanctuary. Sins of a more ceremonial or less egregious nature—such as remaining silent regarding testimony about a crime that has been witnessed, ritual impurity, or making a careless oath—also needed atonement; but the sacrifice depended on the economic status of the guilty party (Lev. 5:1–13).

The so-called guilt offering (*ʾāšām*) was applicable especially in specific cases of sin where the offense was clear and spelled out as opposed to the sin offering which generally dealt with unspecified infractions of covenant law.[55] Moreover, the guilt offering must be accompanied by reparations paid to the offended party, whether the offense be against the Lord (Lev. 5:14–19) or another human being (Lev. 6:1–7). The occurrence of the two terms or their verb cognates in conjunction with one another complicates the issue of their distinction considerably, however, so it is best not to overstate their differences (cf. Lev. 4:22, 27; 5:5–6, 17–18; 6:2–5). Common to both (and to the atoning sacrifices in general in Leviticus 1–7) is the fact that they dealt with the issue of sin against God and man, clear-cut violations of the covenant requirements, describing their means of remedy and offering the promise of forgiveness and restoration.

The fellowship offering, sometimes called the peace offering (*šĕlāmîm*), was a voluntary act designed not to achieve fellowship with the Lord but to celebrate its reality. Sometimes it was an expression of gratitude for some unexpected blessing; sometimes it was attendant to a vow one made to God, promising some gift or act on his behalf if God blesses him in some way; and sometimes it was freely given for

[54] Richard E. Averbeck, חַטָּאת, *NIDOTTE* 2:93–103.

[55] Richard E. Averbeck, אָשָׁם, *NIDOTTE* 1:557–66.

no particular reason, just out of love for and devotion to the Lord.[56] The ritual for fellowship offerings in general appears in Leviticus 3:1–17 and those for various kinds (such as thank, votive, and freewill offerings) are addressed in Leviticus 7:11–18. In any case, an animal without defect was presented, and the offerer slaughtered it after placing his hand upon its head as a symbol of identification with it. Its blood was then sprinkled about the altar by the priest and the choice parts totally consumed on the altar, rising in the smoke, as it were, to the presence of the Lord in heaven. The text goes so far as to say that the sacrifices were like food offered to the Lord by fire (Lev. 3:11).

When fellowship offerings were specified to be thank offerings *(tôdâ),* they must include, in addition to a sacrificial animal, baked goods such as bread and wafers. Though done so in tribute to the Lord, these foods were actually given to the priests who must, however, not hoard them up but eat them that very day (Lev. 7:12–15). If the offerings were votive *(neder)* or freewill *(nĕdābâ),* on the other hand, anything left over could be eaten the next day. Anything beyond that must be burned up because it would have become impure and thus would contaminate anyone who came in contact with it (vv. 16–18).

To sum up the regimen of sacrifices and offerings in Israel as sacred acts, the following points must be made:

1. As a people joined to the Lord by means of a suzerain-vassal covenant, Israel was obligated to appear before him regularly to offer tribute in recognition of his sovereignty and of their dependence on him.
2. This could take place as part of the thrice annual pilgrimage festivals to the place where the Lord "caused His name to dwell" or at local shrines in villages and towns throughout the land.
3. The tribute took the form of sacrifices and offerings of various animals and other materials depending on the situation that prompted the need for an encounter between the Lord and the worshipper.
4. The sacrifices and offerings were made either to atone for sin or otherwise to restore a ruptured relationship between the Lord and

---

[56] Ross, *Holiness to the Lord,* 110–22.

his people; or to celebrate an already peaceful relationship by rendering thanks, making a vow to serve God more faithfully; or simply to express joy at the privilege of knowing and serving such a gracious Lord.

The complexity of the rituals in all of these acts of repentance and devotion tends to overshadow the central premises upon which they were based. While each act and movement was meaningful, what is most important was the purpose behind it and the result it was intended to achieve. And by all means, the paramount, overarching principle is this: sacrifices and offerings and, in fact, all religious activity had no redemptive and restorative value if it was merely pro forma. Such acts must flow out of a truly repentant spirit and a pure devotion if they were to have efficacy. The hymnists and prophets of Israel had much to say on the matter along this line as we shall see.

Miscellaneous Sacred Acts

The book of Numbers draws attention to two special cases of what might loosely be called sacred acts inasmuch as they clearly were religious in nature and required a clearly defined protocol. These involved the test for an unfaithful wife (Num. 5:5–31) and the law of the Nazirite (6:1–21). Our reason for including them is that they are illustrative of the kind of attention to various aspects of Israelite life that assured the purity of the nation as covenant bearer and/or they provide principles of behavior that transcended Israel's historical experience and underscored the interior motives that account for the exterior manifestations of life in all its variety in all people and at all times.

At first glance the test for an unfaithful wife seems to fall into the category of pagan voodoo or witchcraft, but on closer examination it is clear that it makes the connection between the psychological and the physical commonly known in modern psychological terms as the psychosomatic.[57] If this is, indeed, the case, it provides Old Testament evidence for the unitary nature of the human being and also makes the point that sin impacts the total person and that the total person—body and soul—must be redeemed.

---

[57] R. K. Harrison, *Numbers,* WEC (Chicago: Moody, 1990), 112–13.

The hypothetical case presented here is introduced by the important idea that sin against a fellow human being is also sin against God and must be confessed as such (Num. 5:6–7). This lays the predicate for the turn of events that follows and goes a long way toward explaining the strange circumstances that led to the resolution of the matter under dispute. The case involved a woman who was charged with having committed adultery; and though there were no witnesses to the act, her husband had strong suspicion that she had been unfaithful. His concern may or may not have been well-founded, but in any event he was entitled to take the matter to the local priest for his disposition. The priest must take the woman and a grain offering brought by the husband and "have her stand before the LORD" (v. 16). The purported sin, therefore, was not just against her husband but against God, a most serious matter indeed.

After mixing holy water and dust from the tabernacle floor in a clay jar, the priest would make the woman swear before God that she was innocent or, if not, confess that she had sinned. Her guilt would become apparent if, when she had drunk of the water, her thigh wasted away and her abdomen swelled. If no such results occurred, she would be presumed innocent. The physical phenomena that attended her guilt most likely describe sterility since, if she proved to be innocent, she would be able to have children in the future (v. 28).[58]

The oath sworn by the woman would then be written down and the ink washed off the scroll into the water. When she drank the potion, she would, in effect, be ingesting into her being the curse that follows the sin of adultery. The physical effects that followed would make clear to all that she was guilty, and the whole community would view her as cursed before God.

What must be stressed in the example here is that sin ultimately is against God even though an act may be immediately directed toward another human being, and sin brings great harm and pain to both perpetrator and victim. Furthermore, unconfessed guilt impacts the whole person and, if allowed to fester, will at some point manifest itself outwardly and physically. Finally, sin is fundamentally a matter of the

---

[58] Timothy R. Ashley, *The Book of Numbers,* NICOT (Grand Rapids: Eerdmans, 1993), 132–33.

spirit or soul, an inner reaction to impulses that, even if never outwardly exhibited, is nonetheless evil in the sight of the Lord.

The law of the Nazirite deals with an entirely different matter though it too involves an oath or vow (Num. 6:1–21).[59] Should a person wish to devote himself or herself to the Lord in special service or ministry, that person must make a pledge to abstain from alcoholic beverage, to refrain from cutting the hair, and to avoid contact with a corpse. These restrictions must be observed throughout the period of time specified when the vow was made. Should the Nazirite inadvertently come in contact with someone who died without warning, he must offer up appropriate sin and guilt offerings and then renew his vows of separation, beginning all over again (Num. 6:1–12). When the stipulated time was over, the Nazirite could be released from his state of separation by the offering of appropriate sacrifices. He may then cut his hair and drink wine at his pleasure (vv. 13–21).

The theological point to be made here is that service to the Lord is voluntary but once a firm commitment has been made to serve him, that commitment must be kept without fail. This is analogous to the vow that Israel made at Sinai, a promise undertaken voluntarily but one, once made, that obligated her to serve the Lord from that time forward. Israel, like the Nazirite, surrendered herself to a life of separation, vowing to be a people unique and distinct from all others. Very likely, persons who entered into the Nazirite way of life did so as an extension of the covenant commitments made by the nation, portraying by their act the deeper level of consecration they wished for the community as a whole.

---

[59] G. Mayer, נזר, *TDOT* 9:306–11.

Chapter Twelve

Deuteronomy and Covenant Renewal

The Old Testament tradition itself views the book of Deuteronomy as a covenant renewal document composed in Moab some forty years after the giving of the book of the covenant and other revelation at Mount Sinai. Much modern scholarship rejects both the Mosaic authorship of the book and its Late Bronze age setting, preferring to view it as a seventh-century product that Josiah found in his temple restoration project and that formed the basis for the reformation of Judah's faith and life (cf. 2 Kings 27:8–23:25).[1] Though many cogent arguments have been made to refute this hypothesis, there is neither space nor need to do so here.[2] In line with our stated methodology and with current canonical readings of the biblical corpus, we shall understand the text as it stands, that is, as a greatly amended and expanded version of the Sinaitic covenant undertaken with the end in mind of preparing the preconquest community of Israel for life in Canaan as a sedentary people headed eventually toward monarchy.

---

[1] E. W. Nicholson, *Deuteronomy and Tradition* (Philadelphia: Fortress, 1967), 1–17.

[2] Eugene H. Merrill, "Deuteronomy and History: Anticipation or Reflection?" *Faith & Mission* 18/1 (2000): 57–76.

The Pre-Deuteronomic History

Before we address Deuteronomy itself, it will be useful to trace Israel's history for the brief period from the exodus to the conquest in order to understand the context in which covenant renewal became necessary. We have already looked at the exodus event itself and the circumstances that led up to the disclosure of the Sinaitic covenant. During the year or more that the tribes encamped in the Sinai region, Moses had received the covenant, mediated it to the people, and organized them for the journey to the land of promise. The narratives of Leviticus are sparse; and apart from references to such incidents as the ordination of the priests (chs. 8–9), the death of Aaron's sons Nadab and Abihu (ch. 10), and the execution of a blasphemer (Lev. 24:10–23), virtually nothing is known of that period. As for the last of these incidents, it is instructive in pointing out that the law given through Moses was not just a theoretical set of principles but was intended to be taken literally and seriously. It seems that a certain Israelite of mixed parentage had blasphemed the name of the Lord while engaged in an altercation with a fellow Israelite (thus violating the third commandment and Exod. 22:28) and was therefore held in custody until "the LORD's decision could be made clear to them" (Lev. 24:12). This suggests that though the commandment was known and was clear to Israel's leaders, there was nothing so far revealed in the law as to the penalty for such an offense. All that is said is that "the LORD will punish anyone who misuses His name" (Exod. 20:7). It was already clear, therefore, that case law must be developed to deal with legal issues such as this. Having come to know God's will, Moses ordered that the culprit be put to death, thereby adding to the corpus of the book of the covenant the stipulation that "whoever blasphemes the name of the LORD is to be put to death" (Lev. 24:16).[3] One may assume that many other infractions of covenant law like this took place and were redressed by ad hoc declarations by the inspired lawgiver.

Moses' need to deal with this case led him to expatiate on other contingencies, most of which were already covered by the law. He reiterated the fact that murder demanded capital punishment (v. 17; cf. Exod. 21:12) and that personal injury required *lex talionis,* i.e., that

[3] Mark F. Rooker, *Leviticus,* NAC 3A (Nashville: Broadman & Holman, 2000), 296.

the punishment should fit the crime (vv. 19–20; cf. Exod. 21:23–25). However, the law thus far had said nothing about killing another person's animal, so Moses, as in the case of the blasphemer, created a law *de novo* that "whoever kills an animal [belonging to another] is to make restitution for it" (Lev. 24:21). This specific case and its punishment, though strictly speaking not part of the book of the covenant, became enshrined in covenant law and had the same magisterial authority as any other law.

When the time came for Israel to leave Sinai, the Lord directed Moses to make preparation to get underway (Num. 1:1). In order to proceed in an organized and efficient manner, the people must arrange themselves by tribe, clan, family, and individual—an arrangement that provides considerable insight into the nature of the incipient nation's sociopolitical structure. Ever after (and to this day) there was a consciousness of tribal affiliation in Israel, even in the time of the monarchy when the ancient tribal boundary lines were adjusted in view of changing circumstances that seemed to warrant modification. Here in the Sinai deserts Moses distributed the tribes in their encampment according to groups of three tribes on all four sides of the tabernacle. Levi, the priestly tribe, was apart from all this, its tents surrounding the tabernacle for easy access to its ministry there (Num. 1:47–54).

As they camped, so they traveled, the tribes on the east moving first, headed by Judah. The tribes on the south followed, then those on the west and the north. In the midst of the procession was the tabernacle under the watchful care of the Levites who carried it in precise prescription as commanded by the Lord (Num. 3:1–39). This arrangement, both at rest and on the march, drew attention again to the idea of sacred space, sacred persons, and gradations of holiness.[4] It also testified to the role that the tribe of Judah would play in the Davidic-Messianic covenant. Most holy and awesome of all was the presence of the Lord among his people, symbolized by the blazing cloud that stood over the tabernacle (Num. 9:10–23). When the cloud moved, Israel was to break camp and move with it; for in reality the Lord, the great King, was leading the way to the

[4] Philip P. Jensen, *Graded Holiness: A Key to the Priestly Conception of the World* (Sheffield: JSOT, 1992).

place he had promised to the patriarchs as the everlasting possession of his people Israel.

The account of the wilderness travels begins in Numbers 10 with instruction about the blowing of trumpets as a signal to assemble about the tabernacle and prepare to move (vv. 1–7). The same signal would be sounded in time to come when Israel was en route to battle. It would again mark the presence of the Lord who, as the warrior fighting for his people, would lead the way and guarantee them success (v. 9; cf. Josh. 6:2–21; Judg. 6:34; 7:17–18). Sadly enough, however, the people failed to avail themselves of the Lord's power and grace on their behalf, so much so that the dominant theme of the book of Numbers could well be described as failure. Time and again they chafed at his leadership as well as at that of his servant Moses until at last the Lord consigned them to a thirty-eight-year sojourn in the deserts when the journey could easily have been made in weeks (Num. 14:32–34).[5] Those incidents or aspects of the sojourn that are particularly contributory to biblical theology should receive at least cursory attention. Among them is the pericope of the explorers sent out by Moses to reconnoiter the land of Canaan to test its strengths and weaknesses (Num. 13–14). Of the twelve sent out, only two came back with the assessment that though the land was occupied by giants and was well fortified, Israel was well able to conquer it. In Joshua's words, "Don't be afraid of the people of the land, for we will devour them. Their protection has been removed from them, and the LORD is with us" (Num. 14:9).

These words of trust and confidence fell on deaf ears, however, and the people threatened Joshua and Caleb with death. At this point the Lord presented himself in his glory and laid bare the real truth of the matter: the people were not resisting human leadership but that of God himself. "How long will these people despise Me?" he asked. "How long will they not trust in Me despite all the signs I have performed among them?" (v. 11). Then, as he had done following the worship of the golden calf (Exod. 32:9–10), the Lord threatened to dissolve his relationship with Israel and to make Moses founder of a new and greater nation (v. 12). After making the case that such an act on the Lord's part would cause his reputation

---

[5] George W. Coats, *Rebellion in the Wilderness: The Murmuring Motif in the Wilderness Traditions of the Old Testament* (Nashville: Abingdon, 1968).

to suffer among the nations, Moses pleaded that he might forgive the people "in keeping with the greatness of Your faithful love" (Heb. *ḥesed,* "covenant faithfulness," v. 19). The Lord therefore relented; and though he consigned that rebellious generation to wander in the deserts and die there, he pledged to Caleb and those of "a different spirit" (v. 24) that he would see them safely through.

The story provides a parade example of the dynamics of the covenant relationship. God had brought Israel into fellowship with himself with the expectation that they had a mission to accomplish on his behalf. And Israel willingly accepted its terms, understanding full well that they stood to inherit the magnificent promises made to the fathers. The Lord's threat to disinherit Israel notwithstanding, he had committed to them an everlasting faithfulness (Gen. 17:19; cf. 1 Chron. 16:17) to his covenant pledges. The threat of covenant rupture therefore was not that Israel would be abolished in toto but only that one Israelite, Moses, would be left to carry it forward. The truth implicit in this threat—though it was averted thanks to Moses' fervent intercession—is that God always has a remnant people, a residual Israel that must not and cannot fail ultimately to accomplish God's redemptive purpose.

A second story—that of Moses' intemperate striking of the rock (Num. 20:2–13)—makes the same point but in a different way. In response to the people's complaining about a lack of water to drink, Moses encountered the glory of the Lord at the tabernacle who told him to speak to a certain rock that it might provide a miraculous supply of water. Enraged at the Israelites' rebellion, Moses lost his temper; and rather than just speak to the rock, he struck it. Water indeed gushed out, but the dishonor Moses brought upon the Lord in the eyes of the community disqualified him from leading the people into the land. He then, like the unbelieving spies, must die in the desert, never having set foot in the land of promise.

The intent of the narrative is clearly not to suggest that Moses suffered excommunication from the covenant and its promises or even from the covenant nation. His epitaph is sufficient to nullify that idea (Deut. 34:10–12). To be disbarred from the land of promise was not necessarily to be denied what the covenant with Israel entailed in its entirety, but this lapse on Moses' part did reveal that there were penalties for covenant infraction in the here and now. The fact that he continued as the theocratic administrator until his death is sufficient evidence that he enjoyed God's forgiveness, but the privilege of his special access to the holiness of God placed on Moses a heavier weight of responsibility than was accorded to other people.[6] He illustrates well the principle taught by Jesus who said, "Much will be required of everyone who has been given much. And even more will be expected of the one who has been entrusted with more" (Luke 12:48). To dishonor the Lord, as Moses did, carries a high cost (Num. 20:12; cf. Deut. 4:21–24; 32:48–52).

The third narrative in the book of Numbers that yields important theological insight concerns the pagan prophet Balaam whom Balak, King of Moab, hired to curse Israel when Israel was perceived by him to be a threat (Num. 22–25, 31). Besides attesting to the fact that cultures apart from Israel were acquainted with prophetism, the story here emphasizes the sovereignty of Israel's God over even such as these. Though paid a handsome sum to pronounce incantations over God's people, all Balaam could do was utter glorious blessings upon them. Even before he spoke his first words publicly, Balaam was forced to concede to Balak, "I must speak only the message God puts in my mouth" (Num. 22:38). His futile efforts to curse Israel despite employing every known magical device soon gave substance to Balaam's admission. The more he tried, the more glorious were his messages of the blessing and triumph of Israel, culminating in the prophecy that "a star will come from Jacob, and a scepter will arise from Israel. He will smash the forehead of Moab and strike down all the Shethites" (Num. 24:17).

What Balaam could not do in word to curse the Lord's people, he was able somehow to accomplish in other ways, however, for the narrative goes on to describe Israel's engagement in the grossest forms of Baal worship and links it to his influence (Num. 25:1–3; cf. 31:15–16). The Lord let loose a plague against the guilty apostates and had Phinehas the priest not exacted holy vengeance against the leading perpetrators the nation's well-being itself might have been jeopardized. Instead, the Lord blessed Phinehas and his (Aaronic) priestly descendants with a covenant of a lasting priesthood, one that guaranteed that Aaron's line would forever occupy that place of holy privilege (Num. 25:13). Moses had been denied access to Canaan because he had brought dishonor to the Lord (Num. 20:12); Phinehas would enjoy an everlasting priesthood

[6] Martin Emmrich, "The Case Against Moses Reopened," *JETS* 46/1 (2003): 55.

"because he was zealous for his God and made atonement for the Israelites" (Num. 25:13). The usefulness and blessing of the servant of God was inextricably linked to the degree to which he brought glory to God. Underlying this principle is the kingdom idea espoused throughout this theology, namely, that the great King rules through those made as his image and to the extent that they represent him well, to that extent they enjoy his approbation.

The message of Balaam, a message from the Lord despite that prophet's paganism and reluctance, will come in for further notice at the appropriate time. It is an important part of an accumulating body of messianic revelation that pointed inevitably beyond the Old Testament witness to One who embodied all that Balaam and the prophets of Israel could only anticipate.

Deuteronomy as a Covenant Text

The Background of Its Stipulations

After forty years in the Sinai deserts, Israel arrived at the plains of Moab, just east of the Jordan River and Jericho. There they made camp until the time was propitious for them to cross the river and engage in the conquest and occupation of the land that had long been promised to them. Before this could happen, Moses would die, having first delivered to the nation a final address consisting of much instruction and many admonitions, altogether making up what is best described as a covenant renewal document. The need for such a text is apparent. The Sinai covenant, focused on the book of the covenant (Exod. 20–23) but elaborated in the rest of Exodus and in Leviticus and Numbers, had been designed to meet the needs of the desert community in transit to Canaan, though obviously the Decalogue and other bedrock principles had and have ongoing relevance. Now, however, the wandering days were over, and Israel was about to enter a new environment and undertake a manner of life radically different from what they had just experienced. No longer would the lifestyle be almost exclusively pastoral and unsettled. Almost immediately Israel would become an urbanized culture, living in "a land with large and beautiful cities that you did not build, houses full of every good thing that you did not fill them with, wells dug that you did not dig, and vineyards and olive groves that you did not plant" (Deut. 6:10–11; cf. 19:1; Josh. 24:13). Clearly, laws designed for life as they had known it would need to be modified to suit these new, greatly different circumstances.

Even more important, the adult generation to whom the Sinai covenant had been given had passed from the scene, barred from entering the land because of their sin (Num. 14:32; cf. Deut. 2:14–15). A new generation had arisen, one not party to the Sinai covenant arrangement. It too must pledge itself to covenant fidelity to the Lord as He condescended to bring them into the same kind of covenant fellowship and responsibility as he had their fathers. The Lord had promised Abraham that the nation he sired would forever be His servant people, a promise which, to be effective, necessitated its application to every generation of that nation to come.

Moreover, the type of covenant in view here—by form, of the so-called suzerain-vassal genre—required by custom a periodic modernizing and reaffirmation by both parties in order to accommodate the changed conditions that almost certainly would develop since it had first been composed. The great King would expand upon, elaborate, or even reinterpret the text in order to make perfectly clear his expectations of his junior partner; and he would insist that his vassal reaffirm his loyalty and commit himself to full obedience to the demands laid upon him.

All of this attaches to the book of Deuteronomy and provides the insight essential to a proper understanding of the book's function and meaning. In our view this is crucial, for no other book of the Old Testament is as theologically pregnant as Deuteronomy. It may rightly be understood as the charter and confession of Israel's faith to which the poets and prophets most appealed and which formed the basis for the development of the principal themes of the later Old Testament (and New Testament) revelation. This conviction on our part lays the predicate for the use of Deuteronomy as the fountainhead of theological discussion that begins in that book and will be traced throughout the subsequent biblical record.

Having proposed that Deuteronomy, though presented as a series of valedictory addresses by Moses, is in fact a covenant renewal document, it will be helpful to note briefly how its literary structure is informed as a whole by the secular treaty models to which scholars have compared it.

The following outline will suffice, the items marked by an asterisk being those normally found in treaty texts of this kind.[7]

I. The Covenant Setting (1:1–5)
II. The Historical Review (1:6–4:40)*
III. The Preparation for the Covenant Text (4:41–49)
IV. The Principles (or General Stipulations) of the Covenant (5:1–11:32)*
V. The Specific Stipulations of the Covenant (12:1–26:15)*
VI. Exhortation and Narrative Interlude (26:16–19)
VII. The Curses and Blessings (27:1–28:68)*
VIII. The Epilogue: Historical Review (29:2–30:20)
IX. Deposit of the Text and Provision for Its Future Implementation (31:1–29)*
X. The Song of Moses (as a Witness) (31:30–32:44)*
XI. Narrative Interlude (32:45–52)
XII. The Blessing of Moses (33:1–29)
XIII. Narrative Epilogue (34:1–12)

The procedure we will follow in laying bare the theological message of the book is to take up each of these sections seriatim but, at the same time, to determine the central theological premise or premises around which the book as a whole is organized. This mixed approach may at first appear confusing, but it seems on the whole to be the best way to understand the complexity of the book's ideas.

Deuteronomy presents itself as an address by Moses to the nation Israel assembled on the plains of Moab (1:1–5). He repeated the history of the people since they had left Sinai some thirty-eight years earlier, reminding them of both the blessings and the judgments of the Lord but especially of their own failures to love and serve him as the nation chosen to do this thing. Nevertheless, the promise of the land remained for the Lord could not go back on his word to their patriarchal ancestors (1:20–21, 35; 4:1, 21, 37–38, 40). The tension between the ongoing promise of the land and the failure of that generation to inherit it is resolved in the distinction

[7] The rationale for this outline may be found in the author's *Deuteronomy,* NAC 4 (Nashville: Broadman & Holman, 1994), 38–40; cf. K. A. Kitchen, *On the Reliability of the Old Testament* (Grand Rapids: Eerdmans, 2003), 284.

to be made between Israel as a nation, a collective or corporate entity in the abstract, and Israel as constituted by individuals from time to time. Individuals (Moses included) might fall short of a particular blessing, but the nation would inevitably come to the fullness of God's purpose for it. The historical review makes this point in regard to both that generation (Deut. 1:34–36) and to Moses himself (v. 37; cf. 3:23–26; 4:21–22), but it also is replete with assurances that the new generation would not fail to enter the land and would there enjoy great success if it complied with the terms of the covenant about to be made (1:36, 38–39; 3:20–22, 28; 4:1, 22–24). But if they, like their fathers, proved to be disobedient, they too would suffer the consequences of God's judgment (4:25–26). They would be uprooted from the land and remain in another Egyptian bondage until they repented and returned to the Lord with a new heart bent to obedience (vv. 27–30). This was a certain thing for "He will not leave you, destroy you, or forget the covenant with your fathers that He swore to them by oath, because the LORD your God is a compassionate God" (v. 31).

The recital of Israel's recent history was important both as a lesson as to what to expect when covenant norms were ignored and as an incentive to the younger conquest generation to hear and abide by the terms of the covenant about to be revealed. Above all, it was a reminder of the faithfulness of their God to his promises in the past and an encouragement to trust him for whatever lay ahead. On the basis of that faithfulness, Moses exhorted the people to "recognize and keep in mind that the LORD is God in heaven above and on earth below; there is no other. Keep His statutes and commands, which I am giving you today, so that you and your children after you may prosper and so that you may live long in the land the LORD your God is giving you for all time" (Deut. 4:39–40).

The Deuteronomic Decalogue

This profound confession of the nature of Israel's God and of his covenant expectations provides the perfect segue into the fundamental principles upon which the Deuteronomic covenant was based, namely, the Decalogue (Deut. 5:1–21). We noted previously that the Ten Commandments had ancient, pre-Mosaic roots and therefore were not ad hoc laws created for Israel's unique historical situation. They reflect the character of God and were intended to provide timeless guidelines as to how not only Israel but all men are to live before Him.[8] At the same time they were the basis for everything else in the covenant law and, in that sense, were Israel's special property.

That the Decalogue of Deuteronomy is more than just a repetition of the Decalogue of Exodus is clear from certain variations between them (notably in commandments four and ten). At the same time the durability of the Sinai version and its ongoing relevance is equally clear from Moses' introduction to this second law (thus the meaning of the Greek name of the book, *Deuteronomion,* based on a misunderstanding of Deut. 17:18 NIV, "a copy of this law"). He reminded his hearers that the Lord had delivered these commands to them and not to their fathers (that is, the patriarchal progenitors) and that the demands of that covenant had not been altered or rescinded. He exhorted them, therefore, to hear (i.e., obey) "the statutes and ordinances I am proclaiming as you hear them today. Learn and follow them carefully" (Deut. 5:1).

There is no need here to repeat our exposition of the first three commandments since the two versions (Exod. 20 and Deut. 5) are virtually identical.[9] The Sabbath commandment, however, differs considerably from its earlier prototype and in ways that are theologically noteworthy. The prohibition of labor on the Sabbath is common to the two passages, but the rationale (the motive clause) is different. In the Exodus account the remembrance of creation and the fact that God ceased his creative work on the seventh day justified observance of that day as a time of rest. Here, on the other hand, Israel was reminded that they were slaves in Egypt and that God had effected for them a release from their onerous bondage in the exodus (v. 15). For that reason they must allow their slaves to rest; in fact, they themselves, their families, the foreigners among them, and even their animals must be allowed to cease their labor. The great exodus deliverance had therefore come to supplant even creation itself as an event that must be paramount in the thinking and religious observance of the community.

The point here most certainly is that though basic principles of faith and life are inflexibly permanent, the reasons they are recollected and

[8] Terence E. Fretheim, "Law in the Service of Life: A Dynamic Understanding of Law in Deuteronomy," *A God So Near: Essays on Old Testament Theology in Honor of Patrick D. Miller,* ed. Brent A. Strawn and Nancy R. Bowen (Winona Lake, Ind.: Eisenbrauns, 2003), 183–200.

[9] See pp. 331–45.

enacted may vary from time to time. In the developing sacred history of Israel, God's act of redeeming them to be his covenant people took on such immense significance that, after forty years of reflection, creation paled into relative unimportance compared to who and what they now were through God's re-creative grace. And it is not inappropriate to note at the same time that the observance of Sunday as the holy day of the church, an observance based on the triumphant resurrection of Jesus Christ from the dead, is of such powerful significance as to eclipse both creation and the exodus and even the day set apart as a day of commemoration. The truth remains that times and seasons of reflection on God's mighty acts are not only desirable but mandatory; however, what is reflected upon and why are products of the ongoing progression of divine activity and revelation.

The Tenth Commandment betrays a more subtle shift from its earlier rendition but one worth noting as an example of a change of emphasis dictated by a change of context. Exodus 20:17 reads, "Do not covet (Heb. *ḥmd)* your neighbor's house. Do not covet *(ḥmd)* your neighbor's wife," etc., whereas Deuteronomy 5:21 says, "Do not desire *(ḥmd)* your neighbor's wife or covet *(ʾwh)* your neighbor's house," etc. The point worth noting is not so much the Hebrew words employed in each case, for they are essentially synonymous,[10] but the order of the items not to be coveted has a better explanation than only a different text tradition or merely a scribal preference. Some scholars suggest that the Deuteronomy version reflects the tendency of that book to be much more sensitive to women than the tradition behind Exodus.[11] Much more likely is the fact that Israel was about to enter a cultural environment in which sexual restraints were nearly nonexistent and where adulterous relationships would hardly be unusual. The recent events at Shittim, where "the people began to have sexual relations with the women of Moab" (Num. 25:1–3) is sufficient to illustrate what Israel was up against in an environment whose religious practice was saturated in such behavior. In a list of things not to be craved in Canaan, surely the avoidance of desire for another man's wife should be at the top.

---

[10] Moshe Weinfeld, *Deuteronomy 1–11,* AB 5 (New York: Doubleday, 1991), 318.

[11] J. G. McConville, *Deuteronomy,* AOTC 5 (Downers Grove, Ill.: InterVarsity, 2002), 130–31.

General Covenant Stipulations

We have tried to make the case that Israel's covenant law finds its grounds and bearings in the Decalogue, a case accepted by virtually all scholars. We wish now to advance the proposal that even the Decalogue is the fleshing out of even more basic principles, foundational tenets that arise out of the nature of God and that find expression in his relationship with mankind. Jesus, when asked, "Which commandment in the law is the greatest?" answered, "Love the Lord your God with all your heart, with all your soul, and with all your mind. This is the greatest and most important commandment. The second is like it: Love your neighbor as yourself. All the Law and the Prophets depend on these two commandments" (Matt. 22:36–40).

Jesus' response reflected the common Jewish sentiment in the first century, a sentiment rooted in Deuteronomy 6:4–5, the Shema. What he called the second commandment derives from Leviticus 19:18: "Do not take revenge or bear a grudge against members of your community, but love your neighbor as yourself; I am the LORD." We have already reflected on the idea that the Decalogue consists of two major divisions: (1) the first four commandments that speak of mankind's relationship to God, that is, the vertical dimension; and (2) the last six that describe interpersonal human relationships, the horizontal dimension. Jesus no doubt reduced the Ten Commandments to these two categories and said that in each case love must be the driving and energizing factor.

The Shema (so-called because of the first Hebrew word, *šēmaʿ*), though brief, consists of two parts: (1) a declaration of who God is and (2) a command as to how to act in light of that declaration. Nothing could be more cognitively clear and theologically profound than this all-encompassing statement of Israel's foundational confession. To know God and to love him sums up the totality of human responsibility and, for Israel, defined the nature of the covenant relationship between the nation and her God.

At the risk of some repetition, we must engage this text at a deeper exegetical level in order to elicit from it all that it is intended to convey. First, it is directed to Israel, the Lord's covenant partner, on the threshold of the conquest. Israel had already encountered Baalism at Shittim where the Moabites worshipped the "Baal of Peor" (Num. 25:3), and it would not be long before they were immersed in a polytheistic culture where deities of all kinds abounded. The allusion to a "Baal of Peor" already suggests the existence of many Baals or at least the manifestation of Baal at many places (cf. Josh. 11:17; Judg. 3:3; 8:33; 1 Kings 1:2; 18:18; Jer. 9:14; Hos. 2:13, 17). It was therefore important to know not only that the Lord was Israel's God but that he, indeed, was the only God. This apologetic need favors the translation of the first clause as "Listen, Israel: The LORD is our God, the LORD alone," rather than "The LORD our God, the LORD is One" (Deut. 6:4). The idea that the Lord is one, though important (if obscure in this context), seems somewhat irrelevant in view of Israel's situation at the moment.[12]

As for the command, its intent was to enjoin upon Israel a total commitment to the Lord, one involving all that a person is and all he does. The heart *(lēbab)* in biblical physiology refers to the intellectual or cognitive capacity. One must therefore devote one's mental powers to loving the Lord. This means more than mere meditation or contemplation or even theologizing. To love God in the Old Testament sense of the verb was to choose him, a clearly intellectual matter, and to make up one's mind to serve him unreservedly.[13] The soul *(nepeš)* is the person as such, the human being within with the full panoply of feeling and emotion.[14] It includes everything about humanness apart from the cognitive and volitional. The Lord must be loved and served with zeal, compassion, joy, excitement—all the elements and aspects of the psyche that constitute human essence. The strength (*mĕʾōd,* lit., "muchness"), of course, is the physical, the bodily identification and expression of an individual. To love God only in the mind and feelings is not adequate, for the inner impulses must be fleshed out in service. Jesus caught the relationship between profession of love and its reality when he said to his disciples, "If you love Me, you will keep My commandments" (John 14:15). Israel's love of the Lord their God must likewise be characterized by an unstinting and uncompromised obedience to him.

Our proposal is that the Shema is to the Decalogue what the Decalogue is to the whole covenant text, especially in its Deuteronomic rendition. For Israel to obey the Shema perfectly was tantamount to keeping the

---

[12] Peter C. Craigie, *The Book of Deuteronomy,* NICOT (Grand Rapids: Eerdmans, 1976), 168–69.

[13] See p. 62.

[14] D. C. Fredericks, נפשׁ, *NIDOTTE* 3:133–34.

covenant in all its parts and thus to enjoy God's blessing and approval. On the other hand, to fail to conform to the Shema at least placed the individual (and the nation) in danger of covenant violation and hence in need of forgiveness. The apostle James caught the essence of this truth when he wrote that "whoever keeps the entire law, yet fails in one point, is guilty of breaking it all" (James 2:10). Moses thus adumbrated in one easily remembered confession the whole sum and substance of the covenant ethos and law.

The importance of remembering and obeying the covenant requirements is evident from the instructions Moses gave about the pedagogical process of instilling them into the next generation. "These words," he says, "are to be in your heart" (Deut. 6:6). That is, they are to become part of the mental inventory of the people, the basis upon which life decisions must be made (cf. *lēbab,* "heart," in v. 5). This was particularly important in an age of orality when written texts were few and far between. For the Word of God to be retained and to be effective, it must be committed to memory, "incised,"[15] as it were, on the tablets of the mind (v. 7). So vital was this that parents must constantly, by word and deed, repeat the words of the covenant to their children and reinforce the learning by the display of mnemonic devices on their person and on the doorposts of their houses (Deut. 6:7–9). At the minimum, this consisted of the Shema and the Decalogue, the foundational principles of covenant faith and behavior.

A number of scholars have made a convincing case for the argument that Deuteronomy 6–26 consists of an elaboration or interpretation of the Decalogue and in the order of the commandments.[16] We concur and find this observation to be most helpful in both understanding the structure of the book and providing exegetical insight into various problematic texts. However, to demonstrate this here and even to draw overmuch attention to it in the following treatment of the book will unnecessarily distract us from our principal task, which is to grasp the theological intent of the material.

---

[15] Heb. *šnn*; *BDB,* 1042.

[16] S. A. Kaufman, "The Structure of the Deuteronomic Law," *Maarav* 1–2 (1978–79): 105–58; J. H. Walton, "Deuteronomy: An Exposition of the Spirit of the Law," *GTJ* 8 (1987): 213–25.

The Shema, besides distilling the Decalogue as a whole, draws special attention to the first two commandments, that which declares God's demand for exclusive worship and the one prohibiting the fabrication of images either in his likeness or in the likeness of anything in creation (Deut. 5:7–8). The first injunction Moses presented to the people after expounding on the Shema was to "fear the LORD your God, worship Him, and take your oaths in His name. Do not follow other gods, the gods of the peoples around you" (Deut. 6:13–14). He then introduced the policy of holy war, the purpose of which was to destroy totally the wicked Canaanite nations who otherwise "will turn your sons away from Me to worship other gods" (Deut. 7:4). Along with the populace, the structures of pagan cultus and worship must also be eradicated. In line with the second commandment, the Lord ordered Israel to "tear down their altars, smash their standing pillars, cut down their Asherah poles, and burn up their carved images" (v. 5). The reason was that "you are a holy people belonging to the LORD your God," a people chosen "to be His own possession out of all the peoples on the face of the earth" (v. 6; cf. Exod. 19:5). The connection between the first two commandments and Israel's uniqueness as the chosen people of the Lord is patent: if God had recognized only Israel as his people out of all the peoples of the earth, then surely Israel must recognize only the Lord as their God—in fact, as the only God who exists.

Obedience to these commandments would ensure God's blessing and protection. Their crops and livestock would flourish in the land, and they would be free of the diseases they had experienced in Egypt (Deut. 7:12–16). And like his miraculous deliverance of Israel in the exodus, the Lord would deliver them from their enemies in Canaan, driving them from the land and destroying them at Israel's hands (vv. 17–24). Both these positive and negative aspects of God's blessing were attached to the prohibition against the worship of pagan gods, thus linking blessing with uncompromising allegiance to the Lord their God (vv. 16, 25–26).

A principal tenet of Canaanite religion was the belief that Baal, Asherah, and the other deities of their pantheon were responsible for the blessings of nature such as rainfall, the nourishment of the soil, and the fertility of man and beast. It would be tempting in times of drought or other natural disaster for the Israelites to appeal to these gods, especially since, in a sense, they were operating in their own backyard. The Lord, on the other hand, was invisible, aniconic, and in addition was a stranger, having come into Canaan from the deserts where he was most at home. This kind of thinking is implicit in the reference to these gods following the Lord's reminder that all the good things that would come to his people in the land must be attributed not to them or even to the genius and hard work of the people themselves; rather, they must "remember that the LORD your God gives you the power to gain wealth, in order to confirm His covenant He swore to your fathers, as it is today" (Deut. 8:18; cf. vv. 19–20). Once more, adherence to the covenant meant rejection of other gods.

That such a thing as Israel's future apostasy was possible is obvious from a review of its past. No sooner had the Lord revealed the Ten Commandments at Sinai than Israel turned to the worship of a golden calf. Moses recalled this incident at this point of his address precisely in order to warn his hearers that what their fathers had done following the giving of the Sinai covenant they were capable of and most likely to do following the covenant he was making with them now (Deut. 9:7–24). The remedy was clear: "And now, Israel, what does the LORD your God ask of you except to fear the LORD your God by walking in all His ways, to love Him, and to worship the LORD your God with all your heart and all your soul?" (Deut. 10:12–13). The appeal to the Shema, and thus to the first two commandments, is unmistakable. Only by keeping them faithfully could the temptation to worship other gods be averted.

To support this point, Moses spoke in superlative terms of Israel's God as "the God of gods and Lord of lords, the great, mighty, and awesome God" (Deut. 10:17). As the unique and incomparable one, he was worthy of Israel's undivided loyalty. "Fear the LORD your God and worship Him," Moses urged upon his people. "Remain faithful to Him and take oaths in His name. He is your praise and He is your God, who has done for you these great and awesome works your eyes have seen" (vv. 20–21). Then, in a closing exhortation regarding the Lord's solitary existence as God and the need to worship him alone, Moses appealed once more to the language of the Shema. "Love the LORD your God," he exhorted, "and always keep His mandate and His statutes, ordinances, and commands" (Deut. 11:1). Then he added the conditions to be met for God's blessings in the land: "If you carefully obey My commands I am giving you today, to love the LORD your God and worship Him with all your heart and with all your soul, I will provide rain for your land," etc. (vv. 13–14). Here Moses made clear that the Shema was the adumbration of all the commands and that to love him connoted nothing more or less than to serve him (cf. also v. 22).

Specific Covenant Stipulations

The theological concern of Deuteronomy turns now from a preoccupation with the nature and uniqueness of Israel's God and the obligation of Israel to obey him as such to a consideration of his approachability. How, when, and where can he be reached? The Sinai covenant of Exodus treated this theme, of course, making clear the fact that God resided in sacred space, specifically in the tabernacle and most particularly at the ark of the Covenant in the most holy place (Exod. 25:8–9, 22). Like the great kings of the ancient Near Eastern world, he sat there in lofty splendor, guarded by his attendants and ready to receive the tribute of the citizens and subjects of his realm. The book of the covenant had made allowance for God to be worshipped at a multiplicity of sites—"where I cause My name to be remembered" (Exod. 20:24)—but clearly not in opposition to the central sanctuary of the tabernacle. Deuteronomy looks to a future day when pagan shrines and even syncretistic Israelite high places would have to be destroyed, giving way to the one place in the land which "the Lord your God chooses from all your tribes to put His name for His dwelling" (Deut. 12:5; cf. vv. 11, 14, 21, 26).

The linkage of the requirement for God to be worshipped at a central place on the one hand to the Decalogue on the other, though not immediately self-evident, lies in the common reference to the Lord's name. The third commandment warns, "Do not misuse the name of the Lord your God, because the Lord will punish anyone who misuses His name" (Deut. 5:11). The name of God was a metaphor for God himself; i.e., to misuse his name was to do violence to him. The place that God "causes his name to dwell," therefore, is his residence, the one place on earth where he could be approached and the only legitimate place for the theocratic community to meet him and offer him tribute.[17] As the capital of his kingdom, there was no room for other religious centers where other gods held court. They must therefore be demolished (vv. 2–3) lest their continued existence prompt in God's people a curiosity about how other people worshipped their gods, and thus they emulated their detestable behavior (vv. 29–31).

The requirement for God's people to resort to him in a special place has a number of theological ramifications. First, it suggests something of the holiness and transcendence of God himself, for he is not so common as to be found in just any place of human choosing or preference. It is where he chooses to place his name and no other. At the same time, and paradoxically, the existence of God's dwelling place on earth communicates his nearness and accessibility. As Deuteronomy itself asks, "What great nation is there that has a god near to it as the LORD our God is to us whenever we call to him?" (Deut. 4:7). The Lord may be found exclusively in his dwelling place, but God's people are told not to be so overcome by his remoteness that they fail to meet him there (Deut. 12:5).

The questions remain as to who is to meet him at the central sanctuary and when. To take the latter question first, it should be apparent that daily appearance is not in view—at least for the whole nation—because the anticipated occupation of the land would result in an area so large that only a comparative handful of people could live in proximity to the place of worship no matter where it was. Other texts suggest that the only times when the entire community should assemble there—and then only the men by mandate—would be at the thrice-annual festivals already described (cf. Exod. 23:14–17; Lev. 23:1, 4–21; Num. 28:16–29:40; Deut. 16:1–17). Worship and assembly on a lesser scale could be carried out at local shrines also sanctioned by some evidence of God's visitation there (cf. Exod. 20:24; Deut. 12:15–28). This is clear not only from the legislation given here but from subsequent practice as documented in narrative texts (cf. Judg. 6:24–26; 13:18–23; 1 Sam. 9:12–13; 1 Kings 18:30–38).

The matter as to who must participate in worship at the central sanctuary seems best answered by an appeal once more to the nature of

---

[17] Thompson points out that the Akkadian phrase *šakānum šumam,* "to place the name," is exactly equivalent to the Hebrew expression here and means "to assert sovereignty." J. A. Thompson, *Deuteronomy: An Introduction and Commentary,* TOTC (Downers Grove, Ill.: InterVarsity, 1974), 166.

the Deuteronomic covenant. It was a suzerain-vassal type which suggests, therefore, that the Lord, as the great King, held court at his palace, that is, at the place he would choose "to put his name there for his dwelling." Three times a year Israel, his vassal people, must make pilgrimage there to reaffirm their loyalty to him, to repair any broken relationships that may have occurred, and to offer up tributes of praise and thanksgiving. That is, the central sanctuary served as a place of national assembly and of religious activity done on behalf of the nation, whereas local worship centers sufficed to meet the needs of the populace scattered throughout the land.

The instructions regarding the establishment of a place of divine residence on earth and the worship to be carried out there are, not surprisingly, bracketed by references to pagan practices and the need to disavow and eliminate them. This, we have seen, is a regular literary pattern in this section of Deuteronomy where the uniqueness of Israel's God and the need to worship him exclusively is the central theme. The passage begins with the command to destroy all vestiges of pagan worship and to refrain from emulating their ways (Deut. 12:1–4) and concludes with the exhortation that once this has been done, Israel must forever after resist the temptation to revive them again (vv. 29–32).

We earlier gave attention to the fact that all the religions of the ancient Near East were concerned with the means of gaining access to the ways of the gods and trying to make sense of them.[18] This took the form, generally speaking, of divination, the art and science of eliciting from deity the purposes and plans the gods might have for mankind. Insight into these practices has become possible thanks to the recovery of thousands of so-called omen texts that provide detailed prescriptions to be followed in determining the pleasure of the gods. Alongside these have come to light another genre of literature—incantation texts—that were designed to counter or offset ominous reports communicated by divination.[19]

The practitioners of these crafts may, for our purpose, be loosely described as prophets, though in a technical sense prophetism is so far

---

[18] See pp. 88–89.

[19] See especially Walter Farber, "Witchcraft, Magic, and Divination in Ancient Mesopotamia," *Civilizations of the Ancient Near East,* vol. 3, ed. Jack Sasson (New York: Charles Scribner's Sons, 1995), 1895–1909.

attested to only in west Semitic cultures such as Mari and Ugarit, and, of course, the Old Testament.[20] Deuteronomy provides the earliest systematic treatment of the matter, and because of its importance here and in later Old Testament theology, we must devote considerable attention to it. The placement of the topic in the book of Deuteronomy (ch. 13) is strategic because Moses, since the revelation of the Decalogue and Shema, had concentrated almost entirely on the first three commandments, those having to do with the Lord as the only God and the need to worship him exclusively. And just before he addressed the issue of false prophets (Deut. 13) and their detestable practices (Deut. 18:9–13), Moses reminded the people that they "must not do the same to the LORD [their] God, because [the pagans] practice for their gods every detestable thing the LORD hates. They even burn their sons and daughters in the fire to their gods" (Deut. 12:31).

Before he addressed the issue of the prophets of the heathen nations, Moses warned that even from within Israel prophets would rise up who would seek to undermine faith in the Lord. The problem would not be the institution of prophetism itself, for Moses himself was a prophet (Num. 12:2, 7–8; Deut. 18:14–18; 34:10–12) and was preceded already by others who at least evidenced the prophetic gift (Gen. 20:7; 49:1). In fact, the principal means by which God revealed himself in Old Testament times was and would be through the prophets. Like any other good gift, however, prophetism could be corrupted and become the means of communicating not the truth but rather lies. This would be especially reprehensible when done in the name of the Lord (Deut. 18:22), a perversion of divine power and presence linked clearly with a violation of the third commandment (Deut. 5:11).

For an Israelite prophet to urge his hearers to defect from the Lord and worship other gods (even though permitted by the Lord to test his people) was to commit an act of treason against the great King that called for nothing less than the death penalty, for he had "urged rebellion against the LORD your God" (Deut. 13:5). Even family members who did so must be executed without pity because they tried "to turn you away from the LORD your God who brought you out of the land of Egypt, out

---

[20] A. Malamat, "Prophecy in the Mari Documents," *Eretz Israel,* 4 (1956): 74–84; Herbert B. Huffman, "Prophecy in the Mari Letters," *BA* 31/4 (1968): 101–24.

of the place of slavery" (v. 10). This behavior and its results illustrate the underlying struggle for dominion between the Lord God and the invisible hosts of wickedness. At every turn the kingdom is assailed, and tragically enough by fifth-columnists who profess loyalty to the great King while seeking to undermine his sovereignty.

The subtlety of wicked Israelite prophets stood in stark contrast to the open perversity of the Canaanite diviners and enchanters who performed their magical works in public view and with no pretense to be serving Israel's God (Deut. 18:9–13). And yet, remarkably, they would tempt Israel to follow their pernicious ways, a pursuit that sadly enough was often more than successful as the record of Israel's history to the end attests (e.g., 2 Kings 17:7–13). On the other hand, the Lord promised that he would raise up legitimate prophetic spokesmen like Moses who would speak nothing but his word (Deut. 18:18). Their authority as his royal ambassadors would be so great that he would hold accountable anyone who disregarded their words (v. 19). At the same time these prophets' responsibility would be so profound that they must die should they pervert their sacred office (v. 20). The acid test as to the authenticity of their ministry and message would be whether their predicted word came to pass. Even if spoken in the name of the Lord, the message would be invalid if it failed to measure up to that criterion (v. 22).

This anticipated establishment of the prophetic institution gradually found embodiment in a variety of forms and movements ranging from isolated, anonymous individuals who made merely cameo appearances, to highly organized fraternities, to the great canonical prophets, so called because of their inspired writings that make up such a significant part of the Old Testament canon. We shall have occasion to consider these as they appear in the historical record; and we must, of course, incorporate their proclamatory and predictive messages as indispensable elements of a full biblical theology.

We have already given at least passing attention to the prescriptions and laws pertinent to Israel's cultic and social life such as those dealing with sacrifice and offerings (cf. Deut. 14:1–21; 15:19–23; 17:1), issues of purity (cf. Deut. 23:1–14), Sabbaths and festivals (14:22–29; 15:1–18; 16:1–17), and interpersonal relationships (16:18–20; 17:2–13; 19:1–21; 21:1–23; 22:13–30; 24:1–25:19). While these are not to be dismissed as irrelevant to biblical theology, for the most part they are examples or elaborations of foundational principles of theocratic definition and life that were peculiar to Old Testament Israel's historical experience. Consideration of each in detail would not only consume space needed for more comprehensive themes, but it could easily result in a loss of focus on those principles themselves that are the real stuff of transtemporal theological relevance. As a whole, these elements can be gathered around the fourth commandment—observance of the Sabbath, and the fifth—honor your father and your mother.

This latter commandment must be considered more carefully at this point because of its clear ideological connections with the key theological idea of God's reign through chosen instruments in general and the introduction of Israelite kingship in particular. We have proposed from the beginning that the kingdom motif presupposes that the Lord, the sovereign of creation, reigns through his image, the human race, and does so through levels or spheres of regal authority. The fifth commandment is in keeping with the idea that there are structures of government even within the family that are part of a grander scheme of delegated authority. At that microcosmic level it might be said that parents represent God in the home and that children, no matter their age, must honor them as such. The book of the covenant already affirmed that "whoever strikes his father or his mother must be put to death" (Exod. 21:15), and Leviticus decrees that if anyone so much as curses his parents he must die (Lev. 20:9). Deuteronomy carries to a still higher level the notion that parents deserve unquestioned obedience. Should a son be "stubborn and disobedient," he might be hauled before the court of elders who, if they found the allegation true, would stone him to death (Deut. 21:18–21). Such drastic action can be accounted for only on the grounds of the exalted position the parent occupies in the hierarchy of kingdom governance.

The commandment pointed beyond itself, however; and in line with the strategy of Deuteronomy, it led to a consideration of other spheres and levels of administration such as the offices of judge and public official (*šôṭēr,* generic for civil servant of any kind) (Deut. 16:18–20).[21] Above all, it paved the way to the introduction of Israelite kingship in

[21] The root is a verb meaning "to write" (*HALOT* 1475–76), but the office clearly was more than that of a clerk or secretary; see Roland de Vaux, *Ancient Israel,* vol.1 (New York: McGraw-Hill, 1965), 155.

a formal way (Deut. 17:14–20). We stress the adjective *formal* because the prospect of such an institution was already advanced in the days of Abraham who had been told, "I [the LORD] will make you extremely fruitful and will make nations and kings come from you" (Gen. 17:6; cf. v. 16). Then Jacob, on his deathbed, had said of Judah, "The scepter will not depart from Judah, or the staff from between his feet, until He whose right it is comes and the obedience of the peoples belongs to Him" (Gen. 49:10). Even the pagan prophet Balaam foresaw the day when Israel would have a king, a "star" that would come out of Jacob, a "scepter" that would rise out of Israel (Num. 24:17).

Human kingship as an ideal is a reflection of divine kingship and, when exercised in an obedient and godly manner, brings about on the earth God's creation design of filling the earth and having dominion over all things (Gen. 1:26–28). In reality, of course, this has never been achieved because kings, like all human beings, are fallen and flawed, always looking to their own self-interest rather than the Lord's. But kingship nonetheless remains in the scope of God's dominion strategy, exemplified first in the reign of David and his dynasty and then, in the wake of its historical failure, in the regency of Christ, the Son of David and embodiment of all that God intended to do through human agency in establishing a perfect domain.

In the historical development of monarchy in Israel, the initiative for the institution seems clearly to have been crass and self-serving. Three centuries after Moses' time the people demanded of Samuel that he appoint a king to lead them "the same as all the other nations have" (1 Sam. 8:5). We shall return to that crucial passage later and refer to it now only to introduce the Deuteronomic passage that also suggests that the kingship to come would be in response to the people's demands: "We want to appoint a king over us like all the nations around us" (Deut. 17:14). However, the whole tenor of the text implies that though the people would ask for a king, such a request—if even for the wrong motive—was fully within the will of God. There is no rebuke here but only a warning that the king must be one whom "the LORD chooses." Moreover, he must be an Israelite who would recognize his dependence on God alone and who therefore would resist the trappings of large armies, an impressive harem, and abundance of riches (vv. 15–17)—all of which, incidentally, nearly every king of Israel and Judah failed to achieve. More important, the king was to represent the nation, so much so that at stated occasions he must read the text of "this instruction" (no doubt, the book of Deuteronomy) so that he might learn "to fear the LORD his God, to observe all the words of this instruction, and to do these statutes" (vv. 18–19). To the extent the king was loyal to the covenant, to that extent the nation would be blessed and prosper.

Implementation of the Covenant

The specific stipulations of the Deuteronomic covenant (Deut. 12:1–26:15) are followed first by a summary of the covenant's content and an exhortation to obey it (Deut. 26:16–19) and then by lists of curses and blessings typical of covenants of this type. Moses enjoined his hearers to "follow these statutes and ordinances" (that is, the covenant stipulations) and to do so with "all your heart and with all your soul" (v. 16), a statement reminiscent of the Shema, the sum total of all that God demands. He then assured the people that the Lord had declared that day that they were his people, an affirmation not of something new but of his renewed commitment to them to be their God, and, as they were obedient, to make them the most exalted of the nations of the earth.

Part of the ceremony of covenant-making was the invoking of curses upon themselves by the respective covenant partners should its terms be broken. In a remarkable example of this—remarkable because the Lord himself made an oath of self-imprecation—the Lord commanded Abraham to slaughter animals and divide their bodies into two rows, and then he, in a vision, passed between the rows, all the time promising Abraham that he would deliver his descendants from bondage and give them the land of Canaan as an inheritance (Gen. 15:9–21). The astounding thing about this is that the Lord committed himself to a course of action, failing which he would bring upon himself the judgment implicit in the treatment of the animals!

In the suzerain-vassal type of covenant (of which Deuteronomy is an example), only the vassal was placed in a position of jeopardy should he be disobedient and of blessing should he be obedient, though the great King did, of course, obligate himself to punish or reward as the situation required. Deuteronomy contains a lengthy list of curses to become effective in the event Israel broke the terms of the covenant and a much shorter list of blessings for faithful compliance to it. The blessing section

(Deut. 28:1–14) is sandwiched between two sets of curses (27:15–26 and 28:15–68), the shorter of which roughly parallels the commandments of the Decalogue.[22] It merely states in each case that the person who breaks these commandments will be cursed without clarifying the nature of the curse. The longer list of curses presents the covenant requirements in a general way—"if you do not obey the LORD your God by carefully following all His commands and statutes" (28:15)—and then in great detail spells out an enormous array of divine judgments that will follow.

The blessings are conditioned on the proviso that "you faithfully obey the LORD your God and [are] careful to follow all His commands" (28:1), the exact opposite of the attitude that invites God's curses (v. 15). Most of them promise fruitfulness of womb and fertility of soil—appropriate in light of the creation mandate to "be fruitful, multiply, fill the earth, and subdue it" (Gen. 1:28)—but there is also the assurance of victory over enemies that will rise up against them (Deut. 28:7). By fully obeying the covenant, Israel will succeed in being and doing what the Lord had in mind for them when he chose them to be a special nation: "All the peoples of the earth will see that you are called by the LORD's name, and they will stand in awe of [i.e., respect] you" (v. 10 NIV). Moreover, they will become so prosperous that they "will lend to many nations but will borrow from none" (v. 12). Thus they will fulfill the promise to Abraham that in his seed (that is, in Israel) all the nations will be blessed (Gen. 12:3; cf. 22:18; 27:29).

The detailed list of curses, as might be expected, is the reverse of the blessings. Herds, flocks, and produce will fail because of drought and other calamities; deadly epidemics of disease will decimate the population; and fierce enemies will descend upon the land, destroying and deporting the people until there is nothing left of Israel there. The threat of exile is especially prominent here, having been anticipated also in Leviticus 26. There the Lord had promised that violation of the covenant would invite all kinds of calamity including defeat at the hands of brutal enemies (Lev. 26:17). Should that not bring them to their senses, Israel must suffer the fate of utter destruction and removal from the land (vv. 27–33). However, if they repented in their places of exile and turned wholeheartedly to the Lord, he says, "I will remember My covenant with Jacob. I will also

[22] For the rationale behind this arrangement, see Merrill, *Deuteronomy,* 45.

remember My covenant with Isaac and My covenant with Abraham, and I will remember the land" (vv. 40–42). Moreover—and this is a crucial theological point—their repentance would be a certainty; for, as the LORD goes on to say, "In spite of this [the judgment on Israel], while they are in the land of their enemies, I will not reject or abhor them so as to destroy them and break My covenant with them, since I am the LORD their God. For their sake I will remember the covenant with their fathers, whom I brought out of the land of Egypt in the sight of the nations to be their God; I am the LORD" (vv. 44–45). The truth is clear: Israel must repent of its sins in order to be forgiven and restored, but the Lord will guarantee that they do so because his reputation is at stake![23]

The Deuteronomic covenant also predicts that should Israel prove unfaithful to the Lord he will bring against them a mighty nation that will wreak havoc throughout the land (Deut. 28:49–52) and then will uproot them and scatter them "among all peoples from one end of the earth to the other" (vv. 63–64). In a kind of a reverse exodus, "The LORD will take you back in ships to Egypt by a route that I said you would never see again" (v. 68). The curse section proper ends here with no apparent hope for Israel's forgiveness and return; but in his summary of the covenant and its ultimate outcome (Deut. 29:2–30:20), Moses declared that not if but when the nation in exile returns to the Lord, he "will restore your fortunes, have compassion on you, and gather you again from all the peoples where the Lord your God has scattered you" (Deut. 30:3). Then, in a remarkable statement of God's initiative, he went on to speak of Israel's conversion as a circumcision of the heart which the Lord will perform, an act of grace that will enable Israel and its descendants to keep the Shema, that is, to "love Him [the Lord] with all your heart and with all your soul" (v. 6).[24] Thus, as in Leviticus 26:44–45, Israel will repent but will be able to do so as the Lord provides the impetus and means of doing so. Jeremiah made the same point when he foresaw the day when the Lord would put his "law within them [Israel] and write it on their hearts" (Jer. 31:33); and Ezekiel, referring to the same new covenant, says in the word of the Lord to Israel, "I will also sprinkle

---

[23] Mark F. Rooker, *Leviticus,* NAC 3A (Nashville: Broadman & Holman, 2000), 320.

[24] Duane L. Christensen, *Deuteronomy 21:10–34:12,* WBC 6B (Nashville: Thomas Nelson, 2002), 740.

clean water on you, and you will be clean. I will cleanse you from all your impurities and all your idols. I will give you a new heart and put a new spirit within you; I will remove your heart of stone and give you a heart of flesh. I will place My Spirit within you and cause you to follow My statutes and carefully observe My ordinances" (Ezek. 36:25–27).

Both the Leviticus and Deuteronomy curse passages (expanded and clarified by the prophets) speak of the dire consequences to Israel of breaking the covenant with the Lord, but they also make the critical theological point that God's promises to the patriarchs about an everlasting seed have integrity and must be fulfilled no matter how Israel behaves. This should not minimize the culpability of Israel or the justice of the Lord in eradicating the nation from the earth should he so choose. But the great truth that emerges from this apparent quandary is the fact that the Lord is full of *ḥesed,* of grace and covenant loyalty that does not ignore sin, to be sure, but that also provides a way of atonement and renewal so that his covenant pledges can come to pass with no compromise of his holiness and justice. This truth paves the way for the doctrine of grace that is the foundation of New Testament soteriology.

Deuteronomy 29–30 provides a brief review of Israel's history from the time of the exodus to the day of assembly at Moab (Deut. 29:1–8) and then a series of exhortations to keep the covenant that was being offered that day. It is a covenant, Moses declared, "not only with you, but also with those who are standing here with us today in the presence of the Lord our God and with those who are not here today" (vv. 14–15). In other words, the covenant was designed for future generations as well as the present. Should Israel in the future prove unfaithful and God's judgment fall, the curiosity of the nations as to why he dealt with them so harshly would be satisfied by the response that Israel "abandoned the covenant of the Lord" and "began to worship other gods" (vv. 25–26).

The solution to the problem posed by Israel's penchant to disobedience is not difficult, Moses argued, at least in theory (Deut. 30:1–14): it was simply to adhere to the Shema—"to love the Lord your God, to walk in His ways, and to keep His commands, statutes, and ordinances" (v. 16). And the choice to do so was right then, on the day of covenant renewal. "Choose life," Moses pleaded, "so that you and your descendants may live, love the Lord your God, obey Him, and remain faithful to him" (vv. 19–20).

In the future the text of the covenant must be read publicly every seven years as part of the celebration of the Feast of Tabernacles. This must be done "in the presence of the LORD your God at the place He chooses" (Deut. 31:11), thus suggesting that the nation must renew its covenant pledges at least that often. These pledges must be done before witnesses according to normal covenant protocol, but in this case Moses composed a song which, when sung by Israel, would thereafter constitute a confession of their faith and a subtle but real invocation of judgment upon them in the event they disobeyed (Deut. 31:19; 32:5–6, 15–33). Finally, the written covenant document must be deposited in a place of ready access where it, too, could testify against the vassal covenant partner. In the case of Israel, this "Book of the Law" as Deuteronomy is here described, must be placed in the most holy place of the tabernacle beside the ark of the covenant (Deut. 31:26). As we have noted before, the ark represented the presence of the Lord among his people, the palace of the great King where he might be approached and from which he exercised his sovereignty over Israel and the whole world. It is likely that another copy of the text existed as well, perhaps the one the king was to read annually on behalf of the nation to remind him (and them) of his responsibility as vice-regent of the Lord (cf. Deut. 17:18).

After a brief narrative interlude (Deut. 32:45–52), the book closes with Moses' blessing of the tribes of Israel (ch. 33) and an account of his death and burial, along with a fitting epitaphic tribute to this prophet *non pareil,* he whom "the LORD knew face to face" (Deut. 34:10). But the significance of the book does not end here, for as we have already proposed, it is the seedbed for much of the theological truth yet to be discovered.

Chapter Thirteen

The Deuteronomistic History

It is commonplace to refer to Joshua through 2 Kings as the Deuteronomistic History, a term that suggests that these books constitute a theological history written with a view to Deuteronomy and to the extent to which Israel (and Judah) conformed to or departed from the covenant principles of that book.[1] It matters little from a theological standpoint whether Deuteronomy be assigned to Moses and an early date (to which we hold) or not, for the history of Israel covered by Joshua through Kings was, in any case, a product of the late sixth century BC in its final canonical form. It does matter, however, that the historical narrative, though fundamentally theological and interpretive in character, be regarded as an accurate account of events as they actually occurred. That is, the books as sacred history are not thereby disqualified as records of Israel's past in terms of standard definitions of historiographical literature.[2] The theology of these books is developed in both overt statements of a theological nature as well as in the

[1] For the issue and the literature related to it, see Antony F. Campbell and Mark A. O'Brien, *Unfolding the Deuteronomistic History* (Minneapolis: Fortress, 2000).

[2] Eugene H. Merrill, "Old Testament History: A Theological Perspective," *A Guide to Old Testament Theology and Exegesis,* ed. Willem A. VanGemeren (Grand Rapids: Zondervan, 1997), 65–82; "Deuteronomy and History: Anticipation or Reflection?" *Faith & Mission* 18/1 (2000): 57–76.

more subtle accounts of events from which theological deductions can be drawn. Our method will be to trace the history as these books present it but to do so with a sensitivity as to why the authors and editors chose the incidents they did and how the chosen topics relate to the theology of Deuteronomy and, indeed, to that of the whole Torah. We will therefore not discuss Israel's history in detail with all its textual, chronological, cultural, and political complexity—a task better left to a full-fledged treatment of history[3]—but our focus will be on those threads or themes that seem most likely to have theological intent.

The Book of Joshua

Preparations for Conquest

The connection between the Deuteronomistic History and Deuteronomy is not long in coming. Immediately after Moses' death the Lord handed over the reins of theocratic administration to Moses' delegated successor Joshua, and, in words almost identical to those given to Israel and Joshua on the occasion of Joshua's official appointment (Deut. 31:1–8), the Lord acknowledged Joshua's new role and encouraged him to undertake it with great confidence and courage (Josh. 1:1–9). Most important is the injunction to "be strong and very courageous to carefully observe the whole instruction *(tôrâ)* My servant Moses commanded you" (v. 7) and the exhortation that "this book of instruction [Deut.] must not depart from your mouth" (v. 8). All that Joshua and the nation Israel undertook henceforth must be grounded in the Deuteronomic covenant and all the revelation that preceded it.

Joshua's first command to the people—to pack up and prepare to cross the Jordan and occupy the land—was met with a word of compliance indicative of their recognition of his Moses-like authority: "Everything you have commanded us we will do, and everywhere you send us we will go" (Josh. 1:16). It is crystal clear that the community was committing itself to its new leader and, by implication, to the covenant of which he was the administrator.

---

[3] See Eugene H. Merrill, *Kingdom of Priests: A History of Old Testament Israel* (Grand Rapids: Baker, 1987).

Part of Moses' authority lay in the fact that the Lord was with him (Exod. 3:12), and thus Joshua as well was blessed with this assurance of divine presence (Josh. 1:5, 9). But the Lord's accompaniment was not just theoretical; it was demonstrable in his mighty acts on Israel's behalf. In Moses' case it was preeminently the exodus that testified to his presence; in Joshua's case it would be the crossing of the flooding Jordan and the conquest of Canaan that would ensue. We have referred briefly already to the concept of holy war in connection with the exodus, a conflict inspired and led by the Lord as the divine Warrior (cf. Exod. 15).[4] And Moses raised the matter again with reference to the conquest, laying out in effect the principal features of holy war and the results to be expected with its faithful prosecution.

Holy War

It will be helpful to address the question of holy war in greater detail at this point because (1) it raises certain issues vis-à-vis Old Testament ethics and the nature of God; and (2) it is the basis upon which the conquest and, indeed, all war in subsequent history that was sanctioned and justified by the Lord was based.[5] We begin with the instruction of Deuteronomy 7:1–6, 17–26 as to the disposition of the seven nations of Canaan. That this is holy war is clear from the following observations: (1) The Lord himself would lead Israel into the land, and he would drive out the nations (vv. 1–2a). (2) Israel must totally destroy *(haḥărēm taḥărîm)* them, that is, annihilate the people (vv. 2b, 24) and demolish their cultic apparatuses (vv. 5, 25). The verb *ḥrm* in this stem has the twofold idea of devoting someone or something to the Lord for his own special use and/or eradicating it completely so that it no longer existed.[6]

The manual of war (Deut. 20) describes in principial form the ethos and practice of holy war as it was to be waged against distant (that is, non-Canaanite) nations as well as those of Canaan listed in Deuteronomy 7:1. Again, the following points should be noted: (1) Israel must not fear *(lōʾ tîrāʾ)* because the Lord will be present (v. 1). (2) There is a cultic

---

[4] See pp. 111–14 .

[5] For a recent treatment see Stanley N. Gundry, ed. *Show Them No Mercy: 4 Views on God and Canaanite Genocide* (Grand Rapids: Zondervan, 2003).

[6] N. Lohfink, חרם, *TDOT* 5:186–87.

aspect as the presence of the priest attests (v. 2). (3) The battle is not Israel's, but the Lord's (v. 4). (4) In the case of distant lands, the men of a city that will refuse to submit must be slain, though women and children may be permitted to live and livestock and other plunder may be kept (vv. 13–14). (5) In the case of Canaanite cities, all living things must be placed under *ḥērem* and annihilated (vv. 16–17).

The rationale for such drastic action was that the Canaanites, if allowed to survive, will "teach you to do all the detestable things they do for their gods, and you sin against the LORD your God" (v. 18; cf. 7:25). As for its moral justification, the answer is already implicit in the previous sentence. The text does not present the threat of the Canaanite paganization of Israel in hypothetical terms; rather, it is most explicit in affirming that Canaanite survival would guarantee Israelite apostasy. These wicked nations had outrun the extent of God's remedial grace, and there was no hope of their reformation. As Genesis 15:16 puts it: "In the fourth generation they [Abraham's descendants] will return here [to Canaan], for the iniquity of the Amorites has not yet reached its full measure." By Moses' (and Joshua's) day, that full measure had been reached so the seven nations, hopelessly and irremedially unrepentant, must be eradicated for Israel's good and God's glory. The best answer to the moral question, even if apparently simplistic, is that God in his omniscience knows the human heart and even its future potential, and knowing that, he deals with people and nations in his grace or in his wrath according to the just deserts they have willingly brought upon themselves.[7]

The Lord's promise to be with Joshua, given on the eve of conquest, has overtones of holy war, hints understood by the spies who, having just returned from Jericho, said to Joshua, "The LORD has handed over the entire land to us. Everyone who lives in the land is also panicking because of us" (Josh. 2:24). The Lord would prevail and make possible the victory for Israel. The strategy employed against Jericho illustrates the implementation of holy war principles. The priests, bearing the ark of the covenant, must lead the way (Josh. 3:1–4). The ark, of course, represented God's presence, and the participation of the priests suggests

[7] Walter C. Kaiser Jr., *Toward an Old Testament Ethics* (Grand Rapids: Zondervan, 1983), 266–69.

that this was no ordinary human conquest. This kind of war was sacred, undertaken by the Lord and for his glory. This is why the people must consecrate themselves. What they were to be involved in was nothing less than a religious exercise, an act of worship as holy as the offering of animal sacrifices (v. 5; cf. Exod. 19:10).

When the ark reached the edge of the raging torrent of the Jordan, the waters stopped their flow (vv. 15–16). The same God who had separated the primeval ocean from the dry land at the dawn of creation (Gen. 1:9–10) and who had parted the waters of the Red Sea so that his beleaguered people could cross safely into freedom (Exod. 14:21–22), once more demonstrated his sovereignty over the hostile forces represented by these chaotic elements of nature. Like the warrior of the exodus, he now waged battle at the head of his Israelite armies (cf. Exod. 15:3–5). Once across, Joshua neared Jericho, intending to lay siege to it; but before he could go any farther, he was confronted by the "commander of the LORD's army" (Josh. 5:14). This signals again the fact that Israel was engaged in holy war; and in words identical to those spoken to Moses in preparation for the exodus deliverance, the heavenly visitor said to Joshua, "Remove the sandals from your feet, for the place where you are standing is holy" (v. 15; cf. Exod. 3:5). The commander, the people, the occasion, the place—all were holy, and all testified to the religious nature of what was about to take place.

The strategy followed by the priests and people to overcome Jericho was more ritual than military science. The march around the perimeter, climaxed by seven circuits on the seventh day plus the blowing of trumpets, gave a heavily religious tone to the whole scene. And if there remains any doubt as to whether this was holy war, Joshua's command that "the city and everything in it are set apart *(wēhāyētâ ḥērem)* to the LORD for destruction" (Josh. 6:17) should put it to rest. In this instance the treasures of the city were to be devoted to him while all living things—including men, women, and children—were to be slain with the exception of Rahab and her household (vv. 19, 21, 23, 25). Achan's violation of the ban, which caused Israel to be defeated in its first attempt to destroy Ai, resulted in the death of him and his whole family, an application of *ḥērem* to himself, as it were (Josh. 7).

Other instances of *ḥērem,* whether explicitly associated with holy war or not, reaffirm the idea of the Lord's stern justice and his inviolable holiness (cf. Josh. 8:26; 10:1, 28, 35, 37, 39–40; 11:11–12, 20–21; Judg. 1:17; 21:11; 1 Sam. 15:3–21). The fundamental theological truth to be learned in the waging of such war is that God is sovereign over all and that he holds all mankind accountable. To be or do less is to undercut any claims to kingship and to make concessions incommensurate with his standards of righteousness and integrity. No subsequent revelation in either Testament teaches anything to the contrary. The principal difference is that in the New Testament God's justice awaits a future day; but that delay, an exercise of his gracious forbearance, holds every bit as much terror for the unrepentant as the day of his visitation (his *ḥērem)* in Old Testament times.

Covenant Renewal in the Land of Promise

Prior to his death Moses had instructed Joshua that once the conquest had begun he must erect two monuments on Mount Ebal, one a plaster-coated stele and the other an altar (Deut. 27:1–8). On the stele he must inscribe "the words of this law" (v. 3), most likely a reference to the text of Deuteronomy,[8] and on the fieldstone altar offer up fellowship offerings attesting to the covenant harmony that existed between the Lord and his people. The purpose of the inscription, of course, was to provide on a billboard as it were the terms of the covenant to which they had subscribed and which they must keep if they were to enjoy God's blessing. Having arrived now at Shechem, the holy site nearby Mount Ebal, Joshua fulfilled Moses' instructions and undertook a ceremony of covenant renewal (which Moses had not explicitly prescribed) (Josh. 8:30–35). He divided the people into two groups, half at the foot of Mount Gerizim and half at the foot of Mount Ebal, with the priests and the ark of the covenant in the valley between. He then read out the covenant blessings and curses (Deut. 27–28), reminding the throng of the good things that would come for obedience but also the judgment that awaited those who broke covenant with the Lord.

The literary placement of this pericope, as well as its occurrence in the flow of history, is most apropos, for it follows hard upon the narrative of Israel's failure in regard to Ai, a failure directly linked to the breaking of covenant. It was important for Israel to be reminded that sin not

[8] J. G. McConville, *Deuteronomy,* AOTC (Downers Grove, Ill.: InterVarsity, 2002), 388.

only required repentance (cf. Josh. 7:6), but it necessitated renewal of covenant vows as well. A similar ceremony took place toward the close of Joshua's ministry and at the same place, but this time its purpose was to engage in a national renewal of covenant in view of the passing of one generation and the emergence of the next (Josh. 24). We have already noted that covenants of this type had to be restated and reaffirmed, and even amended and updated at times, as new kings and their vassals arose from time to time. This, in fact, was the genius behind the book of Deuteronomy itself, a treaty document appropriate to a nation making transition from the desert to the town and from one generation to the next.

Scholars are generally agreed that Joshua 24 is either a covenant renewal text or the report of one, but there is little consensus as to the delimitations of the various elements.[9] There is clearly a preamble (v. 2a) and a historical prologue (vv. 2b–13), and a loosely organized set of stipulations may also be discerned (vv. 14–25). Verse 26 provides for the deposit of the text, and verse 27 speaks of a great stone as a witness. The curses and blessings are implicitly embedded in verses 14–25 (cf. vv. 19–20). Other elements could also be adduced, but the fact remains that Joshua was rehearsing the mighty acts of God on Israel's behalf and was exhorting the nation to commit itself to faithful compliance to the will of God who had already committed himself to their ancestral fathers with promises that cannot be abrogated (vv. 14, 23; cf. v. 4). This was appropriate because Joshua's impending death as well as that of his contemporaries (vv. 28–31) would mark the end of another era and the beginning of a new one. Each generation must subscribe to the covenant for itself, for the faith of the fathers is never sufficient for the children who follow.

The unity and covenant fidelity of the community was always in jeopardy, a fact borne out by the erection of an altar by the Transjordan tribes that seemed at first to be a challenge to the altar of the central sanctuary (Josh. 22). Moses had permitted Reuben, Gad, and half the tribe of Manasseh to settle on the east of the Jordan provided their men of war joined their brothers in the conquest of Canaan (Num. 32). Now

---

[9] For a helpful overview, see David M. Howard Jr., *Joshua,* NAC 5 (Nashville: Broadman & Holman, 1998), 425–28.

that the conquest was essentially complete, these soldiers returned to the Transjordan. Before they left, however, Joshua exhorted them to keep covenant, the essence of which, again, was "to love the Lord your God, walk in all His ways, keep His commands, remain faithful to Him, and serve Him with all your heart and all your soul" (Josh. 22:5; cf. Deut. 6:4–5). Just as they reached the river, they built a great altar, an act that seemed to Israel's leaders to be a breach of that very covenant. The sense of the solidarity of the nation is seen in the plea of the leaders that "if you rebel against the Lord today, tomorrow He will be angry with the entire community of Israel" (v. 18). They therefore threatened to punish their eastern brothers, perhaps even to engage in holy war as the allusion to Achan suggests (v. 20; cf. v. 12). The leaders of the eastern tribes soon made clear that their altar was not intended for cultic use but, in fact, was a commemorative stela, a reminder to generations to come that they were all one people, the Jordan River between them notwithstanding (vv. 26–27).

At least two lessons of theological import may be gained from this story: (1) As long as Joshua was alive, there was a consensus that the theocratic people were one, though there were fears that that unity was fragile and could easily be undermined. (2) The concept of a central sanctuary—a central place where the Lord was to be worshipped by the community (v. 19)—had taken strong root already and laid the foundation for successive locations of the tabernacle and ark in places marked by the Lord's presence.

Finally, Joshua's valedictory address presented clearly and succinctly the essence of who and what Israel was and what the Lord expected of them (Josh. 23). He reminded them that the Lord, the warrior, had fought for them and made possible their conquest of the land (vv. 3–5). What was encumbent on them now was to "continue obeying all that is written in the book of the law of Moses [i.e., Deuteronomy]" (v. 6), especially the first two commandments of the Decalogue (vv. 7–8) and the Shema (v. 11). Failure to do so would invoke God's judgment, culminating in the curse of exile from the land (v. 13). His final words are worth repeating as a summation of God's requirements of his people: "If you break the covenant of the Lord your God, which He commanded you, and go and worship other gods, and bow down to them, the Lord's anger will burn against you, and you will quickly disappear from this good land He has given you" (v. 16). Like Moses, Joshua exhorted his people to covenant faithfulness, fearing at the same time that his warnings might be in vain (cf. Deut. 31:24–29).

The Books of Judges and Ruth

The Character of the Times

The period covered by the book of Judges (about 300 years; ca. 1350–1050 BC) is a period of transition between the loose-knit federation of tribes commonly known as a theocracy and the emergence of Israel as a monarchic nation. Its transitional nature is clear both from the overlap with Joshua at the beginning of the book (Judg. 1–2) and the hint of the aspiration for kingship from at least some elements of the community long before it became a reality (Judg. 8:22). Moreover, the historian's plaintive remembrance that "in those days, there was no king in Israel" (Judg. 18:1; 19:1), and, in particular, that the absence of a king meant that "everyone did whatever he wanted" (Judg. 21:25), reveals that the era of the judges was one of religious and cultural anarchy that cried out for some kind of solution. The Lord's temporary remedy was to raise up judges, men (and one woman, Deborah) gifted to administer the affairs of the covenant community, sometimes in succession and sometimes contemporaneously and over regional jurisdictions. Though they functioned on occasions in contexts of jurisprudence, the judges for the most part were military leaders whose task was to repel and defeat enemy nations and bring peace and stability to the land—a task that, for the most part, met with only limited success.

The major theological theme of the book of Judges is Israel's covenant disobedience and its repercussions.[10] A subtheme, ironically, is the preparation of a God-given monarchy as a counterfoil to the failure of human government that had no room for God and, at the same time, held a distorted understanding of how he purposed from the beginning to rule through mankind. It is fair to say that the book is an account of how not to live out the creation mandate as it was placed in the custody of God's chosen nation Israel.

---

[10] Daniel I. Block, *Judges, Ruth,* NAC 6 (Nashville: Broadman & Holman, 1999), 58.

Before the conquest was even complete, rebellion had set in. The angel of the Lord chided the people for having broken the Lord's covenant already, though he had kept faith with them (Judg. 2:1–3). The new generation forsook the Lord and went after the gods of the land, to which the Lord responded by allowing surrounding nations to visit judgment upon them. They would repent, and God then raised up judges to deliver them, whereupon they would rebel once more against him, thus repeating the cycle over and over (Judg. 2:10–19). Because of this ceaseless covenant violation, the Lord no longer expelled the wicked Canaanite peoples but allowed them to remain in the land to test the sincerity of Israel's covenant commitment (vv. 20–23).

There is no need here to recount the monotonous and unbroken chain of events that necessitated the call of judge after judge to bring deliverance. Without exception, the historian, introducing each major judge, says, "The Israelites did evil in the eyes of the LORD" or words to that effect (Judg. 3:7, 12; 4:1; 6:1; 10:6; 13:1). By this he means they broke the covenant—in particular the first two commandments—and went after the gods of their pagan neighbors. The judgeship of Gideon in the latter thirteenth century is particularly instructive because it is rather full and provides a window into both the level of unbelief and the idolatry into which Israel had sunk and, at the same time, their sense of a need for revolutionary change on their part if they were to survive as a nation (Judg. 6–9).

Yearnings for a King

Having done evil once more in the eyes of the Lord, the Israelites found themselves under the repressive regime of the Midianites for seven years. As usual, they cried out to the Lord so he sent a prophet to them to put his finger on the problem. The Lord had delivered them from Egypt, he said, and had given them the land. And then he had presented them with a covenant that revealed who he is and what he expected of them: "I am the LORD your God. Do not fear the gods of the Amorites whose land you live in" (Judg. 6:10). As always, the evil they did was to violate the first two commandments, the foundation of the covenant upon which their relationship to the Lord was based.

God then called Gideon to save Israel and by a series of signs persuaded him that he was with him and would bring deliverance through him.

Gideon immediately understood the fundamental theological issue: Who really is God, and how is he to be served? He demonstrated the answer by building an altar to the Lord and destroying those that had been dedicated to the worship of Baal and his consort Asherah (Judg. 6:24, 28). When the angry mobs demanded Gideon's death for this sacrilege, his father Joash, to his credit, zeroed in on the real issue and with impeccable logic asked, "Would you plead Baal's case for him?" (v. 31). He followed this up with the obvious deduction that "if he is a god, let him plead his own case, because someone tore down his altar." By Gideon's act and his father's interpretation of it, Israel was confronted by the need to make a choice as to who God is and what they were to do to those that made claims to deity but in fact were figments of depraved imagination. This is precisely the challenge that Joshua had set before his generation (Josh. 24:15) and that Elijah would repeat more than three hundred years later (1 Kings 18:21).

Gideon's success in defeating the Midianites and driving them from the land led the people to ask him to become their king and establish a dynasty to succeed him (Judg. 8:22–23). He soundly rejected these flattering overtures, affirming to the nation, "I will not rule over you, and my son will not rule over you; the LORD will rule over you" (v. 23). Besides the practical problems of having to contend with a people bent on self-destruction, Gideon seems here to have understood with full clarity the theological implications of the people's request. The Lord himself was king (as Samuel later argued so powerfully); and though he had promised the patriarchs that they would sire a line of kings (Gen. 17:6, 16), the time had not yet come. The problem of the age was not that there was no king but that the true King was ignored in favor of national self-interest. Abimelech's abortive attempt to rule underscores the truth that premature appropriation of the promises of God leads to swift and certain disaster (Judg. 9).

Anticipation of Monarchy

The book of Judges ends with two narratives which, when joined with the book of Ruth, present contrasting insights into life in a community where "everyone did whatever he wanted." Interestingly, all three stories share a Bethlehem connection, suggesting that they had a theological role to play in anticipation of the Davidic monarchy. The first narrative (Judg. 17–18) features a certain Levite from Bethlehem who, in pursuit of a place of ministry, came across an Ephraimite named Micah who needed a priest to officiate at a cult center he had constructed, complete with a silver image and idol (Judg. 17:1–4). Allured by the prestige and emoluments this position would ensure, the Levite accepted the offer and commenced his ministry (vv. 10–13). Meanwhile, the tribe of Dan, unable to settle in its allotted territory, sent a delegation north to find suitable accommodations. En route they encountered the Levite and persuaded him by a better offer to leave Micah and become priest of the tribe. All the Danites then arrived at Laish (later named Dan), slew its inhabitants, and settled there along with their idols and other pagan paraphernalia. In a remarkable literary irony the narrative reveals the identity of the Levite who became the first priest there: He was none other than Jonathan son of Gershom, the son of Moses (Judg. 18:30)![11] He and his descendants served there until the Assyrian captivity hundreds of years later, creating a rival shrine to the central sanctuary that by then had been located in Shiloh (v. 31).

Theological commentary is hardly necessary here, for the story carries on its surface inescapable truths about the slide of Israel into an apostasy from which they would never fully recover. Dan, along with Bethel, eventually served as an official place of calf worship under King Jeroboam I (1 Kings 12:26–33), a sin against which the prophets of the time loudly railed (1 Kings 13:1–3; cf. Amos 8:14). That a tribe of Israel should lapse so quickly into idolatry is astounding enough, but that the shrine there should be headed by a grandson of great Moses himself indicates how narrow indeed was the gap between wholehearted devotion to the Lord and the denial of his uniqueness and incomparability.

The second narrative (Judg. 19–21) also tells of a Levite but one, ironically, from Ephraim who had married a young woman from Bethlehem. Because of infidelity on her part she had returned to her hometown whence, after some time, the Levite retrieved her and set out for the long journey home. Because of a late start, they could get no farther than Gibeah of Benjamin by nightfall, and so they spent the night

---

[11] For the textual and conceptual difficulties of this identification, see Block, *Judges, Ruth,* 511–12.

there. Despite the sanctity of hospitality, wretched thugs from the town demanded that the young woman be released to them whereupon they sexually abused her all night and left her at the threshold for dead the next morning. The Levite, horrified and determined to get vengeance, carved up her body and sent parts to all the tribes so that they could see with their own eyes the unspeakable evil of the Benjaminite mob. The tribal elders convened and demanded that the culprits be punished, but the leaders of Benjamin failed to comply, and thus Benjamin was set upon by the other tribes in a bloody civil war that resulted in the virtual decimation of the tribe. Realizing they had eliminated a tribe from their number (except for six hundred men), Israel set about to find wives for the survivors, some coming from Shiloh, the location of the tabernacle, and the remainder from Jabesh Gilead, a town that had failed to rally to the cause against Benjamin. Thus the tribe was saved from extinction and the promises of the Lord concerning a twelve-tribe people continued to remain in force.

If the central teaching of the first narrative revolves around religious corruption and spiritual apostasy, the second deals with the breakdown of all standards and norms of moral behavior. In this case the Levite, the religious figure, seemed beyond reproach for the most part; but the population at large, especially in Benjamin, was hopelessly hardened to any ethical sensibility, exhibiting to the full the refrain that "everyone did whatever he wanted." Both narratives have little or nothing to say by way of either divine or human assessment of the horrendous deeds they relate, nor do they need to. The stories are laden with theological overtones and implicit self-interpretations that leave little doubt as to the conditions prevailing in the days of the judges and the urgent need to redress them.

The little novella of Ruth begins not with the overt observation that there was no king in Israel but with the much more subdued but equally evocative note that "during the time of the judges, there was a famine in the land" (Ruth 1:1). It ends, however, with a genealogy which, though never uttering the word *king,* concludes with the line "and Obed fathered Jesse, who fathered David" (Ruth 4:21). The lament in Judges that there was no king in Israel and that "everyone did whatever he wanted" seemed at long last to be on the cusp of resolution; there would be a king after all, so there was hope. The reference to a famine, though obviously to be understood in its literal sense, is suitable also to recall the times and situations just described in the book of Judges, three hundred years or more of a dearth of interest in spiritual things and of any general adherence to the covenant requirements mandated for God's people. Ruth, like a refreshing shower, provides relief from the famine, at least for awhile, and illustrates in its principal characters how life ought to be lived as citizens of the kingdom of God.

The story is so familiar as not to require repeating, but its contribution to theology ought not to be ignored.[12] As its genealogical conclusion suggests, the purpose of the book was to link David to the Abrahamic covenant via the Moabite Ruth who, as it turns out, would become David's great-grandmother. This last point is important because it shows, as does the narrative about Rahab the Canaanite (Josh. 6:24–25), that persons outside the blood descendants of Abraham could also enter into the redemptive and dominion purposes of God as they submitted to his lordship (cf. Matt. 1:5–6). As for the connection between Abraham (or Perez here, son of Judah) and David, it is the covenants they respectively represented that are most theologically significant.[13] We shall address this matter at great length in the next section of our study.

Ruth's entry into the covenant nation with all its privileges was prefigured by her status as an alien widow who, in time of desperate need, was rescued from her hopelessness by a redeemer *(gō'ēl)* who paid off the mortgage on her mother-in-law's estate, and, at the same time, took the young woman as his wife. While it is exegetically and even theologically inappropriate to read a New Testament Christological redemption into the text, there is no mistaking the fact that Ruth serves as a model of God's redemptive grace, her ethnicity notwithstanding. It was God's purpose from the beginning to produce a seed from Abraham that would not only model the nature and the ethos of his kingdom (as did Boaz, the *gō'ēl)* but that would attract the nations of the earth to seek and find him and thus become subject to him (as did Ruth).

---

[12] Eugene H. Merrill, "The Book of Ruth: Narration and Shared Themes," *BSac* 142 (1985): 130–41.

[13] Frederic W. Bush, *Ruth, Esther,* WBC 9 (Dallas: Word, 1996), 267–68.

The Books of First and Second Samuel

Only one book (or scroll) in the ancient Jewish tradition, Samuel traces the history of Israel from the birth of Samuel the prophet to the end of David's life and the accession of Solomon to the throne of the united monarchy. There is general agreement that it consists of five major sections—the Samuel narrative (1 Sam. 1–3), the ark narrative (chs. 4–6), the reign of Saul (chs. 7–15), the rise of David (1 Sam. 16-2 Sam. 5), and the succession narrative (2 Sam. 9–20). In addition are the accounts of David's retrieval of the ark (2 Sam. 6), the Davidic covenant (2 Sam. 7), and the list of David's military conquests and heroes (2 Sam. 8). All of these individually and collectively contribute to the unfolding of sacred history with its theological interpretation of events that should be ultimately understood in this light.[14]

The major point of contention in the book is the apparent ambivalence toward the institution of human kingship and whether such kingship was appropriate for the theocratic community of Israel that had been chosen and called by the Lord to acknowledge him as King and to serve him within the framework of covenant. Could the Lord as King coexist with David and his dynastic successors?

The Prophet Samuel: Preparation for Monarchy

The role of Samuel the prophet took multiple forms. He was the founder of institutional prophetism, an office or (better) ministry whose task was to speak on God's behalf against the deviations and excesses of Israel's kings as well as to offer messages of judgment and hope to the nation as a whole, especially in the writings of the canonical prophets. Samuel also marked the transition from rule by the judges, he himself being a judge (1 Sam. 7:15–17), to that by kings. In fact, he anointed both Saul (1 Sam. 10:1) and David (1 Sam. 16:13) to that exalted position. Finally, he provided both political and spiritual leadership over Israel in the interim and was recognized by the people as having at least a quasi-royal function (1 Sam. 8:7).

---

[14] For the canonical placement of Samuel, see William J. Dumbrell, "The Content and Significance of the Books of Samuel: Their Place and Purpose within the Former Prophets," *JETS* 33 (1990): 49–62.

The political and spiritual condition of Israel at the time of Samuel's birth was exceedingly grave. The Philistines were still menacing the existence of the nation despite Samson's heroics, and the priesthood had become so corrupt that the Shiloh tabernacle had become nothing more than a brothel (1 Sam. 2:12–17, 22–25). Such times required strong leadership, both political and religious, for the continuation of Israel as the covenant people of the Lord was at stake. Not everyone was consumed by the corruption of the day, however, and here and there were rays of hope that God would do something to stem the tide and restore the nation to its God-given role as the light of the world. Hannah, Samuel's mother, provided a voice for such hope in her magnificent prayer of thanks for the birth of her son. She exulted that "the foundations of the earth are the LORD's; He has set the world on them. He guards the steps of His faithful ones, but the wicked are silenced in darkness" (1 Sam. 2:8–9). She then continued, uttering one of the most movingly messianic promises in the Bible: "He (the LORD) will thunder in the heavens against [His enemies]. The LORD will judge the ends of the earth. He will give power to His king; He will lift up the horn of His anointed" (v. 10).

Hannah clearly anticipated the rise of a mighty king who would be "His," that is, the Lord's, one who would rule on his behalf. There are, of course, eschatological dimensions to this text as Christian interpretation has long maintained in viewing this as a prophecy of the coming and the reign of Jesus Christ (cf. Luke 1:46–55).[15] But there can be little doubt that she also speaks of a ruler to come in the near future, one who will bring stability to a land that had fallen into a deep slough of apostasy and moral corruption. After all, she, a woman whose devotion to Torah is plainly insinuated (1 Sam. 1:3–11), was well aware of the ancient promises about kings to come (Gen. 17:6, 16) and of the regulations by which they were to be governed (Deut. 17:14–20).

As young Samuel grew up and matured as an apprentice priest under Eli, he gradually came to understand that his life and ministry were not to be confined to the tabernacle and its responsibilities. Rather, he sensed the call of God to lead his people as a theocratic administrator and, more important, as the first in a line of prophets (1 Sam. 3:19–21). Exercising

---

[15] C. F. Keil and F. Delitzsch, *The Books of Samuel* (Grand Rapids: Eerdmans, repr. 1950), 34.

both roles, Samuel successfully challenged the people to forsake their idolatry and to serve the Lord only so that he would bless them with victory over the Philistines (1 Sam. 7:3–4). He then interceded for them with the Lord, offering up both sacrifices and prayers on their behalf (v. 9). Then, in a display of his might as heavenly warrior, the Lord gave victory and enabled Israel to recover territory long lost to the Philistines (v. 14). In this manner Samuel lived out his days as a prophet with a message of exhortation, a priest making intercession for his people as they lapsed over and over again into unbelief and rebellion, and as a judge leading them to triumph in times of national emergency.

Samuel's greatest challenge was over the issue of kingship, an issue that at the same time marked a major turning point in Israel's history and its theological import.[16] That the need for some kind of strong central leadership existed cannot be denied, for the record is replete with instances of both internal and external crisis. The people had abandoned any pretense of covenant fidelity (cf. 1 Sam. 2:12–17, 22–25, 29; 7:1–4; 8:1–3) and hostile powers, in particular the Philistines, constantly harassed and hounded them, going so far as to capture the ark of the covenant itself (1 Sam. 4–6). There is little wonder that Israel's elders at last came to Samuel and demanded that he appoint a king to lead them, "the same as all the other nations have" (1 Sam. 8:5). And the request was all the more urgent in light of Samuel's advanced age and the worthlessness of his sons to take his place as leaders.

Samuel, a devoted theocratist, could not abide such an idea but not for reasons commonly adduced. He (like his mother) surely recalled the Lord's promises about coming kings, so he was not resisting the demand of the people in principle. What was troublesome to him was that the people wanted a king "such as all the other nations have" (1 Sam. 8:5 NIV), that is, a ruler who was autocratic but who could at least provide them with cohesion and security. In any case, it was a rejection of the Lord as King as the Lord himself assured Samuel (v. 7). Moreover, the demand for a king was premature as well. Simply put, the time had not come for the promised line of kings to appear. To this point the Lord had

[16] D. J. McCarthy, "The Inauguration of Monarchy in Israel: A Form-Critical Study of 1 Sam 8–12," *Interpretation* 27 (1973): 401–22; A. D. H. Mayes, "The Rise of the Israelite Monarchy," *ZAW* 90 (1978): 1–19.

not signaled his intentions to move forward on the matter by designating a ruler, but later on he made clear to Samuel that "a man according to His own heart" was in the wings, one of Jesse's sons, as it turned out (1 Sam. 13:14; 16:1).

The persistence of the people in their demand for a king moved the Lord to relent and to grant them their wish. But they must know the serious consequences of their rash appeal, so the Lord outlined in detail the onerous nature of the regime that would come (1 Sam. 8:10–18). The king would rule with an iron hand; and though they may find some solace in a strong central authority, the people would pay the price with loss of personal freedom and appropriation of their assets. The historian makes the point that this foolish demand to be like the other nations was a form of covenant disobedience. In the words of the Lord, "They are doing the same thing to you [i.e., Samuel] that they have done to Me, since the day I brought them out of Egypt until this day, abandoning Me and worshiping other gods" (v. 8). In other words, Israel's insistence on having a human king was a violation of the first two commandments, for it was a rejection of the Lord and a replacement of him by a pagan system of governance that was tantamount to idolatry.

Saul: Failed Monarchy

The inadequacy of Saul is so well-known as to require no comment. What seemed superficially to be an auspicious beginning of his reign soon degenerated into his uncontrollable rage and eventual madness. Samuel continued his warnings about the outcome until the end, urging the people to "fear the Lord and worship Him faithfully with all your heart"—that is, to keep the Shema—and declaring, on the other hand, that if they failed to do all this, "both you and your king will be swept away" (1 Sam. 12:24–25). Two failings on Saul's part were singled out by the historian as especially egregious and contributory to his final rejection by the Lord. One was his hasty offering of a sacrifice at Gilgal despite Samuel's instruction for him to await the prophet's arrival to lead the service. For this arrogance Samuel pronounced the end of Saul's dynasty and informed him that the Lord "has found a man loyal to Him [lit. "according to His own heart"], and the Lord has appointed him as ruler over His people" (1 Sam. 13:14). The Hebrew phrase *(kilbābô)* is best understood not as an approbation of David's heart, that is, his godliness and other qualifications, but rather as a technical term referring to divine election.[17] The choice of David to reign was not ad hoc but had existed in the mind of God for countless ages in the past (cf. Gen. 49:10).

Saul's second misdeed was his refusal to carry out fully the *ḥērem* commanded by the Lord against the Amalekites (1 Sam. 15:1–35). Samuel's response reflects a most important insight into the nature of true Old Testament religion, and that is in the question he posed to Saul and answered for him: "Does the LORD take pleasure in burnt offerings and sacrifices as much as in obeying the LORD? Look: to obey is better than sacrifice, to pay attention is better than the fat of rams" (1 Sam. 15:22). Later prophets, especially Micah, picked up the same theme, going so far as to say that rather than being pleased with countless sacrifices—even of one's child—the Lord required of those who worship him "to act justly, to love faithfulness, and to walk humbly with your God" (Micah 6:8). Saul's disobedience and pro forma religious ritualism cost him not only his kingdom but any more fellowship with the Lord by means of the prophet Samuel (vv. 34–35).

The almost summary disqualification of Saul for what might seem to some to be petty offenses (but remember Moses) underscores not the Lord's untoward vindictiveness but the sanctity of the office Saul held as king of Israel, even if not as the "man according to God's own heart." The king of the covenant nation held a sacred trust as the vice-regent through whom the Lord would reign and, indirectly, through whom he would bless the nations of the earth. Such a king might sin—and indeed invariably did—but he could be forgiven if he repented; and, in any event, the institution itself would continue once founded on the Davidic covenant.

David: The Realization of True Monarchy

We turn now to the earliest stirrings of covenant election that resulted eventually in the installation of David as the first to sit on the throne representative of the sovereignty of the Lord. Saul's rejection paved the way for David's advancement. Samuel, the prophet resistant to the kingship of Saul, responded with alacrity to the command of the Lord to anoint David, the youngest son of Jesse of Bethlehem, and to declare

---

[17] P. Kyle McCarter Jr., *I Samuel,* AB 8 (Garden City, N.Y.: Doubleday, 1980), 229.

publicly that he was the Lord's choice to be the leader of his people (1 Sam. 16:1–12).[18] We should note carefully that the choice ran contrary to normal convention and expectation and for that reason attested to the selection as being divine and not human. David (unlike Saul) was a callow youth, a mere shepherd boy with no experience in leadership and with no physical attributes to commend him (cf. the servant of Isa. 52:13–53:12). If he were to succeed as king, it would be only by God's grace and enablement. That enablement soon followed: Samuel anointed David with oil, and at that moment God's Spirit departed from Saul and came upon David from that time forward. The Spirit was not only a sign of David's election to kingship; it was also an infusion of power and wisdom requisite to the discharge of his high and holy office (v. 13).

Saul, of course, resisted this turn of events and, after an initial and brief period of a modicum of good will toward David, turned against him and sought to do him in. At the same time, he could not escape the realization that his efforts were futile, for David, even Saul must admit, was God's chosen vessel (cf. 1 Sam. 18:12, 28–29; 23:17; 24:20; 26:25). On the other hand, Jonathan, Saul's son and heir apparent to the throne, embraced the news of David's divine appointment and even went so far as to assist David in achieving it. Early in their acquaintanceship "Jonathan committed himself to David, and loved him as much as he loved himself" (1 Sam. 18:1). This went beyond mere friendship for Jonathan, recognizing that God had called David to be king of Israel, surrendered any claims he might have to succeed his father and clothed David with his own royal regalia (vv. 3–4). His later blessing of David—"May the Lord be with you, just as He was with my father" (1 Sam. 20:13)—puts beyond doubt Jonathan's conviction that David would be king and, as well, adds his personal affirmation.

Samuel's anointing of David as king resulted only in a status de jure. As long as Saul remained, David could not assert his rights de facto. His remarkable restraint in preserving Saul's life when he could easily have taken it demonstrated his sensitivity to the sovereign will of God who, David knew, would bring things to pass in his own time (cf. 1 Sam. 24, 26). At last the moment arrived. Saul and three of his sons were slain

---

[18] David M. Howard Jr., "The Transfer of Power from Saul to David in 1 Sam 16:13–14," *JETS* 32 (1989): 473–83

in battle; and the fourth, Ish-Bosheth, went into Transjordanian exile. Meanwhile, David inquired of the Lord whether it was now appropriate to move forward with his claims to kingship, to which the Lord gave an affirmative response, commanding him to go to Hebron where he would be acknowledged formally as king over his own native tribe Judah (2 Sam. 2:1–4). This cemented the connection with dying Jacob's prophetic blessing of Judah that a monarch would arise from that tribe (Gen. 49:10).

Before long and through a series of deft military and political maneuvers on the part of David and his followers, all pretenders to the throne of Saul evaporated, and David alone was left to fill the void. Now even the leaders of the northern tribes were forced to concede the kingship to David, recalling (perhaps grudgingly) that the Lord had said to him, "You will shepherd My people Israel and be ruler over Israel" (2 Sam. 5:2; cf. 1 Chron. 11:2). Representatives of all Israel then assembled at Hebron where David made a covenant with them followed by a formal ceremony of coronation (v. 3). The covenant most likely was a contract between the king and the people committing both parties to mutual obligations and expectations.[19]

David's assertion of strong leadership followed in rapid-fire sequence. He first conquered Jerusalem, a city that to that point in time had belonged to the Jebusites and was therefore on neutral ground between Judah and the tribes to the north. Prior to his taking the city, it had enjoyed no hoary antiquity as far as Israel's history and traditions were concerned. This seemed most appropriate; for with David and the Davidic covenant God was about to do something new, something linked to the past only by the enigmatic reference to Salem (i.e., Jerusalem), the site of the kingship of Melchizedek (Gen. 14:18; cf. Ps. 76:1–2). And yet this connection, as tenuous as it was, might provide an intertextual witness to the Abrahamic and Davidic covenants, a point to be elaborated presently.

Having established Jerusalem as his seat of political power, David now took the unprecedented step of making it also the location of the central sanctuary, the place where the Lord would "put His name for His dwelling" (Deut. 12:5). This consolidation of church and state signaled a

---

[19] Martin J. Selman, *I Chronicles,* TOTC 10A (Downers Grove, Ill.: InterVarsity, 1994), 138.

move whereby government and the cultus alike would operate under the general aegis of the king, if not with his direct participation in the latter. The theological implications of this, which are enormous, will occupy our attention at great length. First, however, we must give consideration to the next stage of David's rule, the granting to him of a special relationship with the Lord commonly called the Davidic covenant.

The Davidic Covenant[20]

After David secured Jerusalem as Israel's capital and completed the construction of buildings—including his own royal palace—suitable for such an important place, he sheepishly came to the prophet Nathan one day and expressed his chagrin that while he lived in a palace of cedar, the Lord lived in a flimsy tent (2 Sam. 7:1–2). This tent was one he had erected himself to house the ark of the covenant since the Mosaic tabernacle seems by then to have been located at Gibeon, just north of Jerusalem (1 Kings 3:4; 2 Chron. 1:3–6). The ark had been separated from its dwelling place for a century or more, having first been stolen by the Philistines (1 Sam. 4:11) who retained it for a short time before sending it on its way back to Israel (1 Sam. 5:1-6:12). It stopped briefly at Beth Shemesh (6:13–21) and then ended up at Kiriath Jearim, fifteen miles west of Jerusalem. Twenty years later it was still there, a reminder to the Israelites in Samuel's time that they were as distant from the Lord as the ark was from the tabernacle (1 Sam. 7:2–4).

Many decades later David, having provided temporary shelter for the ark in his newly established capital, brought the ark into the city with great festivity and fanfare.[21] His joy at that achievement was soon tempered by his comparison of the tent structure with his own glorious palace, thus explaining his desire to erect a temple commensurate with the majesty and glory of God who, in the symbol of the ark, now lived among his people once again. Nathan at first gave his permission to David to build (2 Sam. 7:3), but the Lord interrupted the process with the astounding words that he was satisfied for the moment to dwell in such

[20] See, e.g., Lyle Eslinger, *House of God or House of David: The Rhetoric of 2 Samuel 7*, JSOT Supp. Series 164 (Sheffield: JSOT, 1995); Heinz Kruse, "David's Covenant," *VT* 35 (1985): 139–64.

[21] For the chronology of David's reign, see Eugene H. Merrill, "The 'Accession Year' and Davidic Chronology," *JANES* 19 (1989): 101–12.

humble surroundings and, in fact, would do so until the land was at rest from its enemies. Then he would authorize David's son to build a temple for his name, the central sanctuary of which Moses had spoken centuries before (Deut. 12:5).

The technical term *covenant* (Heb. *bĕrît*) does not occur in 2 Samuel 7, though all scholars agree that the Davidic covenant is its central focus. David himself elsewhere referred to the promises made here as a covenant (2 Sam. 23:5; cf. Ps. 89:3–4, 28, 34). But what kind of covenant was it? How did it relate to those that had preceded it, especially the Abrahamic and the Mosaic? We turn now to these questions and others in order to grasp the profound theological import of David's kingship as an ingredient of the comprehensive creation and kingdom purposes of the Lord.

Studies of ancient Near Eastern treaty and covenant texts have revealed two basic models—the royal grant and the parity, the latter itself further subdivided into bilateral (between equals) and unilateral or suzerain-vassal types (imposed by a superior power upon an inferior). Old Testament scholars have compared these to biblical examples and discovered striking similarities (as well as differences) between the two. There now exists a great deal of agreement across critical and theological boundaries that the Mosaic covenant, no matter its provenance, exhibits the structure of the suzerain-vassal model whereas the Abrahamic and Davidic are examples of the royal grant. This suggests, among other things, that the Mosaic must be viewed in a different light from the other two, not just by form but by function as well. We have already addressed this fact preliminarily and will return to it later.[22] Also, the common nature of the Abrahamic and Davidic covenant structures opens up the possibility that they share conceptual as well as formal features, a matter we shall also shortly explore.

The fundamental premise of the royal grant was its disposition by a superior party to an underling on no other grounds than the good will of the benefactor.[23] The recipient had not initiated the grant, he had no right to expect it, and he had no way of guaranteeing its permanence.

---

[22] See pp. 325–28.

[23] Moshe Weinfeld, "The Covenant of Grant in the Old Testament and in the Ancient Near East," *JAOS* 90/2 (1990): 184–203.

Sometimes in the secular world the grant could be a reward for service and therefore might be conditioned on some kind of response from the grantee. But even these caveats did not bring the grant to pass, nor did they obligate the beneficiary to any kind of reciprocation to ensure its ongoing efficacy. It was fundamentally a matter of grace in both its bestowal and its perpetuation.

We have given some attention to these concepts in our consideration of the Abrahamic covenant and now turn to the Davidic covenant to see if and how they apply to it as well.[24] The first evidence that the Davidic covenant was an unconditional royal grant is that kingship in general and kingship through Judah in particular were integral to the Abrahamic covenant which itself was a royal grant (cf. Gen. 17:6, 16; and 49:8–12 respectively). While not naming David specifically, the narrowing of the scope of Israelite kingship certainly opened the door in that direction. The canonical tradition is much more explicit, for even though Ruth was clearly composed in the era of David, its setting in the time of the days of the judges reveals a desire on the part of Israel's theologians to anticipate David's later importance and his linkage to the patriarchs (Ruth 4:18–21). Then, as we have just seen, Samuel the prophet introduced David, yet unnamed, as "a man according to [the LORD's] own heart," that is, a man whom he has chosen (1 Sam. 13:14; cf. 15:28). Finally, after Jesse had paraded all his sons before Samuel to see which of them would best qualify to be the Lord's anointed, none was suitable until David, unaware of all that was happening at home and certainly in no position to influence the decision, was summoned and selected to be the promised king (1 Sam. 16:2–12).

All these texts point to just one conclusion: the election of David to kingship was a matter entirely outside his own merits or machinations. Centuries before he was born, he was ordained to the office to which in God's time he was eventually anointed. The same is true of the covenant that certified his election and spelled out for him the benefits he could expect and the responsibilities incumbent on him. David had no sooner offered to build a house for the Lord than the Lord declined the offer,

---

[24] E. Theodore Mullen Jr., "The Divine Witness and the Davidic Royal Grant: Ps 89:37–38," *JBL* 102/2 (1983): 207–18; for a criticism of this view, see Gary N. Knoppers, "Ancient Near Eastern Royal Grants and the Davidic Covenant: A Parallel?" *JAOS* 116 (1996): 670–97.

extending to David instead the promise that he would build him a house. To underscore his sovereign and unconditional grace to David, the Lord reminded him of his calling to begin with: "I took you from the pasture and from following the flock to be ruler over My people Israel" (2 Sam. 7:8). There is no hint here of David's having met conditions either to be chosen as king or to receive the covenant about to be spelled out.

The blessings to follow the covenant relationship were many: (1) The Lord would make David's name (i.e., reputation) great. (2) He would provide Israel a safe and secure dwelling place. (3) He would establish a house (i.e., dynasty) for David. (4) David's house and kingdom would be everlasting (2 Sam. 7:9–16). There was only one note of warning—"When he [David's son] does wrong, I will discipline him with a human rod" (v. 14)—but that was quickly followed by the strongest of assurances: "But My faithful love [*ḥesed,* covenant loyalty] will never leave him as I removed it from Saul; I removed him from your way" (v. 15). There would be discipline, indeed, for covenant violation, but the covenant itself would never be annulled no matter the behavior of its royal recipients.

David's response to this unexpected and (to him) undeserved bestowal of grace added its own note to the fact that the covenant bearing his name was unconditional and unending. In utter amazement he asked what there was about himself and his family that made him worthy of such a boon (v. 18). He could only conclude that it was "because of Your word and according to Your will [lit., "heart," as in 1 Sam. 13:14], You have revealed all these great things to Your servant" (2 Sam. 7:21). David confessed that he had brought nothing to the table; all the initiative and all the outworking of the covenant promises were in God's hands and his alone. While he marveled at his own great blessing, David recalled that the selection of his nation Israel was exactly the same. "God came to one nation on earth," he said, "in order to redeem a people for Himself, to make a name for Himself" (v. 23). And he went on to exclaim, "You established Your people Israel [as] Your people forever, and You, LORD, have become their God" (v. 24). He then concluded with words of praise and petition, beseeching the Lord to be true to his word and to bless him and his house forever (vv. 27–29).

The question remains, how does the Davidic covenant relate to the two great covenants that preceded it, namely, the Abrahamic and the

Mosaic? On this question hangs a considerable theological burden. First, we have already drawn attention to the formal or generic connections between the covenant made with Abraham and that with David: Both were unconditional and everlasting, at least in their biblical presentation. The Sinaitic or Mosaic, on the other hand, was conditional in that Israel had the choice whether to subscribe to it and Israel's continuance as a covenant partner and her success in achieving its goals were wholly dependent on her obedience. However, and this is most important, the conditions even in this arrangement were certain to be met because the Lord himself would provide the wherewithal to guarantee it. Thus, even though the Mosaic covenant was conditional by form and even stipulation, its outcome was as certain as if it were a royal grant.

The differences were therefore not so much in form as in function. The Abrahamic covenant was designed to call one man from paganism into worship of the Lord, the one true God, so that he could become the vehicle through whom the Lord would create a nation that would model what his sovereign rule should look like and, at the same time, be the means of blessing the whole earth. The Lord would be the ruler of that nation; but embedded in the covenant was the provision for human kings that would rule on the Lord's behalf, thus fulfilling the creation mandate for mankind to have dominion over all things (Gen. 1:26–28). The Davidic covenant provided that king, guaranteeing an unbroken dynastic line that would (as we shall see) find its climax and perfection in a messianic ruler who will sit on the throne of the kingdom of heaven forever. The Mosaic covenant, between the other two historically and canonically, added nothing to them in substance. Its purpose was not to create a people or nation or king, for that was already provided in Israel's prehistory. Rather, it was crafted to set before Israel an opportunity for service, to be the servant nation promised to Abraham, not in essence only but in actual performance. As Exodus 19:5–6 so succinctly but clearly puts it, "Now if you will listen to Me and carefully keep My covenant, you will be My own possession out of all the peoples, although all the earth is mine, and you will be My kingdom of priests and My holy nation." Israel, already the people of the Lord, now had the opportunity to serve him in bringing to the whole world the message of redeeming grace.

We have argued that the Abrahamic and Davidic covenants were two of a kind, but it is a mistake to view them as being on the same plane as if in a kind of continuum. Instead, it is preferable to see the Davidic as an adjunct to the Mosaic just as the Mosaic was an adjunct to the Abrahamic.[25] To put it in other terms, the Mosaic covenant provided for the nation Israel to assume servant responsibilities as the seed of Abraham, and the Davidic covenant supplied to the servant nation a royal governance that would facilitate that function as well as dramatize the ideal rule intended by the Lord from the day of creation. The genealogy of David in Ruth 4:18–21 makes the Abraham-David connection, bypassing any reference to Israel. The Chronicler's genealogy, on the other hand, recognizes and centralizes the descendants of Jacob, thus including in the map of God's salvific design the servant nation through whom he would bring it to pass (1 Chron. 1:28, 34; 2:1–17). The two together present a full-orbed picture of the distinctive features of each covenant and, at the same time, their interrelationship.

With human kingship in place, there was a fulfillment of the ancient promises that kings would spring from the line of Abraham. Beyond this, the creation mandate that mankind should "be fruitful, multiply, fill the earth, and subdue it" and "rule the fish of the sea, the birds of the sky, and every creature that crawls on the earth" (Gen. 1:28) finds tangible expression even if only in a highly preliminary and anticipatory manner. David and his dynastic successors never exhibited this kind of universal dominion, of course, but the limited success they did enjoy, especially under Solomon (cf. 1 Kings 4:20–34), was a foretaste of the splendor, glory, and power of his descendants yet to come at the end of human history. What the Davidic kings could demonstrate only partially and imperfectly, their eschatological successors would accomplish fully. To be more precise, One would come to occupy David's throne forever, and it is he that will have dominion over all things.

The eschatological king is hinted at already in the context of the Davidic covenant. He is the one called the offspring of David, the one of whom the Lord says, "He will build a house for My name, and I will establish the throne of his kingdom forever" (2 Sam. 7:13). The immediate reference

---

[25] W. J. Dumbrell, *Covenant and Creation* (Nashville: Thomas Nelson, 1984), 89–90, 150–51.

is, of course, to Solomon ("who will come from your own body," v. 12), but the everlastingness of the rule of this scion of David points to One beyond Solomon. This is the messianic king of whom the prophets later spoke with great clarity and conviction. David was only his prototype, but despite his limitations—indeed, his grievous sins—David appears in the accounts of the historian as a king who manifested the traits of the King who is yet to come. He enjoyed success over the enemies of Israel, for "the LORD made David victorious wherever he went" (2 Sam. 8:14). His reign was unchallenged in Israel, at least in the beginning, and he administered "justice and righteousness for all his people" (v. 15). His sins of murder and adultery, with all their awful consequences for his family and the nation, cannot be ignored or excused and were anything but messianic. But he repented and was forgiven and able to resume his responsibilities as the Lord's vice-regent despite fratricide and rebellion among his own children. At the end of his days, he was able to extol the Lord for his grace and faithfulness; and he remained confident that what God had begun in him would never fail of success and fulfillment: "Is it not true my house is with God? For He has established an everlasting covenant with me, ordered and secured in every detail. Will He not bring about my whole salvation and my every desire?" (2 Sam. 23:5).

The Books of Kings

The Deuteronomistic history continues with the books of Kings which, like Samuel, formed a single book in the Jewish tradition. They consist of the account of Solomon's reign (1 Kings 1–11); the history of the Divided monarchy, focused mainly on the Northern Kingdom of Israel (1 Kings 12-2 Kings 17); and the history of the Southern Kingdom of Judah (2 Kings 18–25).[26] As to literary form, the bulk of the literature consists of annalistic records of the reigns of the kings (hence the title), but the biographical accounts of the prophets Elijah and Elisha also occupy considerable attention (1 Kings 17–2 Kings 8). Otherwise, brief prophetic oracles and other messages, frequently delivered by anonymous spokesmen, are interspersed throughout. The purpose of Kings was to

[26] J. G. McConville, "Narrative and Meaning in the Books of Kings," *Biblica* 70 (1989): 31–49.

describe the increasingly downward spiral of the twin kingdoms that resulted at last in their exile to Assyria first and then to Babylonia. What began so well under Solomon ended tragically with the destruction of the city and temple he had built and the dispersion of the nation that God had chosen to be a lighthouse to the other nations of the world. Only at the end, in a kind of postlude, is there any glimmer of hope that the people of the Lord could be revived to resume their God-given task.

The Succession of Solomon

David had prepared for his succession by Solomon (a matter made much clearer in Chronicles), but the transition was hardly smooth. At the moment of Solomon's birth, his parents had named him *šĕlōmōh,* that is, *peace,* no doubt because of the promise of rest contained in the Davidic covenant (2 Sam. 7:11). The Lord, however, named him *yĕdîdyāh* (Jedidiah, "loved by the LORD") because, as the text points out, "the LORD loved him" (2 Sam. 12:24). As we have observed before, the verb *love,* in a covenant context such as this, bears the primary denotation of election or choice. Solomon, though the product of a tawdry relationship, was chosen by the Lord to carry on the messianic role of his father.

David and Solomon's mother, Bathsheba, understood all this, as no doubt did the people as a whole. But this did not stop some of Solomon's older brothers, especially Adonijah, from attempting to usurp the throne in David's dying days. The prophet Nathan, having uncovered a plot by which Adonijah would lead a coup d'état to install himself as king before Solomon's official coronation, was mindful of the will of God in the matter and urged Bathsheba to remind David of the promise he had made that Solomon should reign (1 Kings 1:11–14). David ordered that Adonijah's enthronement be preempted and that Solomon be installed post haste, for, as he put it, "He is the one who is to become king in my place; he is the one I have commanded to be ruler over Israel and Judah" (v. 35). The threat to Solomon's succession thus ended and the line continued according to divine direction.

Before David expired, he left one last word of charge to Solomon in which he clearly articulated the covenant nature of his rule and urged his son to faithful compliance to its principles (1 Kings 2:1–4). "Keep your obligation to the LORD your God," he exhorted, and that meant to "walk in His ways and to keep His statutes, commandments, judgments, and testimonies. This is written in the law of Moses, so that you will have success in everything you do and wherever you turn" (v. 3). If he did so, the Lord would keep his promise to David that he "will never fail to have a man on the throne of Israel" (v. 4). The technical terms by which the Law is described hark back to Deuteronomy, especially to the instructions as to how Israel's kings were to conduct themselves in light of the Mosaic covenant (Deut. 17:14–20). Chief among the stipulations was the need for the king to have at hand a copy of the covenant text so that he might read it regularly and heed its every word (vv. 18–19).

The Establishment of the Temple

This is precisely what David adjured his young son to do; and at the outset of his reign, this is precisely what Solomon did. The narrator observes that "Solomon loved the LORD by walking in the statutes of his father" (1 Kings 3:3). There follows, however, a caveat: "But he also sacrificed and burned incense on the high places." This proleptic addition does not refer to what immediately follows in the text but looks forward to Solomon's dalliances with paganism when he did, indeed, resort to illegitimate shrines, mainly out of a concern to please his heathen wives (cf. 1 Kings 11:1–13). The high place here refers to the location of the Mosaic tabernacle at Gibeon, the only authorized central sanctuary available to him since the great bronze altar was there (1 Kings 3:4–5; cf. 2 Chron. 1:2–6). David had, of course, erected a tabernacle in Jerusalem to house the ark (2 Sam. 6:17), but until ark and tabernacle (that of Moses) were joined, the central sanctuary as envisioned in Deuteronomy 12 could not exist.

The dilemma faced by Solomon—and by his father before him—cried out for resolution. There must be a structure in Jerusalem that would replace both the Gibeon and the Zion holy places and that would consolidate the worship of the Lord at one site. The idea was not new to Solomon or even to David because the Davidic covenant had already made provision for a house of the Lord on a grander and more glorious scale than anything known in the past. Referring to David's son, the Lord had said, "He will build a house for My name, and I will establish the throne of his kingdom forever" (2 Sam. 7:13). In one brief promise the Lord had linked temple and throne together, conveying in it the tantalizing concept of royal kingship which, as we shall see, was clearly understood by David as applicable to himself and his dynastic descendants.

On the basis of such precedent, Solomon undertook plans and preparation for the construction of the temple. In its basic form and function it would differ not at all from the more temporary tent shrines that had preceded it. There must be the outer court, the holy place, and the most holy place, the dwelling place of the Lord as symbolized by the ark. But the dimensions were to be larger, the furnishings and decorations more elaborate, and the structure itself built of stone and not of perishable cloth and skins. The message was clear: The Lord desired to live among his people forever and in the beauty, splendor, and glory appropriate to his person and role as the king of creation. Various decorative motifs such as the cherubim, palm trees, and flowers were reminiscent of the paradisiacal setting of the first holy space, the garden in Eden where the Lord had first made his presence known and where he had provided access to those created as his image to enjoy fellowship with him (1 Kings 6:29, 32). The Jerusalem temple was thus, in a sense, to be a reconsitituted Eden, a symbol that looked forward to a paradise restored (cf. Ezek. 47:1–12; Rev. 22:1–5).

When the temple was finished and everything was in order, Solomon ordered the ark to be transported from its temporary location in the tent structure of David at Zion to the temple on Moriah. Along with the removal of the ark, he authorized the dismantling and retrieval of the holy and venerable tent of meeting (i.e., the Mosaic tabernacle) at Gibeon. The most likely explanation for bringing the tabernacle into the temple to be stored there was the need to preclude its continuation as a central sanctuary in competition with the Solomonic temple. From then on there could be only one place where the Lord would place his name and where he would receive the nation's tribute and worship (1 Kings 8:3–9).

The Dedication of the Temple

Then, just as the Lord had expressed his pleasure at the completion of the tabernacle by filling it with the cloud of his glory (Exod. 40:34–35), so he signaled both his satisfaction with the temple and the fact that he had now taken up residence there by filling it too with his glory (1 Kings 8:10). Solomon followed this by a dedicatory prayer rich in theological insight and expression, one worthy of careful analysis (1 Kings 8:23–61).

But his preface to the prayer, a blessing of the people (vv. 15–21), also merits close attention. He began by acknowledging that the completion of the temple was the fulfillment of a promise by the Lord to David that though he was not the one to bring it to pass he was to be commended for having the heartfelt desire to do so (vv. 17–18) and would see it come to fruition, by faith at least, through the efforts of his son Solomon (v. 19). What the people now saw with their own eyes—Solomon's kingship and the house of the Lord—testified to the covenant faithfulness of the Lord (vv. 20–21).

Solomon opened his prayer proper with a panegyric of praise of God in which he celebrated the uniqueness of Israel's Lord as God and as the one who had kept his promise to David by allowing the temple to be completed (1 Kings 8:23–24). He then prayed that the Lord would keep his promise regarding the unending succession of rulers who would sit on David's throne (vv. 25–26). His central concern, however, was the complex theological question of the compatibility between God's transcendence and his immanence. He had just overseen the construction of a temple in which the dwelling presence of the Lord had been manifest. But how could the God who remains outside of his creation and who cannot be contained by it limit himself to a building made by human hands? He could not, of course, answer this question any more than can we, but he need not do so in order to know that God hears from heaven the prayers of his people directed toward his earthly habitation (vv. 27–30). Therefore, when disaster might strike, even in the shape of national exile from the land, Solomon's prayer was that the Lord would hear and would meet the needs of his people.

Embedded in the prayer are such themes as the temple as the locus of legal adjudication (vv. 31–32); the openness of the Lord to the prayers of foreigners outside the covenant boundaries (vv. 41–43); and his availability to grant success in times of war (vv. 44–45). The inclusion of the foreigner is especially arresting in light of the purpose of Israel in the first place—to be a means of blessing all the nations. Solomon is mindful that people "will hear of Your great name, mighty hand, and outstretched arm" (v. 42); and when the Lord answers their prayers, they will come to know his name and will fear him "as Your people Israel do" (v. 43). Solomon understood the depth and breadth of God's grace and knew the heart of God who desires that all peoples of the earth repent, turn to him, and find reconciliation and restoration.

At the conclusion of the prayer, Solomon blessed the assembly once more. He urged them to reflect back on God's faithfulness to the fathers on the basis of which they could have confidence in him (1 Kings 8:56–57). He prayed that the Lord would turn their hearts to him—attesting to the need for God always to take the initiative in repentance—and that he would enable them to keep all the terms of the covenant (v. 58). Then he pleaded for the Lord to put his prayer on reserve so that it might continue to be efficacious in the future and thereby convince the nations that only the Lord of Israel is God (v. 60). Finally, he drove home the point that the hearts of his hearers must "be completely devoted to the LORD our God to walk in His ordinances and to keep His commands, as it is today" (v. 61). In other words, only faithful covenant compliance could ensure the blessings and favor of the Lord, a point integral to the concept of covenant.

Royal Priesthood

Solomon's intercessory prayer is indicative of the priestly role of the king, a role already hinted at in his offering of sacrifices at the Gibeon sanctuary (1 Kings 3:3–4) and clearly asserted in David's triumphal procession into Jerusalem with the ark of the covenant (2 Sam. 6:12–19). These episodes will receive attention shortly as will their expanded and more theologically driven renditions in the books of Chronicles. First, it is imperative to pay at least brief notice to the concept of royal priesthood in the ancient Near East and to whatever precursors might exist in Israel's premonarchic history.

There is no need to labor the point that kings from most ancient times enjoyed priestly prerogatives in the cultures surrounding Israel.[27] The Sumerians earlier than Abraham practiced a cultus in which their rulers held positions of leadership and the kings of Assyria and Babylonia that followed played an active role in various religious ceremonies including the offering of sacrifices. The same was true of the Hittites of Central Anatolia and the rulers of the petty states of the Levant throughout their

[27] Helmer Ringgren, *Religions of the Ancient Near East* (Philadelphia: Westminster, 1973), 36–42, 79, 169–70.

recorded history.[28] As for Egypt, their pharaohs were not only participants in religious affairs; but as deities themselves, they obviously were at the center of religious life and expression.[29] All of this is amply documented and should not be surprising in an environment in which there was no separation of church and state. It seemed logical that the same hand that controlled the affairs of government should also have oversight of one of its most important components, the realm of the religious life.

We have attempted to make the case already that the earliest Old Testament accounts depict the paternal heads of families not only as fathers but also as priests. Thus, Cain and Abel offered sacrifices not only for themselves but no doubt also on behalf of whatever families they may have had (Gen. 4:2–5). Noah likewise made offerings after the flood as the priest of his family (Gen. 8:20–21). The same is true of Abraham (Gen. 12:7, 8; 22:2–14) and the patriarchs who succeeded him (Gen. 26:25; 35:6, 14). It is true, of course, that these persons were not kings in the strict sense of the terms; but in their premonarchic nomadic or seminomadic culture, they functioned in every respect as kings of their own little domains whether tribes, clans, or a single family.

Clearer evidence of royal priesthood outside the Hebrew tradition and yet contemporary with the patriarchs can be seen in the narrative of Melchizedek (Gen. 14:18–20). The larger context of his life and priestly function is shrouded in mystery, but certain facts are on the surface. First, his name itself is to be translated "righteous king" or the like (cf. Heb. 7:2), and then he is called "king of Salem" (i.e. Jerusalem; cf. Ps. 76:2). He next brought out to Abraham bread and wine, elements of a peace or fellowship offering, a gesture here of friendship and hospitality (Num. 15:8–12; 1 Sam. 1:24; 10:3–4). In doing this, he is called "priest of God Most High" (Heb. *ʾēl ʿelyôn*), thus completing the connection of his dual roles of king and priest. Next, he blessed Abraham, a special function of the priest (cf. Num. 6:24–26), and finally he received Abraham's tithe, again testifying to his priestly office. The New Testament capitalized on this narrative in making a case for the royal priesthood of Jesus, who is

[28] O. R. Gurney, *The Hittites* (Baltimore: Penguin Books), 132.

[29] David P. Silverman, "Divinity and Deities in Ancient Egypt," *Religion in Ancient Egypt,* ed. Byron E. Shafer (London: Routledge, 1991), 64–65.

called "a high priest forever in the order of Melchizedek" (Heb. 6:20; cf. 7:17).

But later Old Testament theology also made use of the Genesis pericope to establish the fact that David, too, was such a priest (Ps. 110:4). In fact, the author of Hebrews quoted Psalm 110 in defense of the royal priesthood of Christ. The psalm was either composed by David or pertains to David as the superscription *(lĕdāwid)* suggests.[30] In it the principal focus is on David's (and his eschatological successor's) triumph over all his enemies, resulting in his universal rule. However, he rules not just as king but as "a priest forever, in the order (*dibrâ,* "manner") of Melchizedek" (v. 4 NIV). That is, he incorporates the twin offices of king and priest into one rule, serving legitimately in both capacities. However, he (David and all who follow him on his throne) will be restricted to a Melchizedekian priesthood and must not intrude into that of Aaron, one limited to the tribe of Levi.

If, indeed, Psalm 110 testifies to David's own consciousness of his priesthood—and there is no reason to think otherwise—then is there any historical evidence that he engaged in priestly ministry; or is the hope of such ministry eschatologically defined and limited?[31] A straightforward reading of the narrative texts favors the former option. David's interest in matters of the cultus even preceded his accession to Israel's throne. He had already visited the tabernacle at Nob where Abimelech was priest in charge, and with a temerity otherwise inexplicable had requested the priest to give him and his starving men some bread (1 Sam. 21:1–6). Abimelech protested that all he had on hand was consecrated bread (the 'bread of the Presence'), available only to persons who were ritually pure. David assured him that his party met these qualifications and without further ado helped himself to the sacred loaves.

While this may be inferential of David's priestly prerogatives, his leadership in building the Zion tabernacle, retrieving the ark of the covenant from Obed-Edom, marching with it in triumphal procession, and installing it in his sanctuary is transparently clear. The Samuel narrative (2 Sam. 6:1–20) provides a number of clues as to the priestly

---

[30] Erhard S. Gerstenberger, *Psalms, Part 2, and Lamentations,* FOTL 15 (Grand Rapids: Eerdmans, 2001), 263.

[31] Eugene H. Merrill, "Royal Priesthood: An Old Testament Messianic Motif," *BSac* 150 (1993): 50–61.

nature of David's superintendence of the whole matter and of his personal participation as well.[32] It was his idea to send for the ark and thus to combine both political and religious centrality in Jerusalem (v. 2). Psalm 132 affirms David's desire to bring this to pass, and the unknown poet prays that the Lord will honor the choice of Zion as his dwelling place.

After a three-month hiatus, David resumed the quest for the ark, this time having it carried on poles as the law demanded (v. 13; cf. Num. 4:15). As for David, the text is clear that "he sacrificed an ox and a fattened calf" (v. 13); he wore a linen ephod and danced before the Lord (v. 14); and, after the ark had been installed in the Zion tabernacle, he "offered burnt offerings and fellowship offerings in the LORD's presence" (v. 17). Finally, he "blessed the people in the name of the LORD of Hosts" (v. 18). Many scholars, in a desire perhaps to safeguard the uniqueness of the Aaronic priesthood or dodge the difficulties posed by a competing priesthood, view David as only an observer of these things or, at most, as a lay participant who, as a Judean not a Levite, could not possibly have ministered as described.[33] But this kind of reading ignores the plain and literal wording of the text whose intent is to give David a central role as royal priest.

This role is suggested elsewhere (1) by his interest in building a temple for the Lord, one more permanent and glorious than the one he had already erected on Mount Zion (2 Sam. 7:2, 5); (2) the appointment of his sons as priests (2 Sam. 8:18);[34] (3) his concern for the ark in his exile from Absalom (2 Sam. 15:24–29); and (4) his purchase of the threshing floor of Araunah the Jebusite as the site for the temple his son Solomon would build, a purchase, incidentally, that was followed by David's priestly act of building an altar and offering sacrifices (2 Sam. 24:18–25). The book of Samuel (and 1 Kings 1–2) says little or nothing more about David's preparation for the temple, a topic left to the Chronicler and to be addressed later. There are, however, brief references to his appointment and supervision of priests and other religious personnel, a fact that can be explained only by David's divine authorization to be involved in such

---

[32] Hans Wilhelm Hertzberg, *I & II Samuel* (Philadelphia: Westminster, 1964), 279–80; Rainer Albertz, *A History of Israelite Religion in the Old Testament Period* (Louisville: Westminster/John Knox, 1992), 121–22.

[33] Roland deVaux, *Ancient Israel,* vol. 1 (New York: McGraw-Hill, 1965), 113–14.

[34] כהן, W. Dommershausen, *TDOT* 7:67.

matters, even if not a royal priest in the sense we are proposing here (cf. 1 Sam. 22:20–23; 23:6, 9–12; 1 Kings 1:32–35).

The record of Solomon as royal priest is, if anything, even more clear and persuasive. We have already noted that among the first things he did was to go to Gibeon, then the location of the Mosaic tabernacle, where he offered sacrifices (1 Kings 3:4). He was not alone in doing so, for a thousand were made on that one occasion. Yet it is difficult to avoid the impression that he personally participated. Moreover, what he did was not illicit or aberrant, for the Lord honored his homage by appearing to him in a dream, offering to the young king whatever he desired (v. 5). Upon his return to Jerusalem, Solomon offered more burnt and fellowship offerings, this time at David's tabernacle where the ark was now housed (v. 15).

Solomon's commission to build the temple also connected king to cultus and under divine direction. Once the project was finished, the king commanded a dedicatory service to be held at which he and all Israel offered innumerable sacrifices (1 Kings 8:1–5). Nothing is said of Solomon's priestly role here, it is true; but following the manifestation of God's indwelling presence, the king turned to the people and blessed them, a distinctively priestly function in the context of the cultus (such as this; v. 14).[35] He then led them in the great dedicatory prayer, an intercessory ministry also closely connected to the office of priest. Before the day was over, Solomon officiated in the sacrifice of still more offerings (vv. 62–63), taking to himself the responsibility of doing so in a temple area large enough to accommodate the thousands of offerings being made (vv. 64–66). After that it became his practice to supervise the offerings made at the thrice annual festivals to which all Israelite males were commanded to appear (1 Kings 9:25).

Sadly, Solomon in his latter years drifted away from the Lord into syncretistic if not pagan ways, still exercising priestly leadership. He built high places for Chemosh, Molech, and various other deities of neighboring lands in an attempt to cater to his foreign wives (1 Kings 11:4–8). As a result, he was informed that his once mighty kingdom would be divided and his dynastic heirs would retain rule over just one tribe, that of Judah from which the royal family sprang (vv. 29–35).

[35] Michael L. Brown, בָּרַךְ, *NIDOTTE* 1:761.

The remainder of the Deuteronomistic history attests only a few examples of royal priesthood, all without exception being negative. They include the double calf shrines established by Jeroboam I of Israel at Bethel and Dan, an undertaking clearly led by the king and including such arrangements as the appointment of priests (many non-Levitical) and the scheduling of festivals (1 Kings 12:28–33). Their illegitimacy is obvious from the prophetic warning that follows; and, of course, Jeroboam had no valid claim to Davidic royal priesthood anyway inasmuch as he was not descended from David. Though King Ahab of Israel is never said to have officiated at a cult site, he was in command of the prophet priests of Baal who tried to lead the people into Baalism at Carmel (1 Kings 18:20). Otherwise the record is silent as to the arrogation of priestly authority by any other rulers of the Northern Kingdom.

The situation in the south was largely the same, a striking fact considering that Judah's rulers without exception were Davidides and might be expected to assume Davidic priestly responsibilities. The two or three instances that are recorded are, as in the case with Israel, cast in negative terms. Ahaz, for example, officiated at a variety of sacrifices but on an altar he himself had built in imitation of an Assyrian model (2 Kings 16:10–14). His wicked grandson Mannaseh also had a direct hand in religious ritual. In an unspeakable concession to heathen practice, he personally sacrificed his own son on a fiery altar and resorted to the occultic arts of sorcery and divination (2 Kings 21:6). Otherwise, the book of Kings has no more to say on the matter of royal priesthood, either overtly or even by innuendo.

In the interest of rounding off our discussion and, at the same time, providing one more bit of evidence for our thesis as to royal priesthood, we dip momentarily into Chronicles, contrary to our usual method of pursuing a canonical sequence. The reference is to the reign of good king Uzziah who, by and large, comes off rather well in the narrative "until he became strong" (2 Chron. 26:15). He then began a downward course, epitomized by his unauthorized attempt to enter the temple to burn incense (vv. 16–21). The Chronicler found no fault with the king's presence in the temple, it seems, for all the priests had to say to him was that it was not right for him to burn incense to the Lord (v. 18).[36] The

[36] H. G. M. Williamson, *1 and 2 Chronicles,* NCBC (Grand Rapids: Eerdmans, 1982), 339.

reason was that this ministry was reserved to the Aaronic priests only and not for others of whom Uzziah may have been but one example (cf. Num. 16:39–40). Rather than acknowledge the limitations of his role as royal priest, Uzziah flew into a rage until he was smitten by leprosy and thus forced to withdraw not just from the temple but also from his kingship and even from society (vv. 20–21).

It is obviously hazardous to try to build a strong case for royal priesthood on the scanty records from the divided monarchy period (931–586 BC). However, enough evidence remains from the reigns of David and Solomon to suggest that the concept was not only known but that it formed an important segment of Israel's theology. Our study of the prophets and of the poetic and wisdom literature (yet to come) will add to and substantiate these claims. It will also document the reasons for the disappearance of the notion in practical terms in the historical period of the Old Testament.

The question remains as to how the notion of Davidic royal priesthood arose in the first place. One suggestion—and with some plausibility—is that David took over a site (Jerusalem) that had for centuries recognized the priestly function of its rulers. Biblically a case can be made for this since, as we saw, Melchizedek, king and priest together, ruled over (Jeru)salem. David, a millennium later, would have been well aware of this and therefore was influenced not just by immediate precedent but, more important, an ancient prototype. This is borne out by Psalm 110 in which David is expressly compared to Melchizedek, sharing with him a common priesthood.

Another proposal, one we think to be preferable, is that the priesthood of David and his royal progeny fits the eschatological, especially New Testament, model of messianic kingship and therefore is necessary as its prototype. For the moment we should resist further attention to the New Testament witness since one could argue that this is methodologically inappropriate at this point. Enough remains in the Old Testament, however, to support the idea that reigning and priestly intercession were compatible ideas. Indeed, Israel was called to be a priestly kingdom, a role that consists of both royal and intercessory components. And Israel was nothing more or less than the national expression of the original creation purpose of God for mankind to reign over all things and to stand between him and all else that he created. The prophets, we shall see, will continue to explore this concept and will shed their light on the proposals advanced thus far.

The Temple and Sacred Space

To return now to Solomon and the Deuteronomistic history, we pick up the story line with a second appearance of the Lord to Solomon immediately after the dedication of the temple (1 Kings 9:1–9). In this vision the Lord renewed his promise to remain always among his people in the temple, clarifying the meaning of this presence with the words "My eyes and My heart will be there at all times" (v. 3). This way of reconciling the otherwise mutually exclusive concepts of God's transcendence and immanence is much like Solomon's own understanding, previously expressed, that prayer should be directed toward the temple since that was the earthly locus of God's presence but that he would hear and answer from heaven, his actual abode (1 Kings 8:29–30).

This insight into sacred space, a theme as old as the garden in Eden, is most useful in tracing that theme through the remainder of Kings.[37] Already in this appearance of the Lord at Gibeon, he threatened, in the language of covenant curses, that if Solomon or his royal descendants were to violate the covenant by serving and worshipping other gods, Israel would be evicted from the land and the temple would be rejected (vv. 6–7). That is, the Lord would no longer live there, thus removing himself from the land itself in a self-imposed exile. Ezekiel later described this as a departure of God's glory from Jerusalem to the east, the ultimate destination of the Jews who were swept away in the Babylonian deportation (Ezek. 11:22–24). The temple in which Solomon took such pride might be imposing now, but the time would come, Solomon was told, when its destruction would be a sign to the nations of God's great displeasure and judgment. And the Lord repeated the reason in order to impress it indelibly on Solomon's heart and mind—"because [the people] abandoned the LORD their God who brought their ancestors out of the land of Egypt. They clung to other gods and worshiped and served them" (v. 9). They will have disobeyed the foundational principle of the covenant, namely, the truth that only the Lord is God and only he is to be worshipped.

---

[37] See the earlier discussion of this theme, pp. 281–92.

In Solomon's latter years he drifted from this principle by (1) giving at least tacit recognition to the existence of other gods (1 Kings 11:4–6) and (2) constructing worship centers where these heathen deities could be worshipped in competition with the Lord (vv. 7–8). Thus, he disregarded the first two commandments and the Shema, which was their theological underpinning. No wonder the Lord was angry and declared to Solomon then and there, "I will tear the kingdom away from you and give it to your servant" (v. 11). At the same time, the unconditionality of the Davidic covenant is also forcibly emphasized. The loss of the kingdom would not take place in Solomon's lifetime "because of David your father" (v. 12), and, in fact, not all would be lost, for one tribe would remain "because of my servant David and because of Jerusalem that I chose" (v. 13). Though blessings of the covenant may be forfeited because of unfaithfulness, God is faithful to his word and will not abrogate a covenant to which he has sworn himself.

The precedent set by Solomon was assiduously followed by all the kings of Israel and virtually all of those of Judah, David's own (and now truncated) kingdom. The central sanctuary as the emblem of sacred space was matched by multiple shrines and temples, and the uniqueness and exclusive claims of the Lord as the only God and the sole deity worthy of worship was scouted by the adoption of the indigenous gods of the land as well as others from afar who were worshipped at these illicit places. All this is to say that the first two commandments, the essence of the covenant law (as we have repeatedly observed), were continuously under assault until God brought both kingdoms to their knees and into the judgment of exile.

Jeroboam I of Israel was first to do this, as we have already noted, worshipping golden calves at Bethel and Dan in imitation of Israel's apostate act at the foot of Mount Sinai centuries before (1 Kings 12:31–33; cf. Exod. 32:2–6). Though these calves were likely iconic representations of the Lord himself, their worship broke the second commandment, and the building of high places as central sanctuaries opposed the clear injunction against worshipping the Lord in any place other than where he would choose as a "place to have His name dwell" (Deut. 12:11).

Rehoboam, son of Solomon, was little better. He permitted the existence of pagan high places even if there is no evidence that he himself participated in the orgies practiced there. In any case, their mere presence in the land evidenced a tolerance for gods other than the Lord, something against which the Decalogue strongly inveighs (1 Kings 14:22–24; cf. Exod. 20:4–6). Of Rehoboam's son Abijah it is said that "he was not completely devoted to the LORD his God as his ancestor David had been" (1 Kings 15:3). It became common from this point forward to refer to David as the paradigm against which royal behavior was to be measured and his name was also invoked as the one for whose sake the Southern Kingdom would continue no matter the sin of its kings. Abijah, his lack of full devotion to the Lord notwithstanding, would have a son to succeed him because "David did what was right in the LORD's eyes, and he did not turn aside from anything He had commanded him all the days of his life" (v. 5). Even the caveat—"except in the matter of Uriah the Hittite"—did not nullify this assessment for David had sought and found forgiveness for the murder of his faithful friend (1 Kings 15:4–5; cf. 2 Sam. 12:13; Ps. 32:1–5). David's obedience therefore counted for something, but the text is nonetheless insistent that it was the Lord's own gracious initiative that ensured the durability of the covenant promises. As for Asa, son of Abijah, his heart "was completely with the LORD his entire life" (v. 14), for he conducted himself as his forefather David had done (v. 11). This approbation came despite Asa's failure to remove the high places, for it seems this was more benign neglect than deliberate toleration of evil.

As for Israel's kings following Jeroboam, their disregard of the Lord and his demand for exclusive worship reads like a tireless litany of rebellious apostasy. Nadab "followed the example of his father [Jeroboam] and the sin he had caused Israel to commit" (1 Kings 15:26), which suggests adherence to the calf shrines of Bethel and Dan. Baasha, founder of a new dynasty, brought no change; for he also "followed the example of Jeroboam and the sin he had caused Israel to commit" (v. 34). His son Elah followed suit (1 Kings 16:13) as did the assassin Zimri (v. 19). Omri, founder of the next dynasty, "did more evil than all who were before him," outstripping even Jeroboam, to whom all kings of Israel were compared (v. 25). His defection from the Lord is seen best in the life and deeds of his son Ahab for whom he seems to have made a marriage relationship with Jezebel, daughter of the pagan king of Sidon, Ethbaal. The name of the king reveals the Baalism to which he was devoted.

Elijah and Elisha: Prophetic Confrontation

Ahab achieved a high-water mark for covenant violation. He built a Baal temple in his capital city Samaria, and there he erected images of Baal and his consort Asherah (1 Kings 16:32–33). Moreover, at the instigation of his wicked wife, he attempted to extirpate the worship of the Lord from his kingdom (1 Kings 18:4) and, when confronted by Elijah the prophet about the matter, blamed him for all the ills of the nation that the Lord had sent. Elijah, however, put his finger on the heart of the matter, offering a rebuttal appropriate to all the kings of Israel: "You have abandoned the LORD's commandments (the covenant) and followed the Baals" (v. 18). At this juncture the prophet sensed the need for a showdown in which the Lord's sole existence as God and his claims to exclusive worship could challenge the inroads of pagan polytheism. The contest at Mount Carmel was arranged accordingly, and the stage was set for the truth to come out.

The pericope of the contest is well worth mining for its insight concerning the nature of Israel's God and the legitimacy of his demand for unrivaled worship.[38] Elijah himself set forth the need for such an encounter in the first place with his question to the people, "How long will you hesitate between two opinions?" and his challenge, "If Yahweh is God, follow Him. But if Baal, follow him" (1 Kings 18:21). The scene is reminiscent of the covenant renewal setting of a similar choice placed before the Lord's people by Joshua: "If it doesn't please you to worship the LORD, choose for yourselves today the one you will worship: the gods your fathers worshiped beyond the Euphrates River, or the gods of the Amorites in whose land you are living. As for me and my family, we will worship the LORD" (Josh. 24:15). More than half a millennium may have passed, but the issue of undivided loyalty to the Lord and to his worship in one place alone had not changed.

The rules of engagement and the criteria for determining the truth of the competing claims were clearly set forth. Each party—the Yahwistic and the Baalist—would offer a bull on an altar but without the advantage of a fire. That must be provided by the deity in whose name the offering was being made. The one who answered by igniting the sacrifice would

[38] Leila Leah Bronner, *The Stories of Elijah and Elisha as Polemics against Baal Worship* (Leiden: Brill, 1968).

be declared the winner and therefore the true God. The prophets of Baal went first; but after crying to their god all day, there was no response. Elijah's suggestion that Baal may have been preoccupied or busy or away or sleeping only intensified the futile efforts of his ministers and served to highlight the irreality of their deity. Elijah then repaired the altar of the Lord that lay in ruins, placed the bull upon it, and doused the whole and a surrounding ditch with water. He then called upon the Lord who ignited the sacrifice and consumed not only it but the altar and the water as well. His appeal was brief but theologically poignant: "Answer me, LORD! Answer me so that this people will know that You, Yahweh, are God and that You have turned their hearts back" (1 Kings 18:37). Once the Lord was vindicated in their eyes, the people responded in kind: "Yahweh, He is God! Yahweh, He is God!" (v. 39). What they could not accept from a review of sacred history they were forced to concede on empirical evidence. In the backyard of the god of thunder and lightning, the Lord had embarrassed him, nullifying any pretense that such a god had power and, indeed, that he even existed.

Such a display of power should have led to national conversion, even to the level of the throne, but such was not the case. Ahab persisted in his unbelief despite the overtures of the Lord who, time and time again, came to his aid (cf. 1 Kings 20:13–14, 22, 28). Even in his final year he relied on false prophets for advice rather than on Micaiah, the prophet of the Lord whom the king had ignored since he spoke nothing but the truth of God (1 Kings 22:5–8). Sadly, King Jehoshaphat of Judah, who was collaborating with Ahab in an impending battle with the Arameans, made no more than a feeble effort to learn the mind of the Lord; and so both kings went off to war with Ahab losing his life and Jehoshaphat having abandoned his theological convictions. The best that could be said was that Jehoshaphat adhered to the ways of Asa his father (but not of David) and to that extent did what was right in the Lord's eyes. But he, like many of his forebears, tolerated heathen high places in direct contradiction to the covenant that insisted on the worship of the Lord and him alone.

Ahab's dynastic successors emulated both him and Jeroboam I, the prototype of anti-covenant ideology and practice. Ahaziah "served Baal and worshiped him. He provoked the LORD God of Israel just as his father had done" (1 Kings 22:53) and even resorted to foreign gods such as Baal-Zebub of the Philistine state of Ekron (2 Kings 1:2), and this despite the counsel of Elijah that there was a God of Israel to whom he could turn in need (v. 6). In an abrupt reversal of this view of things, the foreign commander of the armies of Aram, Naaman, complied with the prophet Elisha's prescription for healing of his leprosy and when cured confessed, "I know there's no God in the whole world except in Israel" (2 Kings 5:15). The irony of a king of Israel turning to a foreign god while a foreign dignitary turned to the God of Israel is striking, but it illustrates at the same time the true basis for covenant inclusion, namely, faith in the living God and obedience to his commands.

Jeopardy of the Kingdom Ideal

The narrative of the Southern Kingdom resumes with brief attention to the reigns of Jehoram and his son Ahaziah. Jehoram had married Athaliah, daughter of Ahab, and conducted himself in the manner of Ahab, so much so that the Lord threatened to have destroyed Judah were it not "because of His servant David" (2 Kings 8:19). Once more the perpetuity of the Lord's commitment to David and his kingdom overrode all other considerations. As the historian puts it, the Lord "had promised to give a lamp to David and to his sons forever" (v. 19). Ahaziah's epitaph is no better—"he walked in the way of the house of Ahab and did what was evil in the LORD's sight" (v. 27).

Things came to such a pass that the Lord called an Israelite general to found a new dynasty in the north, thus terminating that of Omri and Ahab. Jehu executed his task with expedience, removing both Ahaziah, king of Judah, and Joram, king of Israel, from their thrones on the same day (2 Kings 9:24–29) before turning to the rest of their families. He understood his mission to be incomplete, however, until he had rid the land of Baalism, thereby removing the principal threat to the exclusive worship of the Lord. He concocted a scheme to annihilate the Baal priests en masse and then tore down the temple that Ahab had built years before (2 Kings 10:18–27). The extermination of Baalism did not eliminate all vestiges of paganism, however, and Jehu, exercising customary tolerance toward all things Jeroboam, left intact the shrines of Bethel and Dan (v. 29), for which he was condemned and which would bring to an end his own dynasty (v. 30).

That line extended through four more rulers—Jehoahaz, Jehoash, Jeroboam II, and Zechariah—all of whom were evil and none of whom made any effort to lead the nation back to covenant compliance. It seemed in the days of Jehoash that the Lord would have condemned Israel to extinction were it not "because of His covenant with Abraham, Isaac, and Jacob" (2 Kings 13:23). In fact, the historian, at the end of his reflection on Israel's past, comments that "He (the LORD) was not willing to destroy them. Even now [in the historian's own time] He has not banished them from His presence." Appealing next to the Abrahamic covenant (and not the Davidic, which pertained primarily to Judah), the author underscored the permanence of its benefits. The seed of Abraham would, through thick and thin, remain forever as a testimony to God's faithfulness (Gen. 17:7–8).

The assessment of the reigns of the Jehu family is applicable to the last five rulers of the Northern Kingdom as well—Shallum, Menahem, Pekahiah, Pekah, and Hoshea. The only mitigation, if such it is, is in connection with the last of these of whom it is said, "He did what was evil in the LORD's sight, but not like the kings of Israel who preceded him" (2 Kings 17:2)! This faint praise but underscores the spiritual and moral bankruptcy of the nation Israel, the people called to be a "kingdom of priests and a holy nation."

Before returning to the account of the affairs of the Davidic kingdom Judah, it is important to take a careful look at the theological summary of Israel's history in which the narrator went beyond a mere telling of the story—even though with intermittent theological commentary—to an explanation of Israel's present (to him) woeful condition and the inevitable judgment that lay just around the corner. Put simply, "they had worshiped other gods. They had lived according to the customs of the nations that the LORD had dispossessed before the Israelites" (2 Kings 17:7b–8). In violation of the central sanctuary law, they had set up high places and in contravention of the first two commandments had embraced the worship of other gods and set up images to represent them (vv. 10–12). In short, Israel had "rejected [the LORD's] statutes and His covenant He had made with their ancestors and the warnings He had given them" (v. 15). Even Judah had become infected with Israel's debilitating disease; and were it not for the sake of David, as we are constantly reminded, Judah too would have suffered the fate of her northern sister and by then also have gone into captivity (vv. 18–20).

Meanwhile in Judah, the vacancy on David's throne occasioned by Jehu's slaughter of its king Ahaziah was filled by Ahaziah's mother Athaliah who, as we have already observed, was a daughter of King Ahab of Israel. She immediately destroyed all surviving members of the Davidic family—including her own offspring, of course—with the exception of an infant grandson Joash who had been sequestered by his nurse and the high priest Jehoiada (2 Kings 11:1–3). Thus the Davidic dynasty and with it the Davidic covenant came this close to extermination. Six years later the priest instigated a successful plot to assassinate Athaliah, following which young Joash was presented to the public and was acclaimed and anointed as Judah's next king. Of particular interest is the fact that his investiture included the presentation to him of a copy of the covenant (certainly Deuteronomy, at least), which he was obligated to read and obey in line with Deuteronomic prescription (Deut. 17:18–20). Jehoiada then led in a covenant renewal ceremony (2 Kings 11:17), a logical outcome of which was the demolition of the Baal temple and its cultic accoutrements (v. 18).

The removal of these pagan trappings left the Solomonic temple as the sole and central place of worship, but its neglect and abuse over the years necessitated major renovation and repair (2 Kings 12:4–16). The funds for the project poured in, and at last the project was finished, and the temple took its proper place as the unrivaled site for the worship of the Lord. This happy state of affairs did not long endure, however, for King Jehoash of Israel, having defeated in battle Amaziah, the next king of Judah, looted the temple and the royal palace and carried their precious treasures to Samaria (2 Kings 14:11–14). That the dwelling place of the Lord could suffer such sacrilege at the hands of a king of Israel shows how far the Northern Kingdom had fallen away from any semblance of a covenant community.

The reign of Ahaz of Judah in the later eighth century ushered in a period of spiritual decline interrupted briefly and not entirely successfully by the tenures of the godly rulers Hezekiah and Josiah. The implications of these events for the temple as sacred space are enormous; in fact, it is not inaccurate to describe the Deuteronomic account from 735 to 586 BC as the history of the temple, so central were its fortunes to the outcome of the Southern Kingdom. Ahaz, as we noted in another context, embraced heathen worship wholeheartedly, even to the point of constructing an altar modeled after one he had seen in Damascus and elevating it to a place of prominence above that of the great bronze altar of the temple (2 Kings 16:10–14). The latter he relegated to the status of a divinatory tool whereby he could seek divine guidance (v. 15). Whatever that might mean, it at least clearly indicates that Ahaz not only had completely rejected the Deuteronomic statute regarding the place where the Lord would uniquely dwell among his people but had also substituted for it an alien ideology in which the temple came to represent something entirely different. His other adjustments and modifications of the temple precincts displayed his utter disregard of sacred things, an impiety that put at risk the Lord's continued favor toward his chosen nation (vv. 17–18).

The reformation that followed under the leadership of Hezekiah was centered largely around the temple and its covenantal symbolism. The first thing he did was remove the high places and other vestiges of heathen worship (2 Kings 18:4) and then, according to the Chronicler, he refurbished the temple and reinstated the priests, Levites, and other temple personnel to their duties (2 Chron. 29:3–11). The omission of Hezekiah's attention to the temple in the Deuteronomic history is somewhat surprising, though it may be at least partially explained by the historian's preoccupation with the threat of military defeat and destruction by the armies of Assyria.[39] This, in fact, is a feature of this history as compared to that of Chronicles where matters of temple and cultus are much more in the forefront. But Hezekiah's attitude toward the temple and its significance is not entirely lacking in the account. When told of the Assyrian danger, the king "went into the LORD's temple" (2 Kings 19:1) and later, having received a hostile letter from King Sennacherib, took it to the temple and "spread it out before the LORD" (v. 14) as though inviting him to read it as well.

The ground of Hezekiah's confidence in the Lord—and, indeed, of his whole theology—is seen in a number of statements he made in prayer and in public discourse. He addressed the Lord as the "LORD God of

[39] More likely, as Williamson suggests, the Chronicler is attempting to present Hezekiah as a second Solomon, consumed by the desire to place the temple at the center of his royal endeavors. Williamson, *1 and 2 Chronicles,* 350–51.

Israel who is enthroned above the cherubim," who "[alone is God] of all the kingdoms of the earth." The gods of the nations, on the other hand, were to Hezekiah "not gods but made by human hands—wood and stone"—an assessment no doubt originating with his court prophet Isaiah (2 Kings 19:15–18; cf. Isa. 44:9–20). There can be no doubt that Hezekiah saw that the fundamental theological issue was the confession that only the Lord is God and only he was to be worshipped, a confession based squarely on the first two commandments. He was also mindful of his side of the covenant relationship and the obligation to walk before the Lord "faithfully and wholeheartedly," something he said he had done without fail (2 Kings 20:3).

The spiritual slide that was reversed under Hezekiah's reign took a downward turn again under his evil son Manasseh and equally evil grandson Amon. Once again the temple and worship became the center of focus, and how these two kings related to them is the historian's chief theological concern. Manasseh, he says, followed "the abominations of the nations," rebuilding the shrines his father had destroyed and desecrating the temple by placing in its environs altars and other objects devoted to alien gods (2 Kings 21:2–3). Harking back to Deuteronomy 12, the narrator twice refers to the temple as the place where the Lord said he would place his name (vv. 4, 7), thus crystallizing the nature of Manasseh's sin as a violation of the covenant. For this he suffered the curse of that covenant by being handed over to the Assyrians who dragged him off into a personal exile (2 Chron. 33:10–13), foreshadowing that of the nation as a whole (2 Kings 21:14). His son Amon "walked in all the ways his father had walked," a journey into apostasy characterized by the twin themes we have become accustomed to see: he forsook the Lord and worshipped idols, i.e., he violated the covenant at its roots (2 Kings 21:19–22).

The second of Judah's reformer kings, Josiah, commenced his reign at the tender age of eight. When he came of age, his mission in life became crystal clear: he must rid the land of idolatry and rehabilitate the worship of the Lord if his nation was to have any chance of survival. He first addressed the needs of the temple, which had fallen into serious disrepair during the long reigns of his father and his grandfather (2 Kings 22:3–7). Before the work could get well underway, however, it was interrupted by the discovery of a copy of "the book of the law," a document that at the very least included the book of Deuteronomy and more likely was coterminous with that book itself (vv. 8, 11).[40] This becomes virtually certain when it is recalled that the only other places where the term "book of the law" occurs are in Deuteronomy 28:61; 29:21; 30:10; and 31:26. The identification is critical to an understanding of the course of action Josiah took once he had come across the scroll and digested its implications for him and his nation.

A quick glance at its contents was enough to convince Josiah to postpone completion of temple refurbishing in light of the greater need for the rehabilitation of his people. They (and he) had been guilty of gross covenant violation; and if they were to escape the curses attached to such disobedience, there must be national reformation. When the matter was brought to the prophetess Huldah, she delivered the word of the Lord to Josiah that disaster "according to everything written in the book" (NIV) (i.e., the curses of Deut. 27–28) was imminent because of the twofold sin of forsaking the Lord and worshipping other gods (2 Kings 22:15–17). However, because Josiah had repented upon reading the scroll, he would not see the judgment that was about to fall but would be buried in peace (vv. 19–20).

Delaying the project yet longer, Josiah, in accord with the teachings of the scroll, read relevant parts in the hearing of the people and then called them to covenant renewal (2 Kings 23:1–3; cf. Deut. 29:9–15; 31:9–13). The specific appeal—to "keep His commandments, His decrees, and His statutes with all [your] mind and with all [your] heart" (v. 3)—immediately calls to mind the Shema (Deut. 6:4–5) and the covenant stipulations that explicated and applied it. So powerful were the king's example and his words of exhortation that the assembly agreed to the covenant (if only superficially, as it turns out) and committed themselves to the task of purging the land of paganism, the only reasonable response to genuine spiritual awakening (v. 3).

The restoration of the Lord to his rightful place among his people meant that everything that had drawn them away from him in the first place and that had put them in national jeopardy had to be dealt with, and not halfheartedly. First, the temple had to be thoroughly cleared of all the paraphernalia associated with Baalism, for Baal and the Lord

[40] See p. 393.

could not occupy the same sacred space. Next the religious personnel connected to the high places throughout the land must be removed and the shrines where they ministered totally destroyed. These included illicit altars erected by such wicked royal forebears as Ahaz and Manasseh as well as the earlier high places established by Solomon and Jeroboam I. The latter had been prophesied by an anonymous prophet from Judah who had told King Jeroboam in explicit terms that Josiah would demolish the altar he had situated at Bethel (2 Kings 23:15–16; cf. 1 Kings 13:1–3).[41]

Josiah's reformation culminated in a massive celebration of Passover (vv. 21–23). It was appropriate that this particular festival be observed on this occasion (besides the fact it was presumably springtime) for at least two reasons: (1) It provided an opportunity for the whole nation to assemble, thus demonstrating and affirming their oneness as a covenant community, and (2) it signified a deliverance from the bondage of paganism that had all too long held the nation spiritually captive, into the freedom of the pure worship of the Lord in his holy sanctuary.[42] In this sense, the reformation was a second exodus no less miraculous than the first and with the potential to reestablish the nation as the covenant people of the Lord committed fully to worship and serve him alone.

After the brief but regressive reigns of the last three kings of Judah—Jehoiakim, Jehoiachin, and Zedekiah—judgment fell in the form of Babylonian conquest. The holy city and its temple were razed to the ground, much of the population was deported, and the remnant left was thrown into social and political chaos. Strangely enough, the historian reports all this without interpretive comment, as though the tragic events themselves contained their own theological message. At the same time Kings does not end in utter despair and hopelessness; for in a kind of coda, the narrator viewed an event that took place twenty-five years after the destruction of Jerusalem and apparent dissolution of the Davidic kingdom, one that portended the possibility of a better day to come (2 Kings 25:27–30). He informs us that Jehoiachin was released from prison in Babylon; and even though he remained under mild detention, he was elevated by the Babylonian monarch to a place of lofty privilege. This is perhaps the theologian's way

---

[41] D. W. Van Winkle, "1 Kings xii 25—xiii 34: Jeroboam's cultic innovations and the man of God from Judah," VT 46 (1996): 101–14.

[42] T. R. Hobbs, *2 Kings,* WBC 13 (Waco, Tex.: Word, 1985), 337.

of foreshadowing a day when the offspring of David would rise from the ashes of defeat and would lead his chosen people back to the position of privilege and honor for which they had been set apart even from the loins of Abraham.

We may summarize the theology of the Deuteronomistic history as follows:

1. The account of the historian, though obviously based on real and documentable historical events, is concerned not so much with those events per se as with their theological meaning. That is, it is an interpretive historical narrative focusing primarily on the causes and effects of Israel's behavior, particularly that of its kings.

2. The permutations of the record—the shape, form, and emphases of the text—must be read against Torah, especially Deuteronomy, for the historian was concerned to show that to the extent Israel conformed to the covenant principles of that book they were blessed; contrariwise, to the extent they departed from those same principles they were cursed and judged.[43]

3. The principles just alluded to are, throughout the course of this massive history, essentially reducible to the Shema and the Decalogue that elaborates it. In fact, a case can be made that the whole deuteronomic theology revolves around the first two commandments, the first demanding adherence to the idea that there is only one God, viz the Lord of Israel, and the other that only he should be worshipped. This precludes the recognition of other deities as having ontological reality and any attempts to represent them in plastic form.

4. The historical and eschatological success of Israel was bound up with the Davidic dynasty, a line of kings whose permanence was assured but whose every historical representative stood constantly under the judgment of God. The Davidic covenant was the instrument that bound the Lord to that royal succession, guaranteeing that it would achieve its objective of mirroring before the world what divine rule is all about so that mankind could also in its wholeness fulfill the mandate for which it was created. This requires openness to a messianic age when that final David will emerge who can bring to reality what could only be anticipated in the historical context of the deuteronomistic narrative.

---

[43] Gershon Galil, "The Message of the Book of Kings in Relation to Deuteronomy and Jeremiah," *BSac* 158 (2001): 406–14.

Chapter Fourteen

The Books of Chronicles, Ezra-Nehemiah, and Esther

The Deuteronomistic history (Joshua–2 Kings) provides an overview of the period from the conquest to the Babylonian exile from the point of view of a historical reflection on the extent to which Israel (and later, Judah) conformed or failed to conform to the covenant requirements of the book of Deuteronomy. In the language of many scholars, it is *sacred history* or, to use terms we prefer in this work, it is *theological history,* a record whose purpose is not just to recount the major events of that long epoch but to do so interpretively. Such an approach accounts for both the omission of information otherwise attested to as well as the inclusion of material that would generally be considered as inconsequential or irrelevant to normal historiography.

The books of Chronicles and Ezra-Nehemiah continue that tradition of theological history but with a different setting and a different theological agenda.[1] Chronicles, composed in its final form by an anonymous editor conventionally called the "Chronicler," is a postexilic work dating perhaps

---

[1] P. R. Ackroyd, "History and Theology in the Writings of the Chronicler," *CTM* 38 (1967): 501–15; R. L. Braun, "Chronicles, Ezra, and Nehemiah: Theology and Literary History," *Studies in the Historical Books of the Old Testament,* ed. J. A. Emerton (Leiden: Brill, 1979), 52–64.

as late as 400 BC.[2] Ezra-Nehemiah, likely a single work at one time, may have been completed somewhat earlier.[3] Its concern is to trace the fortunes of the postexilic community's efforts—already underway and, in some respects, already concluded—to restore the state to its preexilic condition and status as much as possible so as to enable it to carry out its God-given purpose. On the other hand, Chronicles provides a comprehensive history from creation to the end of the canonical period, with a primary focus on the Davidic dynasty and its rule over Judah, the Southern Kingdom. Even there the emphasis is on the cultic or religious aspects of that reign, an emphasis designed to meld the political and religious role of the king as the vehicle through whom God's creation design will find ultimate fulfillment. The approach here, as always, is to adhere to the canonical order as much as possible while being attentive to chronological concerns. But in this case it seems best to treat Chronicles first since its subject matter antedates Ezra-Nehemiah.

The Books of Chronicles

The books (or book, since they existed originally as a single composition) of Chronicles consist of six major sections: (1) the genealogies and tribal histories (1 Chron. 1:1–9:34); (2) the reign of Saul (9:35–10:14); (3) the reign of David (11:1–29:30); (4) the reign of Solomon (2 Chron. 1:1–9:31); (5) the divided monarchy (10:1–28:27); and (6) the kingdom of Judah (29:1–36:23). All six are integrally connected to one another, revealing the hand of a compiler who has carefully provided a unified theological treatise whose purpose is to link the Davidic covenant to everything that preceded it—including the primeval history of the world itself—and to David's role as priest-king and prototype of a perfect scion yet to come.

Genealogies and Tribal Histories

The genealogies are structured in such a way as to link Adam with the chosen people Israel through Abraham. The patriarch quickly becomes a

[2] David M. Howard Jr., *An Introduction to the Old Testament Historical Books* (Chicago: Moody, 1993), 235.

[3] Ibid., 284.

central figure (1 Chron. 1:27) and the conduit through which Israel and the other offspring of Abraham appear and interrelate (1:28–2:2). The Adam-Abraham nexus draws attention to the fact that God's redemptive purposes for all humanity will find expression in a single individual and his national descendants, the people/nation of Israel. Thus, even the genealogy testifies to the promise of the Abrahamic covenant that in Abraham and his seed all the earth would be blessed (Gen. 12:1–3).

The next stage is the movement from Abraham to David. The historian's strategy to accomplish this is clear, first of all, from the fact that the genealogy of Judah is the first of all the twelve and that it climaxes in the family of David with more than usual detail (2:1–17). After disposing of various non-Davidic branches (2:18–55), the record goes on to list David's children (3:1–9) and then all the kings who descended from him (3:10–16) as well as postexilic leaders of royal blood (3:17–24). What is striking (among other things) is that there is no hint of the Mosaic covenant; and, in fact, Moses himself plays no role whatsoever, merely appearing in the list of names of the genealogy of Levi (1 Chron. 6:3). The intention therefore is most clear: The Mosaic covenant was bypassed for the moment in order to emphasize the Abraham-David linkage, one, we might add, that has already come to our attention in terms of the common royal grant nature of the covenants that they represent.

However, priestly concerns were by no means minimized. Though Moses is only one name among scores in the lineage of Levi, the genealogies of that tribe are as extensive as those of Judah, suggesting the important role of the priesthood and cultus in the Davidic kingdom (1 Chron. 6:1–81). Within the genealogical listing we learn of David's appointment of musicians for his Zion tabernacle (vv. 31–32), and there appears also a list of the chief priests down to David's time (vv. 50–53) as well as the distribution of religious personnel throughout the land (vv. 54–81). Finally, among the lists of returnees from Babylonian exile an inordinate amount of coverage is dedicated to priests, Levites, gatekeepers, and other officiants (9:10–34). Clearly the Chronicler's burden in the genealogies was to make a case for the centrality of the Abrahamic-Davidic connection as an aspect of human redemption, but an aspect that could not be understood apart from the sacral nature of the community over which David reigned.

The Reign of David

Whereas the Deuteronomist devoted several chapters to the reign of Saul (1 Sam. 9–31), the Chronicler dispensed with it in fourteen short verses (1 Chron. 10:1–14) and then mainly to show how Saul's death paved the way for David's accession to the throne.[4] His urgency to move forward from the genealogical introduction of David to the narratives recounting his elevation to kingship is patently obvious. At the outset he also wanted to establish that David was the universal choice of all Israel to be Saul's successor, a device calculated to solidify the legitimacy of his reign (1 Chron. 11:1–2).[5] The narrative then immediately shores up still further that legitimacy by including in rapid succession David's conquest of Jerusalem (vv. 4–9), a list of his mighty men (vv. 10–47), a register of the elements of his fighting forces (1 Chron. 12:1–40), and the story of his retrieval of the ark of the covenant and its relocation to the sanctuary he had built for it (1 Chron. 13:1–14; 15:1–16:3). All of this is put at the beginning of his reign so as to make clear that David was well settled and capable of undertaking his royal responsibilities.[6]

The inordinate attention the account pays to the ark justifies close examination of the Chronicler's intent and purpose in doing so. He is careful to point out that David included all Israel (again) in his plan to send for the ark and that the decision was contingent on God's will (1 Chron. 13:1–4). The disposition of the ark, like everything else to which David put his hand, was not a matter of mere whim or human preference but part of a divine plan sanctioned by the whole nation. Even the debacle of the mishandling of the ark at the threshing floor of Kidon turned out to be a means of blessing the family of Obed-Edom the Gittite who housed the ark until it could be properly transported (vv. 9–14). When three months had passed and it was time to move the ark again, the Chronicler notes—in line with his penchant for the cultic facets of David's reign—that this time it was transported according to the law of Moses which mandated that "no one but the Levites may carry the ark of God, because the LORD

[4] Martin J. Selman, *1 Chronicles,* TOTC 10a (Downers Grove, Ill.: InterVarsity, 1994), 133–34.

[5] Sara Japhet, *I & 2 Chronicles* (Louisville: Westminster/John Knox, 1993), 236.

[6] Eugene H. Merrill, "The 'Accession Year' and Davidic Chronology," *JANES* 19 (1989): 110–11.

has chosen them to carry the ark of the LORD and to minister before Him forever" (1 Chron. 15:2; cf. Num. 4:15; Deut. 10:8).[7]

David himself then assumed responsibility for the protocol of bringing the ark into the city. He summoned the priests to consecrate themselves, chiding them for having failed to follow the law in their first attempt to transport the ark (1 Chron. 15:11–15). He then directed the musicians to sing and pray and the doorkeepers of the tabernacle to be ready to admit the ark to its designated place (vv. 19–24). David had clothed himself with a linen robe and ephod befitting his role as a Melchizedekian priest and with dancing and celebration led the procession to the tabernacle he had built to house it.[8] Continuing his priestly ministry, David sacrificed burnt offerings and fellowship offerings and then "blessed the people in the name of the LORD" (1 Chron. 15:27–16:3). The blending of the regal and religious duties of the king is highly instructive in that it shows David as both the spiritual descendant of the priest-king Melchizedek and the prototype of the One who, in Christian theology, is designated both priest and king (Heb. 7:11–17; Rev. 19:16).

David's understanding of the theological significance of what had just transpired was put to poetry both here in Chronicles (1 Chron. 16:8–36) and in Psalm 105:1–15. After a recital of the Lord's mighty acts in history (vv. 8–13), David recalled the Lord's faithfulness to the Abrahamic covenant in giving Israel the land in which they dwelled that day (vv. 14–22). He then concluded, on the basis of these displays of power and promises, that only the Lord is God and only he is worthy of praise (vv. 23–29). The nations therefore ought to recognize the sovereignty of the Lord and with all creation shout with joy, "The LORD is King!" (vv. 30–33). It is he whom Israel can trust for safety and salvation in the days that lie ahead (vv. 34–36).

The Chronicler's temple-centered theology places David's desire to build a suitable house for the Lord ahead of the account of his success militarily in contradistinction to the order in 1 Samuel. Nevertheless, the text of the ensuing covenant is virtually identical in both sources as is to be expected in a document that must be cast in precise terms in order to ensure its legality. Lacking in the version in Chronicles, however, is

---

[7] Roddy Braun, *1 Chronicles,* WBC 14 (Waco, Tex.: Word, 1986), 188.

[8] See our previous comments on this, pp. 445–52.

any reference to the punishment to be applied should David's son prove to be disobedient (cf. 2 Sam. 7:14). This subtle omission is not to be attributed to manuscript corruption or anything of the kind but reflects a conscious theological movement to the postexilic period where the Davidic monarchy was now oriented to the eschatological age when the misbehavior of a Davidic heir would be unthinkable.[9]

The story of David's purchase of Araunah's threshing floor is also instructive in its Chronicles rendition as compared to that in 2 Samuel 24. Whereas Samuel states that the prophet Gad instructed David to build an altar there, Chronicles originates the command with the angel of the Lord, thus, it seems, lending the command somewhat greater authority (2 Sam. 24:18; cf. 1 Chron. 21:18). When Araunah was aware of the approach of strangers, Samuel says he saw the king and his men (2 Sam. 24:20), but the Chronicler has him seeing the angel first and then David (1 Chron. 21:20–21). Again, there is a presence of deity in Chronicles that is not so apparent in Samuel. This tends to undergird the Chronicler's theology with an angelology much less common in the Deuteronomistic history but increasingly common in the postexilic period when the prophetic ministry was on the wane.[10]

The site having been selected, David continued his all-consuming interest in the temple by (1) challenging Solomon to see to its completion, (2) organizing the priestly and Levitical orders, (3) providing plans and specifications for temple construction, and (4) soliciting gifts from the people to finance the project. Each of these has theological ramifications for the theology of sacred space and the ministries to be conducted in association with it.

After gathering building materials, David charged his "young and inexperienced" son to build the temple he himself had been forbidden to undertake (1 Chron. 22:5). David had been a man of war, and thus it was not appropriate for him to erect the dwelling place of the Lord, whose presence among his people should reflect a time of completed conquest and universal peace. In fact, the Deuteronomic covenant was clear that once the Lord had given rest from all the enemies about, then his people could resort to him in the place he would choose as a dwelling for his

[9] C. F. Keil, *The Books of the Chronicles* (Grand Rapids: Eerdmans, repr. n.d.), 223.
[10] Braun, *1 Chronicles,* 217.

name (Deut. 12:10–11). Solomon's name *(šĕlōmōh)* testified to the peace *(šālôm)* that his reign would inaugurate and that was prerequisite to his task of temple building (vv. 9–10).

More than the right name was required, however, and David drove home the point to Solomon that his success depended on keeping the terms of the covenant, defined here as the "statutes and ordinances the LORD commanded Moses for Israel" (1 Chron. 22:13). The technical terms leave no doubt that the Deuteronomic covenant is in view, the one Moses himself had in mind when he said to Joshua, as David here did to Solomon, "Be strong and courageous" (v. 13; cf. Deut. 31:6).[11] David then turned to Israel's leaders and in the language of the Shema enjoined them to "determine in your mind and heart to seek the LORD your God" (v. 19), the doing of which would result in the building of the sacred site where he would place his name (v. 19).

David's interest in the religious affairs of the kingdom is amply attested to by the sheer fact that four entire chapters (126 verses!) of Chronicles are devoted to the appointment and organization of cultic personnel alone. And his interest was far from a merely detached observation of such matters. The text declares that he "gathered" (1 Chron. 23:2), he "divided" (v. 6), he "instructed" (v. 27), he "divided" (24:3), he "set apart" (25:1), he "dedicated" (26:26), and he "appointed" (v. 32). And what he did not do personally was done in his presence, that is, under his supervision (24:31). There is no way to avoid the clear teaching of these passages to the effect that David not only was ruler of the political and military affairs of the nation (cf. 1 Chron. 27) but was head also of its religious institutions. While this by no means proves his royal priesthood in and of itself, such a role would certainly account not only for his concern for such matters but his hands-on direction and control of them as well.

The focal point of Israel's religious life, however, was the temple itself and not the personnel who ministered there.[12] David's final years, therefore, were dedicated to planning for its construction and instructing young Solomon as to its significance and to the part he must play in

---

[11] Gary N. Knoppers, *1 Chronicles 10–29,* AB 12A (New York: Doubleday, 2004), 777.

[12] Roddy Braun, "Solomon, the Chosen Temple Builder: The Significance of 1 Chronicles 22, 28, and 29 for the Theology of Chronicles," *JBL* 95 (1976): 581–90.

seeing it to completion. The space the Chronicler allots to such matters surely testifies to the enormous theological significance of the temple as sacred space, what David implied to be the royal palace from which the Lord governs the affairs of the nations (1 Chron. 28:2). David throughout his early years as king had collected materials for the temple and its furnishings (1 Chron. 18:7–8, 11; 22:2–5) and now with death approaching made the final preparations for its construction.

David's understanding of the nature and function of the temple is rich with theological implications. He called it "a resting place for the ark of the LORD's covenant and . . . a footstool for our God," and, to repeat the usual formula, "a house for [His] name" (1 Chron. 28:2–3). The focal point was the ark, the temple being considered primarily as its shelter. It was the ark of the covenant, the symbol of the relationship between the Lord and his people, and also the Lord's footstool *(hădōm),* that is, the place of royal presence and power. The imagery here is striking. God had come among his people to dwell in a house in which he could exercise his regal authority over Israel and the nations. He sat upon the ark, testifying to the covenant as the foundation upon which his relationship to Israel and his rule over it found legal justification.

David's role was closely connected to divine kingship and to the temple which represented it. He reflected on God's choice of him to be "king over Israel forever," a choice that began with the selection of his tribe Judah and then increasingly narrowed to his immediate family and, most unlikely of all, to him out of all his siblings (1 Chron. 28:4; cf. Gen. 49:8–12; 1 Sam. 16:6–13). He then hastened to add that this same process of divine election had continued in that out of all his many sons, the Lord had chosen Solomon to be next in line to the throne of Israel (v. 5). To cap it off, David asserted that Solomon, like himself, enjoyed the lofty privilege of a special relationship with the Lord: "I have chosen him to be My son, and I will be his father," the Lord had said (v. 6; cf. Ps. 2:7). The prototypical insinuation of the divine sonship as well as divine kingship of the Davidic dynasty has far-reaching eschatological and messianic ramifications, a matter to be explored more fully at a later point.

After urging Solomon to wholehearted devotion to the Lord and to the temple-building task at hand, David shared with him "the plans of all that the Spirit had put in his mind" (1 Chron. 28:12 NIV). However this is to be understood, it is clear that the temple was not the creation of human architects and builders—despite its superficial resemblance to ancient Near Eastern examples—but was just as much the product of divine revelation as the oracles of the prophets themselves.[13] This being the case, the temple as a whole and in all its parts was of heavenly origin and in its every detail was communicative of some aspect of God's glory and wisdom. Though it may be going too far to embrace the Platonic idea of earthly things being but pale reflections of what exists in heaven as the real, the New Testament (if not the Old) does approach this concept with the observation that earthly priests "serve at a sanctuary that is a copy and shadow of what is in heaven" (Heb. 8:5 NIV; cf. 9:24). This correspondence between the heavenly and earthly dwelling places of the Lord does, at any rate, explain David's insistence to Solomon that he do the work in exact accordance to "the details of the plan," details that were in David's writing and attributable to the fact that "by the LORD's hand on me, He enabled me to understand everything" (v. 19).[14]

David turned next to the entire assembly, urging them to contribute to the project whatever was still lacking and reminding them that "the temple will not be for man, but for the LORD God" (1 Chron. 29:1). He made two points here: (1) the temple would, in fact, be the dwelling place of the Lord, and (2) for that reason alone it must be built and decorated in the finest way possible. As a copy of a heavenly model, it should reflect something of the beauty and magnificence of heaven. David's prayer at the conclusion of the conclave provides warrant for such extravagance as he focused on the transcendent glory of the Lord of the temple: "Yours, LORD, is the greatness and the power and the glory and the splendor and the majesty, for everything in the heavens and on earth belongs to You. Yours, LORD, is the kingdom, and You are exalted as head over all. Riches and honor come from You, and You are the ruler of everything. In Your hand are power and might, and it is in Your hand to make great and to give strength to all" (1 Chron. 29:11–12).

---

[13] For support of the idea that all this took place by divine inspiration, see Wilf Hildebrandt, *An Old Testament Theology of the Spirit of God* (Peabody, Mass.: Hendrickson, 1995), 173.

[14] For the heaven-earth correspondence, see Frank M. Cross Jr., "The Priestly Tabernacle," *BA* 10/3 (1947), 62.

The Reign of Solomon

Solomon's first act following David's death was to retire to the high place at Gibeon to offer sacrifices there on the great bronze altar of the Mosaic tabernacle (2 Chron. 1:2–6). As we noted earlier, that tabernacle had been separated from the ark following the capture of the ark by the Philistines and the subsequent destruction of Shiloh, the old central sanctuary (1 Sam. 4:11). The tabernacle had been spared, eventually ending up at Nob (1 Sam. 21:1–9) and then, perhaps at Saul's initiative, at Gibeon. Meanwhile, the ark had been kept at Kiriath Jearim for many years (1 Sam. 7:2; 2 Sam. 6:1–5) until David brought it into Jerusalem and placed it in the temporary shrine he built for it there (2 Sam. 6:17). Solomon therefore was faced with the problem of a division of sacred space, one at Gibeon and the other on Mount Zion, thus urging upon him all the more the need to build a temple in Jerusalem that would merge sanctuary and ark once again.

Solomon understood perfectly that he had the daunting task of building the temple and leading the nation as its new king, but at his tender age (cf. 1 Chron. 22:5) he knew also that he lacked the wisdom to accomplish either. He therefore prayed for God to gift him with the skills necessary; and because he prayed for this alone, God honored his selflessness by granting him "riches, wealth, and glory" as well (2 Chron. 1:12). Thus equipped, Solomon gave orders to build "a temple for the name of the LORD and a royal palace for himself" (2 Chron. 2:1). The latter was entirely appropriate since it conformed to the theological idea of the Davidic king's role as vice-regent of the heavenly kingdom. It was therefore fitting that both palaces—that of the Lord and that of the Davidic monarchy—should coexist and complement each other to symbolize the respective spheres of royal authority.

Even pagan rulers had come to acknowledge the uniqueness of the Davidic kingship even if their pious platitudes lacked solid substance. Hiram of Tyre, when asked by Solomon for builders and materials, assented with the complimentary tribute that "the LORD God of Israel, who made the heavens and the earth" had given "King David a wise son with insight and understanding, who will build a temple for the LORD and a royal palace for himself" (v. 12). The queen of Sheba came later to visit Solomon and in similar words of praise said to him, "May the LORD your God be praised! He delighted in you and put you on his throne as king for the LORD your God" (2 Chron. 9:8). Her insight that Solomon reigned "for the LORD" is remarkable in its theological incisiveness.

The Chronicler took great pains to describe every facet of the construction of the temple and its furnishings (2 Chron. 3–4) for an obvious reason: Everything about it and in it had symbolic and typical significance. Thus, its measurements, its architectural features, its decorations, and its furnishings were fashioned according to a divine pattern in order that the message communicated through them might be understood as a revelation of God. The specifics of that message are elusive and perhaps even irrecoverable from our vantage point, though the New Testament does offer interpretations of various parts such as the curtain separating the holy place from the most holy place (2 Chron. 3:14; cf. Heb. 10:20). The principal message that emerges from these detailed descriptions is that the God of heaven, who lives in incomprehensible splendor, deserves to abide on earth in such surroundings of beauty and glory as man is capable of creating. The temple, as sacred space, as well as all its furnishings, must be a metaphor for paradise itself, the center of the earth where the LORD could be fitly praised and worshipped.[15]

When the building was finished, Solomon arranged for the ark of the covenant to be brought into it and placed in the most holy place, under the wings of the cherubim (2 Chron. 5:2–14). The cherubim overshadowed the presence of the Lord who sat invisibly in regal splendor in the most holy place with the ark now as his throne and footstool (cf. 1 Chron. 13:6; 28:2). The imagery calls to mind the presence of the cherubim placed outside the garden in Eden "to guard the way to the tree of life" (Gen. 3:24) and clearly also to safeguard the presence of the Lord from fallen mankind's unholy gaze (cf. Ezek. 10:3–5). In the ark were the stone tablets of the Mosaic covenant, in this case the copies to be retained by the Lord as a partner to the covenant made with Israel.

The emphasis on the ark of the covenant at this point was to prepare the reader for the ceremony of covenant commemoration that was about to be elaborated in great detail. This is hinted at, first of all, by the chronological setting of the narrative, "the time of the festival in the seventh month" (2 Chron. 5:3 NIV). This alludes to the Feast of Tabernacles, the time appointed for covenant reaffirmation by the community (Deut. 31:9–13).

---

[15] M. Ottosson, הֵיכָל, *TDOT* 3:387–88.

Later on, Ezra and Nehemiah assembled the postexilic Jewish community and in the seventh month read to them the "book of the law of Moses," climaxed by the observance of the Feast of Tabernacles (Neh. 8:1–3, 13–18). This clearly was in fulfillment of the Deuteronomic instruction as is likely the case in Solomon's temple dedication.

The Chronicler relates a number of stages to this commemoration. First of all, when the priests withdrew from depositing the ark in the most holy place, the Lord "moved in," indicating his residence there by the cloud of his glory (2 Chron. 5:14). Solomon acknowledged this by exclaiming, "I have built an exalted temple for You, a place for Your residence forever" (6:2). He then enlarged on this understanding by quoting the words of the Lord to the assembly that the choice to live among mankind was not of human invention but at God's own initiative: "I have chosen Jerusalem so that My name will be there," He said, "and I have chosen David to be over My people Israel" (v. 6). In one brief statement the rich theological ideas of sacred space and sacred persons are brought together, the temple standing as a microcosm of all creation over which the Lord rules through the representative of all mankind created as his image.

The prayer of dedication of the temple that follows differs little from the version of 1 Kings 8 except for the end where there is a significant advancement of thought because of the different *Sitze im Leben.* In Kings the plea for the Lord to attend to the prayers of his dispersed people is based on his deliverance of them from the iron furnace of Egypt and his choice of them, out of all the nations of the earth, to be his people (1 Kings 8:50b–53). Chronicles, on the other hand, focuses on the ark as the symbol of God's mighty power to save and appeals to his covenant promises to David never to reject him, that is, his people Israel (2 Chron. 6:40–42; cf. Ps. 132:1, 8–10).[16] The two versions complement each other and nicely integrate their respective covenantal bases.

Solomon's amen was immediately punctuated by fire from heaven that consumed the sacrifices prepared for the occasion (an incident omitted in Kings). God's glory again filled the temple, causing the throngs to fall prostrate in worship and thanksgiving (2 Chron. 7:1–3). Their response to this epiphany communicates clearly the people's sense of the presence of the Lord among them, a presence that can be acknowledged only

[16] Raymond B. Dillard, *2 Chronicles,* WBC 15 (Waco, Tex.: Word, 1987), 51.

by obedient submission. All through the Festival of Tabernacles, the celebration continued until at last, on the twenty-third day of the seventh month, the people, who had come from the length and breadth of the land, were dismissed to their homes (vv. 8–10).

The Chronicler's account of the remainder of Solomon's reign largely parallels that of Kings with the glaring omission, however, of any reference to his religious syncretism and even sanction of pagan idolatry, mainly as a concession to his foreign wives (cf. 1 Kings 11:1–8). This is in line with his theological intention to cast the Davidic dynasty in the best light possible without contradicting the truth, an approach famously illustrated by his silence regarding David's adulterous affair with Bathsheba and the disastrous consequences that followed, including the murder of her husband and the near disintegration of David's own family. This way of writing history is seen throughout the narrative of the divided kingdom where the bulk of attention is given to the nation Judah and almost always in a positive vein. We will address some of the highlights of that narrative presently. It might be good first to restate our view of the Old Testament as *Heilsgeschichte* (sacred history) as opposed to history as normally understood, that is, as an objective, dispassionate account of events as they occurred, absent interpretive or evaluative judgments on the part of the historian.

The Nature and Purpose of Sacred History

As we have argued before, the sacred nature of the Old Testament record of the past does not preclude its being founded on actual, even documentable, events. These events, however, were filtered through an ideological (better, theological) grid that offers insight into their causes and effects, especially in the context of the divine plan or purpose to which they contributed and within which they must be interpreted. Sacred history is never content only with what happened. It seeks to explain how and why as well. It is not anthropocentric but theocentric in that everything finds its ultimate explanation in terms of the sovereignty of God who superintends the affairs of nature and nations, leading them to an eschatological objective.

Of most relevance to our present concern, sacred history is selective in what it includes and what it chooses to ignore. Were the biblical history to be viewed as a purely human product, its authors could in all fairness be charged with historical revisionism at the least because of their blatantly obvious sympathy with the subjects of their inquiry, particularly in Chronicles. But the point precisely is that it is not their story in the final analysis but the story of the God of history who, in his omniscience and in line with his purposes, has crafted an account that includes and excludes what is appropriate to those purposes. To deal with the matter at hand—the Chronicler's failure to present the dark side of Solomon—his omission of those sordid details is no denial of their occurrence.[17] The Kings account was well-known to the readers of postexilic Judea so the Chronicler could hardly be trying to conceal this side of the story. Moreover, there was no need, first of all, to repeat what was already known, and, even more important and to the point, to delve into such matters would detract from the main story line which is, after all, not about David and Solomon but the temple and the Lord of the temple who had deigned to inhabit it and dwell among his people.

The Divided Monarchy

The silence on matters unflattering to the Davidic family did not remain unbroken in the reigns of subsequent kings. We need not examine all of these in detail since we have done so in our survey of the books of Kings. It will, however, be of interest to consider the peculiar slant of the Chronicler where it is possible to detect it because that slant will provide insight into the special theology of the book. The first example comes from the reign of Abijah, son of Rehoboam, of whom the Deuteronomistic history says virtually nothing positive. Chronicles, on the other hand, relates Abijah's attempts to use his good offices as a means of enticing Jeroboam and the Northern Kingdom to reenter the covenant fold of Judah (2 Chron. 13:4–12). He reminded them that God had made an irrevocable choice of David to be king and to resist David was to resist the kingdom of God himself (vv. 5, 8). God was with Judah, he said, and to fight against Judah was to fight against the Lord as well (v. 12). While it is possible to look at this cynically as arrogant hubris, it happens that

---

[17] V. Philips Long, *The Art of Biblical History* (Grand Rapids: Zondervan, 1994), 82–86; Long, "Narrative and History: Stories about the Past," *A Biblical History of Israel,* ed. Iain Provan, V. Philips Long, and Tremper Longman III (Louisville: Westminster John Knox, 2003), 75–97; with reference to the question of Solomon, cf. 93–96.

Abijah was more the theologian than even he may have realized, for he correctly connected the Davidic kingdom with the heavenly kingdom of God.

The book of Kings dispenses with the tenure of King Asa in a mere 15 verses (1 Kings 15:9–24), concentrating almost entirely on political and military affairs. Chronicles covers much the same ground (2 Chron. 14:2–15) but much more besides, particularly in the area of cultic reform (15:1–18). Approached by Azariah the prophet, who spoke to him of the sorry fate of the neighboring kingdom Israel during the days they had forsaken the Lord, Asa undertook major reform which attracted new settlers from as far away as Ephraim and Manasseh "when they saw that the LORD his God was with him" (v. 9). The high point was the renewal of covenant vows to the LORD "with all their mind and all their heart" (v. 12), a commitment clearly to the Shema and the commandments associated with it.[18] The result of the reformation was universal joy and "rest on every side" (v. 15).

The reign of Jehoshaphat, though sullied by hints of disobedience in his later years in even the Chronicles account (2 Chron. 17:3), was marked primarily by covenant loyalty. Early on he sent missionaries into various parts of the kingdom, teachers who instructed the populace in "the book of the LORD's instruction" (v. 9). For this and other good works, the Lord blessed Jehoshaphat, so much so that surrounding nations feared him and, more important, feared the Lord (vv. 10–11). In this way the king fulfilled the commission of the Lord to Israel that they should be a means of attracting the nations to him (cf. Deut. 4:5–8). As for Kings Jehoram and Ahaziah, even Chronicles cannot ignore their moral and spiritual bankruptcy (2 Chron. 21:4–22:9), but the reason given in each case was their familial connection to the royal family of Israel. It seems that the historian wanted to highlight the differences between the house of David and the Northern Kingdom by attributing the wickedness of these two Davidic rulers to the baleful influence of the neighboring kingdom.

We turn now to the time of King Uzziah whose reign of fifty-two years occupies but seven verses in Kings (2 Kings 15:1–7) and not much more in Chronicles (2 Chron. 26:1–23). In his later years he was struck with leprosy and forced to live in quarantine for reasons unstated in Kings

---

[18] Selman, *2 Chronicles,* 394.

but brought to light in Chronicles and for obvious reasons. We have already had occasion to note Uzziah's priestly transgression of offering incense in the temple, a rite reserved for only the Aaronic priesthood. The Chronicler's intense interest in the temple and cultus provides a ready explanation for his mention of this negative episode in the life of a king whom, one supposes, he would otherwise have left uncondemned.

The book of Kings, generally careful to praise King Hezekiah for his godly character and accomplishments, omits the narrative of his massive Passover celebration, a matter redressed at length by the Chronicler (2 Chron. 30:1–27). The setting of the pericope reflects both the ruinous spiritual condition of Judah in the wake of the evil reigns of Hezekiah's predecessors Jotham and Ahaz and the sense of revival and reformation engendered by his thoroughgoing consecration to the will of God. Things were at such a pass that there were not enough priests to attend to the Passover sacrifices, nor had the people sufficient time to assemble by the first month of the year when the Passover was to be observed. Clearly with the Lord's sanction (unexpressed but implicit), the king scheduled this important and long-neglected festival for the second month, communicating his desire in a letter widely circulated even in Israel. His appeal to his Israelite kinsmen who had escaped Assyrian exile was to return to Jerusalem and to the Lord lest they suffer the same fate as their countrymen who had already been carried off. At the heart of his exhortation is the invitation to "come to His sanctuary that [the LORD] has consecrated forever" (v. 8). Only there may he be found in residence among his people.

The celebration of this Passover most certainly was designed by Hezekiah to emulate the Lord's gracious and glorious deliverance of his people from Egyptian bondage.[19] They found themselves again in bondage, not to a foreign master but to a spirit of unbelief and disobedience. Their shedding of the blood of the Passover lamb as an act of faith thus resulted in an outbreak of great joy in Jerusalem for there was a consciousness of national cleansing and salvation (vv. 25–27). The genuineness of the reformation was manifested not only in joy but also in the destruction and removal of all the vestiges of paganism introduced by earlier rulers (2 Chron. 31:1). This harks back to the principle enunciated in the first

[19] Dillard, *2 Chronicles,* 245.

two commandments to the effect that a proper recognition of the Lord as the one and only God precludes the possibility of other gods to say nothing of their worship.

After the long period of time embraced by the reigns of the apostate kings Manasseh and Amon, Judah was sorely in need of reformation once again. This time it was under the aegis of King Josiah who, in his eighth year, "began to seek the God of his ancestor David" and in his twelfth year set about to destroy all the high places and other pagan cultic structures (2 Chron. 34:3–7). Again, the impulse was the covenant law of the Decalogue, in particular the first two commandments. This we have come to see as a recurring pattern: What the Lord demands of his people is the confession that only he is God and that there can be no iconic representations of him or of any other being. Covenant renewal and reformation is predicated on this proposition and must inevitably result in the extermination of pagan pretenders.

The Chronicles account of the reign of Josiah and his reformation does not differ materially from that in Kings, so there is no need here to repeat the details. However, as in the case with Hezekiah, the narrator here expatiated on the celebration of a massive Passover, a matter to which Kings gives only summary mention (2 Kings 23:21–23). Of special interest is Josiah's command to install the ark of the covenant in the temple again and to desist from carrying it about (2 Chron. 35:3). This suggests either that the ark had been removed from the temple in the days of Manasseh or Amon or, more likely, that Josiah himself had ordered its removal and subsequent return as a ceremonial reenactment of its original installation in the most holy place by Solomon.[20] The symbolism of this would be powerful, indeed. The Lord had left the holy precincts in the dark days of Judah's apostasy but had now returned in the wake of covenant renewal and reformation. The prophet Ezekiel also recorded the departure of the Lord from the temple at a later time but said nothing of his return (Ezek. 11:22–24).

The Chronicler's interest in the Passover, both here and in connection with Hezekiah's reforms, is best explained by its association with the exodus deliverance which paved the way for Israel's covenant relationship with the Lord at Mount Sinai. It symbolized for him a new exodus, not

[20] Selman, *2 Chronicles,* 538.

an eschatological one such as Isaiah envisioned perhaps but one that was possible, indeed necessary, in Israel's historical existence. Hezekiah's Passover came right on the heels of the corrupt years of his royal predecessors Jotham and Ahaz, and that of Josiah followed the equally paganized reigns of Manasseh and Amon. What was needed in each case was a fresh start, a new beginning of the nation as both a redeemed community and one willing and able to submit once more to the covenant claims and duties made available by a forgiving and gracious God.

The narrative of Chronicles ends, as does Kings, on a note of destruction and despair. Both books alike relate the Babylonian conquest of Judah and the ruin of Jerusalem and the holy temple. But each also offers an addendum of hope. The Deuteronomistic history ties that hope to the survival of the last of the Davidic kings, Jehoiachin, who, though having been taken captive, was at last released and treated by the Babylonians with tender care (2 Kings 25:27–30). The king's release portended the eventual release of the community as a whole at a time and under the circumstances of God's own choosing. The Chronicler, living a century or more later, cited the promise of the prophet Jeremiah that the exile would last for seventy years (cf. Jer. 25:11–12; 29:10–14) at which time the Persian King Cyrus would (and from his vantage point, did already) issue a decree allowing the return only dimly hinted at before. Thus both witnesses attest to the faithfulness of the Lord in regathering his people to the land, enabling them to pick up again the mantle of covenant privilege and responsibility in service to the kingdom of the Lord.

The Book of Ezra-Nehemiah

Ezra-Nehemiah picks up where Chronicles leaves off, quoting more extensively the decree of Cyrus which constitutes the closing of Chronicles (Ezra 1:2–4). Generally speaking, the book of Ezra is preoccupied with the religious life of the restored community whereas Nehemiah gives fuller attention to the political and physical aspects, though clearly in terms of a theocratic community these emphases are not to be viewed as discrete categories.[21] Both leaders were concerned about the well-being

[21] William J. Dumbrell, "The Theological Intention of Ezra-Nehemiah," *RThR* 45 (1986): 65–72; F. C. Fensham, "Some Theological and Religious Aspects in Ezra and Nehemiah," *JNSL* 11 (1983): 59–68.

of the state as a whole and the accomplishments of both provide the raw material from which a theology of the postexilic period can be largely developed.

Ezra was a priest, and therefore matters of a cultic nature were dear to his heart. He recounted the history of temple construction that had commenced prior to his own time by eighty years or so and then described the difficult days of his own leadership when opposition from without and spiritual stagnation from within threatened to abort the existence of the community that had been redeemed from exile to continue on with the ancient covenant traditions. He was not long in getting to his central concern as his quotation of the Cyrus decree makes clear. That decree begins with Cyrus's confession that the Lord God of heaven, who had given him all the kingdoms of the earth as a fiefdom, had commanded him to build a temple in Jerusalem, a work to be undertaken by the Jews whom he would permit to return home from exile (Ezra 1:2).[22] Three times the word *temple* occurs in this brief text; and in the narrative that follows in which the decree is carried out, there are two more allusions to it (vv. 5, 7). In addition to the building itself, Ezra provides detailed lists of its furnishings (vv. 9–11) and sacred personnel (Ezra 2:36–58, 61–63), each, of course, being essential to the reestablishment of the cultus.

In his review of the history of the rebuilding of the temple, which began in 538 BC, Ezra described the erection of the great bronze altar as the first order of the day (Ezra 3:1–6). It was done "as it is written in the law of Moses the man of God" and in conjunction with the Feast of Tabernacles, which was celebrated "as prescribed [in the law]" (vv. 2, 4). Ezra clearly viewed what was done by his priestly predecessor Jeshua as a continuation of the Mosaic covenant tradition. And we should recall as well that the choice to erect the altar coincident with the Feast of Tabernacles implies that the whole series of events was linked to covenant renewal (cf. Deut. 31:10). As for the temple proper, the twenty years between the laying of its foundations and its completion were marked by opposition from surrounding enemies (Ezra 4:1–24) as well as a creeping lethargy within the Jewish community itself, largely because

[22] For the extrabiblical version of this decree, see William W. Hallo and K. Lawson Younger Jr., *The Context of Scripture,* vol. 2 (Leiden: Brill, 2000), 314–15.

of the temple's meager dimensions compared to the glorious Solomonic temple, which some of them remembered (Ezra 3:12; cf. Hag. 2:3).

The various parties that sought to prevent the rebuilding of the Jewish community sent a series of letters to the Persian kings seeking their interdiction. One in particular, that by Tattenai, governor of the entire Trans-Euphrates province of which Judea was a part, is of interest because of the response it elicited from King Darius (Ezra 6:3–12). In it the Persian ruler refers to the original decree of Cyrus that not only permitted the rebuilding of the Jewish temple but also provided the financial wherewithal to make it possible. Darius reinforced this precedent by ordering the Jews' enemies to desist from their hostilities and to allow "the governor and elders of the Jews [to] rebuild this house of God on its original site" (v. 7). Even allowing for the ecumenical outlook of the Persian monarchy, this remarkable reference to the temple as the "house of God" points to the centrality of temple ideology in the thinking of both the Jewish leaders and the Persian king. The latter, moreover, refers to the LORD as "the God of heaven" and the one "who caused His name to dwell" in the Jerusalem temple (vv. 10, 12).

Ezra's passion for the temple and its services was evident in his own day, many years after the previously described events. Armed with a letter of conveyance by King Artaxerxes II, Ezra returned to Jerusalem set on establishing temple worship according to Torah (Ezra 7:10). The king had authorized him to check on the state of the Jewish community as to its understanding of and adherence to the Law and provided him with the financial assets necessary to the functioning of the temple and its ministries (vv. 15–17). Artaxerxes even went so far as to command Ezra to "deliver to the God of Jerusalem all the articles given to you for the service of the house of your God" (v. 19), thus giving tacit recognition to the notion that the LORD lived among his people in the temple and that all tribute and offerings belonged to him alone. Finally, he enjoined Ezra to teach "the laws of your God" to any of the populace who did not know them (v. 25) and to put to death any who would not obey them (v. 26).

Skeptical scholarship refuses to take the texts of the letters of these pagan kings at face value, arguing that they are words put into their mouths (or onto their parchments) by Jewish apologists eager to defend their claim to the land and the reconstruction of their city and its temple.[23] To this date no extrabiblical evidence exists to corroborate the biblical testimony, but that by itself should cast no doubt as to the authenticity of the biblical record. Moreover, and this is important, the effusive praise of Israel's God and the desire to please him by assisting his people is not without self-interest. The letter of Darius betrays his desire for the Jews to pray God's blessing on him for his largess toward them (Ezra 6:10) and Artaxerxes's letter to Ezra openly speaks of his fear that if the God of the Jews is offended, he and his kingdom will be in jeopardy (Ezra 7:23). The bottom line is that the Lord is sovereign over all and uses even the heathen to bless his people and bring glory to his name (vv. 27–28).

Some fourteen years into Ezra's ministry in Jerusalem, Nehemiah, an official high in the Persian court, arrived there and was appointed governor over Judea, a part of the Persian province known as Eber Nahari (across the Euphrates River). Whereas Ezra the priest naturally had the reestablishment of Jewish religious life uppermost in his mind, Nehemiah turned his energies to physical reconstruction though he, too, was not indifferent to matters of the spirit. As for the Persian king whom Nehemiah served, Artaxerxes II, the interest in Israel's God and cultus that he demonstrated to Ezra (Ezra 7:12–26) continued throughout the recorded thirteen-year governorship of Nehemiah. Nehemiah recounts in his journal (an apt description of his book) that God had moved the Persian ruler to allow him to take a leave of absence to return to his homeland (Neh. 2:8) and had impressed him to provide Nehemiah with safe conduct and building materials along the way (vv. 7–9). The point thus far is clear: the God of heaven (a favorite epithet in the postexilic period; cf. Ezra 1:2; 6:9; 7:12; Neh. 1:4; 2:4, 20; Dan. 2:18, 37, 44; 5:23) is sovereign not just over his covenant people but over the monarchs and empires of the whole world.

In spite of intense opposition, Nehemiah was able to build a defensive wall around Jerusalem for, as he puts it, "the gracious hand of my God had been on me" (Neh. 2:18; cf. v. 8). He then repopulated the city and took special care to see to it that the priests, Levites, and other sacred

---

[23] Thus, for example, D. J. Clines, *Ezra, Nehemiah, Esther,* NCBC (Grand Rapids: Eerdmans, 1984), 102. Clines proposes that "the decree was drafted by a Jewish official at the Persian court, possibly even by Ezra himself." For a response to this proposal, see H. G. M. Williamson, *Ezra, Nehemiah,* WBC 16 (Waco, Tex.: Word, 1985), 82.

personnel were duly installed in and about the temple, exercising his prerogative as leader of the community to preclude disqualified priests from participating in its ministry (Neh. 7:1–3, 64–65). The theological high point of the book is the assembly by Ezra and Nehemiah of all the people on the first day of the seventh month (Neh. 8:1). The purpose of the gathering, as the date already intimates, was to read "the book of the law of Moses" preparatory to covenant renewal.[24] All day long Ezra read (thus presupposing the entire Torah) with a cadre of interpreters both translating (from Hebrew into Aramaic) and explaining the text (vv. 2–4). When he finished, the people *en masse* fell on their faces in worship, overcome with both sorrow and joy (vv. 5–12). The sorrow was for the long history of covenant disobedience they and their forefathers had displayed and the joy issued from a sense of forgiveness and new opportunities that lay ahead. The Festival of Tabernacles next ensued, the occasion for covenant renewal as Torah itself prescribed (Deut. 31:9–13). The historian notes that there had been no Festival of Tabernacles like it since the days of Joshua a millennium before (v. 17).

The climax of the ceremony was the reading again of covenant texts—most likely at least Deuteronomy (Neh. 9:3)—followed by a prayer embodying the principal elements of a covenant document (vv. 5–37). This was led by the Levites, who, we should recall, also led the twelve tribes in covenant affirmation at the mountains Gerizim and Ebal in the days of the Conquest (Deut. 27:1–14; Josh. 8:30–35). The highlights of the prayer are (1) a recognition of the Lord as the only God and Creator (vv. 5–6) who (2) chose Abraham and made a covenant with him (vv. 7–8), one that (3) resulted in the deliverance of his descendants from Egyptian bondage (vv. 9–12) into (4) a covenant relationship at Sinai (vv. 13–15). The prayer goes on to catalog the history of Israel's disobedience from the earliest times (vv. 16–25), through the days of the judges (vv. 26–28), and on through the exile of both kingdoms (vv. 29–31). It closes with an appeal to the Lord's covenant love (His *ḥesed)* that he might have mercy on them (v. 32) despite their disobedience and the flaunting of his grace (vv. 33–35). They were in a condition of great distress and could do nothing but leave themselves in his hands (vv. 36–37).

---

[24] Williamson, *Ezra, Nehemiah,* 287.

What they wanted the Lord to do is not explicit but nonetheless most obvious. They wanted him to restore them to covenant favor and to that end pledged themselves to covenant fidelity (Neh. 9:38–10:39). They made a formal commitment, swearing themselves to obedience, putting it in writing, and certifying it by the affixing of the seals of both secular and religious leaders (9:38). What they promised in detail is a concatenation of stipulations occurring in various parts of the Torah, no doubt only examples of their intention to keep it fully (10:28–29). They would no longer intermarry with the heathen (v. 30; but cf. Neh. 13:23–27); they would observe the Sabbath (v. 31; cf. 13:15–22); they would pay the temple taxes (v. 32) and otherwise provide for its services (vv. 33–34); they would faithfully present their firstfruits offerings (vv. 35–36; cf. 13:12–13); and they would provide for the Levites (vv. 37–39); cf. 13:10–13). All these things they had not done; but now, they swore, they would do better. Their summation boils down to the central theme of Ezra-Nehemiah: "We will not neglect the house of our God" (Neh. 10:39). To this Nehemiah added his own testimony when all had been done: "I purified [the priests and the Levites] from everything foreign and assigned specific duties to each" (Neh. 13:30). Like David before him, Nehemiah's burden, in the final analysis, was for the proper functioning of the cultus as the means of glorifying God in service and worship.

The Book of Esther

The book of Esther, technically a part of the Writings, the third great section of the Hebrew canon, is by genre a work of history and thus will be treated as a part of the historical books that have occupied us in this section of our work.[25] Its setting is the royal court of Persia in the early fifth century BC, the king at the time being Xerxes, known in the Hebrew transliteration of Esther as Ahasuerus. The major leitmotif is the peril of the Jewish community in the Persian Empire because of a conspiracy hatched by an anti-Semitic element that persuaded the king of certain nefarious activities by the Jews. Were it not for the good offices of Queen Esther, a Jewess who had become the favorite wife of the king, the plot

---

[25] Forrest S. Weiland, "Historicity, Genre, and Narrative Design in the Book of Esther," *BSac* 159 (2002): 151–65.

would have succeeded and the Jewish population may well have been decimated. Instead, the Jews were authorized to turn on their enemies and with the backing of Xerxes were able to save themselves as well as destroy those who hated them.

It is well-known that the name of God does not occur in the book of Esther, but it is equally clear that the author intends to show at every point that the providential hand of a sovereign God was at work to deliver his exiled people. In fact, it is safe to say that the theology of the book finds its orientation around the idea that the Lord is the God of all the nations and that he works out his purposes among them for their own ultimate good and for the blessing of his chosen people Israel. A secondary purpose of the book is to explain the provenience of the Festival of Purim, a festival first celebrated on the occasion of the Jews' miraculous deliverance from annihilation (Esth. 9:18–28).[26]

Chronologically, the setting of Esther is somewhat earlier than that of Ezra-Nehemiah, but its concern to show that the God of the Jews is the God of the whole world is a concern shared by those books as well. Politically and militarily speaking, Persia was a superpower of the time; and its rulers viewed themselves as invincible potentates living in the lap of opulent luxury. The author of Esther describes Xerxes on one occasion as setting aside a period of six months in which "he displayed the glorious wealth of his kingdom and the magnificent splendor of his greatness," capped off by a seven-day drunken orgy to which his every appetite was pandered (Esth. 1:4–8). The purpose here is clearly to show the heights (or depths) to which human power could rise and by doing so to show by contrast how much greater is the power of Israel's God. That power is evident throughout the book—from the selection of Esther to be queen; the "accidental" discovery by Mordecai, Esther's cousin, of a plot against the king; the elevation of Mordecai to prominence in the court; the successful intervention of Esther on behalf of her fellow Jews; to the triumph of the Jews over their enemies. All of this attests to the hand of a power greater than Xerxes and his minions, that of Israel's God who asserts his sovereignty in history even when and where his name is neither known nor praised.

---

[26] Jon D. Levenson, *Esther* (Louisville: Westminster John Knox, 1997), 18–23.

PART FOUR

THE PROPHETS AND THE KINGDOM

Chapter Fifteen

The Theology of the Eighth-Century Canonical Prophets

At the outset it is important to define the terms used here and to establish the method to be followed in this section. We have already addressed the phenomenon of prophetism in Old Testament Israel against its ancient Near Eastern background but have left unsaid much of anything about the early, preliterary prophets as opposed to those whom we now describe as canonical. By *preliterary* we do not mean illiterate, of course, but only that little of the writings of these prophets is extant in the Old Testament to say nothing of anywhere else—Moses, and perhaps Samuel,[1] being the notable exceptions. The canonical prophets are thus those whose works became recognized early on as sacred Scripture and were therefore incorporated into the gradually expanding corpus of texts regarded as divine revelation. They begin with Amos in the mid-eighth century and end most likely with Malachi in the early fifth century, altogether consisting of four major prophets (including Daniel) and twelve minor prophets.

[1] Talmudic tradition ascribes Judges, Ruth, and Samuel to the prophet Samuel, though clearly not any part of the latter beyond the account of his own death (1 Sam. 25:1). See *Baba Bathra* 14b.

In line with our frequently reiterated method, we shall attempt to blend both a canonical and a chronological approach in an attempt to be sensitive to the impetus lying behind the present (Hebrew) canonical order as well as to the principle of progressive revelation of which, one would think, the prophets themselves were consciously aware.[2] That is, later prophets were in possession of the works of their predecessors and used them, even if not explicitly, as a matrix within which they formulated their own contributions to the emerging collection of inspired works. Thus, we shall commence with Amos, Hosea, and Jonah before engaging Isaiah even though this obviously runs counter to the order of the canon.

We have noted that the primary functions of the Old Testament prophets to this point were to intercede between God and mankind (Gen. 20:7); to serve as spokesmen for the Lord (Num. 12:6–8); to provide counsel or direction (1 Sam. 9:6–9); to confront evil, whether from pagan sources (1 Kings 18) or even that of Israel's kings (2 Sam. 12:1–12); and to speak of things future (Deut. 18:21–22; 2 Sam. 7:4–16). By the time of the rise of canonical prophetism, the prophetic ministry became associated with two basic thrusts: forthtelling and foretelling. The former speaks of ministry and message directed primarily to an audience contemporary to the prophet himself, whereas the latter, while not neglectful of the present, looks forward to the unfolding of future events whether these events threaten judgment or promise salvation and blessing. In any case, the true prophet of God was recognized as such because he stood independent of the religious and political establishments—indeed, in opposition to them if need be—and proclaimed the word of the Lord with authority, conviction, and accuracy of prediction.[3]

The messages of the canonical prophets were invariably in line with Torah. It was the basis of their authority and the fountainhead of their theological reflection. The themes of their writings are therefore Torah themes; and though, indeed, the prophets advanced beyond the substance of the Mosaic revelation, they never contradicted it. Rather, they built upon it, developing its theological ideas with increasingly mature and elaborate insight as the Spirit gave them direction. With this in view, our

---

[2] Walter C. Kaiser Jr. speaks of "an inner center or plan to which each writer consciously contributed." See his *Toward an Old Testament Theology* (Grand Rapids: Zondervan, 1978), 11.

[3] Patrick D. Miller, "The Prophetic Critique of Kings," *Israelite Religion and Biblical Theology,* JSOT Supp. Series 267 (Sheffield: Sheffield Academic Press, 2000), 526–47.

approach in each case will be to isolate those central Torah teachings picked up and elaborated in the prophetic compositions, being mindful, of course, of secondary or subsidiary matters of interest to them. These revolve around the overall theological construct for which we have argued in this work from the beginning, namely, that the purpose of the Old Testament is to reveal God as the Creator and Sovereign of the universe who created mankind as his image and viceroy to rule on his behalf over all things. That rule continues in history, though hobbled and hindered by sin and the fall, and will be consummated in the eschaton as God, by his grace, provides forgiveness and restoration through One chosen in David's royal line to accomplish in his perfection what mankind has failed to achieve. This is the burden of the prophets, a burden that informs the sum and substance of their literary work.

The Prophet Amos

Amos, a native of Tekoa, deep in the territory of Judah, was commissioned by the Lord to minister in the rival kingdom of Israel during the reigns of kings Uzziah of Judah and Jeroboam II of Israel, roughly in the mid-eighth century BC. Though never called a prophet in his book—indeed, disclaiming such a title (Amos 7:14)—Amos bore prophetic credentials and ministered (though only on one recorded occasion) in the tradition and spirit of the great prophets.[4]

He turned first to address the surrounding nations, beginning with those least related by kinship to Israel (Damascus, Amos 1:3–5; Philistia, 1:6–8; Tyre, 1:9–10), then those with roots common with Israel (Edom, 1:11–12; Ammon, 1:13–15; Moab, 2:1–3), and finally to Judah, his own kingdom (2:4–5), and Israel, the special focus of his ministry (2:6–16).[5] He immediately asserted the sovereignty of the Lord who "roars from Zion and raises His voice from Jerusalem" (1:2) and argued that it was in terms of that sovereignty that all the nations must be evaluated. Damascus, because of its mistreatment of Gilead, would go into exile and its king would be destroyed (1:3–5). The Philistines, too, would suffer God's

---

[4] For the theology of the prophet, see Gary V. Smith, *Amos: A Commentary* (Grand Rapids: Zondervan, 1989), 9–14.

[5] Andrew Steinmann, "The Order of Amos's Oracles against the Nations 1:3–2:16," *JBL* 111 (1992): 683–89.

judgment and, for the same reason, the abuse of God's chosen people. And their kings also would perish (1:6–8). The same was true of Tyre, which had broken faith with Israel (1:9–10).

As for Edom (descendants of Esau), it would be ravaged because "he [Edom] pursued his brother [Israel = Jacob] with the sword," a savage betrayal of a kinsman (1:11–12). Ammon, related to Israel through Lot, was no better than Damascus, having dealt with Gilead in the same manner and with the same predicted judgment—"their king and his princes will go into exile together" (v. 15). Moab's sins were also grievous and would result in the destruction of her king and his officials as well (2:1–3). Common to these was the mistreatment of the Lord's own people by the nations and the repudiation and destruction of their rulers. These nations typified the spirit of those who curse the seed of Abraham and thus fall under the curse of the Lord (Gen. 12:3), and their kings reflected the hubris of human rulers who dare to arrogate to themselves the honor and glory that belong to God alone.

The situation of the covenant nation(s) Judah and Israel was, of course, quite different since they were the seed of Abraham. Their mission was to be a kingdom of priests and a holy nation thereby representing the Lord among the nations and attracting them to him for redemption and restoration of fellowship. Theirs was not so much the sin of contending against the sovereignty of God—except in individual and national disobedience—as it was in forsaking him and worshipping other gods in his place. In other words, it was a matter of covenant violation and precisely at its foundational level—disobedience of the first two commandments and the Shema. Speaking of Judah, Amos zeroed in precisely at this point:

> I [the LORD] will not relent from punishing Judah
> for three crimes, even four,
> because they have rejected the law *[tōrâ]* of the LORD
> and have not kept His statutes *[ḥuqqîm]*.
> The lies that their ancestors followed
> have led them astray.
> Therefore, I will send fire against Judah,
> and it will consume the citadels of Jerusalem.
> (Amos 2:4–5)

Israel, if anything, was in even worse straits. Their flagrant disregard of covenant requirements was identified by Amos first as social injustice (Amos 2:6–8; 5:11–13; 8:4–6) and then as a dalliance with foreign cults, even to the extent of engaging in idolatry (3:14–15; 4:4–5; 5:5–6, 21–27; 7:9). These two sins constituted disobedience of the two great pillars of covenant confession: to love the Lord with all one's heart, soul, and strength and the neighbor as one's self. Israel's failure in these respects was all the more heinous—and inexcusable—because, as Amos reminded them, "I have known only you out of all the clans of the earth" (3:2). With covenant privilege comes covenant responsibility, unfaithfulness to which invites swift and certain judgment (3:2b). And judgment was imminent, a fact the Lord disclosed to his prophets (3:7). An enemy was on the horizon who would wreak destruction in the land, including in his scope the ruin of Jeroboam I's Bethel shrine where Israel first defected from the exclusive worship of the Lord (3:14; cf. 4:4; 5:5–6) and where Amos was at that moment delivering his message of woe (7:10–13).

The enemy was Assyria, which by then had risen to a position of world supremacy and had already made threatening moves against the west. Within a generation of Amos's day, Samaria would fall; and much of the Israelite population would be carried off into exile (Amos 3:12; 4:1–3; 5:3, 27; 6:7, 14; 7:11, 17; 8:1–3; 9:1–10). But that was only a portent of what would happen in the more distant future, in 'the Day of the LORD' (5:18–20). This phrase, first occurring here in the prophets, connotes judgment for sinners (as here) but also salvation for the righteous, nearly always in eschatological contexts.[6] Amos refers to "that day" again in 8:3–14, this time in terms of lamentation, cosmic upheavals, and famine, especially for the word of God (v. 12). But he also sees the day as one of restoration of Israel, David's fallen tent, when the LORD "will repair its gaps, restore its ruins, and rebuild it as in the days of old" (9:11). Then God's people will return from exile and work the soil that will be so productive that the plowman will overtake the sower of seed (vv. 13–14). And, the Lord says, "I will plant them [Israel] on their land, and they will never again be uprooted from the land I have given them" (v. 15). Subsequent history, in addition to the eschatological clues in the text, makes clear that this day yet lies in the future.

---

[6] M. Saebø, יוֹם, *TDOT* 6:30–31.

The remedy for Israel's ills lay in repentance, in a positive response to the Lord who says, "Seek Me and live" (Amos 5:4; cf. v. 6). Another way of putting it is to "seek good and not evil so that you may live" (v. 14). To seek good is to become covenant compliant, to know and do the will of God without hypocrisy.[7] The people had been religious enough but in only a *pro forma* way, so much so that the Lord said he hated their festivals, assemblies, and sacrifices (Amos 5:21–23). What he wanted was not a religious charade but the display of authentic justice and righteousness (v. 24). Only then would the glorious promises of the restoration of the house of David become a reality.

The Prophet Hosea

Hosea, a contemporary of Amos, directed his message exclusively toward Israel—a message of unremitting accusation, condemnation, and warning—but one also filled with a strong sense of divine pathos, love, and forgiveness. Employing the imagery of marriage to communicate the Lord's covenant relationship with Israel, Hosea described his own unhappy marriage to a wife who became a prostitute and likened his situation to Israel's unfaithfulness in abandoning the Lord for other gods.[8] By this analogy he, like Amos, arrived at the heart of the real issue: Israel had spurned the Lord and embraced other gods, violating the foundational premise on which the covenant was based, namely, the first two commandments. As the Lord himself declared, "She [Israel] does not recognize that it is I who gave her the grain, the new wine, and the oil. I lavished silver and gold on her, which they used for Baal" (Hos. 2:8).

Prophets, priests, and people alike were guilty. There was nothing but moral chaos and an ignorance of the Lord in the land (4:1–9), a condition both derived from and contributing to the pursuit of other gods. High places with all their sexual immoralities abounded (vv. 13–14), and Israel showed no inclination to repent (v. 17). Though their idols were man-made and therefore powerless, Israel tenaciously clung to them

[7] Francis I. Andersen and David Noel Freedman, *Amos,* AB 24A (New York: Doubleday, 1989), 508.

[8] F. C. Fensham, "The Marriage Metaphor in Hosea for the Covenant Relationship between the Lord and His People (Hos. 1:2–9)," *JNSL* 12 (1984): 71–78.

(8:4–6; 10:5–8; 11:2; 12:11; 13:1–3) and even converted what used to be legitimate places and modes of worship into something displeasing to the Lord (8:11–13).

The root of the problem, as we have suggested, was covenant violation, a point the Lord drove home with the observation that "they [i.e., Israel], like Adam, have violated the covenant" (6:7a). This comparison underscores both the seriousness of their sin and also the fact that there was a certain continuum between the Sinai covenant and the creation mandate.[9] For Israel to break covenant was to endanger and perhaps destroy her capacity to serve as the Lord's channel of redemption by which he intends to restore mankind to its pristine position as God's image. The prophet reiterated the charge of covenant fracture in Hosea 8:1–4, this time attributing it to Israel's rejection of the Lord and his substitution by other gods. Whenever covenant disobedience occurred, it invariably was linked to the rejection of the Lord as the only God and his replacement by other deities physically represented by images and idols.

Such infidelity demanded punishment; and in keeping with the marriage metaphor of the prophet, the punishment most appropriate was divorce (Hos. 2:2), represented in the narrative as Israel's exile from the land (5:14–15; 8:7–10; 9:3–4; 11:5–7). But God's love overrode his judgment; and just as Hosea ransomed his adulterous wife and brought her back to himself (Hos. 3:1–3), so the Lord would honor his covenant commitments (his "marriage" vows) and restore his chosen people to the land (1:7, 10–11). In a second exodus he would bring them through the desert in that eschatological day of salvation (2:14–15). Israel would then no longer refer to the Lord as master *(baʿal)* but as husband *(ʾîš),* emphasizing the intimacy of the covenant relationship (2:16). He would renew his covenant with them, betrothing them to himself in righteousness *(ṣedeq),* justice *(mišpāṭ),* love *(ḥesed),* compassion *(raḥămîm),* and faithfulness *(ʾĕmûnâ),* all terms rich in covenant overtones (2:19–20).

Switching the imagery, the prophet compared Israel's return to the Lord and to the land as a virtual resurrection from the dead (6:1–2).

---

[9] Though most scholars identify Adam as a place name (Edh Damiyeh), Pusey makes a strong case for the personal name. E. B. Pusey, *The Minor Prophets,* vol. 1 (Grand Rapids: Baker, 1950, 1860), 68.

Though he will have destroyed them, he will bring them back just as he brought them out of Egypt where, as his "child" and "son," they were helpless to extricate themselves from oppressive bondage (11:1). That time they had spurned his love and care (vv. 2–4) as they continued to do and would do in days to come, but God's compassion *(niḥûmîm)* would be so powerful that it would overcome any thoughts of eternal retribution that the Lord might have and he would redeem them from their deathly exile (11:8–11). Even in the midst of oracles of doom and judgment (13:1–13, 15–16), the Lord made the remarkable promise, "I will ransom them from the power of Sheol. I will redeem them from death" (v. 14a). Like Ezekiel's dry bones that will come to life again as the Spirit of God quickens them, so dead Israel will rise out of dispersion and return to the Lord and the land he has granted them forever (14:4–8).

Hosea's comparative lack of interest in the nations of the world must be understood in light of his concern for Israel's sinful state, for unless and until his own people repented, turned to the Lord in covenant renewal, and resumed their role as his priestly, mediatorial kingdom, there was no hope for the nations anyway. Warnings of judgment on other nations would ring rather hollow when God's own chosen people lived in such adulterous infidelity. And promises of their redemption seemed rather far-fetched when Israel, the nation elected to proclaim the redemptive message, itself needed forgiveness and restoration to fellowship.

The Prophet Jonah

Jonah ministered in the days of King Jeroboam II of Israel, a fact documented in 2 Kings 14:25. Despite the skepticism of modern criticism as to his actual historical existence—at least as portrayed in the book bearing his name—all we can know of him and his times squares with the account in the canonical book.[10] The problem in many minds, of course, issues from the fact that the narrative is peppered with miraculous events from one end to the other and since, to these same minds, miracle is the stuff of legend and not reality, the account as we have it must be construed as legend, parable, parody, or some other literary genre

[10] C. Hassell Bullock, *An Introduction to the Old Testament Prophetic Books* (Chicago: Moody, 1986), 51.

short of actual historiography.[11] While we contest those views, there is no time or need to offer rejoinders here, for the theology of the book is patently clear no matter how one understands its literary form or the historicity of its events. The book is unique in the fact that it is almost in its entirety a biographical sketch of the prophet himself, his only recorded prophetic message being "In 40 days Nineveh will be overthrown!" (Jon. 3:4). Moreover, it is among only a couple of other books (Nahum and Obadiah) devoted to a single foreign nation, in Jonah's case the Assyrians of Nineveh.

The call of Jonah to go to Nineveh "and preach against it, because their wickedness has confronted Me" (Jon. 1:2; cf. Gen. 18:21) demonstrates at the outset the Lord's intense interest in the nations of the world. This is not surprising in that the Abrahamic covenant itself centers on the idea that in Abraham's seed (i.e., Israel) all the nations of the earth would be blessed. How fitting, then, that a prophet of Israel should bear the message of judgment—and yet of grace—to the greatest nation of the world of the eighth century. At the same time the mission strategy is somewhat different from the normal Old Testament pattern inasmuch as Israel was essentially to be a magnet to which the peoples would be attracted and thus attracted to Israel's God. In Jonah's case the command was to go, anticipating perhaps the New Testament centrifugal model of the church reaching out to the ends of the earth with the gospel message (Matt. 28:19–20; cf. Acts 1:8).

Even before Jonah reached Nineveh, the issue of Israel's God and the gods of the nations came to the fore. In his attempt to flee from the Lord and his call, Jonah boarded a ship heading in the opposite direction. A storm arose, and the ship was in danger of sinking so the sailors "each cried out to his god" (Jon. 1:5). When this failed to still the storm, the sailors cast lots and discovered that Jonah was responsible for their bad fortune, eliciting from him the reluctant testimony, "I am a Hebrew. I worship Yahweh, the God of the heavens, who made the sea and the dry land" (v. 9). The prophet did not limit his understanding of the Lord to be only the God of Israel, but he broadened the horizons to make plain

[11] For a survey of these various options, see Douglas Stuart, *Hosea—Jonah,* WBC 31 (Waco, Tex.: Word, 1987), 435–37; Ernst R. Wendland, "Text Analysis and the Genre of Jonah (Part 1)," *JETS* 39 (1996): 191–206; "Text Analysis and the Genre of Jonah (Part 2)," *JETS* 39 (1996): 373–95.

to these pagan mariners that he was their God as well. Hearing this, the sailors persisted in their efforts to save the ship and cried out to the Lord to forgive them for what they were about to do—throw Jonah overboard (v. 14). When they did so, the sea calmed and all was well, prompting the sailors to fear (i.e., revere and worship) the Lord and make sacrifices and vows to him (v. 16).

Whether true conversion occurred cannot, of course, be known; but the theological points to be made are (1) that Israel's God is indeed the God of creation and the nations, (2) that God cares for all mankind and not just his chosen people, and (3) that God uses even a disobedient Israelite as the channel of his saving grace. The same can be said of Jonah's ministry in Nineveh. He preached to that great city the message of God's judgment to which, most surprisingly, they responded in national repentance from the king to the lowliest citizen. The king then issued an edict that all should call on the Lord for forgiveness so that he would relent of the destruction he had promised to bring upon the city. Jonah's almost predictable response to God's gracious overtures toward Nineveh was to chide him for being more than just his God, the God of Israel. But that reaction elicited from the Lord the key theological idea of the book: "Should I not care about the great city of Nineveh?" (Jon. 4:11). The unlikelihood of a genuine national repentance by Assyria notwithstanding, the fact remains that the book of Jonah adds its witness to the pervasive Old Testament notion that the Creator and Sovereign of the world has no greater plan than to recover the alienated peoples of all nations to their status of unbroken fellowship with him.

The Prophet Isaiah

It is fashionable in contemporary scholarship to deny to Isaiah of Jerusalem the authorship of the entire book that bears his name.[12] The usual consensus is that the prophet wrote most of chapters 1–39, the second part having been composed by an anonymous Second Isaiah (chs. 40–55), and the third by a putative Third Isaiah (chs. 56–66). While not dismissing the critical and even theological importance of the matter,

[12] For a history of "multiple authorship" scholarship, see R. K. Harrison, *Introduction to the Old Testament* (Grand Rapids: Eerdmans, 1969), 764–95.

a work such as ours cannot devote space to it; nor, as with Jonah, is it necessary to do so given our stated method of viewing the Old Testament literature canonically, that is, in its present form. The major deficiency in not addressing the question of the book's unity is that if it is all of one piece and not to be dated later than 700 BC or so, its message must be viewed against that historical, cultural, and theological backdrop. If, however, Second Isaiah springs from the exilic era (ca. 550 BC) and Third Isaiah the postexilic (ca. 450 BC), not only are the respective settings different; but the theological development must also be viewed in a different way. At the least one would have to say that Second Isaiah reflects a more mature theology than original Isaiah and that Third Isaiah's thought presupposes both and moves beyond them. In such a case, proper method demands that Second Isaiah be studied with exilic prophets such as Ezekiel and Daniel and that Third Isaiah finds its place among Haggai, Zechariah, and Malachi, an approach that, in fact, is followed by adherents of the multiauthorship hypothesis.

Our position, already stated, is that Isaiah of Jerusalem was author of the whole book no later than the early seventh century, and our analysis of its theology will proceed on that basis.[13] The descriptor "Isaiah of Jerusalem" suggests the geographical locale of the ministry of this prince of the prophets. As a citizen of Judah, it is not surprising that Isaiah's message is addressed almost exclusively to that nation even though he commenced his ministry at least eighteen years before Samaria's fall in 722 BC. The sheer length of his composition suggests the possibility of a wide variety of themes, but in fact they can be subsumed under just a few headings: (1) the rebellion of Judah, (2) its judgment, (3) its historical and eschatological hope of redemption and restoration, (4) the messianic deliverer, (5) oracles against the nations, and (6) the establishment of the Lord's universal and everlasting kingdom. We shall arrange our discussion around these topics and attempt, at the end, to provide their synthesis.[14]

---

[13] For strong defenses of the unity of the book and common authorship by Isaiah of Jerusalem, see O. T. Allis, *The Unity of Isaiah* (Philadelphia: Presbyterian and Reformed, 1950); Rachel Margalioth, *The Indivisible Isaiah* (Jerusalem: Sura Institute of Research, 1964). Cf. also Robert B. Chisholm Jr., *Handbook on the Prophets* (Grand Rapids: Baker, 2002), 13–14.

[14] For a similar analysis, see John N. Oswalt, *The Book of Isaiah Chapters 1–39,* NICOT (Grand Rapids: Eerdmans, 1986), 31–44.

The Rebellion of Judah

Even before he spoke of his call to ministry (Isa. 6), the prophet addressed the backslidden plight of the Southern Kingdom, his own people. "They have abandoned the LORD," he lamented, and "have despised the Holy One of Israel; they have turned their backs on Him" (Isa. 1:4b). This is clearly the language of covenant unfaithfulness, akin to his contemporary Hosea's comparison of Israel to an adulterous wife. Referring to them as utter pagans (Sodom and Gomorrah, v. 10), the Lord cited their hypocritical worship as something he hates because it was mere playacting (vv. 11–14). It missed the whole spirit of covenant which called for social justice (v. 17) and undivided loyalty to him (v. 29). The remedy was repentance, to which the Lord would respond with forgiveness (vv. 18–19) and restoration (vv. 24–28).

Elsewhere the Lord called his people "obstinate children" (Isa. 30:1 NIV) who, rather than relying on him, would go to Egypt for help, forming covenant alliances with the people from whom he had delivered them to make covenant with him (Isa. 30:1–5). Though they were his servant people, they became deaf and blind to God's will. "They were not willing to walk in His ways," says the prophet, and "they would not listen to His instruction" (*torah,* Isa. 42:24). Moreover, their defection was not of recent vintage. Addressing Israel, the Lord said of them, "Your first father [i.e., Jacob] sinned, and your mediators [the prophets] have rebelled against Me" (Isa. 43:27), setting in train a history of covenant disloyalty. In another place he described his people as "treacherous," "a rebel from birth" (48:8). Finally, in the boldest of terms, he called them "sons of a sorceress" and "offspring of an adulterer and a prostitute," an allusion to their idolatry (57:3), and repeated again the epithet "rebellious children," adding to it "race of liars" (v. 4). Surely such attitudes and actions called for severe response, and it was not long in coming.

The Judgment of Judah

Judah's rebellion against the Lord was prompted by and resulted in a hankering for the gods of the nations and their perverse religious practices. Isaiah listed a number of these early in the book (Isa. 2:6–8) and announced that there would be "a day belonging to the LORD" when the arrogant of Judah, along with their idols, would be brought low and the Lord alone would be exalted (2:12–18). In that day there would be drought, political and spiritual anarchy, and social disintegration (3:1–7), all resulting from God's judgment (vv. 13–14). The tragedy is that the Lord had planted his people like a vineyard in a choice piece of land, hoping for them to produce good fruit. When he came to harvest time, however, he found only rotten grapes (Isa. 5:1–4). The only remedy was to take from around the vineyard its protective hedge so that it could be trampled underfoot by any who passed by (vv. 5–6). Worse than that, the people of Judah would go into exile, leaving the land open for foreign exploitation. The reason for these doleful prospects was that God's people "have rejected the instruction *(tôrâ)* of the LORD of Hosts, and they have despised the word of the Holy One of Israel" (v. 24).

Isaiah's call to ministry came attached with the pessimistic news that no matter how persistent and faithful he was in proclaiming the word of repentance, the people would give no heed (Isa. 6:9–10) and thus would see their cities lie in ruin, without inhabitant, until everyone was spirited away in exile (vv. 11–12). Then, in a specific and identifiable historical setting—the impending invasion of King Tiglath-pileser of Assyria in 735 BC—the Lord warned Isaiah that he would bring against the nation of Judah "the mighty rushing waters of the Euphrates River," referring here metaphorically to the hordes of Assyrian troops that soon would come to overwhelm the land (Isa. 8:6–8). Already the Arameans and Philistines had eaten away at Israel's territory (Isa. 9:12), and Israel's doom had been sealed because of her unrepentance (v. 13). If that be true of her northern neighbor, how could Judah hope to escape? Even Israel would contribute to Judah's downfall before it went into exile (v. 21).

The day of impending devastation is called "a day of tumult, trampling, and bewilderment," one instigated by "The LORD God of Hosts" (22:5). The Lord will play the role of warrior, leading the armies of foreign nations against his sinful nation. No matter what defensive measures are taken, they will be inadequate to forestall certain destruction in the absence of repentance (vv. 12–13). In an oracle addressed specifically to Jerusalem, the Lord points out the irony that even though this is "the city where David camped," it will be besieged and humbled (Isa. 29:1–4). Commanding armies that cannot be counted for number, the Lord will come against his chosen nation with a blitzkrieg of earthquake, storm, and fire (vv. 5–6). The resulting carnage will be so great that Judah, like a collapsing wall, will be shattered in pieces so that "not even a fragment of pottery will be found" (Isa. 30:14). Those who survive will be chased down until nothing remains in the land except a remnant "like a solitary pole on a mountaintop or a banner on a hill" (v. 17).

The judgment just described is not limited to only Israel and Judah but, in the great eschatological day of the Lord, will extend to the whole earth. The opening pericope of the so-called "little apocalypse" (Isa. 24–27) describes it in terms of the chaos that existed at creation before the Lord brought order and structure to bear. Rather than creating in that day, he will be "stripping the earth bare and making it desolate" (Isa. 24:1) until it lies in ruin. The reason is that mankind has "broken the everlasting covenant" (v. 5), the principles of the creation mandate by which the human race was to exercise its authority as the image of God.[15] Beginning with the rebellion of Adam and Eve, the history of the race has been one of ceaseless resistance to the sovereignty of God and to his kingdom design (v. 4). Such insubordination cannot be left unchallenged forever. The day must come when the terrible wrath of the Lord is unleashed and creation, as it were, reverts back to de-creation, to a state where things can and must begin again.

Isaiah put it this way: "For the windows are opened from above, and the foundations of the earth are shaken. The earth is completely devastated; the earth is split open; the earth is violently shaken" (vv. 18b–19).

But the earth alone and its inhabitants are not solely to blame and deserving of divine retribution. The prophet pointed to the underlying issue, that of competing sovereignties whether in the heavens or on the earth (v. 21). From the beginning the demonic hosts headed by the evil one, along with his earthly minions—the evil rulers of the nations—have conspired against the dominion of the Lord. Their day will come, the time of their defeat and confinement, as it were, "like prisoners in a pit" (v. 22). Then "the Lord of Hosts will reign as king on Mount Zion in Jerusalem, and He will display His glory in the presence of His elders" (v. 23). At long last the kingdom of God will be ushered in, and his saints will take their places as his subjects and viceroys.

---

[15] Ibid., 446.

The Restoration of Judah

The eschatological renewal of all things just described had historical, if limited, portents in individual and national restoration in historical times. Judah had sinned grievously against the Lord, but there was still hope of averting his judgment and, beyond that, of a better day in both immediate and more remote times. Early in his ministry Isaiah recorded the plea of the Lord to his people to "discuss this" with him, for there could be forgiveness and cleansing for them (Isa. 1:18–19). Once this happened, Jerusalem could bear the proud label "the Righteousness City, a Faithful City" (v. 26).

The judgment passages we have noted above seem to leave little room for exceptions: Would anyone at all survive, or would God's program for a chosen people come to a dismal and irrecoverable end? The answer is clear: God's covenant promises would stand secure, and there would always be a seed of Abraham to bring them about. Isaiah—as well as other prophets—referred to the faithful minority as the remnant, the few who would remain loyal no matter what. In the day of the Lord's judgment and its aftermath, these would "faithfully depend on the LORD, the Holy One of Israel" and return to "the Mighty God" (Isa. 10:20–21). This return, both physical and spiritual, is, in the context of Isaiah 10, to be understood as a return from Assyrian exile for which there is no historical evidence. The thrust of the passage therefore is eschatological with Assyria representing all forces hostile to the Lord and his people (vv. 24–34). The same setting is in view in Isaiah 11:11–16, which speaks of the return of the remnant from Assyria, Egypt, and a host of other nations (v. 11). From the ends of the earth, God's people will come back to the land of promise as though by another exodus. "The LORD will divide the Gulf of Suez," and there will be a route back from Assyria "as there was for Israel when they came up from the land of Egypt" (vv. 15–16).

That this is intended to be understood as a literal return to a literal land is clear from a number of passages. Isaiah 14:1 declares that "the LORD will have compassion on Jacob and will choose Israel again. He will settle them on their own land," and chapters 26 and 27 end on the triumphant note that "on that day the LORD will thresh grain from the Euphrates River as far as the Wadi of Egypt, and you Israelites will be gathered one by one." Then the exiles who have been confined to Assyria and Egypt (i.e., everywhere) "will worship the LORD at Jerusalem on the holy mountain" (Isa. 27:12–13). They will return to a land almost paradisiacal in productivity, one so blessed by the Lord that the prophet is forced to the language of hyperbole to do it justice. "Streams and watercourses will be on every high mountain and every raised hill," he says, and "the moonlight will be as bright as the sunlight, and the sunlight will be seven times brighter" (Isa. 30:25–26). Their release from bondage and restoration by the Lord will be so magnificent that the land itself will seem like a veritable garden of Eden.

The hyperbole continues and is intensified in Isaiah 35, a passage heavy with eschatological overtones but with its roots in the soil of solid history. The prophet views the land as so transformed that the deserts will burst into bloom and will resemble Lebanon and Carmel in its luxuriant flora (vv. 1–2). Refreshing streams will abound in the dry lands, and everywhere safety will be found, for ferocious beasts will no longer be a threat (vv. 7, 9). The inhabitants of this glorious land will themselves be well and whole, for "here is your God; vengeance is coming. God's retribution is coming; He will save you" (v. 4). Only the redeemed will live there in that happy state. No longer will the trauma of captivity and exile plague them, for "joy and gladness will overtake them, and sorrow and sighing will flee" (v. 10).

These descriptions of God's restoration are greatly expanded in Isaiah 40–66; in fact, they are perhaps the major theme of this whole part of the book. As many scholars have observed, this section of the book is redolent of exodus imagery in which the return of the Lord's people from Babylonian exile is likened to the exodus deliverance of their forefathers from Egypt.[16] Thus, they will make their way across deserts but under the protective care of the LORD who, unlike the dead idols of the nations, has the power to rescue them from bondage and to make a highway over which their trek to the promised land will be safe and easy (Isa. 40). He will take them by the hand like little children and enable them to overcome every obstacle standing in the way of their progress (41:13–16; cf. Hos. 11:3–4). He will do this as the sovereign God compared to whom the gods are nothing (vv. 21–24) and before whom human rulers are but potter's clay to be trodden down (v. 25; cf. 42:10–17).

---

[16] Eugene H. Merrill, "Pilgrimage and Procession: Motifs of Israel's Return," *Israel's Apostasy and Restoration,* ed. Avraham Gileadi (Grand Rapids: Baker, 1988), 268–69.

Isaiah 43 moves beyond Babylonian exile alone to speak of a more general restoration, one with stronger eschatological overtones. The Lord's redeemed will come from all directions, wherever they have been dispersed, and like those from Babylon in historical times will experience the "new thing" (Isa. 43:19 NIV) the LORD will do—"provide water in the wilderness, and rivers in the desert, to give drink to My chosen people. The people I formed for Myself will declare My praise" (vv. 20–21). All this will be done contrary to the impotence of the gods of the nations who can neither effect such deliverance nor even predict it (vv. 9–13).

To accomplish his purposes, the Lord often uses human instruments, even those that do not know him or that might ordinarily be resistant to him. This was true of Israel's restoration to the land from Babylonian exile, a return facilitated by the decree of the Persian king Cyrus in 538 BC who, contrary to the policies of his Babylonian predecessors, adopted the strategy of allowing captive peoples to return to their homelands, hoping thereby to gain their allegiance and also to use them in their own countries as a stabilizing presence in his emerging empire. We have already commented on the effect of that decree in providing hope to the distraught exilic community that the ancient covenant promises would not fail after all (2 Chron. 36:22–28; Ezra 1:1–4). Isaiah here predicted the role that Cyrus would play, a role so important that the heathen king is actually called the anointed of the Lord (Isa. 45:1).

The sovereignty of the Lord is best displayed by his incomparable attributes and his hegemony over the gods, kings, and nations of the world.[17] Isaiah portrayed him as the Creator of all things (Isa. 44:24) whose predictive word is infallible (vv. 25–26) and who commands mighty Cyrus to obey his will (v. 28). He would raise up Cyrus and give him victory over all his foes even though Cyrus would not recognize him as Lord (45:4–5). Yet what the Lord would accomplish through this unwitting instrument would cause people everywhere to know that only the Lord is God (v. 6).[18] And the nations would also come to see that

[17] Eugene H. Merrill, "The Unfading Word: Isaiah and the Incomparability of Israel's God," *The Church at the Dawn of the 21st Century,* ed. Paige Patterson, John Pretlove, and Luis Pantoja Jr. (Dallas: Criswell Publications, 1989), 131–55.

[18] Roy F. Melugin, "Israel and the Nations in Isaiah 40–55," *Problems in Biblical Theology. Essays in Honor of Rolf Knierim,* ed. Henry T. C. Sun and Keith L. Eades (Grand Rapids: Eerdmans, 1997), 249–64.

restored Israel served a God worthy of their worship as well (v. 14). The idols and their devotees would be put to shame in the presence of the Creator and only God (vv. 15–21), but he, in tender love and grace, would extend to them the offer of salvation and submission (vv. 22–24).

The same appeal to the Lord as Creator and the one and only God undergirded Isaiah's urgent, if proleptic, exhortation to Israel to "leave Babylon, flee from the Chaldeans!" and announce to the whole world that "the LORD has redeemed His servant Jacob" (Isa. 48:20). His power and uniqueness are the sufficient grounds upon which the Lord bases his salvific and restorative work. But he would also be moved by strong feelings of love and compassion. The prophet spoke of the Lord of power as the one who "has comforted His people, and will have compassion on His afflicted ones" (Isa. 49:13). He even has a maternal instinct for them, one so consuming that it would not allow him to forget them even though a human mother might forget her newborn child (v. 15). Israel was as deeply engrained on the mind of the Lord as would be a tattoo on the palms of his hands (v. 16). Such covenant love could result in only one outcome—the full and free return of his people to the land and their restoration to the degree that all mankind would confess that the Lord is the Savior and Redeemer of Israel (vv. 22–26).

The covenant love manifested here was founded on the promises made to the fathers in ancient times. The Lord had chosen Abraham, when he was only one individual, to sire a nation without number (Isa. 51:1–2). Surely his purposes could not now be frustrated even though Israel was headed for judgment. To the contrary, the Lord would comfort Zion and "make her wilderness like Eden" (v. 3). The allusion to Eden extends the promise long in advance of Abraham, back to creation itself and all that the creation events meant to the theology that explained Israel's existence. Unless Israel returned to the land and took up its servant ministry, the grand design for human redemption would come to naught, at least as the Lord intended it. They must return to Zion so that there, at the dwelling place of the Lord, it could be said to Israel, "Your God reigns!" (Isa. 52:7). Then, and only then, "all the ends of the earth will see the salvation of our God" (v. 10).

The prophet Hosea had described Israel's return to the Lord as the patching up of a failed marriage, an analogy adopted by Isaiah as well. The Lord would make the barren woman (i.e., Israel) to have many children and (changing the imagery) the widow to be comforted (Isa. 54:1, 4). Then, in a boldly anthropomorphic metaphor, the prophet exclaimed, "Your husband is your Maker—His name is Yahweh of Hosts—and the Holy One of Israel is your Redeemer" (v. 5). Because of her infidelities, the Lord had for a time abandoned her, but (in his words), "I will take you back with great compassion" (v. 7). The Lord then appealed to the Noahic covenant as the grounds for Israel's hopes that her return would come to pass. He had sworn to Noah that never again would a flood cover the earth and now said to Israel, "My love *(ḥesed)* will not be removed from you and My covenant of peace will not be shaken" (vv. 9–10). Continuing the family metaphor, the Lord promised that Israel's sons would be taught by the Lord and her children would be blessed with peace (v. 13).

The covenant in view here is the one made with David, one described as "everlasting" and filled with "promises" (Isa. 55:3). Its purpose, among other things, was, like the others, to draw the nations to Israel's God. When the nation returned from exile and was restored to her glory, "nations who do not know you will run to you," the prophet promised, "for the LORD your God, even the Holy One of Israel, has glorified you" (v. 5). Thus the seed of Abraham would effectively carry out its mission of being the means by which the Lord will bless all the earth. The prophet elaborated on this theme of Israel as the source of blessing in chapter 61 where the language of the original offer of the Sinai covenant appears: "You will be called the LORD's priests; [people] will speak of you as ministers of our God" (v. 6). The Lord would renew his covenant with Israel (v. 8), and "all who see them will recognize that they are a people the LORD has blessed" (v. 9). Thus the seed of Abraham would become a blessing to all nations according to the ancient promise to the patriarch (Gen. 12:3).

The Messianic Servant and Savior

From the beginning of the Old Testament revelation, there were hints, increasingly expanded and clarified, of a special individual whom the Lord would call and empower to deliver the world from its sin and alienation from God. These first appeared in the enigmatic reference to the seed of the woman (Eve) who would crush the head of the serpent (Gen. 3:15), advanced to the royal scion of Judah (Gen. 49:10), the star out of Jacob

(Num. 24:17), on to the anointed one (Heb. *māšîaḥ)* of Hannah's prayer (1 Sam. 2:10), and finally to the offspring of David whose throne the Lord will establish forever (1 Chron. 17:11–14). To this point the figure in view was a royal descendant of David about whom little is said of servanthood or salvation. Amos had nothing to say of a messiah, nor did Hosea except in one place given a messianic interpretation by Matthew (Hos. 11:1; cf. Matt. 2:15). Isaiah, however, is rich in messianic allusion and prediction, beginning in chapter 4 with the reference to "the branch *(ṣemaḥ)* of the LORD" who would be "beautiful and glorious" and would accompany Zion's cleansing from sin and restoration of God's glory (Isa. 4:2–6). The term *branch* as a messianic epithet occurs elsewhere in Isaiah (11:1), Jeremiah (23:5; 33:15), and Zechariah (3:8; 6:12)—all with strong intertextual associations with the ruler from Judah prophesied by Jacob (Gen. 49:11).[19]

Most famous from the standpoint of Christian theology is the Immanuel figure of Isaiah 7 (cf. Matt. 1:22–23). King Ahaz, having refused a sign from the Lord regarding the threat posed to Judah from Aram and Israel, was told by Isaiah that the Lord would nonetheless give him a sign. "The virgin" *(hāʿalmâ),* already pregnant, would give birth to a son and would name him Immanuel ("God with us") (v. 14). The lexicography and grammar certainly favor the idea that a young woman (thus *ʿalmâ)*, well-known to King Ahaz and the prophet, would soon give birth to a child against all odds of it happening naturally. The Greek Old Testament (the LXX) already saw something more to the promise than a historical fulfillment, however, and translated *ʿalmâ* by *parthenos,* "virgin," rather than by its usual *neanis,* "young woman." Matthew, depending on the LXX, also rendered *parthenos* when referring to Mary, the mother of Jesus. This is a classic example of a messianic text which, while having a limited meaning in its historical context, goes beyond that meaning in a future, Christological context.[20] As we shall see, this is by no means true only of this passage.

The unusual—indeed, supernatural—character of the Messiah is borne out by Isaiah's further reference to him as "a child will be born" and "a

---

[19] M. G. Abegg Jr., צֶמַח, *NIDOTTE* 3:816–17.

[20] For the complexity of the passage and its exegesis and meaning, see John H. Walton, "Isa 7:14: What's in a Name?" *JETS* 30/3 (1987): 289–306.

son will be given" who will rule over Israel in the distant future. His epithets—"Wonderful Counselor, Mighty God, Eternal Father, Prince of Peace"—can leave no doubt that this being is more than mortal (Isa. 9:6). And yet, "He will reign on the throne of David and over his kingdom, to establish and sustain it with justice and righteousness from now on and forever" (v. 7). He is human, then, despite the circumstances of his birth (Gen. 3:15; Isa. 7:14) and divine titulary.[21] Moreover, he is royal, a descendant of David (Gen. 49:10; 1 Chron. 17:11–14). The combination of his identity as a Branch and his Davidic descent is clear from Isaiah 11:1–5. Here the offspring of David is called a "shoot" (*ḥōter,* only here) from the stump of Jesse upon whom the Spirit of the Lord will come with a variety of gifts enabling him to carry out his royal functions (v. 2). He will have intuitive insight (v. 3b), will judge equitably (v. 4a), and will inflict judgment on the wicked (v. 4b). There are clearly eschatological overtones in the general context (vv. 6–9), yet Jesus cited this passage as an announcement of his own historical public ministry (Luke 4:18).

In the second part of Isaiah (chs. 40–66), the nature and function of the messianic figure, while still displaying earmarks of Davidic royalty, are dominated by servant motifs, even embracing suffering and death. At the same time, the identity of the servant is frequently ambiguous, sometimes clearly referring to Israel, sometimes to persons such as King Cyrus, and sometimes to a future individual identified in Christian theology as the Messiah, Jesus Christ. This is not surprising because God has called many entities—nations and individuals alike—to serve him, especially, of course, Israel. That call, in fact, is what the Mosaic covenant was all about. God had called his chosen people out of Egypt to become a kingdom of priests and a holy nation precisely to serve him in that capacity (Exod. 19:4–6). But historically Israel failed and thus must be replaced—at least in the interim—by a servant who could and would succeed in carrying out God's grand design of reconciling a lost and alienated world to himself.

The first allusion to a servant figure is to Cyrus, implicitly in view as "from the east" (Isa. 41:2), called to render service to the Lord by defeating and destroying human kingdoms that had stood in the way of

[21] Edward J. Young, *The Book of Isaiah,* vol. 1, NICOT (Grand Rapids: Eerdmans, 1965), 345–46.

the Lord's redemptive program (vv. 2b–4).[22] But this gives way to the explicit reference to Israel, "My servant, Jacob, whom I have chosen" (v. 8). The election of the nation itself was predicated on its descent from Abraham, called here by the Lord, "My friend" (v. 8). In such brief span the Abrahamic covenant was linked to his offspring who would be the servant of the Lord. Isaiah saw a time when that servant would languish in Babylonian exile, but that would not terminate God's plans for the nation. "I have chosen you and not rejected you," he said, so "do not fear, for I am with you" (vv. 9–10). The pericope ends with a resumption of the role of Cyrus, "one from the north" (v. 25), who would tread down the nations to expedite Israel's return (v. 25b).

If the servant of Isaiah 41:8–13 is Israel, the servant of chapter 42 is an individual as both the grammar and the outcome of the servant's ministry make clear. He, like Israel, is chosen (v. 1; cf. 41:9); but like the solitary offspring of David in Isaiah 11:2, he will be invested with God's Spirit to perform judicial (vv. 1b–4) and redemptive functions (vv. 6–7). In himself he will *be* (not bring to pass) a covenant, that is, the means by which God's covenant grace can be mediated to the nations (cf. 49:6). This is what Israel was to do, but the subsequent record bears testimony to their failure. Rather than opening blind eyes, Israel itself was blind and unable to minister to others (Isa. 6:9–10; 42:18–20). The ministry of intercession and redemption was thus left to another.

What fell short of fulfillment in history will succeed in the eschatological day, however. Jacob the servant and Israel the chosen (cf. 41:8) will one day come into their own; and just as the Lord poured out his Spirit on the messianic Servant (42:1), so he will on his servant nation (Isa. 44:3). Once more they will unashamedly confess that they are the people of the Lord, thereby displaying to the world who he is and how they too must relate to him (v. 5). Having been blind to the will of God in history, Israel will, ironically, become "a light for the nations, to be [God's] salvation to the ends of the earth" (Isa. 49:6). He will "restore the tribes of Jacob and bring back those of Israel" (v. 6a NIV), a prerequisite, of course, to their servant function. This will be capped off by the recognition of the

---

[22] Thus Childs and most scholars. Brevard S. Childs, *Isaiah* (Louisville: Westminster John Knox, 2001), 318.

rulers of the world that Israel, the nation chosen by the Lord, is truly his people and worthy of their homage (v. 7b).

Up till now the messianic servant has been viewed primarily in regal and proclamatory terms, but with Isaiah 50:4–11 the scene becomes vastly different. Here he speaks on his own, proclaiming his obedience to the will of God (v. 5) despite cruel treatment at the hands of his enemies (v. 6). Such abuse will, however, give way to the Lord's vindication in a time and place where the servant's accusers will be silenced and reduced to impotence. The New Testament connects the beating of the servant to the affliction of Jesus (Matt. 26:67; Mark 15:19; Luke 22:63), an interpretation certainly in line with the individualized identity of the suffering servant of Isaiah.

Isaiah 50 paves the way for the suffering servant *par excellence* of Isaiah 52:13–53:12. This text, cited many times in the New Testament (Matt. 8:17; Luke 22:37; John 12:38; Acts 8:32–35; Rom. 10:16; 15:21; 1 Pet. 2:22), is used consistently there with reference to Jesus Christ. Other interpretations also abound, however, as to the identity of the servant, the chief being (1) the prophet himself, (2) the nation Israel, and (3) a remnant within Israel.[23] The suffering and substitutionary death of the servant clearly rules out any but an individualistic view, however, since it is both theologically inconceivable and historically nondemonstrable that a nation or even a group could assume atoning and redemptive roles. The identification of the Servant as a single person has enjoyed not only a virtual Christian consensus from the beginning but it is a view embraced historically by some elements of Judaism as well.[24] And as for Isaiah being the servant, there is no evidence in Scripture or tradition that he fulfilled this ministry, nor is there any way to explain what would qualify him to suffer and atone for his own sins, to say nothing of the sins of others.

The prophet described the servant as a figure so terribly maltreated as to be unrecognizable (Isa. 52:13–15). Even before this disfigurement, he was not physically distinguished, having come on the scene with little fanfare, just as a plant emerges unnoticed from the soil. When he did come to human attention, he was shunned and then persecuted, all the

---

[23] Bullock, *An Introduction to the Old Testament Prophetic Books,* 152–54.

[24] Joseph Klausner, *The Messianic Idea in Israel* (New York: Macmillan, 1955), 162–68.

while remaining insignificant to his peers (53:1–3). By reflection on his person and experience, it became clear to the prophet that this servant of the Lord was suffering vicariously for us, that is, for Israel and, by extension, for the whole world (vv. 4–6). He did so without resistance, even to the point of death, at last being consigned to the grave with common humanity even though he was innocent of any wrongdoing (vv. 7–9). Most astounding of all, what he did was in compliance with the will of God who, through the servant's death and subsequent resurrection (thus implicitly in vv. 10b–11a), will justify sinners on the basis of the servant's substitutionary role (v. 11b). Then finally, in God's time, he will reign triumphant, having gained victory over sin and death (v. 12).

The unexpected transition of the messianic deliverer from royal son of David to an innocent suffering servant is troubling; in fact, many Jewish scholars of the postbiblical period argued that the respective roles could be explained only by positing two separate messianic concepts and persons.[25] But the New Testament clearly accommodates both ideas (e.g., Phil. 2:5–11) as do other Old Testament texts as we shall see. The biblical message is univocal: The sin and fall of the human race is so irremediable by human effort and so injurious to the holiness of God that only a perfect atonement effected by a perfect sacrifice could avail to restore humanity to its original state and yet leave the holiness and justice of God unimpaired. And since it is the purpose of God to renew his image as kingly heir of creation, it is most fitting that a redeemer who is both servant and king should be the one anointed to bring it to pass.

Oracles against the Nations

Before the sovereignty of the Lord can be (re)established, the issue of competing sovereignties must be dealt with, especially as they are represented by the kingdoms of the world. From Isaiah's historical purview, the principal and most threatening human power was Assyria, then (in the latter eighth century) at the apogee of its imperial might. Isaiah therefore turned to Assyria early in his book (10:5–19). The Lord had already used Assyria to judge the Northern Kingdom, but Assyria had become boastful of that achievement and had viewed it as part of its

[25] Ibid., 400–403; Helmer Ringgren, *The Faith of Qumran* (Philadelphia: Fortress, 1963), 167–82.

own agenda and not the Lord's (v. 7). Now the Lord would cast Assyria aside once it had completed the Lord's objectives and would punish it for its arrogance (v. 12). By use of a metaphor, the Lord contrasted his sovereignty with that supposed by Assyria. Assyria was only a tool, like an ax, that has no ultimate will or power of its own. It moves and works and is laid aside at the discretion of the woodsman. And should it prove unusable, it can be discarded or destroyed (v. 15). When Assyria had worn out its usefulness, the Lord, like a raging fire, would burn it up so that virtually nothing remained (vv. 16–19). That day came at last with the Babylonian defeat of the Assyrians at Carchemish in 605 BC.

The Babylonians, remote from Isaiah's time and circumstances, would also, like Assyria, be a tool in the hand of the sovereign Lord of Israel but also like Assyria would be judged for its overweening pride (Isa. 13:1–22; cf. 47:1–15). In language reminiscent of the end-times because of Babylon's image as an archetype of all wicked nations, the prophet cast his vision upon both those distant days as well as the nearer future. The Lord, he said, was gathering an army "from a far land, from the distant horizon" that would terrorize haughty Babylon like women in birth pangs (vv. 4–8). This, the "day of the LORD," would be accompanied by cosmic cataclysms (vv. 9–10) and total annihilation at the hands of armies that would accomplish their destructive work so thoroughly that Babylon would resemble Sodom and Gomorrah (v. 19). The beginning of the end was imminent, already at hand (v. 22).

Tyre was also on the Lord's hit list (Isa. 23:1–18) if for no other reason than her pride about her invulnerability (vv. 8–9). Her destruction would be no fluke but part of the plan of the Almighty. Like Assyria and Babylon before her, she would be brought low until she acknowledged the rule of the Lord and paid proper homage to him and his people (vv. 15–18). Isaiah 34 provides a glimpse at the judgment of Edom, a brother nation to Israel which, like Babylon, also typified all kingdoms antithetical to the Lord's purposes and hostile to his people. The universality of the message, though directed to Edom (vv. 5–6, 9, 11), is evident from the appeal at the beginning for all nations to give attention (v. 1) and the declaration that "the LORD is angry with all nations" and will totally destroy them (v. 2). Such a broad vista bears the marks of eschatological orientation so that the judgment on Edom historically anticipated similar judgment on all nations in the eons to come. The stars of heaven would disappear when the Lord wielded his sword against Edom (= the nations), an act of war that would leave the nation depopulated and barren forever except for desert creatures that would become its only citizens (vv. 14–17).

The Establishment of God's Kingdom

The goal of creation was the establishment of a realm over which God could exercise his sovereignty through the mediation of mankind, those made as his image. Man's freedom to sin, which he freely exercised, crippled this goal but by no means brought it to an end. History, especially as narrated and interpreted in the Bible, bears witness not only to the state of ruination precipitated by the fall but also to the measures undertaken by the Lord to rehabilitate the kingdom enterprise and redeem and renew mankind so as to make possible their untrammeled and successful dominion over all things as his viceroys. For this to happen, the kingdoms of the world must be swept aside to make room for his kingdom, one partially exhibited by Israel and the church in history but fully in place only in the eschatological day of the Lord.

The book of Isaiah addresses this glorious theme in a number of places, beginning in chapter 2. The prophet saw in the last days the establishment of the Lord's temple on a mountain that will rise above all others because it will be the Lord's dwelling place (Isa. 2:1–5). Then, not just Israel but all nations will concede his kingship and will make pilgrimage to Jerusalem to be instructed in Torah, to settle disputes, and to enjoy the everlasting *shalom* that he will bring. Gentiles will join Jews in a common acknowledgement of the Lord as God and King. In that day of peace, the antagonisms triggered by the fall will find resolution in a virtual return to Edenic paradise. Animals naturally hostile to one another will become domesticated and live in pastoral harmony. And in a restoration of human domination of the created order, a little child will lead these animals and will be so bold as to play with deadly cobras and vipers (Isa. 11:6–8). Whereas mankind had yielded to the insidious temptations of the serpent in Eden, in the day of the Lord mere infants will show their disdain for such creatures, for there will be intuitive recognition of the spheres of dominion intended by the Creator.

The theme of universalism is picked up again in Isaiah 56. The Lord here looks to the time when no one will be denied access to his saving grace but, with Israel, will enjoy all that kingdom participation means

(vv. 1–3). They will become sons and daughters of the Lord—and even more (v. 5; cf. 1 John 3:2). They will have an everlasting legacy and the priestly privilege of going directly into the presence of the Lord to worship him in prayer and sacrifice (vv. 6–7). Referring to the exiles of Israel, the Lord goes on to say, "I will gather to them still others besides those already gathered" (v. 8).

The reference to the exile locates this oracle solidly in an Old Testament historical context, but it does not remain there. The thrust is forward looking, including in its scope the age of the church, in which all may come to the Lord on an equal footing, as well as a more distant future as the larger context makes plain (cf. Isa. 55:6–13). The same orientation dominates Isaiah 60:1–22. In this remarkable vision the prophet saw Judah as a magnetic light drawing all nations to itself and to the Lord (vv. 1–3). The peoples of the earth are described as sons and daughters of the Lord (v. 4; cf. 56:5) who will come from all nations bringing with them their tributes of sacrifice and praise (vv. 7–9). Then the Lord's sovereignty will be fully acknowledged as earthly kings bow in submission to him (vv. 10–12). As for Israel, any lingering doubts it may have had as to its ongoing relationship to the Lord will be allayed. The nations that then would embrace the Lord as God would honor his chosen people, confirming to them the reliability of his covenant promises (vv. 15–16). Israel would then be secure, never again to be threatened by its enemies and never again to be uprooted from its land (vv. 17–22).

All scholars agree that this passage speaks of a post-Old Testament period, but various eschatological schools of thought disagree as to when and how these promises will come to pass and whether, in fact, a literal Israel is in view at all. Premillennialism understands that Israel, restored and spiritually revived, will reign with the Lord through a thousand-year era (the millennium), and that Isaiah is here (and elsewhere, with many other prophets) describing that period.[26] Other approaches propose that Israel is a code word for the church and that the blessings the prophet refers to are not to be understood literally but are hyperbolic allusions to

---

[26] John S. Feinberg, "Systems of Discontinuity," *Continuity and Discontinuity,* ed. John S. Feinberg (Westchester, Ill.: Crossway, 1988), 83.

the attractiveness of the gospel and the changes that occur in the lives of peoples and nations that embrace its message.[27]

In either case Isaiah concluded his book with a glimpse into a future day when the Lord would destroy the old foundations and create a new heaven and earth (Isa. 65:17–66:24). The Lord's people Israel would be especially singled out for favor. They would know no more sorrow or brevity of life; they would live in security and prosperity; and they would share with all creation the universal peace of such a new environment (Isa. 65:18–25). All this would follow Israel's judgment for sin and the birth of a remnant people from the nation deemed dead and gone. Zion, pregnant with hope, would deliver a nation "in an instant" (Isa. 66:8), a kingdom people to be reared and tenderly cared for by a loving God (vv. 12–13). But God, at the same time, would avenge his people of the wicked kingdoms of the world and display once more his sovereignty over them.

The Prophet Micah

Micah, like his contemporary Isaiah, ministered in and about Jerusalem; but his range of vision extended beyond Judah to include the Northern Kingdom Israel as well. His messages of impending destruction and deportation because of the sins of people, prophets, and rulers alike are balanced by words of both historical and eschatological hope.[28] Judgment was inevitable, but so was God's mercy and grace. The people whom he had chosen and commissioned would undergo severe trial and discipline, it is true, but they would be pardoned in the day of the Lord and restored to their place of covenant privilege.

The prophet cast his message in the form of a *rîb,* that is, a lawsuit with the Lord as prosecutor and judge of wicked Israel whom he had summoned to the bar of justice to render an account.[29] The whole world was aware of Israel's guilt and knew that the awesome ruin that even now appeared on the horizon and would result in Samaria's devastation was

---

[27] J. Ridderbos, *Isaiah,* trans. John Vriend (Grand Rapids: Zondervan, 1985), 536–37.

[28] Kenneth L. Barker, *Micah, Nahum, Habakkuk, Zephaniah,* NAC 20 (Nashville: Broadman & Holman, 1999), 37–41.

[29] For the *rîb*-pattern, see H. B. Huffman, "The Covenant Lawsuit in the Prophets," *JBL* 78 (1959): 285–95.

her fault and hers alone (Mic. 1:1–7). But the prophet found no delight in this, for Israel's sin had become Judah's as well; and the judgment of Samaria would soon be followed by that of Jerusalem, his beloved city (vv. 8–16). Indeed, the Assyrian armies of Sargon and Sennacherib that had sacked Samaria and carried off its citizens in 722 BC returned later to Judah, and though Jerusalem was spared, many of the outlying towns were ravaged.

The sins of Israel and Judah that prompted such divine justice were both social and religious or cultic in nature. The rich exploited the poor and defenseless (Mic. 2:1–5; 6:9–15), the prophets resisted the revelation of the Lord and spouted lies of their own invention (vv. 6–11), and the leaders of the community tolerated the whole, allowing these scandalous affairs to go unaddressed (Mic. 3:14). In a second assize the Lord appealed to the mountains and hills as witnesses to Israel's history of covenant disobedience (Mic. 6:1–2). He had redeemed them from Egyptian bondage and led them safely to Canaan (vv. 3–5), but in the end they had substituted pro forma religious practice for genuine worship. Rather than sacrifices devoid of heartfelt devotion, the Lord wanted his people to "act justly, to love faithfulness, and to walk humbly with [their] God" (v. 8). Their failure to do so demanded the kind of chastening that would awaken them to their hypocrisy and bring them back to a place of integrity and usefulness.

Once judgment was over, there would be deliverance back to the land with the Lord himself leading the way (Mic. 2:12–13). Then the temple mount would be chief among the mountains, for the Lord would reign again from there and would instruct the nations in Torah, administer fair justice among them, and usher in an era of universal peace and prosperity (Mic. 4:1–5 = Isa. 2:3–5). In that day (now heavily eschatological in tone) the Lord would show himself as king and restore to Zion the kingship of David as well (Mic. 4:6–8). The Davidic connection implied in Micah 4:8 is explicitly affirmed in Micah 5:2, which speaks of an individual who would arise in the unlikely village of Bethlehem to become one who will "be ruler over Israel." He would be a shepherd-king empowered by the Lord to bring security and peace to his beleaguered people (vv. 4–5). The messianic character of this ruler has long been recognized, and the New Testament identifies him as none other than Jesus Christ (Matt. 2:3–6; cf. John 7:42).

The prophet closed on a note of confidence that the Lord would show compassion to his chosen people and would forgive them of all their sins (Mic. 7:18–19). This work of grace would not be simply ad hoc, however, but would find its basis in the irrefragable promises of God to the patriarchal ancestors (v. 20).

Chapter Sixteen

The Theology of the Later Preexilic and Exilic Prophets

The Prophet Jeremiah

Jeremiah commenced his ministry in 627 BC and was witness to the rapid political and spiritual decline of his nation Judah; the siege, destruction, and deportation of Jerusalem and its inhabitants; and the dismal days of the early part of the Babylonian exile. His message was laden with indictments for covenant disobedience and the judgment that was already beginning to fall.[1] A lesser, but powerful, theme centers on deliverance and restoration, especially in terms of a new covenant. Strangely, Jeremiah had little to say of a messianic redeemer, but what he did say is theologically noteworthy. He was concerned, finally, to speak of the fate of the nations for, like Isaiah, he saw these as rival kingdoms to that of the Lord, the epitome of human hubris that seeks to rob him of the sovereignty that belongs to him alone.

---

[1] For the theology of Jeremiah, see Robert B. Chisholm Jr. "A Theology of Jeremiah and Lamentations," *A Biblical Theology of the Old Testament,* ed. Roy B. Zuck and Eugene H. Merrill (Chicago: Moody, 1991), 341–63.

Judah's Covenant Unfaithfulness

The litany of Judah's defections from the Lord begins already in Jeremiah 2. The Lord reflected on Israel's early devotion, which before long gave way to idolatry even in the desert sojourn and persisted thereafter (vv. 1–12). He likened their disloyalty to the abandonment of fresh spring water for the turgid, murky water of a cistern, a broken one at that (v. 13). They had made an intentional decision to cease serving the Lord and had become enamored of the idols and Baals despite the lifelessness of these man-made objects (vv. 14–28). Their unfaithfulness was like that of a divorced woman who, having tried another husband, wanted to return to her first one. This was little short of prostitution, the Lord declared (cf. Deut. 24:1–4), so Israel was sent away, divorced from the Lord. Sadly, Judah had followed the perverse ways of her sister and was therefore liable to the same fate absent genuine repentance (Jer. 3:1–10).[2]

Jeremiah described Israel's sin as breaking the yoke (2:20), an apt way of speaking of covenant violation.[3] They also had "torn off the bonds" that joined them to the Lord (5:5 NIV) and in pursuit of other gods no longer confessed the Lord as the God of sustenance (vv. 23–24). Rather than being embarrassed at the futility of these efforts, "they weren't at all ashamed. They can no longer feel humiliation" (Jer. 6:15). Instead, they flaunted their sins even in the sacred precincts of the temple, thinking that their status as God's chosen ones would ensure them immunity (Jer. 7:9–11). They forgot that the odious practices of priests and people at Shiloh had resulted in the capture of the ark there and the subsequent destruction of the place itself (v. 12; cf. 1 Sam. 2:12–25; 4:4–11). Their conduct now was, if anything, even worse, for the Jews were engaged in outright paganism, worshipping the gods and goddesses of the nations around them (vv. 17–18, 30–31; cf. 8:19; 9:14).

The absurdity of worshipping what they themselves had made was not lost on the prophet (Jer. 10:1–16).[4] Like Isaiah (40:18–20; 41:7; 44:9–20), he marveled that the Lord's people (or anyone, for that matter) could bow

---

[2] T. R. Hobbs, "Jeremiah 3:1–5 and Deuteronomy 24:1–4," *ZAW* 86 (1974): 23–29.

[3] William L. Holladay, *Jeremiah 1* (Philadelphia: Fortress, 1986), 97; cf. Jeremiah 5:5; Hosea 10:11.

[4] Philip J. King, "Jeremiah's Polemic Against Idols—What Archaeology Can Teach Us," *BR* 10 (1994): 22–29.

down to images that must be carried about because they could not walk (v. 5) and must be clothed because they could not dress themselves (v. 9). This was an affront in the extreme to Israel's God who is incomparable in his power and wisdom, the only "living God and eternal King" (v. 10). Israel's sin lay not just in the worship of these lifeless frauds, but in their spiritual insensitivity to the actual nature of these objects as creatures of depraved human imagination.

At last the prophet named Judah's sin for what it was—covenant violation (Jer. 11:1–8). Citing the book of Deuteronomy, the Lord declared, "Let a curse be on the man who does not obey the words of this covenant" (v. 3; cf. Deut. 27:26). He then instructed Jeremiah to proclaim its terms and exhort the people to obey them. Their forefathers had not done so and in Israel's case, at least, had suffered the curses of the covenant, including deportation from the land. Judah now was in danger of replicating the sins of her sister to the point of suffering the same judgment. They had already broken covenant by pursuing other gods, filling the land with their idols and altars (vv. 9–13). The prophet could see evidence already of the curse of the Lord in the drying up of fields and pastures (Jer. 23:10), and this was just a portent of worse to come (v. 12). The unrelenting immorality and idolatry of people and prophets alike had turned Judah into another Sodom and Gomorrah (vv. 13–14). Surely they could expect no better outcome than those wicked cities of the plain.

The Judgment of Judah

The first recorded revelation to Jeremiah—one, indeed, accompanying his call to prophetic ministry—focused on the wrath the Lord was about to pour out on the nation to which the prophet was to bear witness. His commission was disarmingly simple—"to uproot and tear down, to destroy and demolish, to build and plant" (Jer. 1:10)—but its implementation was something so distasteful to this sensitive man that he did everything he could to evade it. He saw a nation from the north coming against Jerusalem to destroy the holy city because of its idolatry (vv. 14–16). He must warn the people about it, but warning would be in vain, for the course of retribution was already set. Rather than repent, the people would work out their frustration on the prophet, the bearer of bad news;

nevertheless, the Lord would preserve him until his assignment was over (vv. 17–19).

True to his call, Jeremiah announced the soon coming of the northern hordes, the Babylonian army, that like a lion loosed from its den would wreak great havoc (Jer. 4:5–31; 6:1–8). Waxing poetic, he employed other imagery like whirlwinds, clouds, and eagles to speak of the unstoppable swiftness of the advancing hosts. Dan in the north had already caught wind of their vanguard, and the news would soon spread throughout the land. In its aftermath the land would become "formless and empty" (v. 23), the words *(tōhû wābōhû)* used to describe the earth before its completion at creation (Gen. 1:2). There would be a de-creation, one marked by earthquakes and the absence of life, including mankind and all flora and fauna (vv. 24–26; 9:11).[5] This rather hyperbolic panorama would come about, however, not through unassisted divine interference but through a nation of foreign speech, a myriad of warriors that like a plague of locusts would strip bare the land of all its people and riches (vv. 14–17).

Those who survived the carnage would be exiled from the land, scattered "among nations that they and their fathers have not known" (Jer. 9:16). The thought of all this suffering would call for the services of professional mourners, women employed to express lamentation on behalf of the community (9:17–21). They would shed bitter tears over the masses lying all about unburied (v. 22) and wail the fate of those taken from the land (v. 19). As for the latter, they would be "taken completely into exile" (Jer. 13:19), scattered "like drifting chaff before the desert wind" (v. 24). No longer servants of the Lord, they would become slaves to the enemies who would carry them away, returning to Egyptian bondage (Jer. 15:14).

The question must inevitably arise as to why all this had happened to the chosen people. When the nations of the world inquired, they would be told that Israel had forsaken the Lord and had embraced and worshipped other gods (Jer. 16:10–11; cf. 2 Kings 17:7–20). They had broken the covenant, specifically the first two commandments upon which everything else was founded. The prophet illustrates this graphically

[5] McKane describes the scene as "a reverse creation narrative." William McKane, *A Critical and Exegetical Commentary on Jeremiah,* vol. 1, ICC (Edinburgh: T. & T. Clark, 1986), 108.

through the imagery of pottery manufacture (Jer. 18–19). He paid a visit to a local potter's shop and there saw the craftsman creating a vessel on the wheel. The pot turned out poorly, however, so the potter crushed the clay and remade it into something better (18:1–4). The lesson is clear: the Lord had created Israel to be a vessel of mediation between himself and the nations, but Israel proved to be intractable, resistant, defiant, and therefore of no use. It must be crushed so that it could be reformed and reshaped into an instrument suitable to its Maker's intentions (vv. 11–12). Lest his audience should misunderstand the object lesson, Jeremiah spoke plainly. The people had turned their backs on the Lord and had converted the holy city into a shrine of idolatry (Jer. 19:4–5). Because they had done so, the Valley of Ben Hinnom, lying below the potters' shops, would no longer bear this name but would be called the Valley of Slaughter (v. 6). It would, in the day of judgment, no longer be a dump for broken shards of pottery but a vast cemetery filled with the corpses of Israel's slain (v. 11). And as for Jerusalem as a whole, it would become like Topheth (fireplace), consumed by fire until its idolatry was purged away (v. 13).

The same imagery occurs in Jeremiah's confrontation with King Zedekiah, the ruler in power when Jerusalem fell to the Babylonian siege in 586 (Jer. 21:1–14). Zedekiah, hoping to the end that judgment might be averted, inquired of the prophet whether such a thing could be. The answer was disappointing in the extreme. Not only would the king of Babylon oppose him, but the Lord himself would attack the city, starve it into submission, and take captive Zedekiah and the leaders of the land (v. 7). The city and its environs would be devastated in God's fiery wrath. In his own words he declares, "I will kindle a fire in [your] forest that will consume everything around it" (v. 14).

Zedekiah's three royal predecessors—Jehoahaz, Jehoiakim, and Jehoiachin—also heard a somber and dreadful word of judgment (Jer. 22). Though addressed as those "sitting on David's throne" (v. 4), they needed to understand that this status did not confer upon them exemption from personal and official responsibility nor did it shield them from divine repercussion should they fail to discharge it. Their royal palace—a metaphor for their kingship—would be consumed in the flames, a turn of events so startling to onlooking nations that they would feel compelled to ask how such a thing could happen (v. 8). The answer, as always, would be that God's people had "abandoned the covenant of the LORD their God and worshiped and served other gods" (v. 9). As we have noted over and over, at the heart of covenant violation was the breaking of the first two commandments: (1) There is only one God and (2) only he can be worshipped. As for Jehoahaz and Jehoiachin, they would be taken captive, the former to Egypt (2 Kings 23:34) and the latter to Babylon (2 Kings 24:15). Jehoiakim, mercifully, would be allowed to die peacefully before his city collapsed around him (2 Kings 24:5–6).

The Judgment of the Nations

As the Creator of all things, God has an interest in the nations of the world that is so intense that his ultimate purpose for Israel, the seed of Abraham, was to serve as a redemptive medium to restore all the peoples of the earth to perfect fellowship with him. The message of the prophets is in that respect a universal one, a word of hope if the nations repented but one of condemnation and judgment should they continue in the path of rebellion. Sadly, the latter has characterized the history of mankind, so it is not surprising that the prophetic word more often than not dwelt on the wickedness of the nations and the vengeance of the Lord, whose holiness is offended by the rebellion of his creatures and whose justice demands their punishment.

Jeremiah introduced the topic with a reference to the cup of God's wrath, which the nations must drink (Jer. 25:15–38).[6] This they would do by hearing the word of the Lord through the prophet; and whether they heeded it or not, they would imbibe it, some to their salvation and some to their utter destruction. The wine is here a metaphor for the sword, which in turn is a metaphor for judgment. Having been warned, those who refused to turn to the Lord would taste of his vengeance until the "slain by the LORD on that day will be spread from one end of the earth to the other" (v. 33).

Switching metaphors, Jeremiah next placed on his neck a yoke symbolizing the helpless plight of prisoners of war dragged off into

---

[6] Many scholars liken this drinking of the cup to a trial by ordeal similar to that of the wife suspected of adultery in Numbers 5:11–31; thus Robert P. Carroll, *Jeremiah* (Philadelphia: Westminster, 1986), 501–2; F. B. Huey Jr., *Jeremiah Lamentations,* NAC 16 (Nashville: Broadman & Holman, 1993), 228; cf. 51:7; Isaiah 51:17, 22; Ezekiel 23:31–34; Habakkuk 2:16; Obadiah 16; Zechariah 12:2.

captivity (Jer. 27:1–11). This bit of street theater communicated to the nations—especially those neighboring Judah (v. 3)—that their fate was sealed and that soon Nebuchadnezzar would overrun them and put them in subservience to himself (vv. 6–7). Those willing to submit would remain in their lands, but those who refused to do so would be spirited off into Babylonian exile. The parallels between the Lord's expectations of Israel and Judah, on the one hand, and the nations, on the other, are most instructive as are the consequences when those expectations fall short. With all its focus on Israel, the Old Testament at the same time never ignores God's love for the nations and his desire to redeem them back to himself.

Jeremiah 46–51 provides a catalog of oracles against the nations listed seriatim. Egypt heads the list (46:1–28). This erstwhile superpower had just been defeated by Nebuchadnezzar at Carchemish in 605 BC, the account of which the prophet relates in grand poetic style.[7] Proud Egypt, like its famous Nile, had swollen up with self-sufficiency and imperial ambition, only to fall, not at the hands of Babylonia, but before the Lord Almighty, the divine Warrior taking vengeance on them (vv. 7–10). But that was not the end, for Nebuchadnezzar was about to follow up his victory by invading Egypt itself, there to be the Lord's instrument of punishment on "Amon, god of Thebes, along with Pharaoh, Egypt, her gods, and her kings" (v. 25). In other words, all powers competitive with and hostile to the sovereignty of the Lord could expect his swift and sure retribution.

The Philistines, too, would suffer divine wrath (Jer. 47:1–7) as would Moab. In a lengthy discourse (48:1–47), lengthy because of Moab's status as a brother nation to Israel, the Lord painted a picture of utter destruction because of Moab's idolatry (v. 13), defiance (v. 26), and pride (v. 29). Of all people, those with roots in Abraham should have behaved better. The same was true of Ammon, a nation, like Moab, that sprang from Abraham's nephew Lot, the tawdry circumstances of their birth notwithstanding (Jer. 49:1–6; cf. Gen. 19:36–38). They had become an idolatrous people, worshipping the god Molech rather than the true God (vv. 1, 3). Edom (Jer. 49:7–22) was even more closely related, having

[7] For the background, see Eugene H. Merrill, *Kingdom of Priests: A History of Old Testament Israel* (Grand Rapids: Baker, 1987), 446–50.

descended from Jacob's brother Esau. They had rejected whatever wisdom they once had (v. 7) and had found false security in their fortress-like dwelling among the rocky clefts (v. 16). Their pride would soon turn to abject humiliation, and their latter end would be as final as was that of Sodom and Gomorrah (vv. 17–18). Damascus, next on the list (Jer. 49:23–27), was on the cusp of destruction. Then follow Kedar and Hazor (49:28–33), the former a nomadic tribal people in the Arabian desert and the latter a place so far unidentified in the same area but certainly not the famous city in far north Israel.[8] Though isolated, they too would not escape Nebuchadnezzar's armies but would become desolate forever (v. 33). Finally, distant Elam came in for consideration (Jer. 49:34–39) for undisclosed reasons. Its inclusion may simply be illustrative of the Lord's wide-ranging interest in the nations. Not just his own chosen people or even their near neighbors are in his purview, but all nations everywhere make up his constituency and are accountable to Him.[9]

The list ends, fittingly, with Babylon, to which the prophet devotes more than one hundred verses (Jer. 50:1–52:58). It is fitting because Babylon, like Assyria before it, was the instrument of God's vindication of his righteousness against wicked nations, but at the end it too had become filled with pride and subject to the same fate. The prophet viewed Babylon's violent overthrow as an imminent event, one that would eradicate the paper gods of her pantheon and result in the release of captive Judah (vv. 2–3, 4–10, 18–20). Her sin was that she had "acted arrogantly against the LORD, against the Holy One of Israel" (50:29), not as though she were covenantally related to him as was Israel but that she, representative of all nations, refused to recognize the Lord as God and, moreover, mistreated the seed of Abraham, thus bringing down the curse promised to those who would do so (Gen. 12:3). They had not regarded him as Creator (Jer. 51:15–16) but instead had themselves created worthless images, "a work to be mocked" (vv. 18–19). Babylon's punishment would therefore fall upon her imaginary gods as well as her people (vv. 44, 47), for the real contest of the ages is not between the

[8] By a slight repointing, the word can be read as "enclosure" and thus refer to a settled as opposed to nomadic people. Holladay, *Jeremiah,* vol. 2, 383.

[9] Carroll, *Jeremiah,* 813–14.

Lord and mankind but between him and the demonic spirits that stand behind the fanciful gods and inspire men to worship them.

Restoration and Deliverance

The judgment of God upon his people must always be viewed as a prelude to their forgiveness and restoration. He brings them down in severe discipline in order to raise them up purified and equipped to serve him with the integrity and righteousness intended at the initiation of his kingdom design. Jeremiah is replete with notes of hope despite the throbbing undertones of disobedience and judgment just described. With tender compassion the Lord invited his people to return like a wayward wife to her loving husband (Jer. 3:14). Looking far into the eschatological future as well as more immediate historical times, the Lord foresaw a day when Israel's kings would be like David ("according to My heart"; thus v. 15 literally), the land would be filled with people and worship radically altered. No longer would appeal be made to the ark of the covenant, for the Lord himself would be immediately accessible to his people (vv. 16–17). This anticipates the New Testament teaching that there will be no temple in new Jerusalem "because the LORD God the Almighty and the Lamb are its sanctuary" (Rev. 21:22; cf. John 4:21–24).

There were conditions, of course. Israel must put away its idols (Jer. 4:1) and "break up the unplowed ground" by circumcising their hearts, a sign of covenant renewal (v. 3; cf. Gen. 17:1–14). This rite, used figuratively here, was one of many ways of expressing Old Testament theological development from a cultus based on ritual to a relationship with the Lord founded on faith alone.[10] Even in Jeremiah's time he tried to make the distinction between religion wrapped up in mere symbolism and one of heartfelt devotion to the Lord. He urged his hearers to quit mouthing the shibboleth "the temple of the LORD" and to get busy loving their neighbors and serving God alone (Jer. 7:3–8).

At times Jeremiah despaired of any hope of his people's restoration. "Have You completely rejected Judah?" he asked. "Do You detest Zion? Why doYou strike us with no hope of healing for us?" (Jer. 14:19). The Lord's own reputation was at stake, he argued, and he was duty bound to remember his covenant (v. 21). The Lord's response, as always, was that

[10] G. Mayer, מוּל, *TDOT* 8:161–62; cf. Jeremiah 9:25–26; Romans 2:25–29.

repentance was a prerequisite to restoration, beginning with the prophet himself (Jer. 15:19). He must not condone or cooperate in their sinful ways but live in such a manner that his people would turn to him as an example (v. 21b). And turn they would, not just to Jeremiah but to the Lord. Like a mighty exodus they would return to the promised land and then take up their servant task of attracting the nations to their God. These hitherto pagans would come from the ends of the earth to the Lord and would confess to him: "Our fathers inherited only lies, worthless idols of no benefit at all" (Jer. 16:19). The Lord would then teach them about himself and "they will know that My name is Yahweh" (v. 21).

This is akin to spiritual conversion, what the New Testament describes as the new birth (John 3:3, 7). Jeremiah advanced this concept in his vision of the figs (Jer. 24) where, referring to the exiles in Babylon, the Lord said, "I will give them a heart to know Me, that I am the LORD. They will be My people, and I will be their God because they will return to Me with all their heart" (v. 7). We should note carefully again that the whole process is by divine initiative. The Lord gives the new heart, he (re)makes them his people, and he even guarantees that they will return with all their heart. This raises the conditionality of the Mosaic covenant to the level of unconditionality.[11] The Lord demands of his people that they repent of their sins if they hope to remain his covenant nation, but he provides requisite grace to do so (cf. Deut. 30:1–6; Jer. 31:31–34; Ezek. 36:25–27). In his letter to the exiles in Babylon, Jeremiah encouraged them with the unqualified promise that when the seventy years of exile were over the Lord "will attend to you and will confirm [His] promise concerning you to restore you to this place" (Jer. 29:10). "For I know the plans I have for you," the Lord declared, "plans for your welfare, not for disaster, to give you a future and a hope" (v. 11). There is nothing here but pure, unconditional grace.

The fullest expression of the notion of personal (and national) conversion as a spiritual transformation occurs in Jeremiah 30–31 and in briefer form in Ezekiel 36:24–32. At the outset Jeremiah disclosed God's promise that the days were coming when Israel and Judah would return

[11] As Bright renders it, "I will give them a will to know me." That is, the ability to believe is itself a gift of God. John Bright, *Jeremiah,* AB 21 (Garden City, N.Y.: Doubleday, 1965), 193; cf James 1:18.

from captivity and be restored to the land promised to their fathers (30:3). In the clear language of eschatology, he spoke of a "time of trouble" for Jacob out of which he would be saved (v. 7). The forces hostile to the restoration of the covenant community would be overcome, and Israel would serve the Lord and David redivivus as king (v. 9). This David would be a second David, the messianic offspring of the founder of the chosen dynasty (cf. 1 Chron. 17:11–14). Moreover, Jerusalem would be rebuilt and populated by a joyous citizenry safe and secure from any future threat (vv. 18–21).

The driving force behind this wonderful state of affairs would be the Lord's everlasting love toward Israel, the covenantal *ḥesed* (loyalty) that must find fulfillment if the Lord's reputation is to remain intact (Jer. 31:3). That love would guarantee the renewal of the land as well as their return to it in the first place (vv. 4–9). Just as he had redeemed Israel from Egypt in the distant past, so the Lord would ransom them from the clutches of their taskmasters in days to come (v. 11). Referring to the tragic scene at Ramah from whence many of the Jewish exiles had already been deported to Babylon (Jer. 40:1), the prophet gave comfort to his audience by assuring them that such tragedies would no longer afflict God's people in his day of redemption (vv. 15–17; cf. Matt. 2:18). No longer would there be an uprooting and tearing down of sinful Israel, but the renewed nation will be built and planted (vv. 27–28; cf. Jer. 1:10).

The climax of Israel's return to the land would be the new covenant the Lord would make with them (Jer. 31:31–37). This would be different from the Mosaic in many ways, not least of which because that one could be broken, and, in fact, was broken habitually (v. 32). This new one, to be effected in the eschaton ("after those days," v. 33), would not be engraved on stone tablets but written on the mind and heart of its recipients. There would then be no need for instruction about the Lord and his ways, for all his people would know him innately and experientially. And as for their sins, the Lord would forever forgive and forget them (v. 34). Finally, the covenant relationship would be as everlasting as the laws of nature themselves. If the Lord could forget creation, then perhaps he would forget his covenant commitments to Israel, an absurdity on its face (vv. 35–37).

Ezekiel expanded on this concept and added clarity to it, as we shall see (Ezek. 36:22–31; 37:1–27). For now the question must be asked,

How does the new covenant of Jeremiah relate to the new covenant of the New Testament? Since the whole matter of New Testament revelation as a component of a full biblical theology lies outside the parameters of this work, we cannot address this as fully as it deserves. However, the implications of the question for both Israel and the church are so momentous we cannot ignore it altogether.

This new covenant concept is so important to New Testament theology that the sacred canon of the church has, since ancient times, been called the "New Testament" (Greek *diathēkē,* covenant). In it is wrapped up the whole essence of the Christian faith; for by his incarnation, suffering, death, and resurrection, Jesus Christ introduced and effected a covenant relationship whereby the sins of not just Israel but the whole world could be atoned for and both Jew and Gentile inherit eternal life.

The Synoptic Gospels refer to this covenant on the occasion of Jesus' celebration of the upper room Passover. In Matthew's account, Jesus took up the wine and referred to it as "My blood that establishes the covenant; it is shed for many for the forgiveness of sins" (26:28). Mark's version is essentially the same (Mark 14:24). Luke, however, added the adjective *new* (new covenant), thus, it seems, making unmistakable allusion to Jeremiah and Ezekiel (Luke 22:20).[12] Paul contributed to the discussion in Romans 11 where he cited Isaiah 27:9 to the effect that the Lord's covenant with Israel in the future would result in the forgiveness of their sins (v. 27). His description of the Lord's Supper, reflecting the Gospels' accounts, also focused on the cup as the new covenant (with Luke) (1 Cor. 11:25). That is, just as circumcision symbolized the Abrahamic covenant, so the shed blood of Jesus symbolized the New. Paul elaborated on this in 2 Corinthians 3 where he contrasted the Mosaic and the new covenants (vv. 6–18). His main point is an *a fortiori* argument that if the covenant engraved on stone was glorious (and it was) and yet could not bring life, how much more glorious is the covenant imparted by the Spirit, which could and does give life? He points out that those who continue to adhere to the old covenant remain blind and deaf to its true significance, for only in Christ and by the Spirit can illumination take place (vv. 14–16). The contrast here is between the Mosaic covenant and

---

[12] Darrell L. Bock, *Luke,* vol. 2, *9:51–24:53* (Grand Rapids: Baker, 1996), 1727.

the new one made possible by Christ and available to all people (vv. 16, 18; cf. Gal. 4:24–31).

The epistle to the Hebrews has most to say about the new covenant and its relationship to the old. The author first spoke of Jesus as a Melchizedekian priest who is "the guarantee of a better covenant [than the old, Mosaic one]" (Heb. 7:22). The old one was imperfect for a number of reasons, he said, and to make his case he quoted fully Jeremiah 31:31–34 (Heb. 8:6–12). He then outlined the features of the old covenant with special focus on the tabernacle and its furnishings and services (Heb. 9:1–10), drawing special attention to the Day of Atonement on which the high priest was required annually to enter the most holy place to make atonement for the people. The fact this had to be done over and over again revealed the insufficiency of the old covenant as a whole and underscored the need for something better.

That better thing is the new covenant based on the efficacy of the priestly ministry of Jesus who presented his own blood on the cover of an ark not on earth but in the heavenly tabernacle (Heb. 9:11–14). This made him the mediator of "a new covenant" (v. 15 NIV), better because it made possible the purification of heavenly things whereas the old could purify only earthly things, mere copies of those things that are real in the truest sense (vv. 23–25).

In light of the New Testament data, what are we to make of the "new covenant" of Jeremiah 31? First, it is clear that the author of Hebrews, at least, made use of the Jeremiah passage to set the new covenant in opposition to the old, that is, the Mosaic. But was he thereby interpreting Jeremiah 31:31–34 to be the new covenant inaugurated by Christ? To this we offer a qualified yes. The new covenant will indeed embody all that Jeremiah stated (and more), but that does not preclude the possibility that Jeremiah had in mind first and foremost a new covenant apart from the one Hebrews has in view. This suggestion is supported by a hermeneutic that insists that Old Testament texts are first of all to be understood in their own literary, historical, and theological contexts before they are interpreted retroactively in the light of New Testament usage. Hebrews might well appropriate the Jeremiah passage as the basis for its case for a new covenant in Christ without evacuating it of its meaning for both Old Testament and eschatological Israel.[13]

To that end, the following points should be carefully noted with regard to the setting and meaning of Jeremiah 31:31–34 (and by extension Ezek. 36:24–32):

1. The new covenant is to be made with Israel and Judah. The specificity of the recipients rules out any other party than the literal twin kingdoms unless one is prepared to read "church" or "Gentiles" for "Israel" and "Judah." If this is done, then there is no practical value to the hope of covenant renewal promised here. God's pledges to his chosen people will, in fact, be null and void, at least as far as their identity as a discrete entity is concerned.

2. The covenant is to be made with a people whose forefathers were redeemed from Egypt. Again, a spiritualizing of Israel and Judah would call also for a spiritualizing of Egypt and the exodus.

3. The covenant with "the house of Israel" (v. 33) will differ from the Mosaic only in its being engraved on the mind and heart, making it permanent as well as life changing. There is nothing here suggesting a difference in covenant content.

Jeremiah (and the Old Testament, we might add) has only a renewed Israel in view, and it is highly unlikely that any other interpretation would be conceivable absent New Testament revelation on the matter. But, and this is important, the New Testament does speak and in unequivocal terms uses Jeremiah as an entrée to the magnificent truth that God will restore not only Israel but will, in Christ, provide a way for universal human redemption.[14]

Strangely enough, Jeremiah had little to say about a messianic deliverer whether in connection with a new covenant or not. He did, however, speak of the eschatological ("the days are coming") reign of a "righteous Branch" of David who would rule wisely "and administer justice and righteousness in the land" (Jer. 23:5). His name (among others, to be sure) would be "The LORD Is Our Righteousness," that is,

---

[13] F. F. Bruce, *The Epistle to the Hebrews,* NICOT (Grand Rapids: Eerdmans, 1964), 173–74, 178–79; Walter C. Kaiser Jr., *Toward an Old Testament Theology* (Grand Rapids: Zondervan, 1978), 233–34.

[14] William J. Dumbrell, *Covenant and Creation* (Nashville: Thomas Nelson, 1984), 176–77, 182–84.

the one who would make his people righteous (v. 6). Isaiah also described the messianic descendant of David as a branch (of Jesse, Isa. 11:1; cf. 4:2), and Jeremiah made the connection with David explicit in Jeremiah 33:15. Looking again to the distant future, the prophet spoke of the days that are coming as a time when the Lord "will fulfill the good promises that [He has] spoken concerning the house of Israel and to the house of Judah" (v. 14). Those promises are in regard to one who will sit on David's throne and whose name (as in Jer. 23:6) will be "The LORD Is Our Righteousness" (v. 16).

The king in view here transcends human qualities, and his office is not limited to statecraft. His reign will last forever (v. 17) and will be complementary to the eternal priesthood of the Levitical priests (v. 18). So certain are the covenant promises upon which these declarations are made that only if day and night cease their appointed alternations will a Davidic monarchy and Levitical priesthood be in jeopardy. Linking the promises to the patriarchs and those made to David—and thus their respective covenants—the Lord affirms, contrary to public opinion, that he will restore his chosen people back to their privileges and responsibilities. These, of course, are spelled out in still another covenant, the Mosaic, to which the Lord also has committed himself (vv. 23–26).

The terms *everlasting* and *eternal* (both renditions of the Heb. term *ʿad ʿôlam*) need not mean unending in the absolute sense but lasting into the future as far as the mind can project and/or the context permit.[15] Within the limits of the Old Testament, there is no reason to conclude that the promises of an everlasting Davidic dynasty and Levitical priesthood are not to be taken at face value—that both will in fact continue *ad infinitum.* The New Testament, however, anticipates a time when the rule of David will merge into that of the Lord God or, one may say, will coincide with it (Rev. 21:5–8; 22:1, 3). Jesus, the "Root and the Offspring of David," will reign with the Father (22:16), and in this sense the Davidic dynasty will endure eternally. The Levitical priesthood, however, falls by the wayside, having no role to play once sin is forever a thing of the past. In his vision of the eternal kingdom, John relates, "I did not see a sanctuary in it [the city], because the Lord God the Almighty and the Lamb are its sanctuary" (Rev. 21:22). In that day the temple will have undergone

[15] Anthony Tomasino, עולם, *NIDOTTE* 3:348–49.

transition from a place of appeasement and atonement to a royal palace fit for the God of creation and eternity.

The Prophet Nahum

Nahum, like Jonah, directed a message of judgment to Nineveh, the capital of Assyria, but many years later, on the eve of the collapse of the Neo-Assyrian Empire. The clarity of his vision and the detail of its description of the ferocious attack of the Babylonians against Nineveh leave the impression that it was already underway.[16]

At the outset the Lord pinpointed the fundamental issue at stake: who really is God and what should be done with those who present themselves as divine or human beings in opposition to the God of Israel? The answer is inherent in the Lord's self-description as "a jealous and avenging God" who must and will punish any who resist his claims to sovereignty (Nah. 1:2–6). At that historical moment, it was Nineveh that epitomized human rebellion and arrogance so it was Nineveh that must be judged and destroyed (v. 8). That great city would be eradicated, leaving no record of its historic glory, and all its deities, reputed to be so powerful, would no longer exist (v. 14).

Nineveh's collapse would mean Judah's renewal, at least for a time. The threat of Assyrian conquest would dissipate, the shackles of servitude would be broken, and the wicked nation would no longer invade as it had for two hundred years (vv. 12–13, 15). There would be peaceful respite, times of festivity once more (v. 15a). Judah's splendor would return, and life would be pleasant and productive (Nah. 2:2). The scene here is most likely set in the period of Judah's reformation under the leadership of godly King Josiah (2 Chron. 35:16–19), a time, sadly enough, that was all too brief.[17] The reign of Jehoahaz (609 BC) ushered in the final generation of preexilic Judah, the denouement of the dynasty of David to which wicked Assyria had contributed.

---

[16] Gordon H. Johnston, "Nahum's Rhetorical Allusions to Neo-Assyrian Conquest Metaphors," *BSac* 159 (2002): 21–45.

[17] O. Palmer Robertson, *The Book of Nahum, Habakkuk, and Zephaniah,* NICOT (Grand Rapids: Eerdmans, 1990), 10.

The Prophet Habakkuk

Habakkuk, contemporary with Nahum, entered much more personally into the maelstrom of events surrounding the suffering of his beloved Judah at the hands of the Assyrians. In the spirit of Jeremiah, also a contemporary, he asked how long the Lord would allow repression to go on before he took vengeance (Hab. 1:1–4). And how was it that he could use a nation as evil as Assyria to punish his own chosen people (Hab. 1:12–17)? There is fundamentally a matter of theodicy here, a concern about God's justice in the face of unpunished human sinfulness.

In response, the Lord assured the prophet that in his day he would bring against Assyria the fearsome and irresistible hosts of Babylonia. But Babylonia would prove no more righteous than the Assyrians. Contrary to those who live by faithfulness[18] (i.e., believers in the Lord, Hab. 2:4), the Babylonians were puffed up, arrogant, and greedy (vv. 4–5). Though the instrument of the Lord—as Assyria had been in an earlier time—Babylonia was guilty of unlawful plunder, unnecessary bloodshed, and all manner of debauchery. They resorted to lifeless idols, objects of human manufacture powerless to help (vv. 18–19). In stark contrast was the God of Judah, the Lord who is in his holy temple and before whom all the earth—including Babylonia—must be silent (v. 20).

Habakkuk, apparently satisfied by the Lord's self-defense to this point, burst out into a prayer in which the Lord's sovereignty, despite its seeming tolerance of wicked instruments from time to time, comes to the fore and puts all competing pretenders in their place (Hab. 3:1–19). Rising from the East in ancient times, the Lord came in awesome glory to assert his dominion over the earth (vv. 3–4). Plague and pestilence were his allies (v. 5), and with them he prepared the way for victory over the hostile waters (vv. 8–10). The mytho-poetic imagery here describes the Lord in his existential glory, but careful reading reveals also a historical context.[19] The prophet saw the Lord as the divine Warrior subjugating both man and nature in the redemptive work of the exodus deliverance. He moved heaven and earth to achieve the salvation of his elect people (Hab. 3:11–15). What God did in history he could and would do again

---

[18] For justification of the translation *faithfulness,* see Richard D. Patterson, *Nahum, Habakkuk, Zephaniah,* WEC (Chicago: Moody, 1991), 211–23.

[19] Ibid., 238–39.

and soon. The Assyrians were coming, indeed, but the prophet would "quietly wait for the day of distress to come against the people invading us" (v. 16). Though the Lord's ways are mysterious, he is sovereign and to be trusted. Thus Habakkuk could testify, "I will triumph in the LORD; I will rejoice in the God of my salvation" (v. 18).

THE PROPHET ZEPHANIAH

Zephaniah's message, also from the late seventh century, is almost exclusively devoted to coming judgment in both the near term and more distant future. Moreover, though giving some attention to Assyria, the nation of greatest concern to Nahum and Habakkuk (Zeph. 2:13–15), Zephaniah's range was much broader, including nations as far away as Cush (2:12). His major focus, however, was on his own nation Judah, to which he directed a series of warnings of impending judgment but also words of hope.

The opening oracle is universal in scope, a threat of de-creation resulting in the obliteration of all things on earth. Reversing the creation order of Genesis 1, the Lord said he would sweep away men and animals and then birds and fish (Zeph. 1:2–3). All that would remain would be rubble, a chaos without form and void.[20] This broad sweep laid the predicate for what follows. The God who would in the day of his final judgment pave the way for a re-creation of all things was well able to deal with the nations in the here and now and would not spare even his own chosen people. The prophet then turned to Judah and without naming God's means of doing so (surely Assyria) predicted the punishment of its citizens who, contrary to the covenant prohibitions, had gone after other gods (vv. 4–6). Using the language of sacrifice, the Lord added that he would set Judah apart for sacrifice, viewing their destruction, in a sense, as a means of satisfying his offended justice (vv. 7–13).

This judgment was clearly near at hand, but there was also a day to come in the more distant future ("the great Day of the LORD," v. 14) that would be marked by all the classical signs of the eschatological age—wrath, distress, trouble, ruin, darkness, gloom, clouds, and war

---

[20] Waylon Bailey, *Micah, Nahum, Habakkuk, Zephaniah,* NAC 20 (Nashville: Broadman & Holman, 1999), 411–12.

(vv. 15–18). There was time for repentance, however, before these times of judgment arrived, and Zephaniah urged that his people seek the Lord while they were still able (Zeph. 2:3).

The oracles against Cush (2:12) and Assyria (2:13–15) have little stated rationale except for Assyria's famous pride (v. 15), but those directed to Philistia (2:4–7) and Moab and Ammon (2:8–11) clear the way for Judah's future blessing. Philistia would become part of the inheritance of Judah (v. 7) as would the salty, barren lands of the Transjordan (v. 9). This act of beneficent grace toward the Lord's people would cause all nations everywhere to recognize and extol the God of Israel (v. 11). These blessings would not come without a major turning about on Judah's part. Her people, rulers, prophets, and priests had been disobedient to him, violating the sacred trust of their various offices, and this despite God's endless patience with them (Zeph. 3:1–5). He had warned them over and over again about his day of wrath, but they had given no heed (vv. 6–7).

But Israel's hardness of heart would produce an unexpected result: The nations of the world would see in the Lord's forbearance toward his people something so attractive that they would come to serve him. He even called them "My supplicants, My dispersed people," so thorough and genuine their worship would be (v. 10). This in turn prompted a counterreaction on Israel's part. Seeing the Gentiles coming into covenant faith and compliance would move God's own chosen people, or at least its remnant, to return to him and find forgiveness and blessing (vv. 11–13). Paul, no doubt adopting this text, spoke of the conversion of the nations as a means of engendering in the Jewish people a jealousy that would turn them also to Messiah Jesus (Rom. 11:11–16).

The Prophet Ezekiel

Scholarship is divided on the question as to whether Ezekiel is apocalyptic or contains apocalyptic literature.[21] Most agree, however, that the book embraces apocalyptic themes and imagery even if as a whole it falls outside that category. This is an important issue because apocalyptic requires its own set of hermeneutical and theological methodologies that

---

[21] D. S. Russell, *The Method and Message of Jewish Apocalyptic* (Philadelphia: Westminster, 1964), 88–91.

lead to conclusions often different from those yielded by approaches to prophetic literature in general.[22] Most striking in the book are the visions of the prophet in which he saw objects and beings that were so otherworldly as to defy clear definition and description. They were clearly symbolic of persons and events so transcendent as to require language beyond the inventory of ordinary human speech. Coupled with this was the prophet's playacting, his dramatizing before his hearers of scenes and activities calculated to generate curiosity on their part and an ability through parody and visual allegory to grasp truth that otherwise would be elusive to them.

With these interpretive principles in mind, we see in Ezekiel the same general themes that have characterized most of the prophetic books to this point, namely, disobedience (on both a national and an individual level), addresses to the nations, judgment, and restoration.[23] Remarkably, the prophet omitted any reference to a messianic figure except in two places—34:23–24 and 37:22–25. These by themselves are enough, however, to prove that the messianic hope was alive and well in the dark days of the exile and that restoration of both a historical and eschatological dimension would be wrapped up in a Davidic king who would regather God's chosen people and exercise divinely derived rule over them.

The Disobedience of Israel

In the midst of a series of visions in which he saw "the appearance of the form of the LORD's glory" (Ezek. 1:28), Ezekiel received his call to preach a message of judgment against God's rebellious nation, both the segment that had already been carried away into Babylonian exile and the survivors who still remained in Jerusalem (Ezek. 2:3–8). The oracle is to be dated in 592 BC, five years into King Jehoiachin's captivity and six years before the city and the temple would be destroyed (Ezek. 1:2; 24:2; 33:21). Even with disaster on the horizon, the stubbornness of the people was so ingrained that the prophet's warnings would come to naught (3:7).

---

[22] D. Brent Sandy and Martin G. Abegg Jr., "Apocalyptic," *Cracking Old Testament Codes,* ed. D. Brent Sandy and Ronald L. Giese Jr. (Nashville: Broadman & Holman, 1995), 177–96.

[23] Eugene H. Merrill, "A Theology of Ezekiel and Daniel," *A Biblical Theology of the Old Testament,* ed. Roy B. Zuck and Eugene H. Merrill (Chicago: Moody, 1991), 365–95.

Even those among whom he lived in exile seem to have learned little from it and remained in a mood of obstinate defiance (3:11).

Israel's rebellion was not in the abstract or without definition; it was a rejection of the covenant of the Lord with its various laws and decrees (Ezek. 5:6). Indeed, far from modeling covenant commitment to the Lord, Israel had not even measured up to the minimum standards of the pagans (v. 7)! Transporting him in vision to Jerusalem in his sixth year (591 BC), the Spirit showed him scenes of idolatry in the temple of the Lord (Ezek. 8:1–18). Prominent there was the offensive statue that provokes jealousy (vv. 3, 5), which draws attention to the second commandment that speaks of the fact that "I, the LORD your God, am a jealous God," that is, one who will tolerate no rivals (Exod. 20:5).[24] As we have noted repeatedly, covenant violation finds its essence in the breaking of the first two commandments. It consists of Israel's failure to acknowledge the Lord only as God and turning to creatures rather than the Creator.

Ezekiel 16 and 23 portray Israel as an unfaithful wife whom the Lord had found in an open field, cleansed and purified, and brought into covenant with himself. He had clothed and decorated her with the most expensive and beautiful attire, but she used her attractiveness to lure other lovers with whom she enjoyed illicit relationships. She then entered into their despicable religious practices, behaving even worse than a prostitute, for rather than the heathen coming to her to entice her to sin, she ran to them and did so for free (Ezek. 16:1–34). She was no better than her pagan ancestors, the Hittites and Amorites from whom she sprang (vv. 44–45), and she (Judah) became even more depraved than her sister Samaria who had already gone into Assyrian exile (vv. 46–52; cf. 23:1–21).

In a vision in his seventh year (590 BC), Ezekiel spoke to a gathering of exiles in Babylon and reviewed for them their history since the exodus (Ezek. 20:1–31). The Lord had chosen Israel (v. 5) and made covenant with them to be their God (v. 5). What he required of them was that they recognize only him and that they repudiate the images and idols that stood for other gods (v. 7). But they rebelled, breaking his decrees and laws, and were it not for the sake of his own reputation he would have

[24] Lamar Eugene Cooper, Sr., *Ezekiel,* NAC 17 (Nashville: Broadman & Holman, 1994), 120; Edwin M. Yamauchi, "Tammuz and the Bible," JBL 84 (1965): 283–90.

written them off (vv. 14, 22). Nevertheless, a day of reckoning would come (v. 23) and, in fact, had already come, as they could plainly see.

An advancement in the theology of Ezekiel is the emphasis on personal, individual responsibility in addition to corporate or national. That is, although Israel frequently is perceived in the Old Testament as a community in solidarity, there is also the side, not so much to the forefront, that acknowledges the community to be made up of individuals, each accountable to God. The former point of view was expressed in proverbial form: "The fathers eat sour grapes, and the children's teeth are set on edge" (Ezek. 18:2).

This suggests the distorted idea that children were responsible for the sins of their parents and therefore would be held guilty along with them. This distortion rose, no doubt, from a misunderstanding of the second commandment which states that the children of idolators would be punished "for the fathers' sin, to the third and fourth generations of those who hate Me" (Exod. 20:5). Ezekiel says, to the contrary, that "the person who sins is the one who will die" (Ezek. 18:4). This does not reflect a sociological or even theological maturation, however, but a balance between the concept of corporate identity, on the one hand, and personal identity, on the other (cf. already Deut. 24:16). The Decalogue stresses the *repercussions* of parental sins on generations to come[25] whereas Ezekiel emphasizes *responsibility* for personal and individual transgressions.[26]

The prophet illustrated this principle with a number of examples. First, he described a righteous person who, because of his loyalty to the decrees and laws of the Lord, would live (vv. 5–9). Should he have a wicked son, that son would die for his own wickedness (vv. 10–13). Then he supposed that a son might see all the evil his father had committed but would refuse to imitate him. That son would live, whereas his father would die (vv. 14–18). The bottom line, as Ezekiel reiterates, is that "the person who sins is the one who will die" (v. 20). There was life for the repentant, however; but on the other hand death awaited those who, having been righteous, turned away irrevocably from covenant obedience

---

[25] U. Cassuto, *A Commentary on the Book of Exodus,* trans. Israel Abrahams (Jerusalem: Magnes, 1967), 243.

[26] Daniel I. Block, *The Book of Ezekiel: Chapters 1–24* (Grand Rapids: Eerdmans, 1997), 563.

(vv. 21–24). As to the charge that the Lord was not just in his dealings with sinners and the righteous, the prophet reminded his audience that it was they who were unjust in that their own sense of right and wrong was perverted. His counsel to them was to "throw off all the transgressions you have committed, and make yourselves a new heart and a new spirit" (v. 31), a call to conversion in remarkable anticipation of the gospel.[27]

Judgment on the Nations

With virtually all the other prophets, Ezekiel displayed the Lord's concern for all the nations of the earth since they, too, were his people and he desired their repentance and reconciliation to himself. He first addressed the brother nations Ammon (25:1–7), Moab (8–11), and Edom (12–14; 35:1–15), castigating them for their indifference to Judah's misfortune or even participation in it at the hands of the Babylonians, and warning them that they too would share a similar fate. They then would know that he is the Lord (vv. 7, 11, 14). The Philistines (vv. 15–17) and the Tyrian Phoenicians (Ezek. 26:1–28:26) also must prepare for God's judgment because of their prideful arrogance. The king of Tyre went so far as to claim divinity (28:2); and even though he lived in glorious splendor (vv. 12–16a), he would be cast down in utter ruin and disgrace (16b–19).[28] In the end, Tyre and all of Israel's hostile and sinful neighbors would know that Israel's God is the LORD (v. 23).

Egypt was the focus of much of Ezekiel's attention (chapters 29–32). She had achieved great power and wealth in the decades of Nubian rule, but now her trust in her own resources and her hostility toward the people of the Lord would bring her to her knees in shameful defeat and devastation. Following every hammer blow of God's wrath, Egypt, like other nations similarly treated, would confess that he alone is Lord (29:6, 8, 16, 21; 30:19, 26; 32:15). And that was the purpose of God's judgment of the nations. They must come to realize that he, the Creator of the heavens and the earth, is the sovereign LORD of all, even of them. His desire is that they repent, turn to him in submission, and, with Israel, become part

---

[27] Walther Eichrodt, *Ezekiel* (Philadelphia: Westminster, 1970), 246.

[28] H. G. May, "The King in the Garden of Eden: A Study of Ezekiel 28:12–19," *Israel's Prophetic Heritage,* ed. Bernhard W. Anderson and Walter J. Harrelson (New York: Harper and Brothers, 1962), 166–76.

of the community of faith. Not all nations—in fact, none as such—will come to embrace the Lord as God and submit to his sovereignty. The most that can be said is that individuals from those nations will believe and together will constitute the eschatological kingdom of God, first as the church in history and then as all the people of God in the ages to come. The nations per se will be consigned to ultimate destruction by the Lord, an outcome painted in somber tones in Ezekiel 38–39. Here the prophet saw the nations arrayed against his own special nation Israel, a people redeemed and restored back to their homeland. In that distant day, the whole world will unite as one hostile force against not just Israel but the God of Israel, a final holy war contesting the issue of ultimate sovereignty.

Bearing names of both known and now unknown ancient peoples, these armies will gather in the land of promise where they will find Israel living in peace with no visible means of protection and support (Ezek. 38:10–13). But this is not to say that Israel will be defenseless, for the Lord God will manifest his great power in earthquake and sword, and these mighty human hosts will prove to be impotent in the face of God's anger (vv. 17–22). In this manner, says the Lord, "I will display My greatness and holiness, and will reveal Myself in the sight of many nations. Then they will know that I am the LORD" (v. 23). This will be no surprise, for the promise to Abraham had been that the Lord would bless those nations that blessed Abraham's seed and would curse those that cursed them (Gen. 12:1–3). Gog and Magog represent the climactic epitome of what lay ahead for the nations that would not have the Lord to rule over them (cf. Rev. 20:7–10).[29]

The Lord's powerful work was to be not only on his own behalf and for his own glory, but it would be designed also to restore Israel to its covenant-bearing privileges. "I will make My holy name known among My people Israel," the Lord declared, and as a result "the nations will know that I am the LORD, the Holy One in Israel" (Ezek. 39:7). This is why Israel was called in the first place—to be the Lord's servant in modeling what the kingdom of God should look like and to mediate his saving grace to all peoples. What they failed to do in history they

[29] Leslie C. Allen, *Ezekiel 20-48,* WBC 29 (Dallas: Word, 1990), 210–11; J. Paul Tanner, "Rethinking Ezekiel's Invasion by Gog," *JETS* 39 (1996): 29–45.

will at last accomplish in the day of their renewal and restoration (cf. 39:21–29).

The Restoration of Israel

We have already observed hints of Israel's restoration in the midst of the most severe judgment texts, for the Lord's punishment of the nation was designed for its correction and reinstitution. At the beginning of his prophetic discourses, Ezekiel held out hope for some of the people—those, paradoxically, fortunate enough to have been taken captive (Ezek. 6:8–10). Even in distant Babylonia the Lord would be their sanctuary (Ezek. 11:16), but they would return from there to the land of promise, rid it of all vestiges of idolatry, and undergo a radical renewal of heart (vv. 18–20). The Lord in response would establish with them an everlasting covenant, the nature of which the prophet elaborated later on (Ezek. 16:59–63; cf. 36:24–32).

Addressing the mountains of Israel, the Lord described the paradisiacal conditions that would obtain in his great day of renewal (Ezek. 36:8–15). The population will multiply, flora and fauna will abound, and Israel will no longer be subject to the vagaries of life in an uncertain land but will dominate the land as her own inheritance. This will come to pass not ultimately for the sake of Israel but for the sake of the Lord and his holy name. Israel's regeneration will testify to the nations of the Lord's faithfulness to his promises; and thus, as always, they will know that he is the Lord (v. 23).

The apex of Israel's return to favor would be the cutting of a new covenant, one already described by Jeremiah (Jer. 31:31–34). The Lord would purify his people, cleansing them from all their defilement and idolatry (Ezek. 36:24–25). Most astounding of all, he would remove their stony hearts and replace them with hearts of flesh. They would then be moved by his Spirit to keep covenant with full obedience. This would result in their repudiation of old habits of sin and degradation, freeing them to be the people God called and ordained them to be (vv. 26–32). We must not fail to see in this that the initiative and power to effect this kind of supernatural renewal will lie not in Israel but in the Lord alone. Israel was condemned to be forever written off were she to break covenant and persist in her sin, and everything in her historical experience pointed to this as a foregone conclusion. Humanly there was no prospect of self-reformation and certainly no capacity for spiritual rebirth. Only God could do these things; and for the sake of his promises to the fathers and the integrity of his name, he would and will renew them in the glorious day of salvation.

We have also observed that Ezekiel had little to say explicitly about a messianic figure, but what he did say is of profound theological importance. At the end of the age, he said, the Lord will regather his people to the land and will place one shepherd over them, his servant David (Ezek. 34:23–24). Then the Lord will be Israel's God, and David will be their ruler. The prophet thus culminated previous promises about the continuation of the Davidic line (Gen. 49:10; 1 Chron. 17:11; etc.) and linked Davidic kingship with the exercise of the Lord's own ultimate sovereignty. Ezekiel elaborated on this theme in a clearly eschatological context (Ezek. 37:22–25) where the Lord promised to make Israel an undivided nation in the land with one king over them forever. Never again would they flirt with paganism, for the Lord would purge them thoroughly of any such disposition. In a clear reiteration of mutual covenant commitment, the Lord declared of Israel, "They will be My people, and I will be their God" (v. 23). Lest there be any doubt as to the identity of the king, the prophet named him again—"My [the LORD's] servant David" (v. 24). And the law of the land will be the statutes of the new covenant already articulated (v. 24; cf. 36:24–32). And lest, moreover, there be lingering doubt as to Israel's covenant loyalty in the age to come, the Lord banished such ideas by affirming that "they will follow My ordinances, and keep My statutes and obey them," "I will make a covenant of peace with them; it will be an everlasting covenant with them" and "will set My sanctuary among them forever" (vv. 24, 26).

Chapter Seventeen

The Theology of the Postexilic Prophets

The Prophet Daniel

Since early in the Christian era and especially since the Enlightenment, critics have almost unanimously insisted that Daniel did not write the book that bears his name, nor did it arise in the late sixth century as its contents suggest. Rather, the remarkable precision of its prophecies, especially in chapter 11, presupposes to them a mid-second century provenience.[1] This point of view has become almost a matter of dogma in contemporary scholarship except among those open to the possibility of predictive prophecy and those conversant with the character of the Aramaic in which half the book was written as well as certain other features.[2]

All this apart, there is agreement that the book professes to a setting in sixth-century Babylonia under the lengthy rule of Nebuchadnezzar (605–562 BC); a number of successors, including Belshazzar (562–539); and the

[1] For a strong presentation of this view, see S. R. Driver, *An Introduction to the Literature of the Old Testament* (Cleveland: World, 1956 [1897]), 497–508.

[2] Gleason L. Archer Jr., *A Survey of Old Testament Introduction* (Chicago: Moody, 1985), 387–411; Gerhard F. Hasel, "The Book of Daniel and Matters of Language: Evidences Relating to Names, Words, and the Aramaic Language," *AUSS* 19 (1981): 211–25.

first rulers of the Persian dominion there, Cyrus the Great and Darius the Mede (down to ca. 530). True to our oft-repeated method, we will approach the theological message of the book in light of its own attested setting rather than one determined by historical-critical analysis.

The Contest for Sovereignty

The major theme of the book is the conflict between the kingdom of God and the kingdoms of the world as epitomized primarily by Babylonia and Persia.[3] Daniel had visions and dreams of his own and interpreted those of other persons, especially kings, in which the future course of history would play out, finally culminating in the judgment of the nations by the Lord and their replacement by the Lord's own sovereign rule. The orientation was both historical and eschatological with the latter more dominant, and the presentation was apocalyptic.[4] That is, the scope is panoramic and universal, the language highly symbolic and figurative, and the emphasis on the nations in general with no particular attention to Israel. Messianism is everywhere presupposed, but a messianic figure is at best only hinted at (e.g., Dan. 9:25).

A good place to commence is with Daniel's prayer (Dan. 9:1–27) in which he traced briefly the disobedience of the chosen people (vv. 4–11a), anticipated their judgment (vv. 11b–14), and predicted their forgiveness and restoration (vv. 15–27). They had broken covenant with him and now found themselves scattered from one end of the earth to the other. Citing the curses of the covenant texts (most likely Lev. 26 and Deut. 28), Daniel confessed that he and his people were suffering because of having violated the stipulations of which they spoke (v. 11b). And yet through all the centuries of God's judgment, they had refused to repent and thus deserved the calamitous fate they now endured in exile (v. 14). He concluded his prayer by appealing to the exodus deliverance as a historical precedent for the Lord's acting again in forgiveness and salvation. Urgently he petitioned him to regard the ruined temple with favor, to look with compassion on the holy city that bore his name, and

---

[3] Eugene H. Merrill, "Daniel as a Contribution to Kingdom Theology," *Essays in Honor of J. Dwight Pentecost,* ed. Stanley D. Toussaint and Charles H. Dyer (Chicago: Moody, 1986), 211–25.

[4] John J. Collins, *The Apocalyptic Vision of the Book of Daniel* (Missoula, Mont.: Scholars, 1977).

to do so because of his mercy and in spite of the people's just deserts (vv. 17–19).

The answer to the prayer was not long in coming, at least in terms of what the Lord would do in the future (vv. 24–27). The Jews by then had languished in captivity for seventy years as Jeremiah had predicted (Dan. 9:2; cf. Jer. 25:11; 29:10), but in seven times seventy years the Lord would "put a stop to sin, . . . wipe away injustice, . . . bring in everlasting righteousness, . . . seal up vision and prophecy, and . . . anoint the most holy place" (v. 24). The division of the weeks of years into its various segments—seven sevens, sixty-two sevens, and one seven—has yielded a multiplicity of interpretations depending on one's overall eschatological framework.[5] Certain elements are unambiguous, however, and no exegetical or hermeneutical clues exist to indicate that their descriptions should be taken in any but a literal way: (1) Jerusalem will be rebuilt; (2) an anointed ruler will come; (3) he will be cut off; (4) a hostile ruler will destroy the city and the temple; (5) war will persist during that period; (6) the wicked ruler will make a covenant for one "seven" but will break it halfway through; and (7) he will meet his end after having desecrated the temple (vv. 25–27).[6]

The anointed one *(māšîaḥ),* the ruler *(nāgîd),* is universally regarded as a Davidic Messiah, identified in Christian theology as Jesus Christ. His being cut off *(kārat)* obviously refers to his violent death either "leaving no one/nothing" or "not for his own sake" (thus Heb. *ʾên lô*). It is difficult for the Christian interpreter to see anything else here than the crucifixion of Christ in the first Christian century.[7] But the introduction of the ruler to come who will destroy the city and temple and then make and break a covenant with many points clearly to an eschatological age when righteousness will finally prevail. Daniel deals with this conflict of the kingdoms elsewhere and offers a great deal more information about the evil ruler of whom he speaks here. In the final analysis that ruler epitomizes all the world systems that stand in implacable antithesis to the sovereignty and purposes of the Lord.

---

[5] For the more common options, see Stephen R. Miller, *Daniel,* NAC 18 (Nashville: Broadman & Holman, 1994), 252–57.

[6] Paul D. Feinberg, "An Exegetical and Theological Study of Daniel 9:24–27," *Tradition and Testament,* ed. John S. Feinberg and Paul D. Feinberg (Chicago: Moody, 1981), 189–220.

[7] Christoph Barth, *God with Us* (Grand Rapids: Eerdmans, 1991), 232–33.

The Kingdoms of the World

Ever since the fall, mankind has lived in rebellion against the kingdom of God, seeking to create its own alternative domains and refusing to comply with the creation mandate for which it was created as God's image. The Old Testament as a whole bears witness to this rebellion as it unfolded historically. Daniel's concern, however, was not so much historical as contemporary (to him) and eschatological. He addressed the kingdoms of his own time and those yet to come up to and including the kingdom of God which will, at the end, prevail over all others.

The nature and outcome of human kingdoms was impressed upon Daniel by dreams and visions (as we have already noted), the first being a dream of King Nebuchadnezzar of Babylon. He could not fathom its meaning and refused to divulge its contents to his own diviners; but eventually it came to Daniel's attention, and he offered an inspired interpretation (Dan. 2:36–43). Nebuchadnezzar had seen a great statue made of various metals from top to bottom, ending with feet of clay. The head of gold was Nebuchadnezzar himself, said Daniel, for he was "king of kings" (v. 37). But his kingship was derivative. The God of heaven had entrusted him with it. In words similar to those of the creation mandate of Genesis 1:26–28, Daniel informed the Babylonian king that the Lord "has given you sovereignty, power, strength, and glory. Wherever people live—or wild animals, or birds of the air—He has handed them over to you and made you ruler over them all" (vv. 37–38). Nebuchadnezzar, it seems, symbolized the rule that mankind as a whole was designed to exercise.[8]

The silver, bronze, and iron kingdoms to follow would culminate in a disunited and tenuous government which, though universal, would collapse under the crushing blow of a stone that would "break off from the mountain without a hand touching it" that is, the kingdom of the God of heaven that will never be destroyed (v. 45). Human history and its prideful assertion of rival dominion would give way to the God of eternity.[9]

---

[8] John E. Goldingay, *Daniel,* WBC 30 (Dallas: Word, 1989), 49–50.

[9] C. L. Seow, "From Mountain to Mountain: The Reign of God in Daniel 2," *A God So Near: Essays on Old Testament Theology in Honor of Patrick D. Miller,* ed. Brent A. Strawn and Nancy R. Bowen (Winona Lake, Ind.: Eisenbrauns, 2003), 355–74.

Meanwhile, Nebuchadnezzar seems not to have learned much from his dream, for he set up an image of gold before which he demanded that all people in his realm should bow. Certain citizens of the kingdom of heaven—Shadrach, Meshach, and Abednego—refused to do so, however; for to worship Nebuchadnezzar was to deny the sovereignty of God. The issue at stake could not be clearer: "We want you as king to know," they said, "that we will not serve your gods or worship the gold statue you set up" (Dan. 3:18). For their insubordination they were thrown into a blazing furnace but came forth unscathed, testifying to their faith that "if the God we serve exists, then He can rescue us" (v. 17). God's kingdom, thus, did not need an eschatological day of realization but was already at work in history.

That same demonstration of divine sovereignty in the present is echoed in Nebuchadnezzar's dream about a great tree loaded with leaves and fruit and providing shelter to all the animals and birds of the earth.[10] The tree came crashing down, however, and all the animals scattered. The stump that remained then turned into a beast that foraged about for its survival (Dan. 4:9–16). Daniel revealed to the king that he was the tree and the wild animal. Because of his sinful arrogance he would temporarily be removed from his throne, be afflicted with madness, and then, having recognized the sovereignty of the Lord, be reinstated (vv. 20–27). As Daniel put it, the condition for Nebuchadnezzar's continuing monarchy was for him to "acknowledge that Heaven rules" (v. 26).

Belshazzar, a later successor to Nebuchadnezzar, had to learn the same thing, first by the handwriting on the wall (Dan. 5:18–28) and then in a dream by Daniel that had clear implications for Belshazzar and the kingdoms to follow (Dan. 7:1–14). In it were four animals that emerged from the sea—a lion, a bear, a leopard, and one indefinable. The last had ten horns, three of which were uprooted and replaced by still another. This horn could speak and did so, boastfully (v. 8). The animals, Daniel was informed, were four successive kingdoms that, like the kingdoms of Nebuchadnezzar's dream (Dan. 2), would in the end submit to the kingdom of the Most High (v. 18). The horns of the fourth animal were ten kings, he learned, and the eleventh was a ruler who would "speak

[10] Great trees were metaphors for kings and other rulers in the ancient Near East. See John J. Collins, *Daniel* (Minneapolis: Fortress, 1993), 223–24.

words against the Most High and oppress the holy ones of the Most High. He will intend to change religious festivals and laws" (Dan. 7:25). This ruler is clearly the one referred to in Daniel 9:25–27 who would destroy Jerusalem and its temple and who would make and break covenants with God's people.

This is further clarified by Daniel's vision of the ram and goat (Dan. 8). It seems that a ram in the east with two horns charged toward the west until it met head-on a goat sprouting one horn between its eyes. The ram was soundly defeated, and the goat took its place as a powerful ruler. But at length the goat's horn was broken off and replaced by four others out of one of which still another horn grew. This one came to dominate the earth "toward the beautiful land" (v. 9), going so far as to arrogate to itself the services of the holy temple (v. 12). This time Daniel was left in no doubt as to the identity of the figures in the vision. The ram was Medo-Persia, the goat Greece, and the four horns the nations that would replace the breakup of the Macedonian Empire, the so-called Diadochi. The horn rising out of the four is called here "an insolent king, skilled in intrigue" (v. 23). He would increase in power to the extent that at last he would "even stand against the Prince of princes" (v. 25). He cannot prevail, however, and will be destroyed by the Lord (v. 25; cf. 7:26; 9:27).

This same figure appears once more in Daniel, in chapter 11. This time he is seen as a king who "will do whatever he wants" (v. 36). He will assume a role of superiority above all gods and will dare to blaspheme the Lord God himself. After initial successes in dominating the nations around him, this would-be god will himself be overcome—"he will meet his end with no one to help him" (v. 45).

The figure just described is generally (and correctly) identified as Antiochus IV Epiphanes, king of Seleucid Syria from 175 to 164 BC. But clearly he only anticipated the wicked ruler of eschatological times about whom Daniel had already spoken several times (7:24–26; 8:23–25; 9:26–27). The New Testament knows him as the antichrist, either by that term (1 John 2:18, 22; 4:3; 2 John 7) or by his role as opponent to the Lord and his kingly purposes (cf. 2 Thess. 2:1–12; Rev. 13:1–10; 19:19–21). Old Testament theology alone may not allow such precision, but one thing is clear: The anti-God forces of human government will one day be led, or at least epitomized, by a dictatorial figure who will make a last stand attempt to dethrone the Lord of heaven but who will fail miserably to do so.[11] His defeat and the defeat of godless human institutions that he represents will usher in the glorious Kingdom of God.

The Kingdom of Heaven

In the exilic and postexilic periods of Israel's history, the covenant community no longer lived in relative isolation from the great surrounding nations; in fact, it became absorbed by them. As a result, the Jews thought in much more universal terms, of a world much greater and broader in scope than was formerly the case. This enhanced worldview impacted also their way of understanding and describing their God. He was no longer just the Lord of Israel but the God of heaven and earth. This larger purview is reflected in the divine epithets employed in the later Old Testament literature such as "God of gods" (Dan. 2:47), "the Most High" (Dan. 4:34), and "the God of heaven" (Neh. 1:5; 2:4, 20). The ultimate conflict, then, was not between the deities of Babylonia and Persia on the one hand, and the God of Israel, on the other. Rather, it was the sovereignty of the God of all the universe that was being challenged by human rulers and their gods.

The sovereignty of God (to be considered next) is a prominent theme in Daniel—and certainly presupposes a heavenly kingdom—but the kingdom as such finds clear expressions in only two passages, namely, Daniel 2:44–45 and 7:26–27. The prophet informed Nebuchadnezzar that after the kingdoms of this world had run their course, "the God of heaven will set up a kingdom that will never be destroyed" (2:44). In fact, his kingdom would overthrow all those and put in place God's own perfect rule. Then, in line with his creation intentions, the Lord would put in places of responsibility his special people, "the holy ones of the Most High" (7:27). They would be entrusted with "the kingdom, dominion, and greatness of the kingdoms under all of heaven." The command to mankind to be "fruitful, multiply, fill the earth, and subdue it" (Gen. 1:28) would at last come to realization.

[11] For this view (with qualifications), see Ernest Lucas, *Daniel,* AOTC 20 (Downers Grove, Ill.: InterVarsity, 2002), 290–93, 301–2.

God as Sovereign

The kingdom of God obviously necessitates the concept of God as King, the ruler over all he has created.[12] Daniel, of course, knew him as such, but it is important to note that some of the most potent affirmations of this truth originated from the lips of pagan monarchs. Nebuchadnezzar, having learned the meaning of the image of his dream, confessed to Daniel, "Your God is indeed God of gods, Lord of kings" (Dan. 2:47). And following the miraculous rescue of the three Jewish young men from the furnace, he was constrained to praise their God and to admit that "there is no other god who is able to deliver like this" (Dan. 3:29). Then, in two declarations of gratitude to Israel's God, the same king referred to him as "the Most High God" whose "kingdom is an eternal kingdom" and whose "dominion is from generation to generation" (Dan. 4:2–3). He must "praise, exalt, and glorify the King of heaven, because all His works are true and His ways are just" (v. 37).

King Darius (the Mede; cf. Dan. 5:30) was no less persuaded of the sovereignty of the Lord. Having witnessed Daniel's deliverance from the lions' den, he commanded that Daniel's God alone be worshipped, "for He is the living God" whose kingdom will never be destroyed and come to an end (Dan. 6:26). Whether he, or Nebuchadnezzar for that matter, actually believed what he said and therefore became a convert to Yahwism is pretty much irrelevant to the point that at least they are both on record as having made the declaration that the Lord is God and that they and all mankind must submit to his sovereignty.

The Prophet Joel

The date of Joel's ministry and thus the date of the authorship of his canonical book cannot be determined with precision, but the tone as a whole seems most at home in the period of the exile or shortly thereafter.[13] He describes the denudation of the land because of foreign conquest, a stripping of the countryside so complete that it is as though locusts had swarmed over it, eating up everything in their path (Joel 1:1–7). After

---

[12] For a previous discussion of this aspect of God's role, see pp. 137–42.

[13] For the various arguments see Raymond B. Dillard and Tremper Longman III, *An Introduction to the Old Testament* (Grand Rapids: Zondervan, 1994), 365–67.

enjoining his hearers to lament (vv. 8–12), the prophet called for them to repent for the "Day of the LORD" was at hand, a time of judgment so severe that the recent devastation of the land would pale in comparison (vv. 13–20). The refrain "Day of the LORD" is a hallmark of the book, occurring some nine times in that or a similar form (1:15; 2:1, 2, 11, 31; 3:14, 18).[14] As we have noted earlier, it is a technical term referring usually to God's judgment in eschatological times.[15] Here Joel viewed the destruction of the nation by human armies as a portent of the judgment of the Lord that would surely come and with even greater fury.

In that final day the Lord as heavenly Warrior would lead his armies against his foes, including his own chosen people. No such host had ever been assembled before, nor would there ever be the like again (Joel 2:2). The imagery of cloud, darkness, fire, and earthquake speaks clearly of divine presence, of an awesome display of power and glory associated with the transcendent Lord of creation and consummation. In light of this impending day of reckoning, God's people could only turn to him in sincere contrition, rending their hearts and not their garments (v. 13). Once they did this the Lord would expel the invaders from the land (in the present) (vv. 18–24) and would restore his people to the point that they would recognize that he is among them as their God (to the exclusion of all others) and that they would never again face shame (in the day to come) (vv. 25–27).

That day would also be marked by profound spiritual renewal (vv. 28–29), cosmic upheaval (vv. 30–31), and salvation for all who would call upon the Lord, Jew and Gentile alike (v. 32). On the other hand, the nations would be judged because of their mistreatment of the chosen people (Joel 3:1–3), a curse inherent in the Abrahamic covenant for those who curse his seed (Gen. 12:3). As for Israel, though they would experience the invasion of their land by enemy nations all around, the Lord would deliver them. Then would be ushered in an era of peace and prosperity (vv. 17–18), an unending time in the presence of the Lord who dwells in Zion (vv. 20–21).

---

[14] Ferdinand E. Deist, "Parallels and Reinterpretation in the Book of Joel: A Theology of the Yom Yahweh?" *Text and Context: Old Testament and Semitic Studies for F. C. Fensham,* ed. W. Claassen, JSOT Supp. Series 48 (Sheffield: Sheffield Academic Press, 1988), 63–79.

[15] See p. 495.

The theology of Joel is uncomplicated.[16] It revolves around the idea that the nations, even God's chosen one, are accountable to the Lord and must be judged when they fall short of his rightful expectations. Should they repent, however, they can find forgiveness and in Israel's case reestablishment as his servant people. What is not resolved in history can and will be resolved in the day of the Lord when he makes everything right.

The Prophet Obadiah

Obadiah's provenience, like that of Joel, is unclear but seems best understood in the context of the exile.[17] The prophet was single-minded in his objective to address the nation Edom with a warning of coming judgment. As a brother nation to Israel, Edom could have enjoyed special privileges associated with that relationship, but its history of hostility toward the covenant people bespoke something different. Not only must Edom be punished for its fratricidal behavior, but the name *Edom* itself would become almost a code word for all nations that stand in rebellion against the Lord and his kingdom objectives.[18]

Edom's sin was "violence done to your brother Jacob" (v. 10), a collaboration with invaders who overthrew Jerusalem and carried off its treasures (vv. 11, 13). Instead of coming to Judah's aid, Edom rejoiced in her misfortune and even handed over her refugees to the enemy army (v. 14). Edom thought it could get away with this because of its secure, well nigh invincible location in the clefts of the rocks (vv. 3–4). This engendered a spirit of pompous pride, an attitude that defied not only human attempts at retribution but challenged even the Lord's ability to execute justice. This underestimation of the Lord's might was fatal, however, and would lead to Edom's everlasting downfall (v. 10).

The day of reckoning would be the day of the Lord, the eschatological time when wrongs would be righted (v. 15). Edom and all evil nations would be punished; but Israel, to the contrary, would be saved and, moreover, would become the Lord's instrument of judgment (vv. 17–18).

---

[16] Duane A. Garrett, *Hosea, Joel,* NAC 19A (Nashville: Broadman & Holman, 1997), 304–9.

[17] Thomas J. Finley, *Joel, Amos, Obadiah,* WEC (Chicago: Moody, 1990), 340–48.

[18] Douglas Stuart, *Hosea-Jonah,* WBC 31 (Waco, Tex.: Word, 1987), 404.

Then Edom and other rebel nations would become dwelling places for Israel. Finally, government would be established once more in Jerusalem, the capital of the kingdom of the Lord (v. 21).

The Prophet Haggai

Haggai, the first of the datable postexilic prophets, dedicated himself almost exclusively to the task of rebuilding the Jerusalem temple which, by his time (520 BC), had lain in ruins for sixty-six years. The foundations had, indeed, been laid almost twenty years earlier (Ezra 3:8–13), but the work had come to a halt because of external opposition (Ezra 4:1–5) and, more tellingly, because of the Jews' own self-interest. They had begun to settle into a routine and were so careful to attend to their own needs and desires that they neglected the temple and other matters of the cultus (Hag. 1:4, 9). Haggai's burden was to redress this indifference and to see to it that the people's priorities were put in proper order.

The theology of the book is also temple centered but more from an eschatological than a historical perspective.[19] It was important, of course, for the people to erect a sanctuary then and there that the Lord might dwell among them (Hag. 1:8). But there was a realization already that the project underway was but a pale reflection of God's habitation in the future. Those who had seen the glorious temple of Solomon were especially struck by the comparative meagerness of what now was being done (Hag. 2:3; cf. Ezra 3:12). Yet out of this small beginning would come a dwelling place of the Lord that he would fill with his glory (Hag. 2:7). That glory would far outweigh all the silver and gold in the world, so this latter temple would, after all, outshine the first one.

The phrase "in a little while" (v. 6) suggests not a near historical event but one to take place in the day of the Lord.[20] This is clear from the imagery of cosmic disturbance typical of eschatological texts: "Once more, in a little while, I am going to shake the heavens and the earth, the sea and the dry land. I will shake all the nations" (vv. 6–7; cf. Isa. 2:19, 21; 13:13; 24:18; Amos 9:9). Haggai thus made the transition from the

[19] Richard A. Taylor and E. Ray Clendenen, *Haggai, Malachi,* NAC 21A (Nashville: Broadman & Holman, 2004), 73–83.

[20] Eugene H. Merrill, *Haggai, Zechariah, Malachi* (Chicago: Moody, 1994), 39.

temple of his contemporaries, so small in their eyes, to that temple yet to come which would excel the temple of Solomon in its glory.

In line with temple restoration, the Lord would "overturn royal thrones and destroy the power of the Gentile kingdoms" (Hag. 2:22), all in connection with the shaking of the heavens and the earth that would attend the glorification of the temple (v. 21). And "on that day" Zerubbabel, the governor of Israel and offspring of David, would rule on the Lord's behalf, his derivative power being metaphorically described as the Lord's signet ring (v. 23). That is, whatever he will do will be done on the Lord's behalf and invested with the Lord's own authority. Zerubbabel himself would not, of course, be that messianic ruler in a literal sense but would be only the link between David and the ultimate Son of David who was on the scene in Haggai's day.[21]

The day of the Lord will thus usher in a new permanent residence of the Lord among his people and a scion of David who will exercise sovereignty on his behalf. The New Testament understands this in terms of a messianic temple (Rev. 21:22–25) and a messianic throne (Rev. 22:3), both of which are to be occupied by the atoning Lamb of God.

The Prophet Zechariah

Zechariah was a contemporary of Haggai who, though no doubt concerned about the issues of the day that preoccupied Haggai, communicated visions and oracles of an eschatological nature, both historical (to us) and more remotely future. His language is highly apocalyptic, but this in no way obscures the great theological themes that were close to his heart. These themes may be boiled down essentially to: (1) the disobedience of Israel; (2) the judgment of Israel; (3) the restoration of Israel; (4) the judgment of the nations; (5) the salvation of the nations; (6) the coming Messiah; and (7) the sovereignty of the Lord. We have taken note of these themes over and over again in previous prophetic works, but in Zechariah they achieve a clarity and intensity rare in earlier prophets.

---

[21] Pieter A. Verhoef, *The Books of Haggai and Malachi,* NICOT (Grand Rapids: Eerdmans, 1987), 146–50.

The Disobedience of Israel

This topic was of comparatively little interest to the prophet, perhaps because the exile, the punishment *par excellence* for Israel's long history of sin, was already in the past. He did, however, provide a brief résumé of the people's hypocritical worship even in the seventy years of the exile, an attitude characteristic also of the many centuries prior to it. Their fasting and mourning, their eating and drinking at festival times—all this they did for public display and not as acts of devotion to the Lord (Zech. 7:4–7). What they must do to rectify this was to obey the terms of the Mosaic covenant, especially vis-à-vis the poor and disadvantaged, something their fathers had not done (vv. 8–13). This is why they had ended up in Babylonian captivity (v. 14).

The Judgment of Israel

Zechariah described the exile as a scattering of the Lord's people by the "horns of the nations," as though they were being pushed here and there by cattle or oxen (Zech. 1:21) and by a whirlwind that left the land barren of life (7:14). But judgment was not just a matter of the past. A day yet remained when the unrepentant of Israel would once more experience the Lord's displeasure. This would include wicked rulers who, figuratively at least, would buy and sell their people like so many sheep (11:4–5). All together would go into captivity with not so much as a notice by the Lord (v. 6). The shepherd motif continues in Zechariah 13:7–8 where it is predicted that just as sheep scatter when a shepherd is incapacitated, so two-thirds of God's people would perish in the day when leadership was lacking. Specific fulfillment of these prophecies is most uncertain, but history reveals a number of diasporas from ancient times till modern days in which the Jewish people were scattered among the nations. Even in the eschatological day Jerusalem will be captured, its citizens abused, and many taken into exile (Zech. 14:2).

The Restoration of Israel

These gloomy scenes are more than matched by the prophet's revelation of glorious times to come. The Lord promised that he would come to Jerusalem, rebuild his house, and bless the land with prosperity (Zech. 1:16–17). The city would no longer need walls of protection because the Lord would be a "wall of fire" around it (Zech. 2:5) and he would live among the people (v. 10). Judah would become his inheritance and Jerusalem his chosen city (v. 12). In that Edenic day old men and women as well as children would live in peace and harmony, having come back to the promised land from the ends of the earth (Zech. 8:3–8). Full covenant fellowship would be established, for Israel would become God's people and he their God (v. 8). Whereas they had been an object of cursing by the nations, they would become a means of blessing the nations, a clear and direct fulfillment of the Abrahamic covenant (v. 13; cf. Gen. 12:1–3).

The return of God's people would be at his initiative and not theirs. "I will strengthen the house of Judah and deliver the house of Joseph," he said (Zech. 10:6). Because of his compassion they would be saved, and his gracious favor would be extended to them just as though they had never sinned (v. 6b). He will "whistle and gather them" (v. 8) no matter how far and widely they have been dispersed. Like another exodus they would pass through seas and rivers of opposition until they were safely home (vv. 10–11).

Even so, in the day of the Lord, Jerusalem would once more suffer siege and threat of destruction at the hands of wicked nations (Zech. 12:1–2). However, the Lord would deliver her again, using Jerusalem as his weapon of war (v. 6). The Lord's power and grace on behalf of Judah and Jerusalem would be so persuasive of his sovereignty that the whole nation—from the lowliest citizen to the royal family—would weep in deep repentance for their sin of having spurned him (vv. 10–14). He would then open a fountain of cleansing to purify them (Zech. 13:1), an image reminiscent of Ezekiel's "heart of flesh" that God will place within his people as an act of pure grace (Ezek. 36:26).[22] Once again (cf. 8:8) the Lord would be able to affirm of Israel that "they are My people," and they in full sincerity could say, "The LORD is our God" (v. 9). Never again would Jerusalem be destroyed, for the Lord would make her everlastingly secure (Zech. 14:11).

---

[22] Joyce G. Baldwin, *Haggai, Zechariah, Malachi,* TOTC (London: InterVarsity, 1972), 195.

The Judgment of the Nations

Israel's redemption and restoration oftentimes came and will come at the expense of the nations that suppress and persecute her. But these nations in reality are hostile to the Lord, not his people, for they are motivated by spiritual entities of which they are not even aware. God's creation design was that the nations might rule on his behalf; but because of the fall, they have become co-opted to the service of demonic powers. They therefore must repent or be destroyed so that the kingdom of God can exist alone in unchallenged hegemony.

Zechariah first declared that the horns (i.e., the nations) that pushed Israel into exile would themselves be overthrown (Zech. 1:21). Babylon is an example of an instrument God used to punish his people but to such excess that now Babylon itself must be punished. She had gone beyond reasonable measures and had touched "the pupil of His eye," that is, Israel, his special possession (Zech. 2:8–9). Other nations would also experience the Lord's wrath, especially neighbors to his elect people—Hadrach, Damascus, Hamath, Tyre, Sidon, Ashkelon, Gaza, Ekron, Ashdod, and all the Philistines (Zech. 9:1–8). They had oppressed his nation and now must suffer the curse reserved for those who curse Abraham's offspring (v. 8). The final judgment of the nations would come in the day of the Lord when the Lord as divine Warrior will lead his hosts in holy war (Zech. 14:3–5). With supernatural power he will strike a blow so grievous that the hostile forces of the world will melt away to nothingness (vv. 12–15).

The Salvation of the Nations

At the same time, the grace of the Lord will be extended to mankind—Jew and Gentile alike—to draw them to himself. And these overtures will not go unrewarded, for "many nations will join themselves to the LORD on that day and become My people," he declared (Zech. 2:11). Israel at last would become the magnet to attract them, a role for which God had called them into covenant in the first place. The prophet in most graphic terms foresaw a time when "10 men from nations of every language will grab the robe of a Jewish man tightly, urging: Let us go with you, for we have heard that God is with you'" (Zech. 8:23). In that day they would join Israel in pilgrimage to Jerusalem to celebrate the Feast of the

Tabernacles, the festival associated with covenant renewal (Zech. 14:16; cf. Deut. 31:9–13; Neh. 8:1–18). Those who refused to do so would be marked as rebels, subject to the same kind of discipline that Israel had experienced in her history of disobedience. This is added proof that Israel and the nations will be one people at the end of the ages. No longer will there be anyone considered a pagan Canaanite in the Lord's house, for all mankind will be purified and in common allegiance to the Lord God (vv. 20–21).[23]

The Coming Messiah

Messianism plays a large role in the theology of Zechariah and in familiar terms. The Lord revealed through the prophet that he would bring "My servant, the Branch" (Zech. 3:8) and that this would result in such a massive conversion that He would "remove the sin of this land in a single day" (Zech. 3:9 NIV). The context and technical terminology make clear that this would not be the work of the servant in history (as in Isa. 53) but at the end of the age when, as Isaiah put it, a nation would be born in a day (Isa. 66:8). The coming one would embody two roles—those of priest and king—wearing the mitre of Joshua and sitting on the throne of royalty. His name, the Branch, establishes his messianic credentials; and like the priest-king David, he will exercise God-given dominion over the Lord's people (Zech. 6:9–15; cf. Ps. 110; Rev. 21:22; 22:3).

The most famous messianic text in the book is 9:9–10, which speaks of a king's riding in triumph into Jerusalem. He is righteous and will bring salvation. Then, having established worldwide peace, he will rule over all the earth. The picture is that of a Davidic monarch who comes to assert and establish his universal sovereignty. The Old Testament text alone presents these events as occurring at one time or in rapid sequence; but the New Testament, which views Jesus as the king in question, divides the passage between the triumphant entry (v. 8) and the exercise of kingship that follows (v. 9). In fact, the New Testament citations (Matt. 21:5; John 12:15) allude only to verse 8, suggesting that the ride on the donkey has already (from our perspective) taken place, whereas

[23] For defense of this interpretation, see Merrill, *Haggai, Zechariah, Malachi,* 366.

the assumption of universal sovereignty yet remains to be fulfilled in the day of the Lord.[24]

The Sovereignty of Yahweh

Finally, Zechariah touches briefly on this idea—that the Lord "will become king over all the earth" (Zech. 14:9). There will be only one Lord, he says, and his name will be the only name. The nations that have come to see him will worship him as king, having become, with Israel, one people of the Lord (vv. 16–17). God's original kingdom design—the creation of mankind as his image to rule over all things on his behalf—will at last come to full fruition.

The Prophet Malachi

The major issue confronting the last of Israel's prophets (ca. 470 BC) was the hypocrisy of the Jewish community that was going through the motions of religiosity without genuine and heartfelt commitment.[25] The temple had long since been built and the full apparatus of worship reestablished, but a spiritual lethargy had crept in, and the letter of the law had begun to preempt its spirit. To Malachi it seems as though nothing had been learned through the discipline of exile and that the Jewish state was headed once more for divine judgment. His appeal to his people was that they reorder their priorities and fall in line with the Lord's covenant requirements. Failing that they could expect his displeasure in a day of reckoning. On the other hand, the Lord's covenant promises are forever, and in the end he will save his people from the inevitable curse with which he will afflict the earth.

The Lord's favor toward Israel was established right up front with the remarkable declaration by the Lord, "I have loved you" (Mal. 1:2). This sets the covenant tone of the book, for in biblical technical language for God to love is synonymous with his sovereign election (cf. Deut. 7:7–11).[26] Therefore, He "hated Esau" (or Edom, Mal. 1:3), that is, rejected or failed to choose him. Edom's history of rebellion against the Lord and

[24] Craig L. Blomberg, *Matthew,* NAC 22 (Nashville: Broadman & Holman, 1992), 312.

[25] Taylor and Clendenen, *Haggai, Malachi,* 231–38.

[26] P. J. J. S. Els, אהב, NIDOTTE 1:278–83.

persecution of his brother Israel led the Lord, in fact, to call Edom "a wicked country" (Mal. 1:4), an epithet reflected in the writings of many of the other prophets as well (Isa. 34:1–15; Jer. 49:7–22; Obad.).

The point in establishing the Lord's elective grace here, however, was to highlight by contrast Israel's lack of gratitude for such favor. Priests and people alike despised his name by offering up defective animals as sacrifices, unmindful of the fact that they would never dare offer such gifts to their human governor (Mal. 1:6–8). It would be better to close the temple doors and cease such charades than to continue going through their meaningless rituals (vv. 9–10). Such behavior brought disrepute on thc name of the Lord among the nations (v. 14); and even they, in time to come, would worship him more sincerely than that (v. 11).

The call to the priests was to return to the task to which God had called them by covenant (Mal. 2:1–9). Their ancestors had kept that covenant by and large (vv. 5–6), but now the present generation was in grave danger of being set aside. Already their reputation had been sullied in the eyes of the people (v. 9), and the worst was yet to come because of their violation of the covenant trust handed on to them by their fathers (v. 8). Rather than being blessed for their faithful service, they would be cursed because of their indifference toward the Lord's honor (v. 2).

But the people were no better. They too had broken covenant with the Lord by their mistreatment of one another (v. 10) and, even worse, by their spiritual adultery (v. 11). The two were linked, for the proliferation of divorce in the community went hand in hand with Israel's infidelity toward the Lord, in effect, their divorce from him. The Lord hates divorce, he says, and both kinds: between husbands and wives and between his adulterous people and himself (v. 16). The underlying issue in both cases—and, indeed, throughout the book—was disobedience to covenant commitment whether in the horizontal or vertical dimension.[27]

Turning toward the eschatological age, Malachi foresaw a day when "the Lord," "the Messenger of the covenant," would suddenly appear (Mal. 3:1–5). This messianic figure would purify both Levites and people in that day, and proper worship would be restored to Jerusalem (vv. 3–4). Almost universal Christian consensus identifies the messenger as Jesus Christ, not in his role as incarnate God the Redeemer but as the

[27] Andrew E. Hill, *Malachi,* AB 25D (New York: Doubleday, 1998), 257–59.

Judge who will come at the end of history to restore Israel and to renew the covenant, thereby enabling Israel to worship him in spirit and in truth.[28] This vision clearly matches that of Ezekiel, who also spoke of the cleansing of the chosen people and the Lord's renewal of covenant with them in the last days (Ezek. 36:24–36). Malachi, however, emphasizes more the aspect of judgment as a means of purification, a theme seen elsewhere in the prophets, particularly in Jeremiah (Jer. 30:5–24).

Such glorious prospects, while inevitable because of the Lord's commitment to his covenant promises (Mal. 3:6, 17–18), were predicated nonetheless on Israel's repentance toward the Lord. They must give evidence of a genuine return to him, epitomized here in Malachi by the payment of tithes (Mal. 3:8–11). This is significant because the tithe represents the tribute of a vassal demanded by his suzerain in covenant contexts.[29] This is at the heart of the theology of the annual festivals when Israel, in recognition of the Lord's sovereignty, was to present gifts at the temple, his dwelling place, thus according him the loyal devotion incumbent in their relationship (Exod. 23:14–19). To tithe, then, was to acknowledge covenant compliance and to suggest that all was well between the Lord and the covenant community. When they did this, the Lord would bless them in turn, and all nations would call them blessed (v. 12).

As for the wicked and unrepentant nations of the world, the day of Israel's restoration would also be the day of their judgment and destruction (Mal. 4:1–3). Israel, in an ironic turn of events, would no longer be the oppressed but would be God's instrument of conquest (v. 3). The treading under the soles of the feet evokes the image of the creation mandate that mankind is to subdue the earth and rule over all its creatures (Gen. 1:28). In the end-times Israel will demonstrate God's sovereignty mediated through those created as his image. Thus the kingdom of heaven will prevail over the kingdoms of this world until all rebellion and disobedience everywhere will be put down and he will be King over all (cf. Ezek. 39:7–13).

---

[28] Taylor and Clendenen, *Haggai, Malachi,* 385–86.

[29] Roland de Vaux, *Ancient Israel,* vol. 1 (New York: McGraw-Hill, 1965), 140–41.

PART FIVE

HUMAN REFLECTION ON THE WAYS OF GOD

Chapter Eighteen

The Theology of the Psalms

The Psalms and wisdom literature of the Old Testament open up an altogether different aspect of biblical theology in that they consist primarily of response to the Lord and to the circumstances of life that beset their authors and the communities they represented. This does not affect the fact that their writings were inspired and therefore contribute to the canonical corpus.[1] However, the sentiments expressed may not always be (and, indeed, frequently are not) consistent with the mind of God as expressed in more clearly didactic passages in which "thus saith the LORD" leaves no doubt that he has spoken. This apparently man-originated discourse is particularly true of books such as Job and Ecclesiastes, which will be addressed at a later point. To a lesser extent, even the Psalms betray human attitudes about suffering, vindictiveness, and revenge that seem somewhat less than the ideal reactions to life that should characterize those created as the image of God and called to represent him to the world.[2] They go so far as to question the ways of

---

[1] Benjamin Breckinridge Warfield, *The Inspiration and Authority of the Bible* (Philadelphia: Presbyterian and Reformed, 1948), 150–58.

[2] VanGemeren describes Psalms as "man's word to God and God's Word to man." Willem A. VanGemeren, *Psalms,* EBC 5, ed. Frank E. Gaebelein (Grand Rapids: Zondervan, 1991), 5.

God and even to charge him with attitudes and actions in such a manner as to appear rebellious and agnostic, at least in the case of some of the lament psalms and others that resonate with despair and frustration.

Human responses to life's apparent injustices are still revelatory if only in demonstrating the need for divine wisdom and grace. That is, the reverse side of the coin of God's positive self-disclosure of unambiguous truth is the struggle of mankind, including the saintliest, to understand that truth in the vortex of life's joys and sorrows and eventually to see not just a measure of meaning but meaning in its fullest sense as the Lord bestows grace and help in the here and now and promise of complete resolution of life's mysteries in the day of his coming.[3]

The major theological ideas of Psalms revolve, first of all, around the concept of the Lord's present sovereignty, its exercise in a messianic ruler yet to come, and the role of Zion as the locus of his kingdom. This is the divine side, as it were. The second great complex of themes has to do with human life in both its practical outworkings and in its special meaning for those who know God and find truth and significance in that relationship. The Psalms have much to say about wisdom and ethics and show mankind caught up in circumstances so painful that only profound lament and complaint seem possible. Often this takes the form of lashing out at persecutors in scathing imprecation for their hostility against both the Lord and his chosen ones. But there is also victorious deliverance through his covenant faithfulness, the forgiveness of sins, and cause for thanksgiving and praise. The sorrows and perplexities of human existence must and will give way to eschatological joy in submission to the sovereign Lord of history and of the ages to come.

God as King

This central idea of Old Testament theology is much at home in the Psalms, so much so that those psalms that testify to it can be only representatively treated in any depth. Psalm 9:7, for example, declares forthrightly that "the Lord sits enthroned forever," thus setting the tone for the rest of the collection. David here includes under the rubric of

[3] Patrick M. Miller, "The Psalter as a Book of Theology," *The Way of the Lord: Essays in Old Testament Theology* (Tübingen: Mohr Siebeck, 2004), 214–25.

God's ruling the righteous judgment of the world, the governance of its people with justice, and his protection of the oppressed (vv. 8–10). Psalm 10, joined to Psalm 9 in some Hebrew traditions and in the Septuagint, repeats the note of the Lord's everlasting reign (v. 16) but turns more negatively to the fate of the wicked who, resistant to his kingship, will no longer oppress the disadvantaged of the earth but will, in fact, "perish from [the LORD's] land" (vv. 17–18). He who is in heaven rules also on earth (Ps. 11:4) and sees all men everywhere, both righteous and unrighteous, and will dispense blessing and judgment accordingly. He hates the wicked but loves justice, granting that "the upright will see His face" (vv. 5–7).

Psalm 22, a sustained lament of David quoted by Jesus on the cross (e.g., v. 1; cf. Matt. 27:46), finds resolution in the fact that the Lord is King, no matter the sufferings of life. The time will come, the psalmist says, when "all the ends of the earth will remember and turn to the LORD. All the families of the nations will bow down before You, for kingship belongs to the LORD; He rules over the nations" (vv. 27–28). This is the truth whether or not it seems to have reality in existential moments, and to this the saint of the Lord must cling in faith. Psalm 24, likely a liturgical text accompanying temple worship, celebrates the Lord's present kingship, describing him as "the King of glory" (v. 7). He is, moreover, the divine warrior known to deliver Israel over and over again in the course of her history. Speaking to the gates of the temple, David commands that they be opened to the Lord so that he might take his rightful place as the royal Lord Almighty (vv. 9–10).

The Lord's sovereignty is cosmic in scope, an assertion celebrated in Psalm 29, a poem composed perhaps as a polemic against the Canaanite nature cults.[4] David describes the Lord's thunderous voice as a display of power over the great deeps as well as the lofty mountains (vv. 3–6). It is like lightning or an earthquake, altering the course of natural events (vv. 7–9). All the powerful ones of heaven and earth can do in the face of such awesome majesty is to acknowledge its source, "the LORD [who] sat enthroned at the flood," the one who "is sits enthroned, King forever" (vv. 1–2, 10). Psalm 33 focuses on God's role as Creator, a role that obviously contributes to the theme of Psalm 29, for his rule over all things

[4] Hans-Joachim Kraus, *Psalms 1–59* (Minneapolis: Fortress, 1993), 351.

is predicated fundamentally on his having brought them into existence in the first place. Echoing Genesis 1, the psalmist declares that all things were made by the mere spoken word of the Lord and, having done so, he arranged all things in their proper places (vv. 6–7). This ought to elicit reverence on the part of all people, for though the nations have plans otherwise, the Lord of creation is also the Lord of history, with purposes that cannot be thwarted (vv. 8–11).

Psalm 44, usually regarded as a communal lament, reviews God's mighty exploits in history, especially as Israel's King (v. 4). He, the leader in battle, had conquered foes in the past and is still the source of victory for his people (vv. 5–7). For this he is to be praised (v. 8). But he is not only the aggressor; the Lord also is a refuge from enemy attack from the outside. Should the earth and sea disappear, there is no need to fear for the Creator of both is sufficient to save (Ps. 46:1–3). In him who dwells in Jerusalem, "the city of God" (v. 4), His special people find help. Nations that oppose him will fall (v. 6) as he destroys their instruments of war and establishes universal peace. The Lord's challenge to them is that they "be still, and know that I am God" (v. 10 NIV). In the end he will be "exalted among the nations, exalted on the earth" (v. 10).

In anticipation of his universal rule, Psalm 47 urges the nations even now to do homage to the Lord, "a great King over all the earth" (v. 2). As Israel's God, he has already subjugated nations before them and rightly so, for his realm is not just over his chosen people but over the whole world. In the strongest possible terms, Israel's Lord is confessed as Lord also of the nations: "God reigns over the nations; God is seated on His holy throne" (v. 8; cf. Ps. 22:28; 1 Chron. 16:11). With Israel's kings, the kings of the earth ought to and some day will "have assembled with the people of the God of Abraham. For the leaders of the earth belong to God" (v. 9; cf Pss. 72:11; 102:22; Isa. 49:7, 23; Phil. 2:11; Rev. 19:15–16). Psalm 68:32 adds to this injunction by urging the kingdoms of the earth to "sing to God, . . . sing praise to the Lord."

The blending of the concepts of the Lord as king by virtue of his creation of all things and as ruler of history is clear from Psalm 89. With reference to the exodus of Israel from Egypt, the poet speaks of the crushing of Rahab, the sea monster symbolizing that great nation, and the scattering of enemies (vv. 9–10). This most significant of historical events was possible because the Lord, says the psalmist, owns the heavens and the earth. "The world and everything in it—You founded them," he proclaims, and "You have a mighty arm; Your hand is powerful; Your right hand is lifted high" (vv. 11, 13). Because Israel is the Lord's chosen people, Israel's king also enjoys special privilege in governance. He is the "horn" whom the Lord exalts (v. 17; cf. 1 Sam. 2:10), the shield belonging to the Holy One of Israel (v. 18).

The Enthronement Psalms (47, 93, 97, 99) and those related to them (95–96) are of special interest in terms of divine kingship.[5] Often (but erroneously) associated with a putative annual festival in which Israel's kings served as surrogates for the Lord in a reaffirmation of his kingship,[6] these psalms in fact are hymns of praise designed to celebrate the eternal nature of his rule, one embracing all time from eternity past through all the ages to come.[7] The second of these, Psalm 93, opens with the fiat declaration, "The LORD reigns" (v. 1) and then proceeds to declare that "Your throne has been established from the beginning; You are from eternity" (v. 2). All creation praises him for that reason, for creation itself testifies to his sovereignty. Since this is so, then mankind also must praise him, and especially Israel (Ps. 95:1–2). Having created the depths and heights, the sea and the dry land, the Lord has displayed not only his omnipotence but also that he is incomparable among the gods of imagination (vv. 3–4). In light of this, the psalmist exhorts, "Come, let us worship and bow down; let us kneel before the LORD our Maker" (v. 6).

Psalm 96, a hymn describing the Lord as Creator, continues the appeal. The whole earth is enjoined to praise him and to "declare His glory among the nations, His wonderful works among all peoples" (v. 3). Their idols are to be repudiated; for they represent nonentities, false deities with no power to create (v. 5). To the Lord alone all men should ascribe glory and strength, and to him alone should worship be offered (vv. 7–9). The psalm, like Psalm 93, declares, "The LORD reigns" (v. 10), a statement not so much of a present state of affairs as a confession concerning his

---

[5] W. S. McCullough, "The 'Enthronement of Yahweh' Psalms," *A Stubborn Faith,* ed. E. C. Hobbs (Dallas: Southern Methodist University Press, 1956), 53–61; Roy A. Rosenberg, "Yahweh Becomes King," *JBL* 85 (1966): 297–307.

[6] Sigmund Mowinckel, *The Psalms in Israel's Worship,* 2 vol., trans. D. R. Ap-Thomas (Nashville: Abingdon, 1962).

[7] Erhard S. Gerstenberger, *Psalms, Part 1, with an Introduction to Cultic Poetry,* FOTL XIV (Grand Rapids: Eerdmans, 1988), 198, 258.

nature.[8] He reigns because he and he alone is God. With that truth follows the truth that all mankind is accountable to him. He is coming to judge; and when he does, it will be with equity and righteousness, according to his own character, which is truth (vv. 10–13).

Psalm 97, declaring also at the outset that "the LORD reigns" (v. 1), emphasizes his role of divine warrior, the God whose *mysterium* is hidden in clouds and darkness but whose awesome coming in judgment is displayed in fire and lightning (vv. 2–6). These two facets of the Lord's nature—his transcendence and his immanence—stand in bold relief against the gods of the nations.[9] He is "the Most High over all the earth," the one who is "exalted above all the gods" (v. 9). Psalm 98 begins with a call to praise Yahweh because of all he has done for Israel, works of salvation that have been visible to all the nations (vv. 2–3). With appropriate fanfare he is proclaimed King and not just of Israel but of the whole earth (v. 6). Again picking up the creation motif, the psalmist anticipates the coming of the Lord in judgment, a fitting function of God as Sovereign (v. 9).

Finally, Psalm 99 also utters the majestic exordium, "The LORD reigns" (cf. Ps. 93:1; 97:1) and depicts him doing so "enthroned above the cherubim" (v. 1). This links his kingship with the temple, a connection observed also by Isaiah who, in a vision, saw the Lord "seated on a high and lofty throne, and His robe filled the temple" (Isa. 6:1). The cherubim first appear as guards of the holiness of Yahweh who prevented fallen humanity from entering the garden and illicitly partaking of the tree of life (Gen. 3:24). Their more prominent role, however, was that of hovering over the ark of the covenant in the tabernacle and temple for the ark symbolized the throne of Yahweh who sat invisibly among his people as king over them (Exod. 25:10–22; 1 Kings 8:6–11). In a sense the temple was Yahweh's royal palace, the place he chose to locate his name, that is, his very presence (Deut. 12:5, 11).[10]

Israel as a magnet attracting the nations to the Lord as King is a theme of Psalm 102:12–22. The psalmist looks to the day when the Lord, sitting even now in royal splendor, will restore Zion and, as a result, will cause

---

[8] C. Hassell Bullock, *Encountering the Book of Psalms* (Grand Rapids: Baker, 2001), 196.

[9] Samuel Terrien, *The Elusive Presence* (San Francisco: Harper & Row, 1978), 320–26.

[10] For this psalm and temple theology, see Erhard S. Gerstenberger, *Psalms, Part 2, and Lamentations,* FOTL XV (Grand Rapids: Eerdmans, 2001), 200.

the nations to acknowledge his sovereignty (vv. 12–17). The redemption of his own people from the distress of captivity will be such a display of God's power that the peoples of the earth will be constrained to worship him along with them (vv. 18–22). His universal rule will elicit from angels and men alike outbursts of spontaneous praise (Ps. 103:19–22). Creation itself is at his service, clothing him in majesty and moving at his every command (Ps. 104:1–4).

But even now the Lord as King is attentive to the nations over whom he reigns whether they recognize it or not. From his exaltation over them, he looks down upon them with mercy and compassion (Ps. 113:4–6). The poor and needy he elevates to a princely status, and the barren woman becomes mother of many children (vv. 7–9; cf. 1 Sam. 2:5b, 8). David is so enthralled by these benefits of God's sovereignty that he is compelled to praise him for them. "Yahweh is great and is highly praised," he declares (Ps. 145:3). But the praise is not just in the abstract, not just response to a theological idea. Rather, the Lord must be praised because of his mighty and wonderful works of goodness and righteousness, works that attest to his sovereign power (Ps. 145:4–7).

The kingship of the Lord is clearly a major motif of the book of Psalms; in fact, that aspect of his nature is more abundantly established here than anywhere else in the Old Testament. The creation narratives implicitly make the same point, and obviously the Lord's powerful interventions on behalf of Israel in history add their testimony as well. The psalms, however, speak with loud and clear voice to the truth that the Lord, the God of Israel, reigns over all nations even now. But in the day of his full manifestation, his sovereignty will not only be recognized by Israel and the nations as a matter of dogma but also as a political and sociological reality. Together the peoples of the earth will bow before him and forever offer him tributes of praise and worship.

Mankind as God's Viceroy

We have noted repeatedly that kingdom is a (perhaps *the*) fundamental theological notion in the Old Testament, one introduced by the creation account in which man, the image of God, was authorized to rule on God's behalf, as his surrogate as it were (Gen. 1:26–28). Psalm 8 is devoted to this idea and, in fact, may be viewed as a commentary on the Genesis text. In it David first extols the Lord for the majesty of his name and his transcendent glory (v. 1). Even infants are capable of grasping the sublime truth of God's reality, and their praises are so genuine and powerful as to confound their hard-hearted adversaries (v. 2; cf. Matt. 21:14–16).

The central issue of the psalm is how God can give attention to mere humanity in light of his exalted person and works. The immensity of the creation and the intricacies of the relationship of its parts when compared to the finitude of mankind cause the psalmist to ask in amazement, "What is man that You remember him, the son of man that You look after him?" (v. 4). But it is not just the creation of man that astounds him; it is the exalted role assigned to him. He has been appointed to be a little lower than the *ʾĕlōhîm,* crowned with glory and honor (v. 5). The interpretations of the Hebrew term vary. Some take it to refer to God himself, that is, that man was assigned a role at such an exalted level as to be nearly divine.[11] In favor of this is the fact that man has been crowned in a manner reminiscent of the splendor of God's own status. Against this view is the pervasive biblical truth of the transcendence of God that utterly separates him from all his creation, including mankind. In what sense can man be just a little *(mēʿaṭ)* different from (thus a literal rendering) God and still maintain a necessary ontological distinction from him?

The book of Hebrews, following the Septuagint, understands *ʾĕlōhîm* to be a reference to angels *(aggeloi)* and not to God (Heb. 2:7). Though this might be driven by a theological desire to distance the ineffable Creator from all else, including mankind, it is possible to argue that this was the intention of the psalmist to begin with. That is, it may well be that *ʾĕlōhîm* is to be understood generically as "powerful ones" or the like, a meaning well attested elsewhere (cf. Job 1:6; 2:1; Ps. 82:1).[12] The Greek *aggeloi* would thus be an acceptable interpretation of the identity of the "mighty ones" since no other such superhuman beings are known in the Old Testament. Man therefore was appointed to a position which, though somewhat different from (and perhaps inferior to) that of the "mighty ones," nevertheless authorized him to rule over all things on earth.

---

[11] For a view close to this, see Franz Delitzsch, *Biblical Commentary on the Psalms* (Grand Rapids: Eerdmans, 1955 [1867]), 153–55.

[12] Brooke Foss Westcott, *The Epistle to the Hebrews* (London: Macmillan, 1892), 44.

These things are enumerated in verses 6–8 in reverse order to that found in the creation account (Gen. 1:20–25) and in the creation mandate (Gen. 1:26–28). Here the higher orders (flocks and herds) appear first as just below mankind and then the lower (birds and fish). Over all these God has appointed man as ruler *(māšāl),* having placed all of them "under [man's] feet" (v. 6). The imagery here is exactly the same as in Genesis 1:28 where man is told to subdue *(kbš)* the earth and rule over *(rdh)* everything in it.

As we have seen, the New Testament cites Psalm 8 in support of the idea that mankind, though somewhat lower than the mighty ones (that is, the angels), was nonetheless entrusted with universal dominion (Heb. 2:5–9). The author implicitly admits the limitation to human authority in the present age, however, a limitation to be attributed to human fallenness (cf. Rom. 8:18–21). He implies also that the original intentions of God will be reestablished through the redemptive work of Christ. Jesus, in his incarnation in human form, shared with mankind certain restrictions by virtue of his identification with mortals (cf. Phil. 2:5–11), and those restrictions included his temporary subangelic status (Heb. 2:9a). His substitutionary death for all mankind purchased his absolute sovereignty over all things, including angels, however, and thereby restored the human race to its role as viceroy under God, charged with ruling over all things as God intended at the beginning (v. 9b).[13] Psalm 115:16 adds a footnote to this affirmation by declaring that "the heavens are the LORD's, but the earth He has given to the human race." The angelic hosts may indeed enjoy some kind of superior role in the heavens; but when they move among mankind on the earth, they do so as "ministering spirits sent out to serve those who are going to inherit salvation" (Heb. 1:14; cf. Deut. 33:2–3).

THE MESSIANIC KING

The reinstatement of God's untrammeled sovereignty and the rule of mankind associated with it will be possible only by a work of restoration and redemption through an anointed one who, though the offspring of David, takes on a role in the Psalms that transcends mere humanity and

---

[13] F. F. Bruce, *The Epistle to the Hebrews,* NICNT (Grand Rapids: Eerdmans, 1964), 36–40.

becomes identified with a figure who is nothing short of deity.[14] This bold concept is in line with the revelation through the prophets already addressed (e.g., Isa. 7:14; 9:6–7; 11:1–5; Jer. 23:5–6; Mic. 5:2), and which, if anything, is clarified and enhanced in a number of poetic passages in the Psalter.

The first of these, Psalm 2, a royal (coronation) psalm attributed by the New Testament to David (Acts 4:25), views the nations of the earth as implacably hostile to the Lord and to "His Anointed One" (v. 2, Heb. *mĕšîḥô*). This one, in the historical context of the psalm, is David himself or a Davidic king as the reference to the "King on Zion" in verse 6 makes clear. There follows then the remarkable assertion that the king, the "Anointed One," is nothing less than God's own Son, surely not in an ontological sense in its historical setting but at least in terms of the divine role that David was to play (cf. 1 Chron. 17:11–14).[15] As founder of a line of kings, he and his successors will inherit these same rebel nations as their personal possession *(ʾăḥuzzâ)* (v. 8) and then, in line with Genesis 49:10, Jacob's promise to Judah concerning a coming king from that tribe, will "break them with a rod of iron" and "shatter them like pottery" (v. 9). The only hope for the nations will be to acknowledge the Lord as King and to (lit.) "kiss the Son," that is, to pay homage to the Davidic king who will come to judge and destroy all who remain unrepentant (vv. 10–12).

The linkage of the epithets *anointed, king,* and *son* leads clearly to the idea, seized upon in the New Testament (Acts 13:33; Heb. 1:5; 5:5), of a Davidic ruler of more than mere human nature and capacity. Within the psalm itself, the juxtaposition of "the Lord" and "Anointed One" (v. 2) and "Lord" and "Son" (vv. 11–12) points strongly in this direction.[16] The king to come will sit not just on David's throne but on the throne of the Lord himself, a state of affairs put beyond doubt in New Testament revelation (cf. Matt. 19:28; Phil. 2:11; Heb. 8:1; 12:2; Rev. 19:16; 22:3).

---

[14] Walton views the Davidic Covenant as so central to the book of Psalms as to be the controlling feature of the entire book. John H. Walton, "Psalms: A Cantata about the Davidic Covenant," *JETS* 34 (1991): 21–31.

[15] Peter C. Craigie, *Psalms 1–50,* WBC 19 (Waco, Tex.: Word, 1983), 66.

[16] Christoph Barth, *God with Us* (Grand Rapids: Eerdmans, 1991), 202, 222.

David's hegemony over surrounding nations, a matter established in the historical record (cf. 2 Sam. 8:1–14), is celebrated in Psalm 18:43–50. He had become "the head of nations," and people far off had become subject to him (v. 43). All this he attributes to the power and blessing of the Lord (vv. 46–48; cf. Ps. 2:8–9). But what the Lord had done for him in his own day is but a harbinger of what will come in the future when the Lord will show "loyalty *(ḥesed)* to His anointed *(mĕšiḥô),* to David and his descendants forever" (v. 50). The allusion to Psalm 2 is unmistakable and the character of the messianic king revealed there is most apparent here as well. The ruler to come is Davidic, but more—he is one whose rule is everlasting and therefore divine in nature.

Psalm 45, composed perhaps to celebrate a royal wedding (thus the title *šîr yĕdîdōt*), describes the Davidic king in such extravagant terms as "most handsome of men" (v. 2), "mighty warrior" (*gibbôr*; cf. Isa. 9:6) (v. 3), and even "God" (v. 6). The latter epithet, almost too bold to be ascribed to a mere human being, cannot for that reason be limited ultimately to only a mortal being. Even if it is to be understood as "powerful one," an appropriate rendition of *ʾĕlōhîm* (cf. Ps. 8:5), the truth remains that the king in view transcends mere flesh and blood.[17] His throne is everlasting, and he wields a scepter of perfect justice (cf. Ps. 2:9; Gen. 49:10). He has been anointed to a position superior to all others by God himself (v. 7) and will be acknowledged and praised by the nations forever (v. 17). The New Testament makes use of the psalm, especially verses 6–7, to support the messiahship of Jesus as proof of his superiority to the angels (Heb. 1:8–9).

The king as the adopted son of God, seen already in Psalm 2:7, introduces Psalm 72, by genre a royal psalm (v. 1). His responsibilities include fair judgment and care for society's disadvantaged and oppressed, and his tenure, viewed as a Davidic dynastic succession, will be everlasting (vv. 2–5, 12–15). His presence will guarantee prosperity in the land; indeed, his universal dominion will contribute to it by virtue of the tribute of the nations that will pour into his treasuries (vv. 8–10, 15). As vassal states their kings will submit to his rule (v. 11) and in turn will be blessed by him (v. 17b). This, of course, fulfills the Abrahamic

[17] In the context, of course, the king remains human as the phrase "God, your God has anointed you" (v. 7) makes clear. Delitzsch, *Biblical Commentary on the Psalms,* 82–84.

promise that the Lord will bless those that bless his offspring and curse those that curse them. The messianic king will both hold the nations accountable to the Lord as sovereign and be the mediator of the Lord's gracious benevolence toward them.

The identification of the king to come is made most explicit in Psalm 89 where the covenant made with David (2 Sam. 7:8–16) is cited as the basis for Israel's everlasting kingship (vv. 3–4). The history of his selection from among the people and his anointing to his sacred office is recounted (vv. 19–20), and then the Lord makes promise after promise about his success, promises not limited to David alone but extending throughout his dynasty and fulfilled in the messianic king of the ages to come. His *ḥesed* will be with him, he says (v. 24), for he will know the Lord as Father and, in turn, will be appointed as God's son, his firstborn (vv. 24, 26–27; cf. Ps. 2:7). The relationship between them will endure forever for the covenant loyalty to which the Lord committed himself to David, in the nature of the case, can never fail (vv. 28–29). Individuals in the Davidic dynasty might indeed fall by the wayside—a fact all too well documented in the historical literature—but this could by no means affect the stability and permanence of the commitment to David as a whole (vv. 30–32).[18] "I will not withdraw My faithful love *(ḥesed)* from him," says the Lord, "or betray My faithfulness *(ʾĕmûnâ)*" (v. 33). And in even stronger terms the Lord swears that he does not lie to David when he pledges that "his offspring will continue forever, his throne like the sun before Me" (vv. 35–36; cf. Jer. 31:35–36). The eternality of this avowal presupposes a Davidic descendant whose reign will be unending.

Nowhere is this more clearly developed than in Psalm 110, a text whose purpose is to blend together the two key Old Testament offices, those of king and priest. The messianic ruler, the offspring of David of Judah, will also be a priest forever "like Melchizedek" (v. 4). The Lord is the speaker throughout or is the one spoken of by the psalmist. The identification of the addressee is a matter of disagreement, spoken of only as "my Lord" *(ʾădōnî)*. The lowercase letters suggest the ordinary title of respect accorded a person of great dignity such as a king, so the recipient of the message is a human being, in the context of the psalm a royal figure. As a psalm attributed to David, the "Lord" could

---

[18] Artur Weiser, *The Psalms* (Philadelphia: Westminster, 1962), 592–93.

be Solomon. On the other hand, if the title refers only to the subject of the psalm (that is, "concerning David"), David himself could be the Lord in question. In any case, the dynasty of David is in view.[19] The elevation of the messianic king is evident from the Lord's invitation to him to sit at his right hand, the place of utmost privilege (Pss. 16:11; 80:17; Matt. 20:23; 22:44; 26:64; Acts 2:33, 34; Rom. 8:34; Heb. 10:12). From there he will subdue his enemies and rule over them (vv. 1–3). At the end he will display his wrathful judgment and will "crush leaders over the entire world" (v. 6). But in addition to his regal authority, this Lord will also be a priest, not one descended from Aaron—which necessitated a Levitical ancestry through Aaron (Exod. 29:9)—but one in the order of Melchizedek (v. 4).[20] This enigmatic figure first appears in Genesis 14 as a priest of God most high *(ʾēl ʿelyôn)* and also as the king of Salem, i.e., Jerusalem (Gen. 14:18). Thus he, like the Davidic king, embodied both royal and priestly offices, and both were associated with Jerusalem. We have already noted David's role as priest and the continuation of that role in his successors.[21]

The New Testament, citing Psalm 110 in numerous places (cf. especially Heb. 5:6, 10; 6:20; 7:17), establishes the priesthood of Jesus on that basis. Disqualified from being a priestly intercessor of the Aaronic order because of his Judahite ancestry, his credentials rested in his descent from David, who, according to Psalm 110, was designated a priest of an order that, as it turns out, was superior to that of Aaron. It was necessary that Jesus be a high priest because he must offer, as a high priest, that perfect atoning sacrifice, namely himself, if the human race was to find a permanent solution to the problem of sin (Heb. 2:17–18; 3:3; 4:14–16; 5:8–9). The argument for Jesus' priesthood as superior to the Aaronic continues with the observation that Abraham recognized Melchizedek's priestly authority and, in fact, paid tithes to him. Since Abraham was the ancestor of Levi, founder of the priestly tribe, Levi and all his descendants also deferred to the priesthood of Melchizedek,

---

[19] Herbert W. Bateman IV, "Psalm 110:1 and the New Testament," *BSac* 149 (1991): 438–53; Eugene H. Merrill, "Royal Priesthood: An Old Testament Messianic Motif," *BSac* 150 (1993): 50–61.

[20] P. J. Nel, "Psalm 110 and the Melchizedek Tradition," *JNSL* 22 (1996): 1–14.

[21] See pp. 445–52.

which must be superior because "the inferior [Levi] is blessed by the superior [Melchizedek]" (Heb. 7:7).

The New Testament aside, Melchizedek and his priesthood have been the subject of a great deal of attention in extra-biblical Jewish literature; and Judaism, with Christianity, has always assigned to him an important eschatological and even messianic role.[22] The double office of the coming king is an important advancement in royal theology—one buttressed, as we saw earlier, by the double-crowned Branch of Zechariah 6:9–15 who will also combine royal and priestly functions.

We close our discussion of the messianic King with a brief glance at Psalm 132:1–12. The poet appeals to the Lord to honor David for his desire to build a temple in which the Lord could dwell among his people (vv. 1–5), a request which, as it turns out, was denied (2 Sam. 7:5–11). But something greater was in store for David and his people, for the Lord swore that he would never lack a descendant to sit on his throne (v. 11). The everlastingness of the promise clearly argues for a king to come whose reign, like that of the Lord, would endure forever.

The Kingdom Role of Zion

If the Lord is the great King who exercises his sovereignty through mankind in general and through the Davidic messianic line in particular, over what does he reign and what is the special locus of his administration? The answer, of course, is that his dominion is universal—heaven and earth—and in a sense without the constraints of time and space. In Israel's theology, however, with its concerns about God's presence among his elect people, the place "where He causes his name to dwell," the city of David—Zion as it is called in many of the psalms—is the site from which he holds sway over everything else he has created.[23] And in particular the temple is his capitol, the throne room being the most holy place of the ark of the covenant.

Psalm 46, categorized as a Song of Zion, sets the tone for the whole question of the divine residence. The poet describes "a river—its streams

---

[22] Fred L. Horton, *The Melchizedek Tradition: A Critical Examination of the Sources to the Fifth Century A.D. and in the Epistle to the Hebrews* (Cambridge: Cambridge Press, 1976).

[23] For the political and theological significance of Zion, see Richard S. Hess, *Zion, City of Our God* (Grand Rapids: Eerdmans, 1999).

delight the city of God, the holy dwelling place of the Most High" (v. 4). The river speaks metaphorically of the Lord's presence in Jerusalem, a presence guaranteeing his people security and success (vv. 5–6). "The LORD of Hosts is with us," he exults, "the God of Jacob is our stronghold" (v. 7). The repetition of this line forms a refrain bringing the psalm to a close (v. 11). A similar psalm follows in which Jerusalem is lavishly praised as a city "rising splendidly [which] is the joy of the whole earth" (Ps. 48:2). It is the city of God, the great King, who (as in Ps. 47) fortifies her against all her enemies (v. 3). Those who dared advance against her soon found themselves terror stricken and then destroyed. In the temple in particular the Lord may be found, and from there his praises resound to the ends of the earth, filling Zion with great joy (vv. 9–11). Moreover, what has been true in history will be true forever, for the God of Zion is an everlasting God (v. 14).

As for the nations, they will be accountable to him; for though the Lord resides in Zion, his dominion is universal (Ps. 50:1–2). Should they prove rebellious and resistant to his claims on them, he will call for the elements of nature itself to levy judgment upon them (vv. 3–4). On the other hand, Israel's hope for salvation rests in this same Lord, the God of Zion whom they implore for the restoration of his blessings (Ps. 53:6). That he will do so in the eschatological age is without doubt, for "God will save Zion and build up the cities of Judah" (Ps. 69:35). The diaspora will return, "those who love His name" (v. 36), and they will dwell there.

Psalm 87, another Song of Zion, celebrates the Lord's love for the holy city and says that it is a place praised not just by the Lord's chosen ones but by such erstwhile foes as Egypt, Babylon, Philistia, Tyre, and Cush who, in the day of his coming, will acknowledge him as King (v. 4; cf. Isa. 19:23–25). It will be as though they all had been born in Zion, for all nations will become his chosen ones along with Israel (vv. 5–7). This, of course, anticipates the gospel age when, as Paul puts it, the wall of partition between Jew and Gentile will be broken down and all who call upon the Lord will be one (Eph. 2:14–18). Psalm 102 makes the same point when it suggests that "the nations will fear the name of the LORD, and all the kings of the earth Your glory" (v. 15), a statement made in the context of Zion's restoration and rebuilding as the place of the Lord's enthronement (vv. 12–14). When this takes place, Jerusalem will once more be the point from which radiates the praise of the Lord worldwide and to which the nations will assemble to worship him (vv. 21–22; cf. Zech. 14:16–21).

The significance of the sacred city to the saints of Old Testament Israel is beautifully etched in Psalm 122, a Song of Pilgrimage. Here the psalmist expresses his joy at being able to visit the Lord's temple and there to praise his name according to Torah prescriptions (vv. 1–4). So that this might be done in the future and without hindrance, he urges prayer for Jerusalem; for there the Lord may be found dwelling among his people (vv. 6–9). A psalm composed after the exile (Ps. 126) reflects the longing the captives had for Jerusalem and the joy that overwhelmed them upon their return (vv. 1–3). They had learned, however, that bitter trial eventually gives way to happiness and fulfillment (vv. 4–6).

The Psalter climaxes the importance of Zion for the rule of the Lord and his Davidic surrogates in Psalm 132. Here in unambiguous terms the theologian asserts that "the LORD has chosen Zion; He has desired it for His home" (v. 13). And then the Lord himself confirms this truth: "This is My resting place forever; I will make My home here because I have desired it" (v. 14). But the Lord also reigns through David at this place. He will in days to come raise up a horn for David, a lamp that will radiate the light of God's revelation (v. 17). Horn, of course, is a metaphor for strength (cf. 1 Sam. 2:10; Pss. 18:2; 89:24; 92:10), so the messianic ruler yet to come will exercise his authority with divine enablement. As the poet puts it, "The crown he wears will be glorious" (v. 18).

Life in the Kingdom

Kings and kingdoms presuppose subjects, a truism obviously pertinent to the kingdom of God as well as human principalities. The Old Testament, though focusing on Israel as the Lord's special people, begins and ends with a much larger scope—the entire world and all its inhabitants. Thus all mankind—past, present, and future—constitute in the broadest sense the citizenry of his domain. In a stricter sense, however, the people of the Lord are those who submit to his sovereignty and thus are related to him redemptively. From the vantage point of the sacred texts of Israel, and especially the Psalms, these are first of all the offspring of Abraham, the chosen nation Israel, and then secondarily those responsive to the message of salvation mediated by the servant nation.

Psalms has much to say about the character and conduct of kingdom citizens. As a whole they fall under the rubric of wisdom, an understanding of life principles that issues in proper ethics, morals, lifestyle, and worship. It is fitting that the book should begin as it does, with a statement of what it means to be an obedient member of the covenant community. Psalm 1, a wisdom text, is commonly understood to be an entrée to the whole collection, an introduction to its principal themes and motifs.[24] The psalm draws a sharp distinction between the man who avoids sinful ways and the one who does not. As for the former, he refuses to walk, stand, or sit in the company of wicked men; i.e., he avoids the patterns of life unbefitting the child of God. Rather, he fixes himself on Torah, guiding his life by its principles, and thus he enjoys the blessings that ensue (vv. 1–3). As for the sinner, his life is ephemeral—here today and gone tomorrow (v. 4). On the day of reckoning, he will have no basis for appeal to a just God but rather will perish. The faithful kingdom citizen, to the contrary, will enjoy the watch care of the Lord forever (vv. 5–6).

Psalm 15 echoes this dichotomy but with attention only to the qualities that define those suitable to dwell in the sanctuary of the Lord and "live on [His] holy mountain" (v. 1). Their lifestyle is blameless; they are truthful; they do not injure others with slanderous rumor; they have no patience with evil men but honor only God; they keep their promises, lend money without interest, and refuse to be bribed in a court of law (vv. 2–5). Such traits do not, of course, create kingdom citizens, but they are necessary to the maintenance of good standing before the Lord.

Even King David recognized the need for moral integrity and in Psalm 18 rehearses not only his righteous deeds but lays out principles of behavior that should characterize wise living. He knows full well that God's blessing has come to him because of his upright manner of life (vv. 20–24) and concludes that his own experience is an index as to how the Lord evaluates and responds to human behavior. He is faithful to the faithful, blameless to the blameless, pure to the pure, and shrewd to the crooked (vv. 25–26). In other words, the divine principle is tit for tat or

[24] Leopold Sabourin, *The Psalms: Their Origin and Meaning* (New York: Alba House, 1974), 371–72.

poetic justice. Such a view is typical of the wisdom literature as we shall see; and though it might appear to fall short of New Testament ideas of grace (e.g., Matt. 5:38–48), it does underscore the fact that righteous and evil deeds have their necessary and predictable consequences.

David testifies again to the Lord's faithfulness to him in Psalm 23 and also hints at the demarcation between the righteous and the unrighteous. Like a defenseless sheep depends on the shepherd for nourishment, guidance, and protection, so David acknowledges his vulnerability and need for the heavenly Shepherd to sustain him (vv. 1–4). But the Lord does more than that. He demonstrates the fact that life is not just bearable but, by his intervening grace, can be triumphant. To prepare a table in the presence of one's enemies is to dramatize the ease of life and serenity that the kingdom citizen enjoys even in the face of hostility.[25] And this is not just incidental but an integral feature of life before God. He blesses forever and ultimately opens the doors of his habitation to those who know him as shepherd (vv. 5–6).

Elsewhere, David does not take his status in the kingdom of God for granted. He pleads for the Lord's vindication on the grounds of his upright behavior and unwavering trust in him, challenging the Lord to examine him to see if this is not so (Ps. 26:1–3). As he did in Psalm 18, so here David catalogs his righteous deeds and in so doing contrasts his behavior with that of evil men. He has not sat with them, he says (v. 4; cf. Ps. 1:1), nor does he assemble with evildoers. Rather, he attends to worship in a proper manner, praising God in the process (vv. 6–7). The genuineness of his devotion is expressed as he testifies, "LORD, I love the house where You dwell, the place where Your glory resides" (v. 8). This confession underscores the important idea that righteous behavior in the kingdom cannot be separated from proper attention to the cultus. There is no such thing as righteousness detached from worship; nor, of course, can mere worship unaccompanied by exemplary behavior have any value.

Psalm 34 draws attention again to the bifurcation between the godly and the ungodly and how they are to be distinguished and dealt with respectively. The Lord, the psalmist says, is always attuned to the righteous but turns a deaf ear to the wicked, even so far as to blot out any memory of

[25] For elaboration of this imagery of protected hospitality, see Kraus, *Psalms 1–59,* 308.

them (vv. 15–16). He hears and answers the prayers of kingdom citizens no matter how profound and unsolvable their problems seem to be (vv. 19–20). At the end he redeems them, declaring them exonerated; but evil men, by contrast, will be slain, hopelessly condemned (vv. 21–22).

In any culture there is always the perception that the righteous suffer and the wicked prosper, so much so that the character of God himself may be called into question. This is the conundrum addressed in Job and other wisdom texts, but Psalm 37 also expatiates on it and at great length. In it David cautions against envying the wicked because their days are numbered and they will eventually pass from the scene (vv. 1–2). They will be cut off, he says; and though one looks for them, they will never be found (vv. 9–10). Their day is coming (v. 13), and the harm they thought to do to others will rebound against them (vv. 14–15). Their wealth, so much to be envied, will be worth nothing after all (v. 17); for they will perish and vanish away like wisps of smoke (v. 20). They appear to prosper but will come to nothing but ruin, bereft of goods and any hope of life to come (vv. 35–38).

The righteous, on the other hand, can expect all their heart's desires as they trust the Lord (v. 4). In the day of judgment, their righteousness will shine forth; and their vindication will be as clear as the noonday sun (v. 6). They will inherit the earth and dwell in peace (v. 11; cf. Matt. 5:5), a state of affairs that will last forever (v. 18). In the here and now the Lord shows his favor to the upright. He enables him to make his way through life with safety and stability (vv. 23–24) and never fails to meet his every need (v. 25). All these benefits flow from the Lord's great love for his own (v. 28). The challenge, then, is to manifest the tokens of a righteous life—speak wisdom and justice, meditate on Torah, and live in peace. Those who do will have assurance of deliverance and salvation (vv. 39–40).

Psalm 49, classified by most scholars as a wisdom poem,[26] consists of a series of aphorisms that highlight the difference in fortune between the godly and the ungodly. But it also points to those aspects of human existence that are common to all. First, it is foolish to think that death can be avoided, for there is no ransom sufficient to keep one from its hungry jaws (vv. 5–9). All must die and face endless eons in the grave

---

[26] Bullock, *Encountering the Book of Psalms*, 208.

until at last their names are forgotten (vv. 10–12). This pessimistic view is how life seems from a purely empirical vantage point. However, the truth is that the righteous will survive to have dominion in another day, a hope made possible because of the power of God to pay the ransom price that mankind cannot pay (vv. 14b–15). "God will redeem my life from the power of Sheol," the poet says, "for He will take me" (v. 15). This glimpse into immortality, if not resurrection, marks a high point of Old Testament revelation with respect to the matter of the state of the righteous after death and in the hereafter.[27] A common definition of a sinner in Old Testament wisdom literature is that he is a fool (cf. Ps. 14:1). Conversely, the godly man or woman is wise, for the essence of wisdom is to know God. Psalm 53:1 states, "The fool says in his heart, 'God does not exist.'" This need not carry implications of atheism for a denial of the ontological reality of God or the gods was unthinkable in the world of the Old Testament. What is meant is that fools (= sinners) have no use for God, no place in their lives for his sovereign rule.[28] Seen from this perspective, it seems that the world is populated with fools, for "everyone has turned aside; they have all become corrupt. There is not one who does good, not even one" (v. 3; cf. Gen. 6:11–12; Isa. 53:6). Even the Lord despairs of their ever coming to faith (v. 4); rather, he sees for them only judgment (v. 5).

Psalm 73 reads almost like a poetic version of Job. The psalmist admits his envy of the wicked, observing that they seem always to enjoy life's blessings and always to escape God's wrath even when they shake their fists in his face (vv. 4–11). He laments that he has had misgivings about his own relationship to the Lord, for all his efforts at godliness seem to have availed him nothing but trouble (vv. 13–16). But then came a turning point. He entered the sanctuary of the Lord and in that holy place came to understand God as he is and life from the divine perspective (v. 17). The prosperity of the wicked, he now understood, is only a chimera. Life to them is a fanciful dream, a look through rose-colored glasses. When they awaken, they will see how wasted their lives have been and how hopeless their destinies (vv. 18–20).

---

[27] Oehler is not hesitant to speak of "a rising from the region of the dead to a higher life." Gustave Friedrich Oehler, *Theology of the Old Testament,* trans. George E. Day (Grand Rapids: Zondervan, n. d., 1883), 560.

[28] J. Marböck, נבל, *TDOT* 9:166.

The righteous, though prone to despair from time to time, must, with the poet, see that the Lord is always present. He guides throughout life and then, in a most remarkable affirmation, the writer adds, "You will take me up in glory" (v. 24). Whatever that might have meant in terms of his eternal destiny, the psalmist at least is confident that the Lord is all he needs.[29] If all else fails, he is there (vv. 25–26). The writer concludes with an affirmation of the security he finds in the Lord, and he promises to spread abroad the glorious truth he has come to know (v. 28).

Wisdom themes occur also in Psalm 94:8–15 where the Lord's knowledge is presented as incomparably superior to man's, but he desires to instruct them in his ways so they can enjoy the inheritance he has planned for them. Psalm 112 is a wisdom text in the strict sense and like Psalm 1 draws a sharp distinction between the righteous and the ungodly. The touchstone of blessing for the former is their adherence to Torah (v. 1). Obedience to it will ensure posterity, prosperity, stability, and ultimate triumph. The wicked, on the other hand, will come to no good end, all their hopes and dreams reduced to nothingness (v. 10). Another wisdom piece, Psalm 127, reveals the futility of attempting to build a life without God as the architect (vv. 1–2). What really matters in the long run is a godly line of offspring, for they bring honor to a man (vv. 3–5). Psalm 128 adds to this the blessing of a wife that comes to those who walk in the ways of the Lord (vv. 1–3). And Psalm 133 enlarges the scope to include the extended family. It is good and pleasant, the poet says, for brothers to live together in unity (v. 1), for in such an atmosphere of familial love "the LORD has appointed the blessing—life forevermore" (v. 3).

Finally, the life of the kingdom citizen can be summarized as one of absolute confidence and security in the Lord because he is the infinite God who has created us and who knows all about us. David confessed that the Lord was aware of every facet of his being (Ps. 139:1–4). He is a God of unlimited wisdom (v. 6) and inescapable presence (vv. 7–10) whom one cannot escape (vv. 11–12). Even before he was born, the Lord knew him, for he had created him individually and had already marked

[29] Dahood draws attention to the assumption of Enoch (Gen. 5:24) as analogous on the basis of the same verb (*lqḥ*). Mitchell Dahood, *Psalms II: 51–100,* AB 17 (Garden City, N.Y.: Doubleday, 1968), 195.

out the course of his life (vv. 13–16). And having made him, the Lord will now not leave him to his own devices. He knows David and has him constantly in mind (vv. 17–18). Such certainty is not just imaginary or a pleasant dream to David, for every morning of his life he rises with a fresh sense of the Lord's presence (v. 18).

Difficulties in Kingdom Life

The Psalms, though celebrating the immeasurable joys and blessings of kingdom citizenship, also portray the darker side, the sorrows and tragedies that inevitably afflict all mankind and especially those who suffer for the sake of righteousness. So much is this the case that the so-called lament psalms—those expressing individual and community response to life's many challenges—are the single largest category.[30] The line between the lament psalms composed by individuals to vent their personal complaints and those speaking on behalf of the larger community is often not clear, nor need it be, for the point here is that the righteous in particular and in general are not immune from suffering, persecution, and even death. The theological significance is not in the reality of these things but in how the saint responds to them and is able to accommodate them to his status as a child of God. Related to this is the question as to how lament or complaint can be construed as revelational. Does God speak through human reaction to the vicissitudes of life?

It is impossible here to explore this complex issue in any depth, so it must suffice to say that if one grants that the Bible in its entirety is the Word of God, it follows that all its parts—including human (or even Satanic) responses to God's words and deeds—must also be his Word and thus an aspect of revelation. By incorporating into the sacred text these kinds of questions and challenges to the ways of God, the Lord opens up to the reader the possibility of allowing his own experiences to inform the text and, in turn, to be informed by it. Lament allows for a proper questioning of the purposes of God and, in the Psalms and

[30] For a commonly accepted list, see Hermann Gunkel, *The Psalms: A Form-Critical Introduction,* trans. Thomas M. Horner (Philadelphia: Fortress, 1967), 13–15 (community), 19–22 (individual).

wisdom literature at least, leads to the divine counterresponse that brings satisfying resolution.[31]

The sheer abundance of texts necessitates that only a highly selective and representative number of them can be brought to bear here, and in particular those generally categorized as lament psalms. The first of these, Psalm 3, contains the normal elements of complaint, petition, and confidence in being heard. David, faced with many foes (vv. 1–2), acknowledges the Lord's protective power and calls on him for deliverance (vv. 3–4). Assured of that help, he can now rest in peace (vv. 5–6), for he is confident that even now the Lord is in process of defeating his enemies (vv. 7–8). Though not technically a lament psalm, Psalm 6 also voices David's complaints about life's difficulties, this time unspecified. Body and soul are in agony, and all he can do is ask, how long? He appeals to the Lord's covenant love (*ḥesed,* v. 4); and having gained assurance of it, he bids his enemies to depart (v. 8) and utters imprecation against them that they might be rendered impotent and forced to turn away (v. 10). At another point he wonders if he will ever be free of harassment (Ps. 13). It seems as though the Lord has forgotten him and that he is in danger of being overwhelmed by those who hate him (v. 4). Once more, however, he relies on the Lord's *ḥesed* and concludes that all will be well after all (v. 6).

The depths of despair for David are recounted in Psalm 22, one cited by Jesus on the cross (Matt. 27:46) and by the Gospels with reference to his crucifixion (Matt. 27:35; John 19:24). It seems that God had forsaken him entirely (vv. 1–2) while he suffered the mocking insults of people all around him (vv. 6–8). His enemies—described as bulls, lions, and dogs—tore at him mercilessly until, it seems, his life was ebbing away (vv. 12–18). However, he recalled that the Lord had created him and had been near him in the past (vv. 9–11) and therefore could be counted on again to bring relief (vv. 19–21). When he did so, David pledges to praise him to his friends and publicly in the assembly of God's people. This will inspire others also to turn to the Lord and recognize his sovereignty (vv. 22–31).

---

[31] For a full development of this approach, see Walter Brueggemann, *Theology of the Old Testament* (Minneapolis: Fortress, 1997), especially 117–44.

Employing much the same imagery, David, in Psalm 31:9–24, laments his emotional and physical deterioration at the hands of his enemies (vv. 9–13). But, as before, he trusts God to deliver and preserve him, to put down his foes, even to death (vv. 14–18). He extols the goodness of the Lord (vv. 19–20) and praises him for the salvation that he is confident is already on the way (vv. 21–24). Sometimes it seems that the Lord himself is the enemy. David complains that he has been struck by the Lord's arrows, resulting in his wasting away almost to death (Ps. 38:1–8). Like Job's friends who abandoned him, David laments that his have deserted him and enemies have come instead to make life miserable (vv. 9–12). The problem, it appears, is that David has sinned, and the Lord's attacks are pangs of conscience (v. 4). The remedy is obvious: he must pray a prayer of confession (v. 18) and in so doing invite the Lord to save him not only from his waywardness but also from outside forces that seek to do him harm (vv. 15–16, 19–22). The passage is particularly helpful in showing that much of the cause for human suffering can be attributed to sin and disbelief in the life of the one who utters the call for help.

Psalm 44, a communal lament, complains that the Lord has given the nation over to its enemies for, to them, no good reason (vv. 9–16). "All this has happened to us," they say, "but we have not forgotten You or betrayed Your covenant" (v. 17). They profess fidelity to him, and yet he has crushed them and made their land a wilderness (vv. 18–19). In fact, it is because they have been loyal to him that their enemies attack them, placing them in a constant threat of imminent death (vv. 20–22). In utter frustration they ask why the Lord has forsaken them, and they appeal to him to redeem them because of his covenant love *(ḥesed)* (vv. 23–26). This audacious accusation of injustice on the part of the Lord is hardly mitigated by the prayer for deliverance, for it overlooks the sin of the nation which (though not admitted) surely underlay their present plight. The psalm is helpful, nonetheless, in communicating both a spirit of self-righteousness and, at the same time, a recognition of the need for divine intervention.

David, to the contrary, had no such illusions of innocence in his times of persecution. On an occasion of unknown provenance, he pictured himself as up to his neck in troubles of every kind, beset by "those who hate me without cause" (Ps. 69:4). At the same time he is quick to confess that his guilt lies at the root of his problems (v. 5), some sin he has committed that he prays will not besmirch the glorious name of the Lord (v. 6). Till now he has, in fact, suffered for the sake of that name and in that assertion almost seems overly defensive about his present plight and slightly accusatory. Had he not been such a faithful servant of the Lord, he might not be in such difficulty (vv. 7–12). In any event, David knows that only the Lord can save him, and therefore he calls out to him to do that very thing (vv. 13–18).

Speaking on behalf of the people as a whole, Asaph, in Psalm 74:1–11, asks why the Lord has rejected them "forever," certainly an exaggerated assessment of his nations' plight but one that reveals their sense of desperation (v. 1). The city of Jerusalem and its temple have been reduced to rubble as have all the sacred shrines throughout the land (vv. 3–8). Worse still, the prophets have disappeared so there is no more word from God (v. 9). Why, the psalmist asks, has the Lord allowed this to happen? How long will he allow his name to be slandered before he responds in judgment (vv. 10–11)? At the end his appeal is to the ancient redemptive work of the Lord on Israel's behalf and to his dwelling among them on Zion (v. 2). The plea is that he might move again to deliver them from their present plight.

The same psalmist begs the Lord for the restoration of Israel from destruction—clearly also from the Babylonian conquest—and this time in the garb of a parable (Ps. 80). The petition is to the Mighty One who sits "enthroned on the cherubim," an acknowledgement of his sovereignty despite the nation's dire predicament (vv. 1–2). He laments that his people are fed with "the bread of tears" and that God has given them "a full measure of tears to drink" (v. 5). He reminds the Lord that he had brought Israel like a vine out of Egypt and had planted her in the vineyard of the promised land (vv. 8–11; cf. Isa. 5:1–7). But now the vineyard walls are destroyed, and any passerby who wishes may help himself to its fruit (v. 12). This state of affairs he correctly interprets to be the result of divine judgment (v. 16), but the poet nonetheless pleads with the Lord to return to his people, to restore the Davidic monarchy ("the man at Your right hand") (v. 17), and to reestablish the nation (v. 19). Were he to do this, "we will not turn away from You; revive us, and we will call on Your name" (v. 18). The lament thus moves from complaint to petition to promise of renewed commitment in the aftermath of restoration.

Referring to an event of uncertain historical context, another Asaphic communal lament, Psalm 83, cries out to the Lord not to remain silent in the face of Israel's peril (v. 1). Enemies from all around are plotting its destruction, hostile forces that are the Lord's foes as much as Israel's (vv. 2–8). The theologian thus identifies Israel as God's special people, so much so that an attack on them is an attack on the Lord at the same time. The nation's appeal for help is not necessarily self-serving, then, but is made in the interest of the Lord's reputation as well.

In a much more personal vein, Psalm 88 displays an unremitting complaint about an individual's utter despair. He cries to the Lord day and night, apparently with no success, lamenting that his situation is hopeless and that he is at death's door (vv. 1–6). Like Job, he accuses the Lord of having isolated him from family and friends to the extent that they want nothing to do with him (v. 8; cf. Job 19:13, 19). He knows that those in the grave cannot praise the Lord (vv. 10–12) so why, he asks, will the Lord not listen to his prayers while he yet remains alive (vv. 13–14)? Unlike other lament psalms, this ends with no ray of hope at all.[32] The poet declares that he has known nothing but sorrow all his life; and despite his earnest appeals to the Lord, he has never found relief (vv. 15–18). In fact, the Lord himself has afflicted him, apparently for no good cause (v. 16).

Speaking on behalf of the Davidic king, Psalm 89 accuses the Lord of having broken covenant with him (vv. 38–39), evidence of which is the ruinous condition of his seat of power, Jerusalem (vv. 40–43). The state no longer has an offspring of David on the throne, so what else can one conclude than that the Lord has cast aside his chosen people? How long will this go on? the psalmist asks (v. 46). Will the monarchy, like mortal human life in general, come to an end? If so, how can this be squared with the everlasting promises made to David (v. 49)? He has no answers to these questions and must simply resign himself to the fact that the Lord, though silent on the matter, is still worthy of praise (v. 52).

Our treatment of the difficulties of kingdom life ends with Psalm 102, "a prayer of an afflicted person" (the heading). The piece commences

---

[32] Kraus puts it as follows: "In all its assertions the prayer song is filled with impenetrable darkness. The breath of approaching death drifts through every line. Typical motifs that are otherwise discernible in the prayer songs of the individual are lacking." Joachim Kraus, *Psalms 60–150,* trans. Hilton C. Oswald (Minneapolis: Fortress, 1993), 192.

with an appeal to the Lord to hear and answer prayer (vv. 1–2). The basis for the man's complaint seems to be both physical ailment and emotional distress, a situation so severe that death seems imminent (v. 11). Implicit in his complaint is at least some admission of guilt, for he views his situation as the result of divine wrath against him (v. 10). Here as elsewhere in the psalms of lament there is the frank acknowledgment that kingdom citizenship does not preclude suffering. All the saints of God must recognize and accept that fact and feel free to raise questions and even complaints as to the justice of God. At the same time, there are nearly always statements of hope or at least of confession that the Lord is sufficient to save and make all things right.

Hostility to the Kingdom

Many of the lament psalms just discussed concern the problems and perils of individuals and even the nation brought on by themselves or from unknown causes. Others, however, suggest that such difficulties emanate from hostility to the kingdom itself; that is, they are attacks by enemies of the Lord and of the people Israel who are called by his name to represent him. Psalm 5, to begin with, points up the nature of the conflict: "You are not a God who delights in wickedness; evil cannot lodge with You" (v. 4). Thus the issue is clear: a yawning chasm exists between a holy God and wicked men and nations that are implacably resistant to his sovereignty. The same psalm goes on to describe such enemies as those whose words cannot be trusted, blatant rebels who should be severely punished for their many sins (vv. 9–10).

David, embodying the nation as a whole, prays for the Lord to keep him from "my deadly enemies who surround me" (Ps. 17:9). Like lions they seek his life, and the only hope he has is for the Lord to rise up, confront them, and bring them down (vv. 12–13). Such men know nothing of kingdom hope, for their only reward is in this life (v. 14). That David's enemies are in reality the enemies of the Lord is clear from Psalm 21 where David declares that the Lord will lay hold of his (the Lord's) enemies and will utterly consume them in the furnace of his fiery wrath (vv. 8–9). No matter what plots they lay, they will never succeed, for the Lord will repel them and drive them away (vv. 10–12). Psalm 35 makes the same point. David urges upon the Lord, "Oppose my opponents, LORD; fight those who fight me" (v. 1). That is, the king stands in the place of the Lord, and therefore the enemy of the one is the enemy of the other. He feels comfortable in asking the Lord to come to his defense and to vindicate him (vv. 23–24) while turning the mockery of his foes into their own shame and disgrace (v. 26).

The antagonists of the kingdom focus their attention on its king; hence, David often speaks of his own personal suffering and danger as symbolic of the threats to the kingdom itself. Their desire to inflict harm on him is in the final analysis a veiled attempt to undo his realm and, ultimately, the sovereignty of Israel's God. When they seek his demise, they hope for the collapse of the nation (Ps. 41:5), whether they be foes from without or within (vv. 7–9). David's desire for revenge, then, is not so much personal as it is for the honor of the Lord and his kingdom purposes (vv. 10–12). This connection of David's role in the kingdom with the kingship of the Lord is even clearer in Psalm 52. Here David excoriates an enemy whom he describes as "a disgrace in the eyes of God" (v. 1 NIV). This being the case, God will deal with him, not David, for the real attack is not against David but against the kingdom of the Lord (vv. 5–7; cf. Ps. 54:1–7).

In Psalm 58 David addresses the evil rulers of the nations directly, accusing them of subverting the universal rule of the Lord by their dishonest and unjust ways (vv. 1–5). Hopeless in their rebellion against the Lord, they will be disarmed by him and finally brought to ruin when the Lord avenges those whom they have wronged (vv. 6–10). Then it will be clear that the citizens of the kingdom are indeed the righteous ones and that "there is a God who judges on earth" (v. 11). In the psalm immediately following, Psalm 59, David again appeals to the Lord for deliverance from enemies whom he has not wronged, making clear the point that the real hostility is not against him but against the Lord (vv. 1–4). He therefore urges the Lord to rise up against the wicked nations as a matter of personal honor and to punish them as rebels opposed to his own sovereign design (v. 5). The same theme dominates Psalm 64. David complains about his enemies who seek to do him in (vv. 1–6) but then leaves the matter of retribution in the hands of the Lord since clearly the battle is his. He will strike them down until at last mankind will be forced to acknowledge his wonderful works (vv. 7–9).

The second part of Psalm 83, a communal lament, invokes God's wrath on his enemies (named in vv. 5–8), urging him to do now what he had done to enemies in the past (vv. 9–12). The purpose is not only to punish them but to exonerate the Lord so that they will "know that You alone—whose name is Yahweh—are the Most High over all the earth" (v. 18). This clarifies the point we are seeking to make, namely, that opposition to the king and people of Israel is in fact opposition to the sovereignty of their God.[33]

One of the major moral difficulties in the Old Testament is the use of imprecation by those who wish to avenge themselves upon their enemies or otherwise bring harm to them.[34] These are especially prominent in the Psalms—striking examples occurring in 35:1–9; 58:6–8; 69:22–28; 137:8–9; and 140:9–11. While there may at times be some evidence of personal animosity, it is important to recognize—as we have stressed in this section—that the psalmists by and large are interested not in their own vindication and revenge but in the reputation of the Lord and his kingdom. When they implore him, then, to wreak all manner of havoc upon their enemies, they do so from a spirit of devotion to him. So jealous are they for his glorious name, any assault upon him and his kingdom program elicits from them strong invective and a wish that the evildoers should suffer divine judgment.[35]

Psalm 109 is a classic case in point, though David's words here seem on the surface to be devoid of reference to the honor of the Lord. We repeat, however, the observation that David, as God's "Son" (cf. Ps. 2:7) and surrogate, stands in his place and as such his enemies are the enemies of the Lord. The psalm opens with a complaint about men with "wicked and deceitful mouths" who have maligned David, repaying his good toward them with evil (vv. 1–5). He urges the Lord to appoint legal counsel against them, perhaps Satan himself (cf. Zech. 3:1),[36] so that when they

---

[33] Kraus, *Psalms 60–150,* 162.

[34] Alex Luc, "Interpreting the Curses in the Psalms," *JETS* 42 (1999): 395–410; John N. Day, "The Imprecatory Psalms and Christian Ethics," *BSac* 159 (2002): 166–86; Patrick D. Miller, "The Hermeneutics of Imprecation," *The Way of the Lord* (Tübingen: Mohr Siebeck, 2004), 193–202.

[35] For a helpful understanding of the ethical issues involved, see Bullock, *Encountering the Book of Psalms,* 228–38.

[36] More likely the reference is to any accuser, the primary meaning of Heb. *śāṭān*; cf. Bruce Baloian, שׂטן, NIDOTTE 3:1231–32.

are brought to trial they might be found guilty and lose all they have as a result (vv. 6–15). Their sin is that they have never pronounced blessing on others—only curses—so their punishment ought to fit the crime. As David put it, "Let [curses] be like a robe he wraps around himself, like a belt he always wears" (v. 19). That the wrong has, in fact, been against the Lord is clear from David's insistence that the Lord punish the evil man (v. 20) and, even more to the point, that the sinner come to see that David's ultimate vindication is a work of the Lord: "May [they] know that this is Your hand and that You, LORD, have done it" (v. 27).

Nowhere is the linkage between David and the Lord more clear in respect to their sharing in common the hostility of evil men than in Psalm 139:19–22. Here David pleads for the Lord to slay them; for though they are his enemies (v. 22), they have become such because they "invoke You deceitfully. Your enemies swear by You falsely" (v. 20). Then, in a most telling admission, he confesses that he hates those who hate the Lord (v. 21). David's attitude toward sinners is thus not a personal animus so much as it is a zealous defense of the name and reputation of the Lord.[37] His imprecatory stance is not grounded in petty resentments toward those who have harmed him but in a reverence and love of the Lord that is so deep that, in his view, only their judgment by the Lord can be adequate compensation.

Yahweh's Faithfulness to the Kingdom

In light of the incessant attacks by the evil forces of the visible and invisible worlds against the kingdom of the Lord and its citizens, how does he respond, and what will be the ultimate outcome? More important to the inspired penmen of the Psalms, perhaps, is the question as to their own well-being and that of the nation Israel, which they represented and of which they were a part.

David spoke for himself and his generation when he portrayed the Lord as good and upright, one who lovingly cares for those who are faithful to the covenant (Ps. 25:8–10). Those who fear him will find direction in life, and they and their posterity will enjoy blessing in the land. Moreover, he will continue to disclose himself to them in their

[37] Weiser, *The Psalms,* 807.

times of uncertainty (vv. 12–15). David's own impulse is to seek the Lord, and his fervent prayer is that the Lord will not hide but will turn to him in his hour of need (Ps. 27:7–9). So certain is he of this, he declares that even should his mother and father forsake him, the Lord will receive him (v. 10). Even death will not deny him the Lord's presence for, as he puts it, "I am certain that I will see the LORD's goodness in the land of the living" (v. 13).

The same concept of God's universal care occurs in Psalm 36. Here the psalmist proclaims that the Lord's covenant faithfulness *(ḥesed)* reaches to the heavens and his justice to the great deep *(tĕhôm)* (vv. 5–6). This way of describing the extent of his care suggests that it knows no limits. As Creator, he sustains all he has made, not discriminating between the high and the low or even between man and animal. His special grace rests upon those who know him, however, and David prays that he might continue to display it to them, the upright in heart (v. 10).

The underlying grounds for God's tender love for his people is the covenant he made with them, beginning with Abraham (Ps. 105:9). He remembers his solemn promises to them because he confirmed them to Israel at Sinai as an everlasting covenant (v. 10). Nothing can undermine that pledge, especially as it relates to Canaan, Israel's inheritance forever (v. 11). The land was theirs as the arena in which they could live out the covenant role the Lord had assigned them as a kingdom of priests and a holy nation (Ps. 106:44–46). Psalm 111 is devoted almost entirely to this theme. Here the poet celebrates the wondrous works of the Lord in general and in particular those on behalf of the citizens of the kingdom (vv. 2–4). For those who fear him he provides food, a token of his covenant faithfulness (v. 5). And that covenant issued from the great work of exodus redemption, a work that gives assurance of the Lord's ongoing deliverance. As another psalm put it, "Great is His *faithful love (ḥesed)* to us; the LORD's *faithfulness* endures forever" (Ps. 117:2). These highlighted technical terms put beyond any doubt the Lord's everlasting relationship with his people and his unending care for them.

Psalm 130 begins with the testimony of the individual poet as to his need for a divine hearing from deep within the depths and a note of confidence that he will indeed be heard (vv. 1–4). There is hope in the midst of despair, one more sure than that of the night watchman who waits for the dawning of a new day. The author then applies the confidence of his own experience to the situation of his people Israel. "Put your hope in the LORD," he urges, "for there is faithful love *(ḥesed)* with the LORD, and with Him is redemption in abundance" (v. 7). No matter the plight of the nation at the moment, "He will redeem Israel from all its sins" (v. 8). Again, the kingdom cannot fail because it is founded on the irrefragable promises of God inherent in the covenants made with its founders.

Finally, Psalm 145 culminates the testimony to the Lord's faithfulness to the achievement of his kingdom design by declaring that "the LORD is faithful to all his promises and loving toward all he has made" (v. 13b NIV). He picks up those who fall, provides food for the hungry, and meets the needs of all living things (vv. 14–16). He is righteous in his ways and near to those who call on him, fulfilling their desires and saving them from all their difficulties (vv. 17–20). Promises like these, though addressed to individuals in the kingdom, transcend the particulars and guarantee that the kingdom as a whole will not only survive but will triumph to the glory of God.

The Psalms, like the wisdom literature, consists of the response of the people of the Lord to their life situations as viewed through the lenses of human experience, on the one hand, and by means of the promises and requirements of covenant revelation, on the other. More often than not these perspectives are at radical odds with each other, for the ideals of the covenant relationship between the Lord and his people seem rarely to work out in everyday life. The result is a questioning or challenging of the ways of the Lord, or even, in extreme cases, skepticism and outright disbelief. Thus, many of the psalms seem filled with despair.

At the same time the Lord keeps alive the flame of hope and confidence. Over and over he saves, thus proving in actual experience that he is there and that he cares. Moreover, the theologians and poets of Israel, steeped as they were in Torah, understood fully the nature of God's covenant grace and promises and rose again and again to plateaus of spiritual exuberance. On their own behalf and as the voice of the community, they uttered words of praise and celebration, knowing full well that the God who had constituted them as a kingdom people would carry them and the kingdom through to the end. The ambivalence of the Psalms thus reflects genuine human perplexity and doubt but also supreme confidence in the God whose word cannot fail.

The theology of Psalms can be summarized as a poetic expression of Israel's struggles to be the theocratic covenant people of the Lord in an intensely hostile world, a people who, though often beset by personal and national failure, nevertheless confessed the reality of the Lord and the fidelity of his everlasting promises to their fathers, themselves, and their children yet to come. As we have insisted already, the fact that they are responsive or reflexive does not in any way diminish the revelatory character of the psalms, for the truth of the Lord can be reflected as much in human reaction to his ways as it can be in fiat declaration of propositional dogma.

Chapter Nineteen

The Theology of the Wisdom Literature

Introductory Observations

As with the Psalms, the theology of Old Testament wisdom literature consists largely of the reflections of individuals or communities on their situations in life and their responses to them.[1] As often as not these responses run counter to the normative theology of Israel as articulated in Torah and the Prophets, but they cannot be discounted as valid theology—even revelatory theology—on that account. As we have argued elsewhere, biblical theology is the cohesive integration of all the Bible has to teach about God's revelation of himself and his will as well as the narrative of the historical, social, and religious context in which that revelation occurred. This means, among other things, that the context itself must make its own contribution to theology, for God revealed himself within that context and either in elucidative support of it or, more commonly, in confrontation with it. The challenge to the interpreter of texts is to weigh them against the more propositional

[1] For the peculiar issues relative to the wisdom literature as theological matrices, see Roland E. Murphy, *The Tree of Life: An Exploration of Biblical Wisdom Literature* (New York: Doubleday, 1990), 111–31.

disclosures found elsewhere to see whether what they teach is in accord with the theological consensus that those parts of the record have made normative. Should they fail to do so, the theologian must assess them for what they are, namely, human (or even Satanic) statements of belief that are of theological importance only as such. Should such texts conform to the general theological message of Scripture, they may do so because they issue from an understanding of prior revelation to which the writer and/or speaker makes his contribution or simply because they happen to be right without obvious dependence on antecedent texts and traditions.

The Theology of the Book of Job

The book of Job is particularly illustrative of the tensions just raised. Careful analysis of the composition makes clear that almost all that is said by human speakers is either theologically misleading in light of a meta-theology of the Old Testament or, in some cases, is in flat contradiction to it. Only as God speaks is there any assurance that truth is being spoken.[2] This does not mean, however, that true things are not uttered by others but, as we have already suggested, this may be as much a product of the use of existing normative texts or, at the most, an intuitive insight into truth based on human experience with the true and living God. It is all revelation nonetheless, a record of mankind's struggle with the human predicament, faithfully enshrined in the text, and the divine response that provides its only resolution.

It is unnecessary in a work like this to deal in detail with issues of authorship, dating, and setting of the book of Job.[3] Scholarship agrees that the background is one of patriarchal pastoral nomadism, even ancient, but the time of its composition—to say nothing of its authorship—is a matter of great diversity of opinion. That it emerged in its present form in preexilic times, even as early as the days of Solomon, the golden age of Hebrew wisdom, is not at all unreasonable.[4] The book itself consists

---

[2] Tryggve N. D. Mettinger, "The Enigma of Job: The Deconstruction of God in Intertextual Perspective," *JNSL* 23/2 (1997): 1–19.

[3] For a good review of such matters, see R. K. Harrison, *Introduction to the Old Testament* (Grand Rapids: Eerdmans, 1969), 1022–46.

[4] For various options, see Robert L. Alden, *Job,* NAC 11 (Nashville: Broadman & Holman, 1993), 25–28.

of prologues and epilogues presenting the problem of the book and its resolution between which are lengthy dialogues between Job and his three "theological advisors," a self-righteous monologue by a fourth, and the divine speeches that do not address the issue of the book per se but that lead Job, nevertheless, to an understanding of his problem and thus to the end of his constant striving for answers.[5]

Three main theological themes are brought to the fore: (1) the problem of the human predicament; (2) God and the human predicament; and (3) the resolution of the human predicament. Taken together they address what, in popular understanding, is sometimes phrased in the question, Why do the righteous suffer? or, more technically but accurately, the notion of theodicy. How can a righteous and just God allow, or worse, bring to pass human suffering, especially when it seems that such suffering is for no just cause or good reason? That is, Job has to do with the vindication of God in light of life's imponderable mysteries. To reach a fair verdict in such matters has obvious theological value not only for the theology of Israel but for every man and every woman who struggles with its implications in everyday life.

The Problem of the Human Predicament

The term "human predicament" is not intended to isolate one or even a few of the problems indigenous to human life but to describe the human situation in general with all its moral and ethical dilemmas. Why is it that people suffer and die no matter what they believe or how they live? Is there any hope for correlation between behavior and reward, any possibility that a day will come when the apparent injustices in the here and now will be rectified? Will vindication come at last for the righteous and judgment for the wicked, and if so, how and when?

In his first response to Job, Eliphaz the Temanite makes the observation that the human plight is universal. "Mankind is born for trouble," he says, "as surely as sparks fly upward" (Job 5:7). That is, human trouble is a part of the natural process. Job himself agrees with this assessment, noting that man's service on earth is hard, like that of a hired man (7:1). In the day he wishes for night, and in the night he longs for the day. Life is but a breath to him; and when it is over, there remains nothing but the

[5] A. E. Steinmann, "The Structure and Message of the Book of Job," VT 46 (1996): 85–100.

grave from which no one ever returns (vv. 9–10). All this is a function of man's mortality. They "live in clay houses, whose foundation is in the dust." So fragile are they that they are crushed like mere moths, broken to pieces unnoticed by God and man, until finally they perish forever (4:19–21). Even insensate plants have hope of putting forth new shoots; but mankind is destined to lie down, never to rise again (vv. 10–12).

Death is thus inevitable. Job pleads for at least brief respite before he enters its domain, a gloomy place where even the light is like darkness (10:20–22). But such a place is all he can hope for given his mortal limitations (17:13–16).

The ultimate explanation for man's hopeless condition is his sinfulness. Eliphaz asks, "What is man, that he should be pure, or one born of woman, that he should be righteous?" (15:14). He is "revolting and corrupt," drinking up "injustice like water" (v. 16). Elihu accuses Job and his friends of being sinners but makes the observation that human sin does not and cannot move God one way or another, nor can righteousness (35:1–6). This cynical way of looking at man's standing before God must be understood in light of Elihu's assertion that Job himself is alleging that there is no benefit to him whether he stops sinning or not. God's transcendent sovereignty is so complete that human behavior affects it not in the least and certainly not when it is altered just to gain his attention and obtain benefit from him.

To worsen the sense of life's inequities, it seems to Job that the wicked, if anything, seem even better off than the righteous. They reach old age, enjoy security and peace, prosper materially, enjoy the aesthetic blessings of life, and finally go to their grave in peace (21:1–13). But this is only a chimera. In reality, they too suffer calamity for those who appear to prosper will finally experience the same fate as those who do not (vv. 17–18, 22–26). In fact, Eliphaz observes, the wicked too suffer in this life (15:20–26). Though they seem to escape trouble, they will come to a day of reckoning when all their assets will be stripped away, and they will be left with nothing (vv. 27–35). Bildad the Shuhite adds that the lamp of the wicked is snuffed out, his health declines, he endures irreversible loss, and eventually he perishes, leaving no descent or even memory (18:5–17). "Such is the dwelling of the wicked," he concludes, "and this is the place of the one who does not know God" (v. 21).

Zophar chimes in and notes that whatever joy the wicked knows is ephemeral, and in the end he will perish, never to be found again (20:5–9). What he so much relishes now will become distasteful to his mouth and sour to his stomach. All he has labored to acquire will be lost to him and returned to those whom he has cheated (v. 10). At the end of it all, he will never find satisfaction in all his accomplishments; for just when it seems he is most full of the good things of life, God will bring judgment upon him. God's arrows of retribution will pierce him until he and his house are totally consumed (vv. 20–28). Zophar concludes that "this is the wicked man's lot from God, the inheritance God ordained for him" (v. 29).

Job cites a list of the sins that men commit—removal of boundary stones; theft; abuse of the orphan, the widow, and the needy—and though he wonders why such things are allowed by the Almighty, he, like the others, recognizes that the respite sinners seem to enjoy is only temporary and will be followed by God's judgment (24:1–22). They may have a certain sense of security, but God is not unaware of their sinfulness and in due time will make his displeasure known. Speaking of the wicked, Job observes that "they are exalted for a moment, then they are gone; they are brought low and shrivel up like everything else. They wither like heads of grain" (v. 24).

In even stronger terms, Job, in a reply to Bildad, views the wicked as having no hope (27:7–10). Their offspring will be impoverished, their widows will not mourn them, and all the world's goods they have accumulated will be inherited by the righteous (vv. 13–17). Like a fragile hut in the teeth of a raging storm, they and all they have will be blown away, hooted and hissed off the stage of life (vv. 18–23).

That the wicked should experience final retribution and even in this life be afflicted with trouble should occasion no surprise, but what about the righteous? How is it possible to account for their lot in life that all too often seems radically at odds with any sense of fairness or justice? Job himself is described as "a man of perfect integrity,"[6] one who "feared God and turned away from evil" (1:1). The juxtaposition of this

---

[6] The phrase *tām wĕyāšār* does not, of course, suggest sinless perfection. Rather, it refers to "a discernible group of people to whom adherence to the ethos and social values that clearly distinguish the God-fearing from the wicked is of prime importance." Thus J. P. J. Olivier, תמם, NIDOTTE 4:307.

description with the following note as to Job's prosperity and greatness (vv. 2–3) seems to suggest a direct correlation between his character and the obvious blessings that he enjoyed. Satan makes the same connection, and while conceding that Job is the object of divine favor, he goes on to suggest that the linkage between Job's righteousness and his prosperity is tenuous at best, held together only because God had shielded Job from baleful influences that would undermine the axiom that righteousness always results in blessing (1:8–11).

The narrative goes on to make the point that the innocent can and will suffer reverses for which they can find no good reason. Job loses his oxen and donkeys, his sheep and his servants, his camels, and finally his sons and daughters (vv. 13–19). He himself is not spared, for the Lord allowed Satan to inflict painful sores upon him until all he could do was sit upon an ash heap, scraping the excruciating itch that tormented him day and night (2:7–8). We who can visit behind the scenes are able to see for ourselves that the human condition does not always yield to pat answers. Our predicament is often bereft of any sensible or rational explanation.

The suffering of the innocent troubles modern sensibilities as it did those of Job and his friends. Popular theology taught that such a notion was counter to all human expectation. Eliphaz asks, "Who has perished when he was innocent? Where have the honest been destroyed?" (4:7). Bildad, responding to Job's protestations of innocence, raises the discussion to a more theological level by reminding Job that the Almighty always acts in line with his nature and therefore cannot pervert justice (8:3). What one gets in life is what he deserves. Such a view, he says, rests on ancient tradition to the effect that there is a causal nexus between one's character and his condition (vv. 8–19). "God does not reject a person of integrity," he opines, "and He will not support evildoers" (v. 20). Zophar, tired of Job's self-defense, wishes that God would speak and reveal Job to be the sinner that men know him to be (11:5). The implication is clear: Job's suffering is to be accounted for only by the self-evident fact that he is a sinner in denial.

Job also accepts the premise that the righteous should not suffer, though, of course, this premise contradicts his own experience. What he knows theologically he cannot square with his existential situation. All he wants is an opportunity to encounter God face-to-face, for so sure is he of his innocence he is certain of complete vindication. If his friends can prove otherwise, he is willing to become silent and meet his fate like a man (13:13–19). To this Eliphaz replies that Job is engaged in a game of self-deception and hypocrisy for the accumulated wisdom of the ages teaches that human suffering is a product of sin. Job's own claims to integrity ring hollow in light of such tradition and, in fact, are themselves witness to his sinfulness (15:1–13).

The theological tradition might well make the case that long-standing observation as well as an intuitive sense of justice puts beyond cavil the correlation between the human predicament and its root cause. People suffer because they have offended a holy God and, conversely, are blessed because their manner of life warrants it. But individuals like Job belie the tradition, at least if their testimony is to be believed, because they suffer despite their innocence and therefore unjustly. Either God is unjust, or there is a mystery to his purposes that defies human explanation.

Job persistently and consistently maintains his innocence of sin, at least to the degree that would render unwarranted the severe treatment he has received at God's hands. Even were God to kill him, he would never renounce his integrity (6:10). But what he really wants is for God to lay out the charges against him that have prompted such repercussions (10:2). Is it because God is limited and therefore unable to discern Job's righteousness (10:4–6)? Whatever the case, he asserts that by deed and in thought he has lived in such a way as to deserve better treatment (16:17). Furthermore, no matter what God does in the future, Job will continue the pursuit of righteousness. God might be unfair, but Job will never betray his own integrity (27:1–6).

In a remarkable testimony to his past life and its record of obedience to principles later enshrined in the Torah, Job denies having been lustful (31:1–4); deceitful (vv. 5–8); adulterous (vv. 9–12); abusive to his servants (vv. 13–15); or oblivious to the poor, the orphan, or the widow (vv. 16–23).[7] He has never put his trust in finances (vv. 24–25), nor has he been tempted to idolatry (vv. 26–28). He has never gloated at the

---

[7] Such disclaimers seem to presuppose a post-Mosaic setting for the book of Job by listing covenant stipulations originating in Torah. Archer addresses (without accepting) such a possibility. Gleason L. Archer Jr., *A Survey of Old Testament Introduction* (Chicago: Moody, 1985), 466. More likely, these sins reflect a common wisdom tradition of universally held social norms. See Michael Brennan Dick, "The Legal Metaphor in Job 31," *CBQ* 41 (1979): 37–50. Reprinted in *Sitting with Job,* ed. Roy B. Zuck (Grand Rapids: Baker, 1992), 321–34.

misfortune of an enemy (vv. 29–30), has never failed to provide for his household (v. 31), and has never closed his door to the stranger in need of shelter (vv. 32–34). So persuaded is Job at his own righteousness that he invokes upon himself the curses of God should he be found otherwise (vv. 8, 10, 22). He even challenges the Almighty to write out a summary of his claims against him, promising to put them on public display so the whole world could see if in fact he was deserving of his woeful condition (vv. 35–37).

Smug in his self-righteousness, Job declares that he has a perfect right to complain. God has loaded him down with undeserved misery, shooting him through and through with poisonous arrows of terror (6:1–4). As it is natural for a donkey or ox to voice satisfaction when well fed or for a person to have no appetite for unseasoned food, so Job's complaints do not arise for no reason. Anyone mistreated as he has been cannot restrain himself from lamenting his predicament and demanding that it be adjudicated (vv. 5–7).

Job's friends are not slow to reprimand him for his (to them) aberrant theology. Eliphaz devotes a lengthy discourse (Job 22) to rebuking his suffering friend for his obstinacy in not owning up to his sins (vv. 1–11). He reminds him that God is all-knowing and that it is useless to try to cover up (vv. 12–20), and then urges him to repent and thus be delivered from his sin and its painful consequences (vv. 21–30). He points out that Job could hardly be suffering for his righteousness, so the only reasonable conclusion is that it must be for his wickedness. Then, assuming the role of an omniscient investigator, Eliphaz ticks off a list of sins that Job must have committed to justify such divine displeasure: He had demanded unreasonable security for loans, was lax in the basics of proper hospitality, and neglected widows and orphans (vv. 6–9). He offers not a shred of proof for these allegations, but since the list is almost formulaic as a touchstone of Torah social demands, Eliphaz may be merely saying that Job broke every rule in the book!

Elihu is no kinder. After laying down the principle that unrepented sins cannot go overlooked by God even if the sinner promises never to commit them again (34:31–33), he concludes that Job speaks like a fool if he thinks he can ignore the sins of the past. Indeed, for his self-justifications to both men and God, he ought to be tested still more until he finally comes to terms with his arrogant denials (vv. 34–37). What Job is suffering is only the fruit of his own doing. God has tried to dissuade him of his rebellious course of action but to no avail. Nor will it do for Job to succumb to the bribes of others who might seek from him a halfhearted or insincere confession. No, he must not become even more evil in his attempt to achieve exoneration (36:16–21).

The point thus far is clear: All human beings, by virtue of their sinfulness and mortality, suffer the consequences of their thoughts and deeds; for God cannot hold them guiltless, nor can he let them go unpunished. But he also is a forgiving God; and when sinners repent, he exercises mercy and delivers sinners from their wretchedness. Should they fail to repent, however, they can expect the tribulation to continue. The righteous, on the other hand, enjoy the blessing of a benevolent God. Whatever trials and pains may come their way come as a function of their humanness and not as evidence of divine displeasure. The conclusion of this kind of syllogistic argument is clear: Unexplainable suffering must be attributed to unconfessed and unrepented sin. This is the theology of the sages garnered by empirical evidence over the centuries. Granted its premises, it seems unassailable, but God has not yet spoken.

God and the Human Predicament

The mystery of Job's suffering—and that of all mankind—remains unresolved on the basis of experience and observation alone, for there is often a disjunction between human behavior and its repercussions. The righteous and the wicked appear to share a common misery leaving one to wonder about God's justice on the one hand and the efficacy of proper conduct on the other. The theology of tradition lacks any means of justifying the ways of God in such matters except to assume the simplistic (and understandable) equation that the human predicament is ever and always a *quid pro quo*. We always get what we deserve even if we are convinced of our own innocence.

The book of Job contributes immensely to the discussion by allowing God to speak for himself, in his own defense, thereby bringing to bear a perspective impossible to mere human rationality.[8] It is not as though Job and his companions were oblivious to God and his ways. To the contrary,

[8] Walter Brueggemann, *Theology of the Old Testament* (Minneapolis: Fortress, 1997), 390–91.

in defense of his integrity and character, they responded as they did to the situation at hand. Their problem was not of marginalizing God but rather of failing to see that his dealings with mankind cannot be neatly contained in a theological box of their own design and manufacture.

To human observers, God is elusive.[9] Job lamented, "If only I knew how to find Him, so that I could go to His throne. I would plead my case before Him and fill my mouth with arguments" (23:3–4). Then, he believed, he could present such a strong defense that God would no longer press charges against him (v. 6). But not only God's dwelling place is beyond human reach. So are his ways past finding out. No matter how hard Job tries to enter into the realm of God's mysteriousness, he is stymied at every turn. "He is not a man like me, that I can answer Him," Job complains (9:32). What is needed is an arbitrator, someone who can stand between God's *mysterium* and his own limited perspective (v. 33). Then he could make his case without fear of being misunderstood.

Elihu grasps well this chasm between God's elusiveness and man's ignorance. He rebukes Job for having complained that God will not heed him, reminding him that God does indeed speak. The chasm is bridged by his self-disclosures to mankind whether by dreams and visions, audible sound, or—as in Job's case—by chastisement[10] "on his bed with pain and constant distress in his bones" (33:19). Thus he speaks to Job, but the message he speaks is not what Job wants to hear.

Job himself concludes that the issue at hand is really one of divine sovereignty. He confesses that "wisdom and strength belong to God; counsel and understanding are His" (12:13). Whatever he does cannot be undone. He brings drought to the earth, confounds human wisdom, frees prisoners from their shackles, reduces the proud to nothingness, discloses mysteries to human understanding, makes nations great, and renders human rulers stupid and without direction (vv. 14–25). On the other hand, God's sovereignty is displayed in arbitrary ways, in deeds and actions that appear random, without perceptible purpose. To Job it seems that God regards him as a brute beast and not an intelligent being with

---

[9] For an exhaustive presentation of this as a major theological theme, see Samuel Terrien, *The Elusive Presence* (San Francisco: Harper & Row, 1978), esp. 361–73.

[10] Dhorme insightfully renders the *hofal* of *ykh* here as "salutary correction." Eduard Dhorme, *A Commentary on the Book of Job,* trans. Harold Knight (Nashville: Thomas Nelson, 1984), 69; cf. 497.

whom he should be able to reason (7:12). He finds no ease in sleep, no respite from terror, no meaning in daily existence. To contend with God is vain, for God's wisdom and ways are beyond human comprehension (9:1–4). He controls the forces of nature, manipulating them according to his good pleasure and for purposes he refuses to divulge. And yet, when he is near, it is impossible to see him and to prevent whatever harm he is bent on doing (vv. 5–13). "How then can I answer Him or choose my arguments against Him?" Job asks (v. 14). Even were this possible, it would be dangerous; for God crushes with a storm and multiplies wounds for no reason (v. 17). So apparently illogical are his ways that he can turn Job's heartfelt sense of innocence into a confession of guilt (v. 20). With such a God ordinary dialogue is impossible.

Job's frustration in the face of God's irrational arbitrariness leads him to wonder why God creates only to destroy (10:8–9). Why did he form him with such care and finesse, give him life, and bestow such kindness on him knowing full well the miserable outcome of it all? Whether guilty or innocent of wrongdoing, it seems all the same—God is constantly on the watch for human sinfulness, and claims of innocence are to no avail (10:13–15). Every argument Job advances on his own behalf is countered by God who brings witness after witness against him (v. 17). What hope does he have to find vindication in such unbalanced and unfair circumstances as these?

At the same time, Job and his friends are forced to concede that God's power and wisdom far exceed their own, and there may be reasons for his ways among them that they in their human limitations cannot perceive. Zophar asks Job, "Can you fathom the depths of God or discover the limits of the Almighty?" (11:7). The answer is obvious. God's wisdom is broader and deeper than the universe itself (vv. 8–9), and his power is irresistible (v. 10). He therefore knows the inner thoughts of men even when they—dumb beasts that they be—cannot see their own shortcomings (vv. 11–12). Job concurs, affirming that "wisdom and strength belong to God; counsel and understanding are His" (12:13). As the Creator he understands the ins and outs of the universe, whether the netherworld or the heavens above with all their interconnected bodies (26:5–9). In primeval times he separated light from darkness, split the seas like a monster torn asunder so that dry land appeared, and made the skies above lustrous to the eye (vv. 10–13). And yet these mighty works are only what is visible to human comprehension. How can man know those truly deep things of God that he chooses not to reveal, such things as the mysteries of innocent suffering?

Elihu adds to the theme of divine omniscience by reminding his hearers that God is fully aware of the ways of a man: "He observes all his steps" (34:21). There is no place for the wicked to hide, no need to pump them for information as to their sinfulness (vv. 22–23). Interrogation in a court of law is unnecessary because God already knows the full truth of every case before him. Though he may remain silent in the presence of human evil, his silence should not be interpreted as indifference or inability to act. He is still sovereign and will bring his royal purposes to fruition (vv. 24–30). Elihu also extols God's power, the evidence of which all mankind can see in his mighty work of creation and maintenance of the universe (36:24–26). He brings about the changes of the seasons and the cyclical patterns of the earth's waters, thus making the land fruitful and abundant (vv. 27–33).

Such dramatic displays of God's glory and power cause Elihu to marvel as, indeed, God intends that they should (37:1, 7). The phenomena of the natural elements testify eloquently to his wisdom and sovereign pleasure, moving and acting as they do at his command as obedient servants. Job, says Elihu, should pay special attention to all this, not just to come to an enhanced appreciation of God as Creator but to learn that such a God demands moral accountability. His realm is not just in the visible world but over the thoughts and intentions of the human heart as well. What Job says to God he must say with due respect, for in his majestic transcendence the Almighty does what is right and is answerable to no man (vv. 19–24).

This attribute of God's justice receives further treatment by Elihu in two lengthy passages devoted to it (34:10–15; 36:1–16). At the outset he declares forthrightly, "It is impossible for God to do wrong, and for the Almighty to act unjustly," Job's and his friends' opinions notwithstanding (34:10). Whatever punishment he doles out is fair, for "God does not act wickedly and the Almighty does not pervert justice" (v. 12). It is only his grace that preserves mankind alive, for by a word he could cause all human breath to cease (vv. 14–15). But his justice also calls for judgment upon those who are wicked (36:6). Even the righteous, though blessed and exalted by him, must be mindful of his corrective measures (vv. 7, 8–

10). If they repent and become submissive to his lordship, they will enjoy long days of prosperity; if, however, they fail to do so, they can expect and will well deserve his harsh discipline (vv. 11–12). It is up to Job to respond in an appropriate manner to his own condition, recognizing that his present predicament is of his own making. The remedy is to turn to the God of justice for mercy and forgiveness and thus to be done with his miserable state (vv. 16–17).

As prescient and theologically astute as many of these observations about the human condition and its remedies have been, the matter is not finished until the Lord himself has the final say. Observations about God's ways in the world and speculations as to his nature based on human notions as to how God ought to be may have merit and may actually coincide with reality, but it is only when he discloses himself through spoken and written word that any real sense of theological authority can be achieved. As it turns out, however, it is not so much in what is said as it is in what is left unsaid that resounds with theological power. In four long chapters (Job 38–41) the Lord (now the poet's epithet of choice rather than Elohim or El Shaddai)[11] asks a series of rhetorical questions of Job, (presumably) his companions, and certainly of us and all readers of the book. It is in the asking and answering of these questions that we come face-to-face with the living God in all his power and glory and then find ourselves no longer needing to understand the human predicament.

Hailing Job before him as a man on trial, the Lord proceeds to ask him where he was at the dawn of creation (ch. 38).[12] Who made all things, he inquired, and who set them in their proper place and relationships? Has Job ascended to the heavens, delved into the deep abysses, and learned the mysteries of the elements? Can he control the constellations, command the storms, and provide food for the wild beasts of field and forest? Turning to areas of life where Job might better show awareness through years of observation, the Lord asks about the gestation habits of animals,

---

[11] As Hartley points out, this name is chosen because it evokes the exodus tradition, one of redemption. John E. Hartley, *The Book of Job,* NICOT (Grand Rapids: Eerdmans, 1988), 491.

[12] For the forensic nature of chapters 38–41, see Sylvia Huberman Scholnick, "Poetry in the Courtroom: Job 38–41," Zuck, *Sitting with Job,* 421–39; Kathleen M. O'Connor, "Wild, Raging Creativity: The Scene in the Whirlwind," *A God So Near: Essays on Old Testament Theology in Honor of Patrick D. Miller,* ed. Brent A. Strawn and Nancy R. Bowen (Winona Lake, Ind.: Eisenbrauns, 2003), 171–79.

their freedom from restraint, and how to go about harnessing untamed and unbroken animals to human service (ch. 39). Can he account for the remarkable survival skills of the ostrich which so lacks intelligence as to be a ready victim of every predator? Can Job provide strength to the war horse, teach the hawk and eagle to fly, and give them intuition to build their nests in inaccessible places?

At last Job is allowed to speak in his own defense, but he finds he has nothing to say (40:1–5). But the Lord is not through. Having made the case that only he is God, a case made painfully clear to Job by now, the Lord turns to the matter at hand, namely, divine justice. "Would you really challenge My justice?" He asks. "Would you declare Me guilty to justify yourself?" This, then, is the nub of the issue of the book, the hubris of mankind that not only attempts to know the ways of God but to challenge them as well. Are you God? the Lord is asking (v. 8). If so, then you have a right to assert yourself and the power to save yourself (v. 14). Unless and until he can capture the mighty behemoth and bring to heel the leviathan, mere playthings to the Lord, Job has no legitimate claim to equality with God and therefore no basis for questioning his dealings with him and with humanity as a whole.

Though the pieces are in place for some kind of understanding of Job's dilemma and its ultimate outcome, it remains yet to see how his story—a paradigm for all mankind—can provide the theological resources necessary to meet the profoundest human need, that is, how to make sense of the apparent nonsense of human experience.

The Resolution of the Human Predicament

The narrative prologue to the book is essential to its meaning for it provides to the reader who stands outside the conflictive dialogues of the central section an opportunity to see behind the scenes. From this privileged position it is clear that there are forces at work and decisions made to which the human actors are not privy in the least. They attempt to assess life's situations—especially the miserable condition of Job—without the benefit of hearing for themselves the machinations that set the stage for all that follows.

What is immediately clear is that the struggle of paramount importance in the narrative is not between Job and his counselors or even between him and God but between God and Satan over the issue of sovereignty.[13] Thus Job makes its own peculiar contribution to the major theological theme of the Bible, namely, the rule of God over creation through his designated surrogate, man created as his image. From the beginning this dominion was challenged by the forces of evil, incarnated first as the snake in the garden and now identified as the adversary, the Satan. Job, in a sense, is a mere pawn in the struggle, for he symbolizes all mankind as the agent through which the Lord desires to display his hegemony over all the earth. Satan seeks to subvert that plan by so marring that image that it can no longer be effective and thus of any use to God's kingdom program.

The setting of the contest is the heavenly assembly to which all angelic beings have access and where they render account to the Lord, the great King. Satan is among them, for even he, wicked and fallen as he is, cannot escape the sovereign claims of God over all he has made. One day Satan is asked to report on his activities to which he replies that he has returned "from roaming through the earth and walking around on it" (1:7). The latter verb form *(hithallēk)* is a technical one used here and elsewhere as a way of describing an assertion of control or dominion.[14] The Satan is saying, therefore, that he has been patrolling the earth over which he lays sovereign claim, a state of affairs that came about with the fall of mankind and with which the biblical witness universally concurs (cf. John 12:31; 14:30; 16:11; 2 Cor. 4:4; Eph. 2:2; 1 John 5:19). But his sphere of influence is one permitted to him by the Lord, and it can be exercised to no greater extent than the Lord allows. Thus, when challenged as to his boastful claims by the reminder that Job, at least, has not submitted to him, Satan must concede as much but hastens to point out that it is only the Lord's shield of protection around Job that

---

[13] Most scholars correctly assert that there is nothing in this passage to suggest an enmity of such cosmic proportions this early in the course of revelation and that Satan as a personal name and as God's archenemy is fully developed only much later (1 Chron. 21:1; Zech. 3:1–2). However, the nature of biblical theology is such that ideas introduced only in kernel form in early texts can and do find fuller meaning in light of subsequent revelation. The Satan or devil of the New Testament (Matt. 4:10; 12:26; Acts 5:3; Rev. 12:9; 20:2, 7) is clearly the same person as the figure known as "the Satan" here in Job. See Gustave Friedrich Oehler, *Theology of the Old Testament,* trans. George E. Day (Grand Rapids: Zondervan, n. d., 1883), 448–51.

[14] Eugene H. Merrill, הלך, *NIDOTTE* 1:1032–35.

has precluded Satan's control of him as well (1:10). Remove that shield, he says, and Job too will succumb (v. 11).

The limitations of Satanic dominion are clear from his inaccessibility to Job without divine approval and even the fact that whatever harm does come to Job comes not from Satan himself but ultimately from the Lord. Satan urges the Lord to "stretch out Your hand and strike everything he [Job] owns, and he will surely curse You to Your face" (1:11). The Lord's response is that "everything he owns is in your power," thus delegating to Satan the freedom to put Job to the test (v. 12). It is important to hold in tension the ideas throughout the prologue that Satan is in implacable resistance and hostility to the kingdom of God and yet can never overcome God's sovereignty. But mankind also opposes God's regnal design, choosing to go his own way. Several examples must suffice to make the point.

First, Job's own wife advises him to "curse God and die" (2:9), the very outcome Satan predicted should Job be put to the test (1:11; 2:5). And Job also finds his former friends to be perfidious now that he is in dire straits (6:14–23). He, as a man of God and agent of the kingdom, surely has a right to better treatment. But worse still, his enemies have been commissioned by God to work against him so that God appears to be working at cross-purposes with his own kingdom plans (16:9–17). This, at least, is Job's perception, as misguided as we know it to be. In fact, Job names the Lord as his enemy, the cause of his alienation from his family and community (19:13–20). God has struck him and is responsible for his deplorable lot in life. In the strongest terms possible, Job confesses his frustration that as an innocent citizen of the kingdom he should be rejected not only by its fellow citizens but also by the king himself. "I cry out to You for help," he says, "but You do not answer me; when I stand up, You merely look at me. You have turned against me with cruelty; You harass me with Your strong hand" (30:20–21).

This near blasphemy, designed to put the onus of antikingdom sentiment on God himself, reveals in fact that Job is the archopponent of God's sovereign plans for him and all creation. Over and over he challenges God's kingly rule and rights. His birth, he says, was a tragic mistake (3:1–10), and he would be better off dead than alive (vv. 11–19). Why is it, he wonders, that those like himself who want to die are denied even that blessing from God (vv. 20–26)? He pleads in vain for God to leave him alone or at least to give him the opportunity to exonerate himself (13:20–23). But these reactions are Job at his worst, responses born out of frustration and despair. It is important also to let him speak in times of better mood, times when he sensed that God was on his throne and when he was in submission to him and to the situation in which he found himself, even if with less than perfect understanding and certainly anything but joy.

After the first series of calamities in which he lost virtually all his family and possessions, Job was able to say, "The LORD gives, and the LORD takes away. Praise the name of the LORD" (1:21). Even after he was stricken with painful disease, he could ask, "Should we accept only good from God and not adversity?" (2:10). Even many days later, with no hope of relief in sight, Job could go so far as to affirm that "even if He kills me, I will hope in Him" (13:15). This is not merely blind trust or unthinking emotionalism. There exists in Job's heart not just hope but a growing confidence and not just in God's sovereignty but in his justness and goodness.

He asks the question, "When a man dies, will he come back to life?" and then answers by saying that he will wait for his release to come, a freeing from not only his pain but also from whatever sins may have brought him to this state of physical and spiritual anguish (14:14–17). "Even now my witness is in heaven," he says, "and my advocate is in the heights!" (16:19). Whatever that may have meant to Job, the point is that he anticipates a time of vindication thanks to a heavenly intercessor who will plead his case before God. This same one he calls "Redeemer" *(gōʾēl)* at a later point (19:25), describing him as alive and coming. The purpose of his coming is to stand upon the earth, entering Job's arena in order to take up his cause. Who the redeemer may be is a matter of vigorous debate. Some interpreters understand him to be a supernatural advocate for humans in need whereas others equate him with God himself.[15] The context appears to favor this view though the coming of God to stand upon the earth is a bold theological concept indeed. Whatever the case Job is certain that at some point he will see God with his own eyes and not through the eyes of a mediator. Moreover, he will see him *mibbēśārî,*

---

[15] Marvin H. Pope, *Job,* AB 15 (Garden City, N.Y.: Doubleday, 1965), 146; Hartley, *The Book of Job,* 293–94.

that is, from within or apart from his body, which has already turned to dust (v. 26). Job expects to see God either as a disembodied spirit or from within a new body, one associated with re-creation and resurrection.

In any event, he is confident of ultimate vindication. When God tests him, he will come forth as gold, having nothing for which to be ashamed (23:10). Even popular theology taught that heavenly powers were at work to guide men's steps and provide a means for their reconciliation to God. Through them prayer can be made and God's favor obtained. Then those who are pardoned and cleansed can testify to others of God's saving grace which has spared them from what they deserved and redeemed them from the pit (33:23–28).

But how is vindication to be pursued? The answer it seems lies in God alone and what man needs is the wisdom to grasp who he is and what he can do. So important is this idea to the book that all of chapter 28 is dedicated to it.[16] The central point is that man is incapable of finding wisdom in places that he might expect, for only "God understands the way to it and he alone knows where it dwells" (28:23 NIV). It is therefore only in the pursuit of God that wisdom to know his ways among men can be known. And to know God is to fear him in an awestruck, reverential manner that recognizes and confesses his legitimate claims to sovereignty over all of life, even its mysterious aspects (v. 28). Elihu recognizes the truth that man by himself cannot come to a knowledge of God and his governance of the world. "It is a spirit in man and the breath of the Almighty that give him understanding," he declares (32:8).

God's discipline is also instructive and conducive to the resolution of human dilemma. Eliphaz correctly observes that the person is blessed whom God corrects, for in his chastening he teaches lessons about making one's way through life's vicissitudes and at the end brings rewards that more than outweigh the trials endured in the process (5:17–26). On the other hand, the individual who thinks he or she can solve life's riddle on his own is sadly mistaken. "How can a person be justified before God?" Bildad asks (25:4). If the brightest stars in the heavens are clouded and opaque to the eyes of God, how can a man be pure, he who "is a maggot, and the son of man, who is a worm?" (v. 6).

---

[16] Roy B. Zuck, "Job's Discourse on God's Wisdom: An Exposition of Job 28," Zuck, *Sitting with Job,* 299–302.

The answer lies in repentance, forgiveness, and restoration. Though speaking from a hypocritical and misguided spirit, Eliphaz nevertheless speaks truth when he urges Job to "come to terms with God and be at peace" (22:21). This will effect a transformation of life and fortune so glorious that all that has been missing in Job's life will come back to him in superabundant measure (vv. 22–30). Whether Job was moved by such counsel is impossible to know, but in the end he came to an awareness of God in all his majesty and splendor and having done so saw himself for what he was. He confessed to the Lord that he had spoken of things he did not understand and of things too wonderful for him to know (42:3). "I had heard rumors about You," he said, "but now my eyes have seen You" (v. 5). All he can do and must do, in light of such divine self-disclosure, is to see himself as the despicable creature he is and repent before the Lord in dust and ashes (v. 6).

The theology of Job is not complete without the account of the restoration of kingdom blessing to him. At the beginning he lost sons and daughters, sheep and camels, oxen and donkeys, and at last even his home and health. But at the end, once he had come to confess God as Lord and to recognize his own arrogance in challenging God's sovereign claims, he received back much more than he had lost (42:10–17). More important, he was vindicated not because of the force of his logical or theological arguments but because he had come to know that the ways of God, though mysterious at best, are perfect and designed for the good of the citizens of the kingdom.

How does the wisdom literature, and Job in particular, relate to the whole fabric of Old Testament theology and contribute to the theme we have espoused throughout, namely, the kingdom of God administered through his image, the human race? At first glance it might seem that any connection at all is tenuous and even strained for the notions in Job of dominion and sovereignty, at least on a universal scale, are hardly dominant. God's transcendent power and glory are indeed shown in sharp relief but primarily in terms of his work as Creator and administrator of the physical universe. Little or nothing is said of the nations or of humanity in general and certainly nothing of Israel. And as for man's rule over all things as the vice-regent of the Almighty, not a hint is given.

The most satisfying way to view the contribution of wisdom, including Job, to a larger theology is to see it as a collection of texts designed to help the kingdom citizen orient himself to kingdom life and responsibility. Torah provides covenant stipulations that circumscribe life and give it regulation; the Prophets narrate the history of the kingdom, detailing both its successes and failures and urging conformity to Torah; and the Writings reflect reaction to kingdom realities in everyday life. They reveal the questions, concerns, frustrations, misunderstandings, and triumphs of men and women caught up in everyday kingdom experience, sometimes capturing their total inability to achieve success in mirroring the divine mind and purpose, but at other times, informed by the Spirit, radiating in brilliant light all that it means to be fruitful, to multiply, and to have dominion over all things.

The Theology of Proverbs

Whereas the book of Job is largely narrative and dialogue, Proverbs in an anthology of aphorisms and maxims, described by the book itself as "a proverb *(māšāl)* or a parable *(mĕlîṣâ),* the words of the wise *(dibrê ḥăkāmîm),* and their riddles *(ḥîdōtām)*" (1:6). These are just a few of the technical terms that are sprinkled throughout the book, but all of them zero in on the central theme which is wisdom—its essence, expressions, function, manifestations, and accessibility. The social and historical context for the most part is the united monarchy of Israel under the reign of King Solomon, to whom much of the book is attributed (chapters 1–24). This is not surprising inasmuch as the Israelite tradition roots Israel's wisdom movement solidly in that context.[17] Some parts of the collection are anonymous (e.g., "The Words of the Wise," 22:17–24:34); others are attributed to otherwise unknown individuals such as Agur (30:1–33) and King Lemuel (31:1–9); and still others, while originated by Solomon, were edited by Hezekiah's scribes nearly three hundred years later (25:1–29:27). An unknown hand at a later point compiled the whole and arranged it into its present canonical shape.

The theological function of the book clearly is to provide guidance to the citizen of the kingdom as to how to order his life before God, the king,

---

[17] Duane A. Garrett, *Proverbs, Ecclesiastes, Song of Songs,* NAC 14 (Nashville: Broadman & Holman, 1993), 23–24, 51–52.

and his fellow human beings.[18] The wisdom in view is not essentially of a reflective, philosophical nature but rather one based on and responsive to Torah, observation of the cosmos with all its mysteries and lessons, human experience, and intuitive interaction with all that could and can be known of God in all the ways he chooses to manifest himself. Unlike Job, however, where propositional revelation is scanty to say the least, Proverbs speaks with divine authority in every verse. These are not the mere musings of men but the wisdom of God himself mediated through inspired channels that therefore do not parrot the accumulated wisdom of the sages of antiquity but speak always a current and relevant word of God.[19]

The Essence of Wisdom

Early in the book the assertion is made, "The fear of the LORD is the beginning (or essence, Heb. *rēʾšît*) of knowledge; fools despise wisdom and instruction" (1:7). This becomes almost the leitmotif of the book (cf. 9:10; 15:33; Ps. 111:10), a thread that ties together its parts but that also provides the secret to true wisdom. It comes not by education, observation, philosophizing, or introspection but by recognizing and submitting to the sovereignty of God in all areas of life. To fear him is to obey him, and in obeying him one chooses the true path to wisdom. To choose not to fear the Lord is to despise knowledge (1:29), but to fear him is to find it (2:5).

This kind of wisdom cannot be divorced from proper attitude and behavior. In fact, only the righteous are said to be wise because only they can fear the Lord in truth. Personified wisdom herself says, "To fear the LORD is to hate evil" (8:13), that is, wise men and women show their degree of wisdom by their lifestyle. Another proverb shows the protective value of the fear of the Lord: "One turns from evil by the fear of the LORD" (16:6). But the fear of the Lord is also the source of meaningful life (14:27), satisfaction (15:16), and wealth and honor (22:4). Only he can give wisdom (2:6), for in the final analysis it consists in knowing him personally and intimately (30:3).

---

[18] Bruce K. Waltke, *The Book of Proverbs Chapters 1–15*, NICOT (Grand Rapids: Eerdmans, 2004), 64–65.

[19] Waltke, *The Book of Proverbs Chapters 1–15*, 64–65.

Of all the treasures of heaven and earth, wisdom is most precious. The wise man says of this inestimable gift: "Happy is a man who finds wisdom and who acquires understanding, for she is more profitable than silver, and her revenue is better than gold. She is more precious than jewels; nothing you desire compares with her" (3:13–15). To have wisdom should be one's chief aspiration, for to have her and embrace her will bring honor and glory to her owner (4:7–9).

The Expression of Wisdom

Despite disclaimers to the contrary, the wisdom literature is not unaware of Torah teachings, and certainly Proverbs breathes the spirit of the Mosaic texts, though his name appears nowhere.[20] When the wise man urges his son not to forget his teaching but, to the contrary, to keep his commands, he employs terms (*tôrâ* and *miṣwâ,* respectively) that are abundant above all in Deuteronomy (Prov. 3:1). Then, reversing the terms, he warns, "Keep your father's command, and don't reject your mother's teaching" (6:20). The instructions that follow—to bind them on your heart and fasten them on your neck and to be conscious of them in all places and at all times—is obviously reminiscent of Deuteronomy 6:6–9 and 11:18–20 where parents are commanded to teach their children the covenant stipulations.[21]

Torah referred to in Proverbs 28:4 (forsaking and keeping the law) can be nothing other than the Mosaic writings (so also vv. 7, 9). And in a remarkable equation between revelation *(ḥāzôn)* and law *(tôrâ),* Solomon promises blessing to those who obey it (29:18). Even the oracle taught to King Lemuel by his mother reminds drunken kings not to "forget what the law *(mĕḥuqqāq)* decrees" (NIV), in this case with respect to caring for the needs of the oppressed (31:5).

Wisdom in Proverbs also finds a source in the cultus, regulations for which are obviously Mosaic as well. But as the prophets are quick to condemn pro forma adherence to them (Isa. 1:10–17; Jer. 7:22–23; Amos 5:21–25), so wisdom likewise teaches that mere ritual without inner

---

[20] Scott observes that the teachings of the sages, though not appealing to what he calls "the authority of a revealed religion," nonetheless "presuppose an accepted belief," that is, preexisting revelation. R. B. Y. Scott, *Proverbs, Ecclesiastes,* AB 18 (Garden City, N.Y.: Doubleday, 1965), xvi.

[21] William McKane, *Proverbs* (Philadelphia: Westminster, 1970), 327.

integrity is of no value (15:8). The Lord hears the prayer of the righteous and righteous deeds are, to him, more acceptable than sacrifice (21:3; cf. 1 Sam. 15:22). As for the sacrifice of the wicked, it "is detestable" (Prov. 15:8), especially when done "with evil intent" (21:27 NIV).

The natural order (general revelation) is a third way that wisdom gives expression. For example, the lazy man is advised to look to the ant and gain wisdom in doing so (6:6–8). Lacking any kind of leadership, the tiny creature knows enough to lay up supplies for coming times of want, something indolent human beings often fail to do. Agur observes four earthy creatures that though small are possessed of extraordinary wisdom. The ant provides for tomorrow; rock badgers find dens in which to secure themselves; locusts band together to wreak havoc in the fields; and lizards, tiny enough to be held in the hand, manage to slip into kings' palaces and live the royal life (30:24–28). This kind of wisdom, drawn from careful study of the created world, is the kind that made Solomon famous. His thousands of songs and proverbs were largely based on acute attention to the wonders of the environment surrounding him. Thus, "he described trees, from the cedar in Lebanon to the hyssop growing out of the wall. He also taught about animals, birds, reptiles, and fish" (1 Kings 4:32–34). He did not lecture as a modern botanist or biologist but drew lessons about ordinary life from the characteristics and behaviors of the world in which he lived.

The Function of Wisdom

The role of wisdom in the book of Proverbs operates on two dimensions, the heavenly and the earthly. Wisdom is said to have been the facilitator of God's creation, the instrument by means of which he laid earth's foundations and set the heavens in place (3:19–20). In wisdom's personification in Proverbs 8, she says she was there when God created all things but not just as an observer. "I was a skilled craftsman *(ʾāmôn)* beside Him. I was His delight every day, always rejoicing before Him. I was rejoicing in His inhabited world, delighting in the human race" (vv. 27–31).[22] The personification here brings to mind Paul's description of

[22] Fox takes the term to be an infinitive absolute meaning "being raised"/"growing up," serving as an adverbial complement to the main verb. Michael V. Fox, "*'Amon* Again," *JBL* 115 (1996): 699–702.

Christ in whom "all the treasures of wisdom and knowledge are hidden" (Col. 2:3) and who, in the same context, was the agent of creation. Paul affirms that "by Him everything was created, in heaven and on earth, the visible and the invisible, whether thrones or dominions or rulers or authorities—all things have been created through Him and for Him" (Col. 1:16; cf. John 1:3).[23]

Life also springs from and is enriched by wisdom. She declares that those who find her find life and divine favor, but those who do not find her are destined to death (Prov. 8:35–36). This, of course, is because wisdom proceeds from God who alone is the source of life both here and now and forever.

The Manifestations of Wisdom

We have just noted the personification of wisdom, always as a female. This is because abstract ideas or concepts in Hebrew are commonly rendered in the feminine gender; and, of course, the term *ḥokmâ* itself is feminine.[24] Moreover, wickedness is also in the guise of a woman with heavily sexual imagery, so it is appropriate that her godly counterpart should be seen as a virtuous woman. She is introduced early on as one who "calls out in the street" to encourage the undecided to follow her and thus to fear God and find peace (1:20–33). Those who pay her no heed set themselves up for disaster and will find no sympathy from her in the day of their calamity (vv. 24–26). The entirety of Proverbs 8 consists of a monologue by wisdom who, again, stands in a busy crossroads to make her urgent appeal to fools to forsake their destructive ways and embrace the precious treasures she can dispense. In her they can find prudence, understanding, counsel, and sound judgment. She is the source of proper laws and governance, of riches and honor, and, indeed, of life itself. In another setting, wisdom plays the role of a hostess who, having prepared a sumptuous meal in her palatial house, invites the simple to come and dine with her at her expense (9:1–6). The nourishment they receive will give them abundance of life.

---

[23] Cleon L. Rogers III, "The Meaning and Significance of the Hebrew Word *ḥokmâ* in Proverbs 8, 30," ZAW 109 (1997): 208–21.

[24] E. Kautzsch and A. E. Cowley, ed., *Gesenius' Hebrew Grammar* (Oxford: Clarendon, 1910), ß122q.

The fools and simpletons to whom wisdom appeals are not the intellectually or educationally deficient but people of all kinds who, not knowing God, live in the ignorance of sin. Her invitation, then, is actually an invitation to come to know the true and living God, whom to know is to have a radical change of life and direction. Such persons have succumbed to dame folly, the archenemy and diametric opposite to lady wisdom. She is consistently viewed as a prostitute or an unfaithful wife who is bent on enticing young men by her guileful charms. Wisdom's concern is to warn against the allurements of the adulteress and to offer a better alternative—peace and joy and life (2:16–19).

The warnings to young men to avoid the adulteress do, of course, have literal and practical application, for sexual immorality is a pervasive Old Testament issue.[25] But wisdom texts must also be read figuratively where such sins are in view because of the obvious antithesis being drawn between personified wisdom and her wicked counterpart. When the sage advocates that youth "keep your way far from her" (5:8) and "drink water from your own cistern" (that is, be true to your own wife) (v. 15), he is entreating the kingdom citizen to resist the blandishments of the worldly life and to turn to the Lord for genuine and full satisfaction. This is clear from the end of Proverbs 5 where, having warned against the adulteress, the wise man says, "A man's ways are before the LORD's eyes, and He considers all his paths. A wicked man's iniquities entrap him; he is entangled in the ropes of his own sin. He will die because there is no instruction, and be lost because of his great stupidity" (5:21–23). Clearly the reason to steer clear of dame folly is so that one might escape the terrible consequences of life without God.

Proverbs 7 consists of a lengthy warning against the adulteress in which the spiritual overtones of the sexual imagery are more clearly drawn out. It begins with an appeal to "my son" to keep the commands *(miṣwôt)* and guard the teachings *(tôrâ),* writing them on the tablet of his heart (vv. 1–3). He is to regard wisdom as his sister (v. 4), and therefore the adulteress is folly or ignorance of the Lord and his ways. After reviewing her manifold temptations, the wise man warns his "sons" not to turn after her, for multitudes have done so to their great ruin (vv. 24–26).

---

[25] Robert B. Chisholm Jr., "'Drink Water from Your Own Cistern': A Literary Study of Proverbs 5:15–23," *BSac* 157 (2000): 397–409.

"Her house is the road to Sheol," says he, "descending to the chambers of death" (v. 27). At last she is named—"the woman Folly"—and again the warning to the youth is that "her guests are in the depths of Sheol" (9:13, 18).

Throughout the book of Proverbs, wisdom or the lack thereof is betrayed by speech or even thought. The wise know how to speak aright, but fools do not, often blabbering nonsense and worse. On the other hand, "silence is golden" is an aphorism much at home in wisdom circles. "When there are many words, sin is unavoidable," says the sage (10:19). For one thing, words can hurt or even kill, at least metaphorically. "With his mouth the ungodly destroys his neighbor," we're told, probably through slander and false testimony (11:9). By words the wicked lie in wait to shed blood, but the righteous speak words of deliverance (12:6). That is, words have coercive power either to indict the innocent or to exculpate them.

Sometimes unguarded speech brings unexpected repercussions upon the head of the speaker. Solomon warns that "the one who guards his mouth protects his life; the one who opens his lips invites his own ruin" (13:3), and "the proud speech of a fool brings a rod of discipline, but the lips of the wise protect them" (14:3). It may be better oft times to say nothing at all, for even a fool is thought to be wise if he remains silent (17:28). Otherwise his foolish prattling invites strife and beatings and even complete undoing (18:6–7). What is clear from these passages and others is that not just rebel sinners are guilty of abusing the gift of speech. The wise—the righteous—can also victimize themselves and others by speech that is careless or malicious by design. On the whole, however, the manner and subject of one's speech is an accurate indicator of his wisdom or lack of wisdom and therefore of his status in the kingdom of God.

The clearest manifestation of wisdom and folly is in character and behavior, of which Proverbs has a great deal to say. It can be as subtle as an interior disposition—"the righteous hate lying" (13:5)—or as publicly displayed as acts of murder and mayhem. We have already given attention to speech as an index of the inner person, but a whole lifestyle puts the matter beyond dispute. Proverbs teaches that "the path of the righteous is like the light of dawn, shining brighter and brighter until midday. But the way of the wicked is like the darkest gloom; they don't know what makes them stumble" (4:18–19). There is also a certain stability in the life of the upright that comes from roots planted deep within the soil of godliness that the wicked cannot know (10:30; cf. 12:3, 7).

Persons often reap the fruit of their sowings within their own lifetimes, but if not then, there comes a day when justice will prevail and the righteous and wicked alike will receive their just deserts. This universal biblical principle is nowhere more starkly defined than in Proverbs with its penchant for couplets in antithetical parallelism.[26] Whatever is said about the outcome of the righteous is precisely opposite for the wicked. For example, "the LORD's curse is on the household of the wicked, but He blesses the home of the righteous" (3:33) or "what the wicked dreads will come to him, but what the righteous desires will be given to him" (10:24). More specifically, the righteous arise while the wicked fall (24:16); they succeed while the wicked are brought low (11:5); they gain reward while the wicked suffer loss (11:18, 21, 23; 15:6); they escape trouble while the wicked are full of troubles (12:21); and they find refuge (14:32), joy (10:28), triumph (28:1, 12, 28), and life in its fullest and most satisfying sense (10:16)—none of which the unrighteous can find and enjoy.

Accessibility to Wisdom

The question yet remains, how can wisdom be found? It originates in the Lord, of course, and is revealed in Torah, the cultus, and creation; but how is it mediated or applied at a practical, day-to-day level? Proverbs provides a threefold answer: (1) through parental instruction, (2) through divine discipline, and (3) through the monarchy, God's earthly extension of kingdom rule.

In the hierarchy of the Lord's kingdom administration, the earliest and most basic unit is the family under the headship of the father and mother. At the outset Proverbs underscores this fundamental aspect of the kingdom: "Listen, my son, to your father's instruction *(mûsar)* and don't neglect your mother's teaching *(tôrâ)*" (1:8; cf. 4:1; 6:20; 23:22; cf. Deut. 6:7–9; 11:18–21). Failure to do so results in great loss to the individual himself (20:20; 30:17) and untold sorrow and heartbreak to his

[26] For these and other literary and rhetorical features in Proverbs, see Waltke, *The Book of Proverbs,* 38–63.

parents (10:1; 15:20; 17:21, 25; 19:13, 26; 28:7; 29:3, 15); but obedient compliance to them and recognition of the God-given role of parents brings reward and blessing to them and their children (23:24–25). Those who live within this framework are wise indeed (13:1), but those who refuse to do so are nothing but arrogant fools (15:5).

One of the stated purposes of the book of Proverbs was to facilitate the attainment of "wisdom and discipline *(mûsar)*" and the acquisition of a "disciplined and prudent life *(mûsar haskēl)*" (1:2–3 NIV). The root *ysr* and all its cognate forms has to do with guidance or instruction and the means of bringing it about, up to and including discipline in the punitive sense as well as in the sense of correction.[27] "Fools despise wisdom and instruction," we're told (1:7), for fools (i.e., the ungodly) prefer to live life without constraints and boundaries (5:12; 12:1; 15:5). But life pursued without attention to restriction and instruction will bring sorrow in the here and now to both the errant fool (13:18; 15:32) and to those whom he influences (10:17). More tragic still, the undisciplined life will eventually result in untimely death (5:23; 15:10).

There is a natural tendency on the part of parents to tolerate inappropriate behavior and to withhold discipline under the pretext of love. This, however, is an abdication of kingdom responsibility, an act of disobedience that itself will produce most harmful consequences. Proverbs thus exhorts parents to take whatever measures are necessary to instruct their offspring in the ways of the Lord and to apply correction and even punishment when all else fails. The sage reminds his hearers that "the one who will not use the rod hates his son, but the one who loves him disciplines him diligently" (13:24). When he does so in the proper spirit, he offers hope to his child; but when he fails, he will appear to be intent on killing him (19:18). The rod of discipline has the effect of converting fools to wise men (22:15) and in any case will never be fatal (23:13).

As for children, they should know that godly discipline is from the Lord and is designed for their own well-being (3:11). The father's commands are a lamp and light, and his corrections in discipline "are the way to life" (6:23). The young are, therefore, urged to get "wisdom, instruction, and understanding" (23:23); and when they do, they will bless their parents

---

[27] E. H. Merrill, יסר, *NIDOTTE* 2:479–82.

for discharging their kingdom role and will bring delight to their soul (29:17).

Most striking—and yet not surprising—is the attention to the monarchy in Proverbs, especially as an agent of the Lord in implementing his rule on earth in a wise and just manner.[28] Most of the book is attributed to Solomon, who was certainly keenly aware of the theological significance of the Davidic monarchy, and emphasis on the divinely chosen king and his vice-regency of the rule of the Lord is, of course, consistent with the great theological themes of the Old Testament covered in these pages.

Wisdom personified sets the stage by observing, "It is by me that kings reign and rulers enact just law; by me, princes lead, as do nobles and all righteous judges" (8:15). The Lord controls their heart as they submit to him, controlling it like "a water channel in [His] hand: He directs it wherever He chooses" (21:1). The conjunction of the sovereign purpose of God and human rulership is clear—human kings sit on thrones but only as puppets of an omnipotent God.[29] Since this is true, the kingdom citizen must fear both the Lord and the king because they work in concert (24:21–22). But kings must recognize their own limitations and acknowledge that they reign at the Lord's behest. They must exhibit "loyalty" *(ḥesed)* and "faithfulness" *(ʾemet)* if they hope to secure their throne; that is, they must be sensitive to the covenant terms that allow them this great privilege of serving God in the first place (20:28). There is no place for tyranny (28:16) or the taking of bribes (29:4); nor can a king succeed who lacks equity in justice (29:14), who is unwise with regard to women (31:3), or who is prone to intoxication (v. 4).

The godly ruler, on the other hand, is gifted by the Lord in extraordinary ways. He delights in those who serve him wisely because in doing so they serve God as well (14:35). When he speaks, he speaks as the mouth of the Lord so close is their relationship (16:10); and as a paragon of righteousness, he has no patience with wrongdoing (v. 12) or dishonesty (v. 13). He has the discernment when sitting in judgment to distinguish between right and wrong (20:8, 26); he responds favorably to purity of

---

[28] W. Lee Humphreys, "The Motif of the Wise Courtier in the Book of Proverbs," *Israelite Wisdom: Theological and Literary Essays in Honor of Samuel Terrien,* ed. John G. Gammie, Walter A. Brueggemann, W. Lee Humphreys, James M. Ward (Missoula, Mont.: Scholars, 1978), 180–85.

[29] McKane, *Proverbs,* 559–60.

motive and speech (22:11) and is impressed by those who do their work with skillful competence (v. 29). With uncanny intuition, the wise king can penetrate to the inner core of a matter and in inexplicable ways arrive at an understanding of mysteries inaccessible to other men (25:2–3).

Such assessments of royalty must—in the context of Proverbs and, indeed, of the whole Old Testament—be viewed against the pervasive biblical teaching of the king as the earthly representative of the Lord, the King of heaven, and, more precisely, the royal lineage introduced by David, a role granted to him and his descendants through an irrevocable covenant (2 Sam. 7). The godly king is almost a surrogate of the Lord; and therefore the language used of him approaches the level of the superhuman; for he does, indeed, share in the majesty and glory of God and exercises, at least derivatively, the spiritual gifts that enable him to carry out the responsibilities inherent in the unique office and relationship to which he has been chosen.

The theology of Proverbs revolves around the central theme of wisdom as the fundamental means of access to God and as the secret to living life that is pleasing to him. To be wise is to be godly, but to be foolish is to betray one's absence of a knowledge of the Lord and of submission to his will. With the other Wisdom books, Proverbs constitutes a manual of kingdom citizenship, a guideline for behavior that both pleases the Lord and that enables mankind—and especially Israel—to accomplish the objectives for which they were created and to which, as redeemed and chosen ones, they have been called in the outworking of God's designs for and through history.

The Theology of Ecclesiastes

Though the book of Ecclesiastes itself (Eccl. 1:1, 12) and ancient Jewish tradition ascribe its authorship to Solomon, the majority of modern scholars deny it to him for a number of reasons that little affect its overall theology.[30] Its message is timeless and depends less than most biblical books on any particular *Sitz im Leben* in order for its relevance to be appreciated. The dominant motif of the book is the vanity of life in the

---

[30] See C. L. Seow, "Linguistic Evidence and the Dating of Qohelet," JBL 115 (1996): 643–66; cf. Raymond B. Dillard and Tremper Longman III, *An Introduction to the Old Testament* (Grand Rapids: Zondervan), 248–59.

eyes of "the man under the sun" (Eccl. 8:15), that is, the person whose knowledge of God and his purposes is limited to what he can observe in everyday life in the "here below" in contrast to the unfettered realities discernible to the heavenly realms.[31] For this reason, the theology of Ecclesiastes seems to be like that of Job, largely a response by mankind to the vicissitudes of life and reality rather than a record of truth from the divine vantage point. As we argued already with regard to Job, this is not to say that Ecclesiastes is not revelatory, for how human beings universally think and comport themselves in life's challenging situations provides insight into the human condition, serving as a foil against which to appreciate the Lord's true disclosure of what life ideally ought to be and, indeed, will be in a sinless day to come. As a whole, the book reflects a sound, orthodox view; for at the end it resolves the tensions existent in the competing views of life and reality espoused by those who live under the sun and those who, in a sense, live above it.[32] A secondary theme of the book is well summarized in Ecclesiastes 12:8: "'Absolute futility,' says the Teacher. 'Everything is futile.'" The term translated *futile (hebel)* can also be understood as "empty or worthless," but in the context of wisdom or its lack, *futile* seems most appropriate.[33] What the Teacher *(Qohelet)* is saying is that mankind, unaided by special revelation, can make little or no sense of the world and of its own existence. To the "man under the sun" (8:15; cf. 1:3, 9, 14; 2:17–20, 22; etc.), that is, the man whose knowledge is circumscribed by his own limited perspective and experience, life is a riddle, a conundrum in which things more often than not seem rationally and morally inverted.

To the human eye, the course of life is cyclical, nonteleological. There is nothing new under the sun, nor is there any hope of anything different in the future (1:3–11). Everything has its time, but everything moves mechanically, aimlessly (3:1–8). One can only conclude that man is no more special than anything else in creation, that he is caught up in the same randomness as are brute beasts (3:18–22). The dead are better off than the living (4:1–3), the laborer than the rich man (6:12), and the

---

[31] Ardel B. Caneday, "Qoheleth: Enigmatic Pessimist or Godly Sage?" *GTJ* 7 (1986): 25–26.

[32] Tremper Longman III, *The Book of Ecclesiastes,* NICOT (Grand Rapids: Eerdmans, 1998), 37–39.

[33] Gordon H. Johnston, הבל, *NIDOTTE* 1:1005–6.

righteous person seems to have no advantage over the sinner (9:1–8). One can only conclude that "man is unable to discover the work that is done under the sun" (8:17).

Nevertheless, the human spirit craves meaning and seeks to ferret it out no matter the cost. Qohelet testifies that he himself made assiduous effort to search for the truth but after great investment of time and energy came to realize that whatever insights he had gained yielded little profit—it was, as he put it, "a pursuit of the wind" (1:17). He does come to see that wisdom is better than folly and light is better than darkness, but the wise and the foolish eventually experience the same fate (2:12–16). "Who can straighten out what [God] has made crooked?" (7:13).

One thing is clear: pleasure and the acquisition of wealth are not the key to unlock life's mysteries. It is an exercise in futility, "a pursuit of the wind" (2:1–11). We come into the world with nothing and shall leave with nothing (5:8–17). A stillborn child is better off than a man who accumulates wealth but does not live to enjoy it or who has many children but is so unloved by them that they do not even accord him a proper burial (6:1–11; cf. Jer. 20:14–18). Power and position are no more rewarding than wealth. Even a king who is not open to advice is worse off than a poor youth who, by his shrewdness, eventually sits on the throne (4:13–16). Nor does life find meaning in work that has no raison d'être. All one gains by labor may be squandered by heirs who have come about their good fortune the easy way and therefore have no appreciation of its value—"this too is futile" (4:13–16).

Qohelet's message is not one of unrelieved pessimism, however, for he clearly sees that there is a way out of the shadowy realm of meaninglessness and that is to (1) come to a knowledge of God, (2) experience the wisdom of God, and (3) enjoy a relationship with God. In line with Old Testament thought in general, Qohelet teaches that "the fear of the LORD is the starting-point of wisdom." Without him, the author asks, "Who can eat and who can enjoy life?" (2:25). God gives wisdom, knowledge, and happiness to those who please him and the assets of sinners will be turned over to them as well (2:26). People can know him because "he has . . . set eternity in the hearts of men" (3:11 NIV),[34] having given them an instinctual awareness of his existence and a feeling

[34] For defense of this translation, see Garrett, *Proverbs, Ecclesiastes, Song of Songs,* 299.

of emptiness without him. All the good and beautiful things God has done have been done so men will revere him (v. 14), and yet his works are so profound and limitless that mankind is incapable of fathoming them from beginning to end (v. 13b).

As always, entrée to God and his purposes is through the wisdom that he imparts. Qohelet says that he had determined on his own to be wise but discovered the futility of such a quest (7:23). "What exists is beyond reach and very deep. Who can discover it?" he asked (v. 24). He therefore sought other avenues of enlightenment in pursuit of his goal. He knew full well the value of wisdom, for it is "as good as an inheritance, and an advantage to those who see the sun. For wisdom is protection as money is protection, and the advantage of knowledge is that wisdom preserves the life of its owner" (7:11–12). He had observed life's paradoxes and apparent injustices and had come to see that only wisdom could help him sort things out and give him balance (vv. 15–18).

As an example, Qohelet relates the anecdote of a city under siege by a powerful king and his army. Its deliverance came by the wisdom of a poor man in the city, but his wisdom was unappreciated, and he was soon forgotten (9:13–15). Qohelet's conclusion is that wisdom is better than strength but is undervalued by the world at large. "Wisdom," he says, "is better than weapons of war, but one sinner can destroy much good" (v. 18). That is, the good that wisdom can accomplish is easily eroded away by a spirit of unbelief and cynicism that attributes success in life to blind chance or anything else apart from God. Just as a few dead flies can spoil the exquisite aroma of a costly perfume, so a bit of folly can outweigh wisdom and honor (10:1). The principle being addressed here is that access to truth is a precious thing, but it is difficult to achieve because all the wicked forces of heaven and hell are opposed to it.

The reason, fundamentally, is man's natural proclivities to folly and wickedness given his fallenness. In a remarkably astute observation about the human condition, Qohelet comments that "there is certainly no righteous man on the earth who does good and never sins" (7:20; cf. 1 Kings 8:46).[35] Though perhaps not articulating the doctrine of original sin, the sentiment expressed here at least recognizes its universality. In

---

[35] Franz Delitzsch, *Commentary on the Song of Songs and Ecclesiastes* (Grand Rapids: Eerdmans, n. d.), 327.

the same passage Qohelet says that after intense investigation he found not one upright man or woman. God had made them to be so "but they pursued many schemes" (vv. 28–29). His justice must interpose itself, however, and thus the sage has room in his theology for retribution (3:17). The God fearers need not fear the day of God's wrath, but it will not go well with the wicked (8:12–13).

The theme of God's judgment is expanded in Ecclesiastes 11:9–12:7. There Qohelet encourages the young to give themselves fully to the opportunities for joy and fulfillment that come their way but to do so with an eye to the day of reckoning when they must appear before God (11:9). Life, then, must not be lived with reckless abandon but with wisdom and discretion. Old age with all its infirmities will come soon enough, and then it will be too late to remember the Creator and live life to his glory (12:1–7).[36]

As for the present, how shall we live? Qohelet's advice is multiplex but consists in the main with the notion that one must learn to be content with his lot in life and take advantage of the blessings that come his way. "There is nothing better for a man than to enjoy his work," he says, "because that is his lot" (3:22 NIV). More than that, he should enjoy food and drink, wealth and possessions, for these are all gifts of God, meant to be received and used with gladness (5:18–20). There is no spirit of hedonism or profligacy here but an exhortation to live out one's days to the optimum, cherishing every moment and relishing every God-given favor. To "eat, drink, and be merry" is part and parcel of God's creation design (8:14–15 NKJV). In fact, whatever one does, he should do with all his energy, for in this is to be found joy and contentment (9:9–10). "If a man should live many years, let him rejoice in them all," Qohelet concludes (11:8).

Especially precious are family and friends. The wise man appeals to his hearers to "enjoy life with the wife you love all the days of your fleeting life, which has been given to you under the sun" (9:9). Such feelings of affection may not clarify all of life's conundrums but will give at least some measure of significance to an otherwise inchoate existence. Persons who try to live with no human companionship of kinfolk can make no

---

[36] Barry C. Davis, "Ecclesiastes 12:1–8—Death, an Impetus for Life," *BSac* 148 (1991): 298–318.

sense of life, for they have no one with whom to share its bounties (4:8). And in times of difficulty, they have nowhere to turn, no one who can help them bear the inevitable burdens and sorrows of life (vv. 9–12).

Despite the uncertainties of life, it is incumbent on those under the sun to plan for tomorrow. Those who invest wisely their time and treasure will find a return beyond measure (11:1). Besides that, the unknowns of tomorrow demand that the resources of today be seen for what they are—blessings of God, the stewardship of which is a hallmark of true wisdom and godliness (vv. 2–6).

Finally, life in the here and now must be sensitive to the kingdom hierarchy, a matter that finds its roots in the creation mandate and its fullest historical expression in the Davidic monarchy. The tradition of Solomonic authorship of the book of Ecclesiastes provides ample reason for the book's interest in such matters as, indeed, was the case with Proverbs as well. Mincing no words, Qohelet instructs his hearers to "keep the king's command. Concerning an oath by God [to do so], do not be in a hurry" (8:2).[37] The king's word is supreme, he goes on to say, and whoever obeys it will come to no harm; but clearly those who do not obey can expect to suffer the consequences (8:5). Obedience must be to the extent of even one's attitude, so much so that evil thoughts toward him, if found out, will have severe repercussions (10:20). The wise man or woman, then, is the one who understands the role of the king in God's program of redemptive governance and who gladly submits to him as he would to God himself.

Ecclesiastes, like Job, consists of the musings of "the man under the sun" (cf. Eccl. 1:3; 2:19, 22; 5:18; 6:12; 8:9, 15, 17) who, unaided by direct, propositional revelation, does his best to make sense of suffering and death, misunderstanding and irrationality, but often to no avail. He raises questions that he is not equipped to answer except with stock clichés born of a theology based on common sense and the traditions of the fathers. The resolution of the dilemma in both instances is the interruption of human discourse by a word from God, in the case of Job a lengthy monologue delivered by the Lord himself, and in Ecclesiastes

[37] This may refer to putative annual covenant renewal ceremonies in which the people of Israel pledged their fealty to the LORD and to his vice-regent, the Davidic king (cf. 2 Chron. 23:3, 16; Neh. 9:38). Though silent as to such a possible context, Longman correctly observes that to Qohelet "the king's authority is virtually godlike." Longman, *The Book of Ecclesiastes,* 212.

the communication of God's mind on the matter by Qohelet, words that he testifies are "given by one Shepherd" (12:11).

Qohelet says of himself that he was wise and was commissioned to teach "delightful sayings" and "to accurately write words of truth" (vv. 9–10). This is tantamount to a declaration that his words—those that reported the philosophizings of the man under the sun as well as his own closing exhortations—are, indeed, the very word of God. He has said all that needs to be said and now presents "the conclusion of the matter," namely, "Fear God and keep His commands *(miṣwôt),* because this is for all humanity" (v. 13).[38] God himself will evaluate human thought and deed, good or evil, and will bring them to light on the day of judgment (v. 14).

Ecclesiastes contributes to Old Testament theology in two basic ways: (1) It records the reactions of men and women to the vagaries of life as they experience it and as they attempt to derive meaning from it on the basis of observation and of the accumulated wisdom of the ages; and (2) it shows the deficiency of human reason alone to come to terms with the most fundamental issues of life and the need, therefore, to hear a word from God. Human existence is meaningless without that word so man must, above all, fear God and thereby acquire the wisdom essential to a full understanding of who he is as the image of God and what is expected of him as a kingdom citizen and servant.

The Theology of the Book of the Song of Songs

The famous first-century rabbi Akiba, while debating the canonicity of the Song of Songs, observed that "the whole world is not worth the day on which the Song of Songs was given to Israel; for all the Hagiographa are holy, but the Song of Songs is the holy of holies."[39] This obviously hyperbolic assessment reveals both the struggle the book encountered in terms of its status as sacred Scripture and the resolution of that struggle—that the book, as problematic as it is in certain respects, is

---

[38] Garrett characterizes this last admonition as "the book's final look at Gen 2–3," an apt observation in light of the teaching of the whole book. Garrett, *Proverbs, Ecclesiastes, Song of Songs,* 344.

[39] Quoted in Roger Beckwith, *The Old Testament Canon of the New Testament Church* (Grand Rapids: Eerdmans, 1985), 323.

of profound theological value. Its bold, graphic imagery of lovemaking between the Shulamite maiden and her beloved came to be understood in Jewish exegesis as a parable depicting the Lord's love for Israel and, in Christian hermeneutics, a picture of Christ's love for the church.

Modern scholarship has forged a majority consensus that the book should be taken as a poetic rendition of a literal human relationship, whether fictional or actual. Its purpose is to glorify romantic love and to celebrate the purity of sexual intimacy within the bonds of married life.[40] Theologically, the message is that what God has created is intrinsically good and beautiful and that man and woman, in their love for and admiration of one another, are fulfilling the creation mandate that imparts to the two of them together the authority to have dominion over all things and to "be fruitful, multiply, fill the earth, and subdue it" (Gen. 1:28). It depicts the ideal, what man and woman were created to be and, indeed, will be absent the corrupting influences of sin, which has transmuted love to lust and distorted the nobility of sexual expression into a vile and perverted caricature that bears no resemblance to the creation design.[41]

Having said this, it is not exegetically or theologically inappropriate to understand the Song as a paradigm or template by which to gain access to a greater love and intimacy, that of the Lord for his creation and, in particular, for mankind created as his image.[42] We have made the point time and again that God's nature as the altogether transcendent One precludes human understanding of him and access to him unless and until he deigns to disclose himself by whatever means he chooses—by creation, by deed, by history, or, most unmistakably and unambiguously, by word. In any case, such disclosure is necessarily metaphorical, for the thoughts and intentions of God exist on a plane utterly elusive to mankind and communicable only in the language of analogy. God's love—with all his other attributes and characteristics—may be declared in word, and, indeed, is repeatedly affirmed in biblical texts; but it is most easily grasped when draped in imagery common to human experience. Thus,

[40] Tremper Longman III, *Song of Songs, NICOT* (Grand Rapids: Eerdmans, 2001), 58–62; for a helpful study on the practical value of the book, see Greg W. Parsons, "Guidelines for Understanding and Utilizing the Song of Songs," *BSac* 156 (1999): 399–422.

[41] Roy B. Zuck, "A Theology of the Wisdom Books and the Song of Songs," *A Biblical Theology of the Old Testament,* ed. Roy B. Zuck (Chicago: Moody, 1991), 253.

[42] Longman, *Song of Songs,* 67–70.

the innocence, purity, and wholesomeness of the love between the man and woman of the Song open the window to an insight—no matter how inadequate or deficient—into God's indescribable and inexhaustible love for all beings in all places and at all times.

Chapter Twenty

Conclusion

The presentation of Old Testament theology recounted in the foregoing pages has attempted to view that part of the Bible holistically, synthetically, and analytically, bearing in mind the enormous diversity and complexity of the material and the literary garb in which it finds expression. In conclusion, we will touch upon four major issues by way of summary, reinforcement, and proposals for moving beyond the efforts made here: (1) the premises that have informed our approach; (2) the method adopted and applied throughout; (3) the proposed center, themes, and motifs that have provided structure to the work and that seem best able to accommodate the varying data; and (4) the theological, hermeneutical, and practical relationship of the New Testament to the Old and its indispensability for a full-orbed biblical theology.

Theological Premises

At the outset we have, without apology and equivocation, undertaken our work with the settled conviction that the Old Testament is the written word of God, revealed by him to the prophets of old, preserved from error in matters of fact and doctrine, and authoritative for both Israel and the church. We have made no effort to argue the point or provide evidence for it except to remind the reader that this is the Bible's own understanding of itself and the studied opinion of virtually all pre-Enlightenment Jewish and Christian scholars and laity alike. How one views the question of bibliology has obvious consequences for his theology so we have not on purely a priori grounds adopted one stance as opposed to another. Indeed, the position advocated here is the fruit of many years of careful and prayerful consideration of all the issues involved and reflects more than just a casual acquaintance with the difficulties inherent in any evaluation of Scripture.

That said, it is important also to recognize the human side of inscripturation, something the Bible also does with its hundreds of "thus saith the LORD's" in the Old Testament and its explicit affirmations in the New Testament (2 Tim. 3:16; 2 Pet. 1:21). God revealed and inspired his word but mediated it through prophets and poets whose gifts and faculties he left intact, accommodating his thoughts to the several and varied experiences and abilities they brought to their task. All this, of course, is well-known to students of bibliology, but to this must be added the complicating factor that much of what human authors wrote was either a record of uninspired utterances by other men or women or the reflections and responses of the authors themselves to what they knew or did not know of the mind of God. This notion is troubling to many at first glance, for it seems to admit the possibility of material other than divine revelation in the sacred text. In a sense this is true, but God's revelation takes a variety of forms, going so far as to allow ideas inconsistent or even contrary to the normative truth derivative from him alone. That is, the ruminations, meditations, rationalizings, and opinions of men—unorthodox or misguided as they might be—are permitted to have their say if for no other reason than to reveal how deficient they are and how much they are in need of divine correction.

In the final analysis, the whole corpus—the Word of God and the words of men—is revelatory, the product of a process of divine redactionism that guarantees that every part is precisely as it ought to be, contributing to the redemptive message for which it is intended. This lends to it a cohesion, a united and self-consistent presentation from beginning to end that cannot be explained by any number of documentary or redactionary theories of human creativity but only by the self-evident fact of the originating and controlling work of the Spirit of God. This leads to a further premise, one that logically follows—the expectation that a single Author has a single overarching message that can be readily detected. Moreover, that message itself, if it is to be understood in any meaningful way, must be informed by a central theme or themes, a story line that leaves no question as to the Author's intentions and desired effects.

Theological Method

The term *story line* suggests narrative, and indeed the Bible is narrative if nothing else. That does not mean, of course, that it is narrative as the term is commonly understood—an unbroken rendition that has a beginning, a plot development, a climax, and a dénouement—for it is a story constantly interrupted by this or that digression and consisting of a wide variety of genres not commonly at home in narratives, genres such as genealogies, poetry, proverbs, and prophetic oracles. At the same time, the serious reader of the Bible knows he is reading a story, one with a beginning and end and traceable events in between. In other words, the Bible, and especially the Old Testament, is diachronic, panoramic, sweeping across the ages from creation to the final consummation of time and history.

In light of this, we have adopted a diachronic method and have begun where the narrative begins, with Genesis 1. From there we have moved forward, trying as best we can to be alert to the chronology of events as presented by the sacred historians themselves. Sometimes the time line is explicit and apparent; at other times it goes underground, reappearing at critical moments to carry the story forward. The problem is particularly acute when it comes to the Psalms and Wisdom literature for as often as not these writings are anonymous, and there is no clear indication of their *Sitzen im Leben.* Rather than speculate or, worse, try to manufacture some kind of chronological setting based on subjective notions of religious evolutionism and the like, it seems best for the moment to set aside the diachronic scheme and let the texts speak for themselves in nonspecific terms, the reason, no doubt, they were left without chronological anchorage in the first place.

Besides the common sense inherent in reading a story from beginning to end as it was intended, there is in the case of the Old Testament a further justification for the diachronic approach, namely, the principle of progressive revelation. This more theological term has to do with the idea observable in the Bible itself that it is not just a story but God's story, his account of reality, design, and purpose. No author lays out before his readers the full narrative at the beginning, robbing them of the excitement of discovering the ins and outs of the plot as they make their way through it. Should we expect the biblical narrative to be any different? Added to this is the fact that the Old Testament is not just a story for readers from the time of its finished form, but it is a record of God's revelation of himself over the course of millennia. And what he has revealed is of such a transcendent nature and of such theological complexity that it had to be communicated gradually, carefully, patiently lest its hearers and readers be exposed to depths of truth they were unable to grasp and assimilate. In other words, the Bible is sensitive pedagogically, teaching at first in germ form what would eventually be fleshed out in full maturity of spiritual and intellectual understanding. In this process there are no alterations, corrections, or contradictions from era to era, but there clearly is organic development. What begins in seed form is perfect but incomplete. When it comes to fruition, it is both perfect and complete. What the early pages of the narrative could only dimly anticipate finds both literary and theological completion and resolution at the end.

One would reasonably expect, given the narrative nature of the biblical revelation, to find the initial key statements of theological significance to be precisely at the beginning of the canonical collection. A quick glance there will find the first of a number of major turning points in the form of covenants of various kinds that build upon those that precede, and without running counter to them, embellish and amplify them with greater and greater detail, precision, and clarity. Thus the creation account followed by a statement of its meaning, particularly with reference to the creation of the human race (Gen. 1:26–28), marks the point of departure for all subsequent revelation. It provides all the key elements for what follows and itself is fleshed out by the ever-enlarging accumulation of data that at the end forms the totality of God's self-disclosure.

The second critical moment is the fall, man's exercise of free will in opposition to the sovereignty of God. One might view this insubordination as anticovenant, a flagrant disregard of the covenant mandate which forever altered the kingdom purposes of God and called for still a new direction, one still involving covenants, to be sure, but covenants now no longer primarily regnal in character but salvific or redemptive. The first of these, the Abrahamic, addresses the need for reconciliation between God and mankind, a need made emphatically clear not only by the fall but also by its horrendous aftereffects—murder, hubris, and a bent toward sin in general that seemed irremedial. The flood narrative followed by that of the tower of Babel bears eloquent testimony both to the dissolution of human culture and to the judgment of God that must come to bear in the interest of his own holiness and justice.

The covenant with Abraham, an exhibition of pure grace on the part of the Lord, set in motion a plan whereby God could implement his creation design despite the human condition and do so without compromising his own integrity or coercing compliance on the part of those whom he desired to restore to fellowship and servanthood within the kingdom framework. From it emerged gradually and with ever-increasing transparency further elements of the saving design, elements that traced the agency of the Lord's reconciling work to a nation descended from Abraham through Isaac, Jacob, and his twelve sons, a people called into still another covenant relationship, this one not redemptive in nature but functional. The nation, Israel, would transmit the means of divine salvation to all the world and, at the same time, would model for the nations God's ideal of what the kingdom should look like and how it should operate in the world. But the ideal was never translated into historical reality and thus was postponed to a day when one would come who would embody perfect Israel and would, in Israel's place, achieve restoration of the nations to fellowship with God and to his service as citizens of the kingdom.

The next turning point—the selection of David as the messianic king and forebear of the Redeemer of the nations—solidifies Israel's role as the kingdom of priests and elevates the theme of restoration to the kingdom level where Israel, individualized in her monarchy, is not only the repository of the saving message but the embodiment of the means of its implementation. Or, to put it more precisely, Israel becomes the earthly expression of the kingdom of heaven, an imperfect and, in fact, a failed expression, to be sure, but nevertheless the matrix from and through which both David and his greater Son would and will emerge to achieve the saving and royal purposes of the Lord.

Israel's historical failure to serve the Lord in the capacity of a servant people, seen over and over again in her violation of the Mosaic covenant, led to the need for a new covenant, one oriented to the distant future. That covenant, articulated most clearly by Jeremiah and Ezekiel, would be made with eschatological Israel, but it would be different in that it would become internalized, no longer inscribed on tablets of stone but impressed indelibly into human hearts. Israel's failure to keep the old covenant would be overcome by the energizing work of the Spirit who would provide the capability of keeping it in perfect obedience. Coupled with this new covenant is the gradually emerging concept of a messianic figure known variously as the seed of Abraham, the son of David, and the suffering servant. In the latter role he would effect the reconciliation of all humanity to God and his sovereignty by his vicarious suffering on their behalf, and as the royal descendant of David he would rule over not just revived Israel but over all the nations of the earth.

The Theological Center

The fact of creation alone—to say nothing of the "creation mandate"—is sufficient to show that the sovereignty of God is a major theme of Old Testament revelation. Indeed, it is not inaccurate to consider it *the* major theme, the overriding principle of biblical thought around which everything else revolves. Any view of God that assigns him any role other than that of sovereign over all creation results either in an ontological dualism in which he is coequal with the material and/or spiritual universe or at least renders him limited in some aspects of his nature and work. That is, God by definition is Lord of all, certainly God as he discloses himself in Scripture.

The assertion of the kingship of God presupposes, of course, a realm over which he has dominion and a narrative explaining or recounting the implementation of his relationship to it. The realm is all that exists save God himself and the narrative—insofar as he chooses to reveal it—is the written Word of God augmented and reinforced by what can be learned from the natural order. It is not enough merely to assert that God himself is the center of biblical theology, for such a center is only an abstraction, a theological datum devoid of purpose and lacking in any kind of perceivable rationale. The human mind demands to know not just the what of theology but the why as well and so a meaningful center must show God in action as well as in existential reality. This is precisely what the record recounts: God at work in time and space, bringing to pass in history his eternal and inevitable purposes.

His strategy in carrying out these programs is to do so through the agency of the human race, the highest order of creation and his image and likeness. Mankind is thus brought into the equation and not just as an afterthought. Indeed, his role as vice-regent of the Lord, the one created and chosen to represent him, elevates him to such an esteemed status that proper definition of a center must incorporate the human dimension as well. We propose the following as a suitable, if succinct, synthesis of what we perceive the theological center of the Old (and New) Testament to be: God, the sovereign Lord of all that is, created the universe for his own glory, displaying that glory through what is made and what he does in nature and history. Man, created as God's image, is the channel and agent chosen by God to mediate his revealed will and to implement his sovereign purposes. In our view, this encapsulates the essence of the biblical message. All else relates to the impairment of this grand design by the opposition of wicked spirits to the sovereignty of God, an opposition that resulted in man's sin and fall and thus the crippling of his capacity to fulfill the mandate for which he was created. But there is also the word of redemption and reconciliation, the gracious program of God whereby all creation will be renewed and mankind will be restored to his glorious position as God's earthly surrogate.

The creation account is thus the beginning of the sacred narrative, and it is there that the central theological theme is introduced. The fall and its tragic consequences become the sotto voce of everything that subsequently follows in the narrative; but the notes of divine redemption, growing ever more audible and clear, eventually drown out the despair of the human dilemma and point to the triumphant day of full restoration of God's eternal and glorious designs.

Biblical history is thus the vehicle that communicates the divine and human drama in both its events and its telling. This is why the oft-used term *Heilsgeschicte* is so appropriate to describe it, for the history recounted in the Bible is fundamentally not an objective recitation of brute facts (as though such were possible in any history) but an interpretation of events that themselves were ordained by God, the relating of which is from his perspective and not that of even the human writers whom he used as his amanuenses. The Lord supplies his own version of the historical narrative precisely because only he understands its dynamic reality and only he, the omniscient God, can interpret its permutations in light of its eventual outcome.

That outcome, of course, lies always in the future from the Old Testament perspective; that is, it is eschatological, a history of events that have not yet transpired. The sovereign reign of God through human agency fails miserably in the history of the past whether the history of the pre- and postflood patriarchs, the days of Egyptian bondage and exodus deliverance, the era of the united monarchy, the period of the divided kingdom, or the epoch of postexilic Judea. That dominion must await a future day, one inaugurated by the scion of David, the suffering servant, and one to be consummated by that same Messiah who will come in power and great glory. Mankind, fully redeemed and restored, will then take up the privileges and responsibilities of reigning for which he was created, and at last the kingdom of earth will also become the kingdom of heaven.

The Old Testament and the New Testament

This work has been undertaken consciously and deliberately as an Old Testament theology, fully mindful of the limitations, liabilities, and even misleading nature of that term. We have labored to make the point that a work that seeks to embrace the fullness of God's revelation, that is, the canon in its totality, must be properly labeled a "biblical theology," for to the Christian the Bible is not limited to the Old Testament. To call it an "Old Testament theology" then is to be imprecise, again from a Christian perspective, for it suggests both the possibility that biblical theology can be done absent the New Testament and the fact that this is precisely what we have done. Neither is correct. In its truest sense, biblical theology—as a term denoting content—cannot be confined to either testament alone. Nor have we attempted this work as though the New Testament does not exist. Our use of the term has to do not with the subject matter of theology so much as it does with theological method. That is, our Old Testament theology, while limited for the most part to the Old Testament material, has attempted to view that material biblically as opposed to dogmatically, systematically, philosophically, or any other way. To approach it biblically means to allow the text to speak for itself in each of its parts (exegetically), intertextually (hermeneutically), and synthetically or integratively (theologically).

This said, and to repeat, it is impossible for the Christian theologian to ignore the New Testament for even if he does not (or in our case *cannot*) continue the pursuit of biblical theology to the conclusion of the whole canon, he cannot escape his tradition and the conscious or even subconscious baggage that that entails. He cannot read the Old Testament apart from the deep impress and impact of the New Testament upon his psyche to say noting of trying to present a coherent, objective theological construct devoid of any input from the New Testament. We confess, then, to having done an Old Testament theology through a Christian New Testament lens and for this offer no apology. What is required in the ideal is that a work like this should move beyond the Hebrew Scriptures to trace the theological themes that have been surfaced to their logical, theological, and canonical conclusions in the Greek Bible, the two parts thus yielding the fullness of the saving message.

The reader will observe that the present work is sprinkled liberally with New Testament references and allusions, both implicit and explicit. This alone confirms the convictions just expressed, but it also reveals the fact that the Old Testament recognizes its own incompleteness, its own openness to the future. Judaism fills this longing for conclusion in the Mishnaic and other extra-canonical literature whereas the church reopens the canon (at least in its view) and brings it to a glorious and triumphant finality in Christ and the New Testament Scriptures.

How this is done lies outside the purview of this work. Suffice to say, the hermeneutics involved seem, from the standpoint of modern hermeneutical theory, arbitrary and self-serving though the principles at work are precisely those employed by the rabbis in the composition of Jewish literature contemporary to the New Testament. We say arbitrary and self-serving because there often appears to be no persuasive connection between New Testament texts and those from the Old Testament that are cited as allusive, referential, or even predictive. That is, it seems that the evangelists and apostles (and Jesus himself) take liberties with the Old Testament passages in order to provide evidence or proof for some point or other that they are trying to establish. Is this hermeneutic defensible; and if so, on what grounds other than the fact that it was sanctioned by common use in the first century? If not, the implications of the New Testament for biblical theology are enormously problematic.

Fundamentally, the issue of the relationship of the testaments—whether theologically or hermeneutically—boils down to the nature of the whole. If one is of the conviction that the Old and New Testament alike are the Word of God, revealed and inspired by him, the difficulties largely dissolve, for the authorship and, hence, the intertextual connections of its various parts (both testaments) not only find theological justification but hermeneutical warrant as well. Authors of texts have dominical rights to those texts and from their privileged position can employ whatever devices or methods they choose to communicate and interpret their own writings. Who, then, can question the Holy Spirit of God on the matter and charge him with hermeneutical impropriety should he "violate" modern rules of hermeneutical theory?

Finally, of what use is a theology of the Old Testament to the Christian believer? Is not the Hebrew Bible irrelevant to the Christian faith, and if that be too extreme, is it not of only marginal interest and importance in the light of the finished work of Jesus Christ? To these and similar questions we offer the following observations in bringing this work to a close.

1. The New Testament and the gospel never claim to have superseded the Old Testament in terms of its canonical status. Over and over again and until the end of the apostolic age, it is cited as the Word of God, inspired and authoritative in its parts and in the whole. The testimony of Jesus and the early church in the matter is sufficient proof that the Old Testament is not only the continuing Word of God, but it has lost nothing of its magisterial character for the Christian believer.

2. The Old Testament constitutes over 75 percent of the biblical text and therefore its denial as Christian Scripture or even its benign neglect as a work worthy of theological investigation constitutes a repudiation of a significant portion of divine revelation. Some central doctrines—for example, the nature and character of God—find scant treatment in the New Testament. Old Testament theology, then, is crucial to the full elaboration of this foundational truth as well as many (if not all) others.

3. The New Testament presupposes the Old at every point, so much so that one can say that the New Testament is largely meaningless apart from its Old Testament orientation. The life, ministry, and teachings of

Jesus as well as apostolic preaching and pronouncements betray on every hand their indebtedness to the Old Testament which, after all, was their only Bible. It is as though one should begin reading any book three-quarters of the way through it and claim to have full understanding of its message and meaning. So it is with the Bible. The Christian who shuts himself up to the New Testament alone and who has no interest in or concern for the theology of the Old is hardly in step with Jesus on the road to Emmaus who, "beginning with Moses and all the Prophets, . . . interpreted for them the things concerning Himself in all the Scriptures" (Luke 24:27).

Name Index

Allis, O. T. . . . 53n, 501n
Ammon, C. F. von . . . 9 (2)
Anderson, A. A. . . . 28n
Anderson, Bernhard W. . . . 288n, 543n
Astruc, Jean . . . 7
Averbeck, Richard E. . . . 46n, 131n, 219n, 229n, 237n, 273n, 352n, 358n, 378n (2)
Baab, Otto . . . 14, 14n, 15 (2)
Baloian, Bruce E. . . . 72n, 597n
Barr, James . . . 7, 7n
Barth, Christoph . . . 85n, 252n, 549n, 578n
Bauer, G. L. . . . 9 (2)
Beckwith, Roger . . . 28n, 638n
Beecher, Willis Judson . . . 80n
Block, Daniel I. . . . 190n, 311n, 421n, 424n, 542n
Braun, Roddy L. . . . 167n, 465n, 469n, 470n, 471n
Breasted, J. H. . . . 261n
Bruce, F. F. . . . 28n, 229n, 534n, 577n
Brueggemann, Walter . . . 18 (3), 18n, 37n, 285n, 591n, 611n, 631n
Buchanon, G. W. . . . 201n
Bullock, Hassell C. . . . 93n, 140n, 318n, 319n, 498n, 513n, 574n, 587n, 597n
Bultmann, Ruldolph . . . 25n
Burden, J. J. . . . 28n
Carpenter, Eugene . . . 160n, 222n
Carroll, Robert P. . . . 80n, 526n, 528n
Cassuto, Umberto . . . 40n, 84n, 271n, 288n (2), 339n, 366n, 542n
Childs, Brevard S. . . . 17 (2), 17n (3), 21, 85n, 212n, 344n, 347n, 512n
Chisholm Jr., Robert B. . . . 179n, 262n, 501n, 521n, 627n
Clements, Ronald E. . . . 157n, 160n, 187n, 255n
Clendenen, E. Ray . . 557n, 563n, 565n
Clines, David J. A. . . . 215n, 485n
Collingwood, R. G. . . . 10n, 26n
Cölln, D. G. C. von . . . 10 (2)
Cross, Frank M. . . . 84n, 134n, 265n, 473n
Darrell, Bock L. . . . 173n, 304n, 532n
Dawn, Marva . . . 111n
Day, George E. . . . 12n, 200n, 316n, 588n, 617n
Deist, Ferdinand . . . 25n, 555n
Delitzsch, Franz . . . 108n, 144n, 210n, 212n, 428n, 576n, 579n, 636n
Dempster, Stephen G. . . . 17n
DeWette, W. M. L. . . . 10 (2)
Dhorme, Eduard . . . 214n, 612n
Dorff, Elliot . . . 32n, 507n
Doria, Charles . . . 39n

Dorsey, David A. 148n
Dumbrell, William J. 17, 17n, 46n, 160n, 239n, 297n, 327n, 427n, 439n, 482n, 534n
Durham, John I. 160n, 331n, 343n, 360n
Dyrness, William. 79n, 344n
Eades, Keith L. 32n, 507n
Eichhorn, J. G. 7, 9
Eichrodt, Walther 14 (3), 14n, 15 (2), 45n, 56n, 81n, 282n, 316n, 543n
Eissfeldt, Otto 13 (2), 14
Ellis, E. Earle 3n, 28n
Elwell, Walter A. 205n, 231n
Enns, Peter 60n
Ernesti, J. A. 8
Feinberg, Charles Lee . . . 228n, 549n
Feinberg, John S. 228n, 517n, 549n
Feinberg, Paul D. 228n, 549n
Fields, Weston W. 102n, 131n
Foh, Susan. 203n
Foster, Benjamin R. 132n
Freedman, David Noel 80n, 134n, 153n, 265n, 496n
Fretheim, Terence E. 51n, 64n, 393n
Frymer-Kensky, Tikva. 32n
Gabler, Johann P. 5, 5n, 6 (3), 6n, 7 (3), 7n, 8, 8n, 9, 9n, 12, 21, 30
Gaffin, Richard B. 1n,
Garrett, Duane. 38n, 556n, 622n, 635n, 638n
Gelston, A. 140n
Gerstenberger, Erhard S. . . 141n, 319n, 447n, 573n, 574n
Gilbert, Allan S. 188n
Goldingay, John 25n, 241n, 247n, 550n
Gordon, Robert P. 205n
Gramberg, C. P. W. 10, 10n
Greenberg, M. 270n, 282n
Greengus, Samuel 185n
Grogan, Geoffrey W. 216n
Gundry, Stanley N. 111n, 415n
Gunkel, Herrman. 77n (2), 590n
Hamilton, Victor P. . . . 115n, 150n (2), 205n, 233n, 295n, 327n
Harner, Philip B. 107n
Hasel, Gerhard F. 1n, 5n, 8n, 9n, 27n, 266n, 547n
Hävernick, H. A. C. 12
Hayes, John H. 5n, 9n (2), 11n, 12n, 14n
Hegel, Georg 10 (2), 11, 12
Heidel, Alexander 102n, 209n
Hengstenberg, Ernst W. 12 (2), 12n
Hess, Richard S. 582n
Hort, Greta 158n
House, Paul R. 97n
Höver-Jahg I. 201n
Howard, Jr. David M. 196n, 419n, 432n, 466n
Hubbard, Jr. Robert L. 115n, 121n
Huffman, Herbert B. 80n, 403n, 518n
Hufnagel, W. F. 8n
Jacob, Benno 85n, 336n
Jacob, Edmund Edmond 15, 15n, 119n, 176n
Kaiser, G. P. C. 9 (2)
Kaiser, W. Walter C. 16 (3), 16n, 19, 416n, 492n, 534n
Kalimi, Isaac 32n
Kitchen, K. A. 196n, 328n, 391n
Kline, Meredith G. 239n, 348n
Koch, K. 221n
Köhler, Ludwig 14 (2)
König, Eduard 13 (2)
Kraus, Hans-Joachin 49n, 318n, 571n, 586n, 594n (2), 597n
Kruger, Paul A. 95n
Laetsch, Theo 90n, 95n

Lamberty-Zielinski H.. . . . . 176n
Lehmann, M. R. 55n
Lewis, Jack P. 246n
Lind, Millard C. 265n
Lindblom, Joh 99n
Lipinski, E. 128n, 270n
Lohfink, Norbert 112n
Ludwig, Theodore M. 107n
Malamat, A.. . . . . 88n, 403n
Martens, Elmer A... 5n, 16, 16n, 295n
Martin, Jaines D.. . . . . 187n
Martins, Elmer A. . . .5n, 16n (2), 295n
Mathews, K. Kenneth A. 65n (2), 103n, 106n, 193n, 224n, 234n, 281n (2), 297n
Matthews, V. Victor H. 188n
McConville, Gordon J. 238n, 376n (2), 394n, 418n, 440n
Melugin, Roy F. 507n
Mendenhall, George E. . . . 188n, 239n, 270n, 327n
Merrill, Eugene H. 25n, 45n, 91n, 103n, 134n, 153n, 156n, 192n, 194n, 195n, 206n, 207n, 252n, 313n, 337n, 340n, 369n, 383n, 408n, 413n, 414n, 426n, 434n, 447n, 468n, 506n, 507n, 521n, 527n, 540n (2), 548n, 557n, 562n, 581n, 617n, 630n
Milgrom, Jacob 99n
Miller, Patrick D.. . . . 45n, 265n, 393n, 492n, 550n, 597n, 615n
Moberly, R. W. L. 69n
Moriarty, Frederick C.. . . . . 135n
Morus, S. F. N. 7, 8 (3)
Mulzac, Kenneth 152n
Murphy, Poland E. 51n, 603n
Naudé, Jackie A. 56n
Nielsen, Kristen. 145n, 205n
Nissinen, Martti. 78n
Noss, John B. 108n
Noth, Martin 189n, 344n (2)
O'Connell, Robert H. 187n
Oehler, Gustave F.. . . . . . . 12, 12n, 13, 14, 16, 200n, 316n, 588n, 617n
Ollenburger, Ben C. 5n, 28n (2)
Oswalt, John N.. . . . 135n, 300n, 501n
Otto, E. 225n
Pannenberg, Wolfhart 32n
Pantoja, Luis 507n
Pardee, Dennis 133n
Patterson, P. Paige 507n
Patterson, R. Richard D. 537n
Payne, Barton J. 81n, 238n
Pretlove, John 507n
Preuss, Horst Dietrich 215n
Priest, James E. 152n
Prolcsch, Otto 15, 15n
Prussner, Frederick . . . 5n, 9n (2), 11n, 12n, 14n
Rad, Gerhard von . . . 15 (3), 15n, 26n, 45n, 50n, 111n, 147n, 170n, 202n, 217n (2), 337n
Ramsey, George W. 45n
Reid, Daniel G. 111n
Reimer, David J. 58n, 60n
Ringgren, Helmer 252n, 445n, 514n
Robinson, H. Wheeler. 76n (2)
Rooker, Mark M.. . . . . 131n
Rosenberg, Roy A. 140n, 319n, 573n
Ross, Allen P. 38n, 131n, 177n, 237n, 298n, 338n, 354n, 377n (2), 379n
Sailhamer, John. 9n, 17n
Sakenfeld, K. D. 67n
Sandys-Wunsch, John . . .6n, 7n, 8n (2)
Seebass, Horst. 70n
Sellin, Ernst. 14 (3)
Semler, J. S.. 8
Skinner, John. 176n (2)

Smith, Mark S. 37n
Soggin, Alberto J. 203n
Speiser, E. A.. . . . . 232n, 282n
Sproul, Barbara 39n
Stern, H. S. 201n
Steudel, J. C. F. 12
Stol, Marten. 185n
Strong, Augustus H. 169n
Sun, Henry T.C.. . . . . 32n, 507n
Taylor, R. Richard A. 557n, 563n, 565n
Taylor, S. Sophia 144n, 210n
Tromp, Nicholas J. 209n
Tsevat, Matitiahu. 32n
Van, Dam Cornelis 100n, 361n, 362n
Van, Leeuwen Raymond C. 39n, 101n, 168n
Van, Ruler A. A. 25n
Vanderkam, James C. 78n, 88n
VanGemeren, Willem A. . . . 25n, 181n, 413n, 569n
Vatke, J. K. W.. 11
De, Vaux Roland . . . 185n, 223n, 256n, 367n, 374n, 405n, 565n
Verhoef, Peter A. 86n, 92n, 558n
Vos, Geerhardus 16 (2), 16n, 84n, 200n, 210n, 240n
Vriezen, T. C. 15, 15n, 38n (2)
Wagner, S. 63n, 136n
Wakeman, Mary K. 268n
Waldman, Nahum 201n
Waltke, Bruce K. . . . 170n, 230n, 242n, 623n (2), 629n
Waschke, E. J. 235n
Watson, Francis. 32n
Weinfeld, Moshe . . . 239n, 242n, 294n, 394n, 435n
Weiser, Artur 66n, . . 322n, 580n, 598n
Wellhausen, Julius. 7, 7n, 11
Wenham, Gordon J.. . . . . . . 41n, 105n, 144n, 169n, 194n, 203n, 230n, 236n, 355n
Westermann, Claus 25n, 104n, 115n, 143n, 144n (2), 194n, 228n, 233n (3)
Wilson, G. Gerald H. 51n
Wilson, J. John A. 260n, 332n
Wolff, Hans Walter . . . 105n, 169n (2), 176n, 180n, 258n
Wright, G. Ernest 48n
Young, Edward J. . . 125n, 173n, 511n
Zachariä, G. T.. . . . . 8n
Zimmerli, Walther. 243n

Subject Index

Aaron. 86–87, 171, 210, 261, 263, 273, 350, 354, 360–363, 376, 447, 581

Abrahamic covenant 155, 239, 253, 254, 269, 299, 326, 426, 436, 438, 458, 467, 469, 499, 512, 532, 555, 560

Adam. 113, 129, 146, 149–151, 154, 162, 167, 172–173, 177, 183–185, 200–205, 207, 210, 217–220, 234, 246, 280–283, 286, 295, 312, 466–467, 497, 504

Adultery 60, 63, 92, 342–343, 345, 381, 440, 526, 564

Ammon 302–303, 308–309, 493–494, 527, 539, 543

Angel of Yahweh (or the Lord) 77–78, 80–83, 145, 243, 291, 422, 470

Angelology 144, 146, 316, 470

Anthropology 9, 106, 169, 174, 176–177, 184

Apocalyptic. 215, 299, 303, 539, 548, 558

Apostasy 63, 399, 416, 424–425, 428, 454, 461, 481

Ark of the covenant. 116, 141, 291, 321, 334, 355, 357–358, 400, 411, 416, 418, 429, 434, 445, 447, 468, 472, 475, 481, 529, 574, 582

Atonement. 60, 99, 122, 150, 218, 228–230, 233–234, 237, 246, 283, 347, 353–354, 357–358, 372–373, 376–378, 389, 410, 514, 533, 536

Assyria 97, 213, 302–310, 440, 445, 460, 495, 500, 503, 505, 514–515, 528, 536–539

Baal. 79, 388, 395–396, 398, 423, 450, 455–457, 459, 462, 496

Babel. 43, 110, 113, 153, 156, 188, 192–194, 224, 288, 298–299, 303, 306–307, 645

Babylon. 306–307, 309, 311, 313, 334, 440, 445, 463, 507–508, 515, 525–528, 530–531, 537, 541, 545, 547–548, 550, 553, 561, 583

Babylonian exile 46, 51–53, 58, 90, 118, 120, 124, 332, 465, 467, 506–507, 512, 521, 527, 540

Bethel 77–79, 82, 93, 191, 231–232, 289–290, 424, 450, 453–454, 457, 463, 495

Blessings, covenant. . . . 244, 248, 299, 326, 328–329, 391, 399, 407–408, 418–419, 437, 445, 453, 585

Blood in making covenant 237, 273, 349–350, 375, 532–533
Blood in sacrifice 218, 228, 230, 237, 240, 295–296, 354, 358, 363, 368, 375–376, 378–379, 480, 628
Book of the covenant . . . 64, 186, 272, 328, 345, 347–348, 350, 365, 367, 375, 383–385, 389, 400, 406
Breath of life 105, 150, 168, 171, 174, 176, 179, 239, 293

Canaan. 113, 155, 159, 242, 244, 325, 346, 350, 386, 402
Canon 2–4, 17, 20–22, 28–29, 32, 39, 42, 86, 92, 235, 404, 487, 492, 532, 638, 648–649
Center, theological 14, 20–21, 27, 641, 646–647
Central sanctuary 346–347, 400–402, 419–420, 424, 433, 435, 442–443, 453, 458, 474
Chronicler, the. . . 48, 55, 74, 290–291, 448, 450, 460, 465, 468, 470, 472, 475–476, 478, 480, 482
City, the 188, 223–225, 298, 310–311, 535, 572, 582–584
Community 167, 178, 184, 292, 326, 343, 345, 347, 350, 359, 369, 374–375, 377–378, 401, 419–421, 427, 459, 463, 467, 475, 483, 531, 542, 544, 565, 585, 590, 600
Covenant renewal 288, 295, 350, 366, 383–384, 389–390, 410, 418–419, 455, 459, 462, 481, 483, 486, 498, 529, 534, 562, 637
Covenant violation 72, 397, 422, 437, 455, 462, 494, 497, 522–523, 526, 541
Creation mandate 17, 43, 76, 105–106, 136–137, 140, 149, 151, 156, 171, 173, 192, 203, 216, 223–224, 234, 239–241, 243, 247–248, 284, 293–294, 298, 300–301, 306, 313, 319, 323, 341, 366, 408, 421, 438–439, 497, 504, 550, 565, 577, 637, 639, 646
Creation narratives 44, 50, 53, 55, 75–76, 102, 129–130, 310, 351, 575
Cultus 229, 248, 287, 351, 365–366, 374–376, 398, 433, 445, 447, 449, 460, 467, 480, 483, 485, 487, 529, 557, 586, 624, 629
Curse, covenant. 113, 174, 184, 205, 281, 285, 307, 408, 420, 461, 494, 523, 528, 561
Cyrus. . . . 46, 53 (2), 53n, 63, 108 (3), 482 (2), 483, 484, 507 (5), 511 (2), 512, 548

Dan, city of 424, 450, 453–454, 457, 524
Davidic covenant. 69, 358, 427,431–441, 453, 459, 464, 466, 578
Davidic dynasty. . . . 69, 190, 321–322, 406, 437, 459, 464, 466, 372, 477, 531, 535–536, 580–581
Davidic kingdom. 285, 458, 463, 467, 479
Day of Atonement 99, 354, 357, 372–473, 533
Day of the Lord. . . . 63, 120, 132, 134, 139, 215, 299, 495, 504, 515, 516, 518, 538, 555–558, 560–561, 563
Decalogue, the. . . . 335, 345, 353, 366, 389, 392–393, 395–398, 400, 403, 408, 420, 454, 464, 481, 542
Deuteronomic covenant 366, 392, 402, 407, 409, 414, 470–471
Deuteronomic history 413–414, 440, 450, 452, 464–465, 470, 478, 482

Diachronic method . . . 2–4, 11–12, 15, 17, 21, 29–30, 643
Divination 88–89, 98, 402, 450
Divine warrior. . . . 116–117, 139, 265, 386, 415, 417, 420, 429, 503, 527, 537, 555, 561, 571, 574, 579
Dreams 48, 77–80, 87, 100, 215, 313, 315, 548, 550, 589, 612

Edom. 191, 213, 301–303, 305, 308–310, 494, 515–516, 527, 543, 556–557, 563–564
Egypt. . . . 49–50, 62–63, 96, 108, 110, 116, 120, 123–124, 134, 138, 156, 158–160, 195–196, 213, 253–256, 258–269, 298, 305, 307, 310, 327, 330–331, 336, 366, 368–370, 373, 393, 409, 445, 476, 498, 526–527, 531, 543, 572, 583
Election 70, 139, 336, 431–432, 436, 441, 472, 512, 563
Elijah. 86, 92–93, 423, 440, 455–457
Elohim. 39–41, 84, 86, 105, 174–175, 329, 615
El Shaddai 84–86, 242, 260, 339, 615
Enlightenment, the . . . 6, 97, 547, 642
Eschatological age 161, 470, 538, 549, 564, 583
Evolution(ary). . . . . 11–13.
Exile, the 98, 306, 309, 366, 482, 486, 517, 540, 554, 556, 559, 584
Exodus, the 134–135, 158–159, 194, 253–255, 257–259, 264, 266–268, 307, 310, 326, 331, 349, 367, 369, 384, 393–394, 398, 410, 415, 417, 481, 506, 534, 537, 541, 548, 572, 615

Fall, the 199–200, 203, 206–210, 216, 218, 220, 223, 238, 240–241, 246, 249, 280, 283, 286, 292, 295, 326, 377, 493, 516, 550, 561 617, 644, 645, 647
Festivals. 54, 76, 142, 289, 316, 348, 366–367, 370–372, 379, 401, 404, 449–450, 496, 552, 565

Gad, the prophet 91–92, 291, 470
Garden, the 40–41, 50, 106, 143, 147, 149–150, 162, 185, 203, 206, 217–218, 220, 281–282, 286–288, 292, 312, 322, 351, 356, 443, 475, 574, 617
Genealogies. 446–467, 643
God as Creator 39, 41–42, 45–46, 52, 54, 76, 84, 107, 109, 130–131, 136, 139–140, 143, 154, 158, 174–175, 177, 199, 207, 238, 278, 298, 304, 307, 319–320, 322, 329, 339–341, 486, 493, 500, 507–508, 516, 526, 528, 541, 543, 571–573, 576, 599, 613–614, 621, 636
God as gracious. . . . 41, 64, 68–69, 71, 94, 115, 117, 119–120, 122, 125, 166, 222, 380, 482, 485
God as Redeemer 115–118, 123, 508–509
God as Savior 55, 121–122, 124, 214, 235, 426, 508–509, 514, 521, 564, 619, 645
God's compassion. 63–68, 72–74, 123–125, 182, 396, 409, 497–498, 505, 508–509, 520, 529, 548, 560, 575
God's covenant faithfulness 67, 69, 122, 211, 387, 421, 444, 570, 590

God's forgiveness . . . 67, 73, 121, 148, 219, 364, 493, 505, 529, 532, 539, 621
God's grace 65–66, 220, 432, 444
God's holiness. . . 14, 56–58, 128, 364, 388, 514
God's immanence . . 39, 105, 175, 277, 444, 452, 574
God's love 62–63, 66–67, 497, 527, 639
God's omnipotence 44–47, 49–50, 135, 137, 279, 573
God's omniscience . . 50–53, 114, 201, 204, 262, 279, 288, 416, 478, 614
God's patience. 71, 539, 585
God's pity 63–64, 66
God's righteousness 57–63, 72, 108, 110, 320, 418, 440, 497, 511, 528, 534–535, 574–575
God's sovereignty 41–42, 135, 155, 173, 186, 223, 259, 262, 297, 304, 311, 315, 322, 477, 494, 504, 551, 553, 623, 644, 646–647
God's transcendence 277, 357, 401, 444, 452, 574, 576, 614
God's wrath. . . . 47, 62, 64, 67, 71–73, 111, 135, 152, 213, 234, 236, 301, 303, 305–307, 311, 322, 336, 416, 504, 523, 525–527, 538–539, 543, 561, 588, 595, 597, 636
Good and evil 50, 54, 131, 150, 183, 200–201, 207, 209, 216, 281, 283, 294
Government. 83, 152–154, 156, 296–297, 306, 308, 342, 344, 405, 421, 433, 446, 550, 552, 557

Hebrews, the 78, 111, 113, 194–197, 243, 254
Hezekiah 43, 97, 117, 139, 459–461, 480–481
Hierarchy, kingdom. . . . 144, 146, 279, 317, 341, 405, 629, 637
High places 231, 298, 307, 400, 442, 449, 453–454, 456, 458, 460, 463, 481, 496
Holiness. 14, 27, 56–59, 72, 103, 128, 140–141, 158, 233, 266, 270, 277, 352, 357, 360, 364, 377, 385, 388, 401, 410, 418, 514, 526, 544, 574, 645
Holy war 47, 110–111, 114, 116, 265, 301, 398, 415–417, 420, 544, 561
Humanity. 56, 141, 148, 167, 173, 185, 190, 243, 273, 292–293, 322, 354, 467, 514, 574, 576–577, 616, 621, 638, 664

Idolatry . . . 49, 51, 64, 67, 72, 74, 114, 305, 320, 332, 334–336, 346, 422, 424, 429–430, 461, 477, 495, 502, 522–523, 525, 527, 541, 545, 609
Image of God 31, 105–106, 130, 136, 143, 152, 169–172, 174, 177–178, 200, 203, 208–209, 217, 219, 239–2400, 281, 292, 295–297, 342, 504, 569, 575, 638
Immortality 126, 210, 214, 588
Individual, the 139, 167, 178–179, 183–184, 190
Israel as God's own possession. . . . 49, 123, 128, 159, 160, 166, 255, 269–270, 398, 438, 561
Israel as God's son 63, 256

Jerusalem. 55, 59, 73, 90, 98, 109, 117, 121, 173, 211, 291, 301, 306, 313, 347, 352, 369, 433–434, 442–443, 445–446, 448–449, 451–453, 463, 468, 474, 476, 480, 482–485, 493–494, 500–501, 503–505, 516, 518–519, 521, 523,

525, 529, 531, 540–541, 549, 552, 556–557, 559–562, 564, 572, 581, 583–584, 593–594
Jesus Christ 13–15, 17, 81, 84, 97, 126, 156, 172, 215, 248, 394, 406, 428, 447, 511, 513, 532–534, 549, 552, 564, 577, 626, 649–650
Joshua 74, 96, 146, 194, 210, 280, 288, 386, 414–421, 423, 455, 471
Josiah. . . . 97, 289, 383, 459, 461–463, 481–482, 536
Judgment by God 110–111, 263, 291, 302, 307, 335, 366, 392, 410, 420, 500, 503, 543, 548, 555, 607, 636

Kingdom of God 142, 148, 155, 222–225, 258, 264, 273, 278, 292, 297–298, 306–307, 309, 317, 329, 343, 426, 478–479, 504, 544, 548, 550, 553–554, 561, 584, 586, 618, 621, 628
Kingdom of heaven. . . . 151–152, 298, 313–314, 317, 342–438, 551, 553, 565, 645, 648
Kingdom of priests 38, 152, 159–160, 269–271, 323, 326–327, 340, 343, 359, 438, 458, 494, 511, 599, 645
Kingship, divine 43–44, 135, 138–141, 151, 154, 159, 207, 278, 318–321, 406, 421, 472, 516, 562, 571, 573–575, 580, 596, 646
Kingship, human. 57, 91, 123, 199, 251–252, 405–406, 418, 421, 427, 429, 431–433, 435–436, 439, 442, 444, 451, 468, 474, 519, 525, 546, 550

Lex talionis 152, 296, 342, 384
Light and darkness 103, 108, 130–131
Lots 98–100, 499
Levites. . . . 55, 99, 355, 357, 360, 370, 376, 385, 460, 467–468, 485–487, 564

Melchizedek 154, 196, 359, 433, 446, 447, 451, 469, 580–582
Messiah 156, 190, 510–511, 539, 549, 558, 562, 648
Messianic king 63, 440, 577, 579–582, 645
Method, thelogical 2–3, 7–8, 21, 28, 32, 648
Moab 82, 88, 182, 303, 305, 308–309, 388, 394, 493, 527, 539, 543
Mosaic covenant 259, 245, 255–256, 258, 270, 294, 300, 326–327, 340, 348, 355, 435, 438–439, 442, 467, 475, 483, 511, 530, 532, 559, 645
Mount Zion 62, 99, 291, 448, 424, 504
Murder. . . . 60, 92, 109, 219, 296, 342, 345, 384, 440, 454, 477, 628, 645
Myth 26, 132, 140
Mythology. 108, 132–133, 212

Narrative 2, 20, 25–27, 31–32, 37–38, 84, 130, 149, 166–167, 210, 283, 413, 464, 477, 482, 603, 622, 643–648
Nebuchadnezzar 44, 55, 78, 313–314, 527, 547, 550–551, 553–554
New covenant 63, 239, 521, 531–534, 545–546, 646
New Testament 3–5, 9, 11, 13–15, 17, 19, 25, 32–33, 44, 97, 103, 106, 115, 122, 135, 142, 145–146, 172, 176, 179, 203, 215–216, 224, 229, 235, 238, 246–247, 257, 300, 317,

340, 358, 376, 390, 410, 418, 426, 446, 451, 473, 475, 499, 513–514, 519, 529–530, 532–535, 552, 558, 562, 577–579, 581–582, 586, 641–642, 647–651
Noahic covenant 241, 284, 296, 342, 509

Offering, burnt. 83, 231, 233–234, 236–237, 291, 356, 358–359, 363, 376–377
Offering, fellowship (or peace). 233, 237, 364, 376, 378, 446

Passover 49, 235, 260, 263, 349, 367–371, 375, 463, 480–482, 532
Persia. 108, 305, 307, 316–317, 487–488, 548, 552–553
Philistines 118, 196–197, 246, 302, 304, 308–309, 428–429, 493, 503, 527, 543, 561
Pilgrimage. 348, 370–372, 379, 402, 516, 561, 584
Pillar, sacred 232, 289
Prediction 90–92, 97, 243, 492, 510
Presuppositions 7, 12–13, 20–23
Progressive revelation . . . 3, 12–13, 21, 29–30, 218, 302, 492, 644
Priests 100, 271, 273, 289, 305, 355–357, 359–360, 362–364, 370, 376, 377, 379, 384, 416–418, 446, 448, 450–451, 460, 467, 469, 473, 476, 480, 485–487, 496, 509, 522, 535, 539, 564, 645
Prophetism 79, 87–91, 93, 364, 388, 402–403, 427, 491, 492
Prophets, canonical 80, 87–88, 94, 404, 427, 427, 491–492
Psalms of Yahweh's kingship 44, 139, 318, 321

Rahab, the monster 133, 267–268, 322, 572
Rationalism 6–7, 10, 97
Rebellion. 41, 67, 71–72, 74, 89, 109, 136, 150–151, 155–156, 160, 170, 192, 196–197, 199, 204, 207, 217–218, 222–223, 225, 248, 268, 280, 282, 299–300, 303, 308, 317, 354, 387, 403, 422, 429, 440, 501–502, 504, 526, 536, 541, 550, 556, 563, 565, 596
Resurrection 125, 214–216, 248, 394, 497, 514, 532, 588, 620
Restoration 68, 102, 114, 118, 120–121, 124, 126, 162, 165, 173, 210, 212, 215–216, 249, 444, 493–496, 498, 501–502, 505–508, 510, 516, 521, 529–531, 540, 545, 548, 558–559, 561, 565, 577, 583, 593, 621, 645, 647
Revelation 7, 16, 27, 75, 77–78, 80, 146, 603, 642, 644, 648
Ritual. . . . 99, 128, 140, 218, 222, 232, 287, 346, 354, 355, 359–361, 364, 369–372, 374–379, 417, 450, 529, 624
Royal grant 239, 241–242, 245, 248, 294, 326, 435–436, 438, 467
Royal priesthood 445–451, 471

Sabbath 105, 186, 229, 330, 340, 348, 355, 365–367, 372–374, 393, 405, 487
Sacred history 26, 69, 85, 209, 264, 349, 367, 394, 413, 427, 456, 465, 477
Sacred space 281–282, 284, 286–292, 351, 353–354, 359–360, 363–364, 374, 385, 400, 452–453, 459, 463, 470, 472, 474–476

Samuel, the prophet 43, 59, 80, 86, 88, 90–93, 117–118, 158, 406, 423, 427–432, 436, 470, 491
Satan 41, 135, 145–146, 162, 205–209, 283, 300, 304, 311–312, 317, 323, 597, 608, 617–618
Saul 91–92, 97, 100, 118, 427, 430–433, 437, 466, 468
Seed of Abraham, the 190, 192, 194, 242–244, 253, 271, 273, 299, 307, 323, 325, 327, 343, 408, 410, 426, 439, 458, 467, 494, 499, 505, 509, 526, 528, 544, 555, 646
Seed of the woman, the. 115, 205, 236, 246–248, 283, 509
Servant of the Lord, the. . . . 45, 53, 62, 124, 432, 511–514, 562
Shechem 77, 112, 231, 288, 418
Shema, the. 395–400, 407, 409–410, 420, 430, 453, 462, 464, 471, 479, 494
Sheol 125–126, 210, 212–213, 215, 303–304, 310, 498, 588, 628
Shrines. 282, 287, 321, 347, 379, 400–401, 442–443, 450, 453–454, 457, 461, 463, 593
Signs 76, 88–89, 91, 95–98, 142, 157, 260–262, 351, 365, 386, 422, 538
Sinaitic covenant. 38, 186, 346, 350, 365, 383–384
Solomon 61, 63, 68, 72–74, 211, 291, 347, 352–353, 358, 427, 439–445, 448–449, 451–453, 460, 463, 466, 471–476, 478, 481, 557–558, 581, 604, 622, 624–25, 628, 631–632
Sons of God. 144–145, 312
Sons of the prophets 86, 92–93
Soul, the 124, 176, 330, 380, 382, 395–396, 399–400, 407, 409, 420, 495, 591, 631
Spirit of God 19, 246, 266, 496, 642, 650
Suzerain-vassal treaty 239, 270, 294, 327, 371, 379, 390, 402, 407, 435
Synchronic method 2–3, 14, 21

Tabernacle, the 98, 104, 141, 292, 321, 347, 352–361, 364–365, 381, 385–387, 400, 411, 420, 425, 428, 434, 442–443, 447–449, 467, 469, 474, 533, 574
Tabernacles, the Feast of 349, 411, 475–476, 483
Ten Commandments 330, 342, 346, 392, 395, 399
Theocracy/theocratic. 153, 171, 251, 292, 326, 341, 359, 361, 364, 374, 387, 401, 405, 414, 420–421, 427–428, 482, 601
Theophany/theophanic 255, 272, 288
Torah 18, 28, 37–38, 99, 107, 161, 222, 233, 239, 271, 287, 366, 371, 376, 414, 428, 464, 484, 486–487, 492–493, 502–503, 516, 519, 584–585, 587, 589, 600, 603, 609–610, 622–624, 629
Tree of the knowledge of good and evil . . . 50, 150, 183, 200–201, 207, 209, 216, 281, 294
Tree of life. . . . 54, 141, 150, 209–210, 356, 475, 574
Tribalism 24, 188–189, 385
Tyre 206, 302, 305, 309–312, 474, 493–494, 515, 543, 561, 583

Unleavened bread 49, 348–349, 367–371
Urim and Thummim 98, 100, 362

Vice-regent, man as. 41, 173, 186, 292, 342, 411, 431, 440, 474, 621, 637, 647
Vindication 24, 60, 213, 513, 528, 586–587, 597–598, 605, 608, 613, 619–620
Visions. 77–80, 87, 315, 540, 548, 550, 558, 612
Wise, the 622, 624, 627–628, 632, 634, 636–637

Yahweh 39–40, 81, 84–86, 105, 174–175, 260, 329, 339

Scripture Index

Gen 1:1 . . . . 39, 42, 44 (2), 142, 168, 278
Gen 1:1-5 131
Gen 1:1-31 130
Gen 1:1–2:3. . . .40, 130, 142, 167
Gen 1:1–2:4a. 39
Gen 1–11. . . . . .15, 76
Gen 1:2 . . . . . .102, 142, 266, 524
Gen 1:3 . . . . .75, 279
Gen 1:3-14 365
Gen 1:4 . . . . .40, 50, 201
Gen 1:5-7 75
Gen 1:6 279
Gen 1:6-10 132
Gen 1:9 279
Gen 1:9-10 75
Gen 1:9-11 . . .158, 264, 322, 417
Gen 1:10 . . . . .40, 50, 201
Gen 1:11 279
Gen 1:12 . . . . .40, 50, 201
Gen 1:14 . . . . .75, 76, 279
Gen 1:14-15 142
Gen 1:18 . . . . .40, 50, 201
Gen 1:20 . . . . .75, 176, 279
Gen 1:20-25 . . . . .105, 577
Gen 1:21 . . . . .40, 50, 201
Gen 1:22 . . . . .75, 301
Gen 1:24 . . . . .75, 176, 279
Gen 1:25 . . . . .40, 50, 201
Gen 1:26 . .75, 135-136, 144, 147, 170, 219, 279, 286
Gen 1:26-27 . . . . .168, 184
Gen 1:26-28 . . 42, 104, 147, 155, 203, 234, 279, 313, 406, 438, 575, 577, 644
Gen 1:26-30 . . . . . . .40, 167, 203
Gen 1:27 168
Gen 1:28 . . . . 40, 43, 76, 105, 110, 140, 143, 149, 151, 153, 183, 184, 224, 259, 284, 408, 439, 553, 565, 577, 639
Gen 1:28b 240
Gen 1:28-30 . . . . .149, 183
Gen 1:29-30 . . . . .280, 295
Gen 1:31 . . . . . . .40, 50, 199, 201
Gen 2. 339
Gen 2:2 . . . . .281, 365
Gen 2:2-3 . . . . .229, 339
Gen 2:3 281
Gen 2:4-6 143
Gen 2:4-25 . . . . 40, 130 (2), 142, 167
Gen 2:4b–3:34. 225
Gen 2:5 . . . . .105, 204, 280
Gen 2:7 . . . . 105, 169, 174, 179, 205, 208
Gen 2:8 204
Gen 2:9 . . . . 50, 54, 201, 204, 220, 282
Gen 2:15 204
Gen 2:16-17 . . . . .76, 183
Gen 2:17 . . . . .200, 209, 216, 218
Gen 2:18 . . . .
Gen 2:19 . . . . .105, 106, 147, 176
Gen 2:19-20 . . . . .171, 183
Gen 2:20-23 203
Gen 2:21 . . . . .106, 179
Gen 2:24 . . . . .107, 184, 185
Gen 3:1 41
Gen 3:1-2 205
Gen 3:1-15 146
Gen 3:3 . . . . .76, 218
Gen 3:4 205
Gen 3:5 . . . . . . .50, 217, 283, 351
Gen 3:7 . . . . . . .50, 202, 203, 228
Gen 3:8-9 . . . . .41, 189, 283
Gen 3:8a 286
Gen 3:9-19 76
Gen 3:13 219
Gen 3:13-14 . . . . .41, 205
Gen 3:14 285
Gen 3:15 . . . . .509, 511
Gen 3:16 . . . . .115, 184, 202
Gen 3:17 . . . . .204, 234
Gen 3:17-19 . . . . .136, 218
Gen 3:18 204
Gen 3:19 . . . . .204, 216
Gen 3:20 184
Gen 3:21 . . . . .150, 218, 228
Gen 3:21-23 . . . . .41, 177
Gen 3:22-24 209
Gen 3:22 . . . . . . .54, 76, 201, 283
Gen 3:23 219
Gen 3:23-24 286
Gen 3:24 . . . . .141, 353, 475, 574
Gen 4:1 185
Gen 4:1-5 287
Gen 4:2 . . . . .143, 219
Gen 4:2-5 446
Gen 4:3 229
Gen 4:5 229
Gen 4:6 76
Gen 4:8 210
Gen 4:12 143
Gen 4:14 . . . . .220, 287
Gen 4:15 115
Gen 4:17 . . . . .185, 188, 223
Gen 4:19 185
Gen 4:20 283
Gen 4:26 . . . . .43, 85, 224
Gen 5:1 169
Gen 5:1-3 200
Gen 5:3 169
Gen 5:5 210
Gen 5:11 210

Gen 5:14 210
Gen 5:17 210
Gen 5:20 210
Gen 5:24 589
Gen 5:27 210
Gen 5:29 136
Gen 5:31 210
Gen 6:2 145
Gen 6:4 145
Gen 6:5 . . . . . . 180, 220, 221, 234
Gen 6:7 . . . . 210, 293
Gen 6:8 65
Gen 6:8-10 115
Gen 6:11-12 . . . . 109, 588
Gen 6:13 76
Gen 6:17 . . . . 176, 210, 293
Gen 6:17-18 239
Gen 7:2 284
Gen 7:11 142
Gen 7:15 176
Gen 7:21-23 210
Gen 7:22 168
Gen 8:20 . . . . 233, 284
Gen 8:20-21 . . . . 230, 446
Gen 8:20-22 288
Gen 8:21 . . . . 180, 220, 234, 297, 298, 369
Gen 9:1 . . . . 151, 240, 295
Gen 9:1-7 . . . . 284, 293
Gen 9:1-17 234
Gen 9:2 . . . . 171, 284
Gen 9:3 . . . . 95, 152
Gen 9:4 296
Gen 9:5 296
Gen 9:5-6 152
Gen 9:6 . . 152, 200, 219, 296, 342
Gen 9:7 . . . . 110, 295
Gen 9:10 176
Gen 9:10-16 106
Gen 9:12 176
Gen 9:15-16 176
Gen 9:17 366
Gen 9:18 153
Gen 9:18-27 153
Gen 9:19 192
Gen 9:20 151
Gen 9:24-27 297
Gen 9:25-26 . . . . 113, 194
Gen 9:26 339
Gen 10:1-32 153
Gen 10:5 . . . . 188, 192
Gen 10:8-12 193
Gen 10:10 278
Gen 10:18-19 . . . . . 113, 193–194
Gen 10:20 192
Gen 10:21 . . . . 113, 194, 241
Gen 10:25 194
Gen 10:31 192
Gen 11:1-4 153
Gen 11:1-9 . . . . 43, 110, 223, 298
Gen 11:4 . . . . 43, 188, 288
Gen 11:6 . . . . 192, 224
Gen 11:9 . . . . 113, 188, 193
Gen 11:10-26 241
Gen 11:27-31 188
Gen 11:27-32 186
Gen 11:31 303
Gen 12:1 241
Gen 12:1-3 190, 325, 467, 544, 560
Gen 12:2 . . . . . . 84, 154, 160, 254
Gen 12:2-3 . . . . 241, 251, 269
Gen 12:3 . . . . 128, 159, 253, 299, 308, 326, 408, 494, 509, 528, 555
Gen 12:4-5 186
Gen 12:7 . . . . . . 77, 231, 288, 446
Gen 12:8 . . . . 289, 338, 446
Gen 12:13 195
Gen 12:16 186
Gen 12:16-20 154
Gen 13:1-18 224
Gen 13:3-4 289
Gen 13:4 . . . . 231, 338
Gen 13:14-15 194
Gen 14:1-24 154
Gen 14:13 194
Gen 14:14 186
Gen 14:18 . . . . 359, 433, 581
Gen 14:18-20 446
Gen 14:19-20 154
Gen 14:22 339
Gen 15. 242
Gen 15:1 80
Gen 15:1-21 175
Gen 15:2 339
Gen 15:5 . . . . 84, 253
Gen 15:5-7 325
Gen 15:8 339
Gen 15:9-21 . . . . 350, 407
Gen 15:13 . . . . 195, 258
Gen 15:13-14 . . . . 128, 254
Gen 15:14 . . . . 259, 367
Gen 15:18 113
Gen 15:18-19 325
Gen 15:18-20 194
Gen 15:19-21 112
Gen 16:1-6 81
Gen 16:2 339
Gen 16:10 191
Gen 16:14 84
Gen 17:1 . . . . 84, 326
Gen 17:1-3 175
Gen 17:1-14 529
Gen 17:2 253
Gen 17:3-8 325
Gen 17:4-5 154
Gen 17:4-6 . . . . 160, 254
Gen 17:6 . . . . 138, 245, 251, 406, 423, 428, 436
Gen 17:7-8 458
Gen 17:8 256
Gen 17:9-14 241
Gen 17:11 366
Gen 17:16 . . . . 138, 191, 245, 251, 254, 406, 423, 428, 436
Gen 17:17 180
Gen 17:18-19 257
Gen 17:19 . . . . 234, 387
Gen 18:10 77
Gen 18:13 77
Gen 18:16–19:26. 110
Gen 18:16-19 244
Gen 18:17 77
Gen 18:18 . . . . 154, 160, 191, 251, 254, 326
Gen 18:19 108
Gen 18:20 . . . . 77, 221, 225
Gen 18:21 499
Gen 18:24 73
Gen 19–20. 112
Gen 19:4-9 225
Gen 19:15 221
Gen 19:36-38 527
Gen 20:2 197
Gen 20:3-7 78
Gen 20:7 . . . . 86, 403, 492
Gen 20:9 278
Gen 20:17 326
Gen 21:17 . . . . 81, 112
Gen 21:22-34 197
Gen 21:22-27 326
Gen 21:33 . . . . 54, 338, 339
Gen 22. . . . . 234, 244, 257
Gen 22:2 . . . . 231, 290
Gen 22:4-14 446
Gen 22:7 235
Gen 22:8 236
Gen 22:9 347
Gen 22:11 81
Gen 22:14 . . . . 236, 339
Gen 22:15-18 . . . . 175, 327
Gen 22:17-18 . . . . 155, 325
Gen 22:18 . . . . 159, 191, 241, 269, 326, 408
Gen 23:1-4 112
Gen 24:1-4 . . . . 186, 187
Gen 24:12 339
Gen 24:27 68
Gen 24:38 . . . . 185, 187
Gen 25:8 . . . . 192, 210

Gen 25:16 189
Gen 25:23 . . . . 191, 254
Gen 26:1-7 197
Gen 26:2 77
Gen 26:3-4 155
Gen 26:4 . . . . 269, 326
Gen 26:4-5 327
Gen 26:5 . . . . 244, 245
Gen 26:24 77
Gen 26:25 . . . . 338, 446
Gen 26:26-31 326
Gen 26:34-35 186
Gen 27:29 . . . . 241, 245, 408
Gen 27:39-40 303
Gen 27:46–28:5. 186
Gen 28:3 85
Gen 28:10-14 289
Gen 28:10-15 . . . . 78, 145
Gen 28:12 232
Gen 28:13-15 155
Gen 28:17 78
Gen 30:27 326
Gen 31:10-11 79
Gen 31:11 82
Gen 31:13 289
Gen 31:20 180
Gen 31:22-50 237
Gen 31:34 331
Gen 31:51-54 347
Gen 32:1 145
Gen 32:14 229
Gen 32:19 229
Gen 32:21 77
Gen 32:22-28 155
Gen 32:28 . . . . 289, 338
Gen 32:30 . . . . 78, 338
Gen 33:11 65
Gen 33:18-20 288
Gen 33:22-32 77
Gen 35:1 77
Gen 35:1-7 289
Gen 35:2-5 331
Gen 35:6 446
Gen 35:7 . . . . 78, 232
Gen 35:9-10 77
Gen 35:11 . . . . . 85, 191, 251, 254
Gen 35:11-12 155
Gen 35:14 . . . . 78, 446
Gen 35:29 192
Gen 37:26-27 189
Gen 37:27 179
Gen 38:1-26 189
Gen 39:2-5 326
Gen 39:5 253
Gen 39:9 221
Gen 39:21 68
Gen 40. 78
Gen 41. 78
Gen 41:33 236
Gen 41:45 359
Gen 41:46-57 253
Gen 41:50 359
Gen 43:8-9 189
Gen 43:11 229
Gen 44:5 221
Gen 44:14-20 189
Gen 45:8 203
Gen 46:1-4 80
Gen 46:3 . . . . 160, 185, 191, 253, 254
Gen 46:3-4 245
Gen 46:4 128
Gen 46:5-7 186
Gen 46:20 359
Gen 46:26-27 186
Gen 46:28 189
Gen 47:7 253
Gen 47:11 253
Gen 47:12 . . . . 185, 186
Gen 47:13-27 326
Gen 47:22 359
Gen 47:26 359
Gen 47:29-30 210
Gen 48:3-4 . . . . 77, 85
Gen 48:5-6 186
Gen 48:14 256
Gen 48:18 256
Gen 49:1 403
Gen 49:8 252
Gen 49:8-12 . . . . 436, 472
Gen 49:10 . . . . 156, 252, 406, 431, 433, 509, 511, 546, 579
Gen 49:11 510
Gen 49:16 189
Gen 49:25 85
Gen 49:29 192
Gen 50:15 221
Gen 50:17 221

Exod 1:7 253
Exod 1:8 254
Exod 1:11-14. 195
Exod 1:13 259
Exod 2:1-2. 361
Exod 2:11-15. 259
Exod 2:15 156
Exod 2:16 359
Exod 2:24 157
Exod 2:24-25. 259
Exod 3:1 359
Exod 3:2 . . . . 78, 82
Exod 3:4 77
Exod 3:5 . . . . 78–79, 159, 417
Exod 3:7 255
Exod 3:7-10. 110
Exod 3:8 128
Exod 3:10 255
Exod 3:11-12. 260
Exod 3:12 . . . . 96, 143, 159, 268, 374, 415
Exod 3:16-17. 110
Exod 4:1-8. 96
Exod 4:11 180
Exod 4:14 . . . . 72, 361
Exod 4:16 87
Exod 4:17, 21, 28, 30 96
Exod 4:21 . . . . 157, 263
Exod 4:22 108
Exod 4:22-23. . . . . 122, 128, 160, 256
Exod 4:23 143
Exod 5:1-2. 110
Exod 5:2 . . . . 43, 157, 260
Exod 5:3 375
Exod 5:22–6:8. . . . . 16, 27
Exod 5:23 255
Exod 6:1-8. 367
Exod 6:2-5. 85
Exod 6:3 339
Exod 6:4-5. 260
Exod 6:6 . . . . 122, 128
Exod 6:6-7. 159
Exod 6:16-25. . . . . 360, 361
Exod 7 86
Exod 7:1 . . . . 157, 171, 261
Exod 7:3 . . . . 96, 263
Exod 7:4 255
Exod 7:5 . . . . 43, 157
Exod 7:7 361
Exod 7:13 263
Exod 7:17 261
Exod 7:23 180
Exod 8:10 261
Exod 8:15 263
Exod 8:19 . . . . 43, 96, 111, 158, 331
Exod 8:21 255
Exod 8:26 375
Exod 9:14 . . . . 261, 331
Exod 9:16 . . . . 48, 158
Exod 9:34 263
Exod 10:1-2. 96
Exod 10:2 262
Exod 10:9 375
Exod 10:16 43
Exod 10:25 375
Exod 11:1-10. 368
Exod 11:5 257
Exod 11:7 262
Exod 11:9-10. 96
Exod 12. 235

Exod 12:1-11. . . . . .368, 375
Exod 12:2 368
Exod 12:2, 6 367
Exod 12:11 368
Exod 12:12 . . .257, 260, 307, 331
Exod 12:14 375
Exod 12:14-20. 368
Exod 12:29 . . . . .111, 257
Exod 12:39 368
Exod 13:1 123
Exod 13:2 257
Exod 13:3 368
Exod 13:3-4. 368
Exod 13:3-10. . . . . .349, 367
Exod 13:7-10. 367
Exod 13:13 235
Exod 13:14-15. 368
Exod 13:14-16. . . . . .123, 375
Exod 13:15 . . . . .257, 264
Exod 13:20–14:4. 264
Exod 14. 133
Exod 14:4 . . . . 158, 263 (2)
Exod 14:13 . . . . .116, 264
Exod 14:17 . . . . 263 (2)
Exod 14:18 158
Exod 14:19 82
Exod 14:21 . . . . .158, 263
Exod 14:21-22. 417
Exod 14:30 116
Exod 14:31 49
Exod 15. . . . . .134, 265, 310, 415
Exod 15:1-18. 265
Exod 15:1-21. . . . . .133, 158
Exod 15:2 116
Exod 15:3-5. 417
Exod 15:6 . . . . .49, 111
Exod 15:8 134
Exod 15:11 . . . . .56, 159, 266
Exod 15:13 . . . . .68, 122
Exod 15:21 49
Exod 16:8 268
Exod 16:21-26. 365
Exod 17:1-4. 268
Exod 18:1 359
Exod 18:4 . . . . .106, 177
Exod 18:12 361
Exod 19:3-6. . . . . .175, 269
Exod 19:4 128
Exod 19:4-6. . . 39, 128, 129, 159, 165, 270, 511
Exod 19:5 . . . .166, 255, 327, 398
Exod 19:5-6. 438
Exod 19:6 . . . .254, 323, 326, 359
Exod 19:8 . . . . 161, 272, 329, 330, 350
Exod 19:10 417
Exod 19:14-15. 329
Exod 19:14-19. 272
Exod 19:16-19. 351
Exod 19:22 359
Exod 20. . . . . .348, 393
Exod 20–23. . . . 328 (2), 350, 389
Exod 20:1-17. 345
Exod 20:1–23:33. 272
Exod 20:2a, 2b 329
Exod 20:3-17. . . . . .330, 331
Exod 20:4-6. . . . . .333, 454
Exod 20:5 . . . . . 335 (2), 541, 542
Exod 20:6 . . . . .68, 337
Exod 20:7 . . . . . . 57, 337 (2), 384
Exod 20:8 340
Exod 20:8-11. . . . . .105, 339
Exod 20:10 340
Exod 20:12 . . . . 186, 341 (2)
Exod 20:13 342
Exod 20:14 342
Exod 20:15 343
Exod 20:16 344
Exod 20:17 . . . . .345, 394
Exod 20:18-21. 346
Exod 20:18–23:33. 345
Exod 20:24-26. 231
Exod 20:24 . . . . 237 (2), 346, 400, 401
Exod 20:25-26. 347
Exod 21–23. 186
Exod 21:2-11. 348
Exod 21:12 384
Exod 21:15 . . . . .186, 405
Exod 21:17 186
Exod 21:23-25. 385
Exod 21:24 296
Exod 22:9 222
Exod 22:27 64
Exod 22:28 384
Exod 22:29 257
Exod 23:10-11. 373
Exod 23:11 348
Exod 23:14-15. 369
Exod 23:14-17. 401
Exod 23:14-19. 565
Exod 23:15 . . . . . . .349, 367, 371
Exod 23:16 . . . . .370 (2), 349
Exod 23:17 . . . . 371 (2)
Exod 23:20 317
Exod 23:21 . . . . .74, 82, 222
Exod 23:23 317
Exod 24. . . . . .272, 376n
Exod 24:1 361
Exod 24:1-4. 328
Exod 24:3 330
Exod 24:4 349
Exod 24:4-8. 375
Exod 24:5 . . . . 237 (2),
Exod 24:9-11. 361
Exod 24:10 352
Exod 24:11 . . . . .350, 355
Exod 25:1-9. . . . . .104, 357
Exod 25:8 352
Exod 25:8-9. 400
Exod 25:9 356
Exod 25:10-22. . . . . .141, 574
Exod 25:22 . . . . .353, 400
Exod 25:23-30. 355
Exod 25:31-36. 356
Exod 25:31-40. 355
Exod 25:40 356
Exod 26:30 357
Exod 26:35 355
Exod 27:8 359
Exod 27:1-8. 358
Exod 27:21 . . . . .356, 361
Exod 28. 361
Exod 28:1 360
Exod 28:1-5. 104
Exod 28:2 363
Exod 28:12 362
Exod 28:29-30. 100
Exod 28:30 362
Exod 28:40 363
Exod 28:41 363
Exod 29 . . . . .361, 362
Exod 29:1 363
Exod 29:1-43. 376
Exod 29:9 581
Exod 29:18 363
Exod 29:27-28. 364
Exod 29:28 237
Exod 30:1-10. 358
Exod 30:17-21. 359
Exod 31:12-13, 16. 355
Exod 31:13 . . . . .241, 366
Exod 32:1-6. 256
Exod 32:2-6. 453
Exod 32:4 332
Exod 32:6 237
Exod 32:9-10. . . . . .245, 386
Exod 32:10 254
Exod 32:10-13. 72
Exod 32:15 . . . . .340, 353
Exod 32:30 353
Exod 32:32 73
Exod 33:2 82
Exod 33:12-13. 65
Exod 33:13 . . . . .254, 256
Exod 33:19 65
Exod 34:6 . . . . .65, 66, 71
Exod 34:6-7. 222
Exod 34:7 73
Exod 34:9 73
Exod 34:15-16. 187

Exod 34:20 ....235, 257, 371
Exod 34:22 ....349, 370
Exod 34:23 ....371 (2)
Exod 34:29 353
Exod 35:34 180
Exod 40:10 289
Exod 40:34-35.............443

Lev 1 233
Lev 1–7...................378
Lev 1:9, 13, 17 377
Lev 3:1-17................379
Lev 3:11 379
Lev 4:4 378
Lev 4:10 ....233, 237
Lev 4:18-19...............230
Lev 4:20, 26, 31 353
Lev 4:22, 27 378
Lev 5:1-13................378
Lev 5:5-6, 17-18 378
Lev 5:14-19...............378
Lev 6:1-7.................378
Lev 6:2-5.................378
Lev 6:12 233
Lev 7:2-3, 33..............230
Lev 7:11-18...............379
Lev 7:12-15...............379
Lev 8:8 ....100, 362
Lev 9:7 233
Lev 9:22 233
Lev 9:23 78
Lev 10:3 377
Lev 10:1-3................111
Lev 10:11 161
Lev 11 233
Lev 11:10 176
Lev 11:10-46..............106
Lev 11:44 377
Lev 11:44-45...........56, 271
Lev 12:8 233
Lev 14:19-20..............233
Lev 15:15 233
Lev 16 353
Lev 16:1-2.................99
Lev 16:1-34...............372
Lev 16:2 354
Lev 16:7-10................99
Lev 16:16, 21 222
Lev 17:11 ....240, 295
Lev 19:2 ....56, 271, 377
Lev 19:3 186
Lev 19:3, 30 366
Lev 19:18 ....330, 395
Lev 20:7-8................377
Lev 20:9 405
Lev 20:26 ....57, 377
Lev 21:8 57
Lev 22:32 ....57, 377
Lev 23 366
Lev 23:1, 4-21.............401
Lev 23:4-8................369
Lev 23:5 367
Lev 23:7-8................367
Lev 23:11, 15-16...........370
Lev 23:16 370
Lev 23:18 369
Lev 23:18-19..............233
Lev 23:20 370
Lev 23:23-25..............372
Lev 23:28, 30 372
Lev 23:33-36..............371
Lev 23:43 371
Lev 24:8 ....355 (2)
Lev 24:10-23..........111, 384
Lev 24:12 384
Lev 24:16 384
Lev 24:21 385
Lev 25 279
Lev 25:2 373
Lev 25:8-55...............373
Lev 25:27 354
Lev 25:49 188
Lev 26 408
Lev 26:3-13...............328
Lev 26:12 261
Lev 26:14-43..............328
Lev 26:17 ....279, 408
Lev 26:44-45..............409

Num 1:1 385
Num 1:2 185
Num 1:47-54...............385
Num 3:1-39................385
Num 4:15 ....448, 469
Num 5:5-31................380
Num 5:6-7.................381
Num 5:11-31..............526n
Num 6:1-12................382
Num 6:1-21................382
Num 6:14 233
Num 6:24-26...............446
Num 6:25 66
Num 9:10-23...............385
Num 10 386
Num 11:1-3................111
Num 11:16-17, 25............87
Num 11:25 91
Num 11:31-34..............111
Num 12:2 87
Num 12:2, 7-8..............403
Num 12:6-8............79, 492
Num 12:10 111
Num 13–14 386
Num 14:9 386
Num 14:10 78
Num 14:11 96
Num 14:18 ......67, 71, 73, 222
Num 14:19 ....68, 73
Num 14:22 96
Num 14:32 390
Num 14:32-34..............386
Num 15:8-12...............446
Num 15:32-36..............366
Num 16:19, 42 78
Num 16:22 179
Num 16:25-33..............335
Num 16:28-35..............111
Num 16:39-40..............451
Num 18:17 230
Num 20:2-13...............387
Num 20:6 78
Num 20:12 ....388 (2)
Num 20:16 317
Num 20:24-26..............210
Num 21:1-3................111
Num 21:11-26...............99
Num 22–24 88
Num 22–25, 31 388
Num 22:22 82
Num 22:38 388
Num 24:4 ....80, 86
Num 24:16 86
Num 24:17 ....388, 406, 510
Num 24:17-19..............138
Num 24:19 279
Num 25:1-3...........388, 394
Num 25:3 395
Num 25:4 72
Num 25:6-9................111
Num 25:13 ....388, 389
Num 26 98
Num 27:11 188
Num 27:21 ....100, 362
Num 28 369
Num 28:9-10...............366
Num 28:12-38..............371
Num 28:16–29:40...........401
Num 28:26-31..............370
Num 29:1-6................372
Num 29:7-11...............372
Num 31:2 210
Num 31:15-16..............388
Num 32 419
Num 32:22 280
Num 33:39 361
Num 36:6 188

Deut 1:1...................38
Deut 1:1-2.................38
Deut 1:34-36..............392
Deut 1:36.................134

Deut 1:37 . . . 72
Deut 2:14-15 . . . 390
Deut 2:30 . . . 114
Deut 4:5-8 . . . 479
Deut 4:7 . . . 401
Deut 4:8 . . . 59
Deut 4:21 . . . 72
Deut 4:21-24 . . . 388
Deut 4:31 . . . 66
Deut 4:34 . . . 96, 265
Deut 4:35, 39 . . . 331
Deut 4:37 . . . 62
Deut 4:39-40 . . . 392
Deut 5 . . . 393
Deut 5:1 . . . 393
Deut 5:1-5 . . . 175
Deut 5:1-21 . . . 392
Deut 5:7-8 . . . 398
Deut 5:11 . . . 57, 337, 400, 403
Deut 5:12-15 . . . 366
Deut 5:15 . . . 265
Deut 5:16 . . . 186
Deut 6–26 . . . 397
Deut 6:4 . . . 396
Deut 6:4-5 . . . 330, 395, 420, 462
Deut 6:6 . . . 397
Deut 6:6-9 . . . 624
Deut 6:7-9 . . . 397, 630
Deut 6:10-11 . . . 390
Deut 6:13 . . . 143n
Deut 6:13-14 . . . 398
Deut 6:22 . . . 96
Deut 7:1 . . . 415
Deut 7:1-2 . . . 221
Deut 7:1-5, 26 . . . 112
Deut 7:1-6 . . . 112, 114, 194, 415
Deut 7:3-4 . . . 187
Deut 7:4 . . . 398
Deut 7:6 . . . 128n, 255, 270
Deut 7:7-8 . . . 108, 270, 336
Deut 7:7-11 . . . 563
Deut 7:8 . . . 62, 122
Deut 7:9 . . . 68
Deut 7:12-16 . . . 398
Deut 7:13 . . . 62
Deut 7:17-26 . . . 415
Deut 7:19 . . . 96, 265
Deut 7:25-26 . . . 112
Deut 8:18-20 . . . 399
Deut 9:7-24 . . . 399
Deut 9:8, 19-20 . . . 72
Deut 9:14 . . . 245
Deut 9:26 . . . 49
Deut 9:29 . . . 49, 265
Deut 10:4 . . . 330
Deut 10:8 . . . 469
Deut 10:12-13 . . . 399
Deut 10:15 . . . 62
Deut 10:17 . . . 265, 399
Deut 10:18 . . . 60
Deut 11:1 . . . 399
Deut 11:2-9 . . . 96
Deut 11:18-20 . . . 624
Deut 11:18-21 . . . 630
Deut 11:24-25 . . . 134
Deut 12 . . . 141, 442, 461
Deut 12:1–26:15 . . . 407
Deut 12:1-4 . . . 402
Deut 12:5, 11 . . . 141, 574
Deut 12:5 . . . 401, 433, 435
Deut 12:5-7 . . . 346
Deut 12:5, 14 . . . 79
Deut 12:5, 11, 14, 21, 26 . . . 400
Deut 12:8-11 . . . 347
Deut 12:10-11 . . . 471
Deut 12:11 . . . 453
Deut 12:13 . . . 236
Deut 12:15-28 . . . 401
Deut 12:31 . . . 403
Deut 13 . . . 88, 90, 403 (2)
Deut 13:5 . . . 122, 403
Deut 13:17-18 . . . 67
Deut 14:1-21 . . . 404
Deut 14:1-22 . . . 233
Deut 14:2 . . . 70, 128n, 255, 270
Deut 14:22-29 . . . 404
Deut 15:1-18 . . . 404
Deut 15:15 . . . 122
Deut 15:19-23 . . . 404
Deut 16:1-8 . . . 369
Deut 16:1-17 . . . 401, 404
Deut 16:10 . . . 370
Deut 16:13-15 . . . 371
Deut 16:16 . . . 369, 371
Deut 16:16-17 . . . 371
Deut 16:18-20 . . . 404, 405
Deut 17:1 . . . 404
Deut 17:2-13 . . . 404
Deut 17:6-7 . . . 344
Deut 17:10-11 . . . 161
Deut 17:14-20 . . . 406, 428, 442
Deut 17:14 . . . 406
Deut 17:18 . . . 393, 404
Deut 17:18-20 . . . 459
Deut 18 . . . 87, 89
Deut 18:9-13 . . . 403, 404
Deut 18:10-11 . . . 89
Deut 18:14-18 . . . 403
Deut 18:14-19 . . . 89
Deut 18:18 . . . 404
Deut 18:21-22 . . . 492
Deut 18:22 . . . 403
Deut 19:1 . . . 390
Deut 19:1-21 . . . 404
Deut 19:15 . . . 344
Deut 19:21 . . . 296
Deut 20 . . . 116, 415
Deut 20:16 . . . 176
Deut 20:17 . . . 112
Deut 21:1-23 . . . 404
Deut 21:8 . . . 122
Deut 21:15-17 . . . 256
Deut 21:18-21 . . . 186, 405
Deut 22:13:30 . . . 404
Deut 23:1-14 . . . 404
Deut 23:5 . . . 62
Deut 24:1-4 . . . 522
Deut 24:1–25:19 . . . 404
Deut 24:16 . . . 335, 542
Deut 24:18 . . . 122
Deut 26:16-19 . . . 161, 407
Deut 26:18 . . . 128n
Deut 27–28 . . . 418, 462
Deut 27:1-8 . . . 418
Deut 27:1-14 . . . 486
Deut 27:6-7 . . . 233
Deut 27:16 . . . 186
Deut 27:26 . . . 523
Deut 28 . . . 548
Deut 28:1, 13 . . . 161
Deut 28:1-14 . . . 408
Deut 28:7 . . . 408
Deut 28:49-52 . . . 409
Deut 28:61 . . . 462
Deut 29–30 . . . 410
Deut 29:1-8 . . . 410
Deut 29:2-6 . . . 96
Deut 29:2–30:20 . . . 409
Deut 29:9-15 . . . 462
Deut 29:20 . . . 74
Deut 29:21 . . . 462
Deut 30:1-6 . . . 530
Deut 30:1-14 . . . 410
Deut 30:3 . . . 67, 409
Deut 30:10 . . . 462
Deut 31:1-8 . . . 414
Deut 31:6 . . . 471
Deut 31:9-13 . . . 376, 462, 475, 486, 562
Deut 31:10 . . . 483
Deut 31:11 . . . 411
Deut 31:15 . . . 78
Deut 31:19 . . . 411
Deut 31:21 . . . 298
Deut 31:24-29 . . . 421
Deut 31:26 . . . 411
Deut 32 . . . 60
Deut 32:5-6, 15-33 . . . 411
Deut 32:8-9 . . . 113
Deut 32:12, 39 . . . 331
Deut 32:15 . . . 117

Deut 32:32 225
Deut 32:40 55
Deut 32:44-48 38
Deut 32:45-52 411
Deut 32:48-52 388
Deut 32:50 210
Deut 33:2-3 577
Deut 33:5 138
Deut 33:7 . . . . . 106n
Deut 33:8 362
Deut 33:10 161
Deut 33:21 236
Deut 33:29 177
Deut 33:27 54
Deut 34:10 411
Deut 34:10-12 . . . . . 387, 403
Deut 34:11-12 96

Josh 1:1-5 194
Josh 1:1-9 414
Josh 1:3-5 134
Josh 1:5, 9 415
Josh 1:16 414
Josh 2:24 416
Josh 3:1-4 416
Josh 5:14 417
Josh 6:2-21 386
Josh 6:17 417
Josh 6:24-25 426
Josh 7 417
Josh 7:6 419
Josh 7:10 77
Josh 7:24-26 335
Josh 8:26 418
Josh 8:30-35 . . . . . 376, 418, 486
Josh 10:1, 28, 35, 37, 39-40 . . 418
Josh 10:24 247
Josh 11:11-12, 20-21 418
Josh 11:17 396
Josh 14:1-2 99
Josh 15:1 99
Josh 16:1 99
Josh 17:1, 14, 17 99
Josh 18:1 . . . . . 252, 280
Josh 22 419
Josh 22:5 420
Josh 22:21-34 231
Josh 23 420
Josh 24 419
Josh 24:1-27 288
Josh 24:8-13 194
Josh 24:15 . . . . . 423, 455
Josh 24:13 390
Josh 24:16-20 96
Josh 24:19 74
Josh 24:25-27 376

Judg 1–2 421
Judg 1:17 418
Judg 2:1-3 422
Judg 2:7 . . . . . 143n
Judg 2:10 210
Judg 2:10-19 422
Judg 3:3 396
Judg 3:7, 12 422
Judg 4:1 422
Judg 5:11 59
Judg 5:14 252
Judg 6–9 422
Judg 6:1 422
Judg 6:10 422
Judg 6:11-24 82
Judg 6:12 78
Judg 6:14 116
Judg 6:15 185
Judg 6:17 . . . . . 65, 97
Judg 6:24 231
Judg 6:24-26 401
Judg 6:24, 28 423
Judg 6:34 386
Judg 7:2, 7 116
Judg 7:13 78
Judg 7:17-18 386
Judg 8:22 . . . . . 138, 421
Judg 8:22-23 . . . . . 43, 423
Judg 8:33 396
Judg 9 . . . . . 138, 423
Judg 10:6 422
Judg 13:1 422
Judg 13:1-5 83
Judg 13:3, 10 78
Judg 13:18-23 401
Judg 17–18 424
Judg 17:1-4 424
Judg 18:1 421
Judg 18:30 424
Judg 18:31 252
Judg 19–21 424
Judg 19:1 421
Judg 21:11 418
Judg 21:25 421

Ruth 1:1 425
Ruth 1:20-21 86
Ruth 4:18-21 . . . . . 436, 439
Ruth 4:21 425

1 Sam 1–3 427
1 Sam 1:3 252
1 Sam 1:3-11 428
1 Sam 1:24 446
1 Sam 2:1 120
1 Sam 2:2 57
1 Sam 2:3 51
1 Sam 2:5b, 8 575
1 Sam 2:8-9 428
1 Sam 2:10 . . . . . 510, 573, 584
1 Sam 2:12-17, 22-25 . . . 428, 429
1 Sam 2:12-25 522
1 Sam 2:13-15 179
1 Sam 2:29 429
1 Sam 2:34 97
1 Sam 3:1 . . . . . 80, 88
1 Sam 3:1-18 77
1 Sam 3:1-21 . . . . . 88, 90
1 Sam 3:15 80
1 Sam 3:19-21 . . . . . 88, 428
1 Sam 4–6 429
1 Sam 4:3 117
1 Sam 4:4 321
1 Sam 4:4-11 522
1 Sam 4:11 . . . . . 434, 474
1 Sam 4:20 180
1 Sam 5:1-5 334
1 Sam 5:1–6:12 434
1 Sam 6:20 271
1 Sam 7:1-4 429
1 Sam 7:2-4 434
1 Sam 7:2 474
1 Sam 7:3-4 429
1 Sam 7:8 118
1 Sam 7:15-17 427
1 Sam 8–12 429
1 Sam 8:1-3 429
1 Sam 8:5 . . . . . 138, 406, 429 (2)
1 Sam 8:7 . . . . . 43, 427
1 Sam 8:10-18 430
1 Sam 9–31 468
1 Sam 9:6-9 492
1 Sam 9:9 91
1 Sam 9:12-13 401
1 Sam 9:16 118
1 Sam 10:1 427
1 Sam 10:1-7 91
1 Sam 10:3 289
1 Sam 10:3-4 446
1 Sam 10:5 . . . . . 92 (2)
1 Sam 10:7, 9 97
1 Sam 10:19 117
1 Sam 12:7 59
1 Sam 12:24-25 430
1 Sam 13:13 190
1 Sam 13:14 . . . . . 430, 436, 437
1 Sam 14:6 117
1 Sam 14:23 117
1 Sam 15:1-35 431
1 Sam 15:3-21 418
1 Sam 15:22 . . . . . 431, 625
1 Sam 15:28 436
1 Sam 16:1 . . . . . 190, 236, 430
1 Sam 16:1-12 432

1 Sam 16:2-12 . . . 436
1 Sam 16:6-13 . . . 472
1 Sam 16:12-13 . . . 190
1 Sam 16:13 . . . 427
1 Sam 16:13-14 . . . 432n
1 Sam 16–2 Sam 5 . . . 427
1 Sam 17:32 . . . 180
1 Sam 17:47 . . . 117
1 Sam 18:1 . . . 432
1 Sam 18:12, 28-29 . . . 432
1 Sam 19:18-24 . . . 91
1 Sam 20:13 . . . 432
1 Sam 21:1-6 . . . 447
1 Sam 21:1-9 . . . 474
1 Sam 22:5 . . . 92 (2)
1 Sam 22:20-23 . . . 449
1 Sam 23:6, 9-12 . . . 449
1 Sam 23:17 . . . 432
1 Sam 24 . . . 432
1 Sam 24:6 . . . 180
1 Sam 24:20 . . . 432
1 Sam 25:1 . . . 491n
1 Sam 26 . . . 432
1 Sam 26:25 . . . 432
1 Sam 28:6 . . . 100, 362
1 Sam 29:9 . . . 145

2 Sam 2:1-4 . . . 433
2 Sam 3:18 . . . 118
2 Sam 4:9 . . . 124
2 Sam 5 . . . 427
2 Sam 5:2 . . . 433
2 Sam 6 . . . 427
2 Sam 6:1-5 . . . 474
2 Sam 6:1-20 . . . 447
2 Sam 6:2 . . . 321
2 Sam 6:12-19 . . . 445
2 Sam 6:17 . . . 291, 442, 474
2 Sam 7 . . . 427, 434n, 435, 632
2 Sam 7:1-2 . . . 434
2 Sam 7:2 . . . 92, 291, 448
2 Sam 7:3 . . . 434
2 Sam 7:4-16 . . . 492
2 Sam 7:5 . . . 448
2 Sam 7:5-11 . . . 582
2 Sam 7:5-16 . . . 92
2 Sam 7:8 . . . 437
2 Sam 7:8-16 . . . 190, 580
2 Sam 7:9-16 . . . 437
2 Sam 7:11 . . . 441
2 Sam 7:12 . . . 211
2 Sam 7:12-16 . . . 69
2 Sam 7:13 . . . 439, 442
2 Sam 7:14 . . . 470
2 Sam 7:15 . . . 68
2 Sam 7:21 . . . 437
2 Sam 7:23 . . . 123
2 Sam 8 . . . 427
2 Sam 8:1-14 . . . 579
2 Sam 8:11 . . . 280
2 Sam 8:14 . . . 440
2 Sam 8:18 . . . 448
2 Sam 9–20 . . . 427
2 Sam 12:1-12 . . . 492
2 Sam 12:7-12 . . . 92
2 Sam 12:13 . . . 454
2 Sam 12:22 . . . 65, 68
2 Sam 12:23 . . . 211
2 Sam 12:24 . . . 441
2 Sam 12:24-25 . . . 63
2 Sam 12:25 . . . 92
2 Sam 13:33 . . . 180
2 Sam 14:17, 20 . . . 145
2 Sam 15:24-29 . . . 448
2 Sam 17:10 . . . 180
2 Sam 19:27 . . . 145
2 Sam 22:3 . . . 117
2 Sam 22:16 . . . 145
2 Sam 22:39 . . . 247
2 Sam 23:3 . . . 203
2 Sam 23:5 . . . 435, 440
2 Sam 24 . . . 470
2 Sam 24:1-17 . . . 291
2 Sam 24:10 . . . 180
2 Sam 24:11 . . . 91, 92 (2)
2 Sam 24:14 . . . 104
2 Sam 24:18 . . . 470
2 Sam 24:18-19 . . . 92
2 Sam 24:18-25 . . . 448
2 Sam 24:20 . . . 470
2 Sam 24:25 . . . 292

1 Kings 1–2 . . . 448
1 Kings 1–11 . . . 440
1 Kings 1:2 . . . 396
1 Kings 1:8-10 . . . 92
1 Kings 1:11-14 . . . 441
1 Kings 1:22-24 . . . 92
1 Kings 1:29 . . . 124
1 Kings 1:32-35 . . . 449
1 Kings 1:32-40, 45 . . . 92
1 Kings 2:1-4 . . . 441
1 Kings 2:10 . . . 211
1 Kings 3:3 . . . 442
1 Kings 3:3-4 . . . 445
1 Kings 3:4 . . . 434, 449
1 Kings 3:4-5 . . . 442
1 Kings 3:5 . . . 78
1 Kings 3:8 . . . 70
1 Kings 4:20-34 . . . 439
1 Kings 4:32-34 . . . 625
1 Kings 5:3 . . . 247
1 Kings 6:29, 32 . . . 443
1 Kings 8 . . . 476
1 Kings 8:1-5 . . . 449
1 Kings 8:3-9 . . . 443
1 Kings 8:6-11 . . . 141, 574
1 Kings 8:10 . . . 443
1 Kings 8:23 . . . 68, 180
1 Kings 8:23-24 . . . 444
1 Kings 8:23-61 . . . 443
1 Kings 8:24 . . . 353
1 Kings 8:29-30 . . . 452
1 Kings 8:30, 34, 36, 39, 50 . . . 73
1 Kings 8:46 . . . 73, 636
1 Kings 8:50b-53 . . . 476
1 Kings 8:56-57 . . . 445
1 Kings 9:1-9 . . . 452
1 Kings 9:2 . . . 78
1 Kings 9:25 . . . 449
1 Kings 11:1-8 . . . 477
1 Kings 11:1-13 . . . 442
1 Kings 11:4-6 . . . 453
1 Kings 11:4-8 . . . 449
1 Kings 11:9 . . . 72, 78
1 Kings 11:43 . . . 211
1 Kings 12:25–13:34 . . . 463
1 Kings 12:26-33 . . . 424
1 Kings 12:28-33 . . . 450
1 Kings 12:28-29 . . . 289
1 Kings 12:31-33 . . . 453
1 Kings 13:1-3 . . . 289, 424, 463
1 Kings 13:1-5 . . . 97
1 Kings 13:18 . . . 145
1 Kings 14:20 . . . 211
1 Kings 14:22-24 . . . 454
1 Kings 15:3 . . . 454
1 Kings 15:4-5 . . . 454
1 Kings 15:9-24 . . . 479
1 Kings 15:26 . . . 454
1 Kings 15:29 . . . 176
1 Kings 16:13 . . . 454
1 Kings 16:32-33 . . . 455
1 Kings 17:17 . . . 176
1 Kings 18 . . . 492
1 Kings 18:3-4 . . . 93
1 Kings 18:4 . . . 455
1 Kings 18:16-40 . . . 88
1 Kings 18:18 . . . 396
1 Kings 18:20 . . . 450
1 Kings 18:21 . . . 423, 455
1 Kings 18:30-38 . . . 401
1 Kings 18:37 . . . 456
1 Kings 20:13-14, 22, 28 . . . 456
1 Kings 22:5-8 . . . 456
1 Kings 22:19 . . . 144
1 Kings 22:53 . . . 456
1 Kings 12–2 Kings 17 . . . 440
1 Kings 17–2 Kings 8 . . . 440

2 Kings 1:2 . . . 457

2 Kings 1:16 93
2 Kings 2:3 . . . . 93 (2)
2 Kings 2:5 93
2 Kings 2:12 93
2 Kings 2:19 . . . . 93 (2)
2 Kings 5:14 179
2 Kings 5:15 457
2 Kings 6:1-6. 93
2 Kings 8. 440
2 Kings 8:19 457
2 Kings 9:1-10. 93
2 Kings 9:24-29. 457
2 Kings 10:18-27. 457
2 Kings 10:29 290
2 Kings 11:1-3. 459
2 Kings 11:17 459
2 Kings 12:4-16. 459
2 Kings 13:23 . . . . 66, 67, 458
2 Kings 14:11-14. 459
2 Kings 14:25 498
2 Kings 14:27 117
2 Kings 15:1-7. 479
2 Kings 16:10-14. . . . . . . 450, 460
2 Kings 16:15b 231
2 Kings 17. 440
2 Kings 17:2 458
2 Kings 17:7-13. 404
2 Kings 17:7-20. 524
2 Kings 17:7-22. 332
2 Kings 17:7b-8. 458
2 Kings 17:36 266
2 Kings 18–25. 440
2 Kings 18:4 460
2 Kings 19:1 460
2 Kings 19:15 . . . . 44, 321
2 Kings 19:15-18. 461
2 Kings 19:19 117
2 Kings 19:22 57
2 Kings 20:1-11. 97
2 Kings 20:3 461
2 Kings 21:2-3. 461
2 Kings 21:6 450
2 Kings 21:14 461
2 Kings 21:19-22. 461
2 Kings 22:3-7. 461
2 Kings 22:15-17. 462
2 Kings 22:30 210
2 Kings 23:1-3. 462
2 Kings 23:15-16. . . . . 97, 463
2 Kings 23:21-23. 481
2 Kings 23:34 526
2 Kings 24:4 74
2 Kings 24:5-6. 526
2 Kings 24:15 526
2 Kings 24:20 73
2 Kings 25:27-30. . . . . . . 463, 482
2 Kings 27:8–23:25. 383

1 Chron 1. 167
1 Chron 1:1–9:34 466
1 Chron 1:27. 467
1 Chron 1:28, 34 439
1 Chron 2:1-17 439
1 Chron 6:1-81 467
1 Chron 6:3 467
1 Chron 6:54-81 99
1 Chron 10:1-14 468
1 Chron 11:1-2 468
1 Chron 11:2. 433
1 Chron 12:1-40 468
1 Chron 13:1-14 468
1 Chron 13:1-4 468
1 Chron 13:6 475
1 Chron 15:1–16:3 468
1 Chron 15:2. 469
1 Chron 15:11-15 469
1 Chron 15:27–16:3 469
1 Chron 16:8-36 469
1 Chron 16:11 . . . . 140, 572
1 Chron 16:17 387
1 Chron 16:35 117
1 Chron 16:36 55
1 Chron 17:11 546
1 Chron 17:11-14 . . . . . 510, 511, 531, 578
1 Chron 17:21 123
1 Chron 18:7-8, 11 472
1 Chron 21:1 . . . . . 146, 205, 206, 304, 617
1 Chron 21:18 470
1 Chron 21:20-21 470
1 Chron 21:26 292
1 Chron 21:29 291
1 Chron 22:1 291
1 Chron 22:2-5 472
1 Chron 22:5 . . . . 470, 474
1 Chron 22:6-10 347
1 Chron 22:13 471
1 Chron 22:18 280
1 Chron 23:2. 471
1 Chron 24:5, 7, 31 99
1 Chron 25:5 92
1 Chron 27. 471
1 Chron 28:2-3 472
1 Chron 28:2. . . . . 472, 475
1 Chron 28:4 472
1 Chron 28:9. 298
1 Chron 28:12 . . . . 352, 472
1 Chron 29:1-5 104
1 Chron 29:1 473
1 Chron 29:11 48
1 Chron 29:11-12 473

2 Chron 1:1–9:31 466
2 Chron 1:2-6 . . . . 442, 474
2 Chron 1:3-6 434
2 Chron 1:12. 474
2 Chron 2:1 474
2 Chron 3–4. 475
2 Chron 3:1 290
2 Chron 3:14. 475
2 Chron 4:1 358
2 Chron 5:2-14 475
2 Chron 5:3. 475
2 Chron 5:13. 68
2 Chron 5:14. 476
2 Chron 6:36. 73
2 Chron 6:40-42 476
2 Chron 7:1-3 476
2 Chron 7:3, 6 68
2 Chron 7:14. 74
2 Chron 9:8 475
2 Chron 13:4-12 478
2 Chron 13:8. 278
2 Chron 13:11 356
2 Chron 14:2-15 479
2 Chron 17:3. 479
2 Chron 18:18 144
2 Chron 20:6 48
2 Chron 20:6-9 325
2 Chron 20:21 68
2 Chron 21:4–22:9 479
2 Chron 23:3, 16 637
2 Chron 25:8. 48
2 Chron 26:1-23 479
2 Chron 26:15 450
2 Chron 29:3-11 460
2 Chron 30:1-27 480
2 Chron 30:6 325
2 Chron 30:9 66
2 Chron 31:1 480
2 Chron 32:24 97
2 Chron 33:10-13 461
2 Chron 34:3-7 481
2 Chron 34:28 210
2 Chron 35:3 481
2 Chron 35:16-19 536
2 Chron 36:15 64
2 Chron 36:22-28 507

Ezra 1:1-4 507
Ezra 1:1-5 557
Ezra 1:2-4 482
Ezra 1:2 . . . . 483, 485
Ezra 2:36-58, 61-63 483
Ezra 2:63. 362

Ezra 3:1-6 483
Ezra 3:8-13 557
Ezra 3:12. . . . . 484, 557
Ezra 4:1-24 483
Ezra 6:3-12 484

Ezra 6:9 . . . 485
Ezra 6:10 . . . 485
Ezra 7:10 . . . 484
Ezra 7:12 . . . 485
Ezra 7:12-26 . . . 485
Ezra 7:23 . . . 485
Ezra 9:15 . . . 59

Neh 1:1 . . . 80
Neh 1:4 . . . 485
Neh 1:5 . . . 69, 553
Neh 1:10 . . . 123
Neh 2:4 . . . 485, 553
Neh 2:8 . . . 485 (2)
Neh 2:18 . . . 485
Neh 2:20 . . . 485, 553
Neh 4:22 . . . 177
Neh 5:5 . . . 280
Neh 7:1-3 . . . 486
Neh 7:65 . . . 362
Neh 7:64-65 . . . 486
Neh 8:1 . . . 486
Neh 8:1-3, 13-18 . . . 476
Neh 8:1-18 . . . 562
Neh 9:3 . . . 486
Neh 9:5 . . . 55
Neh 9:7-8 . . . 325
Neh 9:17 . . . 65 (2), 67, 71
Neh 9:19, 27-28 . . . 67
Neh 9:31 . . . 65, 66
Neh 9:32 . . . 69
Neh 9:33 . . . 70
Neh 9:38 . . . 637
Neh 9:38–10:39 . . . 487
Neh 10:39 . . . 487
Neh 13:23-27 . . . 487
Neh 13:30 . . . 487

Esth 1:4-8 . . . 488
Esth 9:18-28 . . . 488

Job 1–2 . . . 157, 205
Job 1:6 . . . 312, 317, 576
Job 1:6-7 . . . 304
Job 1:7 . . . 206, 208
Job 1:8 . . . 207
Job 1:12 . . . 145
Job 2:1 . . . 317, 576
Job 2:1-2 . . . 304
Job 2:2 . . . 206
Job 3:8 . . . 133
Job 3:17 . . . 212
Job 4:15 . . . 179
Job 4:18 . . . 145
Job 5:7 . . . 605
Job 5:15 . . . 117
Job 5:17 . . . 86
Job 5:20 . . . 125
Job 6:4, 14 . . . 86
Job 7:6 . . . 145
Job 7:17 . . . 180
Job 7:21 . . . 73, 211
Job 8:3 . . . 61, 86
Job 8:5 . . . 86
Job 9:4 . . . 47, 51
Job 9:8 . . . 133, 266
Job 10:4 . . . 179
Job 10:16 . . . 47
Job 11:7 . . . 86
Job 12:10 . . . 176
Job 12:25 . . . 131
Job 13:3 . . . 86
Job 14:14 . . . 214
Job 16:13 . . . 64
Job 19 . . . 214
Job 19:13, 19 . . . 594
Job 19:25 . . . 122, 124, 214
Job 19:27 . . . 180
Job 21:22 . . . 51
Job 21:26 . . . 212
Job 22 . . . 610
Job 22:29 . . . 117
Job 26:12 . . . 46, 133, 322
Job 26:13 . . . 146
Job 30:18 . . . 47
Job 30:27 . . . 182
Job 33:4 . . . 45
Job 36:22 . . . 47
Job 37:23 . . . 59
Job 38–41 . . . 615
Job 38:7 . . . 144
Job 38:8 . . . 266
Job 41:1 . . . 133

Ps 1 . . . 585, 589
Ps 1:1 . . . 586
Ps 2 . . . 321, 322n, 578, 579 (2)
Ps 2:1-2 . . . 319
Ps 2:6 . . . 257, 291
Ps 2:7 . . . 472, 579, 580, 597
Ps 2:8-9 . . . 579
Ps 2:9 . . . 579
Ps 2:12 . . . 257
Ps 3 . . . 591
Ps 3:7 . . . 118
Ps 3:8 . . . 117
Ps 4:1 . . . 59
Ps 5 . . . 595
Ps 5:2 . . . 139
Ps 6 . . . 591
Ps 6:4 . . . 119
Ps 6:5 . . . 68
Ps 7 . . . 119
Ps 7:5 . . . 181
Ps 7:9 . . . 59
Ps 7:11 . . . 59, 180
Ps 8 . . . 575, 577
Ps 8:4 . . . 178
Ps 8:4-6 . . . 137
Ps 8:5 . . . 579
Ps 9 . . . 61, 571
Ps 9:5 . . . 319
Ps 9:7 . . . 55, 570
Ps 9:8 . . . 59
Ps 9:11 . . . 291
Ps 9:14 . . . 120
Ps 10 . . . 571
Ps 10:14 . . . 177
Ps 11:4 . . . 571
Ps 11:7 . . . 59, 63
Ps 13 . . . 591
Ps 13:5 . . . 120
Ps 13:6 . . . 68
Ps 14:1 . . . 588
Ps 14:7 . . . 118
Ps 15 . . . 585
Ps 16 . . . 181
Ps 16:7 . . . 180
Ps 16:9-10 . . . 210
Ps 16:10 . . . 213
Ps 16:11 . . . 581
Ps 17:7 . . . 265
Ps 17:9 . . . 595
Ps 18:2 . . . 584
Ps 18:8 . . . 141
Ps 18:27 . . . 119
Ps 18:28 . . . 103
Ps 18:43-50 . . . 579
Ps 18:50 . . . 68
Ps 19:1-6 . . . 76
Ps 19:14 . . . 122, 124
Ps 20:9 . . . 118
Ps 21 . . . 595
Ps 22 . . . 571, 591
Ps 22:3 . . . 57, 271
Ps 22:28 . . . 140, 572
Ps 23 . . . 586
Ps 23:6 . . . 68
Ps 24 . . . 265, 571
Ps 24:7 . . . 137
Ps 25:6 . . . 66
Ps 25:7 . . . 68
Ps 25:8-10 . . . 598
Ps 25:10 . . . 69
Ps 25:11 . . . 73
Ps 25:16 . . . 66
Ps 25:22 . . . 126
Ps 26:1-3 . . . 586
Ps 26:2 . . . 181
Ps 26:11 . . . 124
Ps 27:7-9 . . . 599

Ps 27:9. 177
Ps 29 .571
Ps 29:1. 144
Ps 29:2. 56
Ps 29:10. 55
Ps 30 .181
Ps 31:5. . . . . .70, 124, 177
Ps 31:9-24 592
Ps 31:16. . . . . .68, 119
Ps 32:1-5 454
Ps 32:5. 74
Ps 32:10. 68
Ps 33 .571
Ps 33:4. 70
Ps 33:5. 63
Ps 33:7. . . . . .133, 266
Ps 33:22. 68
Ps 34 .586
Ps 34:7. 146
Ps 34:18. 117
Ps 35 .595
Ps 35:3. 117
Ps 35:24. 59
Ps 35:28. 60
Ps 36 .599
Ps 36:5. 69
Ps 36:6. 61
Ps 37 .587
Ps 37:28. 63
Ps 38:1-8 592
Ps 40:10. 60
Ps 40:10-11 69
Ps 40:11. . . . . .67, 70
Ps 40:12. 180
Ps 41:5. 596
Ps 41:13. 55
Ps 43:3. 70
Ps 44 . . . . .139, 572, 592
Ps 44:3. 266
Ps 44:26. . . . . 124 (2)
Ps 44:27. 68
Ps 45 .579
Ps 45:5. 319
Ps 45:7. 63
Ps 46 .582
Ps 46:1-3 572
Ps 47 . . . . 44, 139, 140, 318, 572, 573, 583
Ps 47:3. 247
Ps 47:4. 62
Ps 47:8. 137
Ps 48 .139
Ps 48:2. 583
Ps 48:10. 59
Ps 49 .587
Ps 49:15. 126
Ps 50:1-2 583
Ps 50:3. 141
Ps 51:1. . . . . .67, 68
Ps 51:14. 60
Ps 52 .596
Ps 53:1. 588
Ps 53:6. . . . . .118, 583
Ps 54:1. 120
Ps 54:1-7 596
Ps 54:5. 70
Ps 55:16. 117
Ps 55:19. 55
Ps 56:4. 179
Ps 57:3. . . . . .69, 117
Ps 57:8. 181
Ps 57:10. 69
Ps 58 .596
Ps 59 .596
Ps 59:5. 319
Ps 61:7. 69
Ps 62:1. 117
Ps 63:2. . . . . .47, 179
Ps 64 .596
Ps 64:3. 68
Ps 65:5. 59
Ps 66:6. . . . . .134, 267
Ps 66:7. 55
Ps 67:1. 66
Ps 68 47
Ps 68:14. 86
Ps 68:19. 117
Ps 68:32. 572
Ps 69:4. 592
Ps 69:13. . . . . .68, 70
Ps 69:18. 124
Ps 69:35. . . . . .118, 583
Ps 71:2 .59
Ps 71:22. 57
Ps 71:24. 59
Ps 72 . . . . .63, 579
Ps 72:1. 61
Ps 72:8-9 280
Ps 72:11. . . . . .140, 572
Ps 72:13. 119
Ps 73 .588
Ps 73:21-22 180
Ps 74 . . . . .133, 139
Ps 74:1-11 593
Ps 74:2. . . . . .123, 291
Ps 74:12. 117
Ps 74:13. . . . . .46, 266
Ps 76:1-2 433
Ps 76:2. . . . . .291, 446
Ps 76:6-9 111
Ps 77 . . . . .49, 134, 267
Ps 77:9. 67
Ps 78 . . . . .49, 49n
Ps 78:35. 122
Ps 78:38. 67
Ps 78:39. 179
Ps 78:40-56 96
Ps 78:68. 62
Ps 78:70. 70
Ps 79:5. 73
Ps 79:8. 67
Ps 80 .593
Ps 80:17. 581
Ps 82:1. . . . . .144, 576
Ps 83 . . . . .594, 597
Ps 84:11. 66
Ps 82:5. 103
Ps 85:6. 73
Ps 85:7. 68
Ps 85:11. 70
Ps 86:15. . . . . . . 64, 65 (2), 66, 71
Ps 86:16. 118
Ps 87 .583
Ps 88 . . . . 211 (2), 212n, 594
Ps 88:1. 117
Ps 89 . . . . 45, 268, 322, 572, 580, 594
Ps 89:3-4 435
Ps 89:5. 70
Ps 89:9-10 266
Ps 89:10. 133
Ps 89:11-13 45
Ps 89:14. 61
Ps 89:15. 103
Ps 89:16. 60
Ps 89:18. 57
Ps 89:24. 584
Ps 89:26. 117
Ps 89:28. . . . . .69, 435
Ps 89:34. 435
Ps 89:35. 56
Ps 90:2. 54
Ps 91 .119
Ps 91:1. 86
Ps 91:4. 70
Ps 91:11. 146
Ps 92:8. 55
Ps 92:10. 584
Ps 93 . . . . 44, 139, 140, 141, 318, 319, 573 (2)
Ps 93:1. . . . . .141, 574
Ps 93:2. 54
Ps 94:8-15 589
Pss 95–99 . . . . .44, 139
Ps 95 .319
Ps 95:1-2 573
Pss 96–99 318
Ps 96 . . . . .140, 320, 573
Ps 96:13. . . . . .59, 61, 70
Ps 97 . . . . 140, 141, 320, 573, 574
Ps 97:1. . . . . .141, 574

Ps 98 . . . . 141, 320, 574
Ps 98:9. . . . . 59, 61, 140
Ps 99 . . . . 57, 140, 141, 321, 573, 574
Ps 99:2. 141
Ps 99:4. 61
Ps 99:8. 73
Ps 101:1. 61
Ps 102 . . . . 583, 594
Ps 102:12. 55
Ps 102:12-17 225
Ps 102:12-22 574
Ps 102:13. 67
Ps 102:22. . . . . 140, 572
Ps 103 145
Ps 103:3. 73
Ps 103:4. 125
Ps 103:6. 59
Ps 103:8. . . . . 64, 66, 71
Ps 103:11. 68
Ps 103:13. 67
Ps 103:17. 68
Ps 103:19. 278
Ps 103:19-22 575
Ps 104 45
Ps 104:1-4 575
Ps 104:4. 145
Ps 104:24. 51
Ps 104:25-30 45
Ps 104:26. 133
Ps 105:1-15 469
Ps 105:5. 96
Ps 105:9. 599
Ps 105:20. 203
Ps 105:26. 70
Ps 105:27. 96
Ps 105:31. 135
Ps 106 . . . . 50, 54, 120
Ps 106:1. 68
Ps 106:9. . . . . 134, 267 (2)
Ps 106:11. 267
Ps 106:44-46 599
Ps 106:47. 118
Ps 107 124
Ps 107:1-2 125
Ps 107:1. 68
Ps 107:13. 117
Ps 108:1. 181
Ps 108:6. . . . . 118, 265
Ps 109 597
Ps 109:21. 68
Ps 109:26. 119
Ps 110 . . . . 322, 447 (2), 451, 562, 580, 581 (2)
Ps 110:2. 280
Ps 110:4. 447
Ps 111 599
Ps 111:3. 60
Ps 111:4. . . . . 65, 66
Ps 111:7-8 70
Ps 111:10. 623
Ps 112 589
Ps 112:3. 60
Ps 112:4. 131
Ps 112:9. 60
Ps 113:4-6 575
Ps 115:9. . . . . 106n
Ps 115:11. . . . . 106n
Ps 115:16. 577
Ps 116:5. . . . . 59, 65, 66
Ps 117:2. 599
Ps 118:1-4 68
Ps 118:7. 177
Ps 118:14. 117
Ps 118:21. 117
Ps 118:25. 118
Ps 118:29. 68
Ps 119:29. 66
Ps 119:41. 68
Ps 119:58. 66
Ps 119:86. 70
Ps 119:90. 70
Ps 119:137. 59
Ps 119:138. 70
Ps 119:142. 60
Ps 119:156. 66
Ps 119:166. 117
Ps 121:2. . . . . 106n
Ps 122 584
Ps 124:8. . . . . 106n
Ps 126 584
Ps 127 589
Ps 128 589
Ps 129:4. 59
Ps 130 . . . . 126, 599
Ps 132 . . . . 448, 584
Ps 132:1. 476
Ps 132:1-12 582
Ps 132:8-10 476
Ps 132:13. 291
Ps 133 589
Ps 135:4. . . . . 128n, 270
Ps 135:8-12 96
Ps 136 68
Ps 139:1-4 589
Ps 139:13. 180
Ps 139:19-22 598
Ps 141:2. 358
Ps 143:6. 176
Ps 143:11. 59
Ps 145 600
Ps 145:3. 575
Ps 145:4-7 575
Ps 145:6. 49
Ps 145:8. . . . . 65, 66, 71
Ps 145:9. 66
Ps 145:11-13 278
Ps 145:13. 55
Ps 145:17. 59
Ps 145:19. 119
Ps 146:6. 70
Ps 146:8. 63
Ps 146:10. 55
Ps 147:11. 68
Ps 148:2. 145
Ps 149:4. 119
Ps 150:2. 49
Ps 150:6. 176

Prov 3:1. 624
Prov 3:19. 51
Prov 3:34. 66
Prov 4:18-19 103
Prov 5 627
Prov 5:11. 179
Prov 7 627
Prov 7:23. 181
Prov 8 . . . . 625, 626
Prov 8:35-36 626
Prov 10:8. 180
Prov 13:9. 103
Prov 14:30. 179
Prov 15:8. 625
Prov 20:22. 119
Prov 21:12. 59
Prov 22:17. 180
Prov 23:15-16 180
Prov 28:4. 624
Prov 28:15. 203

Eccl 1:1, 12 632
Eccl 1:3 637
Eccl 2:13 131
Eccl 2:19, 22 637
Eccl 3:21 177
Eccl 5:18 637
Eccl 6:12 637
Eccl 8:9, 15, 17 637
Eccl 8:15 633
Eccl 10:4 203
Eccl 11:9–12:7 636
Eccl 12:7 177
Eccl 12:8 633

Song of Sol 5:4 182

Isa 1:1 80
Isa 1:4 271
Isa 1:4b 502
Isa 1:10-17 624
Isa 1:18-19 505

Isa 1:27 . . . 126
Isa 2:1-5 . . . 516
Isa 2:3-5 . . . 519
Isa 2:6-8 . . . 502
Isa 2:9 . . . 74
Isa 2:19, 21 . . . 557
Isa 2:22 . . . 176
Isa 3:8-9 . . . 225
Isa 4:2 . . . 535
Isa 4:2-6 . . . 510
Isa 5:1-4 . . . 503
Isa 5:1-7 . . . 593
Isa 5:16 . . . 59, 62
Isa 5:20 . . . 103, 131
Isa 5:24 . . . 72
Isa 6 . . . 502
Isa 6:1 . . . 141, 574
Isa 6:1-3 . . . 352
Isa 6:1-7 . . . 57
Isa 6:3 . . . 271
Isa 6:5 . . . 137
Isa 6:8 . . . 104n
Isa 6:9-10 . . . 503, 512
Isa 7 . . . 510
Isa 7:3-17 . . . 97
Isa 7:14 . . . 510, 511, 578
Isa 8:3-4 . . . 97
Isa 8:6-8 . . . 503
Isa 8:18 . . . 98
Isa 9:3 . . . 579
Isa 9:6 . . . 54, 511, 579
Isa 9:6-7 . . . 578
Isa 9:12 . . . 503
Isa 9:17 . . . 67
Isa 10 . . . 505
Isa 10:5-6 . . . 303
Isa 10:18 . . . 179
Isa 10:20 . . . 271
Isa 10:20-21 . . . 505
Isa 11:1 . . . 510, 535
Isa 11:1-5 . . . 511, 578
Isa 11:2 . . . 512
Isa 11:5 . . . 70
Isa 11:6 . . . 148, 173
Isa 11:6-8 . . . 516
Isa 11:6-9 . . . 285
Isa 11:8 . . . 148
Isa 11:9-10 . . . 173
Isa 11:11-16 . . . 505
Isa 11:14 . . . 161
Isa 12:1 . . . 73
Isa 13:1-22 . . . 515
Isa 13:1–14:23 . . . 303
Isa 13:5 . . . 303
Isa 13:6 . . . 86
Isa 13:9 . . . 309
Isa 13:13 . . . 557
Isa 14:1 . . . 67, 505
Isa 14:2 . . . 161
Isa 14:3-23 . . . 311
Isa 14:4b-20 . . . 212
Isa 14:19 . . . 304
Isa 14:26-27 . . . 303
Isa 14:29 . . . 304
Isa 16:6 . . . 305
Isa 16:11 . . . 182
Isa 17:1-3 . . . 305
Isa 19:4 . . . 305
Isa 19:23-25 . . . 583
Isa 20:1-5 . . . 98
Isa 23:1-18 . . . 515
Isa 24 . . . 299
Isa 24–27 . . . 504
Isa 24:1 . . . 504
Isa 24:16 . . . 59
Isa 24:18 . . . 557
Isa 25:9 . . . 119
Isa 26:4 . . . 55
Isa 26:9 . . . 176
Isa 26:19 . . . 215
Isa 27:1 . . . 46, 133, 134, 146, 266
Isa 27:9 . . . 532
Isa 27:11 . . . 67
Isa 27:12-13 . . . 505
Isa 29:1-4 . . . 503
Isa 29:22-23 . . . 325
Isa 29:22-24 . . . 125
Isa 29:23 . . . 56
Isa 30:1 . . . 502
Isa 30:1-5 . . . 502
Isa 30:14 . . . 504
Isa 30:18-19 . . . 66
Isa 30:25-26 . . . 506
Isa 31:2 . . . 51
Isa 31:3 . . . 179
Isa 33:2 . . . 66
Isa 33:22 . . . 118, 139, 252
Isa 33:24 . . . 74
Isa 34 . . . 515
Isa 34:1-15 . . . 564
Isa 34:12 . . . 301
Isa 35 . . . 506
Isa 35:4 . . . 118
Isa 35:9 . . . 126
Isa 37:36 . . . 146
Isa 38:1-8 . . . 97
Isa 38:18 . . . 70
Isa 38:19 . . . 70
Isa 40 . . . 506
Isa 40–55 . . . 45, 46n, 102, 500
Isa 40–66 . . . 506, 511
Isa 40:5 . . . 179
Isa 40:10 . . . 47
Isa 40:18 . . . 169, 333
Isa 40:18-20 . . . 522
Isa 40:25 . . . 58
Isa 40:26 . . . 45, 107
Isa 40:28 . . . 54
Isa 41:2 . . . 511
Isa 41:7 . . . 334, 522
Isa 41:8-9 . . . 325
Isa 41:8-13 . . . 512
Isa 41:14 . . . 122, 124
Isa 41:20 . . . 45, 107
Isa 41:21-24 . . . 52
Isa 41:22-24 . . . 52
Isa 42:1 . . . 62
Isa 42:1-9 . . . 45
Isa 42:5 . . . 107
Isa 42:5-6a . . . 46
Isa 42:18-20 . . . 512
Isa 42:24 . . . 502
Isa 42:25 . . . 180
Isa 43 . . . 507
Isa 43:1 . . . 46, 108
Isa 43:3 . . . 123
Isa 43:4 . . . 63
Isa 43:11-12 . . . 118
Isa 43:14 . . . 122
Isa 43:15 . . . 139
Isa 43:19 . . . 507
Isa 43:27 . . . 502
Isa 44:3 . . . 512
Isa 44:6 . . . 139
Isa 44:6-8 . . . 53
Isa 44:9-11 . . . 334
Isa 44:9-20 . . . 461, 522
Isa 44:20 . . . 334
Isa 44:22 . . . 125
Isa 44:24 . . . 507
Isa 44:28–45:1 . . . 53, 63
Isa 45 . . . 108
Isa 45:1 . . . 507
Isa 45:7 . . . 132
Isa 45:9-10 . . . 46
Isa 45:12 . . . 46
Isa 45:20 . . . 118
Isa 45:21 . . . 59
Isa 46:7 . . . 118
Isa 46:13 . . . 59
Isa 47:1-15 . . . 224, 515
Isa 47:5 . . . 304
Isa 47:13 . . . 118
Isa 47:15 . . . 118
Isa 48:14 . . . 63
Isa 48:14-15 . . . 224
Isa 48:20 . . . 125, 508
Isa 49:1-6 . . . 120
Isa 49:6 . . . 189, 512
Isa 49:7 . . . 70 (2), 140, 572
Isa 49:10 . . . 66

Isa 49:13 . . . . .67, 508
Isa 49:23 . . . . .140, 572
Isa 49:24-26 120
Isa 49:25 120
Isa 50. 513
Isa 50:4-11 513
Isa 51:1-2 508
Isa 51:1-3 325
Isa 51:4 322
Isa 51:9-10 267
Isa 51:11 126
Isa 51:17, 22 526
Isa 52:5 203
Isa 52:7 508
Isa 52:9 125
Isa 52:13-15 513
Isa 52:13–53:12. . . . . . . .432, 513
Isa 53. 562
Isa 53:6 588
Isa 53:7 235
Isa 54:1, 4 509
Isa 54:5-6 343
Isa 54:7-8 67
Isa 54:8 68
Isa 54:10 66
Isa 55:3 . . . . .69, 509
Isa 55:6-13 517
Isa 55:7 . . . . .67, 74
Isa 56. 516
Isa 56–66. 500
Isa 56:2 366
Isa 56:10 79
Isa 57:15 55
Isa 59:1-2 119
Isa 59:13 180
Isa 60:1-22 517
Isa 60:10 67
Isa 60:14 . . . . .223, 225
Isa 60:20 55
Isa 61:8 . . . . .63, 71
Isa 62:12 223
Isa 63:1 117
Isa 63:4 180
Isa 63:7 66
Isa 63:9 123
Isa 63:15 . . . . .67, 182
Isa 63:16 . . . . .55, 108
Isa 63:17 189
Isa 64:8 175
Isa 65:17-18 109
Isa 65:17–66:24. 518
Isa 65:18-25 518
Isa 65:25 285
Isa 66:8 . . . . .518, 562

Jer 1:10 . . . . .523, 531
Jer 2 .522
Jer 2:27-28 118
Jer 3:1-5 522
Jer 3:1-10 522
Jer 3:6 343
Jer 3:8 343
Jer 3:14 . . . . .343, 529
Jer 3:16 180
Jer 3:20 343
Jer 4:1 529
Jer 4:5-31 524
Jer 4:19 182
Jer 4:23 102
Jer 5:5 522
Jer 5:7 . . . . .73, 343
Jer 5:22 . . . . .133, 266
Jer 6:1-8 524
Jer 6:15 522
Jer 7:3-8 529
Jer 7:9-11 522
Jer 7:22-23 624
Jer 7:24 180
Jer 7:31 180
Jer 9:2 343
Jer 9:14 396
Jer 9:16 524
Jer 9:25-26 529
Jer 10:1-16 522
Jer 10:3-9 334
Jer 10:6 48
Jer 10:7 137
Jer 10:10 55
Jer 10:11 334
Jer 10:12 . . . . .47, 51
Jer 11:1-8 523
Jer 11:12 118
Jer 11:20 181
Jer 12:1 59
Jer 12:2 180
Jer 12:15 67
Jer 13:14 67
Jer 13:19 524
Jer 13:27 343
Jer 14:14 . . . . 80 (2)
Jer 14:19 529
Jer 15:14 524
Jer 15:19 530
Jer 15:20 119
Jer 15:21 125
Jer 16:5 67
Jer 16:10-11 524
Jer 16:19 530
Jer 17:10 181
Jer 17:19-22 366
Jer 18–19. 525
Jer 18:1-6 175
Jer 19:4-5 525
Jer 20:12 181
Jer 20:14-18 634
Jer 21:1-14 525
Jer 22. 525
Jer 23:5 . . . . .510, 534
Jer 23:5-6 578
Jer 23:6 535
Jer 23:10 523
Jer 23:14 225
Jer 23:16 . . . . 80 (2)
Jer 23:25-28 79
Jer 24. 530
Jer 25:11 549
Jer 25:11-12 . . . . .90, 482
Jer 25:15-38 526
Jer 27:1-11 527
Jer 27:5 266
Jer 28:1-7 90
Jer 28:16-17 90
Jer 29:10 . . . . .530, 549
Jer 29:10-14 482
Jer 30–31. 530
Jer 30:5-24 565
Jer 30:10-11 120–121
Jer 30:18 67
Jer 31 533
Jer 31:3 . . . . .63, 531
Jer 31:7 118
Jer 31:11 126
Jer 31:20 182
Jer 31:29-30 335
Jer 31:31-34 . . . . . . 530, 533 (2), 534, 545
Jer 31:31-37 531
Jer 31:32 343
Jer 31:33 409
Jer 31:35-36 580
Jer 32:17 47
Jer 33:15 . . . . .510, 535
Jer 33:23-26 325
Jer 33:26 67
Jer 34:11, 16 280
Jer 34:18 350
Jer 36 .94
Jer 36:3 74
Jer 40:1 531
Jer 41:10-15 308
Jer 42:12 67
Jer 46–51. 527
Jer 46:10 307
Jer 46:18 137
Jer 46:27 120
Jer 47:1-7 . . . . .308, 527
Jer 48:1-9 308
Jer 48:15 137
Jer 49:1-6 527
Jer 49:7-22 . . . . .527, 564
Jer 49:18 309

Jer 49:23-27 528
Jer 49:34-39 528
Jer 50–51. 224
Jer 50:1–52:58. 528
Jer 50:1-3 306
Jer 50:40 309
Jer 51:11 307
Jer 51:15 51
Jer 51:15-16 528
Jer 51:57 137

Lam 1:18. 59
Lam 1:20. 182
Lam 2:2, 17, 21 64
Lam 2:11. . . . . 182 (2)
Lam 3:2. . . . . .103, 132
Lam 3:13. 181
Lam 3:22. 66
Lam 3:22-23 71
Lam 3:32. 68
Lam 3:34. 247
Lam 3:43. 64
Lam 5:19. 54

Ezek 1:1 . . . . .78, 80
Ezek 1:2 540
Ezek 1:4-25. 317
Ezek 1:5 169
Ezek 1:10 169
Ezek 1:13 169
Ezek 1:16 . . . . .78, 169
Ezek 1:22-28. 352
Ezek 1:24 86
Ezek 1:28 540
Ezek 2:3-8. 540
Ezek 4:1-3. 98
Ezek 5:6 541
Ezek 5:11 64
Ezek 6:8-10. 545
Ezek 6:9 343
Ezek 7:4, 9 64
Ezek 8:1-18. 541
Ezek 8:3 80
Ezek 8:18 64
Ezek 9:10 64
Ezek 10:3-5. 475
Ezek 10:5 86
Ezek 11:16 545
Ezek 11:19 179
Ezek 11:22-24. . . . . .452, 481
Ezek 12:14 177
Ezek 12:24 80
Ezek 13:6-9. . . . . 80 (2)
Ezek 13:16 80
Ezek 13:23 . . . . 80 (2)
Ezek 16 541
Ezek 16:1-34. 541
Ezek 16:32 . . . . 343 (2)
Ezek 16:46-48. 225
Ezek 16:59-63. 545
Ezek 18:1-4. 335
Ezek 18:2 542
Ezek 18:4 542
Ezek 20:1-31. 541
Ezek 20:12 366
Ezek 20:17 64
Ezek 20:41 58
Ezek 21:29 80
Ezek 22:14 180
Ezek 22:28 . . . . 80 (2)
Ezek 23 541
Ezek 23:31-34. 526
Ezek 23:37-45. 343
Ezek 24:2 540
Ezek 24:14 64
Ezek 24:15-27. 98
Ezek 25:3 309
Ezek 25:15 . . . . .246, 309
Ezek 26:1–28:26. 543
Ezek 26:7-14. 311
Ezek 27:1-36. 311
Ezek 28 206
Ezek 28:1-19. 311
Ezek 28:2 . . . . 312 (2)
Ezek 28:11-19. . . . . .259, 312
Ezek 28:12-15. 317
Ezek 29:1–32:32. 310
Ezek 29:3-5. 46
Ezek 31:18 310
Ezek 32:1-2. 46
Ezek 32:2 310
Ezek 32:17-21. 213
Ezek 33:21 540
Ezek 34:22 121
Ezek 34:23-24. 546
Ezek 34:25 285
Ezek 35:1-15. 309
Ezek 35:5 247
Ezek 36:8-15. 545
Ezek 36:22-31. 531
Ezek 36:23 56
Ezek 36:24-25. 545
Ezek 36:24-32. . . . .530, 534, 545
Ezek 36:24-36. 565
Ezek 36:25-27. . . . . .410, 530
Ezek 36:26 . . . . .179, 560
Ezek 37:1-14. 215
Ezek 37:1-27. 531
Ezek 37:9 45
Ezek 37:19 189
Ezek 37:22-25. 546
Ezek 37:23 121
Ezek 38–39 544
Ezek 38:10-13. 544
Ezek 38:16 58
Ezek 38:23 56
Ezek 39:7 544
Ezek 39:7-13. 565
Ezek 39:25 67
Ezek 39:27 58
Ezek 40:2 80
Ezek 43:3 80
Ezek 43:3-17. 358
Ezek 44:13 360
Ezek 45:8 189
Ezek 47:1-12. 443
Ezek 47:9 . . . . .106, 176
Ezek 47:13 189
Ezek 48:1-35. 189
Ezek 48:15-35. 223

Dan 1:8 313
Dan 1:15 179
Dan 1:17 80
Dan 2. . . . . .78, 224, 551
Dan 2:18 485
Dan 2:20 48
Dan 2:36-43 550
Dan 2:37 485
Dan 2:37-38 313
Dan 2:44 485
Dan 2:44-45 553
Dan 2:47 . . . . .313, 553, 554
Dan 3 314
Dan 3:18 551
Dan 3:28-29 313
Dan 3:29 554
Dan 4. . . . . .78, 224
Dan 4:2-3 554
Dan 4:3 . . . . .44, 55
Dan 4:5, 10, 13 80
Dan 4:9-16 551
Dan 4:22 314
Dan 4:34 . . . . .44, 55, 553
Dan 4:34-35 313
Dan 4:34-37 78
Dan 4:37 . . . . .44, 313
Dan 5:18-28 551
Dan 5:30 554
Dan 6:7 314
Dan 6:22 314
Dan 6:26 554
Dan 6:26-27 44
Dan 7:1-14 551
Dan 7:1-28 315
Dan 7:10 141
Dan 7:25 552
Dan 7:26-27 553
Dan 8. 552
Dan 9:1-27 548
Dan 9:2 . . . . .90, 549

Dan 9:4 .69
Dan 9:14 59
Dan 9:19 73
Dan 9:25 548
Dan 9:25-27 552
Dan 10 317
Dan 10:13, 20 300
Dan 11. 552
Dan 11:4 203
Dan 12:1 317
Dan 12:2 . . . . .216 (2)

Hos 1:2-9. . . . . .496n
Hos 1:6 . . . . .67, 74
Hos 1:7 . . . . .67, 118
Hos 2:2 497
Hos 2:4 .67
Hos 2:8 496
Hos 2:13 396
Hos 2:16 343
Hos 2:17 396
Hos 2:18 285
Hos 2:19 . . . . .67, 68
Hos 2:20 70
Hos 2:23 67
Hos 3:1-3. 497
Hos 4:8 221
Hos 4:15 343
Hos 6:1-2. 215
Hos 7:4 343
Hos 8:1-4. 497
Hos 8:13 221
Hos 9:9 221
Hos 10:11 . . . . .522n
Hos 10:15 290
Hos 11:1 . . . . .63, 510
Hos 11:9 271
Hos 11:3-4. 506
Hos 12:3-4. 338
Hos 13:9 177
Hos 13:12 221
Hos 13:14 . . . . .125, 215, 215
Hos 14:4 63

Joel 1:1-7. 554
Joel 1:8-12. 555
Joel 1:13-20. 555
Joel 1:15 . . . . .86, 555
Joel 2:1 555
Joel 2:2 555
Joel 2:11 555
Joel 2:13 . . . . .66, 67, 555
Joel 2:18-19. 63
Joel 2:18-24. 555
Joel 2:25-27. 555
Joel 2:28-29. 555
Joel 2:28-32. 299
Joel 2:30-31. 555
Joel 2:31 555
Joel 2:32 555
Joel 3:1-3. . . . . .299, 555
Joel 3:12-13. 299
Joel 3:14 555
Joel 3:14-16. 299
Joel 3:17 299
Joel 3:18 555

Amos 1:1–2:3 302
Amos 1:3-5 493
Amos 1:6-8 302
Amos 1:9-10 302
Amos 1:11-12 302
Amos 2:4-5 494
Amos 2:6-8 495
Amos 3:12. 495
Amos 4:1-3 495
Amos 4:11. 309
Amos 5:3. 495
Amos 5:4. 496
Amos 5:6. 496
Amos 5:8. 133
Amos 5:11-13 495
Amos 5:20. 132
Amos 5:21-23 496
Amos 5:21-25 624
Amos 5:27. 495
Amos 6:7, 14. 495
Amos 7:7-11 290
Amos 7:11. 495
Amos 7:14. . . . . .93, 493
Amos 7:17. 495
Amos 8:1-3 495
Amos 8:4. 280
Amos 8:4-6 495
Amos 8:14. 424
Amos 9:1-10 495
Amos 9:6. 133
Amos 9:9. 557

Obad 16. 526

Jonah 1:2. 499
Jonah 1:5. 499
Jonah 1:9. 499
Jonah 1:14. 500
Jonah 1:16. 500
Jonah 3:4. 499
Jonah 4:2. . . . . .65, 66, 67, 71
Jonah 4:11. 500

Mic 1:1 80
Mic 1:1-7. 519
Mic 2:1-5. 519
Mic 2:12-13. 519
Mic 3:14 519
Mic 4:1-5. 519
Mic 4:6-8. 519
Mic 4:8 519
Mic 4:10 126
Mic 5:2 . . . . .519, 578
Mic 6:1-2. 519
Mic 6:8 431
Mic 6:9-15. 519
Mic 7:8-9. 132
Mic 7:18 73
Mic 7:18-19. 520
Mic 7:19 67
Mic 7:20 69

Nahum 1:2-3 305
Nahum 1:2-6 536
Nahum 1:3. 71
Nahum 1:4. . . . . .133, 267
Nahum 1:8. 536
Nahum 1:12-13 536
Nahum 1:14. . . . . .305, 536
Nahum 1:15. 536
Nahum 1:16. 267
Nahum 1:19. 267
Nahum 2:2. 536
Nahum 2:5-7 305
Nahum 3:8. 305
Nahum 3:17. 305
Nahum 3:18. 305

Hab 1:1-4 537
Hab 1:2 118
Hab 1:12 54
Hab 1:12-17 537
Hab 2:4 537
Hab 2:16 . . . . .526n
Hab 3:1-19 537
Hab 3:2 67
Hab 3:11-15 537
Hab 3:15 134

Zeph 1:2-3. 538
Zeph 2:3 539
Zeph 2:4-7. 308
Zeph 2:13-15. 538
Zeph 3:1-5. 539
Zeph 3:5 59
Zeph 3:15 139
Zeph 3:17 . . . . .117, 139, 265

Hag 1:4 557
Hag 1:8 557
Hag 1:9 557
Hag 2:3 . . . . .484, 557
Hag 2:7 557
Hag 2:22 558

Zech 1:8 . . . 80
Zech 1:9 . . . 145
Zech 1:12 . . . 67
Zech 1:13-14 . . . 145
Zech 1:16 . . . 67
Zech 1:16-17 . . . 559
Zech 1:19 . . . 145
Zech 1:21 . . . 559, 561
Zech 2:3 . . . 145
Zech 2:4 . . . 223
Zech 2:5 . . . 560
Zech 2:8-9 . . . 561
Zech 2:11 . . . 561
Zech 3:1 . . . 597
Zech 3:1-2 146, 205, 206, 617n
Zech 3:2 . . . 267
Zech 3:8 . . . 510, 562
Zech 3:9 . . . 562
Zech 4:1, 4-5 . . . 145
Zech 5:5, 10 . . . 145
Zech 6:4-5 . . . 145
Zech 6:9-15 . . . 582, 562
Zech 6:12 . . . 510
Zech 7:1-3 . . . 290
Zech 7:4-7 . . . 559
Zech 8:3 . . . 223, 225
Zech 8:3-8 . . . 560
Zech 8:7 . . . 121
Zech 8:8 . . . 59
Zech 8:13 . . . 121
Zech 8:21 . . . 223
Zech 8:23 . . . 561
Zech 9:1-8 . . . 561
Zech 10:2 . . . 80
Zech 10:6 . . . 121, 560
Zech 10:8 . . . 126
Zech 10:11 . . . 135
Zech 11:6 . . . 64
Zech 11:10 . . . 300
Zech 12:1 . . . 176
Zech 12:1-2 . . . 560
Zech 12:2 . . . 526
Zech 13:1 . . . 560
Zech 13:7-8 . . . 559
Zech 14:2 . . . 559
Zech 14:3 . . . 301
Zech 14:3-5 . . . 561
Zech 14:9 . . . 137, 140, 563
Zech 14:11 . . . 560
Zech 14:16 . . . 138, 562
Zech 14:16-19 . . . 58
Zech 14:16-21 . . . 584

Mal 1:2 . . . 62, 563
Mal 1:3 . . . 563
Mal 1:4 . . . 564
Mal 1:6-8 . . . 564
Mal 1:9 . . . 66
Mal 1:14 . . . 137, 140
Mal 2:1-9 . . . 564
Mal 2:11 . . . 63
Mal 3:1-5 . . . 564
Mal 3:6 . . . 565
Mal 3:8-11 . . . 565
Mal 3:11 . . . 267
Mal 3:17 . . . 128, 270
Mal 3:17-18 . . . 565
Mal 3:18 . . . 270
Mal 4:1-3 . . . 565

Matt 1:1 . . . 190
Matt 1:5-6 . . . 426
Matt 1:22-23 . . . 97, 510
Matt 2:3-6 . . . 519
Matt 2:15 . . . 510
Matt 2:18 . . . 531
Matt 3:17 . . . 77
Matt 4:10 . . . 617n
Matt 5:5 . . . 587
Matt 5:9, 45 . . . 257
Matt 5:27-28 . . . 345
Matt 5:38-48 . . . 586
Matt 8:17 . . . 513
Matt 8:20 . . . 172
Matt 9:6 . . . 172
Matt 10:23 . . . 172
Matt 11:19 . . . 172
Matt 11:24-27 . . . 173
Matt 12:26 . . . 617n
Matt 19:5 . . . 185
Matt 19:28 . . . 189, 578
Matt 20:23 . . . 581
Matt 20:30-31 . . . 190
Matt 21:5 . . . 562
Matt 21:9 . . . 190
Matt 21:14-16 . . . 576
Matt 22:36-40 . . . 395
Matt 22:40 . . . 330
Matt 22:44 . . . 581
Matt 23:35 . . . 229n
Matt 25:21, 23 . . . 281
Matt 26:64 . . . 581
Matt 26:67 . . . 513
Matt 27:35 . . . 591
Matt 27:46 . . . 571, 591
Matt 28:19-20 . . . 499

Mark 10:7-8 . . . 185
Mark 11:2 . . . 173
Mark 12:31 . . . 330
Mark 14:24 . . . 532
Mark 15:19 . . . 513

Luke 1:19, 26 . . . 317
Luke 1:46-55 . . . 428
Luke 4:18 . . . 511
Luke 5:1-11 . . . 511
Luke 9:51–24:53 . . . 304
Luke 10:18 . . . 304
Luke 12:48 . . . 388
Luke 22:20 . . . 532
Luke 22:37 . . . 513
Luke 22:63 . . . 513
Luke 24:27 . . . 651

John 1:3 . . . 626
John 1:12 . . . 257
John 1:14 . . . 44, 353
John 3:3, 7 . . . 530
John 4:21-24 . . . 529
John 5:19 . . . 617
John 7:42 . . . 519
John 12:15 . . . 562
John 12:19 . . . 300
John 12:31 . . . 617
John 12:38 . . . 513
John 14:15 . . . 396
John 14:30 . . . 617
John 16:11 . . . 617
John 19:24 . . . 591
John 20:20-31 . . . 172
John 21:1-6 . . . 173

Acts 1:8 . . . 499
Acts 2:1 . . . 349
Acts 2:33-34 . . . 581
Acts 4:25 . . . 578
Acts 5:3 . . . 617n
Acts 5:19 . . . 146
Acts 8:32-35 . . . 513
Acts 9:4-6 . . . 77
Acts 12:8 . . . 146
Acts 13:33 . . . 578
Acts 17:26 . . . 113

Rom 1:18-23 . . . 76
Rom 1:22-23 . . . 285
Rom 2:25-29 . . . 529n
Rom 7:5, 18 . . . 179
Rom 8:1, 3-5 . . . 179
Rom 8:16 . . . 257
Rom 8:18-21 . . . 205, 577
Rom 8:19-21 . . . 284
Rom 8:34 . . . 581
Rom 9:18 . . . 262
Rom 9:21 . . . 175
Rom 10:16 . . . 513
Rom 11 . . . 532
Rom 11:11-16 . . . 539
Rom 12:19 . . . 297
Rom 13:1-5 . . . 297

Rom 13:4. 342
Rom 15:21. 513

1 Cor 5:5 179
1 Cor 6:3 146
1 Cor 6:16 185
1 Cor 11:1-10 203
1 Cor 11:25 532
1 Cor 15:22 286
1 Cor 15:45 286
1 Cor 15:55 . . . . .125, 215
1 Cor 15:50-57 216

2 Cor 3. 532
2 Cor 4:4 617
2 Cor 10:2 179
2 Cor 11:14 317

Gal 4:24-31 533

Eph 2:2 . . . . .300, 617
Eph 2:14-18. 583
Eph 3:10 300
Eph 6:10-18. 259
Eph 6:12 300

Phil 2:5-11. . . . . .514, 577
Phil 2:11 . . . . .140, 572, 578

Col 1:16. 626
Col 2:3. 626

2 Thess 2:1-12. 552

1 Tim 2:11-15 203

2 Tim 2:8. 190
2 Tim 3:15-17 642
2 Tim 3:16. 642

Heb 1:5 578
Heb 1:8-9 579
Heb 1:14 . . . . .146, 577
Heb 2:5-9 577
Heb 2:7 576
Heb 2:9a 577
Heb 2:17-18 581
Heb 3:3 581
Heb 4:14-16 581
Heb 5:5 578
Heb 5:6 581
Heb 5:8-9 581
Heb 5:10 581
Heb 6:20 . . . . .446, 581
Heb 7:2 446
Heb 7:7 582
Heb 7:11-17 469
Heb 7:17 . . . . .446, 581
Heb 7:22 533
Heb 8:1 578
Heb 8:5 473
Heb 8:6-12 533
Heb 9:1-10 533
Heb 9:11-14 533
Heb 9:24 473
Heb 10:12 581
Heb 10:20 475
Heb 11:4 219
Heb 11:9-10 225
Heb 11:24-26 156
Heb 12:2 578

Jam 1:18 530
Jam 2:10 397

1 Pet 1:18-19. 123
1 Pet 2:22 513

2 Pet 1:20-21. 24
2 Pet 1:21 642
2 Pet 2:4 144
2 Pet 2:6 225
1 John 2:18, 22 552
1 John 3:2 . . . . .257, 517
1 John 4:3 552

2 John 7. 552

Jude 6 . . . . .144, 317
Jude 7 .225
Jude 9 .317

Rev 5:5 190
Rev 5:8 358
Rev 5:9-10. 305
Rev 7:4 189
Rev 8:3-4. 358
Rev 11:8 225
Rev 12:7-9. 317
Rev 12:7 317
Rev 12:9 . . . . .135, 146, 617n
Rev 12:15 . . . . .135, 146
Rev 13:1-10. 552
Rev 13:1, 2, 4, 11 135
Rev 16:13 135
Rev 17–18. 224
Rev 19:15-16. . . . . .140, 572
Rev 19:16 . . . . .469, 578
Rev 19:19-21. 552
Rev 20:2 . . . . 41, 135, 146, 304, 617n
Rev 20:7 . . . . .617n
Rev 20:7-10. 544
Rev 21:1-2. 142
Rev 21:5-8. 535
Rev 21:12 189
Rev 21:22 . . . . .529, 535, 562
Rev 21:22-25. 558
Rev 21:22-27. 142
Rev 22:1 535
Rev 22:1-5. 443
Rev 22:3 . . . . .535, 558, 562, 578
Rev 22:16 190